OPERATION LOST TRUST
AND
THE ETHICS REFORM MOVEMENT
1989-1999

Published by the Crangle Company

BY
JOHN V. CRANGLE

ISBN 978-0-692-69798-6

PROFESSIONAL PRINTERS
WEST COLUMBIA, S.C.

ABOUT THE AUTHOR

John V. Crangle served as Executive Director of Common Cause/South Carolina from 1986 until 2016 during the period when the Operation Lost Trust investigations and prosecutions eventuated. He was a participant in the ethics reform efforts which produced the 1991 Ethics Act.

He received his BA in History from the University of South Dakota (1962), MA in History for the University of New Hampshire (1964), PhD in History from the University of South Carolina (1969), and J.D. from the School of Law of the University of South Carolina (1985).

He is the author of numerous articles and reviews on the history of British anti-imperialism and reform movements. He is a contributor to *The Biographical Dictionary of Modern British Radicals, The Historical Dictionary of Tudor England, 1485-1603*, and *The Biographical Dictionary of Modern Peace Leaders*.

He has received grants for graduate studies from the Ford Foundation and the National Defense Education Act. He also engaged in post-doctoral studies at the Catholic University of America, University of Wisconsin—Madison, University of Virginia, and the University of California—Berkeley.

He is a member of the South Carolina Bar and admitted to practice in the Commonwealth of Pennsylvania.

TABLE OF CONTENTS

CHAPTERS	PAGE	

PREFACE

A Note from the Author

The purpose of the author in writing this book is to present a comprehensive historical account of Operation Lost Trust and the ethics reform movement as a contribution to the historical record of the State of South Carolina. No previous writings on the subject have tried to provide a complete picture of the origins, events, and results of Operation Lost Trust. The author has also tried to include some new information based on interviews undertaken in 2014 and 2015 of persons who were major players in the drama of Lost Trust, including state legislators, journalists, activists, state constitutional officers, lawyers, and prosecutors.

The history of Operation Lost Trust and the ethics reform movement are closely related and interactive. The scandal drove political demand for ethics reform from the time it became public on July 18, 1990.

The narrative of this book is formatted to show the interactions between law enforcement, the courts, the politicians, the defendants, the citizenry, the media, and the shaping of ethics reform legislation. Therefore, a chronological format is used which traces the progress of the sting, the prosecutions, and ethics reform movement from the beginning in 1989 until the last three defendants were convicted in 1999.

The author has included some analysis of the various aspects of Lost Trust and ethics reform. Many questions can be raised about the legitimacy of the sting, the prosecutions, and the results of Lost Trust.

Writing a history of Operation Lost Trust and the ethics reform movement is a complicated task. First, the criminal prosecutions were directed toward a total of 28 defendants. Second, a variety of crimes were indicted, including extortion, bribery, obstruction of justice, witness tampering, false statements to the FBI, racketeering, criminal conspiracy, and cocaine and marijuana violations. Third, the defendants all hired attorneys to handle their trials, motions, pleas and appeals and some defendants employed more than one attorney. Fourth, the prosecutions were handled by three U.S. Attorneys for South Carolina—Bart Daniel, John Simmons, and Pete Strom, Jr.,—who in turn had many assistant prosecutors. In addition, U.S. Department of Justice prosecutors intervened in 1995 to handle the final cases until 1999. Multiple judges handled the trials, pleas, motions, bond hearings, and appeals from 1990 until 1999 in U.S. District Court in South Carolina as well as at the 4th Circuit and U.S. Supreme Court.

The ethics reform movement and reactions of the political class, the media and general public were also complex. Many candidates, elected officials, journalists, citizen activists and others became involved in the effort to promote ethics legislation and regulations to clean up the corruption and abuses in South Carolina's government.

Fearing that the reader could easily become confused and even frustrated by the large numbers of participants and events in Lost Trust and the reform movement, the author has taken pains to make the historical narrative and analysis as clear and concise as practicable. In some cases, the author has erred on the side of repetition and restatement in hopes that the reader will be able to recall who the historical actors were and what they did during the period from 1988 until 1999.

Finally, the author has tried to point out some controversial issues and questions about both the scandal and the prosecutions as well as about the ethics reform movement, inviting the reader to make his own judgments about the events described in the book. Some readers may conclude that the Lost Trust prosecutions were marked by abuses and misconduct while other readers may conclude that the government did what was needed to expose and attack public corruption and drug crimes in South Carolina's political class.

Readers may form differing opinions about the ethics reform movement and the 1991 Ethics Act which came out of it. Some may regard the new law as an overreaction while others may conclude that the law was too permissive and left major abuses in place.

Acknowledgments by the Author

The author would like to acknowledge the outstanding journalists of *The State* newspaper who covered Operation Lost Trust so well for such a long time. The author relied very heavily on the archive of *The State* newspapers on file in the South Carolina State Library in Columbia. The author would also like to recognize the capable journalists and academics who assisted interviewing persons for the book. Rick Bundrett of *The Nerve*, Eva Moore of *The Free Times*, Henry Eichel retired from *The Charlotte Observer*, Corey Hutchins and Dr. Robert J. Moore of Columbia College all helped the author with the interviews published herein.

The author would also like to thank those persons who sat for interviews about their role in Operation Lost Trust. Their comments based on their direct experience of events of Operation Lost Trust were most helpful in preparing an accurate and realistic historical account of the scandal and of its many consequences, including the ethics reform effort which culminated with the passage of the 1991 Ethics Act.

The author refers to himself in the third person as John Crangle the Executive Director of Common Cause/South Carolina rather than in the first person. This book on *Operation Lost Trust and the Ethics Reform Movement* is a chronological and narrative history. All of the quotations attributed to the author are found in the archives of *The State* newspaper. A few matters covered in this book are based on the author's memory as a person involved in the events surrounding Lost Trust and the ethics reform movement during the entire period from 1987 until the present.

The author would like to thank Columbia attorney Herb Louthian, Greg Harruff and Dr. Moore for reviewing the manuscript.

CHAPTER ONE

THE BACKGROUND OF LOST TRUST

State House Culture of Corruption

Operation Lost Trust was the product of an FBI drug and bribery probe and sting operation starting in 1988 which bought votes of legislators and which exposed a widespread drug culture at the South Carolina State House in Columbia. The deeper roots of the scandal drew from a political culture dating back into the nineteenth century in which state politicians and office holders had long financially exploited the state's political, legal and ethical systems which not only tolerated but actually promoted self-serving and corrupt behavior. There were no state laws which effectively restricted campaign financing and lobbying nor were there ethics laws which significantly limited the ways in Which public officials at the State House could profit from their office.

The South Carolina General Assembly passed an ethics act in 1975 which was little more than a cosmetic reaction to the Watergate scandal in Washington, which had played out from 1972 until the resignation of President Richard M. Nixon in 1974. The 1975 Ethics Act allowed the most abusive behavior to continue unabated and even its feeble requirements were generally unenforced.

Legislators Exploit Lobbyists

Long before Operation Lost Trust was revealed by the media on July 18, 1990, when the FBI served subpoenas, it was obvious to journalists, reformers, lobbyists, and politicians that lobbyists thrived in an out-of-control State House culture as did legislators who brazenly exploited the opportunities to line their own pockets. It was common practice for politicians to shake down lobbyists for money, free meals, liquor, and free trips. The "Fat and Ugly Caucus," a group of over a dozen members of the South Carolina House of Representatives, would, as common practice, break for lunch and go into the lobby of the State House and demand that a lobbyist surrender his credit card which the caucus would use to buy lunch and drinks. In some cases the caucus would invite staff, friends, pages and others to join them for lunch, often running up bills for several hundred dollars on the lobbyist who feared retaliation if he refused. Shake downs demanding free trips to Mexico and other locations were inflicted on State House lobbyists as well. Legislators were not above demanding cash to buy a car or other personal items.

As many of the candidates who raised so-called campaign money had no primary or general election opposition, they often had to spend almost nothing to get re-elected and were free to spend funds on themselves at will including on personal expenses. Uncompetitive legislative districts gerrymandered by incumbents made it easier to abuse campaign accounts without electoral consequences.

1975 Ethics Act Allowed Abuses

The 1975 Ethics Act merely required public officials to disclose the campaign contributions which they received (8-13-620). But there was no actual monitoring of compliance with the law and no enforcement by the State Ethics Commission which was supposed to receive disclosure filings from statewide candidates such as governor, attorney general, secretary of state, lieutenant governor, comptroller, commissioner of agriculture, superintendent of education, and adjutant general. Neither did the House and Senate ethics committees enforce compliance with the toothless disclosure and reporting provisions of the 1975 Ethics Act which applied to legislative candidates and legislators.

At least as bad was the fact that the 1975 Act allowed those who received campaign contributions to use them for personal expenses unrelated to their campaigns. And officials could accept and keep unlimited gifts of goods, services, and cash from any sources and use such gratuities without restriction for personal purposes. In fact, as Operation Lost Trust clearly demonstrated, some legislators took cash from donors such as lobbyists and put it in their pocket for personal use without ever reporting the money on their campaign disclosure forms.

Ethics Act of 1975

The major South Carolina Code provisions of the 1975 Ethics Act were as follows:

8-13-110—created the State Ethics Commission to monitor statewide and local officials, but not legislators;
8-13-260—empowered the Senate to take disciplinary actions against senators indicted or convicted of felonies;
8-13-420—prohibited bribery and banned the giving and acceptance of campaign contributions on condition of recipient taking an official action;
8-13-520—empowered the Attorney General to take action and sue to recover the value of something received by an official in violation of the Act;
8-13-530—provided that a bribe or kickback was recoverable by the state from the recipient;
8-13-610—required the filing of statements of economic interest by public officials;
8-13-620—required that candidates keep records of contributions received;
8-13-810—required that officials file mandatory disclosure reports
8-13-1010—imposed penalties for violation of the 1975 Act of misdemeanor on conviction and up to 90 days in jail and a fine of $1,000.

CHAPTER TWO

ORIGINS OF THE STING

Ron Cobb Arrested

The triggering event of Operation Lost Trust was that a former Democratic House member from Greenville, Ron Cobb, who was a registered lobbyist at the South Carolina State House, was arrested for selling cocaine to an undercover federal agent in April, 1989. The FBI then made a deal with Cobb when he revealed that as a lobbyist he had a list of some eighty legislators in the past and that he thought he could bribe them. The deal required Cobb to serve as a sting agent to bribe legislators to vote for a horse racing betting bill in return for which he would not be prosecuted for federal drug charges under an immunity deal.

Cobb Gives Cash to Legislators

Legislators proved eager to take the bait and before long a number of them had taken amounts running from as little $300 to as much as $4,300 in handouts from Ron Cobb in connection to the betting bill. The FBI recorded the transactions in which the cash was handed by Cobb to individual legislators at various locations including Cobb's suite at the Town House Hotel in Columbia and his office in the AT&T high-rise near the State House; money was also handed out on a boat anchored at Hilton Head, South Carolina, which was called "The Tally Ho." The FBI captured all such cash handouts on videotape and audiotape which was later played in court to convince juries and judges of the defendants' guilt of crimes including extortion, conspiracy, and bribery.

The FBI sting also utilized Rep. Robert Kohn (R-Charleston), a corrupt House member, as a sting agent after he was caught taking a bribe. Rep. Kohn eagerly assisted the FBI in luring legislators to make contact with Rob Cobb in order to have Cobb give them money in connection with the betting bill.

Capital Gains Tax Bill Discovered

Federal prosecutors also discovered evidence of corruption which had eventuated before the FBI staged its sting operation. This corruption actually dated from 1987 and involved a tax break bill which was promoted and passed by the South Carolina General Assembly and signed into law by Gov. Carroll Campbell.

The tax bill involved a retroactive tax break for capital gains which had the result of cutting the taxes of a group of Greenville, South Carolina, businessmen who saved a total of $8,500,000.

Several of the businessmen had hired Ron Cobb as their lobbyist to move the tax cut bill through the General Assembly.

Cobb said he paid two highly influential legislators for their help in passing the tax cut bill, giving $75,000 each to Speaker Pro Tem Jack I. Rogers, (D-Marion) and Sen. Jack Lindsay, (D-Marlboro) who moved the bill to passage with almost no notice even to other legislators. Rogers was later indicted for bribery for taking the payoff from Cobb, but Lindsay died in January, 1991, and was never charged.

Cases Taken to Trial

Of the total of 28 defendants charged with felonies in Operation Lost Trust, only eight of them chose to go to trial. All of them were legislators, including seven House members and one senator, Bud Long (D-Horry). No lobbyists, executive branch officials, nor the single university administrator and the lone businessman chose to go to trial.

Those who chose to go to trial and who were convicted:

Rep. Luther Taylor (D-Richland)
Rep. B.J. Gordon (D- Williamsburg)
Rep. Larry Blanding (D-Sumter)
Rep. Ken Bailey (D-Orangeburg)
Rep. Ennis Fant (D-Greenville)
Rep./Judge Tee Ferguson (D-Spartanburg)
Sen. Bud Long (D-Horry)

The only person who went to trial and was acquitted was Tim Wilkes (D-Fairfield).

1990 Elections

With all House members and all constitutional officers, including Gov. Campbell, up for election in 1990, but no senators up until 1992, the Operation Lost Trust scandal did not impact all state elections immediately. However, Democrats thought they might use the scandal against Gov. Campbell and Republicans thought their candidate for Secretary of State, Jim Miles, could use the scandal against incumbent John Campbell, Democrat.

Democratic State Chairman, Albert McAlister, vainly called on Gov. Campbell to remove Dick Greer as Development Board Chair as he was a suspect. Governor Campbell announced in late July that he would make reform a key plank in his re-election campaign, by which he meant reorganizing government to give the governor more power and the legislature less. But Gov. Campbell did not put forward a major ethics reform package during the 1990 campaign or afterward.

In the Jim Miles-John Campbell race, Miles' campaign manager, Bob Knight, said he was happy to see the scandal come up just before the election and appear to be related to Campbell's failure to supervise lobbyists' registration. Campbell's manager, Frank Knapp, conceded—"It's bad timing for the secretary." It was, indeed, and Jim Miles made the scandal the only real issue in the race and defeated Campbell in November.

The Cobb-Lindsay Nexus

The media was intrigued by the unclear relationship between Cobb and Sen. Lindsay brought to light by Lost Trust and the tax break scheme. Both were known to have helped Hitachi Corp. in its fight with IBM to obtain millions of dollars of mainframe computer contracts with the state government.

Cobb and Lindsay dropped out of sight after July 18, 1990, and sources said Cobb was out of state in FBI protective custody while Lindsay had a lung disease which impaired his speech. Even so, sources said that Lindsay was like a hero to Cobb and Lindsay had helped Cobb with his lobbying of bills. Friends said that even if Cobb knew of wrongdoing by Lindsay, Cobb would not tell prosecutors.

And it was known for several years Cobb had worked for National Advanced Systems, an arm of Hitachi, to get contracts for equipment purchases with the state. In fact, the Budget and Control Board, Clemson University, the Highway Department, and the departments of Social Services and Education had bought millions of dollars worth of Hitachi equipment.

Cobb appeared at an April 18, 1987, hearing for National Advanced Systems in a contested sale to Clemson objected to by IBM, and Jack Lindsay appeared as well for Hitachi. Cobb was hired by a Myrtle Beach group to lobby for a gasoline tax increase and Lindsay helped to pass a gas tax increase which would produce up to $10 million for an Economic Development Account under a group of agency heads chaired by Dick Greer, a friend of Cobb, Lindsay, and Gov. Campbell.

Cobb Nexus to Lindsay, Greer and Rogers

Jack Lindsay and Jack I. Rogers helped get $3.9 million from the Economic Development Account to build state roads in Marlboro County where Lindsay and Rogers lived.

Cobb was employed by the S.C. Housing Authority as a lobbyist. At the same time, Cobb worked for Interstate/Johnson Lane, one of four underwriters employed by the Authority.

Cobb lobbied for Cray Research, Inc., which was trying to sell supercomputers to the state while Lindsay promoted the buying of supercomputers in the Senate Finance Committee. Dick Greer supported the buy which fell through on objections by Fred Sheheen, Higher Education Commissioner.

Rogers, Cobb, and Lindsay worked together on the retroactive $8.6 million tax break for 21 taxpayers with Cobb being recommended to lobby the tax break by Dick Greer.

FBI Special Agent Scandal Erupts

Operation Lost Trust had just been revealed on July 18 when it came out that the probe's FBI special agent, Fred Verinder, had been stopped on March 22, 1990, by the Highway Patrol for drunk driving, but Verinder had been able to use his influence to get the charge reduced to speeding with the help of Highway Patrol Chief J.H. Red Lanier who came to the scene of the stop. At the same time, the FBI was investigating the corruption at the S.C. Department of Highways. SLED Chief, Robert Stewart, told U.S. Attorney Bart Daniel on April 24 about the matter, but federal agents did not investigate until July 25, 1990. Verinder was reassigned to Washington and the media did not report the ticket until July 24, 1990, a week after Verinder and Daniel broke news about Lost Trust.

Daniel said he reported the incident to FBI headquarters on July 6 and closed the matter. Red Lanier retired abruptly August 4, 1990, amid an investigation of his role in the Verinder traffic ticket.

Failure of the State to Prosecute

The State of South Carolina never prosecuted any of the same defendants charged by the federal grand jury. This was due in part to the lack of meaningful restrictions and penalties in the meretricious 1975 Ethics Act, but also because of the decisions of state officials at the time, including the Attorney General of South Carolina, Travis Medlock, and the 5th Circuit Solicitor, James Anders of Columbia.

The weakness of state enforcement of corruption and ethics was not only due to the permissive features of the 1975 Ethics Act, but also to the decision made by state law enforcement not to pursue separate state level prosecutions for the same corrupt actions being prosecuted by the federal authorities.

CHAPTER THREE

THE LAW, COURTS, PROSECUTORS, AND ISSUES IN LOST TRUST CASES

U.S. Grand Jury Procedures

A federal grand jury has power to investigate and to indict. It has 23 members and a quorum of 16. It needs 12 grand jurors to formally indict. A grand jury meets once per month but more often if necessary. Two or more grand juries may be at work at the same time. The grand jury can subpoena documents and witnesses.

The suspect can go into the grand jury and face the U.S. Attorney and three or four assistants. Prosecutors can ask the suspect any questions. Suspects can invoke the Fifth Amendment and not answer but are told the likely charges and often given an offer of immunity for full cooperation. Accepting immunity waives Fifth Amendment rights and refusal to cooperate and answer can result in contempt charges, and a U.S. District Judge can order jailing until cooperation. Immunity includes (1) use immunity which means what the defendant says can't be used as evidence to convict, but other evidence can be used, and (2) blanket immunity (transactional immunity) which means the prosecution agrees not to prosecute the defendant on the suspected crime.

Venue of Cases in Lost Trust

Most Operation Lost Trust trials were conducted in the United States District Court for The District of South Carolina—Columbia Division—in Columbia, at the federal courthouse located on the corner of Richland and Assembly streets in the downtown area of the city. That was the appropriate venue for federal crimes committed in the State of South Carolina. Several cases were handled in Charleston, S.C.

The Grand Jury

The jury pool from which the grand jury was drawn consisted of South Carolina residents in the U.S. District Court for the District of South Carolina. The district court's jurisdiction includes all of South Carolina.

Trial Juries

The jury pool for the trial juries called to Columbia came from all South Carolina counties, a total of 46 counties.

The 28 Indictments in Lost Trust

The FBI raids on the South Carolina House of Representatives on July 18, 1990, were quickly followed by the filing of federal grand jury indictments starting on August 24, 1990, against the first defendants. From that time forward and continuing to September, 1991, the U.S. Attorney for South Carolina, Bart Daniel, would hold periodic news conferences to announce new indictments and prosecutions. A total of 18 legislators and 10 others were indicted.

The Trials in Lost Trust

The first trial began in October, 1990, when Rep. Luther Taylor (D-Richland) was prosecuted in Columbia and convicted. The last trial would be held in November, 1991, when Sen. Bud Long (D-Horry) was convicted. Both were found guilty of crimes constituting public corruption. Eight defendants elected trials.

The conviction of Long marked the end of the first round of trials in the Lost Trust prosecutions. By that time a number of defendants had entered guilty pleas, and some of those convicted at trial began to file appeals which were successful and resulted in new trials, the last of which ended in 1999.

The Guilty Pleas

The FBI conducted corruption probes in Arizona, Kentucky, and California in which state politicians had almost always been convicted. This pattern or prosecutorial success was replicated in South Carolina where only eight defendants chose to go to trial and where only one of them, Rep. Tim Wilkes (D-Fairfield), would be acquitted by the jury.

A total of twenty of the defendants entered guilty pleas in the South Carolina Lost Trust case. This was a result, in part, of the fact that some defendants quickly pled guilty and that the earliest cases taken to trial, starting with the trial of Rep. Luther Taylor (D-Richland) had ended in guilty verdicts and prison sentences. Six convictions in trials followed and later defendants realized that the videotaped evidence of cash being handed to legislators during the defendants' conversations about voting for a horse racing bill with lobbyist Rob Cobb was too over powering for many jurors to resist.

Those who pleaded guilty all had legal representation in court by prominent members of the South Carolina Bar who concluded with their clients that the evidence of bribery would likely produce a guilty verdict from the jury and that a guilty plea with offer of cooperation would result in a lesser sentence on the recommendation of leniency by the U.S. Attorney's Office.

Of the twenty who pleaded guilty, the number included 10 legislators, six lobbyists, three state employees, and one businessman. Rep. Bob Kohn (R-Charleston) was the first to make a deal with the prosecution and he was the only defendant to become a sting agent himself.

The Prosecution

The U.S. Attorney who began the Lost Trust prosecutions was Bart Daniel, a Republican appointee, who served as U.S. Attorney for South Carolina until his resignation in March 8, 1992.

Daniel's assistants in the Lost Trust cases were John McIntosh, Sherry Lydon, John Barton, and Dale DuTremble, Scott Schools and "Buddy" Bethea.

Upon Daniel's resignation, the new U.S. Attorney was John Simmons who served until after Bill Clinton defeated President George H.W. Bush and then resigned.

Pete Strom, Jr., became the U.S. Attorney upon his appointment by President Bill Clinton in 1993.

The U.S. Department of Justice took over the remaining Lost Trust trials in 1995 and prosecuted them until the last three convictions of Rep. Larry Blanding, Rep. Paul Derrick, and Sen. Bud Long in 1999. The Department sent in new attorneys from Washington to prosecute those last cases. The new attorneys included Richard Pilger and Robert Meyer.

The Judges

Most of the cases in Lost Trust were tried by U.S. District Court Judge Falcon Hawkins, a veteran jurist who announced his retirement as the last cases were being appealed and retried.

Judge Henry Simon handled a few of the cases. And a U.S. Judge from West Virginia, Charles Haden, in 1999, was brought in to retry the last cases in the Lost Trust prosecutions after Hawkins dismissed all charges in 1997 against the last five defendants but was overturned on appeal in 1998.

U.S. Magistrate, Charles Gambrell, handled some matters related to the Lost Trust cases but did not conduct any trials or impose any sentences.

Most appeals were taken to the 4th Circuit in Richmond, Virginia.

Hobbs Act

The criminal statute on which most Operation Lost Trust cases rested was the federal Hobbs Act (18 U.S. Code § 1951). The Hobbs Act is an anti-corruption law which applies to state and local officials as well as federal officials. The Act defines bribery as an illegal gratuity given, offered, or promised to a public official "for or because of any official act performed or to be performed by such public official." Both the donor and recipient are criminally liable under the statute. The Hobbs Act has harsh penalties.

Ron Cobb's payments of cash to legislators to vote for a bill pending in the legislature were violations of the law. The cameras caught both the images and the words on tape. In all but one case the evidence was sufficient to induce a plea or produce a conviction at trial.

RICO—Racketeer Influenced and Corrupt Organizations Act

RICO prosecutions are based on the authority of the United States government to regulate interstate commerce provided by the United States Constitution's commerce clause (US Constitution, Article I, Section 8, Paragraph 3). RICO carries severe criminal penalties and the forfeiture of assets illegally obtained. RICO is also enforceable civilly, but was not so enforced in the Operation Lost Trust criminal prosecutions.

RICO (18 U.S.C § 1961-1968) is a statute passed by Congress in 1970 to give federal law enforcement more severe and favorable laws with which to prosecute organized crime, especially the Mafia.

RICO requires that the defendant commit two or more predicate crimes of certain types (bribery and extortion are such crimes) in a period of ten years acting in conspiracy with one or more co-conspirators.

Speaker Pro Tem Jack I. Rogers was the only defendant in Lost Trust who was prosecuted under RICO and convicted of racketeering for taking bribes.

Issues in the Lost Trust Corruption Cases

The central issue of fact in the Lost Trust prosecutions for corruption at trial was not whether the defendants had taken cash from lobbyist Ron Cobb. Videotapes made at the Town House Hotel and Cobb's AT&T building office clearly showed Cobb handing cash to the accused. The legal issue was whether the cash was given and taken as a bribe to influence the official actions of a state legislator, in particular, his vote on the pari-mutuel bill then pending in the General Assembly.

The Hobbs Act requires to convict a quid pro quo transaction in which something of value is given to a public official in return for his taking action in his official capacity. The central problem in the Lost Trust was the problem of proving that the officials took the money to cause them to promote and to vote for the betting bill in a certain way. However, some of the legislators had an established position in favor of the betting bill long before taking any money from Cobb. They had openly declared that they intended to support the bill and vote for it whether or not they took any money from Cobb. This was especially true of a number of African-American legislators who had regarded the betting bill as a jobs bill for low income black citizens of South Carolina. Perhaps some or all who took money did not decide to vote for the bill because of Cobb's money—they were very likely, if not certain, to vote for the bill regardless of the money.

Purpose of Anti-Bribery Laws

The purpose of anti-bribery laws of South Carolina in effect in 1990 (S.C. Code 8-13-420) which was part of the 1975 Ethics Act (which was not used in Lost Trust) and the Hobbs Act was to prohibit and prevent public officials from taking action in their official capacities which they would not otherwise take if they had not been bribed to do so. The ethical principle behind anti-bribery laws is that they ban payments for official actions on the theory that such actions would cause the public official to act against the public interest as he sees it and do something that benefits him personally instead.

McCormick v. U.S. Disrupts Lost Trust Prosecutions

The process of indicting and taking pleas or conducting trials went forward after the conviction of Taylor from late 1990 into 1991. It appeared that the U.S. Attorney was running up an unbroken string of victories as the number of guilty pleas and convictions at trial mounted up.

But the U.S. Supreme Court disrupted the prosecutions when it ruled on May 23,1991, in the case of *McCormick v. U.S.* (500 U.S. 257 (1991) that the Hobbs Act (18 U.S.C. Section 1951) required that the prosecution prove that the defendant accused of taking a bribe took an official action in return for the bribe. However, the U.S. Attorney in the first Lost Trust trials had not met that burden of proof.

Therefore, the convictions obtained at trial prior to May 23, 1991, were invalidated when the first defendants to be convicted at trial took their appeals to the 4th Circuit Court of Appeals in Richmond, Virginia. The Court ordered the cases retried by the U.S. District Court in South Carolina.

CHAPTER FOUR

THE YEAR 1990 BEGINS

The year 1990 can be divided into two distinct phases. In the first half of 1990 dating to July 18th, Operation Lost Trust was conducting a secret sting operation and an investigation of corruption in South Carolina's state government dating back to 1987. In the remainder of the year after July 18th, Operation Lost Trust was revealed to the public as the subpoenas were delivered, the indictments handed up, the guilty pleas were entered, and the first trial was held.

In the period before July 18th, the South Carolina General Assembly met and continued to wrestle with problems left over from the previous session, including ethics and lobbying reforms. And the candidates for the state offices in the House of Representatives and in all of the constitutional offices, including governor and Secretary of State, began their campaigns in anticipation of the general elections slated for November, 6th.

Aside from the FBI, the U.S. Attorney for South Carolina, and FBI sting agent Ron Cobb, there were few people who knew that Operation Lost Trust was being conducted right under their noses. It appears that few, if any, legislators and executive officials knew about the FBI sting and investigation. Even the Attorney General of South Carolina, Travis Medlock, did not know of the probe until just before it became public on July 18th.

1990 Legislature Opens Session

On opening of the session of the General Assembly in Columbia on January 9, 1990, ethics reform was not considered a major issue at the time. Other proposals got more attention.

Sen. Rick Lee (R-Spartanburg), who would be one of the first indicted in Lost Trust was arguing at the start of the session that the session should be cut short by six weeks and Lee and Sen. Thomas Pope (D-Newberry) joined in proposing a bill to cut the length of the session. Lee had served as the chairman of a committee in 1987 which had proposed a failed scheme to cut the session down by one month. The 1990 session ended in the first week of June, 1990. Lee was indicted on August 24 for taking a bribe from Cobb on May 24, 1990, in the final days of the session.

The State Lists Major Issues in 1990 Session

The State published a list of the major issues facing the new session of the General Assembly. Among the chief subjects identified were bills to deal with racial discrimination in public places, auto inspection fees being raised from $3.50 to $5.00, allowing auto dealers to hold tent sales, and requiring that those riding motorcycles under age 21 wear helmets and goggles. In addition, a bill to shorten the 1991 session of the General Assembly was up for consideration. But the subject of ethics and lobbying reform was not on *The State's* list.

General Assembly Convenes

Among the real issues facing the session were long-standing problems with lobbyists' abuses and legislators' parasitical relationships with lobbyists and campaign donors. The more general problem was that the state's ethics laws, especially the 1975 Ethics Act, were extremely permissive and unenforced by the responsible entities, including the State Ethics Commission, the House and Senate ethics committees, and the Attorney General.

There were a few legislators who were actually interested in ethics and lobbying reform issues. Jim Miles, the Republican candidate challenging for Secretary of State, began his campaign early in 1990 by chastising the incumbent, John Campbell, for failing to register and report lobbyists and their spending. But aside from Miles, about the only people who seemed much concerned about ethics issues were Speaker Bob Sheheen (D-Kershaw) and Reps. Malloy McEachin (D-Florence) and Candy Y. Waites (D-Richland). Gov. Carroll Campbell seemed ignorant about and indifferent to the abuses of lobbyists and legislators going on in the State House where he shared space for his office on the ground floor with the House and Senate above him on the second. Campbell had served in the South Carolina House and later the U.S. House before becoming governor.

Black Caucus Demands Positions

The Legislative Black Caucus demanded early in the 1990 session of the General Assembly that they be given more of a role.

Rep. Ennis Fant (D-Greenville) said in the days before the session started in mid-January, that the Caucus had approached Speaker Sheheen (D-Kershaw) with its proposals, and had also contacted Speaker Pro Tem Jack I. Rogers (D-Marlboro) as well.

The Caucus wanted the General Assembly to elect a black judge and provide blacks with more leadership roles in the House, including committee chairmanships. The Caucus also wanted the Legislature to create a new congressional district gerrymandered to elect a black member of the U.S. House from South Carolina. But the 1990 session ended with the indictment of eight Black Caucus members, all of whom would be found guilty by 1991, including Fant.

CHAPTER FIVE

ETHICS REFORM ISSUE EMERGES

Senate Judiciary Ethics Bill Still in Preparation

The Senate Judiciary Committee chaired by Marshall Williams (D-Orangeburg) moved the ethics bill sponsored by Sens. Williams and Ed Saleeby (D-Darlington), which had been introduced in 1989 and carried over to the 1990 session.

Ethics reform proposals and talk about ethics reform had been in the air in the late 1980s but there seemed to be little serious interest in the subject prior to the revelation of the Lost Trust scandal by U.S. Attorney Bart Daniel on July 18, 1990.

Those persons interested in ethics reform, led by Speaker Bob Sheheen and Rep. Malloy McEachin along with Williams and Saleeby, seemed to be keeping the subject of ethics reform alive but only on life support as the 1990 session began. Common Cause/South Carolina and the media, especially *The State* newspaper, the major daily in South Carolina, also joined in trying to keep the ethics reform issue alive in the 1990 session.

In the middle of 1990, however, the Lost Trust scandal delivered a jolt of electricity to the political class and the citizenry which finally galvanized the General Assembly to take decisive action to promote and pass ethics reform legislation.

Editorial on Secretary of State

The State published an editorial on March 2, 1990, criticizing Secretary of State, John Campbell, for asking lobbyists to donate to his re-election campaign fund at the same time that he was supposed to be regulating lobbyists according to the 1975 Ethics Act. The editorial rejected Campbell's protestations that he had no authority over lobbyists.

The State wrote: "Secretary of State, John Campbell, has been rightly criticized for soliciting campaign contributions from lobbyists—especially since he also is responsible for certain regulatory functions related to their activities."

The editors pointed to a letter of January 5, 1990, in which the Campbell campaign asked a lobbying group, the S.C. Society of Association Executives, to donate $1,000 to a fund-raising dinner for Campbell. "Those same lobbyists are required by law to register with the Secretary of State and to submit to his office annually 'a complete and itemized sworn statement of all contributions and expenditures'."

Quoting John Crangle of Common Cause/South Carolina who called it a "conflict of interest," *The State* went on to note that Campbell "has taken a hands-off approach" and had allowed lobbyists to ignore the disclosure requirements of the 1975 Ethics Act.

Legislators Party With Lobbyists

The South Carolina Textile Manufacturers held its 14th annual weekend event for legislators at Hilton Head, South Carolina, starting on Friday, March 9, 1990. A third of the legislators in the General Assembly attended the festivities, enjoying free rooms, free food, free drinks, and gratuities including golf and tennis. Some 84 members were entertained against the backdrop of a pending ethics reform bill recently passed 109-0 by the House to impose at least new disclosure requirements on such schemes.

Jerry Beasley, the lobbyist of the Manufacturers, reveled in the middle of the partying and entertainment saying it was necessary to help employees in the textile industry get to know legislators. But he refused to tell the media which legislators were in attendance.

Cindi Ross Scoppe of *The State* contacted the offices of all 170 legislators and found out who went to Hilton Head and also contacted the Hyatt Regency Hotel in Hilton Head and found out that 10 of 46 senators and 54 of 124 House members attended.

Beasley finally admitted that 84 state officials came to the event. John Crangle, of Common Cause/South Carolina, derided the Hilton Head largesse saying "What's really going on is an effort to obtain influence and access by giving members of the General Assembly favors—free food, free liquor, free trips." He pointed to the Manufacturer's gratuities as concrete evidence of the need to ban such practices and, at a minimum, to require full disclosure and reporting.

At least the public had a right to know which public officials attended the Hilton Head bash, Crangle asserted, adding that if anyone wanted to keep their identity secret it was Common Cause's position that "the taxpayers and the voters have a right to know what their employees are doing down there. If the public officials don't like that, then they need to find a new job."

Rep. Joe McElveen (D-Sumter), a leader of the House ethics reform movement, predicted that "I think the day is coming that those kind of things are going to end. The impression is once somebody gives you something, it's hard to be against them."

Some of those at Hilton Head partying and golfing would later be convicted in Operation Lost Trust, including Rep. Frank McBride (D-Richland), Rep. Donna Moss (D-Cherokee), and Rep. Danny Winstead (R-Charleston). On the other hand, a future governor, Rep. Jim Hodges (D-Lancaster), was also at Hilton Head and Lt. Gov. Nick Theodore, Secretary of State John Campbell, and Treasurer Grady Patterson were also in attendance.

Miles Blames Secretary of State on Lobbying Issue

Jim Miles, the Republican candidate for Secretary of State, was hitting his incumbent opponent, John Campbell, for failure to enforce the weak lobbyist disclosure provisions of the 1975 Ethics Act well before Operation Lost Trust exposed the outrageous antics of lobbyist Ron Cobb in mid-July, 1990. At the time, of course, Miles could not know that his criticism of Campbell's failings would be given a huge boost by the FBI sting which seemed to prove that Campbell had been negligent.

In mid-March, 1990, Miles was publicizing his determination to also crack down on securities frauds and con artists, if elected. He further stated his determination to make lobbyists file and disclose and repeatedly blamed John Campbell for his failures to enforce the law, saying lobbyists should be forced to file and disclose and that Campbell should refuse to register lobbyists who failed to complete their annual disclosure forms.

Miles said that Campbell had the power to compel compliance, claiming that "he has life or death" control of lobbyists because he could refuse to re-license lobbyists. But Campbell protested, lamely, that, in fact, he had no enforcement powers. Miles countered that Campbell had "chosen not to enforce the law."

South Carolina Ethics Law Worthless

In the months leading up to the public revelations of Operation Lost Trust, the failings of the 1975 Ethics Act became even more obvious. In comparison with the ethics laws of other states, the Act was one of the worst and most permissive of every sort of abuse, conflict of interest, and corruption.

In an extensive research-based article on March 26, 1990, published on the front page of *The State*, staff writer Cindi Ross Scoppe detailed how bad the 1975 Ethics Act really was. She started out by showing that the Act was little more than a relaxed disclosure law which allowed lobbyists to report undetailed and vague uses of money to try to influence legislators. Itemization of the actual amounts and uses of the money was not required.

By way of comparison, Oregon, Texas, and Wisconsin completely banned lobbyists from giving campaign contributions, while Minnesota banned contributions during legislative session. In 1990, Minnesota had just seen its House ban state representatives from inviting lobbyists to political fund-raisers during the legislative session.

The spending of money by lobbyists on handouts to legislators was limited in Nevada to $100 per year per legislator while several states limited lobbyists' spending on legislators to maximum amounts each month.

Wisconsin had the most stringent limits on lobbyists' gratuities, banning them completely. But some other states had weak disclosure laws. Still other states, 20 of them, required anyone spending money on legislators to file disclosures, and 30 states required lobbyists to itemize their spending on public officials.

The executive director of the Alabama Ethics Committee told Scoppe that the national trend was toward mere disclosure laws, not restrictions and limitations on the use of money in politics and lobbying. The Assistant Secretary of the State of Wisconsin, Tom Hecht, explained that Wisconsin had strict laws and that "In the Midwest, particularly Wisconsin, there's a long history of ethics in government that goes back 150 years." But Hecht did not think that strict laws would work in the south, remarking, "A Wisconsin-type law I don't think would work in South Carolina. You're coming from a different history, a different way of running state government."

Lobbying Bill Stalled—Ethics Committee Does Nothing

A lobbying reform bill, strongly opposed by lobbyists, was stalled in a subcommittee of the Senate Judiciary Committee, chaired by Sen. Ed Saleeby, who had not moved the bill, but it would have been the most significant lobbying reform bill since 1975.

Even so, the Senate seemed complacent about the inactivity of the Senate Ethics Committee. Sen. John Land (D-Clarendon) remarked of the committee of which he had been a member since 1985, "It's not a very active committee.... Since I've been on it, we've had very few meetings and had very few pieces of legislation."

The legislative ethics committees had been created in 1975 by the Ethics Act of that year in response to the Watergate scandal. The committees were supposed to oversee legislators and the law also created the State Ethics Commission. The committees had not functioned as investigative arms and were content to do nothing more than rarely receive ethics complaints against legislators. Neither did they introduce new ethics bills and did little to act on bills sent to them.

Gary Baker, director of the State Ethics Commission, understated the case when he said of the Senate and House ethics committees, "They've been fairly inactive over the years." Noting the lack of legislative initiative in the committees, Baker added, "Virtually all of the legislation has come from the Commission or individual legislators. The committees themselves have not taken the lead in ethics legislation."

Ethics Committees Inactive

The House Ethics Committee met once in 1990 and six times in 1989. The Senate Ethics Committee met once in 1990 and not at all in 1989. At the 1990 meeting of Senate Ethics only the chairman, Ed Saleeby, showed up. The committee had polled members in 1989 about appointments to the State Ethics Commission but might have violated the Freedom of Information Act by not conducting the polling in public. And, when ethics bills had come to the Senate panel, it had shown even less interest than in the House, said Baker of the Ethics Commission, who blamed Saleeby for doing less than the House.

Although Sen. Phil Leventis (D-Sumter), a member since 1985, said the committee had dealt openly and timely with complaints filed, the records of the committee were secret and not open to the media or public. Leventis admitted, "I think we should have more initiative."

On the other hand, Sen. Sherry Martschink (R-Charleston) thought the legislative ethics committees should be abolished and their duties shifted to the Commission, pointing out that

"You've got legislators making decisions on ethics for legislators." The conflict of interest was glaring.

The chair of Senate Ethics was a dubious figure. Sen. Ed Saleeby not only played cards with lobbyists for money, he also took multiple favors from them. A member of the committee since 1985, Saleeby took trips paid for by lobbyists but did not report them on his disclosure reports, claiming that he only took one such trip. When asked by the media about the matter he refused to talk and then made a speech in the Senate complaining, "I am sick and tired of everybody jumping on me.... And so for some little pipsqueak reporter to infer that I'm over here just to get free liquor and motel rooms, to me, makes him crazy as hell."

<u>Senate Ethics Committee Ineffective</u>

The Senate Ethics Committee was little more than a pious fraud, pretending to concern itself with its mission but, in fact, doing nothing. Scathing articles by Cindi Ross Scoppe and Trip DuBard of *The State* and *Associated Press* ripped off the mask on March 26, 1990. The two reporters revealed that the Committee had only met once in the two years before April, 1990. The committee had never proposed a single piece of ethics legislation in the entire time the committee had existed since 1975. And of six members of the committee, four of them had had their own ethics put in doubt in recent years. The fecklessness of the Senate Ethics Committee mirrored that of the House Ethics Committee as both committees were almost purely cosmetic in purpose and function.

John Crangle of Common Cause/South Carolina told the reporters, "The committee is about the least likely group in the state Legislature to become concerned about state ethics that you can find." Lt. Gov. Nick Theodore also recognized the paralysis of the committee when he wanted quick action on an ethics reform bill and sent it instead to the Senate Judiciary Committee. The same bill had passed the House in 1988 but had died in the Senate Ethics Committee, at the time chaired by Sen. Ed Saleeby (D-Darlington), a man known by Theodore for playing poker with lobbyists at the Town House Hotel where Rob Cobb was also bribing legislators.

The dubious conduct of prominent senators was exemplified by the way they used their public offices to gain advantages for themselves and their associates. In addition to taking handouts from lobbyists and special interests, some of them took actions which might be seen as tainted by personal interest and conflicts of interest.

Sen. Marshall Williams (D-Orangeburg), one of the most powerful senators, was exposed by *The State* in an *Associated Press* article as having helped to secure funding from the S.C. Highway Department to build roads around his church at a cost of $105,000. On the Senate floor, Williams defended his actions by saying on March 19, 1990, that "Yes, I'm proud. I paved them around my church, and I told them and I'll tell them now; I'll do it again."

Two prominent senators, John Land and Isadore Lourie, frequently represented clients before the Workers' Compensation Commission whose members had to be confirmed by the Senate after their appointment by the governor. But the House Labor, Commerce, and Industry subcommittee had warned in 1987 that such activity was improper. Land and Lourie protested that there was nothing wrong with practicing before such state agencies.

Common Cause's John Crangle faulted the Senate Ethics Committee for limiting its activity to handling ethics complaints against senators if any ever came in and asserted that the Committee should be pushing new ethics legislation and was not. He derided the committee saying, "I think that you could argue, based on the composition, that the committee is designed to be a good ol' boy do-nothing committee that is designed to tolerate business as usual."

House Ethics Bill Passed

The House passed H.4613, its new ethics reform bill, by vote of 109-0 in the early days of the 1990 session and sent it on to the Senate. The bill required more disclosure of lobbyists' spending on legislators in cases where a lobbyist spent more than $100 in one day on a legislator. The bill also required the disclosure of spending by clients who spent more than $500 on contributions. In addition, lobbyists were required to report on spending and activity relating to efforts to influence legislation and all branches of state government. Finally, lobbyists would be required to report all income and expenses.

John Crangle, of Common Cause/South Carolina, ventured muted praise for the House bill, saying that, "We would not be at the cutting edge of reform with this legislation. It's catch-up type of legislation that would put us where a lot of states were 15 years ago." The weakness in the bill was that it was merely a disclosure bill and did not place any prohibitions on lobbyists and their gratuities to public officials.

Senate Committee Rejects Lobbyists Bill

The Senate Judiciary Committee acted on April 10, 1990, to reject a bill which would have moved jurisdiction over lobbyists from the Secretary of State to the State Ethics Commission. However, Judiciary did agree that disclosure laws should be changed to require more information from lobbyists, but less than that required by the House bill which had been passed and sent to the Senate.

The Senate lobbying bill would give jurisdiction to enforce the lobbying bill to the Attorney General. Critics complained that both the Secretary of State and the Attorney General took campaign donations from the very lobbyists they were supposed to have jurisdiction over.

The Judiciary passed the lobbying bill out on April 10, 1990, and sent it to the full Senate for consideration. Weak as it was, the bill did advance the idea of independent enforcement and investigation.

Lobbying Disclosure Bill

As the 1990 session of the General Assembly was drawing to a close, a lobbying disclosure bill was still in limbo. H. 4613 proposed to move the oversight of lobbyists from the Secretary of State's office to the State Ethics Commission. By mid-April the House had passed the bill, but the Senate had a bill which would leave control with the Secretary of State.

The Senate Judiciary Committee did report H. 4613 out to full Senate, but it was unclear as to whether the Senate would do anything about lobbyists in the 1990 session.

The supporters of H. 4613 were Speaker Robert Sheheen and Rep. Malloy McEachin. The bill sought to force more complete disclosure of lobbyists' expenditures on public officials. In addition, the bill would compel lobbyists to report their business dealings with officials.

South Carolina had one of the weakest lobbying laws in the nation and even its feeble requirements were not enforced. In fact, wrote John Crangle of Common Cause in an op ed on April 11, 1990, the state's lobbying law was almost worthless. The op ed was entitled, "Lobbying Law Needs Teeth," and was published by *The State*.

Tee Ferguson Runs for Judgeship

Democrat House member Tee Ferguson appeared to have the votes lined up in the General Assembly to win election to the circuit court bench on April 11, 1990. He sought a seat in the 7th Circuit of Spartanburg and Cherokee counties. (Ferguson had recently taken a bribe from Ron Cobb and possessed cocaine on five different dates.)

Ferguson represented a House district in Spartanburg County. At the time, only one of the 31 circuit court judges was black, even though nearly one third of the population of South Carolina was black.

The Legislative Black Caucus was pushing hard for the election of Ferguson. Sen. Kay Patterson, chair of the caucus, reported just before the election that he had lined up some 120 of the 169 sitting legislators to vote for Ferguson. This was more than enough to beat the sole challenger for the seat, Family Court Judge Thomas Foster of Spartanburg.

Ferguson had problems when he was screened by the Judicial Screening Committee as the committee held an extra day of hearings on the dubious history and qualifications of Ferguson. The committee chairman, Rep. Jack I. Rogers (D-Marlboro), who had been taking bribes, remarked that certain allegations against Ferguson were not proved and, "I feel that he was slighted."

Elected to the House in 1983, Ferguson had a major advantage over his non-legislator opponent. At the time, a total of 22 of 31 circuit judges were former legislators.

Tee Ferguson Elected Judge

On April 11, 1990, the General Assembly elected Spartanburg Democratic House member James Cleveland Tee Ferguson to the Circuit Court bench. At the time, it was permissible for sitting legislators to run for and be elected to judgeships without having to resign their seats before their election, a great and unfair advantage.

At the time, Ferguson was 39 years old and was slated to replace a retiring judge on the 7th Circuit as of May 7, 1990, when he would be sworn into office serving Spartanburg and Cherokee Counties in upstate South Carolina.

Ferguson was elected without opposition as his three opponents in the race all withdrew before the vote. Ferguson scared off his opponents because he had support from the Democratic Party and unanimous backing from the Legislative Black Caucus.

Ferguson had his problems as a candidate for the bench. The Judicial Screening Committee found Ferguson and the other three candidates qualified, but in the hearings it came out that Ferguson had a bad reputation. He had money problems and he had been accused of making threats against his wife's ex-husband. He had had harsh words with a former client, and, allegedly, he had punched a man outside of a Greenville nightclub. The committee accepted Ferguson's explanation of his financial problems and found the other allegations to be unproven.

During the committee proceedings on the Ferguson application for judge, Ferguson had kept his distance from the media. On his election, he said he intended to work very hard to justify the confidence shown in him.

Ferguson joined Judge Richard Fields as the only two black circuit judges in South Carolina. Sen. McKinley Washington (D-Charleston), a black legislator, commented after Ferguson's election that, "No question about it, it's a great day for us." Washington pointed out that the committee had heard opposition to the election of a black judge from people in the upstate region but, "We were determined to break that."

Ferguson's tenure on the bench would be very brief, and on August 23, 1990, Ferguson would be forced by the exploding Operation Lost Trust scandal to take a voluntary leave of absence without pay, which was followed on July 7, 1991, with his conviction for taking a bribe from Ron Cobb to support the betting bill. On August 26, 1991, Ferguson would resign from the bench. Later he would plead guilty to cocaine possession.

Miles-Campbell Race

As the primary elections neared in late April, 1990, the contest for Secretary of State between challenger Jim Miles and incumbent John Campbell appeared destined for a general election shootout.

Gov. Carroll Campbell, of the same party as Republican Jim Miles, seemed reluctant to get involved in the harsh criticism which Miles was dropping on John Campbell early in the campaign cycle.

Miles promoted his candidacy as a populist attack on the incumbent, saying that he would put the public interest ahead of that of the corporations. Miles also promised not to take any campaign donations from any companies or organizations which hired lobbyists because if elected to the office of Secretary of State, he would have authority to receive lobbyists' disclosure reports, which would be a conflict of interest. By contrast, it was known to the public that John Campbell solicited and took campaign donations from the same group of lobbyists he was supposed to regulate, but did not.

The failure of many lobbyists and their employers to register and disclose with the Secretary of State, Campbell, was a topic of increasing attention in the spring of 1990. As the lobbyists ran rampant, the media was focusing more stories on Campbell's refusal to regulate lobbyists. Critics of the abusive behavior of the lobbyists were pointing out that the lobbyists were not registering and reporting in addition to indulging in the most outrageous schemes to use money and gratuities to control legislators. It all made Campbell look very bad.

Republican challenger, Jim Miles, saw from the start of his campaign that the incumbent, John Campbell, could be attacked as failing to make lobbyists register and disclose with his office. Reform organization, Common Cause/South Carolina, and the media combined to publicize the fact that the Ethics Act of 1975 had disclosure requirements that were being violated even while Campbell did nothing.

By late April, 1990, Secretary of State, John Campbell, was finally beginning to feel the heat. It was increasingly obvious that Campbell's major vulnerability was that he was soft on lobbyists at a time when the lobbyists were under increasing public scrutiny for their undue influence and corrupting conduct at the State House. The media and Common Cause/South Carolina intensified hostile attention on the antics of out-of-control lobbyists until Operation Lost Trust went public exposing the corrupt dealings of lobbyist Ron Cobb and 17 legislators. Thereafter, Jim Miles went for the kill in the general election and reformers convincingly demanded reforms.

Secretary of State Campaign Reacts to Criticism

Campbell's political consultant, Lois H. Pope, felt that something had to be done to counteract the criticism and bad publicity in the media. On April 27, 1990, Pope published a letter to *The*

State arguing that the criticism of Campbell for not doing his job was wrong because Campbell had no power over lobbyists. Pope wrote, "The truth of the matter is that the Secretary of State's office had no enforcement authority over lobbyists." Pope went on to assert that the law said, "Lobbyists are required to register with the Secretary of State, and that he is to publish a list of all lobbyists.... His other duty concerning lobbyists is to accept annual reports from each.... This is merely a filing, nothing else."

Pope went on to criticize John Crangle of Common Cause for saying that, "Mr. Campbell should not accept money from a group over which he has enforcement authority." Pope also blamed Jim Miles, who she said, "quickly jumped on the bandwagon regarding Mr. Campbell's asking lobbyists to support his re-election effort with a contribution."

Pope tried to praise Campbell "as a true servant of the people of this state, one who is not only sensitive and caring about the welfare of South Carolina, but who displays a rare sense of honesty." Pope deplored the sharp accusations against Campbell. And she pointed out that, "the public should be aware of the tremendous amount of money required to win any election now." On November 6, 1990, the voters of South Carolina found Pope's argument unconvincing and elected Jim Miles.

Lobbying Regulation Bill Stalled

Lobbyists were certainly spending money at the State House to influence legislators and legislation. In late April, 1990, Common Cause/South Carolina released a research report which found that lobbyists had spent $3.7 million in 1989 to influence the Legislature. $577,000 of that was for meals, entertainment, lodging, and travel for lobbyists and legislators and the remaining $2.8 million was for lobbyists' salaries.

As the 1990 session of the General Assembly came to an end on June 7th, the lobbying reform bill was caught in a conflict between the House and Senate over the question of who would enforce the new law, if passed. The House proposed to transfer jurisdiction over lobbyists to the State Ethics Commission while the Senate favored the status quo with the Secretary of State in charge.

On June 6th, a conference committee on the lobbying reform bill entertained a Senate proposal to assign to the Attorney General the responsibility for reviewing lobbyists' disclosure reports. But House conferees rejected the proposal on the grounds that officials such as the Attorney General and Secretary of State should not have authority over lobbyists because they took donations from lobbyists, an obvious conflict of interest, if such contributions were to be allowed in the future.

After the House rejected the Senate proposal, the Senate President Pro Tempore, Marshall Williams, told the Senate from the floor that if the lobbying reform bill died then the House would be at fault. But House Judiciary Committee Chairman, David Wilkins, rebutted Williams' charge by saying the House had made more concessions than the Senate. Sen. Don Holland (D-Kershaw) then alleged that the House wanted the bill to die, but Speaker Bob Sheheen said he would push a deal and felt the House had "met them more than halfway."

The 1990 session of the General Assembly expired on June 7, 1990, at 5:01 p.m. without passing an ethics reform bill or lobbying regulation bill. The Senate stalled the legislative process in the struggle to limit the participation of Gov. Carroll Campbell in the reapportionment process. Lobbying reform was one of several important bills that failed to pass before the session ended. Senate President Pro Tem Marshall Williams deplored the end of the session remarking, "We're through for the year, everything down the drain." Gov. Campbell rejected a request that he authorize the session to continue.

Interview
Rep. Candy Y. Waites (D-Richland)

By Eva Moore and John Crangle
August 29, 2014

Summary of the interview with Ms. Waites

Waites became concerned about the tactics that were used against her in her first campaign for the House in 1988. She won the election over her opponent, Ray Rossi, but the false and unattributable allegations made against her caused her to seek ethics reform. Her only recourse had been to enlist large numbers of volunteers to contact voters in the district to provide them with accurate information.

After her election, Waites met with Gary Baker, Executive Director of the State Ethics Commission. Her experience had shown her that more regulation of campaigns and candidates was needed. Early in her first term in the House, Waites became fully aware that the existing 1975 Ethics Act allowed unlimited campaign contributions and unlimited use of campaign funds. She was also concerned that the law did not require identification of the sources of campaign funds or published materials.

After she entered the House, Waites introduced four reform bills to deal with the problems she had identified in campaign practices. She also became aware of the blatant practice of lobbyists offering free meals, drinks, trips and gifts to influence legislators to support legislation they desired. She observed the control lobbyists had over many members of the General Assembly. She became aware of the large sums of money that a waste management company was spending to influence legislation.

Waites was shocked by the fact that many legislators did not know the contents of the bills before voting. Instead, they simply followed the party leadership's directions on how to vote. She began to share her observations with the press in order to inform the public. Some legislators objected to her openness with the media and were concerned that their actions might be reported. Waites believed that votes were public record and the public had the right to know what was going on in the legislature.

Even before the FBI sting became pubic in July of 1990, Waites introduced an ethics bill, H.3521. Four legislators objected immediately to the bill which killed it on February 16, 1989. She introduced four additional bills dealing with ethics and campaign finance reform, none of which passed. Among those who objected to her bills were House members who were later convicted of public corruption. Representatives Bob Kohn and Danny Winstead were convicted in the Lost Trust prosecutions. Charles Sharp was convicted years later as Commissioner of Agriculture for taking bribes to protect cock fighting in Aiken County.

After Lost Trust became public, many legislators jumped on the ethics reform bandwagon and introduced reform bills. In the 1991 session, there were 25 ethics reform bills introduced in the House and 49 in the Senate. Many of the bills dealt with limiting the amount and source of campaign contributions that could be made. It soon became obvious that many of the Republican members wanted no limits or high contributions limits while many of the Democrats favored limits which were low.

The compromise over the conflict about campaign contribution limits was reached by Rep. Tim Rogers (D-Richland) and Rep. David Wilkins (R-Greenville) when Rogers wrote Wilkins proposing limits of $3,000 per donor to statewide campaigns and $1,000 per donor for all other candidates, including legislators. Waites also wrote Wilkins a letter proposing limits.

CHAPTER SIX

LOST TRUST GOES PUBLIC

First FBI Raids

At 11:00 a.m. on Wednesday, July 18, 1990, forty FBI agents began the raids of the offices of 18 members of the South Carolina House of Representatives in Columbia. The FBI executed search warrants to seize evidence of bribery and related crimes, thus opening the public phase of Operation Lost Trust, the largest public corruption scandal in state history.

The sudden descent on the 18 offices was sprung without any prior warning and the target representatives were shocked to learn that their campaign finance reports had been seized by federal agents.

Lost Trust triggered a flood of media coverage from newspapers, radio, and television, not only in South Carolina, but all over America. The scandal would create an upheaval in the political class of state government and politics that would continue from 1990 for years. And the criminal prosecutions would continue from August, 1990, until the final two retrials and convictions in 1999.

Personal Service of Subpoenas Is Tip-off

Most of the 124 House members whose records were subpoenaed by the FBI did not receive personal service but had their records seized at the House Ethics Committee office in the Blatt Building, the House office building on the State House grounds. The FBI came to the office and took the records from the staff on duty at the time.

However, a select few were also served personally with subpoenas. This was a tip-off that they were the special focus of the Operation Lost Trust probe, and all of those who were personally served were soon indicted. Another tip-off was that only one state senator, Sen. Bud Long (D-Horry), was personally served with a subpoena. He was the only senator indicted in the probe except for Sen. Rick Lee (R-Spartanburg) who by that time was already cooperating with the FBI prior to his indictment and guilty plea.

Among those to take personal service was the worst of the lot, Rep. Jack I. Rogers (D-Marlboro), Speaker Pro Tem, whose law office was served in Bennettsville. However, he was not there, but in Berlin, Germany, at the time, and his records were seized from the office by the FBI.

On the first day of the public part of the probe, FBI agents not only seized records of all House members, but also interviewed some of them about their campaign funds even before demanding campaign documents.

Speaker Bob Sheheen admitted his surprise, saying he had no direct knowledge of the probe, but only conversations with two members who had talked to the FBI. He said the two had been asked about taking cash donations and whether they had reported them on disclosure forms. Sheheen said his first impression was that the agents were trying to find out if any cash was given as a bribe. Sheheen also said that, "The one guy who said he took the money was of the opinion that he wouldn't be surprised if pictures had been taken." But Sheheen said his records were not taken by the FBI.

However, John Barton, head of the criminal division of the U.S. Attorney's office in South Carolina, would not confirm or deny that a grand jury probe was in progress. His name was on the subpoenas. "This one is close to the vest," Barton told the media.

Personal Service

Among the others taking personal service of subpoenas were Reps. Thomas Limehouse (R-Dorchester), Larry Blanding (D-Sumter), Luther Taylor (D-Richland), Frank McBride (D-Richland), James Faber (D-Richland), Paul Derrick (R-Lexington), Tim Wilkes (D-Fairfield), Daniel Winstead (R-Charleston), and Robert Kohn (R-Charleston). All of them would be indicted.

Sen. Bud Long said that he took a personal service on July 18, but would not have to turn over his records until 10 a.m. on July 19, 1990. However, Long's records had not been seized from the Senate Ethics Committee files, unlike those of the House. Long told the press, "I don't know what it's about.... They've asked for my records of campaign contributions and gifts."

Subpoenas Reveal Operation Lost Trust

Next, FBI agents served subpoenas on all of the 124 members of the South Carolina House of Representatives on the afternoon of Wednesday, July 18, 1990. This expanded the public phase of the massive investigation conducted by the FBI and the U.S. Attorney, Bart Daniel, into rampant corruption at the State House in Columbia. And the media was quick to grasp the fact that they had a huge scandal to cover in the coming months involving "an apparent investigation of cash contributions for legislative favors," as *The State* wrote in its July 19, 1990, front page story on shocking revelations.

Ethics Committee Chairman, Pat Harris (D-Anderson), expressed complete surprise when federal agents came to the office and demanded records for all House members since 1988. "I have no idea what this is about," he exclaimed to *The State* reporter, Clark Surratt. But Surratt did, writing, "The investigation apparently involves possible violations of the Hobbs Act, a federal anti-corruption law that prohibits legislators' acceptance of money or gifts in return for promised performance." Surratt went on to say, "The lawmakers were targets of a federal sting operation in which a person acting as a lobbyist offered money for legislative favors," according to an attorney he interviewed.

Pat Harris told reporters, "I've been on the Ethics Committee since its inception (in 1975) and we never have had anything like this." Of course, Harris, as chair of the committee, might also have said that since its creation by the 1975 Ethics Act, the committee had done almost nothing to enforce the feeble provisions of the Act.

The FBI asked for records of members for 1988, 1989, and 1990, including statements of economic interest listing all gifts of $100 or more from lobbyists along with their business dealings with public entities. The other document seized for each member was their campaign finance disclosure form listing all donations received of over $100 and the use of that money.

S.C. Ethics Act Worthless

The FBI seizure of legislative records and the July 18, 1990, first revelations of Lost Trust by the media triggered attention of television and the press to issues of the use of money by special interests to buy votes a the State House. On July 20, 1990, John Crangle, of Common Cause/South Carolina, responded to inquiries from *The State* by saying that he was not surprised that legislators were in trouble over taking campaign contributions. Blaming the 1975 Ethics Act's failure to limit or regulate campaign money, Crangle said of such laws, "They're so relaxed that almost anything is permitted as far as contribution amounts and uses."

The 1975 Act only required candidates to keep records of contributions over $100 and to file records within 30 days after elections. But the money could be used for any purpose. Crangle said, "You can buy clothes, cars, wedding gifts, football tickets—any use is legitimate.... You can also walk off with it." He pointed out that federal campaign laws are much more restrictive, banning corporate donations, and limiting the amounts given from any one source to any one recipient.

Many states had more restrictive laws than South Carolina. Crangle pointed out that, "What's defined as legal in South Carolina is defined as illegal in a number of other more progressive states and should be illegal in South Carolina." He also said that South Carolina's 1975 Ethics Act, which allowed unlimited campaign contributions, gifts, and conversion of campaign funds to personal use facilitated "de facto bribery" and that the fake law "creates an atmosphere of tolerance for improper and unethical behavior."

Ron Cobb as "Wheeler Dealer"

The central character in the morality play of Operation Lost Trust which opened to the public on July 18, 1990, was Greenville lobbyist, Ron Cobb, drug dealer turned FBI sting agent. Although Cobb had flown beneath the radar of the press for years, he had been on the radar of state and federal law enforcement for months before he was exposed as the chief FBI informant who had handed out intended bribes to legislators in 1989 and 1990.

Former Rep. Lewis Phillips (D-Greenville), described Cobb, his former desk mate when Cobb served as a House member from Greenville in the years 1977 to 1984, as "a well-liked young man" before Cobb lost his 1984 re-election bid. But another witness, a lobbyist who knew Cobb, said of Cobb, "He has a reputation for being a high flyer and a wheeler-dealer."

At first, federal authorities would not tell the media if Cobb was cooperating with them in the probe. But interviews by *The State* clearly found that legislators believed that Cobb was in the middle of the scandal. 5th Circuit Solicitor, James Anders of Columbia, said that Cobb was a focus of a criminal investigation being conducted by his office. Anders told the media that Cobb had received checks which may have been used to pay off legislators.

Cobb's Web Entangles Politicians and Operatives

A distracting factor was the relationship of Cobb to the former Executive Director of the S.C. Petroleum Marketers Association, David W. Reed, who was fired on March 15, 1990, after the discovery of missing money at the Association. Reed was known to have a relationship to Cobb and that Cobb had received money from the Association. Reed's conduct had triggered an investigation and a person in that probe told of Cobb's involvement with the betting bill.

Cobb's relationship with the Alpha Group, for which he registered as a lobbyist for the first time in January, 1990, was a puzzle to journalists. Rumors held that the FBI had approached Cobb and proposed to fund an effort to pass the betting bill. But Cobb did not file required disclosure forms on his work with the Alpha Group, even while he did file for his other clients.

Sen. Theo Mitchell (D-Greenville), underfunded as the Democratic candidate for governor in 1990, told the media that Cobb had asked Mitchell to come to Cobb's office in the AT&T building where Cobb said that his client would make a campaign contribution to Mitchell, but wanted support for the betting bill. Mitchell said of the encounter, "I told him I couldn't take a donation with any strings attached. I said my vote is not for sale."

Cobb Dangles Cash

Cobb's offerings of money to legislators in return for their vote on the betting bill was quickly perceived by reporters as the key to the exploding scandal. And they soon identified the major legislators who would be indicted shortly afterward, starting on August 24th of 1990.

One of the first suspects was former House member Tee Ferguson (D-Spartanburg), who had just been seated on the circuit court bench in late May, 1990. Speaker Bob Sheheen revealed that Ferguson had come and told him that he had refused money from Cobb and that Ferguson had also told the State Law Enforcement Division (SLED) of Cobb's offer.

Paul Derrick (R- Lexington) made surprising admissions only a day after the sting went public when he told *The State*, after the subpoena of his campaign records, that he had taken money from Cobb at the Town House Hotel, but that Cobb did not solicit Derrick's vote on any bill. Also, Derrick said the amount was $1,000 in cash, adding, "It is unusual to get a cash contribution. It's the first one I've ever got." Derrick also revealed that Rep. Thomas Limehouse (R-Charleston) had told him that he, too, had taken $1,000 from Cobb.

Other legislators identified as having taken money from Cobb included Rep. Robert Brown (D-Marion), chair of the House Labor, Commerce, and Industry Committee, who took $1,000 from Cobb. The committee reported out the betting bill in April, 1989, but it did not pass the House.

When the first word of the federal probe hit on Wednesday, July 18, 1990, the centrality of Ron Cobb was obvious. He was known to be soliciting votes for the betting bill and handing out money in 1989 and 1990 to legislators.

Even so, his friend, Robert Kohn (R-Charleston), denied Cobb was assisting federal agents in a sting probe of legislators. Kohn told reporters on July 19, 1990, that, "I don't buy that; I don't believe it." Kohn was one of those known to have been questioned by the FBI and to have had his campaign records subpoenaed by the government. What was not known in the first days of the public phase of the scandal was that Kohn had also been an FBI sting agent during the 1990 session of the General Assembly and that, in fact, he had been collaborating with Cobb in catching legislators ever since Kohn himself was fingered by the FBI for corruption and drugs.

Ron Cobb's Dubious Career

At the time that Lost Trust became public, Rob Cobb was 41 years old. He had been elected to the House in November, 1976, as a Democrat from Greenville at the age of 28. At the time, he listed his occupation as a builder and real estate agent. He had a wife and two children and lived in Piedmont. He had graduated from Carolina High School but did not attend college.

Upon his election to the House, he was elected chair of the freshman caucus and he was appointed to the Labor, Commerce, and Industry Committee, the same committee that would later handle the betting bill when Cobb was pushing it with cash payoffs. He also served on the State Housing Authority where he met Sen. Jack Lindsay (D-Marlboro), one of the most powerful and, as it turned out, one of the most devious legislators in the state.

Then his marriage fell apart in 1984 and he was defeated badly in his re-election bid.

Cobb then turned to lobbying state government. His income in 1989 was only $30,000, but in 1990, it was reported as $89,000 in the forms he filed with the Secretary of State's office. In 1990 he added a client, Hitachi Data Systems, which paid him $46,760, and he had five other clients who paid a total of $42,300. He also listed as a client the Alpha Group, but filed no disclosure form, indicating the Group was pushing the betting bill. One lobbyist registered for the betting bill was Elliott D. Thompson, who said that the bill was used as a front by the government sting because, "there's a lot of money involved, and it involves interstate business."

Gov. Campbell's Statement on Lost Trust

Reacting to the exploding scandal on July 19, 1990, Gov. Carroll Campbell admitted in his first news conference on Lost Trust that he was first briefed on the investigation by federal authorities on the evening of Tuesday, July 17, 1990, the day before the first batch of campaign records were seized by the FBI from the House Ethics Committee office in the Blatt Building.

Campbell tried to reassure the reporters and the citizenry of South Carolina that, "I think that the vast majority of the members of the General Assembly are honest and hard-working and dedicated people." Even so, he had to admit, "There are some that will spoil the whole barrel for everybody by their actions, and we are seeing them in the papers now and we will see more."

Campbell took some assurance that it seemed no one party or race was targeted in the probe, saying, "It is very important to me to note that this investigation evidently cuts across all lines—political, racial and otherwise—and therefore there should never be any question raised about it being anything other than aimed at each individual because of that individual's action."

Lost Trust Sting Fits National Pattern

The FBI sting in South Carolina fit into the mold used by federal authorities in other states. Such stings offered bribes which were captured on videotape. And they were conducted over an extensive period of time targeting state and even federal officials.

U.S. Attorney, David Levi, of California commented on July 20, 1991, just after the revelation of Lost Trust, that, "Bribery is a crime of intent, but hearing the words that are spoken, it can be difficult to prove. That's why we like to do sting operations."

One of the most notorious stings was directed toward Congress in the early 1980s when Operation ABSCAM stung members of the House using fake Arab businessmen handing out bribe money for favors to congressmen, including Rep. John Jenrette of South Carolina.

In California, the FBI set up fake shrimp processing companies and federal sting agents offered payoffs to members of the General Assembly to vote for bills purportedly advocated by the companies. Those taking bribes were prosecuted for violating the Hobbs Act, the same as in South Carolina. California state senator, Joseph Montoya, was caught on videotape taking $3,000 and went to prison for extortion, racketeering, and money laundering.

Videotapes and fake companies were deemed essential to prove that money was taken to buy votes, otherwise the culprits could claim the money was a legal campaign donation, not a bribe. Distinguishing bribery from the common practice of pressuring lobbyists to attend campaign fund-raisers for legislators was difficult in practice.

The FBI sting operation in South Carolina also was similar to that not only of California, but also of Tennessee, which had preceded Lost Trust by only five years. In all three states, federal investigators learned of corrupt dealings between lobbyists and high level public officials and launched sting operations aimed at bribery involving legislation. Lobbyists' use of cash payoffs was the central fact pattern in the probes conducted in the three states.

Assistant U.S. Attorney of Tennessee, Robert Washko, told *The State* that, "We had real bona fide lobbyists here convicted. It appears there may be a lot of similarities in what they're looking into (in South Carolina)." The Tennessee probe was called "Operation Rocky Top" and focused on illegal gambling and corruption between top state officials and persons associated with bingo or pari-mutuel betting. In the "Rocky Top" sting, more than 40 persons in Tennessee were indicted, including a state representative who was implicated in a scheme involving illegal bingo and efforts to get his help. In that case, the legislator approached the lobbyist, but the lobbyist agreed to help the investigation against the legislator.

A bingo operator also pleaded guilty to bribery for trying to pay a state senator $10,000 to vote for a betting bill. The senator then helped the investigation. Two public officials were suspects, but killed themselves.

Alpha Group—FBI Front

The sudden revelation of the hitherto unknown Alpha Group funding the bribes handed out by Ron Cobb caused I.S. Leevy Johnson, a prominent Columbia attorney representing Rep. Frank McBride and Rep. James Faber in Democratic seats in Richland County, immediately to conclude that the Alpha Group was a fake created by the federal investigators. Although Johnson did not comment about the role of his clients in the growing scandal, campaign disclosure forms revealed that Faber took $1,100 and McBride took $1,100 from the Alpha Group.

A member of the Georgia Horse Foundation, Miles Gammage, told the media that he had never heard of the Alpha Group. And South Carolina's most prominent lobbyist for the pari-mutuel bill, Elliott D. Thompson, said he knew nothing of the Group either. Rep. Tim Rogers (D-Richland), a major supporter of the betting bill also confessed ignorance of the Alpha Group. But Rogers told the media that he had reported to law enforcement that he had heard rumors that, "some members, and now former members, had engaged in activity that I considered to be illegal or unethical." And Rep. David Beasley (D-Darlington), future governor of South Carolina (1995-1999), said that as to the Alpha Group, "My suspicion is that it is a dummy setup by the FBI."

The Alpha Group, which lobbyist Ron Cobb served as the sting agent, was an FBI front organization, handing money to Cobb with which to bribe legislators purportedly to promote the Alpha Group's goal of passing a pari-mutuel betting bill for horse racing. But the Alpha Group was not known to any other lobbyists who represented real organizations trying to pass pari-mutuel bills in other states or even in South Carolina. Furthermore, the same legislators who took bribes from Cobb acting for the Alpha Group had never heard of the Alpha Group before 1990, and some of them who took bribes did not know there even was an Alpha Group, let alone that it was the source of the bribe money they took.

Rep. Paul Derrick (R-Lexington), a golf partner and friend of Ron Cobb, said that he never heard of any Alpha Group until the sting was announced in the newspapers on July 19, 1990. Derrick denied that Cobb had asked him to vote for the betting bill. When asked by reporters if Derrick's meeting at the Town House with Cobb was a sting, Derrick said, "It is very discouraging to think that someone who was a friend...would intentionally try to set you up. I would hope that is not the case.... Why have I been singled out, with my reputation for being 100 percent straight-arrow?" In fact, at his trial, it would be exposed that Derrick was notorious for demanding free handouts from lobbyists at the State House. Derrick would be convicted at trial in 1991 and on retrial in 1999 of taking bribes from Ron Cobb.

Sen. Rick Lee Takes $3,000

Sen. Rick Lee (R-Spartanburg) took $3,000 in cash from Ron Cobb at his office on the 11th floor of the AT&T Building across from the State House near the end of the 1990 session. He said that even though he had never received a contribution so large and did not usually get cash contributions, he raised no questions about taking the money in $100 bills from Cobb when he pulled it out of his desk drawer and handed it to Lee. Lee called the cash from Cobb as "his business."

Sen. Marshall Williams (D-Orangeburg) remembered that, at the end of May, Sen. Lee had asked him to move the betting bill from the Judiciary Committee which Williams chaired. At that point, the bill had gone nowhere for 15 months. "He was anxious, for some reason, to get the bill on the roster." The committee did move the bill to the Senate, but it failed to pass before adjournment on June 6, 1990.

Lee explained himself to the media by saying that he had supported the betting bill for a long time, alleging, "It was something I'd worked on for 18 months.... I'd already committed to that long before Ron's interest." But other committee members said that Cobb was trying to buy support for the bill.

Lee had a campaign debt of $17,000 leftover from his 1988 race and wanted money from lobbyists to pay it. He did, in fact, report the $3,000 from Cobb on his disclosure forms with the Senate Ethics Committee. Lee pointed out that under South Carolina's meaningless campaign finance laws it was legal to take unlimited cash from lobbyists.

Officials React to Lost Trust

As soon as the U.S. Attorney announced the sting, politicians reacted. "It came like a damn bolt of lighting," said Sen. Marshall B. Williams, the most senior member of the Senate after 44 years in the body. The sting shocked the whole of state government, but most of all, the General Assembly with its cozy symbiotic relationship between legislators and lobbyists. The utter lack of laws limiting the flows of money from special interests and their lobbyists to public officials was obviously a major factor in the scandal which needed to be corrected by new legislation in the coming 1991 session. Lost Trust made the point as sharply as possible.

The chief sting agent, Ron Cobb, was known to frequent local nightspots with powerful legislators like Sen. Jack Lindsay, a major fixer at the State House. This made the issue of regulation of lobbyists more central than it had ever been. Rep. Malloy McEachin (D-Florence) noted that in the 1990 session, his efforts to pass a lobbyists regulation bill had failed and legislators felt there was no public concern or pressure to do anything. McEachin said at the time he told a colleague that the only thing that would move the bill was a scandal. Reacting to the sting, he said, "I think that we've got more than that. This shatters what little confidence people had."

Officials Shamed by Lost Trust

Speaker Bob Sheheen quickly realized the sting was a game-changer: "The institution is damaged; the process is damaged; the professions (legislator and lobbyist) are damaged.... It tends to confirm in the minds of skeptics what they thought was the truth."

Sen Ernest L. Passailague (D-Charleston) added: "The perception with the public is that the whole system stinks.... The public bundles us all together as rotten." Passailague would be a major advocate for ethics reform in 1991.

The vulgar spectacle at the State House was worsened when 5th Circuit Solicitor, James C. Anders, revealed that Rep. Ennis M. Fant (D-Greenville) was trying to set up an escort service at the State House in the 1990 session. Furthermore, Rep. James Faber (D-Richland) was known to be under investigation for questionable business dealings in the town of Eastover, S.C.

Speaker Sheheen, who had tried and failed to pass reform bills prior to the scandal admitted: "I'm mad because some people who participate in the process have chosen to abuse the process and have found willing participants on the other side."

Unanswered Questions Raised by Lost Trust Revelations

Journalists and the public were struggling to figure out what was going on with the Lost Trust corruption scandal. The government released just enough information by serving subpoenas for legislative records to trigger speculation based on fragmentary evidence.

It did come out within the week after the first subpoenas were executed that lobbyist Ron Cobb, not yet known as an FBI sting undercover agent, was a suspicious central figure in what was happening and that he was involved in more than one dubious transaction with multiple officials and some private actors.

Several legislators told the media that they had contacts with Cobb and a mysterious man, "Mr. Williams," who was represented as a client of Cobb from Atlanta. It eventually came out that "Williams" was, in fact, an FBI sting agent working with Cobb.

Sen. Theo Mitchell, Rep. Paul Derrick, and Sen. Rick Lee were exposed as having had contacts with Cobb in which they were offered money. Derrick admitted taking $1,000 while Lee said he took $3,000. Three other legislators conceded they had taken contributions from Cobb or the Alpha Group.

It also came out on July 20, 1990, that David W. Reed, a former lobbyist for the oil jobbers, had given Cobb $20,000 for some unknown reason. On that date, Reed was indicted for improper uses of funds of his former employer, the S.C. Petroleum Marketers Association.

Editorial on Scandal

Within a week, *The State* published an editorial on July 24, 1990, confronting the scandal entitled: "Federal probe shatters confidence in Capitol." The editorial read: "The 1990 General Assembly toyed with a bill that would have prohibited candidates from converting campaign contributions to personal use and...the measure died as did one mandating more detailed disclosure of lobbying expenditures."

The editorial went on to say: "Common Cause, the citizens watchdog group, has correctly pointed out the existing laws invite de facto bribery and create an atmosphere of tolerance for unethical behavior." The editorial further said of Common Cause: "It has served the public interest well this year and in previous years by lobbying hard, albeit, in vain, for needed reforms in laws governing campaign finances and lobbying."

The State called upon the General Assembly in the 1991 session to attack the reform problem at a time when more corruption would be exposed. "In six months, we should know more clearly how many rotten apples are in the barrel" and what reforms were needed "in the interlocking issues of campaign funding and lobbying reform."

Common Cause Reform Proposal

In fact, the day of the editorial, Common Cause/South Carolina released a nine point reform proposal demanding that the General Assembly clean up the mess: "The public—the citizens, taxpayers and voters—of South Carolina will no longer tolerate the irresponsible refusal of the General Assembly to clean up its own house." The nine reforms demanded in the July 24th proposal included:

1. A total ban on cash campaign contributions.

2. A total ban on conversion of campaign money to personal use by candidates.

3. A ban on campaign contributions made during the legislative session.

4. A ban on campaign contributions from corporations, partnerships, law firms, and labor unions (out of their own funds).

5. A limit on contributions from political action committees (PACs) of $250.

6. Full disclosure of all campaign contribution receipts and expenditures 10 days before the elections.

7. A tax on all contributions to pay for enforcement of regulations on campaigns.

8. Comprehensive lobbying regulations legislation including transfer of lobbyists' regulation to the State Ethics Commission.

9. Partial public financing of legislative and statewide campaigns, with funds generated by a tax on campaign contributions, unspent campaign funds, and a tax check off for taxpayers.

Chief Suspects Identified in Lost Trust

As rumors and more disclosures of suspects spread, some of those under fire tried to avoid blame. House Speaker Pro Tem Jack I. Rogers (D-Marlboro) refused to answer media questions but it was known that he had hired attorneys Robert Simpson and Tim Rogers (D-Richland), both of Columbia, and that he had tried in April, 1990, to push the betting bill. Rep. Robert B. Brown (D-Marion) admitted he took $2,500 from Cobb at the Town House but denied a deal to support betting.

It also became known that the government had subpoenaed not only the records of 170 legislators, but also of 15 others. Cobb was also increasingly reputed to be a sting agent who handed out money to legislators while the FBI videotaped the bribery as evidence.

The question also arose as to whether Cobb was running the sting to avoid prosecution on his income taxes.

The antics of Jack I. Rogers especially provoked attention because on April 12, 1990, he had led an energetic attempt to leapfrog the stalled betting bill, which had languished for a year, over other contested bills on the agenda by adjourning debate on them to get to the betting bill. But Speaker Sheheen recognized Rep. Mike Fair (R-Greenville) on an anti-abortion bill and blocked the betting bill. On the other hand, Rogers had co-sponsored the betting bill before Cobb started to lobby for it.

Rep. Brown also had supported the betting bill since the start and denied taking cash later on from Cobb to vote for it. While saying, "I have nothing to hide, and I don't think I've done anything illegal," Brown sent his secretary to the House Ethics Committee to amend his campaign disclosure form to show a $2,500 donation from Cobb.

Suspect Number One—Jack I. Rogers

By late July, 1990, the centrality of Jack I. Rogers to the scandal was sensed by reporters who continued to focus on his actions. Ron Cobb was reported to have requested that two other betting bill lobbyists give Rogers campaign money. Elliott L. Thompson and Ernie Nunnery reported that around April 1, 1990, they met with Cobb who sought money for Rogers, including $2,000 from Cobb and $1,000 from the pro-betting Tourism Council represented by Thompson and Nunnery. Both refused to give cash and their contacts with Cobb ended. And at the time it was not known, but increasingly suspected, that Cobb's pro-betting Alpha Group was an FBI front, which of course, it was.

The fact that Rogers appeared under special scrutiny by the federal government worried the House. Speaker Bob Sheheen remarked, "When you've got people involved in leadership who are under scrutiny, that reflects not only on them but on the institution." House leaders and 30 members were reported as talking with Sheheen about calling a meeting to damage control the crisis. The problem was, Sheheen said, "you don't know what's coming next." Sheheen denied rumors he was working with federal authorities.

It was also known that Rep. Tee Ferguson, about May 1, 1990, told Sheheen he had been offered cash campaign money by an unidentified lobbyist and, on the advice of Sheheen, had rejected the money by certified letter sent to Cobb, which Cobb turned over to the FBI.

CHAPTER SEVEN

NEW SCANDALS PROLIFERATE

Verinder Scandal Embarrasses the Prosecution

While the Lost Trust scandal was just getting started, other scandals were breaking out. On July 25, 1990, Highway Patrol Chief, Col. J.H. "Red" Lanier, a 34 year veteran, announced his 5 day suspension relating to his intervention in the arrest of the FBI's chief agent in Columbia, Special Agent Fred Verinder, for drunk driving. 5th Circuit Solicitor, Jim Anders, said he was studying whether to charge Verinder for DUI and Lanier for obstruction of justice. A trooper, Johnny E. Osborne, testified that Lanier had asked him to help Verinder. Gov. Carroll Campbell had directed the State Law Enforcement Division (SLED) to gather evidence because he was concerned that Lanier's actions and Verinder's traffic stop might taint a federal probe of payoffs at the South Carolina Highway Department.

The FBI Chief Agent in Columbia, South Carolina, was stopped on S.C. 277 by State Trooper W.D. Herring on March 22, 1990, on grounds of driving under the influence of alcohol. When the head of the Highway Patrol, Col. "Red" Lanier, found out about the stop, he got the trooper to reduce the charge to speeding, the trooper later testified. The trooper was Johnny Osborne.

On or about April 12-13, 1990, state officials found out about the stop and Lanier's intervention in the case after Lanier casually mentioned the arrest in a conversation with the head of the State Law Enforcement Division, Chief Robert Stewart. Then on April 17th, Stewart met with Gov. Carroll Campbell and told the governor about the incident. Stewart and Campbell decided to seek legal advice from high level sources in the federal government as to what to do about the matter. Campbell then met with Stewart and Lanier on April 23rd and told them to report the facts to the U.S. Attorney.

At the time, Verinder was investigating suspected bribery and payoffs at the South Carolina Highway Department. Even so, U.S. Attorney Bart Daniel, having just taken the job, called Washington at the insistence of Gov. Campbell to inform officials in the federal government about the Lanier and Verinder situation. 5th Circuit Solicitor James Anders and S.C. Attorney General Travis Medlock advised Daniel before he made the call.

After the elapse of some three months, federal agents arrived in Columbia July 25th to investigate, but only after a delayed response by the U.S. Department of Justice Office of Professional Responsibility.

Then in late July, Gov. Campbell ordered Chief Stewart to take the deposition of trooper Osborne who said that he did, in fact, arrest Verinder for driving under the influence and called a wrecker to tow Verinder's car. But then Col. Lanier came to the scene, after a call from Verinder, and the trooper then wrote a speeding ticket instead of the DUI citation.

Verinder-Lanier Scandal Worsens

The media dug into the way in which Lanier intervened with one of his state troopers to prevent Verinder from being arrested for drunk driving. Sen. Sherry Martschink (R-Charleston) told the media on July 25, 1990, that she knew that Lanier had bragged about his ability to block persons from being charged with drunk driving even if they were driving drunk. Martschink had been trying to pass a bill which would have moved control of the South Carolina Highway Patrol to the State Law Enforcement Division to which Lanier had strongly objected.

A local radio station, WOMG, claimed to have found evidence in a trooper's log book to show that Lanier had also told the arresting officer to drop charges against a person who had been stopped for drunk driving and that that person was a high school friend and former banker of Lanier.

Verinder-Lanier Scandal Worries Gov. Campbell

Public outrage over the special treatment accorded the FBI Special Agent Fred Verinder by Col "Red" Lanier of the Highway Patrol triggered the decision of Verinder to remove himself from the probe of corruption at the Highway Department.

Gov. Carroll Campbell held a news conference on July 26th urging that federal investigators report the facts of the probe to the public as soon as possible to discourage the spread of false rumors.

In fact, callers were bombarding the headquarters of the Highway Patrol and complaining of favored treatment for Verinder.

Campbell said there was no agreement with the Executive Director of the Highway Department, Joe Rideouette, as to exactly what to do. Lanier had imposed on himself a one-week suspension which Rideouette thought sufficient and felt that Lanier should not be terminated.

Multiple Probes Going On in 1990

At his news conference in Columbia on July 26, 1990, a week after the story about Lost Trust broke, Gov. Carroll Campbell bemoaned the large number of probes in progress in South Carolina. He worried that the growing number of scandals would discourage new businesses from expanding or even locating in the state. Development chairman, Dick Greer, had told reporters that economic development prospects had "expressed alarm" at the breaking FBI expose of corruption at the State House.

"This is making me sick," Gov. Campbell told the media. Surrounded by multiple probes and exposés, he could not stop the scandals from being exposed but he deplored the constant din of new reports of corruption crises popping up around the state, saying, "What is hard to deal with is disclosure by drips. It's approaching the time to turn the faucet wide open." He said he had hoped the federal probes would move more rapidly and get to the bottom of the corruption as soon as possible. Campbell also said that federal authorities might help clear up the situation by revealing more about the matters being investigated.

Campbell was joined at his news conference by SLED Chief, Robert Stewart, who provided little information about the SLED probes being conducted which the governor had mentioned to reporters. The Chief did say that the link between Cobb and the misused money at the S.C. Petroleum Marketers was being examined. Campbell said that while SLED was probing Cobb, it found out that the federal authorities were also doing so.

Gov. Carroll Campbell worried that the sting scandal was already hurting economic development. He noted a few days after the revelation of Lost Trust that Hitachi Corp. had just postponed plans to build a $150 million factory in Greenville, although State Development Chairman, Dick Greer, who would later be convicted of cocaine violations, denied that the project had been scrapped. Greer conceded that two other industrial projects expressed alarm over stories of public corruption. Hitachi was a client of Cobb.

The Greenville News broke stories in late July that Cobb had been arrested for cocaine and started helping the FBI and, further, that Cobb was providing cocaine and prostitutes for legislators.

Campbell told reporters that he asked U.S. Attorney Bart Daniel to speed up the probe because it was hurting the state's image. Campbell deplored the continuing series of new scandals.

He deplored the wild rumors triggered by news stories that were accurate at the start. Campbell hoped the federal authorities would tell more. He further worried over a SLED probe of Santee Cooper over dubious coal purchases at the state-owned utility and a probe of money from the Petroleum Marketers Association related to Cobb. And a Patriot's Point Authority hotel and marine complex failed, triggering another SLED probe. Campbell acknowledged that a SLED probe of Cobb accidentally ran into an FBI probe of Cobb and SLED backed off.

Major Investigations in Progress in 1990

At the time of Gov. Carroll Campbell's news conference on July 26, 1990, there were eight known probes of public corruption and abuse of office in progress in South Carolina. They were published by *The State* as including:

Operation Lost Trust—the FBI was known to be interviewing and investigating 15 state legislators for public corruption.

Highway Department—Federal authorities were probing possible corruption involving the department and its personnel and construction companies.

Agent Verinder-Col. Lanier—the FBI internal affairs division was studying the fact that Col. "Red" Lanier, Chief of the S.C. Highway Patrol, had directed a state trooper to not write a drunk driving ticket on FBI Special Agent Fred Verinder, who was in charge of FBI units probing Lost Trust.

Patriot's Point—SLED was looking into financial and legal issues relating to the corruption of a hotel and marina complex at Patriot's Point which failed.

S.C. Petroleum Marketers—SLED was digging into the use of $100,000 of discretionary funds of the S.C. Petroleum Marketers Association by its former executive director.

Rep. Ennis Fant—5th Circuit Solicitor James Anders was studying Rep. Fant's operation of an escort service out of his office in the Blatt Building on the State House grounds. (He would be convicted in Lost Trust.)

Rep. James Faber—SLED was probing his sale of a backhoe to the Town of Eastover. (He would later be convicted in Lost Trust.)

State Aeronautics Commission—SLED was concluding a probe of the Commission which had resulted in 10 charges against the former director.

Verinder-Lanier Scandal Grows

Public outrage over the apparent ticket-fixing done by Col. "Red" Lanier for FBI Special Agent Fred Verinder triggered unexpected fall-out. While officials having authority over the matter seemed puzzled about what to do, public indignation swelled.

On the one hand, the Chairman of the S.C. Highway Department board, Charles B. Dalton, told the media that he thought the self-imposed five day suspension of Col. Lanier was enough punishment for him and that the public reaction was more directed against Agent Verinder. Dalton thought that the opinion of the general public and the General Assembly would influence the outcome of the crisis. And Highway Department Executive Director, Joe Rideoutte, tried to minimize the matter, saying that the suspension of Lanier was enough and that he did not think the ticket-fixing would hurt the Operation Lost Trust probe.

But some in the public were not satisfied. Three calls from two men came in to the S.C. Highway Patrol office on July 27, 1990, threatening the lives of both Col. Lanier and Director Rideoutte. In response, the Patrol posted two officers at the entrance of the Highway Department office on Park St. in Columbia and SLED agents were put on standby status. Rumors even floated that a bomb threat had come in.

Mitchell Blames GOP Plot for Lost Trust

Sen Theo Mitchell (D-Greenville), the Democratic candidate for governor against Gov. Carroll Campbell, said on July 26, 1990, that the FBI sting at the State House was inspired by the Republican interests in South Carolina. Mitchell alleged that Gov. Campbell knew about the sting before it went public by more than one day as Campbell had said in a news conference on July 26th.

In fact, Campbell had told the news conference that he had some awareness of the probe already in 1989 but did not get precise information until the evening of July 17, 1990, the day before the first subpoenas for legislative records were served. And Campbell denied Mitchell's charge that the sting was inspired by the Republicans. Even Democratic national committeeman, Donald Fowler, said there was no evidence behind Mitchell's allegations and noted that one of the biggest payoffs given by Ron Cobb went to Republican Sen. Rick Lee. S.C. Democratic Chair, Albert McAlister, said he had reason to suspect the FBI was moved by partisan pressures.

Dick Greer, Campbell's economic development chairman, was at pains to deny a rumor that Ron Cobb had bribe money stashed on Greer's boat at Hilton Head Island. Greer called Mitchell's allegations of the probe as a partisan sting "absurd." Of course, in fact, Greer had been doing cocaine with Ron Cobb even as Greer sent new clients to Cobb for help.

Cobb Exposed As Financial Basket Case

The financial fortunes of Ron Cobb at the time of Operation Lost Trust were unstable. Although his lobbying income in 1990 was $90,000 the year before it was only $30,000 and that was the year in which Cobb was stung by an FBI informant in a drug deal and went undercover for the government as a sting agent, thereafter being paid large sums by the FBI.

Cobb's second wife left him and filed for divorce, but not until after she had shot herself on July 18, 1988, and run up $120,000 in medical bills which exhausted the Cobb's marital assets. And he supported his wife until May, 1989.

But Cobb tried to hide his problems. And he appeared to his associates as a different person than they thought they had known.

Rob Cobb became a lobbyist soon after he lost his 1984 re-election and he easily connected with the former legislators he had known during his eight year tenure in office. Cobb also became more cozy with the lobbyists at the State House and more dependent of their financial support. One State House observer said that Cobb spent too much time on helping other lobbyists and not enough time and effort on building ties with legislators.

His financial situation had deteriorated in the early 1980s as his brief legislative career was coming to an end. In 1982, his business, Cobb Builders, Inc., was in trouble and his wife left him and divorced him in 1983. Ten days later he remarried. These disasters hurt his standing, said Molony, "he really lost his prestige," and his life hit bottom.

Then in 1985, Cobb opened Government Business Associates, Inc., a lobbying shop. By 1988 he had landed nine clients, including state associations of professional groups such as the trial lawyers and chiropractors. Hitachi Data Systems hired Cobb as its lobbyist in 1988 and by 1990 Hitachi was Cobb's biggest client, paying him $46,760 for the year plus expenses of $12,640. Development chairman, Dick Greer, a poker partner, old friend and golf buddy, steered clients to Cobb, including Greenville businessmen who needed to pass a tax break bill. Even so, Cobb failed to build a solid client base and remained a "pick-up" or contract lobbyist who was hired off and on to do some lobbying work.

Cobb's Struggle With Failure

Hit hard by adversity in the 1980s, including the failings of his business, his marriage, and his political career, Ron Cobb seemed to rebound and to act like a fun-loving, joking, and back-slapping type of man. He also hid his private life and sorrows from his friends and the politicians he dealt with. One friend said of Cobb, "He's not going to let on a lot about his life."

What was known about Cobb as the Lost Trust scandal became public was that he was suspected of being an FBI sting agent who bribed politicians at his office at the AT&T Building and at his suite of rooms at the Town House Hotel. Some rumors held that Cobb was a crook. And there seemed to be evidence that he was a snake who bit his friends in a sting operation. But others thought more highly of Cobb; one fellow lobbyist said of him, "He's probably the most loyal person you ever met. When he's your friend, he's your friend for life."

One thing was obvious about Cobb—he loved being a big shot at the State House. A lobbyist said, "He loved being in the General Assembly. He was devastated when he was defeated." In fact, his tenure in the House seat for District 25 was brief—he was elected in 1977 and he was defeated in 1984.

His abilities were limited and some were dubious. Lawyer Michael Molony, who was staff council for the Labor, Commerce, and Industry Committee on which Cobb served, said of him as the sting broke, "He was smart, but I wouldn't say he was intelligent. He had tremendous street smarts."

Editorial Points to Lawyer-Legislator Fees

On July 29, 1990, *The State* published an editorial focused on the contentious issue of legislators who were also lawyers with clients who had business before the General Assembly, presenting possible conflicts of interest. *The State* thought that Lost Trust emphasized the problem of legislators getting money from interest groups and their lobbyists, which was similar to legislators getting money directly from the interest groups for real or fictitious legal work.

The issue of lawyer-legislators was foremost in the mind of Gov. Carroll Campbell, one of the very few non-lawyers to become governor of South Carolina to that point in time. Campbell rejected the call of Common Cause/South Carolina for a special session of the Legislature to pass the ethics reform bill, but *The State* argued that Campbell "acted wisely rejecting Common Cause's request for a special session.... Gov. Campbell said the 1991 General Assembly should go beyond reform of lobbying and campaign finance laws and address the lawyer-legislator issue as well." *The*

State praised Campbell for his wisdom saying, "He and a lot of other people correctly perceive that as an area of greater abuse than those alleged in the FBI's sting operation."

<u>*The State* Editorial Predicts Reform Bill in 1991</u>

The State editorial of July 29th agreed that action was needed to deal with multiple problems and predicted "the General Assembly will move with shame-faced alacrity next year to tighten disclosure laws governing campaign financing and lobbying." But, the more important corruption was the "conflicts of interest that involve much more money than the amounts appearing in the fed's current sting operation."

The editors pointed out that "It is reasonable to assume that many lawyer-legislators or their law firms are on lucrative retainers from businesses and individuals which would have an interest in countless pieces of legislation that flow annually through the General Assembly." Lawyer-legislators taking fees from those pushing bills might have serious conflicts of interest but they were hidden from public view because "there is no requirement that a lawyer-legislator or any other lawmaker, for that matter, disclose either the client or the amount received...that data should be available to the public."

To address the lawyer-legislator problem and the secrecy surrounding it, "The Legislature that convenes in January [1991] must move with purpose and dispatch and enact whatever stringent reforms are needed to restore confidence in the General Assembly."

<u>List of Suspects Identified by *The State*</u>

By late July, *The State* had fingered most of the suspects and all of them listed in an article of July 29, 1990, except Rep. Tim Wilkes, would be convicted. The list included all of the following:

Rep. Ken Bailey (D-Orangeburg)..........$450 from Alpha Group
Rep. Paul Derrick (R-Lexington)..........$1,000 from Cobb
Judge Tee Ferguson (ex Rep. D-Greenville)........Offered bribe money from Cobb
Sen. Rick Lee (R-Spartanburg)..........$3,000 from Cobb
Rep. Frank McBride (D-Richland)..........$1,300 from Alpha
Rep. Danny Winstead (R-Charleston)..........$200 from Cobb client
Rep. Larry Blanding (D-Sumter)..........$100 from Cobb
Rep. James Faber (D-Richland)..........$1,100 from Alpha
Rep. B.J. Gordon (D-Williamsburg)..........$1,000 from Cobb Associates
Rep. Tom Limehouse (R-Dorchester)..........$1,000 from Business Associates (a former Cobb lobbying group)
Rep. Jack I. Rogers (D-Marlboro)..........$250 from Cobb

Rep. Robert Brown (D-Marion)..$2,500 from Cobb
Rep. Ennis Fant (D-Greenville)...$1,300 from Cobb
Rep. Robert Kohn (R-Charleston)...$150 from Cobb
Sen. J.M. "Bud" Long (D-Horry).......................Amount unknown as of 7/29/1990
Rep. Tim Wilkes (D-Fairfield)..$1,500 from Cobb

The State reported that the FBI had contacted all of the above but may also have contacted others, which, in fact, it had. The list did not include Rep. Donna Moss (D-Cherokee) and Rep. Luther Taylor (D-Richland) who would later be indicted and convicted.

Impact of Sting on State House

Senior Writer, Clark Surratt, of *The State*, published an article in the July 29, 1990, edition of the paper speculating on the likely consequences of the Operation Lost Trust scandal on State House politics. He pointed out that the most common reaction to the spreading cloud of the crisis was fear and even horror. He also predicted that there would probably be a change in the behavior and practices of legislators and lobbyists. At the time, Surratt did not know how long the scandal would last and how many people would eventually be implicated.

He wrote that, "Gov. Carroll Campbell last week practically proclaimed this era as political doomsday for South Carolina and its people." The governor had even stated that a prospective new business was scared off by the negative publicity about the state's government and political system.

With remarkable prescience, Surratt saw the scandal would cause big changes. Surratt thought that in the end, "The federal investigation of Capitol corruption may serve as a big dose of laxative for a bloated system of too-close relationships between people with money and those who make decisions that might be influenced by that money."

Noting that "most lawmakers have been moaning and groaning," there was at least one who thought the sting was a blessing in disguise. Sen. Sherry Martschink (R-Charleston) told the media, "The revelations bring out into the open practices that should never happen."

Surratt also felt that the FBI exposure of State House corruption would have further benefits, predicting that "Chances will never get better than in January to get action rolling on reform of campaign disclosure, lobbyist disclosure, and ethics law. Everybody is saying that, including us pontificators in the news media."

He also believed that even without any new ethics legislation, "Special interest groups will be careful for a while about the people they hire to look out for them in the State House." He thought that special interests would "be careful about how much money they contribute to campaigns."

Surratt Predicts Reforms After Scandal

Based on his long experience covering state government and politics, veteran *The State* writer, Clark Surratt, saw that changes would surely result from the inchoate Lost Trust scandal which would get much worse in later 1990 and 1991. Some of the changes seemed almost inevitable, but the degree of reform was hard to predict in such a fluid situation at a time when no indictments had yet been handed down for the public to see.

Surratt did see that, in the future, legislators would be more circumspect about the lobbyists they dealt with. And "there will also be a period when there won't be as many parties and a lot less wining and dining at nightspots and dayspots. State House folks will be talking about a new era."

Surratt also tried to "look two or three years down the road" and made some clairvoyant predictions, saying that in the near future, "Strict ethics laws will be in place. South Carolina may even be looked to as an example."

But he worried that there would be decline and "the cycle will start over again." Surratt thought that "Ron Cobb won't be there by name—presumably. But his spirit will live on in some lobbyists...[and] willing legislators will be around who are ready to relax and enjoy a good time with the folks with the money to pick up the tab." In time, "Some big businesses...will shell out the money to influence the Legislature. By this time, everybody will have figured out how to get around those nice new laws. Or probably just ignore them. And South Carolina will be back to normal."

Poll Negative on Lobbyists

The Associated Press published a poll in *The State* on July 29, 1990, that asked respondents what they thought of lobbyists. At the time, of course, the people of South Carolina were increasingly sensitized to the activities of lobbyists at the State House because of a lobbying reform bill being dragged down by opposition in legislative hearings during the 1990 session and by the erupting scandal of Lost Trust revelations.

The *AP* poll showed that 81% of the respondents thought that state legislators sometimes voted the way lobbyists wanted them to in exchange for gifts from lobbyists. Only 9% thought they did not. The poll also showed that 51% thought that lobbyists had too much influence on shaping laws in the South Carolina General Assembly. Only 10% thought that lobbyists had too little influence, and 27% thought they had the correct amount.

The poll also posed a question about the problem of campaign finance of candidates in state government and found that 89% of respondents thought the state should limit the amount of money candidates could spend while only 7% opposed and 4% had no opinion.

Lanier Case Provokes Anger

The State published a survey on July 29, 1990, about the public's view of the way in which Col. "Red" Lanier had intervened to prevent FBI Special Agent Fred Verinder from getting a drunk driving ticket. The reaction was by a margin of three to one that the public thought that the five days suspension of Lanier from his job as head of the South Carolina Highway Patrol was too little punishment.

One respondent to the survey said, "Off with red's head." Another thought that Lanier had been a bad example to young people. Still another thought the problem was more widespread remarking, "There is too much corruption in the state and not enough punishment for those higher-ups who are digging in the public pocket and causing others to be punished for things that the higher-ups are getting away with."

But Lanier had his defenders, too. One told pollsters that, "I think we need more people to get involved with helping friends. I don't drive drunk, but we do need friends helping friends and in that respect, I think Col. Lanier did his job." Another woman blamed the trooper, not Lanier, saying the trooper was "just a smart aleck."

The general reaction was negative with 1,572 respondents favoring more punishment for Lanier and only 467 who thought the suspension of Lanier was sufficient.

Scoppe Outs Culture of Town House

In a penetrating Sunday article in *The State* of July 29, 1990, staff writer, Cindi Ross Scoppe, painted a lurid picture of the dim, smoke-filled rooms of the Town House Hotel, a place of legislators and lobbyists eating, drinking, playing poker and doing deals every year during the legislative session from January to early June.

"The place fills up by 6, and liquor mixes easily with talk of politics, of coalitions and deals, as the men who write the laws mingle with the lobbyists who make sure the laws are written the way they want." After the schmoozing is finished "the crowd clears out, by 8 or so, action moves to the hidden, all-night poker game, where the men who run the state of South Carolina, such as Sens. Jack Lindsay and Ed Saleeby, State Development Board Chairman, Dick Greer, and House Speaker turned lobbyist, Rex Carter, are regulars."

As Jack Lindsay was in poor health in the legislative session of 1990 and would die in January, 1991, he did some of his legislative work at the Town House Hotel where agency heads and legislators went to deal with him. But almost everybody who was anybody in state politics came to the hotel as well to be seen and work the system. "It's like a college dormitory—of graduates," observed lobbyist Tom Smith, a former state senator, adding, "If you hang out there long enough, you'll run into 80% of the people in the General Assembly. Everybody's down there for something."

The Town House as a Center of Political Fixing

Ron Cobb had a big presence at the Town House Hotel. Not only did he hang out in the bar and play poker with legislators and other lobbyists, but he actually lived there and in 1990 and 1991; his rent was paid for by the FBI while he lured legislators to his suite of rooms and bribed them one after the other. Scoppe observed, "Ron Cobb turned the place to be into the place to be stung." Cobb would often sit at a corner table in the hotel bar and even before the poker games started he would go to his suite and hand out money.

"At the Town House, most of the people have some sort of connection with government and can talk about things and laugh...that's why most people go," said lobbyist Steven Smith. The hotel was the place to get things done quick, unlike the State House with its tedious committee meetings and long sessions where the real business of framing and passing laws was seldom being done.

Some 15 or more legislators had rooms at the Town House during the session. They would talk and deal at breakfast in the restaurant and pick up again in the evening after leaving the State House. "Business is conducted there," said Rep. Robert Kohn, a resident himself who had already been indicted for corruption and turned into an FBI undercover sting agent. As a disclaimer, Kohn told Scoppe, "I'm not trying to imply that it's illegal, unethical or immoral. It's transactions that could stand the scrutiny of federal agents or even the press. Of course, I'm also sure that stuff goes on that ain't supposed to happen." And, of course, he knew there was.

Not all legislators and lobbyists and their hangers-on congregated at the Town House, mostly the older crowd. The younger set hung out at Beau's, a bar and restaurant at the Radisson Hotel on Assembly Street across from the State House. It was at Beau's that big money special interest groups kept open bar tabs for all legislators and their friends to eat and drink as much as they liked without paying. An it was at Beau's, it would later be exposed, that hard drugs were being dealt from behind the bar by one of the bartenders.

The Town House Hotel was a parallel state legislative committee room where the bills were cooked up and passed before they were done at the State House. One legislator told Scoppe, off the record, "Budget bills have been worked out there. Conference committee disputes. Major legislation. You establish the dialogue to get it worked out. Sometimes 30 minutes in the Town House lounge can accomplish more than 30 days at the State House."

Yet one legislator, Doug Hinds, a Georgetown Democrat, explained that he lived at the Town House because "it's almost a family atmosphere." It would soon be shown to be a crime family.

Town House Deal-Making, Drinking, and Poker Playing

But the family atmosphere at the Town House had some bad family secrets. One House member told Scoppe on background that as the poker games progressed into the night and the liquor consumption soared along with the poker pots, "I've seen times when there's eight at the table playing and you have to wait in line to get a spot at the table. One time there was $1,000 on the table, (a lobbyist) won the hand and he was so drunk he didn't even know he won."

Not all legislators went to the Town House and some loathed the place and the good ol' boys that played politics and poker in a cloud of smoke and a flood of booze. Sen. Sherry Martschink, one of the very few women in the Senate, expressed her disdain, telling Scoppe that she stayed away from the hotel "because of the parties, the poker, the other activities that went on around the Town House—the wine, the women, and song, minus the song." Perhaps the senator had heard that Cobb dealt in money in his lobbying business.

But Robert Kohn took off his hat as an undercover puppet of the FBI and defended what was going on and said, "It's not a heavy drinking kind of crowd. They're more interested in doing business and getting information as opposed to chasing women and getting drunk."

The legislative life for all too many at the State House was a life of ease, even pampering, by not only the staffers but even more so by groveling lobbyists always eager to please. Cindi Scoppe sketched the day of such persons, writing of the culture of living off the lobbyists, "The opportunities are endless, if you're a lawmaker. Spend an hour or two in the morning making laws, then head over to the Capital City Club or the Alumni House (at the University of South Carolina) for lunch. A lobbyist tags along and picks up the tab. Or perhaps you'll see a lobbyist across the room and just tell the waitress to charge it to him." Of course, the easy life stretched into the afternoon and the legislator would "then [go] out to the Columbia Country Club for a round of golf. Again, take a lobbyist along, and he'll pay. Or charge it to a lobbying firm."

But the day was still not done, for more mooching off the special interests was in store. "After the late-afternoon Town House visit, it's often out to a reception, put on just about every night by some group that wants to influence the Legislature. Many of those are held right down the hall (from the bar at the Town House). Then, if you're not invited to the poker game...drop by Beau's, where you can shag and drink and, if you didn't get enough to eat at the reception, pick up dinner. Courtesy of the lobbyists who showed up." Sen. Martschink observed that sweetheart dealing between legislators and lobbyists was not confined to the Town House, remarking, "That is not where it stops or starts."

At a House subcommittee meeting on a lobbyist reform bill in the 1990 session, not long before the sting went public, lobbyists said that they did not know how much money they spent on individual legislators because legislators just told waitresses to put the bills for dinner and drinks on the tab for lobbyists to pay.

The manager of the Town House said that he did not allow open bar and restaurant tabs, but one legislator said that he went to the hotel for entertainment and "When I got up to leave, I asked the waitress for the check, and she said, 'Oh, it's already covered.'" Another legislator said, "You don't pay for anything at the Town House. Lobbyists pay for it." The waitresses knew who the legislators were and put the bills on the tab. At the end of the night, the lobbyists split up the bills.

But not all lobbyists thrived in a world of parasites and some tried to avoid going to the watering holes like Beau's so that they would not be hit with big bills run up and dumped on them by free-loading pols. This was true of lobbyists for clients who did not have the money to try to buy access and influence.

Fourth Circuit Errs in *McCormick* Case (896 F. 2d 61 (4th Cir. 1990))

The 4th Circuit Federal Appeals Court gravely blundered when it changed precedent and handed down a ruling on February 12, 1990, which soon would have an impact on the Lost Trust bribery cases which were filed in South Carolina starting on August 24, 1990. The ruling applied to a case in which a West Virginia official was charged with violating the Hobbs Act, the same statute which would be used to indict all but Donna Moss of the 18 legislators caught up in bribery charges in Lost Trust. The new case misconstrued 18 U.S. Code Section 1951 (Hobbs Act).

The court wrongly held that in Hobbs Act cases alleging bribery, "Prosecutors do not need an explicitly 'quid pro quo' exchange to prove that money received was never intended to be a legitimate campaign contribution." Prosecutors hailed the case as making it easier for them to prove that defendants took bribes. The U.S. Attorney in Memphis, Tenn., opined that the main fact to be proved in bribery cases was "whether this public official is using his position to get money."

U.S. Supreme Court Upsets Convictions with *McCormick* Decision

The prosecution of Lost Trust cases in the last half of 1990 and before May 23, 1991, was based on the ruling of the 4th Circuit in the *McCormick* case which was handed down in 1990. But the decision was appealed by the U.S. Department of Justice to the U.S. Supreme Court which quickly reversed the 4th Circuit ruling.

In *McCormick v. U.S.* (500 S.C. 257 [1991]), the Supreme Court held on May 23, 1991, that it was not enough to show that an alleged bribe-taker merely had taken money as the 4th Circuit had held. The Supreme Court ruled that the prosecution must also show that the person taking the alleged bribe took some official action in return for the consideration received. A showing of quid pro quo was essential to convict.

As the first cases tried in Lost Trust under the Hobbs Act had been based on the erroneous ruling of the 4th Circuit in the *McCormick* case, the prosecution had not even tried to prove a quid pro quo and, of course, had *not* proved a quid pro quo. The instructions of the trial court had not told the jury that it was essential to prove a quid pro quo and the jury did not use the quid pro quo standard to decide to convict.

The Supreme Court ruling, therefore, made all of the early convictions at trial defective prior to May 23, 1991, and subject to successful appeals with the result that retrials were ordered on appeal for those found guilty under the defective standard.

Summary of Major Points of *McCormick v. U.S.* Case
500 US 257
May 23, 1991

Opinion of the United States Supreme Court

"We thus disagree with the Court of Appeals' holding in this case that a quid pro quo is not necessary for conviction under the Hobbs Act when an official receives a campaign contribution.

The receipt of such contributions is also vulnerable under this Act as having been taken under color of official right, but only if the payments are made in return for an explicit promise or undertaking by the official to perform or not to perform an official act. In such situations, the official asserts that his official conduct will be controlled by the terms of the promise or undertaking. This is the receipt of money by an elected official under color of official right within the meaning of the Hobbs Act."

Summary of Major Points of the *Hobbs Act*
(18 U.S. Code Section 1951)

(a) Whoever in any way or degree obstructs, delays, or affects commerce or the movement of any article or commodity in commerce, by robbery or extortion or attempts or conspires to do so, or commits or threatens physical violence to any person or property in furtherance of a plan or purpose to do anything in violations of this section shall be fined under this title or imprisoned not more than twenty years, or both.

(b) As used in this section—

(2) The term "extortion" means the obtaining of property from another, with his consent induced by wrongful use of actual or threatened force, violence or fear, or under color of official right.

Summary of Major Points

Racketeer Influenced and Corrupt Organizations Act

(18 U.S. Code Section 1961)

As used in this chapter—

(1) "racketeering activity" means, (a) any act or threat involving murder, kidnapping, gambling, arson, robbery, bribery, extortion...which is chargeable under State law and punishable by imprisonment for more than one year; (b) any act which is indictable under Title 18, U.S. Code Section 1961;

(3) "person" includes any individual or entity capable of holding legal or beneficial interest in property;

(4) "enterprise" includes any individual, partnership, corporation, association, or other legal entity;

(5) "pattern of racketeering activity" requires at least two acts of racketeering...and the last of which occurred within ten years...after the commission of a prior act of racketeering activity.

RICO Prohibited Activities

18 U.S. Code Section 1962

(c) It shall be unlawful for any person employed by or associated with any enterprise engaged in, or the activities of which effects interstate or foreign commerce, to conduct or participate, directly or indirectly, in the conduct of such enterprises affairs through a pattern of racketeering activity or collection of unlawful debt;

(d) It shall be unlawful for any person to conspire to violate any of the provisions of subsection (a), (b), or (c) of this section.

RICO Criminal Penalties

18 U.S. Code Section 1963

(a) Whoever violates any provision of section 1962 of this chapter shall be fined under this title or imprisoned not more than 20 years...and shall forfeit to the United States...

(3) Any property constituting or derived from, and proceeds which the person obtained, directly or indirectly, from racketeering activity...in violation of section 1962.

Interview
Cindi Ross Scoppe

By Eva Moore and John Crangle
July 28, 2014
Columbia, S.C.

Cindi Ross Scoppe

Cindi Ross Scoppe wrote as much or more than any other journalist in South Carolina about Operation Lost Trust and the ethics reform effort. She was a staff writer for *The State* newspaper in Columbia, S.C., during the time that the scandal was revealed and played out in guilty pleas, trials, convictions, appeals, retrials, and convictions. Scoppe refused to testify for the prosecution and was jailed for contempt by Judge Falcon Hawkins in 1991. She is currently the Associate Editor of *The State*.

Interview

Cindi Ross Scoppe graduated from college in 1985 and joined the news staff of *The State* in the fall of 1986. One of her major areas of assignment was state government and politics. She spent considerable time at the State House during the legislative sessions from 1987 onward during which she attended sub-committee, committee, and floor proceedings of the General Assembly. She also interviewed numerous public officials and activists involved in state government during Lost Trust.

Scoppe became suspicious that there were corrupt dealings in state government during the period before Operation Lost Trust was exposed, but she had no idea that the corruption was so commonplace as was later revealed by the scandal.

Once the scandal broke, the task of covering it became very difficult because there were so many criminal defendants, public officials, and others involved and because events had to be covered both at the State House and at federal courthouses in Columbia, Charleston, and Richmond, Virginia. *The State* devised a strategy for coverage which assigned certain reporters to specific tasks. For example, Margaret O'Shea was assigned to cover court proceedings while Jeff Miller was assigned to write about the U.S. Attorney's office and the indictments handed down by the grand jury. Cindi Scoppe was assigned to write explanatory articles probing what was actually going on at the State House and in state government and politics. Other reporters were assigned to various tasks as needed.

The State also adopted a strategy of investigative reporting which relied on reporters' access and contacts with marginal figures on the edges of the Lost Trust scandal who knew what was going on in the scandal. But some of the most important players in Lost Trust also provided off-the-record information, including U.S. Attorney Bart Daniel, who informed Scoppe of matters related to the scandal.

Scoppe's view of the causes and background of Operation Lost Trust was that corruption was facilitated and even fostered by the fact that the 1975 Ethics Act was extremely permissive allowing unlimited campaign contributions, free gifts, and unrestricted dealings between legislators and lobbyists at the State House. In time, the line between free gifts and bribery was blurred so badly that officials and lobbyists lost all sense of the difference between the normal symbiotic dealings of legislators and lobbyists and outright corruption and misuse of public office.

One of the questions that remains puzzling to Scoppe is the question of how widespread corruption actually was in state government and how many culpable parties were not caught in the Lost Trust sting and prosecutions. There seemed to be a focus on a number of small fry legislators who were lured into taking money from Ron Cobb, but, perhaps, some bigger fish got away.

A question that Scoppe does not seem to have a disapproving view of is whether the use of the pari-mutuel betting bill was a legitimate way for the FBI to try to capture corrupt officials. Scoppe says that the federal investigators and prosecutors had to have an issue involving interstate commerce to assert federal jurisdiction and that the betting bill provided such jurisdiction. She does not seem to feel that it was unfair to use the betting bill as the issue with which to catch officials committed to the bill before they took money from Ron Cobb.

Scoppe is not sure whether the FBI aborted the sting process of giving money to legislators to obtain their vote on the betting bill. One rumor at the time was that the federal authorities became concerned that so many state legislators were quickly taking bribes and that a very large portion of the General Assembly was going to be indicted for bribery and that the legislative process would be disrupted by the removal of so many officials charged with crimes.

Scoppe believes that the ethics reform movement relied on two theories of reform in framing its proposals for new ethics legislation—disclosure and limitations. Some reformers stressed the need and value of passing disclosure laws to force the exposure of campaign contributions, uses of political money, and conflicts of interest affecting officials. Another view was that some behavior of lobbyists and officials was so bad that it should be outlawed completely. In time, the two approaches were combined in the 1991 Ethics Act.

CHAPTER EIGHT

THE LOST TRUST SCANDAL SPREADS

Dick Greer Exposed by the Media

Although it would not be exposed by the federal authorities until after the November 6, 1990, general elections, Gov. Carroll Campbell's chief confidant, old friend, and chairman of the board at the South Carolina Economic Development Office was gradually found out by the media. On July 31, 1990, *The State* reported that Dick Greer had been steering business to FBI sting agent and super lobbyist, Ron Cobb.

Greer had been a key ally of Campbell since his entry into the State Legislature and had chaired Campbell's campaigns for the U.S. House and for governor in 1986 and 1990. He was well positioned to help Cobb, his cocaine using buddy, get lobbying clients among the businesses seeking legislation and regulatory favors.

Nucor Corp., a large steel firm, acknowledged on July 30, 1990, that Greer had suggested that Nucor pay Cobb a $100,000 lobbying fee to help resolve an electricity rate dispute. Greer reacted by denying any wrongdoing and said that he was afraid the media would mislead readers and "take something I did that I thought was honorable and right and make it sound sleazy." Greer then alleged a conspiracy against Campbell, saying, "I am firmly convinced that there is a group, a person or someone trying to use me and my friendship with Ron Cobb to get to Carroll Campbell. They are using every contact I ever had with Ron Cobb to make it appear like guilt by association."

Ken Iverson, president of Nucor, said that Greer contacted Nucor in June, 1988, and said that the company needed a lobbyist to handle its rate dispute with Carolina Power and Light, but Iverson did not recall at the time if Greer had suggested Cobb. But Nucor did not hire Cobb and used its general manager to deal with the rate matter. *The State* reported on July 31, 1990, that Iverson and the plant manager met with Gov. Carroll Campbell and Greer on July 1, 1988, to promote an effort to reduce the rate increase. The two from Nucor did not ask advice on how to deal with the rate issue. Greer then called later to offer gratuitous advice about hiring Cobb. Iverson thought the call from Greer was unusual and that it was strange for Greer to suggest that the regulatory issue be handled by legislation.

Nucor sources told the media that Greer had mentioned a fee of $100,000 to be paid to Cobb. Then Cobb called Nucor and said that he was following up on Greer's recommendation of him. But Nucor declined to hire Cobb because, one Nucor official later said, "he was not the kind of person Nucor wanted to be associated with."

Given the later revelations about Ron Cobb in July, 1990, a former Nucor official remarked, "We decided that we did not want to be involved with Mr. Cobb at all, and we were disturbed that the chairman of the State Development Board would have recommended him. In the light of what is happening now, we are very glad to have dodged that bullet."

In response to the sudden exposure of the Nucor account of Greer's behavior, Greer at first denied that he had ever referred anyone to Cobb, but after a series of five telephone calls with *The State* in late July, 1990, Greer admitted that he had contacted Nucor and said that *The State* would probably find out about other cases in which he had also recommended Cobb's lobbying services.

Gov. Carroll Campbell's office released a statement saying that the governor thought that Nucor had contacted the Board for help and that, "The governor has complete confidence that Dick Greer has explained this incident to the best of his recollection." It was well known that Campbell and Greer were long-time friends and business associates before Campbell's election in 1986 which discounted Campbell's words.

Greer tried to justify his recommendation of Cobb by saying that his memory was hazy until refreshed by *The State*. He had previously said that, "I did not refer anybody to Ron Cobb. I never accepted a dollar from Rob Cobb. I never gave a dollar to Rob Cobb. I never did anything but my job. People came to me with problems, and I tried to help them work their problems out if it was for the economic good of the state. That's all I ever did. If legislation was involved, I might have recommended a lobbyist. I might have recommended Rob Cobb."

Greer Denied Probe Focused on Him

Under increasing public scrutiny and suspicion, State Development Board Chairman, Dick Greer, denied that the Lost Trust investigation was directed at him. On July 31, 1990, Greer denied knowing of any probe of his ties with corrupt lobbyist Ron Cobb.

It was well known that Cobb had been subject to state drug investigations since 1988 and that he had ties to Greer. Greer admitted, "Ron Cobb was my friend—is my friend" in a meeting with the editors of *The State* newspaper at that time. Then he added that, "Everybody talks about him like he's dead because nobody can find him." Greer also complained that some of those being examined by the FBI were "trying to throw the heat off themselves by saying, 'You think I'm in trouble, look at Dick Greer. Look at what he did with Ron Cobb.'" Full of self-pity, Greer protested that "people like me get smeared with the same brush he is."

Greer asked for a meeting with the editors after *The State* reported that Greer had recommended Ron Cobb as a lobbyist to Nucor Corp. to help with an electricity rate dispute and had also recommended that Nucor pay Cobb $100,000 for the job. Greer admitted that he did recommend Cobb to Nucor but denied proposing any lobbying fee amount. Nucor officials said that Greer had stated a figure for Cobb's help in its struggle with Carolina Power and Light.

Cobb's Tentacles Exposed

The Charlotte Observer reported several legislators had said they were approached by Rep. Bob Kohn in the spring of 1990 on behalf of Cobb, who was promoting the betting bill. *The Spartanburg Herald-Journal* also reported that Cobb was having tax problems with the Internal Revenue Service.

The editors of *The State* wrote on August 2, 1990, that although there was no evidence that Greer knew Cobb used "unsavory tactics" when he referred Nucor to Cobb, that Greer's Development Board should have tried to help Nucor rather than refer Nucor to Cobb. The editorial concluded: "Mr. Greer believes he has been unfairly tarred. Perhaps so. But the chairman's coziness with the lobbyist and his handling of the Nucor incident have damaged his credibility and effectiveness."

The State did not know the full dimensions of the criminality of both Cobb and Greer at the time the editorial was published. It would soon be revealed by the prosecution that Greer not only had dubious dealing with Rob Cobb, but also that Greer had ties to other suspects in the Lost Trust probe, including Sen. Jack Lindsay.

The State editorial did point out the suspicious fact that, "To Mr. Greer's embarrassment, officials of a steel manufacturer, Nucor Corp., said he proposed they hire Mr. Cobb for a whopping $100,000 to push a legislative proposal.... Mr. Greer denies he quoted the fee but concedes he touted Mr. Cobb for the job."

Greer Admits More Dubious Conduct

Gov. Campbell denied any previous knowledge of Greer's advocacy for Cobb, according to Tucker Eskew, the governor's spokesman. Greer eventually admitted that he had, in fact, referred both Tom Roe, a Greenville businessman seeking tax break legislation, and Nucor, to Cobb.

Greer was also at pains to tell the public that he was not a target of the FBI probe into influence peddling. He admitted it was a mistake to refer prospects to Cobb.

Greer also said that he got Sen. Jack Lindsay (D-Marlboro) to help with a resolution against the electricity rate increase. Such a resolution was documented in Senate records of June 21, 1988. But Greer regarded the resolution as a stopgap and that legislation was needed.

The State editors wrote that Greer's referrals to Cobb were a big mistake, "Cobb's influence peddling involved, at the very least, passing out cash to legislators. Cash donations, unfortunately still legal in this state, are suspect enough," and Cobb was handing out bribes. Greer should have been trying to help Nucor himself and his actions "have damaged his credibility and effectiveness."

Cobb as Sting Agent Becomes Apparent

Cobb's close ties with Rep. Luther Taylor and Rep. Bob Kohn were subject of speculation before they were indicted, including questions of whether the three were all FBI sting agents to direct friends to bribe money. Rep. Jimmy Bailey (D-Charleston) said that Kohn had approached him earlier in the year 1990 about a lobbyist who wanted to donate $500 in cash, but Bailey had said he would report it as a campaign donation on his forms. Kohn said the donors did not want the money reported.

Black Caucus members said, off the record, that Taylor had approached black legislators about helping Cobb with the betting bill and that Cobb and Taylor had been close as well as Cobb and Kohn.

Reps. Frank McBride and James Faber admitted that they had been notified that they were targets of the probe. Such letters, Assistant U.S. Attorney John McIntosh said, were notices that the targets were likely to be indicted.

Senators Make Reform Proposals

Within only two weeks it became obvious that the Lost Trust scandal had become a major political crisis and might get much worse in the near future. State public officials did not know how bad it would become, but it was almost certain that state legislators would be blamed by the media and the public.

It was only to be expected that legislative leaders would be forced to take action to make it look like they were not to blame and that they were also trying to clean up the mess. Major political leaders quickly came forward with ethics reform ideas which they said they would push in the 1991 session of the General Assembly set to convene in the following January.

Two of the most powerful senior senators stepped forward on August 1, 1990, and announced that they would take the lead on ethics reform. The two had been the chief obstacles to ethics reform legislation coming over from the House to the Senate in the 1990 session. "I think we've got to do something," admitted Sen. Ed Saleeby (D-Darlington), the chairman of the moribund Senate Ethics Committee. Joining with Sen. Marshall Williams (D-Orangeburg) who had also obstructed the House ethics bill, Saleeby sent a letter to the remaining 44 senators in the South Carolina Senate which outlined their reform package proposal.

The major ethics reform proposals set forward by Sens. Saleeby and Williams only two weeks after Operation Lost Trust became public on July 18, 1990, included some drastic changes in the way business was done at the State House. Williams said he viewed the scandal as "a good opportunity now, while everyone is awake and listening, to go ahead and do something about a problem our government has."

Sen. John Courson (R-Richland) also announced that he would move to ban cash contributions. And in the House, leaders spoke of the fact that Operation Lost Trust made it almost inevitable that major ethics reforms would be promoted in the legislature.

The Saleeby-Williams proposals were the first major legislative schemes put forward after Lost Trust was revealed. The two said they would file their bill as soon as possible to assure early consideration in the 1991 session in January.

The chief reform proposals were:

A ban on all cash campaign contributions over $100.
A ban on conversion of campaign funds to personal use.
New disclosure laws to ensure prompt and accurate reports on the sources, amounts, and uses of campaign funds.
A ban on campaign contributions during the legislative session.
A cap on the amount of political action committee contributions.
A disclosure requirement for lobbyists spending.

Public Outrage Comes Quickly

Public reaction and attention to the growing scandal provoked a letter to the editor printed in *The State* from Carl Dubose of Dalzell, S.C., published on August 2, 1990, in which he accused politicians of trying to stop the FBI probe and protect both politicians and lobbyists. Dubose wrote: "The reins of government have increasingly come under control of lobbyists" and further said that officials at the State House were "puppets" of lobbyists and that the failure of legislators to pass legislation to control lobbyists "has helped to contaminate our state government." Dubose concluded by saying, "This investigation needs to be expanded rather than hastened to end the orgy of graft between powerful lobbyists and elected officials."

Officials Briefed on Lost Trust

The Lost Trust scandal seemed to be exploding like a chain reaction as more reports came out about suspects being probed. In Washington, D.C., the South Carolina congressional delegation was briefed on the scandal by federal authorities at the end of July.

"It's a lot worse than I had thought," said one member off the record. "It was sobering," said Rep. Arthur Revenel, Jr. The briefing by Bart Daniel and Fred Verinder, followed a briefing earlier of senators from the state. Daniel said that he was not favoring any suspects regardless of who they were.

"May God in heaven, the reporters don't know how bad this thing is going to be," said one. "This thing will live in infamy," said another.

Indictments were expected by mid-September. "They told us the worst is yet to come, that the trials will be unpleasant," said Rep. John M. Spratt of York. Rep. Floyd Spence of Lexington said, "they weren't on a fishing expedition."

Members came away with the impression that between 15 and 25 people would be charged. The U.S. Attorney also briefed Speaker Bob Sheheen. In addition, more information that Rep. Luther Taylor had taken money from a Cobb firm had come out.

FBI Videotapes Used to Coerce Pleas

The federal videotapes, in grainy black and white, were subjects of intense interest and were believed to implicate both legislators and agency heads. Federal agents told attorneys that the tapes were damning evidence of payoffs. In one tape, Cobb was seen handing cash and drugs to an official and talking about hiring a prostitute or groupie for the official.

Prosecutors were showing the tapes privately before the three-day grand jury sessions, set to start on August 21, 1990, to elicit pleas and cooperation from legislators. Three attorneys said that prosecutors warned that there would be no lenient deals for defendants after their indictments and that they had better plead and agree to cooperate with the investigation.

Former U.S. Attorney Henry McMaster, then a candidate for Lt. Governor, said that it was common practice to grant full or partial immunity to suspects for cooperation in exposing others: "They start with two or three little people, and they tell on the bigger people, and they keep on telling on up the line.... It's like a forest fire that spreads along one limb and out one branch and then another until you have the whole tree on fire and then the forest." McMaster said it was common practice to show damning evidence before indictments to coerce pleas. And the grand jury was an investigative agency that gathered more evidence of crime as it went along.

Cobb Pushed Tax Break on the Sly For His Clients

The role of Ron Cobb in obtaining a tax break of $8.6 million for some 21 people without the matter being debated and hardly even noticed was exposed by *The State* on August 5, 1990, in an investigative article by Cindi Ross Scoppe and Jeff Miller. It came out that one of the 21 beneficiaries of the tax break had come to suspect that the tax break was obtained by bribery, even though he could not prove it.

Sen. Ernest Passailague (D-Charleston), an accountant, pointed out the suspicious legislation, observing that, "It was clear the way the thing evolved that this was targeted, special-interest legislation aimed at selected people." He observed the progress of the special tax bill even before he was elected to the Senate and took office in 1989. Sen. Tom Moore (D-Aiken) also thought the bill was suspicious, saying that "it did not wash, and it just would not set well." Moore was one of a group of senators who tried to reverse the tax break after he found out about it a year after it passed.

The tax break legislation was the result of an effort to lower the tax rate on capital gains which had been increased due to a change in the federal tax law which South Carolina had adjusted to.

Tax Break Skullduggery of Cobb Exposed

Tom Roe, a Greenville businessman who had a major interest in a business called Builder Marts, sought to get the tax break after he was hit by a retroactive tax increase imposed by the General Assembly. He joined with another Greenville businessman to hire lobbyist Ron Cobb to secure the tax break. Cobb was hired on the recommendation of Dick Greer, Chairman of the State Development Board. They agreed to pay Cobb a fee of $25,000.

The result of Cobb's lobbying was a proviso in the state budget revealed in May, 1988, to allow any person who had to pay state capital gains in 1987 or January, 1989, to pay the older rate of only 2.8%, a benefit which applied to 60,000 people who could save some $22 million in state capital gains taxes. But $8.6 million of the tax break's benefit would go to Tom Roe and another 20 people. The proviso was not debated and almost nobody knew about it. Gov. Carroll Campbell signed the bill, but his office disclaimed that the bill had been originated by him.

After the bill was signed, then Ron Cobb came back to Tom Roe and demanded more money, some $80,000, telling Roe that some people had to be paid off for helping with the bill. Roe refused to pay Cobb any more money but another real estate developer did pay Cobb.

Sen. Frank Gilbert (D-Florence) pointed out the beneficiaries of the bill. Sen. Moore, Sen. John Land (D-Manning), and Sen. Peden McLeod (D-Colleton), then joined to try to repeal the retroactive tax plan. But Sen. Jack Lindsay (D-Marlboro), a close friend of Cobb, tried to keep the tax break. Then the Senate decided to allow everybody who had capital gains from January 1 to June 22, 1987, to have the lower tax rate which also benefited Roe. It later came out that Cobb had bribed Lindsay to smuggle the bill through.

Videotapes on Boat Found Out by *The Charlotte Observer*

By mid-August, it came out that the FBI videotaped Rep. Robert Brown (D-Marlboro) on board a cabin cruiser provided to Ron Cobb by the FBI sting. Cobb moored the 45 foot boat at the Heritage Golf Classic tournament at Hilton Head Island in April, 1990. In addition to Brown, *The Charlotte Observer* reported others on the boat, including Sen. Jack Lindsay (D-Marlboro), lobbyist Steve Smith of the S.C. Savings and Loan League, and Tom Collins, an employee of Hitachi Data Systems and an old friend of Cobb.

Vote on Betting Bill Exposed as Abnormal

It also came out that the betting bill had been polled out of the Senate Judiciary Committee even though only eight senators, rather than the usual ten, had signed the poll in voting for the bill to go forward. Sen. David Thomas (R-Greenville), an opponent of gambling, called the abnormal poll "outrageous."

Jack Lindsay's Last Days

One lobbyist told John Crangle of Common Cause in the lobby of the State House in early 1991 that, "They will never catch Jack Lindsay." Rumors swirling about Lost Trust and newspaper articles made it very clear that the ultimate fixer and legislative strategist was one of the main targets of the federal prosecutors and would soon be indicted. Lindsay had been out of control for many years.

Cobb's dealings with Lindsay ran the gamut from playing cards for money at the Town House to Lindsay pushing bills favored by Cobb in the Senate. In the end, the probe discovered bribery and that Lindsay had taken $75,000 from Cobb to slip through a tax break bill for Greenville businessmen worth $8.6 million.

But Lindsay's health was failing. A heavy smoker and boozer, Lindsay would pull an oxygen bottle on wheels with one hand around the State House with the mask held to his mouth alternating with a cigarette in the other hand, puffing away. Lung disease was eating his life away and in August, 1990, he was confined to his home in Marlboro County, relying on an oxygen bottle 24 hours a day. He needed a lung transplant, but was perhaps too weak to endure the process.

It seemed that Lindsay might be indicted at any time, but he never was, perhaps because prosecutor Bart Daniel expected Lindsay to die very soon, which he did on January 11, 1991.

Interview
Jack Kuenzie, WIS-TV

By John Crangle
September 9, 2014
Columbia, S.C.

Jack Kuenzie

Jack Kuenzie was a news reporter for WIS-TV, an NBC affiliate, during the years 1990 and thereafter when Operation Lost Trust was one of the most important new stories of the time. WIS-TV devoted a great deal of time and attention to covering the scandal and the criminal prosecutions and political reactions to the large number of state legislators and lobbyists who were convicted of corruption, conspiracy, obstruction of justice, drug crimes, and related offenses.

Kuenzie was one of the several WIS-TV reporters assigned to cover various aspects of Lost Trust. Lou Fontana, Jerry Adams, Ed Carter, and David Stanton were also involved in the work of reporting on Lost Trust.

One of the problems faced by WIS-TV was the fact that beginning in July, 1990, when the sting became public, there were so many different events and topics to cover, including news conferences, indictments, trials, pleas, appeals, retrials, and the political reaction to the growing scandal, including the ethics reform struggle at the State House.

Summary of Interview with Jack Kuenzie—WIS-TV

Television had problems covering some aspects of Lost Trust, especially the trials because federal judges would not allow television crews and equipment into the courtrooms. As a result, WIS-TV had to hire artists to do sketches of the judges, lawyers, witnesses and defendants and the artists needed sufficient time to prepare their work for the camera causing delays in production and presentation of the news.

In order to cover Lost Trust and other new stories, WIS-TV divided the assignments up among its reporting staff. Lou Fontana was assigned to cover the State House, where he was in contact with a number of legislators and lobbyists directly involved in Operation Lost Trust or in the political reform movement. Jerry Adams was assigned as a political reporter in the field covering the political fallout of Lost Trust as well as many other news stories. Jack Kuenzie was assigned to cover the workings of the criminal justice system and, therefore, dealt with the prosecutors, lawyers and defendants in Operation Lost Trust cases over the course of the early trials in 1990 and 1991 and the appeals and retrials which lasted until 1999.

WIS-TV relied on walk-in and walk-out footage and interviews of the lawyers and their clients at the federal courthouses in Columbia and Charleston. Crews and reporters would stand ready before and after trials began and adjourned to get footage of the participants, and in some cases, interviews with the lawyers and defendants as they passed into and out of the courthouse building. In some cases, the scenes captured included defendants trying to elude coverage and slip out the back doors. In one such instance, Rep. Luther Taylor (D-Richland), a huge black man of some six feet and seven inches in height, came out of his trial in late October, 1990, and tried to run away from reporters but when he could not escape he put his hand over the lens of a television camera operated by the WIS-TV crew.

In another instance, one of the defendants had a car waiting outside the courthouse to spirit him away after his trial. A WIS-TV cameraman came up to the car just as the defendant was getting in but the driver accelerated the car backwards, hitting the cameraman and rolling him over the trunk of the car onto the pavement. Even so, the camera was running all the while and captured footage which conveyed the spinning and tumbling of the cameraman as he was hit and rolled over the top of the trunk onto the ground.

Kuenzie was impressed by the fact that the U.S. Attorney, Bart Daniel, who handled the prosecutions in 1990 and 1991, was very accessible to the media and granted interview requests liberally. This was also true of his assistant prosecutors Scott Schools, John Barton, Dale DuTremble, and Sherri Lydon who were willing to talk to television and print reporters.

Kuenzie believes that Bart Daniel thought of himself as a clean government crusader who was out to purge South Carolina government of corruption at a time when it was infested with crooked politicians and lobbyists.

Kuenzie is of the opinion that the reason Gov. Carroll Campbell was not contaminated or discredited by Lost Trust was that, in addition to the lack of evidence that he was involved in the scandal, Campbell's reputation in 1989 and thereafter had been greatly enhanced by his handling of the state emergency caused by Hurricane Hugo in late September, 1989. In the crisis, Campbell had called for coastal evacuation in a timely manner and had handled the aftermath of the hurricane providing emergency assistance and relief for those affected.

Even though two close confidants (Dick Greer and David Hawkins) of Campbell were convicted in Lost Trust, the governor was never perceived as having any connection to either the drugs or the bribery which was the core of the scandal. His economic development chairman, Dick Greer, and his assistant, David Hawkins, both pleaded guilty in federal court.

Kuenzie thinks that television coverage of government and politics at the state level in South Carolina was greater during the Lost Trust era than in more recent years. In the 1990s, journalists relied on authorities as sources of information and thought that the information they got from official sources could be believed and used in news stories. But in 2014, television coverage is more episodic and superficial rather than focused and penetrating on the topics covered. Furthermore, current television methodology likes to do stories on little people and their lives and problems.

As to the long term consequences and results of Operation Lost Trust in the years since 1990, Kuenzie believes that the scandal had the beneficial result of causing the General Assembly to pass the 1991 Ethics Act which imposed a number of restrictions on public officials and lobbyists. Kuenzie thinks the establishment of limits on campaign contributions and the ban on lobbyists giving gifts to legislators were badly needed and beneficial reforms which helped to reduce the use of political money and gratuities to influence politicians and policy-making. Kuenzie is concerned, however, by the fact that candidates for state offices are raising a larger proportion of their campaign funds from outside of South Carolina than was the case in previous years.

CHAPTER NINE

LOST TRUST PROVOKES REFORM MOVEMENT

Lt. Governor Forms Ethics Reform Committee

Campaigning for re-election, Lt. Gov. Nick Theodore saw the need to push reform as a way of winning votes and cleaning up the mess at the State House.

On August 9, 1990, Theodore announced he was forming a new ethics reform committee as a way of proposing new ethics and campaign finance reform bills prior to the new legislature set to convene in January, 1991.

The ideas under consideration were banning cash contributions, banning use of campaign funds for personal use, and requiring more disclosure by lobbyists. A proposal to have the state fund primary elections was also on the docket.

The committee included five senators, four House members, and one person each from the S.C. Chamber of Commerce, the governor's office, and Common Cause/South Carolina. Rep. Candy Waites (D-Richland) said all the ideas should be considered and "People are very sensitive right now to this whole situation."

Theodore's group planned to meet once a month until the new session of the General Assembly began in January, 1991 and to present a reform proposal at that time.

Lobbying Exposed

Until Lost Trust exposed lobbyist Ron Cobb as the central figure in a massive bribery and drug scandal, the lobbyists of South Carolina had flown under the radar. But aside from desultory if controversial consideration of a weak lobbying bill in 1989 and 1990, not much was said or done about lobbying and lobbyists.

Cobb and the sting changed that. Lost Trust exposed the big money paid to lobbyists, the free food, free liquor, free trips, and free money and drugs that lobbyists handed out to politicians to buy access and votes. Even so, lobbyists tried to defend themselves against critics. Steve Smith, a lobbyist with the S.C. League of Savings Institutions, minimized the evils of lobbying: "A lobbyist is just like any salesman...a salesman had to be likeable socially." He said that without lobbyists, the state would have to pay for "funding a multimillion dollar research arm of that General Assembly, and then you can kick all the lobbyists out."

Rep. David Beasley (D-Darlington), a governor-to-be, defended lobbyists: "You always have to remember that lobbyists' information is in many respects beneficial to their perspective. And you can take that all into account." Lynn Stokes of Laidlaw, a waste management company, said lobbyists provided information to busy legislators about their side of the issues.

Citizen Anger Mounts

More letters to the editor came in as the scandal spread. Dillard Thompson of Columbia wrote in *The State*, "Concerning the alleged payoffs to state legislators, I have wondered why someone would spend $5,000 to win an election for the Legislature when the salary of legislators is only $10,000 a year." Thompson also blamed Gov. Campbell for being more concerned with the bad publicity to the state: "It seems that his main concern should be how to clean up state government."

R.A. Harris from Camden, S.C. wrote: "I was saddened [at]...the continued decline of the ethics of elected and appointed officials.... The recent assaults upon our sensibilities may provide the impetus for action." Harris blamed the apathy of the people, "cash handouts and the lack of courage of officials and self-serving statements of politicians.

Lee R. Gandee of West Columbia, S.C., laced into both state and congressional members, denouncing traffic ticket fixing by Highway Patrol Chief Lanier and Solicitor Jim Anders for dropping criminal charges against Lanier's son. Gandee hoped the voters would clean house in the nearing elections on November 6th.

House Ethics Reform Rockets Forward

The stalled and weak ethics reform movement which had started in 1989 with a very unambitious lobbying control bill in the House took off almost as soon as the first media exposés about the FBI sting hit the news stands and television screens of South Carolina.

"Leaders from Gov. Carroll Campbell on down seem to be falling all over themselves to get behind ethics legislation. The few lawmakers who pushed reforms in the past wonder where everyone has been," wrote the *Associated Press* in mid-August, only a month later.

Rep. Malloy McEachin (D-Florence) who had fought in vain for lobbying reform the previous eight years mused, "I sure would have loved to have this kind of help eight years ago...even this year." Not much interest had been shown in ethics reform and lobbying reform until the scandal hit.

Speaker Bob Sheheen adverted to the out-of-control lobbyists at the State House, the worst of whom was Ron Cobb, saying, "Everybody's going to be for correcting it." But McEachin pointed to the Senate as a huge obstacle to reform, dismissing the protests of Senate Pro Tem Marshall Williams (D-Orangeburg) who had said he had "always been for reform." McEachin said, "Give me a break," for, in fact, Senate leaders "were like a stone wall" blocking reform.

Reform Tide Mounts in Mid-1990

Sen. Joe Wilson (R-Lexington) said that his suspicions about abuse of office were confirmed by the sting. He said that Senate leaders did not perceive the problem before the scandal as he did.

The State editorialized on August 12 and called for action, blaming the legislature for failing to pass a reform bill in the most recent session ended in June that "would help to prevent the kind of graft targeted in the recent FBI 'sting'." The editors blamed Sens. Marshall Williams and Ed Saleeby for "derailing legislation to subject lobbyists to stricter disclosure and accountability."

But Williams and Saleeby had now repented and "have unveiled a package of ethics and campaign finance reforms," *The State* wrote. "It would ban cash contributions over $100, bar conversion of campaign funds into personal assets... and prohibit campaign contributions during the legislative session." In addition, Sen. Williams wanted to revive bills to require more disclosure by lobbyists, *The State* pointed out.

Rep. Candy Waites (D-Richland) was pushing a campaign disclosure bill and Sen. John Courson (R-Richland) wanted to ban cash contributions. Gov. Campbell promised a reform agenda and Lt. Gov. Nick Theodore convened a committee to propose an ethics package.

The State predicted that the sting would "reveal a level of scandal unprecedented in this century." This would drive reform.

President Holderman in Trouble at USC

Among the proliferating scandals hitting South Carolina in 1990, another shocker was exposed by the media at the University of South Carolina in Columbia. Dr. James B. Holderman, a high-flying celebrity president for 13 years, accepted an honorary doctor of human letters from the University in the late summer commencement of 1990 after his resignation on July 1.

Along with Sen. Jack Lindsay, who was not able to attend because of his lung disease, and professor James Dickey, author of *Deliverance*, Holderman was on the edge of a cliff when they all received honorary degrees at the same time.

Holderman was leaving under a cloud after his lavish spending of university money was exposed by aggressive reporting by the biggest newspapers in the state, including *The Greenville News*, *The Charlotte Observer*, and *The State* of Columbia. Holderman would be convicted later.

Lobbyists' Income and Clients

The major lobbyists among the 260 registered in South Carolina in 1990 earned as much as $205,000 in the case of Ed Yarborough, who had nine clients. Four received $100,000 in round numbers for the year, according to an article in *The State* published on August 12, 1990.

The entertainment budgets of the major lobbyists ran as high as $37,621 in the case of Jerry Beasley of the South Carolina Textile Manufacturers Association. Six lobbyists had budgets of $10,000 or more.

SLED Probes Hitachi Deal

As the Lost Trust scandal got worse, the Budget and Control Board ordered SLED to probe the purchase of Hitachi computers for which Rob Cobb had worked as a lobbyist. The salesman on the deal was Tom Collins and the lawyer was Jack Lindsay. The three had been working for Hitachi to sell Japanese-made computers in spite of the state's buy-American policy.

Records in the Budget and Control Board office seemed to indicate that the specifications written by the state were tailored so that only Hitachi computers met them and that Sen. Jack Lindsay contacted the director of the Highway Department during the procurement process to try to influence the framing of the specifications to favor Hitachi. The sale was for $3.3 million.

IBM complained that the purchase of a computer by the State Department of Education was slanted so that Hitachi made the sale for $1.9 million. Both IBM and Amdahl complained that Hitachi's NAS got a sale to Clemson even though their bid was higher and the equipment was inferior. When questioned about the matter, the salesman for NAS fainted on the witness stand and fell off the stand, ending the inquiry.

Ironically, the state procurement code at issue was written in response to a 1979 procurement scandal involving a free trip to Europe for the person who signed the purchase agreement to buy a computer for the state university.

Lobbyists' Freebies

Shortly after he was fingered in the sting, the media exposed that Rep. Robert Kohn recruited four legislators to go on an all-expense paid trip to New York for which the Teachers Insurance and Annuity Association picked up the tab.

Linda Walker, the lobbyist for TIAA, said that Kohn invited himself and the four to go on the New York trip and the lobbyist felt pressured to pay for it all. "We felt like we were being used, but we couldn't afford to get these people mad at us."

The company provided air fare, rooms for two nights at the Waldorf-Astoria Hotel at $159 per night plus tickets to a Yankees baseball game and to the Broadway musical *Les Miserables*, at a cost of some $2,000 in all.

Walker said that an attorney for TIAA had mentioned a trip to Kohn who served on the House insurance study committee and that Kohn called to say he wanted to go on the trip.

Four of the five who went on the trip acknowledged that they had been questioned by the FBI since the trip, including Luther Taylor, Robert Brown, and Tom Limehouse, and Alex Harvin

(D-Clarendon) also was interviewed, but denied taking any cash when offered by Cobb. All except Harvin and Walker would later be convicted in Lost Trust.

Ron Cobb Gets Immunity

A month after the sting broke, it leaked out that the federal prosecutors had given lobbyist Ron Cobb immunity for helping the sting and that he would also be given immunity by the state. 5th Circuit Solicitor, Jim Anders, told the media that Cobb's cooperation with the sting warranted immunity by the state, but that SLED would interview Cobb in relation to whether Cobb received money from the executive director of the S.C. Petroleum Marketers Association to pay off legislators to pass a 1986 bill favoring oil jobbers. Allegedly, $22,500 of the $110,000 missing from the association account went to Cobb.

Secretary of State Campbell Keeps Lobbyists' Gifts

The State Ethics Commission ruled that the Secretary of State could in the future take no more than $10 from lobbyists or businesses he regulated. Campbell said that in the past he had thought nothing wrong in taking larger amounts even though critics thought otherwise. He said that he would not return any money, unlike Treasurer Grady Patterson, who said he would. The Commission found ambiguities in the law and in regulations in that the law said that gifts could not be taken from regulated persons by the public officials who regulate them.

Jack I. Rogers Fate Dangling

As of mid-August, Jack I. Rogers, Speaker Pro Tem, had not received a target letter. Tim Rogers, his attorney, expressed some hope that his client would not be charged even though his campaign records were seized by the FBI on July 23, 1990.

Rogers was reported to have volunteered to help the probe. At the same time, he hired criminal attorney, Thomas P. Simpson of Columbia.

Rogers was known as an associate of Jack Lindsay, who in turn was a friend of Ron Cobb and Wade R. "Ronnie" Crow, a lobbyist for the S.C. Thoroughbred Association, which was pushing the betting bill. Crow was interviewed by the FBI at least three times.

Cobb's Defenders Speak Up

The U.S. attorney asked the South Carolina Attorney General to excuse the fact that Ron Cobb did not file a lobbyists' disclosure form for the Alpha Group, the FBI sting front handing out bribes for votes on the betting bill.

A letter dated August 13, 1990, from Bart Daniel addressed to the Attorney General's assistant, James G. Bogle, Jr., read: "Please be advised that pursuing this complaint has the potential of compromising and interfering with a federal law enforcement investigation."

Ron Cobb's brother, Herritt Cobb, said of Ron: "He's not a man in trouble," saying that Cobb was helping to catch criminals.

The action against Ron Cobb was one of nine complaints the Secretary of State sent on July 30, 1990, to the Attorney General against lobbyists who failed to file timely disclosure forms. Only Cobb failed to comply with the demand for reports.

Rep. Bob Kohn Goes Down

Rep. Bob Kohn (R-Charleston) called a news conference in Columbia on August 16, 1990, to announce his plans. It was known that he viewed tapes on August 14, 1990, with the U.S. attorney and was trying to work out a plea bargain. The grand jury was set to meet the following week on August 21 to consider evidence against Kohn, who was reputed to be taking drugs, women, and money from Cobb. Kohn had hired no attorney at that time. Rumor was that he would resign.

It was also reported that other lawyers and their clients were reviewing tapes, too, before any grand jury indictments. Prosecutors had said that there would be no plea deals after indictments.

The FBI was believed to have contacted Sen. Bud Long, Rep. Luther Taylor, Sen. Rick Lee, and Rep. Robert Brown. Of course, in the end, they would all be indicted.

At the news conference on August 16th, Kohn announced his resignation after 16 years in the House and also said he had been undercover for the FBI in the vote-buying scandal at the State House. Kohn was reputed to be asking legislators to take money from Cobb. Kohn admitted: "When the FBI wants you to cooperate, you will cooperate."

Speculation was that the news conference was called by the FBI to force the others to come forward.

Bob Kohn—Profile in Crime

Kohn, age 45, said that he came to the State House in 1974 "to change the way business was done...the good ole boy system," but became part of the system instead. Kohn said that by helping the FBI he was helping reform, remarking that, "The irony is that by cooperating with the FBI, I am indeed facilitating change, but in a much different and more drastic manner than I had ever imagined."

But skeptical colleagues saw Kohn as a wheeler-dealer out for himself. "I've never seen Mr. Kohn in his service as an agent of change or a person who has tried to change the system," mused

Speaker Bob Sheheen. Another legislator dismissed Kohn: "He's never had an idealistic bone in his body."

Kohn was on the Labor, Commerce, and Industry Committee which passed the betting bill. Rep. Larry Martin (R-Pickens) said Kohn and Cobb were close. Other members of the committee were Paul Derrick, Tom Limehouse, and Tee Ferguson, all of whom would go to jail in the end.

Rep. Tom Limehouse Drops Out

Rep. Tom Limehouse, age 31, stood in front of his law office in Summerville in the hot sun on August 18, 1990, and with sweat pouring down his face, announced the end of his political career. Admitting he took $1,000 from Cobb, Limehouse said: "I have not sold my vote," although he said his reputation was "tainted." He intended to fight. "If indicted, I would plead not guilty, and hope that a jury would clear my name."

Limehouse's attorney, Andy Savage, said, "Speculation that has been reported in the press doesn't apply to Tom Limehouse."

Although S.C. Republican Party executive, Tony Denny, said the party had not urged Limehouse to resign, Sen. Mike Rose (R-Dorchester) from the same town said, "Good riddance." Rose said Limehouse "operates out of self-interest instead of the public interest. He has one of the worst characters of any person I've had the displeasure of knowing."

Speaker Sheheen said that other House members would also resign based on questions directed to his office about resignations. Sheheen had some insight that the Lost Trust scandal was going to become much worse in the near future.

Sales for Jobs at DSS?

As the first indictments came in on the Lost Trust probe, the FBI and SLED began to look into the question of whether state officials who were offered money and new jobs by the Hitachi Corp. were also the officials who bought millions of dollars of computers from Hitachi.

The allegations were that a person from Hitachi offered consulting jobs of $2,000 per month to three top DSS officials, including the Commissioner, James L. Solomon, Jr. A source said Solomon was offered the use of a beach condominium. But there was no evidence that the offers were accepted.

Hitachi sold $7 million worth of computers to DSS since 1987. Hitachi said the corporation never authorized offers of payments. Records of the State Ethics Commission indicated that the Executive Director of the Commission, Gary Baker, advised two DSS officials not to take any consulting work from Hitachi.

Gov. Campbell Calls for Change

Like other candidates for state-wide office, Gov. Campbell joined Jim Miles and Lt. Gov. Nick Theodore in trying to get ahead of the scandal.

Campbell told a rally of his supporters in Columbia on August 18, 1990, that he would make reform and reorganization of state government a major theme in his re-election campaign. He did not cite ethical rot as the major problems, but blamed the "arrogant" bureaucracy for its lack of accountability and inefficiency and impugned the part-time boards that controlled and protected them.

End of "Business as Usual" Predicted

On August 20, 1990, a month into the public phase of Lost Trust, Cindi Ross Scoppe predicted a big change in the culture of the State House in an article entitled, "Business as Usual a Certain Casualty of Probe." Her opinion was that corruption and a sprawling bureaucracy would finally be attacked as a result of all the scandals being exposed.

Reciting all of the suspects who had been fingered by the media for taking money from super lobbyist Ron Cobb, Scoppe wrote: "It can be said with near certainty that some legislators will go to jail." She also predicted urgent reforms: "It can be said with near certainty that the General Assembly will move swiftly in January to tighten South Carolina's ethics and lobbying laws, among the weakest in the nation." She also predicted reorganization of state government.

Scoppe saw new leadership coming in, noting that "the leadership of the Senate has been deteriorating" and that Jack Lindsay was nearing the end, and Ways and Means chairman, Bob McLellan, had lost his primary. The good ol' boy system was blown open by the sting exposing what Republicans had been saying about the State House for years, with good reason, because they were good ol' boys, too, and knew the political culture of the State House was rotten.

Scoppe Lists Evidence of Corruption in State Government

Scoppe pointed to cozy relationships of legislators and lobbyists, shakedowns by freeloading politicians living off lobbyists, poker games at the Town House played by legislators with lobbyists, and Dick Greer hustling business for his buddy Ron Cobb. Scoppe also noted such evidence as Sen. Jack Lindsay helping Hitachi hustle state business while serving as Hitachi's lawyer, big computer sales for Hitachi to state buyers, a sweetheart $8.6 million tax break for 21 rich businessmen in Greenville, and polling out a betting bill in Senate Judiciary without enough votes.

Reciting all the politicians implicated in the sting probe and all of the money changing hands, Scoppe believed that the 18 month old probe would claim more victims among those who hung around with Cobb, taking money from him at the Town House Hotel and the AT&T Building and floating on his boat at the Heritage Golf Tournament in Hilton Head.

She was later proven right. Almost everything she said came true and almost every person she listed as contaminated by the scandal was convicted within less than 18 months.

Solicitor's Probe Collides with FBI Probe

5th Circuit Solicitor, Jim Anders, found out about the Lost Trust FBI probe when he contacted the FBI with information about Ron Cobb, particularly about money from the S.C. Petroleum Marketers Association that went to Cobb. Anders then found out that the FBI had a file on Cobb.

Anders' probe was instigated by Speaker Robert Sheheen, who heard that money was being shifted around in accounts at the Petroleum Marketers Association when auditors contacted and asked staff at Sheheen's law firm, which handled legal work for the Association. Sheheen asked Anders to check out the matter because Sheheen had heard rumors that some of the missing money had been used to pay off legislators.

Anders then reported the matter as a Hobbs Act violation and thought the FBI should know. Anders' interest was whether the money had been used to pay off legislators and whether Cobb had a 1986 lobbying deal with the oil jobbers, but the Association said that Cobb had not been employed since 1985. The former executive director of the Association, David W. Reed, was indicted by the Richland County grand jury on July 20, 1990, for misusing some $2,000 to pay his daughter's tuition at the University of South Carolina.

Interview
Robert Sheheen

By John V. Crangle
November 17, 2014
Camden, S.C.

Robert Sheheen (Dem.)

Robert Sheheen was Speaker of the South Carolina House of Representatives from 1986 to 1994 at the time of Operation Lost Trust. Prior to the public revelation of the scandal in late July, 1990, Sheheen had been pushing for reforms in the House and had banned the notorious "Fat and Ugly Caucus" in the House. Sheheen retired from the House in 2000, having served since 1977 as a Democrat from Kershaw County. He practices law in Camden, S.C.

Interview

Q1. Looking back on the effect and consequences of the 1991 Ethics Act, what is your opinion of the law?

A. The best part of the 1991 Ethics Act was the ban on lobbyists giving gratuities and campaign funds to politicians and public officials. In years since the Act took effect in 1992, lobbyists have actually praised the bans on gifts and donations. The limits on the amounts of campaign donations from non-lobbyists have also been beneficial and the limits were both reasonable and practical and have remained unchanged for almost a quarter of a century.

Q2. What is your opinion of the enforcement provisions of the Act regarding the regulation of legislators?

A. The House favored transfer of the investigation of violations by legislators to the State Ethics Commission. The Senate opposed. The Senate argued that the South Carolina Constitution might have to be amended to allow the State Ethics Commission to go beyond investigation into the disciplining of legislators for violations of the Act.

Q3. What was Gov. Campbell's role in the ethics reform effort after Operation Lost Trust?

A. Gov. Campbell did not promote any specific ethics reform proposals aside from disclosure proposals. But in time the Republicans did come around to supporting the "no-cup-of-coffee" rule, although the Republicans did not favor the rule at first. I myself refused corporate donations from any corporation that was not located in my House district.

Q4. What reforms and improvements would you suggest to modernize the Ethics Act at this time?

A. I think the use of campaign funds should be restricted to actual campaign expenses and should not be used for any other purposes. I also think that some limits should be placed on the amounts of campaign funds donated by corporations and political action committees. With regard to the use of multiple LLCs to avoid contribution limits, I think that contributions should be attributed to any person who owns a 5% interest in the LLC.

Q5. What other reform ideas do you have to improve government in South Carolina?

A. I doubt that public financing of elections could pass the Legislature. But term limits on the Speaker would be beneficial. I do think the Speaker should appoint the members of House committees but the committees should elect their chairs. The House budget should be a program budget and results of government expenditure should be measured and evaluated.

Q6. What is your view of the issue of whether some violations of the Ethics Act should be decriminalized and made strictly civil violations while others should remain criminal?

A. It might be practical to draw a line in the law such that any violation of the Ethics Act involving more than $2,000, for example, might be considered criminal while anything less should be civil. But there should be no new amendments of the Act to require proof of criminal intent which, in fact, is often very difficult for prosecutors.

Q7. Any other reform proposals?

A. Yes. I think there should be periodic audits of campaign finance disclosure reports to detect errors and violations.

Q8. As a former Speaker of the South Carolina House, what is your opinion of the scandal involving Speaker Bobby Harrell?

A. I was amazed at the toleration shown for the abusive conduct of Bobby Harrell.

CHAPTER TEN

CRIMINAL INVESTIGATION PRODUCES INDICTMENTS

Grand Jury Probe Digs Deeper

On August 21, 1990, the federal grand jury was gaining momentum. Meeting at the U.S. Courthouse in downtown Columbia starting at 10 a.m. and holding its sessions in secret, the media was left to rely only on rumors and situational evidence from outside the grand jury room as to what the 23 grand jurors were doing.

Michael Spears, attorney for Sen. Rick Lee (R-Spartanburg), came to the courthouse but said he was there on tax business; Spears claimed he knew nothing about the grand jury, and Spears said he did not know whether Sen. Lee would be indicted. "We can't even find out the time schedules.... The lid is on everything."

Speaker Bob Sheheen said on August 20, 1990, that he expected 9 or 10 legislators to be indicted in the near future. By that time, some 15 legislators were known to be targets and subject to investigation of the grand jury. The fact that John Barton, chief of the criminal division of the U.S. Attorney's Office, came to the grand jury was clear evidence that the probe was going forward. And the withdrawal of Reps. Kohn and Limehouse as candidates indicated their likely fate. Furthermore, Speaker Sheheen said that he would move to suspend any House members who were indicted and expel any convicted in the scandal.

Cobb Raises Political Money

The long tentacles of Ron Cobb seemingly reached everywhere into the state's government. As the election for governor neared, it came out that Cobb had held a fund-raising event for Sen. Theo Mitchell in his Democratic primary race for governor. Cobb had also offered Mitchell money in March or April of 1990 to vote for the betting bill, but Mitchell refused, so the senator told the media later.

On May 29th, Cobb and four other lobbyists put on a fund-raising event at the Town House Hotel at the behest of other legislators. Cobb sent out the invitations. However, not many contributors showed up at the event, probably because Mitchell was widely seen as having no chance against Gov. Campbell. At the time, it was common practice for lobbyists to sponsor campaign fund-raisers for legislators.

Indictments Expected

By August 22, 1990, reporters expected indictments would come out on August 24th. U.S. Attorney Bart Daniel called a news conference for that date to discuss the probe, announcing beforehand, "We're working hard, and I hope we're making progress." The scheduled conference was only the second such event informing the pubic, following the first news release by Daniel and the FBI on July 20th acknowledging the investigation.

Rumors were flying that the probe would expand, after Solicitor James Anders said Cobb had been granted federal immunity, to include executive and judicial branch officials, which proved to be true. Lobbyists were worried that the immunized Cobb might point at them. "You've got Ron Cobb sitting up there with immunity, and if he sees anything in the papers he don't like, he might point fingers and say anything," one lobbyist said off-the-record.

Waiting for indictments, lobbyists said that fund-raising since the scandal broke had dropped. "It's been almost nil," said Richard Davis, lobbyist for the S.C. Association of Realtors.

Meanwhile, State Republican chairman, Barry Wynn, asked Democratic Attorney General, Travis Medlock, to act on his statutory power and seize campaign contributions of Secretary of State John Campbell and Treasurer Grady Patterson, in view of a State Ethics Commission ruling that Campbell should return contributions from cemetery owners his office regulated.

Racial Targeting Raised

The Democratic candidate for governor, Sen. Theo Mitchell, complained that the FBI probe of vote-buying in South Carolina was like other federal probes in implicating a disproportionate number of black officials. He pointed to the fact that nearly half of the suspects were black.

Republican candidate for Lt. Governor, Henry McMaster, a former U.S. Attorney who had once unsuccessfully prosecuted Mitchell for food stamp fraud, denounced Mitchell: "It is difficult to imagine a more irresponsible, nonsensical statement by a public official."

Mitchell, in return, blasted McMaster and charged that "political careers are built on the backs of the poor. He [McMaster] tried to build one on my back...." But Lt. Governor Nick Theodore spurned Mitchell's statements about bias based on race. Theodore also said he wanted to change Senate rules to require suspension of indicted senators and removal on conviction.

Cobb's Web Stretches Everywhere

The web of personal and financial relations of Ron Cobb became more and more obvious as the scandal progressed. It came out that S.C. Highway Department Director, Joe Rideoutte, had helped Cobb get a $15,000 lobbying fee from the Horry County transportation council in 1987 to help the Highway Department lobby. The deal was that Cobb would get $10,000 to lobby for a gas tax increase plus a $5,000 bonus if the bill passed.

It also came out that Lost Trust suspect, Sen. Bud Long (D-Horry), had helped Cobb to get access to county transportation and water public authorities. Long said Cobb bragged that he helped Rideoutte get his job, which he denied.

The Days Before the First Indictments

On August 23, 1990, Rep. Robert Brown (D-Marion), resigned and Judge Tee Ferguson took a leave from the Circuit Court bench. Brown gave Speaker Bob Sheheen his resignation after a meeting on that evening. Sheheen said Brown expected indictment within two days.

Brown reported taking $2,500 from Ron Cobb and said of his resignation, "I regret any appearance of impropriety and any negative reflection on the House of Representatives or citizens of Marion County." However, in July he had denied taking the money as a bribe from Cobb at the Town House Hotel. Brown did file an amended report of the money from Cobb only after the FBI seized his campaign records on July 17th.

Judge Tee Ferguson told S.C. Supreme Court Chief Justice, George Gregory, in a letter dated August 22, that he wanted to be relieved "until such time as the matter concerning alleged votes for cash is resolved in so far as it seeks to implicate me." Ferguson added, "I feel that it is imperative that a judge, at any level, must sit in an unquestioned posture." In a one sentence order, Gregory relieved Ferguson as a circuit court judge until January 7, 1991, with full pay at an annual rate of $82,877. Ferguson had reported to Speaker Sheheen an offer of money made to him but did not identify the source. He said he rejected the money.

The First Indictments Released by U.S. Attorney

On Friday, August 24, 1990, the first 5 indictments of Operation Lost Trust were announced; in the next year another 23 would be announced. The 5 charged were Sen. Rick Lee, Reps. Robert Brown, Bob Kohn, Luther Taylor, and Danny Winstead.

Sen. Rick Lee (R-Spartanburg)

Lee was a 37 year old who had served in the House from 1979 to 1984 and in the Senate since 1985. He held a bachelor's degree from the University of South Carolina, was married and had two children. He served on Banking and Insurance, Judiciary, and three other committees. He was accused of taking a $2,000 cash bribe from lobbyist Ron Cobb to vote for the pari-mutuel betting bill. Lee would plead guilty.

Rep. Robert Brown (D-Marion)

Brown was elected to the House in 1982. He was a 34 year old real estate broker and president of TBA Management, Inc. He was a graduate of the University of South Carolina, was married and had one child. He was chair of the House Labor, Commerce, and Industry Committee which passed the pari-mutuel betting bill. Charged with taking a $2,000 cash bribe to vote for the betting bill, Brown would plead guilty.

Rep. Bob Kohn (R-Charleston)

Kohn was elected to the House in 1975. He was 45 years old and the sole employee of Kohn and Associates, a commercial property casualty insurance consulting firm. He was married and had two children. He was assistant minority leader for House Republicans and became floor leader in the House for Gov. Carroll Campbell's auto insurance reform package in 1989. Charged with taking a $2,500 bribe, Kohn cooperated with the probe and pleaded guilty.

Rep. Luther Taylor (D-Richland)

Taylor was elected to the House in 1983. He was 40 years old and held a bachelor's degree from Clemson University. He had no wife and one child. He ran for the Senate in 1985 and lost to Kay Patterson. He was charged with taking $4,000 in bribes from Ron Cobb and with criminal conspiracy. Taylor would be convicted at trial but have his conviction reversed on appeal. He died in 1997 before retrial.

Rep. Danny Winstead (R-Charleston)

Winstead was elected to the House in 1979. He was 44 years old and had attended Carson Newman College. He was married and served in the South Carolina National Guard. He was a conferee on the 1990-1991 budget. He was a member of the House Ethics and Ways and Means Committee. He was charged with taking a $1,000 cash bribe and pleaded guilty. He was also charged with obstruction.

The Federal Prosecutors

The federal agents and criminal prosecutors in Lost Trust included the following:

FBI Agents:

Fred Verinder—FBI Special Agent
Career Investigator of public corruption in New York.
Tommy Davis—FBI Spokesman
25 year veteran of the FBI from Rockingham, North Carolina.
Mike Clemens—FBI Special Agent
Pottstown, Pennsylvania
Charles Sheppard—FBI Agent
Mike Morehart—Lead Working Agent
Petersburg, Virginia
John Harley—The top FBI Agent in South Carolina.

Attorneys:

Bart Daniel—U.S. Attorney for South Carolina (35 years old). Graduate of the Citadel and University of South Carolina School of Law. Assisted U.S. Attorney Henry McMaster in Operation Jackpot, a major drug smuggling case.
John Barton—Chief of the U.S. Attorney criminal division (38 years old). A 1977 graduate of the University of South Carolina and USC School of Law. Served as a prosecutor in the S.C. Attorney General's Office.
John McIntosh—Assistant U.S. Attorney (51 years old). Graduate of Presbyterian College and USC School of Law, 1965. Number two attorney in the office.
Dale DuTremble—Assistant U.S. Attorney (42 years old). A 1978 graduate of USC and the USC School of Law. Served in office (1983-1986, 1989 -)
Scott Schools—Assistant U.S. Attorney (27 years old). AB Duke & J.D. USC (1987)
Sherri Lydon—Assistant U.S. Attorney (27 years old). JD, USC (1987)

Interview
Travis Medlock

By John V. Crangle
July 1, 2015
Columbia, S.C.

Travis Medlock

Travis Medlock was Attorney General of South Carolina at the time of Operation Lost Trust but he was unaware of the FBI sting and probe until July 18, 1990, when the FBI served the first series of subpoenas on state legislators seeking their campaign finance forms.

Interview

Medlock was satisfied that the federal investigation was "thorough and competent" and there was no need for the state to conduct a similar probe.

Medlock is of the opinion that the main failing of the 1975 Ethics Act was that it did not require income disclosure of the personal income of officials and "the Act was grossly inadequate. Income disclosure is the core to a meaningful Ethics Act." Medlock did not comment on the question of whether the 1975 Act was defective because it allowed officials to take unlimited gifts of free meals, free drinks, free trips and cash from any and all sources, including lobbyists.

Medlock had had a role in the discussion of the Senate bill which later became the basis of the 1975 Ethics Act. Medlock said that at the time he was a member of the Senate and was "embattled with the Senate establishment due to my strong efforts for reform. It became almost physical."

Although in the year 2015 Medlock said, "I do not recall the Ethics Act debate but certainly would have voted for the strongest version if present the day of the vote." Medlock recalled that "I led the ethics reform in 1969-1970 and pushed then a rules change in the House setting up the first ethics law—with personal income disclosure included.

Medlock said that, "I believe I was the first legislator in the history of S.C. to lead a successful effort resulting in an Ethics Act. It was a rule of the House change. It was a hard fight."

Medlock also pushed to establish the state grand jury system, noting that "I am credited by some as the 'Father of the State Grand jury system'." Medlock added, "We wrote it, lobbied for it, (and) campaigned statewide for it and set it up."

CHAPTER ELEVEN

WORSENING SCANDAL PROVOKES REFORMERS

Hope for a New Day After the Sting: Calls for Reform

Responding to the first indictments on August 24th, Gov. Campbell saw value in the sting: "None of us want it. But I would a whole lot rather have it purging itself than us go on with it existing in state government.... I think that's the good side."

Speaker Sheheen added: "Yes, the House as an institution is damaged.... What we will see though is a great majority of House members working hard to restore public trust." The Speaker predicted a reform agenda to include a ban on officials taking handouts from lobbyists like Ron Cobb.

Reform laws to stop cash campaign donations and laws to stop the abuses of lobbyists like Ron Cobb were obviously needed. Thus even Sen. James Waddell (D-Beaufort), known for his enjoyment of the good life as chairman of the Senate Finance Committee admitted, "We've got to move to remove the cloud." Waddell proposed some drastic reforms, including banning campaign contributions during the legislative session, the time during which most legislators raised a great deal of their funds from special interests and lobbyists with interest in pending bills. Waddell wanted more donor source disclosure and ordered his staff to examine lobbying regulations from other states.

Calls for Reform Grow Louder

The senior member in the Senate, Marshall Williams (D-Orangeburg), said from the disaster of the scandal a better world could be made. He thought reform could purify corruption, echoing the remarks of Gov. Campbell, Speaker Sheheen, and Sen. Waddell. "Sickening would be a good word," he said of the criminal charges spreading like a disease. "When it's all over, when the purifying takes place, we might have a better General Assembly." With the right reforms, obstacles to abuse of office could be set up. "I think you'll find that some who would be tempted in the future might not fall as quick."

Rep. David Beasley (D-Darlington), who would later in 1994 win election as governor as a Republican, demanded reform: "It won't stop this kind of activity from happening. But our laws are too loose. We need to tighten them up as much as possible." But on the day of the first five indictments, Beasley admitted it was "a very sad day in South Carolina's history. It's disheartening, disillusioning to see it occur."

Impact on the 1990 Elections

As the first five indictments were revealed by U.S. Attorney Daniel and the FBI, *The State*, in an editorial worried that more indictments were predicted by the U.S. Attorney and that the probe would affect the November, 1990, elections for the Senate, House, the governor, Secretary of State, treasurer, and perhaps others.

Noting that "Mr. Daniel said there is no timetable for future indictments," *The State* said "the functioning of state government is impaired. A long delay could affect the outcome of a number of political races this fall." *The State* hoped for a quick end of the process and then a "move forward with comprehensive reforms in campaign financing and lobbying laws that helped create this sorry mess."

Sen. Mitchell Denies Corruption

Sen. Theo Mitchell (D-Greenville), the struggling Democratic candidate for governor, rejected the notion that corruption was a major problem at the State House, a view which fewer and fewer South Carolinians were inclined to accept as the number of indictments and guilty pleas piled up in the first weeks after the scandal became known to the public.

Rather than capitalize on the issue and champion reform ideas, Mitchell said, "It's so unfair to think corruption is rampant. Graft is not the call of the day in the General Assembly I serve in."

Mitchell continued to raise questions about the many black legislators implicated in the scandal in South Carolina and in similar scandals in other states. "Who pointed them in that direction, and why were they pointed out? What reason were they pointed out?"

Former U.S. Attorney, Henry McMaster, dismissed Mitchell's insinuation of racial bias, saying, "It's a straightforward investigation into crime and corruption."

First Shock of the Sting Embarrasses South Carolina

The first indictments on August 24, 1990, sent a shock wave through state's leadership as well as the public. Reaction ran the gamut from anxiety over how far the scandal would spread to what damage it would do to the state's economic development efforts. As the indictments piled up in groups for the next year and the trials and appeals continued into 1999, the toll on the state's image and morale got worse and worse.

Speaker Bob Sheheen took a somewhat fatalistic view of the corruption: "Regardless of what we do up here, it can't stop a bad person from coming here." On the other hand, he saw the need for legislative reform: "We can just make it easier to find these people out by stronger disclosure and conduct laws." Even so, Sheheen concluded: "You can't ever prevent people who want to exercise bad judgment from using it."

Gov. Carroll Campbell worried: "The state's image in the midst of something like this obviously is not going to be enhanced." Campbell took consolation in the prospects of reform, saying, "The system is purging itself," and adding, "We watched this happen in West Virginia, we watched it in Tennessee, we watched it in California, and now it is happening in South Carolina." The governor worried that other states would use the sting to scare off economic development from the state.

Rumors—True and False—Subject to Truth-Testing

The secrecy of the federal sting and of the grand jury and the piecemeal disclosures made over a period of months by authorities, combined with the proliferating number of indictments produced a storm of rumors and half-truths amid the actual facts of Lost Trust.

A month into the scandal, Clark Surratt of *The State*, tried to find out what was myth and what was true about the scandal at that point among 14 major rumors then spreading over the State House.

On Friday, August 24, 1990, perhaps the most shocking day in a scandal which would produce new crimes for over a year into late 1991, Bart Daniel and John Harley, the top FBI agent in South Carolina, held a news conference to tell the public what was true and false about some rumors.

Daniel and Harley said that there were no sex and drug tapes, aside from a few mentions on the tapes. No drugs nor sex was offered by the probe as a bribe, only money. But it was true that Cobb was an FBI stooge and undercover lobbyist. Cobb did have immunity and would keep it as long as he cooperated. The Alpha Group was an FBI front promoting the betting bill with bribes to legislators.

At his news conference on August 24, 1990, U.S. Attorney Bart Daniel revealed important facts: The mysterious figure of Joe Williams of the Alpha Group luring the bribe-takers with Cobb was an FBI agent; Ron Cobb was in protective custody since July 18, 1990; the FBI had a boat at the Heritage golf tournament in April, 1990, called the 'Tally Ho' which was used to videotape vote buying by legislators, and a room at the Town House Hotel and Cobb's office at the AT&T Building were both bugged for videotape.

On the other hand, some rumors were false. There were no videotapes of poker games and gambling at the Town House Hotel involving Sens. Jack Lindsay, Sen. Ed Saleeby, and Development Chair Dick Greer.

To clear up rumors, Daniel and Harley revealed that the probe started in April, 1989, on local federal initiative and was not originated and planned in Washington to target corruption in South Carolina. The probe followed a drug investigation, but turned into a sting when federal investigators learned that some legislators were prone to bribery.

Solicitor Jim Anders claimed that he called the federal authorities to report information from a legislator who saw bribes being handed out, but the news conference could not confirm more than the fact that they that they received several phone calls about vote selling in state government.

As to early suspects, Daniel told reporters that Rep. Robert Kohn was co-opted as a sting agent after he was discovered in vote-buying. Kohn was allowed to hold a press conference.

The FBI plan was to force suspects to turn themselves in for fear of being caught. Finally, Rep. Luther Taylor was not cooperating in the probe, as had been erroneously reported in the media.

U.S. Attorney Puts Indictments in Context

The indictments of the first five legislators were the result of some 16 months of prior investigative work by the FBI, starting in April, 1989, even before Bart Daniel became U.S. Attorney for South Carolina. The probe started out as a drug investigation and turned into a bribery and public corruption sting operation known as Operation Lost Trust.

FBI agents and federal prosecutors indicated in announcing the first indictments that many more would come as the federal grand jury continued digging out evidence and handing up indictments. Speculation was that in addition to elected officials, some other non-legislator defendants would be named.

The lost Trust charges were just the most recent corruption scandals in a state long plagued with officials abusing public office for illegal personal profit.

Scandal Disrupts Elections

With incumbent legislators starting to drop like flies, the state's political parties tried to replace them with new candidates after the June primaries had been held.

The State Election Commission voted on August 23, 1990, to allow the Republican Party to have its executive committee pick a new candidate to replace Rep. Bob Kohn, who resigned. The Dorchester County Election Commission had already authorized the Republican Party to replace resigned Rep. Tom Limehouse.

The Democratic Party protested the actions violated state law and both commissions split in the vote on the matter. A lawsuit was contemplated.

Charleston County Republicans nominated Stephen Gonzalez to run for Kohn's seat and Dorchester County Republicans nominated Annette Young to replace Limehouse.

Meanwhile, a scramble in the House followed Robert Brown's resignation as chair of Labor, Commerce and Industry with five representatives seeking the post.

Lost Trust—Latest Corruption Scandal in S.C.

By the end of August, after the first indictments, *The State*'s Margaret O'Shea wrote an article putting the latest scandal in historical context of a sordid record of abuse of power and dishonesty stretching back over twenty years in South Carolina.

Denouncing the Lost Trust sting as the worst in history, O'Shea wrote, "No darker cloud ever gathered over South Carolina state government, and a greater number of officials ever was caught in the storm."

Deploring the sorry chronicle of corruption, she wrote that the indicted officials "can draw a little hope and a lot of despair from legislative history" of official crimes. Pointing out that "this is not the first time members of the General Assembly have been indicted while in public office."

Pointing to 11 legislators since 1970, O'Shea began with Sen. Ralph J. Gasque, a 24 year incumbent, who was indicted for fraud and conspiracy in 1977. He was accused of using federal Manpower funds in his law office and use of a bogus corporation to acquire property from the U.S. Department of Housing and Urban Development. He resigned after six months, was convicted in U.S. District Court and sentenced to a maximum of five years.

Rep. Joe Holland was indicted on six counts while representing Laurens County as a Democrat. He resigned, saying he had a nervous breakdown after being charged with grand larceny, breach of trust, conspiracy, and filing a false insurance claim related to a robbery of his grocery store. He was convicted in state court and given five years in prison and five years probation.

Sen. John D. Long, III, a senior Democrat for Union County, was convicted in 1980 of racketeering for taking bribes and resigned his seat the day before he was sentenced to 10 years in prison.

Sen. Eugene Carmichael (D-Dillon), was convicted of voting fraud along with 30 others for trying to rig the Democratic primary in Dillon County. A millionaire oil broker, tobacco warehouse owner, farmer, and president of a textile mill, he was found guilty of criminal conspiracy, obstruction of justice, and 12 counts of vote-buying. He was sentenced to 10 years in prison and $20,000 fine. He appealed all the way to the U.S. Supreme Court and held his seat until 1983. His appeals failed.

Rep. Danny Bundrick, a Democrat from Orangeburg County, was a successful farmer who was charged with filing false claims with the Federal Crop Insurance Corp. for $126,267 and a fraudulent $48,232 claim for low-yield disaster payments. He also converted his own crops to personal use when pledged to the Farmers Home Administration. Pleading guilty in federal court, Bundrick resigned, received a five year sentence, and agreed to pay $700,000 in restitution for fraud. He was paroled in 1984 with terminal cancer.

Rep. James Kinard served 7 years in the House before his 1984 indictments on five counts of failing to keep proper firearms records at his gun shop in Columbia. He resigned, pleaded guilty and received five years probation, 1,000 hours of community service, and a $12,000 fine.

Rep. Chris Pracht, IV, was elected to the House in 1977 at the age of 22 and named as 'Outstanding Young Man of America' in 1979. In 1980, he was picked as 'Legislator of the Year' by Young Democrats. A son-in-law of U.S. Rep. William Jennings Bryan Dorn, he served Anderson County briefly before he was indicted in 1984 with possession of 1,000 pounds of marijuana with intent to distribute in West Palm Beach, Florida. The drugs were smuggled from Jamaica. He was suspended and then resigned and received 10 years in prison. *The State* headline captioned the article about Pracht's demise, "Pracht's Promising Start Ends Sadly."

Rep. Sterling Anderson became Speaker Pro Tempore of the House in 1986 when he was charged with conspiracy, wire fraud, and lying to lenders relating to loans to customers at his Spartanburg mobile home business. He was convicted in federal court during a trial in which employees detailed loan applications using false names and social security numbers. After indictment, he suspended himself and then went to prison.

Rep. Robert Woods from Charleston represented himself and took the witness stand in federal court in 1985. He was convicted of fraud in misusing federal day-care funds in a church he operated. A 14 year House member, he was sentenced by a jury conviction on 18 counts of fraudulent claims to the U.S. Department of Agriculture. He got 10 years in prison.

Two legislators got off easy. Democrat Rep. Herbert U. Fielding of Charleston pleaded nolo contendere for failure to file an income tax return for 1967 and similar charges for 1969 and 1970 were dropped. He resigned his seat in 1973, served 90 days in prison, and was elected to the Senate in 1982.

Rep. Theo Mitchell, a Democrat of Greenville, was indicted for food stamp fraud in 1982 when nabbed by an undercover agent at his law office. He was one of 33 charged, but the charges were dropped on technical grounds after a mistrial. He held his seat during the trial and was later elected to the Senate.

Fears for the Future

As the first indictments were disclosed by the U.S. Attorney on August 24, 1990, the prospect of many more falling to criminal charges became clearer than before. Bart Daniel made it evident at his news conference on that date that the probe had discovered many more culprits who would be revealed to the public in the near future.

Jeff Miller in *The State* wrote that "More legislators will undoubtedly fall to Operation Lost Trust. And it's entirely possible that even some non-elected officials and others will be caught in the largest investigation of public corruption in modern state history." This proved to be true.

The tapes promised to paint a shocking picture of corrupt officials taking bribes of cash, even though no drug or sex tapes had been made as no such bait was offered by the FBI. The tapes produced in trials all showed Cobb giving money to legislators in the context of incriminating conversations.

Hope for Reform Provides Some Reassurance

The first five indictments did offer some consolation that the scandal would force reform by self-interested and some sincere politicians eager to distance themselves from the scandal and appear to be part of the solution and not part of the problem.

Speaker Bob Sheheen said at the time of the first indictments that those who had been advocating campaign finance and lobbying reform in the late 1980s would now have a better chance of passing their bills. At a minimum, Sheheen said that the House should adopt rules to control campaign funds.

It was expected that a number of reform proposals would be filed and Daniel said that Operation Lost Trust was about good government and he was doing his best to clean out the crooks.

However, John Crangle of Common Cause/South Carolina worried about the sincerity of the political class and their inclination to try to put the scandal behind them without making real changes. Crangle said:

> Too many members of the Legislature regard the current scandal as a public relations problem, not an institutional problem. Unless the people of South Carolina and the newspapers, television stations and radio stations keep a constant, critical watch on the General Assembly, the legislators will do little, if anything, to correct the fundamental institutional corruption in South Carolina.

FBI Denies Entrapment in Sting

In the news conference held on August 24, 1990, U.S. Attorney Bart Daniel denied any illegal means were used to catch corrupt officials: "We were extremely careful to avoid the notion of entrapment.... None of the defendants was entrapped."

Daniel anticipated a defense which sting defendants often used to defeat prosecutions based on stings—the entrapment defense. It was a defense raised without success by South Carolina Congressman John Jenrette in the ABSCAM bribery case in Washington, D.C., and by Mayor Marion Barry in the same city in a drug sting a few years before.

The entrapment defense is based on the theory that the defendant who did the illegal act was not predisposed to the crime but was lured into the crime by unfair and even irresistible means. But Prof. Eldon D. Wedlock, Jr., of the University of South Carolina School of Law, a board member of Common Cause/South Carolina, told the media that the entrapment defense was a "two edged sword and very dangerous" because it would open the door for the prosecution to present more evidence of the defendant's bad character and predisposition to commit the crime charged.

Daniel, however, said that the defendants targeted for bribes had been identified as persons who had previously committed similar crimes in the past based on evidence collected by local federal authorities. The sting originated in South Carolina and was not instigated in Washington.

Little Sympathy for Officials Charged in Sting

The protests of innocence and entrapment uttered by the defendants in Lost Trust received little or no resonance with the public, and few officials except for a couple of black politicians prone to play on racial paranoia as a way of trying to appear as spokesmen of the black community, such as Sen. Kay Patterson (D-Richland), tried to claim that the sting was racially motivated to destroy black politicians. Few blacks protested.

Republicans were loathe to make excuses for Republican legislators indicted. At a GOP campaign rally in Columbia on August 24, 1990, State GOP Executive Director Tony Denny joined Republican candidates and said that Gov. Carroll Campbell and other Republican candidates denounced those who took bribes and that such corrupt officials had no place in the Republican Party. Denny noted: "There wasn't a lot of sympathy here for the people who were indicted.... The attitude is basically, if there are people selling their votes, they ought to get out." 750 attended the rally and paid $10 per person to lunch on Beaufort stew—shrimp, sausage, and corn—and meet candidates and luminaries such as Sen. Strom Thurmond, Rep. Floyd Spence and Rep. Arthur Ravenel.

Sen. Lee Pleads and Resigns

Sen. Rick Lee (R-Spartanburg), the sanctimonious legislator who, at a Senate committee hearing on April 10, 1990, had denounced Common Cause Executive Director John Crangle, as a liar for defaming the Senate and Lee himself for testifying that there was a practice of payoffs and shakedowns at the State House, resigned his seat and announced his guilty plea on August 27, 1990, to bribery in selling his vote on the betting bill. He was the first Senator and one of only two, along with Sen. Bud Long, to be convicted of bribery. Oddly, the federal grand jury charged Lee with accepting a bribe on May 24, 1990, almost exactly the same time as Lee castigated Crangle for making allegedly false allegations of corruption.

At the hearing, several senators were so incensed by Lee's attack on Crangle that one of them, Sen. John Courson (R-Richland), came up to Crangle after the hearing and asked to join Common Cause, a non-profit public interest group, and wrote a $50 check to do so, handing it to Crangle in the hallway. After the indictments Courson championed reforms.

Lee admitted he took a $2,000 cash bribe on May 24, 1990, to vote for the betting bill, having previously told the media that he took $3,000 from Ron Cobb in the AT&T Building. Lee's resignation saved the Senate the ordeal of having to vote to expel him.

Lee's Resignation Begins Exodus at State House

Comments about Lee after his news conference at the Spartanburg County Administration Building included those of Sen. David Thomas (R-Greenville) who said, "He saved himself and he saved the whole Legislature a lot of grief.... The Senate rules go into a protectionist mode, where they defend someone who is indicted.... The Senate rules are flawed."

Lee and Reps. Brown, Kohn, Taylor, and Winstead were all indicted on the same day, August 24, 1990, and set for arraignment on August 29, 1990, in Columbia before U.S. Magistrate Charles Gambrell. They, too, would leave the General Assembly a short time later and would be convicted.

Rep. Ennis Fant Reprimanded

The virtually defunct House Ethics Committee shook off the dust 14 years after its creation by the 1975 Ethics Act, and finally issued a public reprimand to Rep. Ennis Fant (D-Greenville), a Baptist minister, for trying to set up an escort service and run it from his House office in the Blatt Building on the State House grounds.

The unanimous opinion chastised Rep. Fant because he "used his official position... to obtain financial gain for himself." The committee could have recommended expulsion.

Chairman Pat Harris (D-Anderson), said that the penalty was not related to the fact that Fant had been contacted by the FBI as a suspect in the Lost Trust scandal. Harris also said that he proposed to transfer jurisdiction over ethics to the State Ethics Commission in the future and would introduce a bill in the 1991 session to do that.

The committee said that Solicitor James Anders in Columbia had found that Fant did not violate any law. The public reprimand did not require anything beyond a majority vote of the Ethics Committee; an expulsion would have required a vote by the full house. Speaker Sheheen had requested a SLED probe in May, 1990, and the SLED report of July, 1990, found Rep. Fant to have set up an escort service run out of his official House office in The Blatt Building which paid girls $75 for their work and ran ads in newspapers for job applicants whom he later interviewed.

Chairman Harris said he was glad that Speaker Sheheen had asked SLED to investigate Fant, otherwise, "we probably would have had another bad situation in the Blatt Building...he never used his office for solicitation, but I think that given time, it would have happened."

Two of the six members of the House Ethics Committee that reprimanded Rep. Fant were absent—Danny Winstead and Larry Blanding. Both were convicted of corruption in Lost Trust along with Fant himself soon after the reprimand.

Miles Urges Prosecution of Campbell

Jim Miles, the Republican challenger of Democratic incumbent Secretary of State John Campbell, came out in late August and urged that the state should prosecute Campbell for refusing to return some $23,000 he had accepted in 1990 as campaign donations from people his office regulated.

Based on an August 15, 1990, ruling by the State Ethics Commission which held Campbell should not take money from those he regulated including lobbyists and cemetery owners, Miles, a Greenville attorney, saw the opportunity to drive still another nail in Campbell's coffin and said: "You have [Sen.] Rick Lee, who admits he illegally took $3,000, facing 20 years in prison and you have Secretary of State John Campbell, who has illegally taken $23,000—not $3,000, but $23,000." Miles blamed Travis Medlock, the Democratic Attorney General, for not taking action. However, Medlock's office said the ruling of the Commission did not have retroactive application, and Frank Knapp, Campbell's campaign manager, said taking money prior to the ruling was legal and no prosecution was justified.

Lobbyists Flout Disclosure Laws

Not only did South Carolina have weak ethics laws but they were not even enforced. Margaret O'Shea and *The State* reviewed the filings of 290 registered lobbyists with the Secretary of State and found that only 9 of them filed disclosures with the House Ethics Committee as required by House rules.

The House had never made an effort to make sure that lobbyists knew about lobbyists disclosure laws and rules and never enforced the same. The Senate had no such disclosure rules at all.

Even the Chairman of the House Ethics Committee, Patrick B. Harris, claimed not to know the committee was supposed to collect and monitor such disclosure forms. "If we have a duty, we have been derelict, and something should be done about it." Harris said that his committee should not be required to handle lobbyists and that the duty should go to the State Ethics Commission.

The House rule that both legislators and lobbyists had been ignoring provided that any person found in violation was guilty of contempt of the House and "may be ordered into custody by the House and dealt with as it deems proper."

Ruth Muldrow, Executive Secretary of the House Ethics Committee, said the committee had never enforced the disclosure rules and usually fewer than 10 lobbyists or so did file disclosure forms each year.

Speaker Sheheen Demands Ethics Reform

Overwhelmed by criminal charges and the exposure that the House was not enforcing its own ethics rules to force lobbyists' disclosure, Speaker Bob Sheheen said that the rule itself was too vague, but he did think new legislation was needed: "I think the time is right to get even greater disclosure and limit expenditures by lobbyists for the benefit of individual members.... For example, all these dinners, golfing, trips and things like that—the time is right to outlaw all of that."

Of course, Speaker Sheheen was right that the House had been derelict in both violating and not enforcing the weak provisions of the 1975 Ethics Act and the rules of the House. In fact, Sheheen's actions in the months before Operation Lost Trust was revealed to the public indicated that he had started to move to deal with the most outrageous abuses in his own chamber. By the time of Lost Trust, Sheheen had already suppressed the parasitical "Fat and Ugly Caucus" and had also reported rumors about Ron Cobb's uses of money at the State House to SLED. Furthermore, Sheheen had found out about Rep. Fant's use of his Blatt Building office to run an escort service and had notified law enforcement about Fant's conduct. Sheheen also alerted SLED about issues at the S.C. Petroleum Council related to Cobb.

Ethics Committees Exposed as Failures

In an editorial on August 31, 1990, *The State* ridiculed the House Ethics Committee, noting that among the six man committee which blamed Ennis Fant for ethics violations in trying to set up a prostitution ring in the House office building, were two members charged with felonies in Lost Trust.

In fact, *The State* noted one, Danny Winstead, had resigned and did not handle the Fant reprimand and neither did the indicted Larry Blanding. The four left voted to reprimand Fant.

Chairman Pat Harris promised to introduce a bill in 1991 to transfer ethics enforcement over to the State Ethics Commission which *The State* strongly endorsed saying: "Mr. Fant's reprimand could be the last official act of the House Ethics Committee." Sen. Sherry Martschink (R-Charleston) said she would introduce a bill to transfer to the Ethics Commission jurisdiction over both House and Senate ethics matters.

The State urged that jurisdiction over lobbyists should be shifted to the Ethics Commission as well as from the Secretary of State. The 1991 Ethics Act would include such a jurisdictional reform.

Failure of Ethics Enforcement Denounced

The State's editorial of August 31, 1990, went into a harsh indictment of the failure of state government in South Carolina to establish and enforce ethics standards and operate a clean political system. The editors wrote: "The widening trail of corruption offers shameful proof of the absolute necessity of South Carolina to change. Change might even be wrought by the artistry of a new constitution. USC academicians Walter Edgar and Blease Graham—both long-time students of South Carolina—argue for this."

The State noted that various groups were organizing to propose a number of reforms to strengthen ethics oversight, to control political contributions, to control elections, and even to examine the excessive power of the legislative branch.

"There are signs that your entrusted public servants are attuned. Some are long-time advocates of good government," and should be re-elected, but many were insincere opportunists who "will rush to to the table, throw a few crumbs and hope we don't reach the meat of the problem."

The editorial concluded: "Once more we implore you to raise your voice.... In the name of good South Carolinians, it can be done."

Five Post Bonds in Sting

On August 30, 1990, the first five defendants in the Operation Lost Trust cases posted their bonds before U.S. Magistrate Charles W. Gambrell in Columbia after being photographed and fingerprinted by U.S. marshals. It was their first court appearance since indictment the previous week.

The five defendants arraigned in court were:

Rep. Luther Taylor (D-Richland)—charged with four counts of selling his vote and one count of conspiracy to recruit other legislators to take bribes in violation of the Hobbs Act. Maximum sentence of 20 years in prison and a fine of $250,000 for each violation.

Rep. Daniel E. Winstead (R-Charleston)—charged with taking a bribe and obstruction of justice. Maximum sentence of 30 years in prison and $500,000 in fines.

Sen. Rick Lee (R-Spartanburg)—charged with one count of bribery. Maximum sentence of 20 years in prison and a fine of $250,000.

Rep. Robert Brown (D-Marion)—charged with one count of bribery. Maximum sentence of 20 years in prison and a fine of $250,000.

Rep. Robert A. Kohn (R-Charleston)—charged with conspiracy to violate the Hobbs Act and bribery (combined into one count). Maximum sentence of 20 years in prison and a fine of $250,000.

Of the five arraigned, only Sen. Rick Lee announced his intention to plead guilty as charged. His plea hearing was set for September 10, 1990. However, due to the fact that federal magistrates were not allowed to take guilty pleas, all five defendants entered not guilty pleas on August 30, 1990.

The court released all five legislators on unsecured bonds subject to restrictions, including that none of them could travel outside of South Carolina without court permission. Of the five defendants, only Luther Taylor would elect for a trial. The rest would enter guilty pleas according to plea bargains.

Fat and Ugly Caucus Members Caught in Lost Trust

Although the "Fat and Ugly Caucus," formed by Rep. David Hawkins in 1980 in the House, had only 30 members at its apex, a very large proportion of them were charged and convicted in the Lost Trust prosecutions in 1990 and 1991.

Caucus members who were eventually convicted were the following:

Rep. David Hawkins
Sen. Rick Lee
Rep. Robert Brown
Rep. Danny Winstead
Rep. Robert Kohn
Rep. Luther Taylor
Rep. Jack I. Rogers
Rep. Paul Derrick
Rep. Tom Limehouse
Rep. B.J. Gordon
Rep./Judge Tee Ferguson

Lost Trust indicted and convicted other legislators who were not Caucus members as well, including:

Sen. Bud Long
Rep. Ken Bailey
Rep. James Faber
Rep. Frank McBride
Rep. Ennis Fant
Rep. Donna Moss
Rep. Larry Blanding

Rep. Tim Wilkes was also indicted, but was acquitted in September, 1991. Wilkes did not belong to the Caucus.

Fat and Ugly Caucus—Origins of Corruption

Cindi Ross Scoppe raised the question in an article in the September 2, 1990, edition of *The State* as to whether the "Fat and Ugly Caucus" in the South Carolina House of Representatives was an ancestor of the massive corruption exposed by Operation Lost Trust not long after the Caucus was closed down by Speaker Bob Sheheen in 1987. The Caucus included a number of House members who would regularly demand that lobbyists buy them free food, drinks, and trips.

Ms. Scoppe's investigative article examined the backgrounds of the 17 legislators interviewed by the FBI in the Lost Trust probe and found that five of those indicted as of September 1, 1990, had been members of the "Fat and Ugly Caucus" charged with vote selling. She found that only ten percent of those remaining in the House who had once been members of the Caucus had not been questioned by the FBI.

One of the Caucus' former leaders was the notorious chameleon, Rep. Robert Kohn (R-Charleston), who was indicted on August 24, 1990, as one of the first officials charged with corruption in the scandal. Kohn was the first after Ron Cobb to go undercover and help the FBI catch other crooked legislators.

One of the founders of the Caucus was Rep. David Hawkins, who left the House in 1987 to join the staff of Gov. Carroll Campbell. Hawkins was later convicted on plea of obstruction in Lost Trust.

The disbanding of the House "Fat and Ugly Caucus" in 1987 after Bob Sheheen was elected as Speaker and Rep. David Hawkins left both the Caucus and the House to work for Gov. Campbell may have triggered even more aggravated abusive behavior by those who had once been members of the Caucus. One former House member said that once Hawkins left, the discipline that he had imposed in limiting the abuses disappeared and those who had been in the Caucus went out on their own to hustle whatever they could from lobbyists and, the source added, "that's when everything went wrong."

But David Hawkins denied after Lost Trust broke that the Caucus served as a causal factor in the Lost Trust scandal, saying, "What they did or didn't do had absolutely nothing to do with our little group.... I don't see the connection between what we were doing and this."

The foundation of the Caucus dated back to about 1980 and was started by Hawkins and other House members who had little influence in the chamber. It started out as a social group which would go out to lunch on Tuesday and coerce lobbyists into paying the bills.

CHAPTER TWELVE

PROSECUTION MOVES FORWARD

Criminal Investigation Produces Indictments

The federal investigations included not only a sting operation to lure public officials into taking bribes, but also a drug investigation which used a sting operation to catch Rob Cobb; however, it did not use a sting to gather evidence on the other defendants indicted in the Lost Trust prosecutions for drug violations.

The indictment of Rep. Jack I. Rogers for RICO crimes was based on evidence, in part, obtained without a sting operation as to Rogers taking bribes to fix the capital gains tax reduction bill before Operation Lost Trust stings began. However, Rogers was also charged with bribery for taking a bribe on the betting bill, which was being undertaken as part of the sting operation. In addition, Rogers was charged with extortion for shaking down lobbyist Ken Kinard for part of Kinard's lobbying fees, but the FBI did not use a sting operation to catch Roger's shaking down Kinard on videotape.

The drug crimes of lobbyists were not captured on tape so far as can be determined, in that none of the drug defendants went to trial on their drug charges and the government did not have to present any videotaped evidence to the court showing that any drug sting had been used to catch any drug defendants. However, it is known that Cobb himself was caught in a drug sting operation in 1989, which triggered Operation Lost Trust as a bribery sting.

Robert Brown—First to Appear in Court

Rep. Robert Brown (D-Marion) became the first defendant in the Lost Trust series of prosecutions to appear in federal trial court. He was ordered to appear before Judge Falcon Hawkins on September 2, 1990, at the U.S. District Court in Columbia, S.C. His attorney was Cam Littlejohn.

Brown was the first of the five legislators indicted in August, 1990, for selling their votes to Rob Cobb in connection with the pari-mutuel betting bill. The order to appear was unusual in that it required Brown to present himself in court so soon after he was indicted by a federal grand jury. However, defendants announcing their intent to plead guilty commonly were called to court after only a brief interlude.

Brown had resigned his seat in the House the day before he was indicted on August 24, 1990, on an indictment alleging that he took a bribe of $2,000 from Rob Cobb. Brown had served as chair of the House Labor, Commerce, and Industry Committee, an important position dealing with business and economics.

Sen. Rick Lee (R-Spartanburg) was also called to appear in court on September 10, 1990, on allegations that he took a bribe of $2,000 in cash from Rob Cobb. Lee had resigned immediately on his indictment for corruption intending to plead guilty.

Brown Enters Not Guilty Plea

Robert Brown (D-Marion) appeared in federal court September 2, 1990. Brown entered a not guilty plea in response to his corruption indictment on August 24, 1990. Brown's guilty plea was mandatory in that defendants were prohibited by law from pleading guilty to felonies before federal magistrates and Brown and four other Lost Trust defendants had all appeared before magistrates, not district court judges.

The issue of videotapes in the Lost Trust cases was unclear in that it was a matter of discretion with federal judges and prosecutors at to whether they would release videotapes of corrupt transactions in cases where the defendants pleaded guilty. As such, the question of whether the tapes would be exposed to the public was a matter which could be negotiated by defendants and the prosecutors. Defendants commonly prefer not to have such tapes publicized after they plead guilty.

Brown, along with Rep. Robert Kohn (D-Charleston), faced maximum sentences of twenty years and fines of $250,000 each.

Kohn had been working undercover for the FBI for several months prior to the indictments.

Other legislators charged in the first round of indictments on August 24, 1990, included Rep. Luther Taylor (D-Richland) and Rep. Danny Winstead (R-Charleston). Taylor was charged with selling his vote four times and faced a huge total of 120 years in prison and $1.5 million in fines. Taylor was not set for immediate appearance in court.

Winstead Indicted for Bribery and Obstruction

Rep. Danny Winstead (R-Charleston) was charged with accepting a bribe of $1,000 from Ron Cobb and also with obstruction of justice. He faced up to 30 years in prison and a fine of $500,000.

Winstead was indicted among the first five defendants charged in Lost Trust on August 24, 1990. He was not set for an expedited or immediate appearance in federal court following his indictment. Winstead did not immediately plead guilty, but did so later.

Luther Taylor Motions Criticize Prosecution

Rep. Luther Taylor (D-Richland), who was suspended from the House after indictment for bribery and conspiracy, filed motions on September 4, 1990, alleging that the prosecution had created a circus atmosphere and made it impossible to give Taylor a fair trial.

Attorney Joel S. Collins, a former federal prosecutor himself, criticized Bart Daniel, his staff, and the FBI for briefing the state's congressional delegation about the sting before holding a major news conference after indictments were handed down. Such actions denied Taylor a fair trial, Collins alleged.

Taylor faced a maximum of 120 years in prison and a fine of $1.5 million at the time the motions were filed.

The motions indicated that the U.S. Supreme Court should dismiss all charges due to too much publicity by the government. Collins wrote that the court had said there was a "need in certain circumstances to protect a defendant from massive, pervasive, and prejudicial publicity."

Collins asked for a gag order on both the government officials and those indicted in the Lost Trust scandal.

Collins demanded full discovery of evidence to be used by the prosecution and for disclosure of witnesses to be called by the prosecution at the trial. The demand included all video and audiotapes to be used as evidence.

The motions asked for documents about drug charges against Ron Cobb and Bob Kohn, both sting agents. The motions also sought to learn who started the contacts during the sting and sought information which might impeach Cobb and Kohn as witnesses.

Robert Brown Pleads to Bribery

On September 4, 1990, Rep. Robert Brown, (D-Marion) became a convicted felon, pleading guilty to bribery in U.S. District Court for selling his vote on the betting bill. He became the first legislator to plead guilty, followed by Sen. Rick Lee, who also admitted vote selling on the same bill.

Brown was the most powerful of the five legislators indicted to that point in time as he was chairman of an important committee; the Labor, Commerce, and Industry Committee in the House through which the betting bill passed under his leadership.

At age 34, Brown, upon conviction, could no longer vote nor hold public office under state law. He also faced up to twenty years in prison plus a fine of $250,000.

Rep. Brown entered his plea but did not watch the grainy and muffled videotape which showed him taking cash from sting lobbyist Ronald Cobb, who pulled the crisp $100 bills from a wad of cash, a total of $2,000. The tape revealed a discussion of strategy for passing the betting bill in which Brown indicated his complicity.

In the audiotape, Brown mentions the name "Joe" without a last name, perhaps the mysterious "Joe Williams," an accomplice of Ron Cobb pushing the betting bill who was, in fact, a secret FBI agent for the FBI front, the Alpha Group. "Joe" is seen in the videotape in which Brown takes the money from Cobb.

Cobb says: "Robert's with us, hook, line. I mean sinker, he's our man," commenting to "Joe" in front of Brown who had put the $2,000 in cash into his pocket.

The bribe was paid on the FBI fishing boat "Tally Ho" at Hilton Head, South Carolina, on April 14, 1990.

FBI Agent, Mike Clemens, testified that Brown actually took two handouts of cash, one for $2,000 and the other for $500.

On the "Tally Ho," Cobb asked Brown what it would take to get his help on the betting bill. Brown replied, "I think you know where my motivation is," followed by Brown's indication that he wanted money. He said he wanted the "biggest number you can get," according to Clemens.

When the sting broke after the seizures of campaign records in late July, Brown amended his campaign report belatedly after the June deadline to report the money taken in cash from Cobb.

At first Brown said, "I've never taken a dime with strings attached." But at the plea hearing, Brown told Judge Hawkins when asked by the judge if he was guilty of bribery on the facts presented by the prosecution, Brown said, "Yes, Your Honor, it is [sic]."

The plea agreement for Brown required him to fully cooperate with the prosecution and name other lawmakers who had also sold their vote and to testify before the grand jury and tell everything he knew about the scandal. Bart Daniel said that he had other tapes of Brown and that more charges might be made against Brown if he failed to fully cooperate and reveal more details about public corruption, narcotics, money laundering, and obstruction of justice. Daniel said that all of those violations were being probed by the government.

Brown was represented by attorney Cameron B. Littlejohn, Jr., who worked in the same law firm as Judge Hawkins' son.

Daniel said the recommended sentence would be 33 to 37 months in federal prison, but with a recommendation of lenience for full cooperation which the judge was not bound to show in sentencing. Another judge other than Hawkins would impose sentence later. Brown was on bond until sentencing.

Sen. Rick Lee revealed that he would plead guilty September 10, 1990, for taking $2,000 from Cobb.

Brown—Who Was He?

The Robert Brown who pleaded guilty to bribery on September 4, 1990, seemed to be a different person from that described by his friends and associates. Rep. Larry Martin (R-Pickens) and Speaker Bob Sheheen found Brown a capable committee chairman of LCI. "Robert was anxious to work real hard," Sheheen said. But five other members of LCI were also implicated in the scandal; one was Rep. Robert Kohn, who had been turned as a sting agent after being caught.

Rep. Hicks Harwell (D- Florence) described Brown as having "as much potential politically as anybody in this area," the same region of South Carolina which Harwell represented.

Brown started out as a college page in the state Senate and rose to Chairman of LCI in a little over a decade. Elected to the House in 1984 at age 27 from his town of birth, he joined the family business in 1978.

The Mayor of Marion where Brown lived, Bobby Gerald, said, "He was an excellent representative.... When it came to grants and other help for the county, he was Johnny on-the-spot." Brown's minister, Rev. Wayne Roe, said of Brown, "He's been a faithful church member.... I hate to see him end his career. I support Robert Brown, and we all stand behind him."

Speaker Sheheen said that after a slow start in the House, Brown got more serious. In 1988, Brown was elected to chair LCI, a job that required "a lot of political maneuvering and arm-twisting," according to Rep. Martin who also sought the job.

Harwell said Brown may have gotten in trouble because he had too much power too young and too soon, "So much, so soon."

Jack I. Rogers Exposed for Racketeering

Speaker Pro Tem of the House, Rep. Jack I. Rogers (D-Marlboro), became more and more the focus of the Lost Trust scandal. In the end, he would be hit the hardest by the courts and convicted of racketeering for brazen and persistent corruption in office.

Although not caught in the first round of five indictments which caught smaller fish, the media clearly showed that Rogers had been a major player in the struggle to pass a betting bill and might well be a suspect in the matter.

By September 5, 1990, it became clear that Rogers had led the doomed effort to "charge the hill" on April 25, 1990, the same day that LCI Chair Robert Brown tried to win passage of the betting bill under the auspices of the Alpha Group, the FBI front. All 15 of the current House members then known to have been contacted by the FBI were voting for the bill as a group.

Rep. Terry Haskins (R-Greenville), who led the fight to stop the betting bill, said he had been warned that Rogers was going to try to bring the bill up for a debate on the House floor. And it was known that Rogers took $250 from Ron Cobb. Further, the main point of the Robert Brown case was that Brown took money from Cobb to pass the betting bill.

Rogers Took Money to Move Betting Bill

The deal with Cobb that Brown made required Brown to move the betting bill forward ahead of other pending bills by moving to adjourn debate. In fact, Brown did not move to adjourn debate, but Rogers did;,the very act that Brown was paid a bribe to do on the day of April 25, 1990. And previously on April 12, Rogers did not move to adjourn debate, but tried to direct others to do so without his action.

Rogers made 7 of the 8 motions to adjourn debate on April 25, 1990. All 15 suspects joined Rogers in voting for the motions, except Reps. Tee Ferguson and Tom Limehouse who abstained on such votes. Up to that time among the 15 from the General Assembly, all would later be indicted and all but one would be convicted of crimes related to the betting bill at issue in the Labor, Commerce, and Industry Committee.

Rep. Terry Haskins (R-Greenville) led a group fighting the betting bill which included Reps. Wes Hayes (D-York), David Beasley (D-Darlington), and later Mike Fair (R-Greenville). Hayes forced a vote on Rogers' motion to adjourn debate and won 46-44, stopping the betting bill by keeping a "boating while intoxicated" bill on the floor for debate and pushing the betting bill off the floor.

California Legislator Caught in Reverse Sting

As the Operation Lost Trust was reaching a crescendo in Columbia, *The Los Angeles Times* reported that Sen. Paul Carpenter of the California General Assembly took $20,000 from an undercover FBI sting agent on a bogus bill planted by the FBI.

Sen. Carpenter claimed at a jury trial that he took the money to trap the bribe-giver in a "reverse sting." But he never actually conducted an investigation of the money given and never told any law enforcement agency about taking it and keeping it.

Under cross examination, Carpenter admitted he lied to the California Fair Political Practices Commission when he said that he notified the FBI sting agent about state campaign finance laws. He further admitted that he gave $17,000 of the money to three senators who voted in favor of the bill.

Carpenter was charged with four counts of racketeering, extortion, and conspiracy in connection with a corruption sting in which an FBI operative posed as an Alabama businessman trying to bribe votes for a shrimp plant near Sacramento.

Thomas Winstead Pleads to Bribery

The defendants indicted on August 24, 1990, fell quickly to convictions following the plea entered by Rep. Robert Brown. Convinced of his guilt, by early September Rep. Thomas E. Winstead of Charleston was admitting in federal court that he took a bribe of $1,000 from Ron Cobb.

A videotape at the plea hearing showed corruptionist Rep. Bob Kohn as sting agent on June 21, 1990, handing Winstead an envelope from Ron Cobb which Kohn said was related to voting on the betting bill. Winstead responded to Kohn's question of whether the amount of money was enough by saying, "Yeah...he gave me a nice contribution." The camera showed Winstead putting the envelope in his hip pocket. The money was handed out at the Shoney's Restaurant in North Charleston, unlike most other bribes paid out at Hilton Head or Columbia.

Winstead admitted he took $2,500 from Kohn to support the betting bill and that he had obstructed justice. Judge Falcon Hawkins pronounced him convicted. He faced up to 30 years in prison and a $500,000 fine. Winstead had agreed to fully cooperate in a plea agreement he had signed on August 23, 1990, just before his indictment. He was also promised use immunity that whatever he told the FBI would not be used as evidence against him in court. And he further agreed to resign from the House which he did prior to his conviction.

Winstead Tried to Obstruct FBI Investigation

Winstead's obstruction was based on his efforts to influence Bob Kohn to stonewall the FBI probe. Unknown to Winstead, of course, Kohn had recently become an undercover stooge of the FBI.

FBI agent Mike Clemens testified at the Winstead plea hearing prior to conviction that in January, 1990, Kohn, not yet aware of the sting, told Cobb that Rep. Winstead would support the betting bill if paid off. On January 23, 1990, Winstead told Cobb that he would push the bill but did not want the payoff until afterward so that it would not look like he was paid in advance to vote. Winstead thought that would look less like a bribe.

Taking the money on June 21, 1990, Winstead later said on July 20th that he thought the Mafia was behind the betting bill and would silence anybody who implicated the mob.

Then after he heard of the FBI probe and the subpoenaed records, Winstead told sting agent Kohn on July 20, 1990, to "deny everything" setting up his obstruction charge, adding that, "Yes, sir. You're dealing with the Mafia. You're dealing with the families." Of course, the FBI recorded Winstead's remarks to Kohn as evidence, making Winstead look both guilty and stupid.

Winstead warned Kohn against amending his campaign reports after the subpoenas had seized them, saying it would arouse suspicion: "They'll jump right on that like a June bug." Winstead then added: "Like I told 'em, [the FBI] what I got is what I reported. That's it. I deny everything else. I ain't never got nothin' from nobody."

Not saying who advised him, Winstead said to Kohn, who, like Winstead, was not a lawyer but a crook turned informant, "Make them prove everything; don't give 'em anything and don't admit anything... Let it roll and deny everything." Then he told Kohn to deny that they had met to discuss the sting and the two agreed to notify each other if contacted by the FBI. "I hope I don't hear from you." Then Winstead replied: "No, no. I hope I don't hear from you either.... Even if you do, we ain't done nothing, said nothing, or meant nothing."

The prosecution did not play the tape in its entirety because other portions contained information used in the ongoing probe. Yet enough of the tape was presented in court to show there was adequate factual evidence to justify Winstead's guilty plea.

Winstead, Kohn Scheme Over Wrong Problem

When Reps. Danny Winstead and Bob Kohn met on July 20, 1990, they erroneously thought the FBI was after them for a bill being pushed by the S.C. Credit Union League, not the betting bill. Ron Cobb was lobbying for both bills. And the credit union bill was supported primarily by Reps. Robert Brown, Luther Taylor, Tom Limehouse, Bob Kohn, and Tee Ferguson, all of whose records had been seized by the FBI.

Rep. Larry Martin remembered that all of them were pushing at the end of session to move the credit union bill which would have legalized automobile tent sales. Taylor was the floor leader pushing the credit union bill in the LCI. Committee, which was opposed by the Auto Dealers Association which disliked tent sales.

In fact, the FBI was taking action on the betting bill which happened to involve all of the persons also promoting the credit union bill. The FBI was not investigating or running a sting on the credit union bill.

Who Was the Real Danny Winstead?

Like some of the others caught in Lost Trust, Winstead had an alter ego as a private person quite different from his corrupt persona as a politician.

Those who knew Winstead said they were shocked. Sen. Sherry Martschink, also from Charleston, said, "When I first heard the names of those supposedly involved, he was the one I was most surprised at. He and his wife, Iris, are the kinds of people you'd want to live next door to."

His officemate in the House, Rep. John Rama (R-Charleston), said that he was very disappointed and embarrassed, noting that "he seemed to know the ins and outs of the Legislature, and I looked to him for advice."

Known as a quiet and easy-going politician, Winstead had represented District 117 in North Charleston since 1979 and had served on the Ways and Means Committee, a major panel shaping the state budget. Sen. Martschink said that Winstead was known as a person who got things done on the committee. He was also chairman of the roads committee of the Charleston County Legislative Delegation which controlled the paving of roads.

Age 44, Winstead had been born in Ridgeland, S.C., but moved to Hampton and finished high school there. He attended, but did not finish, Carson-Newman College in Tennessee. Later moving to Charleston, he worked for the Southern Bell Telephone Company and was employed by the Medical University as a communication consultant for five years, but resigned as of October 1, 1990, apparently due to his indictment.

He also served as a deacon in the Hillcrest Baptist Church and had been a member since 1969.

Gov. Campbell Pushes Reform Ideas

With the November 6, 1990, general elections nearing, Gov. Carroll Campbell felt compelled to step forward with proposals to clean up the mess at the State House. Until his Development Board Chairman, Dick Greer, was charged with cocaine, Campbell's administration had not been in any way implicated in Lost Trust so far as the public and voters knew. Greer would be charged April 10, 1991, after the re-election of Campbell.

Campbell's response to the crisis was, however, not congruous with the problems revealed by the growing scandal which were primarily based on bribery, abuse of office, and drug use. Campbell argued, instead, for proposals to reorganize state government to give himself more power by consolidating the work of state boards and commissions to provide more accountability.

In an early September interview with reporter Jeff Miller of *The State*, Campbell said that since taking office in 1987, he had concluded that all state agencies should be directly responsible to the governor for budget and operations, which was not the case at the time. Boards and commissions were elected by the Legislature and were responsible to nobody. Campbell thought some constitutional amendments were needed, but Campbell did not favor calling a state constitutional convention to restructure for fear of making things worse. But Campbell's proposals really did not address the problems exposed by the scandal.

Campbell noted that campaign finance was in the spotlight because of the scandal, and public support for reform was growing as to limiting cash contributions and improving disclosure of funds.

As to cash contributions, he proposed a limit of $100 per donor. But the governor opposed other types of contribution limits.

He also advocated that the election process was in need of improvements and wanted responsibility for state elections, including primaries, shifted to the State Election Commission which should also collect and hold campaign disclosure forms. Gov. Campbell urged filing of campaign financial reports 30 days and 10 days before elections, and amounts of $2,500 or more should be reported 24 hours after receipt. He favored disclosure of all contributions by candidates.

In addition, he favored shifting oversight of all public officials to the State Ethics Commission. He felt the legislative ethics committees were not effective, but, if not eliminated, should at least be modeled on those of Congress, which Campbell had learned about while in the U.S. House. Such committees should have three Democrats and three Republicans, Campbell reasoned, and "that way you'd never have a cover-up." Even so, Campbell's plan was much less than what was needed to deal with out-of-control lobbyists and campaign financing.

Campaign Money Conflicts of Interest

In addition to Secretary of State John Campbell, who took half of his campaign funds from lobbyists and cemeteries he regulated, State Treasurer Grady Patterson had the same contribution problem in the amount of $92,000 from banks he regulated. Patterson said he would return $20,000 from banks which were direct corporate donations but not the rest from bank PACs which the Ethics Commission had ruled were legal donations.

Attorney General Travis Medlock took $11,500 from the law firm McNair, one of the largest lobbyist firms. He also took $9,350 from Nelson Mullins Riley and Scarborough which was a major lobbyist contract firm. Of course, Medlock was responsible for enforcing lobbying laws.

Prof. Blease Graham of the University of South Carolina Political Science faculty said, "I think he [Medlock] is in a very shaky boat...in the public's eye it doesn't look right." But Bob Sheheen said, "I'm not going to make a judgment.... A conflict of interest situation is one that each person has to decide for himself." However, Sheheen added: "I think the appearance would be better" if Medlock stopped taking money from lawyers.

Attorney General Travis Medlock was responsible for enforcing the law against all lobbyists, but at the same time, he was taking campaign money from them.

Prof. Eldon Wedlock, a specialist in legal ethics and constitutional law and Chairman of the Board of Common Cause/South Carolina, pointed out that Medlock was "in a position of conflict of interest, to be taking contributions from people he might have to investigate and prosecute."

Rep. Joe McElveen (D-Sumter), an advocate of lobbying law reform in the 1990 session of the General Assembly, agreed: "If it were me, and it were someone whom I had direct regulatory power over, I would not accept the contributions."

The issue had been raised when the State Ethics Commission told Secretary of State John Campbell that he could not take money from lobbyists because his office had jurisdiction over them without violating a state law limiting to $10 contributions from the regulated to the regulator. In fact, Campbell had taken half of all his money from regulated parties, an amount of nearly $10,000. This would prove a huge liability for Campbell's re-election campaign and a major reason for his defeat by Jim Miles.

Speaker Bob Sheheen fought in the 1990 session of the Legislature to shift jurisdiction over campaign finance and ethics rules from the Attorney General to the State Ethics Commission. Pointing to the conflict, Attorney General Medlock said: "It would certainly put the Attorney General or any elected official who was in charge of prosecuting someone in a difficult situation if he had received a $1,000 campaign contribution from that person."

Regulating lobbyists who gave the Attorney General campaign money presented the same conflict problem. It was a real problem because about one third of all 290 registered lobbyists in the state did not report their lobbying income as required by law. But Medlock, in charge of enforcement, said the law was too vague to enforce.

Sen. Phil Leventis (D-Sumter) complained and, after two weeks of public criticism, Medlock changed his mind and ordered all lobbyists to disclose their income or be brought into court. "You can't hold a different standard for Travis than you can do for John Campbell," Leventis said of campaign contributions. Political money created conflicts.

Rick Lee Bites Dust

The third official to plead guilty in Lost Trust was Sen. Rick Lee (R-Spartanburg), who announced his intent on September 9, 1990, to join Robert Brown and Danny Winstead who had already done so. Lee said he sold his vote on the betting bill.

He entered his plea on September 10, 1990, at the U.S. Courthouse in Columbia, but he had actually cut a deal before July 18th.

New Charges on Horizon

Speculation was growing about a possible new charge of money laundering raised by prosecutors for the first time in early September. Laundering is a scheme to make money obtained illegally look like it was obtained by legal means.

Former U.S. Attorney, Henry D. McMaster, responded to an inquiry from the media by telling Clark Surratt of *The State* that, "It is laundering money if a legislator takes a bribe and reports it as a campaign contribution."

Drug charges were also rumored to be announced in mid-September, 1990, although no such charges had yet been filed in the first five indictments, but it would soon be revealed that an extensive drug probe and prosecution was a major part of Lost Trust.

Taylor Doing "Business as Usual"

The video and audiotapes of Luther Taylor caught him telling Ron Cobb about the corruption in the old days at the rundown Jefferson Hotel located near the State House where bribery and prostitution in Columbia had been entrenched for decades. Taylor said: "They say a man, a lobbyist, knew what hotel room a man was in. He'd come and knock on the door. And when the man came to open the door, there'd be a grocery bag full; full of capital."

However, it came out that on May 9, 1990, lobbyist Linda Walker told Taylor that the FBI was investigating Ron Cobb and that Taylor should be careful in dealing with Cobb. However, Walker denied that, saying: "I did not warn him of anything. I had heard there was an investigation, but I didn't really know there was. I was just talking to Luther Taylor walking down the street and I just said to him, 'I hope you're not involved'. I thought it was pretty common knowledge."

Walker was most likely worried about obstruction of justice issues related to the notice she gave to Taylor. Walker was never charged in relation to Lost Trust.

Taylor Case Near Trial

In the month before the start of the Luther Taylor trial set for October 8, 1990, the discovery process in which attorney Joel Collins forced out prosecution evidence was complicated by the fact that although Collins wanted the evidence, he did not want it published. In fact, he asked the court to seal the case files to prevent public prejudice against Taylor.

Collins even suggested that the trial might have to be moved outside of South Carolina because, "There won't be 12 citizens who can read and write, who keep up with the news in any fashion, who have not read or heard about this case.... The U.S. Attorney General is fanning the flames."

Collins told Judge Hawkins that the court should stop disclosure of information from the cases of other defendants who had pled guilty in previous days which were reported by the press. Bart Daniel opposed, saying that some of the facts must be disclosed to the public. It was a classic conflict over the right of a criminal defendant to a fair trial pitted against the public's right to know what their government was doing.

Taylor Took Payoff in Computer Deal

The long arms of 6 foot 7 inch Rep. Luther Taylor could reach into pockets with ease and he grabbed money not only on the betting bill but also on computer deals for the sale of nearly $3 million of computers to Clemson University. The probe found that Taylor took another $2,000 to help seal the deal in a disputed appeal involving National Advanced Systems, a Hitachi appendage. Taylor was on the State Procurement Panel from 1986 and into 1990, which dealt with state government purchases.

Although not indicted on the matter when it was discovered, the FBI concluded that Taylor was prone to take a bribe and an easy target for the sting according to documents filed in U.S. District Court September 10, 1990, which related to Taylor's nearing trial set for October 18, 1990.

The documents were revelatory and named those expected to be charged as implicated in the bribery, including Kohn, Ferguson, Blanding, Fant, Gordon and McBride; all members of the Black Caucus in the House. All would, in fact, be charged.

Taylor was identified as having taken bribes in 1988 and 1989 leading up to the sting. The prosecution seemed to have plenty of evidence against Taylor ready for his trial.

Hitachi denied any knowledge of corruption by their lobbyist Ron Cobb involving Taylor, saying, "Illegal activity of this nature is expressly prohibited in our contract with Mr. Cobb."

Taylor's attorney, Joel Collins, protested Taylor's rights. He insisted that Judge Hawkins take action to stop such leaks in the future.

Taylor Implicated in Corruption in Computer Buys

The federal prosecutors alleged that Taylor was entangled in payoffs in the computer purchases sold by National Advanced Systems (NAS) to Clemson University because the matter was appealed to the Procurement Review Panel [PRP] on which Taylor had served since 1986 as one of three legislative members.

Cobb as lobbyist for NAS asked Taylor to help NAS defeat the appeal by an unsuccessful vendor to the PRP. Taylor demanded one percent of the contract amount—$2,800. Although the PRP records do not show any action by Taylor, the appeal was rejected in favor of NAS. Cobb did pay the amount in installments ending June 1, 1988.

The prosecution wanted to use the computer bribes to show that Taylor took the $4,300 bribes on the betting bill with full "knowledge, intent, and lack of mistake" when Taylor asked for a payoff of $2,500 from an FBI sting agent on January 16, 1990. The picture was that Taylor had been crooked prior to the deal and was again doing the sort of payoff he had a pattern of doing.

The government alleged that the old Jefferson Hotel on the corner of Main and Laurel streets in downtown Columbia had been a traditional place for corruption of officials.

Pre-Indictment Publicity Protested

Andy Savage, attorney for bribery suspect Rep. Thomas Limehouse, was concerned about media speculation that his client might be indicted for corruption. Savage said, "we are facing some serious questions about when the public's right to know comes in conflict with the right to a fair trial." Savage worried that the public might think that everybody rumored to be involved might be seen as guilty because some had pleaded guilty already.

Savage said that clients might be suspects and indicted even though they had not received target letters. Seven legislators were identified as being entangled with Luther Taylor and many more indictments were expected.

The canons of ethics of the South Carolina Bar said that lawyers are not supposed to discuss in public evidence which likely might be challenged in court. But prejudicial information was leaking out about the defendants and suspects.

Critics said that Bart Daniel was saying too much about the Lost Trust cases in public and that evidence was being released that was too prejudicial to suspects who might be charged. But the leaks were not stopped.

Push-Back Against Ethics Reform

Proposals to limit government payments and stop gambling involving legislators ran into opposition from members of Lt. Gov. Nick Theodore's ethics reform committee when Sen. Kay Patterson and Sen. John Courson objected to a proposal to stop legislators living in Richland County from getting state payments for living expenses while in legislative session. The payments were approved to offset expenses for lodging and meals of legislators from distant places who had to rent motel rooms and pay for food while away from home.

A proposal was made to ban gambling by legislators, a common practice exposed in the Lost Trust scandal, which often involved lobbyists throwing poker games with legislators and deliberately losing substantial sums of money in the process. Sen. Courson and Rep. Candy Y. Waites of Columbia complained that they were insulted by the proposed ban which they said was not needed because state law already banned gambling by anybody in the state. "It's there and it's the law," said Waites, "I resent the implications." Courson said there was no proof that legislators and lobbyists played poker together at the Town House Hotel, saying, "I don't know it's going on." In fact, it was.

Racism Alleged v. Sting

On September 17, 1990, two back bench black senators complained that the vote-buying scandal at the State House was designed to catch a disproportionate number of black legislators. In a news conference, the chairman of the Legislative Black Caucus, Sen. Herbert Fielding (D-Charleston), and Sen. Kay Patterson (D-Richland) accused the FBI and the U.S. Attorney's office of improper tactics to sting blacks. Patterson said the FBI tried to bribe a black official five times before he took $450, but refused to identify the alleged target.

Eight of 17 reported targets were black. The Greenville branch of the NAACP had said the same sort of thing at about the same time, alleging a plot against blacks by federal officials.

Fielding said, "there is no reason for any investigation to focus disproportionately on blacks." Patterson claimed views expressed by the two represented the opinion of the whole caucus. Patterson, who had a long history of making an issue of black victimization, alleged:

"If anyone argues with the fact that this sting is not targeted on blacks and that blacks are way out of proportion—a disproportionate number—then they need their heads examined."

Daniel denied the charge saying, "We didn't target whites; we did not target blacks." He completely rejected the charges.

Fielding said that in Alabama and Atlanta, the FBI had gone after black officials without probable cause.

Capital Gains Tax Scandal Appears

Obscured by the media focus on indictments for bribery on the betting bill were charges of bribery related to a 1989 capital gains tax break bill to help 21 people save $8.6 million in taxes.

The issue was raised in public by Sen. Ernie Passailague (D-Charleston) who said the FBI was asking him about the role of State Economic Development Chair, Dick Greer, in getting the tax break bill passed. On September 16, 1990, Sen. Passailague said the FBI interviewed him the previous week about another effort by two powerful senators to remove the tax break with no success.

Dick Greer, in return, lashed out at Passailague on the tax break issue, resenting the implication that he was involved.

An undisclosed source also said that Attorney General Travis Medlock's office had turned over to the FBI a probe of capital gains tax break by SLED, a claim the office denied. The Attorney General's office said the probe was still going on.

The probe had been started by Medlock in August, 1990, his office said, along with Gov. Carroll Campbell's office in response to an article in *The State* about a payoff to lobbyist Ron Cobb for the tax break.

Tax Break For Businessmen Probed

The SLED probe was looking into a report that Ron Cobb was trying to collect more money from clients for payoffs given to legislators to obtain the tax break bills passage. The clients were those who benefited from the tax break bill passed in 1988, but partially reversed in 1989 when one client refused to pay.

Greer, chairman of Gov. Campbell's re-election campaign committee in 1990, and Chairman of the Economic Development Board under Campbell, reportedly directed a person seeking a tax break bill to lobbyist Ron Cobb.

Campbell's spokesman impugned Sen. Passailague by saying that he approached the FBI, but that they were not interested in the tax matter. Tucker Eskew of Campbell's staff said: "Ernie and the truth are real strangers."

Passailague said that the FBI was probing the relationships between the tax bill, campaign contributions, the beneficiaries of the tax bill, and legislators, looking for evidence of Hobbs Act bribery.

The 1988 bill gave over $20 million in tax breaks to 60,000 people, but that a select group of 21 taxpayers saved $8.6 million.

Greer allegedly sent Greenville businessman Tom Roe to Cobb and Roe also gave $6,000 to Campbell's first campaign for governor in 1986. Later, Sen. Jack Lindsay and Sen. James Waddell tried and failed to rescind the tax break act, perhaps in retaliation for the fact that Cobb's clients refused to pay any additional money to Cobb when Cobb demanded a second payment to reward him for his success.

Passailague Defended in Greer Matter

Democratic senators defended Sen. Ernie Passailague who had raised questions about Dick Greer's ties to the tax cut bill and Rob Cobb.

Sens. Jim Bryan, Herbert Fielding, John Land, Isadore Lourie, and Nell Smith issued a news release saying:

> Senator Passailague has made no public statements concerning the governor's role, and for the governor's office to hysterically and harshly impugn Senator Passailague's credibility and make a personal attack on his integrity is an insult to the senator and his office.

Capital Gains Tax Bill Probed

In late September 1990, *The Spartanburg Herald-Journal* reported a probe of the role of Dick Greer in the capital gains tax cut bill, and that $150,000 was offered to key legislators and lobbyists to pass the tax cut bill.

David Hawkins Rumored To Be Involved With Cobb

The Charlotte Observer newspaper in late September, 1990, reported that Ron Cobb tried to get David Hawkins to help with the pari-mutuel betting bill and that the FBI had taped at least two meetings in which Cobb requested Hawkins help with the bill. Hawkins was Gov. Campbell's Director of Legislative Affairs. Cobb reportedly offered Hawkins money in return.

Hawkins would later plead guilty to obstruction of the FBI investigation in the Lost Trust cases. Hawkins also had a dubious reputation stemming from his previous service in the South

Carolina House of Representatives where he was the foremost leader of the notorious "Fat and Ugly Caucus" which had lived off the lobbyists at the State House in the 1980s.

The Caucus was suppressed by Speaker Robert Sheheen prior to the revelations of the Lost Trust scandal. Sheheen reached the point where he concluded that the "Fat and Ugly Caucus" was abusing its power and demanding handouts from lobbyists as part of a pay-to-play scheme in the House.

Taylor Alleges Prosecutorial Misconduct

Taylor's pretrial motions alleged that the government tried to trick him into obstructing justice too. Taylor claimed that Rep. Robert Kohn, turned FBI sting agent, met with Taylor at McDonald's restaurant near the USC football stadium to incriminate him.

The grand jury was never told that Taylor and the Black Caucus had been supporting the pari-mutuel betting bill before the sting began. The grand jury was not told how the legislative process worked or that there was nothing Taylor or others could have done to ensure the bill would pass.

In an affidavit filed on September 19, 1990, indicted Rep. Luther Taylor charged that the FBI plied him with a liter of Scotch alcohol and kept him in a room for questioning for some 25 hours on July 17 and 18 at the Ramada Inn on Two Notch Road. He also filed a motion to dismiss criminal charges against him because of prosecutorial misconduct.

The charges were extortion and conspiracy, a total of six charges in all.

As the grand jury continued to meet and handed down new indictments periodically, Taylor also accused the government of selective prosecution in that the sting agreed in advance with undercover FBI lobbyist Ron Cobb that, "its sting operation would specifically exclude, avoid, and not target a certain senior senator, a member of the General Assembly of South Carolina." The senior senator, it was later revealed, was Sen. Jack Lindsay.

Taylor's attorneys also demanded that the judge make Cobb available for discovery. (Cobb was believed to be under protective custody by the FBI.) Taylor asked for discovery of evidence of racial targeting based on a purported "Fruhmenschen" policy predicated on the theory that blacks were innately corrupt. (Fruhmenschen means "primitive man" in German.)

Defendants in Scandal Get Help—But Not Much

The efforts to portray the defendants and suspects in Lost Trust as victims of crooked tactics and racial targeting received a little reaction, but not much.

Efforts to raise money for black Reps. Luther Taylor, Frank McBride, James Faber, and Ennis Fant from constituents ended up with little in their defense funds in spite of allegations that they were the victims of racial targeting.

Jeff Simons set up a fund-raising plan claiming that, "Everybody is on the same wave length. We feel it's entrapment and it's racially motivated." But the opinion in the black community that the FBI was trying to wipe out black legislators got a cynical reaction from some blacks. Dr. Willease Sanders, a Benedict College English professor for some 30 years, remarked at the time that even if the sting forced blacks out of their positions, their heavily gerrymandered massively black House districts would produce black replacements and that she knew some of the suspects herself, and would not put it past them to take money on the side.

Simons claimed that the "strength of the black community is those lawmakers with experience... If we keep throwing them out, we'll never get the seniority." Even so, few blacks showed evidence that they felt sorry for the accused and few donated to defense funds.

Simons said in raising money for the defense fund of three blacks—Taylor, McBride, and Fant—that he knew James Faber was fully supported by House District 70, in lower Richland County, a predominantly black area. He said that "We don't think Mr. Faber's done anything wrong." At the time, Faber was being challenged by Rev. Joe Neal in the Democratic primary election. In the end, Rev. Joe Neal would replace Faber after his conviction for bribery. It turned out that all convicted blacks would be replaced by blacks.

Simons kept complaining of racist plotting, saying, "When you think about this situation of entrapment, even animals sometimes get treated better. It's against the law to bait a field for birds or deer, but it seems like it's open season on black politicians." Simons continued and said all the money was raised through church and community meetings promoted by blacks to be used for legal defense costs.

Rev. Joseph H. Hollis in Taylor's district said money had been raised at one or two meetings at churches to help Taylor. I.S. Leevy Johnson, attorney for both Faber and McBride, said the effort was a "vote of confidence in their innocence" and he alleged that in the black community, there was a "deep-seated feeling that there's a pattern of prosecutorial misconduct to single out black elected officials."

Six More Indicted

On Friday, September 21, 1990, six more criminal defendants were added to the list bringing the total to 11 officials charged in Lost Trust.

The most serious charges were directed to Rep. Thomas Limehouse (R-Summerville), an attorney accused of conspiracy, extortion, taking a $2,000 bribe, and witness tampering. Limehouse took money, saying he would "mortgage his office" for money and that he had done it before and would do it again. Limehouse allegedly said he would sell his support for the betting bill for "a couple of suits and five or six shirts."

The FBI may have picked Limehouse because he had been paid off by Ron Cobb in the past. Limehouse met Cobb and another undercover FBI agent at the Town House Hotel three months before taking a $2,000 bribe and told them he was satisfied with Ron Cobb's payoffs in the past and that he expected more money "at the end of the rainbow."

In addition to Rep. Limehouse, a white legislator, three Democrats in the Black Caucus were indicted, too, on September 21, 1990. Reps. Ennis Fant (Greenville), Larry Blanding (Sumter), and B.J. Gordon (Williamsburg), were all charged with conspiracy to violate the Hobbs Act in taking bribes to support the betting bill.

The other official indicted was Rep. Donna Moss (D-Cherokee), for possession of cocaine during the 1989 legislative session. Moss resigned the day she was indicted. She was the only woman ever charged in Lost Trust.

The first lobbyist was also indicted. James Brown V, who represented the Credit Union League was charged with possession of marijuana. Brown was known as a member of the fast crowd at the State House and the Town House bar.

At the announcement of the indictments, U.S. Attorney Bart Daniel and FBI agent John Harley, the top FBI agent in South Carolina, promised more indictments in the future. At the same time as all the disclosures of public corruption, Daniel said, "In our public officials we repose a sacred trust... to represent the public and obey the law... in some, that public trust has been misplaced."

Charges Lodged Against Six Defendants

Indictments against the six filed on September 21, 1990, charged the following criminal defendants:

Rep. Thomas Limehouse (R-Charleston) (Age: 31)

Elected to the House in 1985, he was the youngest member of the House. He would pose many questions to legislators about bills being debated. He championed the Freedom of Information Act. He sometimes blocked bills for no apparent reasons. He had an antagonistic relationship with Sen. Mike Rose of Dorchester County where he lived, and Rose welcomed his demise.

Although able to influence the movement of bills on the House floor, he was not regarded as a rising star in his party.

He graduated from the University of South Carolina in 1979 and the USC School of Law in 1982.

Limehouse was charged with conspiracy, bribery, witness tampering, and extortion.

Rep. Rev. B.J. Gordon (D-Williamsburg) (Age: 57)

By occupation, Gordon was a minister, car salesman, and licensed auctioneer. Gordon was a minister at several Williamsburg churches, including Piney Grove Baptist Church, Bethlehem Baptist Church and Wilson Chapel Baptist Church.

Gordon had a history of problems. In 1988, *The State* reported alleged irregularities in the use of federal funds channeled through the Gordon Development Center, a facility for retarded adults in the county. The matter included a $12,000 grant from the state for a new heating system for the Center. However, the grant funds were not deposited in the Center's account. *The State* reported that Gordon used $4,000 of the money as a loan to buy a truck, but later returned the money to the Center. He served for 17 years.

Rep. Larry Blanding (D-Sumter) (Age: 37)

Elected to the S.C. House in 1977, Blanding was a real estate agent and a 1975 graduate of Claflin College where he was president of the student body. He took a master's degree in education from South Carolina State College in 1977.

Active in the youth program of the Black Political Caucus, he was a delegate to the 1972 Democratic National Convention in Miami Beach, Florida.

In the House he served on the Ethics Committee and on Ways and Means where he was on the subcommittee dealing with law enforcement funding for prisons and police. He was popular in his district.

He was charged with taking two bribes in total of $1,300.

Rep. Donna Moss (D-Cherokee) (Age: 36)

She was elected in 1988 with the votes of 9 Republicans as chair of the Medical, Military, Public and Municipal Affairs Committee to oust African-American legislator Rep. Juanita White (D-Jasper). But she provided poor direction and did not originate major legislation in her committee. She was also accused by a fired staffer in 1990 or making racist remarks about blacks.

She was a 1977 graduate of the College of Charleston.

She had no opposition in the November, 1990, election but resigned on indictment for possession of cocaine. She was not a major target of the sting. Moss was the only woman charged with crimes in Operation Lost Trust and would become the only woman convicted. Her cocaine charges were based on the government's incidental discovery of her possession.

Rep. Ennis Fant (D-Greenville) (Age: 29)

Elected to the House in 1988, he had a brief but troubled career. He was a Baptist minister.

He pushed passage of a bill to prohibit discrimination in the hotels and restaurants in late 1989 after he was refused service in a white singles club in Greenville.

Fant accused Speaker Bob Sheheen of neglecting the effort to elect a black committee chairman and criticized Sheheen's early re-election efforts.

In May, 1990, SLED investigated Fant based on a tip from Sheheen that Fant was trying to organize an escort service out of his House office in the Blatt Building. No criminal charges resulted but the House Ethics Committee required an apology.

Fant was unopposed in the November, 1990, election.

He was charged with vote selling.

James Brown, V (Lobbyist) (Age: 30)

Brown was the first lobbyist charged.

A Republican, he began as a page in the House while in college. He worked as legislative aide of Reps. Danny Winstead and Bob Kohn before becoming a lobbyist. All three were later charged in Lost Trust.

Brown lobbied for the S.C. Credit Union League which also hired Ron Cobb. He was a regular patron of the Town House bar, along with Ron Cobb and lobbyist Tom Collins, who worked for Hitachi and lobbyist Randy Lee, a buddy of Cobb. Brown used to talk about his partying with legislators.

Brown was subpoenaed in the Luther Taylor trial in October, 1990, and later pled to marijuana possession. He died a few weeks later of lung disease on November 30, 1990.

Criminal Charges Pile Up

Because the U.S. Attorney did not file all indictments at one time and the grand jury was continuing to probe the corruption in state government, batches of new indictments were handed down every month or two after the first charges were filed on August 24, 1990. With the next six indictments handed down on September 21, 1990, the public reactions varied from those who were concerned to those who felt that the matter had become almost routine. Some citizens expressed anger at the unending indictments.

On the one hand, Sen. Herb Fielding (D-Charleston) of the Black Caucus thought the second round of indictments in which three of six defendants were black was more evidence of racial targeting which he and Kay Patterson both alleged.

On the other, Tony Denny, Executive Director of the S.C. Republican Party, said that although "[i]t's still pretty shocking stuff..I'm ready for the criminal justice system to work its way and get this over with." Gov. Carroll Campbell felt assured that the "system is working to purge itself."

But Democratic Chair Albert McAlister admitted: "I'm sort of getting used to it...it's not as exciting as it was the first time." The shabby and pedestrian bribe-taking and drug use of the defendants seemed to vary little from case to case.

Cesspool of State House Corruption Provokes Indignation

Prof. Earl Black of the University of South Carolina worried that the scandal could continue to entangle more officials, saying, "If we get 15 or 20 legislators, that's really going to be embarrassing.... It's going to contribute to more of voter disgust." This prediction, of course, came true, and in the November, 1990, general elections many new legislators were returned by the voters.

The fact that three of the indicted—Donna Moss, Larry Blanding, and Danny Winstead—had served on the House Ethics Committee seemed most disconcerting, prompting Ethics Chair Pat Harris to complain: "It would seem that when you're elected to a committee like this by the entire House, you're held in high esteem." Harris said, "This gives me a real bad feeling."

The drug charges against Rep. Moss and lobbyist Brown were bemoaned by David Jameson, director of the Richland-Lexington Alcohol and Drug Abuse Council for 12 years who said: "When you get someone in a decision-making position, it really makes a problem for those of us trying to fight substance abuse. It gives a real mixed message, particularly among young people."

Racial Bias Issue

Indictments of three more black House members, Gordon, Blanding and Fant, aggravated the battle over alleged racial bias in the sting. Some 40 percent of the criminal defendants were black, but only 12 percent of legislators were black and 30 percent of the total population of South Carolina was black.

The sudden revelation that a deal had been cut with Ron Cobb to the effect that he would not have to try to sting white Sen. Jack Lindsay (D-Marlboro), a high-profile politician with a bad reputation, provoked more questions because the reason given was that Lindsay was Cobb's mentor and close friend. This type of deal with a criminal defendant seemed to show that certain politicians were getting extremely favorable treatment by the prosecution without any real justification whereas other defendants were getting hammered.

Bart Daniel denied bias, saying, "No single group or individual was targeted." He claimed the government was "not...keeping any sort of score card." Pushing back on the matter, Daniel said: "There has been some discussion that it might be politically or even racially motivated. Neither is true.... The indictments speak for themselves and will continue to do so over the next several months. They demonstrate that this investigation crosses all political, racial, and national lines."

Cobb Denies Bribing for Petroleum Association

5th Circuit Solicitor James Anders of Columbia said that Ron Cobb had denied that he offered money to legislators to back a bill in 1988 sought by his client, the S.C. Petroleum Marketers Association.

Anders said that Cobb had been granted state immunity from prosecution for his lobbying on behalf of the oil company bill related to the fact that Cobb took a contingent fee. Cobb had an agreement that said he would be paid more or less depending on how successful his lobbying was in moving the bill at the State House. Such contingent fees were illegal as they were based on a percentage of the profits his clients expected to receive from whatever provisions of the bill were actually passed.

Anders said that Cobb admitted he got paid $22,000 from a total of $114,000 reported as missing from the Association after an audit.

The Richland County grand jury indicted the Association's executive director, David W. Reed, on 43 counts of breach of trust with fraudulent intent. Reed allegedly took the money and put it in his own personal bank account or used it to pay his personal debts, including some $2,111 of Association money to pay his daughter's tuition for the full semester of 1987 at the University of South Carolina. Reed's lawyer, Jack Swerling, denied that Reed had done anything illegal.

Cobb Entangles in Web of Suspicion at Marketers Association

Cobb said that he had agreed with the Association director to lobby for a bill in 1985-1986 to increase the oil jobbers' share of gasoline taxes collected at gas stations where the jobbers delivered bulk fuel from major oil companies to the stations. The bill was expected to produce $600,000 for the jobbers and Cobb was to be paid a total of $100,000 in monthly payments for one year.

Cobb complained that David Reed did not, in fact, pay $77,500 of the fee owed to Cobb for his lobbying. Cobb claimed he was owed the unpaid amount, although it could be viewed as an illegal contingent fee.

The Association denied agreeing to the lobbying deal with Cobb, although it admitted to hiring Cobb in the 1984-1985 session of the General Assembly to lobby for a bill that failed.

Solicitor Anders said that Speaker Bob Sheheen asked SLED to look at Reed based on Cobb's lobbying for the Association and the misuse of Association funds.

Indicted Blacks Pushed to Door

In late September, Jesse Jackson's former South Carolina presidential manager in his 1988 bid for president called on indicted black legislators to resign to make way for replacement candidates who would run in the November, 1990, elections.

Those indicted would likely not be around in the new 1991 session of the General Assembly and would not be able to deal with the important redistricting process after the 1990 federal census.

It was unknown at the time what final effects the sting would have on the political system in the near future. But by late September, 1990, Reps. Donna Moss, Robert Brown, Robert Kohn, and Danny Winstead had resigned along with Sen. Rick Lee and would have to be replaced by elections. Further, Thomas Limehouse had withdrawn his re-election bid. The consequences of these vacancies would cause committee shake-ups and other dislocations in the legislature.

Convicted Could Hold Office

South Carolina law did not bar convicted felons from holding office after completing sentences. This contradicted advice that Judge Falcon Hawkins was giving defendants that they would give up their rights to vote and hold office during and even after sentence served. No federal law applied to the matter as only the state controls voting eligibility by criminals according to the United States Constitution Article I, Section 2, para. 1.

Some state legislators believed the bars to voting and office holding were longer, and continued even after the convicted party had completed their sentence in full. Judge Hawkins seemed to reflect that erroneous opinion.

Sequence of Events

April, 1989	Federal agents apprehend Donna Moss for possession of cocaine.
September, 1989	Lobbyist James Madison Brown, V, apprehended with marijuana.
January 11, 1990	Rep. Tom Limehouse informs federal agent that he is ready to deal on the pari-mutuel bill.
January 25, 1990	Limehouse tells Rob Cobb that he will back the pari-mutuel bill in return for clothing.
February 1, 1990	Rep. Ennis Fant talks with Ron Cobb about betting bill.
February 14, 1990	Fant agrees to mobilize support on the betting bill from the Freshman Cau cus and the Black Caucus.
February 15, 1990	Fant accepts $1,000.

March 7, 1990	Rep. Larry Blanding and Rep. B.J. Gordon meet with Cobb at State House and agree to back betting bill in return for money.
March 8, 1990	Gordon accepts $1,000, as does Blanding, in return for their support of the betting bill.
April 12, 1990	Supporters of betting bill including Limehouse, Blanding, Gordon, and Fant try to get betting bill to a vote in the House.
April 25, 1990	Proponents of betting bill again try to to get the betting bill to a vote.
May 8, 1990	Blanding accepts another $300 from Cobb, as does Fant
May 18, 1990	Limehouse tried to influence Cobb's communications with the federal investigation to hide criminal information.

Interview
Bart Daniel

By Corey Hutchins
May 8, 2014
Bart Daniel's law office, 7 State Street, Charleston, S.C.

Summary of Interview with Bart Daniels

Bart Daniel vividly remembers the phone call 25 years ago that changed his life. A Saturday morning at his Charleston home, his two young girls playing in the den. Spirits were up in the Daniel household that weekend. On Monday, the young lawyer—he was just 33—would be sworn in as South Carolina's newest U.S. attorney under President George H. W. Bush. But the real work that would come to define his professional career and legal legacy in the Palmetto State would begin that Saturday with a ringing telephone. When he answered it, he heard the voice of Fred Verinder, the state's new director of the Federal Bureau of Investigation.

Verinder, the new FBI special agent in charge, was not from South Carolina. The no-nonsense G-man with a background in public corruption had come to South Carolina on the urging of U.S. Sen. Fritz Hollings. Before taking on his new office in the South he'd worked stints in New York and Chicago, where he brought down powerful mob bosses and drug lords. He was not, as Hollings had once told Daniel, a typical FBI chief known among government prosecutors unflatteringly as a "desk agent" who spent his afternoons dreaming of a peaceful retirement on the South Carolina coast or on Lake Murray. In the short time Verinder had been in South Carolina, he'd already gained a reputation as a serious ball buster.

The reason the new FBI director was dialing up Daniel on a Saturday morning was because he had some important news. Daniel excused himself to the laundry room and took the call on a different line.

"Bart," Verinder told him, "We've been working on a drug case, and we've jammed up, and now caught, a lobbyist with a kilo of cocaine. And we know we can get a legislator who has a cocaine problem."

The new FBI director told Daniel that if they wanted to prosecute, the news would make a big splash. They could collaborate on a simple bust like that together, Verinder said. Or they could try something different.

Daniel was listening.

The FBI director explained how a typical case like this could go down: Bust the cokehead lobbyists and make newspaper headlines. A big press conference with mountains of white powder on the table. The TV news crews, and all of that. As a former state prosecutor, Daniel knew the rigamarole well enough. He'd been through such busts himself and had played his part plenty as ringmaster for the media circus. During his previous time in the U.S. attorney's office Daniel had worked on the famous Operation Jackpot, a big-time marijuana trafficking investigation and prosecution that stretched from the South Carolina coast to South America with big yachts, piles of pot, and cash.

Yes, nailing a few lobbyists for cocaine would make a splash. But both Verinder and Daniel seemed to be thinking at the same time about how running the familiar old plays never really did that much in the grand scheme of things. They might yank some crooked politicians out of the Statehouse and a few small-time dope dealers off the streets, but not much more. After a while, they knew, everyone would forget about the scandal, and people would settle back to their normal nefarious ways.

"We can do that," Verinder said over the phone that night. "Or we can go for the longer term."

Nothing might ever come of trying to play a long game with this lobbyist whom they had on the hook for a serious drug charge. A flamboyant huckster named Ron Cobb, their perp, came from the Upstate and was known as a wheeler and dealer with probably a little too much dirt under his fingernails.

Now, backed in a corner on a drug charge following his arrest around 2 a.m. the prior morning, Cobb was singing to the FBI about a cesspool of public corruption he could help expose under the copper-domed Statehouse where he'd ingratiated himself with the Palmetto State's political elite. If the FBI and U.S. Attorney's Office could team up and get Cobb to work for them by infiltrating the Statehouse as a paid government informant, it was anyone's guess what this character might come up with.

"That may or may not pay off," Verinder warned Daniel over the phone. But he wanted to check the pulse of this young man before Monday when Daniel would officially become the new U.S. attorney and be working as the federal government's prosecutorial arm on cases like this one that the FBI would investigate.

Daniel liked the idea, and he immediately liked Verinder. Both of them probably had the same initial concerns about the other. Was this guy serious or a typical career type waiting for a pension who might be skittish about taking big risks or rocking the boat?

"Let's go for something more longer term," Verinder said.

Warding off the background noise of his two kids playing in the den, Daniel made the decision that would alter the course of his career, not to mention South Carolina history.

"Fred, I'm with you 100 percent," he said. "Let's do it."

Interview

"Without Fred Verinder, Lost Trust never happens," Daniel recalled 25 years later in an interview at his downtown Charleston law office.

The following are portions of a conversation, the questions and answers edited for clarity, about what happened after the phone call between Daniel and Verinder on that day in April, 1989, and about Daniel's role as the chief prosecutor in what would then become the largest legislative vote-buying scandal in American history.

Corey Hutchins: You were very young for a U.S. attorney. How'd you get the job?

Bart Daniel: I got hired off the street by a guy named John W. McIntosh, who later on plays a significant role in Lost Trust. I served as his law clerk, and then he went to the Attorney General's office. I sort of followed him over there. I then worked for two years as a law clerk. When I graduated, John McIntosh was the head of the criminal division. He hired me on an economic crime grant. He hired me and John Barton who had already been out in private practice for three years. John Barton was later one of the chief prosecutors in trying the cases with us.

CH: When you were in the AG's office then, were you aware of the level of corruption going at the Statehouse?

BD: While we were there we were right in the capital complex. You can't be in that small of a complex with having politics all around you when you're trying to be a professional objective lawyer and not get frustrated when some of the corruption is just flouted at you. It really was a climate of corruption in a lot of ways. You had such cozy relationships. I was an Assistant State Attorney General one and two years out of law school and we saw this, and it was frustrating. There were a lot of good 'ol boys, and you saw it wasn't the way the system is supposed to work. But as state prosecutors there really was nothing we could do. Because you have to have somebody inside and have wiretapping authority. And you have to have some investigative capabilities that the state didn't have—and still doesn't have to a large extent.

CH: How widely known was this culture of corruption? Just among insiders like yourself, or did the general public know?

BD: I don't think the general public had a clue. Insiders. And lawyers that dealt within the confines of the Statehouse grounds. Any sort of agency on the Statehouse grounds. You could see it. Back then many were long-serving members who made a living off the influence and had for many years. So that was the initial backdrop.

CH: You then followed McIntosh to the U.S. attorney's office and became a white-collar prosecutor. He also hired your friend John Barton, and also a man named Dale DuTremble. You all worked there together for a couple years, then you left for a brief stint in private practice. Not long after that, on Dec. 22, 1988, U.S. Sen. Strom Thurmond sent a letter to the president recommending you to run the U.S. attorney's office. So you were back with your old crew. The weekend before you were sworn in, you got that phone call from Verinder. You decided to play the long game with the lobbyist they'd busted, Ron Cobb. What happened next?

BD: The FBI guys, they tell Cobb, "Look, here's what you can do. You can either work for us and maybe this whole thing goes away—we're not making any promises—but depending on what you can do, or, you can go ahead and get jammed up on this kilo-plus of cocaine." And Cobb said, "OK, I'll work with you." Once he got into it, man, he was a showman. He's flamboyant, he's colorful, but he really got into it. He got into the role. The role was really himself.

CH: Did Cobb come up with the idea to wear a wire and become a rat, or did the government?

BD: Cobb probably told them that he could help them with a corruption case, I don't know the answer to that. They knew Cobb could do stuff. Whether the agent says it to Cobb or Cobb says it to the agent, both sides knew what Cobb could do, there's no doubt about that.

CH: You didn't meet Cobb at first, the FBI handled him. How come?

BD: There are reasons for that. You don't want the prosecutor to meet the informant. So they start working with Cobb. And what we do then is, we're racing against the clock. I got sworn in May 1st. The legislative session ends the second Tuesday in June. From the time I get sworn in we're working because we had to get permission to tape people.

CH: Describe that process.

BD: You have to get someone in there to talk dirty with Ron Cobb about something they've done together in the past. You don't have permission to talk dirty about something in the future. This avoids entrapment. Given that Cobb, the free-flowing nature, the flamboyant guy he was, the kind of people he hung around with, they started talking dirty almost immediately about stuff they did in the past and about stuff they wanted to do in the future—about scams.

CH: What kind equipment was the FBI using to tape these guys?

BD: Back then it was supposed to be state of the art. DuTremble resigned twice, you know. One time Dale DuTremble was so mad over the equipment that the FBI was using. Just shoddy. Not that the agents were shoddy, they weren't. They were the best. But the videos came out grainy, and the sound initially wasn't very good. It was very frustrating.

CH: Throughout the sting did you ever worry that Cobb might become a liability?

BD: He became a liability. I got back [from a vacation] and it was a firestorm. They were waiting on me in my office when I came in early on a Monday morning. John McIntosh and John Barton with Mike Clemmons. I said "Well, this ain't good," and they said to me, "Cobb's been using cocaine. He went to Jack Lindsay's funeral, he says he used cocaine after that." I think he'd tested positive or something. And we had to use him as a witness. So we talked about it. You have to disclose it. Your star witness is using cocaine. How does that play over with a jury? So we charged Ron Cobb. We talked about not calling Cobb as a witness.

CH: Did you think that it could blow the case?

BD: Yeah. But, I knew one thing. We had gotten past July 17th. Look, man, you take a risk. What you want is the potential benefit to outweigh the potential harm. You're dealing with a snake. He could blow up on you at any time.

CH: You said you were running against the clock because the session was ending. Why was the end of session, and July 17th specifically, significant?

BD: We're hurrying between May 1st and that second Tuesday, because what happens is everybody goes back home. There's no business going on and you don't really have an opportunity to do anything undercover. We had a couple little tapes early. Several tapes of Robert Kohn, and I think we had, even that early, something on Luther Taylor.

CH: Did the government direct who Cobb would try to reel in?

BD: No. We had an open-door policy. When someone knocked on that door we didn't look in some peephole to see if they were Democrat or Republican or white or black. If they wanted to sell their vote we opened that door and let them in and let them talk.

CH: Ron Cobb used a betting bill to bribe lawmakers. Who decided what kind of bill to use for bait?

BD: DuTremble and the FBI. There had been something introduced before, and I think they had found out that word was there was going to be a lot of money.

CH: How did you spend the off season before the next session?

BD: I know Cobb talked to and taped Kohn once or twice in the off-session and I'm pretty sure he talked to Luther Taylor, who was right in Columbia. And from those two guys—oh, and people say "How come you had so many African-Americans?" Well, Luther Taylor was African American and he recruited his friends. "How come you had so many Republicans?" Can you imagine me, a U.S. attorney, the first person we had was Kohn and all he's bringing us is Republicans and I'm thinking "Boy,"—laughing—"there are some people who will give me hell now." And then all of a sudden we start getting some Democrats. We were really, really, surprised at some of the people who knocked on that door. We had one guy show up, we didn't even know who he was. The FBI didn't know who he was. His name was Ken Bailey, from Orangeburg. He'd been in one term or two terms. This was in the following session. He came and knocked on that door. We didn't even have permission to talk dirty to him because Cobb had never done anything with him before. We would have to send these tapes up to Washington for the FBI public corruption team up there to give us permission.

CH: Where was Cobb taping the lawmakers?

BD: We arranged to get the AT&T building, which was across the street at the Statehouse. And we got a nice, sort of a big-shot kind of thing befitting of someone like Ron Cobb. It perfectly fit his image. And we were able to have several different cameras in there. It was all hardwire[d]. We would watch on closed-circuit TV at the FBI office in Columbia while these bribes were going down. We'd watch in real time, and so we started getting permission, and sometimes, no kidding, poor Ron Cobb is sitting there ready to make a payoff, but we have not gotten permission from the FBI in Washington to do it. And right when the guy is sitting in the office on videotape Cobb takes a phone call and it's the FBI saying "We got it, go for it." Cobb says, "It's a business doing pleasure," and starts making a payoff to the guy. Before that he was stalling and stammering and all that.

CH: Why was cash used instead of checks?

BD: No one would ever accept a check because of the paper trail.

CH: All in all 18 lawmakers were offered and accepted money. Only one refused? Theo Mitchell?

BD: Theo Mitchell was a little bit different. Yeah, he did.

CH: Anyone else refuse to take money?

BD: No. Because remember now, anybody we gave the money to, we had at least three or four steps, we'd already talked dirty about past stuff, and you had to tape each one and send each one up, so you'd already laid such a foundation by the time you're ready to give him the money the guy's already agreed to take it.

CH: Why were lawmakers offered varying amounts for their vote?

BD: Some people demanded more. The standard was $500, but one of them suggested like $300. One of them suggested like $300 and a couple of suits and shirts. One of the guys wanted golf clubs. One of them wanted a Mercedes or something.

CH: Were any lawmakers who accepted bribes not prosecuted?

BD: No. Every single one of them who took the money was prosecuted.

CH: In addition to Donna Moss, Dick Greer, and lobbyists indicted, were there any other drug suspects found during the sting?

BD: We prosecuted everybody. I can't think of anyone we didn't prosecute. I caught hell because there were a lot of very powerful people that got prosecuted. And, you know, you just do your damn job. We had people that were very close to the governor. We had David Hawkins who was his legislative director, we had Dick Greer who was just really a fine guy. He was using cocaine. You can't ignore it, he was a public official. He was chairman of the State Development Board. A very successful business person.

CH: So the session ended. You had some initial tapes of lawmakers pledging to sell their votes for dirty money. What were you thinking at the time?

BD: The hardest thing you learn when you're working as a federal prosecutor, or a state prosecutor when you're doing an undercover operation, especially in an area with the kind of volatility and sophistication and talk of Columbia and the Capitol, you always wonder about people finding out about you. We were worried to dickens that someone was going to find out about us.

CH: How many people in the U.S. attorney's office knew about the sting before it was public?

BD: Dale DuTremble, John Barton, John McIntosh, and myself were the original ones. Then we added the young people about two or three months before it went public, and that was Sherri Lydon and Scott Schools. At the FBI they probably had more people. The two lead agents were Mike Clemmons and Tommy Davis. And then the tech guy was Bob Johnson. You had federal prosecutors hand-typing and carrying memos and stuff over to the FBI.

CH: During the sting, where there any scares?

BD: Yeah there were some scares. The best James Bondish kind of scare was, we were so worried, it's springtime in the legislative session, maybe April or May in '90. This was when things were rolling, and we were really busy. Representative Limehouse was with Cobb, and we had this undercover agent from Washington, or wherever he's from. His name is Joe Williams and he's supposed to be this big monied guy. So he meets at the hotel at night for drinks, it's he and Cobb. Limehouse, Cobb and the undercover agent, and maybe Limehouse has someone else with him. But what happens is the undercover agent Joe Williams has got [a tape recorder] in his jacket pocket. And for some reason the jacket comes open and the red light gets shone. And boy, Tom Limehouse takes Cobb aside and says "Ron, we gotta talk, that son-of-a-bitch, your goddam friend, he's got some kind of recorder, I saw the red light." So Cobb says "No, man, you're mistaken." They'd already broken up by the time this happened. Right then Cobb and the agent talk. That agent gets with our agents, they get with Quantico, Virginia, where the FBI lab is. They concoct, overnight, and build, a little transmitter about the same size as the one he's got, with the red light in the same place. So at breakfast the next morning the guy's there and Ron Cobb says to him, "Hey, look, Tom's concerned that you've got some kind of tape recorder there in your breast pocket, what's going on there?" He says, "Oh, this is my remote-controlled garage door opener, they got these new things, this is nice!" It was an exact replica. They did it overnight and got it back there in time.

CH: That's a good one. Did the press ever catch on to the undercover sting?

BD: No. We never really had that. We didn't let secretaries type anything. We did our own typing, and then we would take it over to the FBI.

It was something else that happened though. Something earlier on. There was some kind of word getting around that something was going on, and it just sort of died out. This is springtime, it's getting warm. I go to a hotel room to meet the FBI agent up there. Kohn is meeting with Tee Ferguson. And they're hearing rumblings at this time there's some kind of investigation going on. This is May of 1990, before we take things down in July. So Kohn turns it around. He's working for us at this time. See, we ended up later—fascinating from a cloak-and-dagger standpoint of what the FBI was able to do—we end up taking Kohn in first, and Kohn works for us for a long time starting in January. With Cobb. At some point in time Kohn agrees to join our side, just like Cobb. He's recruiting people because he gets paid by the head. So we got all these payoffs to Kohn. And he's saying "I can get this guy for cheap, so-and-so wants some of this." He's not working for us at that time, but later on he does work with us. But the whole time he's bringing his guys to Cobb, and Luther is bringing his guys to Cobb. So, something happens—it's being taped—and T. Ferguson says something.

CH: Did Cobb ever refuse to roll over on Jack Lindsay?

BD: He probably said that, and the agents told him, "Look, you're not in charge and that's not going to happen." The truth of the matter is, all the action in the bill was in the House, because remember, all spending bills start in the House. We don't get to the Senate about legislation like that until the very end if it's involving money.

CH: Did the FBI know at the time that Jack Lindsay had allegedly taken money from Ron Cobb to fix a tax cut for Greenville businessmen?

BD: No. There was that information, but it's much different to have information [than] for us to be able to prove something. There's no way in the world you could have charged Lindsay with something like that. I'm not even sure—because it wasn't on tape—that we could have gotten anything to start a conversation with Lindsay. But we were so busy. We ultimately end up getting Lindsay, but he passes away.

CH: Would he have been indicted if he didn't die?

BD: He had already signed a plea agreement.

CH: What did you have on him?

BD: The same kind of public corruption, I can't remember the specifics. Not taking a bribe, not related to the bill, but some unrelated stuff but similar stuff.

CH: If he had lived would he have gone to a grand jury?

BD: Yeah. We were going to go to court. But when he signed the plea agreement, he had bad cancer, he was dying then. But he's a tough guy, man.

CH: Some of the tapes make mention of someone named "Warren" and "The Big Man." Who were they?

BD: I can't remember if they do or not. There was a lot of talk on those tapes.

CH: Did the grand jury find any evidence of crimes that were not made public?

BD: No. Just because a guy gets charged with this thing you had to have some things leading up to that, or at least talk about some past things. And that's when you talk about Hitachi, about the capital gains bill. There were two capital gains bills, and this was just a mess. There were people out there who wanted to say we were trying to protect Governor Campbell, which was so absurd because we prosecuted Dick Greer, who was his very best friend in life. And we prosecuted his legislative director, David Hawkins. But that said, there were two capital gains bills. One, the general capital gains bill that cut capital gains taxes for everybody and that was endorsed by the Chamber of Commerce. Governor Campbell had made it his top legislative priority. There was a different capital gains bill that really impacted six very wealthy people, among others, involving a tremendous amount of money. And that was the one where there was illegal activity. What had happened was—and I might get this technical part [wrong]—the federal tax code had changed, but the South Carolina tax code, some of which mirrored it, had not changed. There were six people that were cited because they were raising hell about it. Six people agreed to get together and hire Ron Cobb. I can't remember how much they paid him. But it wasn't, my recollection now, it wasn't anything more than normal—those lobbyists make a lot of money. Cobb was trying to bribe people unbeknownst to them.

CH: How do you handle doing an investigation and being ready to go public without influencing an election?

BD: Theo Mitchell was running for governor. He gets charged with something unrelated to Lost Trust later on. He gets convicted. I know we had something on Theo Mitchell. But specifically we all agreed we don't screw around and mess with the elective process. If you've got a case and it's ready to go, you bring it. You don't go out and indict a half-baked case. You don't go out and try to say "We can't let this guy get elected governor, we can't let this guy get elected to the House," or whatever the case may be. You can't do that. And we didn't do that. We had experienced people.

CH: What's that like for you when you have information on a candidate, and you know the public doesn't, and you know the press doesn't, and you see that they might win another election. What's that feel like?

BD: That really is a hard thing. We faced some of that, but not nearly as much as you'd think. It was not during an election year. It was May 1, 1989, until July 19th, 1990. But there weren't any elections yet. The only one I can think of was Theo Mitchell, but that case wasn't all the way ready, and that case wasn't a Lost Trust case.

BD: Down here in Charleston, Tee Ferguson had been elected as a state court judge. But he'd taken his bribe when he was a legislator. Now, we didn't stop that judicial election. We weren't ready to take the thing down yet. I'd never thought about it until you mentioned that thing about races and stuff; that was a race there was nothing we could do about.

I've never told anybody this, I hardly remember it, but there was a retired state court judge here. And he was so beloved and respected. He stopped me in front of Washington Park on Broad Street when I was the U.S. attorney, and he said, "Bart, I gotta tell ya. I told my friends that we would rue the day that the Legislature elected Tee Ferguson to be a circuit court judge. Bart, I'm just telling you, his character is not fit." And I went, "Wow, he knows something." Most of these guys, people felt like were somewhat sleazy or something, and Tee was one of those guys. But legislators elected him. There were some suspicions that Tee did things fast and loose. But he did get elected [judge] and there wasn't anything we could do about that.

CH: What about Jim Miles' defeat of Secretary of State John Campbell?

BD: That doesn't have anything to do with anything.

CH: Did the prosecution hold off on the indictment of Dick Greer until after the November, 1990, election for governor?

BD: That's true, but something really not related to Lost Trust other than it's corruption at the Statehouse.

CH: Was there any evidence that Governor Campbell knew of Greer's cocaine use with Ron Cobb?

BD: No, no, no. Absolutely not.

CH: How did you decide when to stop the sting?

BD: That decision gets made for you. Cobb ran out of people that he was influential with. Cobb's finishing up all the people he knows and stuff. We still got Jack Lindsay hanging out there. But Cobb goes to all the people he'll be able to pay off. And we had developed a game plan that we would not do anything publicly. We would do two things that were really important from an evidentiary standpoint. We wanted to go until the end of the legislative session, the date legislators had to file their campaign disclosure reports. Must have been July 17. So we waited until that happened because then they would have had to declare if they'd gotten any money from Ron Cobb. Any campaign contributions from anybody else. So these guys had to declare. It was put in writing and it was filed under oath.

CH: Were you worried that some of these guys just might disclose that they took money from Cobb?

BD: Hell yeah we worried about that. And 18 filed and none of them claimed it.

CH: Do you think if the sting had gone on longer you would have nailed more lawmakers?

BD: Not with Cobb. Because we got his people, quite frankly, the people he had good relationships with.

CH: What if you'd gotten another lobbyist to work for the government like Cobb?

BD: Sure, you could have.

CH: How many more?

BD: Probably a few more. But you know, like I used to say, the vast majority of the men and women in the Legislature were honorable people and honest people, and doing it all for the right reasons. I don't think you would have gotten another dozen. I really don't. I'd be really surprised.

CH: In your opinion, if this thing was drawn out and you had everything at your disposal, how many people do you think you could have nailed for corruption? Was the entire Legislature corrupt, basically?

BD: Let me tell you something. Think about where we were back when we started. They kept coming and they kept coming. We weren't crazy. We realized, "oh, we got something big, big, big."

CH: Were you worried that you might cripple the entire government of South Carolina?

BD: That's exactly right. There was a lot of talk when we came out public. Even my father-in-law was mad at me. He said, "Here we are in South Carolina trying to recruit industry and business and good paying jobs, and you guys do this?" There was some real resentment about that. And I think the governor resented it greatly. I'm not sure if he ever spoke to me again. And I had worked on his campaigns before being appointed U.S. attorney. There was a lot of resentment in a lot of quarters.

CH: So what happened after July 17th when the lawmakers who accepted bribes didn't disclose them?

BD: After those were nailed down we had a team meeting in John Barton's office. After July 17 we'll go out and interview everybody that took money. And ask them, "Did you take money, cash campaign contributions?" John Barton is the chief of the criminal division and one of the lead lawyers in the case. He says "Bart, you're absolutely crazy. These guys, almost every one of them are lawyers. They're not going to talk to the FBI." I shook my head and said, "John, they're politicians first and lawyers second. And they'll talk." Every single one of them that was interviewed talked. Bud Long didn't because he wasn't there, he was out of town.

CH: Talk about the day of the raids, the day Lost Trust officially became public.

BD: We had 70 FBI agents from around the country come in. We went over a script with them. They went to [the lawmakers] offices in their hometown and said they were doing a survey or whatever it was. But they did identify themselves as FBI agents. Then basically questions get harder and harder. They're back in their law offices, their pharmacies, their optometry offices, all those kinds of things. So [the agents] go all at the same time so that nobody can tip off anybody else.

BD: That morning, while they were doing that, the FBI director had requested that we come up to Washington, me and Fred Verinder. The night before, John McIntosh, Fred Verinder and I went out to dinner. Fred Verinder looked at me and said, "Your life will change forever tomorrow. It's going to be a firestorm." I said, "Oh, I've already figured that one out." He said, "Bart, I'm going to leave the state eventually. But you're going to be here." He said, "I'm not trying to put pressure on you, but you guys better not lose these cases." Next morning, according to plan, while the agents were fanned out, he and I flew to Washington. We met with the FBI director, met with the Attorney General and then the Attorney General or the director suggested that, while it was going down, to tell the congressional delegation. Just that something was getting ready to go public and was happening real soon, and you want to reassure them that everything is going to be OK and state government is not going to come crumbling down, because it's been limited and it's been confined. It's an extensive number, but it's been confined. And that's what we told them.

CH: How did the media react?

BD: They put it together in two days. Who had been interviewed? They didn't get them all, but they got a remarkable number of those who had been interviewed by the FBI. We only interviewed the guys—we didn't go out and interview 10 other guys to throw anybody off—we put all our resources into interviewing the guys who had taken the money.

CH: Were you worried about leaks in the aftermath?

BD: Oh, no. We'd kept it a secret for 15 months. I wasn't worried about anybody talking. My secretary didn't know.

CH: Do you think the Lost Trust scandal was one of the main reasons for the passage of the Ethics Act in 1991?

BD: It might have been the only reason.

CH: Do you believe the sting helped clean up corruption in South Carolina government?

BD: Yeah. When people talk now about corruption, the kinds of things people look at now—they're important, don't get me wrong—but when people throw around the term Lost Trust, which we hear now, I mean they don't have a clue.

CH: What's changed?

BD: Back then, what we learned early on, it was astounding to me. I thought I knew there was a bunch of no good going on. But when you learned the specifics of it you'd shake your head. Here's what would happen, and it happened all the time: lobbyists would take you for drinks, take you out to dinner. Next time the guy can't make dinner, so the guy says to the lobbyist "I'll just need your credit card up at—what was the place called, not the Townhouse, there was another place on Assembly Street right across from the capitol. So the guy would leave his credit card there. So the legislator drank all damn night. What they would do toward the end of the session: Lobbyists would have clients, I'm talking national clients who wanted to educate, if you want to call it that, so they would have a meeting at some really nice resort or some place. The legislator would go and the lobbyist would pay for everything for three days. But it gets worse. What if one guy couldn't make the trip? So he says, "Hey, you owe me a trip. How about you just give me your credit card and I take my girlfriend and I go to Las Vegas." That's the kind of stuff that was going on. It was a climate for corruption, it really was.

CH: Had this major event not happened do you think it would have gotten worse or better?

BD: Worse.

CH: How did you decide who to indict and try first?

BD: It used to be considered that the FBI and the DEA or Customs, they investigate and the U.S. attorney prosecutes. What we did is we got together early on. Now that does become important because it's a real hard conversation. A lot of bitterness sort of emanated from this. We went to a public corruption seminar the next June, before it because public. It was out in Phoenix. So we're up there and we were talking to each other about how we were going to indict the cases. This is where a big disagreement came in. One of the unwritten rules you have is that during the investigation stage, if the U.S. attorney and the FBI have a disagreement we defer to the investigators. They investigated it, they're the experts, we have to defer to them. That's just the way the rules work. So it comes down to—Fred Verinder thinks, his game plan is he's got a giant indictment with 18 legislators and we've got 18 legislators going to trial in a courtroom. And the trial's going to last six months. We'd been around the block. We knew that wasn't the way to do it. And boy, I was sitting in the back seat of Fred Verinder's car, and he was in the front and an agent was driving—in Phoenix—and Mike Clemmons the case agent was in the car with me. Verinder says "Well, when we do these indictments, Bart how long do you think the trial will last." I said, "Well, Fred, We're not going to indict them all at once." I said, "That doesn't make any sense from a tactical standpoint because you want to indict your strongest cases first." He said "What the hell do you mean?" I said, "It's South Carolina, we don't have six month trials, a jury ain't going to listen for six months, there's all sorts of problems with that. Nothing good comes of that. You lose people you shouldn't lose. You've got to basically take your time, develop the evidence, line it up, go strong all the way down."

CH: So you tried your strongest cases first. How did that affect the rest of the trials?

BD: The federal sentencing guidelines when Luther Taylor gets convicted are 63 months to 78 months. And his lawyer, Joel Collins, comes in and argues something less than the federal guidelines, which back then the judge couldn't do. The judge had to give him no less than 63 months. Judge Hawkins, after a two or three hour hearing gives him 78 months. And I get on the way back from Charleston, I had my own cell phone, not a government cell phone, and Tom Limehouse's lawyer called me. We'd already met with Limehouse's lawyer in my office in Charleston—DuTremble and I, trying to work something out with him—and he pretty much told us to go jump in a lake, and was really pretty arrogant when he did that—but his lawyer called me on the way down to Charleston and said "We really want to talk. We really want to work something out." Now, we ended up not immediately working something out. DuTremble got so mad when we finally did work something out—and he was pleading guilty to what he was charged with, which was obstruction and the Hobbs Act, extortion—DuTremble got so mad I had to take the plea and do the sentencing, DuTremble wouldn't do it. He was a piece of work, man. Great guy.

CH: What was it like losing the Tim Wilkes trial?

BD: We wouldn't have charged him and we wouldn't have tried him if we didn't think we could win. The jury said otherwise. I think he had an excellent lawyer, and I think they learned from all the previous trials. Our case wasn't as strong, I think it was the second to last case.

CH: So, why did you leave the U.S. attorney's office when you did?

BD: I had always planned on leaving early. I had three young children. My wife and children did not move to Columbia because we had a house and we'd have had to sell the house and then three years later buy a new house and put them in school. Financially I couldn't afford it. I had to get back to support my family. I had young kids. I couldn't have afforded to stay much longer.

CH: How do you think your visibility with Lost Trust helped your career?

BD: Sure. Reporters said to me, "Bart, you came out of nowhere." Truth of the matter is I really didn't. It's like anybody else. I'd been a state prosecutor, I'd been around the Statehouse, I used to get McIntosh's coffee. You do all those things and you work your way and you learn. As an assistant U.S. attorney I had some high-profile cases. I came in and we did Operation Jackpot. I went to Australia, the Jersey Channel Islands, the Bahamas, all chasing drug assets. I'd prosecuted and lost cases. You have to lose. You have to get the shit kicked out of you, your teeth kicked in, you get knocked down, you get back up. All those guys, DuTremble, McIntosh, Barton, we'd all lost cases. Won plenty, but lost, too, and you learn. At that point in time, by the time I'd left being an assistant U.S. attorney in 1985 I went into private practice, I'd built a real good practice. I'd already bought this building. In the three and a half or four years I'd been in private practice, I'd done well. So when I took the job as U.S. attorney it was a big financial [hit].

CH: Did you ever worry the sting might negatively affect your career?

BD: When you go after powerful people, for every action there's going to be a reaction. I'll never forget my good friend is Gedney Howe—he still is my good friend—and he told me at the time when it became public, he said one of his friends who had business at the Statehouse said to him, "Does Bart realize what he's doing? Is he just too damn young to know better? Because this is going to be hell to pay for him." What if everything had blown up? Then I'd be run out of the state.

CH: Who came up with the name Lost Trust?

BD: There was a name; the FBI supervisor, he has this damn—I can't even remember it—it was some Greek something name that stood for something. None of us ever called it that. We really didn't call it anything early on. Eventually we started talking about it—we had to figure out some kind of name for it. We called it Broken Trust. And when it actually came out, a newspaper called it Broken Trust, somebody else used the name Lost Trust. Lost Trust stuck. It was initially named after some Greek horse or something. It was difficult to pronounce and it made no sense.

CHAPTER THIRTEEN

THE PLEAS AND TRIALS BEGIN

Pretrial Hearing in Taylor Case

The trial of Rep. Luther Taylor was set for October 15, 1990, but he seemed unstable. The FBI Special Agent Mike Clemens said that they stayed with Taylor in July because they were afraid he would kill himself, fearing the ruin of his political career. They stayed with him for over a day and bought him a bottle of alcohol but did not read him his rights.

Taylor then said he would help the sting, but changed his mind and got ready for trial. Later he turned prosecution witness.

On September 4, 1990, Judge Falcon Hawkins held the first pretrial hearing in any of the Lost Trust cases. Taylor appeared first but 10 other indictments were pending. Taylor's lawyer, Joel Collins, had asked for dismissal on grounds of prosecutorial misconduct.

FBI testimony and documents at the hearing revealed that when the FBI picked up Taylor on July 17, 1990, on the driveway of his house, he held up his arms and opened his coat to reveal a .38 caliber revolver, which he was allowed to lock in the trunk of his car. Taylor was told that he was in trouble, had a "strong case" against him, and could plead to one count of bribery under the Hobbs Act.

Gag Order in Taylor Case

Distressed by media reports of misleading accusations by lawyers outside of or in his courtroom, Judge Falcon Hawkins ordered a gag on both prosecution and defense on September 24, 1990. No media communication was allowed.

Taylor's attorney wanted a complete gag on releasing any information about the sting and Lost Trust, including documents.

In three situations the prosecution had revealed guilty pleas and then provided the media with videotapes and audio transcripts. Such documents and evidence were so popular with the many reporters assigned to cover Lost Trust that they were standing in line to get them.

Taylor's lawyers brought six large black binders to court containing newspaper articles on Lost Trust since the story broke on July 18, 1990.

Joel Collins told reporters that, "I can't tell who's putting out more information, you or the government." Daniel asked for sanctions on Collins for trying to prejudice the prospective "jury panel by having the media report incorrect, misleading, inaccurate, and legally insufficient information in the newspapers." Daniel alleged that defense motions "are without merit, fly in the face of established case law, and should be dismissed."

Motion for Change of Venue Made in Taylor Case

Taylor moved a change of venue on grounds of pretrial prejudice. Hawkins delayed ruling, saying, "We may have to move it to Kalamazoo, Michigan. I don't know where we're going to have to go." (The trial was held in Columbia.)

Collins also argued the name "Lost Trust" was prejudicial to Taylor and asked why it was used. U.S. Attorney Dale DuTremble said the name had not been used before and the U.S. Justice Department picked the name. Hawkins saw no bias in the name.

The prosecution denied showing tapes to the South Carolina congressional delegation related to the indictments in a briefing.

Allegations of targeting black officials were denied.

Prosecution said it would provide receipts of all reimbursements to Ron Cobb and Rep. Robert Kohn, but denied paying money to Shelly Adams, who may have been with Cobb in FBI custody. Kohn and Cobb were paid to help the sting.

Prosecution admitted they had agreed with Cobb that he would not have to testify against Sen. Jack Lindsay, an old Cobb legislative ally and mentor.

U.S. Justice Fears Bias Label

The large number of black legislators caught in the early phases on the Lost Trust scandal caused worry among senior officials at the U.S. Department of Justice according to a highly placed federal source, the *Associated Press* reported.

Sources told *The Greenville News* that Justice was worried of accusations of selective prosecution in view of the fact that in the first two months of time since public notice of the sting, 8 of 18 legislators indicted and/or interviewed by the FBI were black.

However, Attorney General Dick Thornburgh and his senior aides denied telling Daniel to change the course of the probe to avoid bias.

Daniel said he had evidence to show no racial bias and that there was none.

The implication of a large number of whites, 10 of 18 suspects, eased anxiety over racial bias claims by blacks.

The Justice Department offices of Public Integrity and the Executive Office of U.S. Attorneys registered concern in Washington about the bias issue.

The problem arose, one source said, because "word got out among legislators that somebody was dangling money out there, and the first people to nibble were a group of black legislators." Eventually whites took the bait: "You had other members of the South Carolina Assembly who wanted to get a piece of the action."

Party Files Suit on Elections

The removal of legislators caused by Lost Trust required special elections and the Democratic Party filed suit over the setting of the date.

The seat of Sen. Rick Lee (R-Spartanburg) was one of those to be filled.

Pretrial Proceeds in Taylor Case

In pretrial proceedings in the Luther Taylor case held on September 24, 1990, the FBI said they stayed with Taylor to prevent suicide because they had seen cases of suicide by those faced by ruin. They also wanted to prevent Taylor from warning others who were to be subpoenaed the following day, July 18th.

A listening device was placed on Taylor's telephone to catch calls from others in the scandal, but rather than cooperate, Taylor retained Joel Collins and decided to fight. At the hearing, Collins blamed the FBI for not reading Taylor his rights and for bringing Taylor a liter of whiskey.

Agent Clemens replied that he knew what kind of scotch he wanted because Taylor told him so. Bart Daniels said that Taylor asked for the liquor and was not compelled to drink, saying, "Taylor asked the agent to obtain the whiskey for him."

The government denied it gave Taylor drinks to get him to talk. The prosecution said, "Taylor was not interrogated at the Ramada Inn.... Taylor makes no claim that he was under the influence of alcohol during his debriefing or grand jury appearance on July 17, 1990."

Collins asked the judge to have Daniel's top assistant, John Barton, to testify, but dropped the idea when Judge Hawkins said that he would allow it, but then disqualify them from trying the case.

Hitachi Sues to Stop Computer Probe

The role of the chief bribes-man Ron Cobb in Lost Trust was paralleled by continuing questions about his role in the purchase of $2.7 million of computers by the S.C. Department of Social Services from Hitachi Corporation.

On September 27, 1990, it was reported in the media that Cobb was believed to be in protective custody by the FBI in the Lost Trust scandal and was suspended by Hitachi as their lobbyist because, it's spokesman said, "He's not doing any work for us."

The S.C. Procurement Review Panel, chaired by Sen. Hugh Leatherman (D-Florence), also announced that the Panel had just been sued by Hitachi to stop the review and therefore the Panel would not hold a hearing at which Hitachi local sales representative, Tom Collins, was set to testify. Hitachi alleged that the Panel had "no authority for the type of investigative hearing the review panel seeks to hold."

Leatherman said he believed the Panel had broad authority to investigate on its own motion without an outside complaint being made, and he said a circuit judge had already ruled that way.

The Panel was probing the apparent rigging of the requirements of the computers to be bought so that Hitachi's offering would match the most closely. Hitachi had a history of winning six other contracts for sales to S.C. state government.

South Carolina Press Association Appeals Gag Order

Jay Bender, attorney for the South Carolina Press Association, continued his running battle with Judge Falcon Hawkin's gag orders issued in response to the requests of Joel Collins in the Luther Taylor case. With the Taylor trial docketed for October 15, 1990, Bender took the gag order to the U.S. 4th Circuit Court of Appeals seated in Richmond, Virginia on October 1, 1990.

The appeal pitted the usual issue in such cases of the rights of the criminal defendant to a fair trial free of pretrial prejudice caused by massive negative news coverage against the interests of the media and the public in knowing what their courts and public officials were doing. In a case involving the alleged public corruption of elected officials paid by the taxpayers to act honestly in the public interest, the appeal of the gag order by the Press Association presented a conflict of a high profile case of the defendant's right to a fair trial and the public's right to see their government in action.

Rep. Donna Moss Announced Guilty Plea

Rep. Donna Moss (D-Cherokee) joined the growing list of legislators lining up to plead guilty in Lost Trust even before a single defendant had gone to trial. It appeared that the evidence was so strong and the dangers of going to trial were so great that the prudent thing to do was to negotiate the best possible deal before a disastrous conviction at trial and a resulting aggravated sentence.

So on October 1, 1990, Moss announced that as of October 12, 1990, just days before the start of the Luther Taylor trial, she would plead guilty to the charge of possessing illegal drugs while in public office.

Lost Trust Special Elections Set

Each one of those who pleaded guilty also resigned from the legislature. This triggered a landslide of special elections to fill the vacated seats in the House and the single seat in the Senate resigned by Rick Lee (R-Spartanburg).

A special election to replace Rep. Robert Brown (D-Marion) was called after Brown resigned his seat in the House.

As the Senate would not stand for general election again until 1992, a special election to replace Sen. Rick Lee in his upstate district was called for January 2, 1991, with a nine candidate primary for the seat set for November 13, 1990.

USC Students Write Ethics Code

The outrageous conduct of so many corrupt and drugged legislators at the State House only one block away from the University of South Carolina campus in downtown Columbia spurred the USC Student Government Association to decide to write its own new code of student conduct.

Led by SGA President Steven K. Benjamin, its primary mover, the Code was designed as a student ethics code to define standards of behavior for the student body as a whole.

The USC SGA took the action in early October and was moving the code forward in the two week period before the Luther Taylor trial was set to begin on October 15, 1990.

Lobbyist Brown Pleads Guilty

Just two weeks before the start of the Luther Taylor trial, lobbyist James Brown, V, who had lobbied for credit unions in South Carolina at the State House, announced that he would plead guilty to illegal drug possession.

Brown would later appear as witness in the Taylor case in the federal courthouse in Columbia which ended in Taylor's conviction on October 24, 1990.

Brown died the next month of lung disease.

Lobbyist James Brown, V, pleaded guilty to illegal drug use on October 3, 1990, and signed a court approved plea agreement to cooperate with the federal prosecution.

Brown promised to testify against legislators on drug charges.

Brown was the first non-legislator to plead guilty in Lost Trust and would be followed in subsequent months by other lobbyists and Dick Greer, Gov. Campbell's economic development chairman, who would also plead to drug charges.

Brown admitted to using marijuana at a party in September, 1989, and pleaded to illegal possession of the drug. He also said that he had used drugs with a number of lobbyists, legislators, and appointed officials and agreed to testify against them, said FBI agent Tommy Davis in court when the judge accepted the plea. U.S. Attorney Bart Daniel said that others implicated in drug abuse would be revealed.

David Hawkins Rumors Spread

In early October, 1990, rumors were spreading to the effect that David Hawkins, a former House member and legislative assistant to Gov. Carroll Campbell, was believed to be entangled with lobbyist Rob Cobb and the betting bill. It was believed that Hawkins had met with Cobb about the bill, but the details were obscure when the matter was first reported by the media.

Hawkins was well known in the House as the primary founder of the notorious "Fat and Ugly Caucus" in the South Carolina House which was created in the early 1980s to coerce lobbyists to give caucus members free food and free drinks and to use lobbyists' credit cards as they wanted.

Hawkins was also reputed to be a business associate of the shady Rep. Jack I. Rogers (D-Marlboro) in a water plant in Spartanburg, S.C.

Hawkins would later be charged in the Lost Trust scandal for obstruction.

Rep. Fant Makes Excuses for Bribery

Rep. Ennis Fant (D-Greenville), a part-time Baptist preacher, reacted to his indictment under the Hobbs Act by arguing that the Legislative Black Caucus, of which he was a part, had taken a position in favor of a bill to legalize betting on horse races in South Carolina. The alleged bribe given to Fant by lobbyist Cobb was based on Cobb's desire to get Fant to vote for the betting bill. Fant said he had been backing the bill long before taking the money.

Fant, who had reported taking only $100 from Cobb as a so-called campaign contribution, had, in fact, taken two bribes of $1,300 in total from Cobb according to the indictment against him.

Fant said the legislators in the Black Caucus were all targeted by the Lost Trust sting and that the sting agent, Ron Cobb, had asked Rep. Luther Taylor to contact other Black Caucus members about taking money to vote for the bill.

Fant was represented by attorneys Tommy Thomason and William A. Coates of Greenville, S.C.

Big Money Goes to Gov. Campbell

As the 1990 campaign came to its last four weeks, the money poured into Gov. Carroll Campbell's campaign chest.

As there were no limits on the amounts and sources of campaign donations, donors could give huge amounts.

Campbell's disclosure forms revealed a total of some 5,812 donors of whom 122 gave $5,000 or more to help his re-election.

The biggest donors included:

Dr. Morikazu Sasaki of Greenville who gave $30,000
Wm. Gregg (Springs Industries) gave $25,000
Bowater Corp. gave $11,000
South Carolina Chamber of Commerce gave $10,000
Merrill Lynch gave $10,000
Policy Management gave $10,000
Fifteen corporations and political action committees gave $5,000 each

Theodore Donated Money to Gordon

As the campaigns for Lt. Governor reached within a month of the November 6th general election, the advertising war between Lt. Gov. Nick Theodore and challenger Republican Henry McMaster heated up.

In early October, McMaster ran an ad linking Theodore to one of the defendants indicted for bribery in the sting—Rep. B.J. Gordon.

The ad revealed that Theodore gave a total of $26,000 to Gordon of funds that Theodore had received from lobbyists' contributions and that he also gave $2,500 to Gordon in 1986.

In the end, the charge did not affect the results of the election, for the voters returned Theodore to office.

Greer Threatens Slander Suit

Dick Greer, Gov. Campbell's close associate, threatened to sue Sen. Ernest Passailague (D-Charleston) for slander alleging that Greer had helped promote the controversial tax break for Greenville businessmen which was being lobbied by Ron Cobb, another crony of Greer.

In fact, it was known that Greer had recommended that Cobb be hired by the businessmen to push the bill at the State house.

Although it was not known to the public at the time Greer threatened a slander suit, Cobb had, in fact, paid bribes to get the bill passed in the House and Senate and, further, Greer had been discovered by the FBI to have been using cocaine.

No lawsuit was ever filed in the matter by Greer and he eventually pleaded guilty to drug offenses.

Four Defendants Hire Lawyers

Rep. Thomas Limehouse (R-Dorchester) hired attorney Andy Savage of Charleston, S.C., as his attorney. Savage responded by arguing that the anti-bribery Hobbs Act under which the four were charged on October 5, 1990, was not applicable to the betting bill because the Act did not apply to transactions solely within one state. As the federal law was, in fact, based on the commerce clause in the United States Constitution, the facts of the bribery on the betting bill would have to be based on interstate commerce. (The bill would have only put the betting issue on a referendum ballot. The defense would fail in court later on.)

Others hiring lawyers were Rep. B.J. Gordon (D-Williamsburg) who retained attorney Lionel Lofton, and Rep. Larry Blanding (D-Sumter) who hired Danny Martin, himself a Democratic representative from Charleston.

Blanding denied the money he took was a bribe and said it was a campaign donation.

At the time that the three House members of the Black Caucus, Blanding, Fant, and Gordon were indicted, four of the ten charged at that point were black.

Lack of Real Jobs Made Legislators Easy Targets

In an extensive article published in *The State* on October 7, 1990, journalist Cindi Ross Scoppe published her investigation of the economic and financial backgrounds of legislators accused of taking bribes and found that many of them were living by their wits and had no real full-time jobs and regular sources of income.

Even their legislative jobs were low-paying, part-time positions, and seasonal offices at which they worked three days per week from mid-January to the first week in June each year. On Mondays and Fridays during the legislative session, they did not have to report for duty at the State House. And even then, the legislature convened at noon on Tuesday when in session and usually adjourned by mid-day on Thursday.

The compensation package for legislators included a base annual salary plus additional payments for travel mileage, per diem, and retirement benefits. Aside from this income which varied from the early part of the year when they were paid more while in session to the last half of the year when they seldom convened, many legislators lived off of part-time jobs or were self-employed.

This lack of a steady and substantial income made legislators prone and vulnerable to take bribes and handouts from lobbyists and others seeking favors at the State House.

Legislators as Hustlers

The problem of part-time legislators being placed in a position where they were poorly paid for spending more and more time in public service and the power they had to pass laws made them prone to take bribes to supplement their meager incomes.

Prof. Glen Broach, a political scientist at Winthrop College, told Cindi Scoppe of *The State* that "it puts them in a situation where the temptation to abuse is pretty intense."

A political consultant, Bud Ferillo, who had worked in the House and Lt. Governor's office for 14 years, said the pressures of lost time from the growing demands of legislative work and poor pay made corruption more likely. Ferillo said the danger was becoming worse: "We have seen the climate evolve that's more conducive to venial corruption than in past years."

The danger that such financially marginal lawmakers would try to capitalize on their powers was very real. The danger that they would shake down lobbyists and take bribes was a natural consequence.

John Crangle of Common Cause/South Carolina, a political reform organization at the State House, said that based on his experience as a lobbyist since 1987: "I think that anytime you have part-time, semi-professional legislators as we do, you're going to have a situation in which some individuals are going to have rather tenuous occupations, low-income occupations, and they're going to regard their government positions as a source of income they need to pay their bills."

Ms. Scoppe's review found a number of retired persons under 65 years of age and ten House members with no jobs and no sources of income indicated on their official disclosures.

S.C. Legislators' Tenuous Incomes

Scoppe pointed out that without a real full-time job with a company or government, most legislators had to fend for themselves in a harsh economic environment in one of the poorest states in the country. Coming from small towns and rural districts, lawmakers found the slim $10,000 per year base salary paid by the state for their seasonal job as state legislators put them below the poverty line without outside income such as a self-employed business or pension.

Sen. Jack Lindsay, a target of the FBI probe, said based on his experience as a small town lawyer in Bennettsville, South Carolina, and a state senator for 38 years that, "I guess everyone that runs for the Legislature, young lawyers, think they'll go serve a term or two, get themselves known, help establish their law practice."

Lax Disclosure Laws for Legislators Cause Little Disclosure

The disclosure provisions of the 1975 Ethics Act which applied to legislators were so lax that they allowed legislators to file reports which failed to show their actual sources of income and employment. The law required legislators to complete statements of economic interest but the information required on the forms was scanty, inconsistent, and often not complete.

Although 34 states required legislators to disclose all of their assets and income, the Act allowed legislators to check "not applicable" to portions of the disclosure forms that asked about business transactions with government and lobbyists. Further, the forms allowed legislators to not report potential conflicts between their official positions and business associations. In fact, some legislators were lawyers on retainer to companies with interests in legislation, but often did not disclose their sources of fees.

Common Cause/South Carolina Executive Director John Crangle derided the disclosure requirements of South Carolina, arguing that "it allows a lot of either actual or possible conflict of interest situations to go undetected by the press or public." Crangle noted the result was, "Nobody knows the individual has a conflict of interest except the person himself." Prof. Glenn Broach of Winthrop College added the state needed better disclosure laws to help in "determining the extent to which this use of office for personal gain is occurring."

Black Targeting Charge Rebutted

The repeated charges that the black legislators caught up in Lost Trust had been targeted by the FBI sting were rebutted by Gene L. Sansbury of Columbia in a letter to the editor of *The State* on October 7, 1990.

"Much ado has been made lately (especially by black political leaders Messrs. Kay Patterson and Herbert Fielding) about unfair targeting and prosecution of certain black officials in accepting bribes for votes." However, Sansbury felt their protests were evasions and blamed any blacks who might make excuses for crooked black politicians, saying, "I find it strange that their constituents are so supportive."

Blaming the crooked politicians for betraying those who elected them in the black community, Sansbury impugned the integrity of those black officials who seemed to be in politics to make money, charging that, "While many black politicians talk a good line and do a lot of grandstanding, their votes will be with their own pocketbooks and not with the voters who elected them."

Corruption at Economic Development Office Charged

Struggling Democratic challenger, Sen. Theo Mitchell, became more desperate as the general election neared and incumbent Carroll Campbell had a huge lead in the polls and in fund-raising.

Three weeks before the election, Mitchell launched an attack on Campbell alleging that the Governor's Economic Development Office was corrupt and a scandal in itself. The charge, which was not convincing without any corroborating evidence from Mitchell, did, in fact, have at least some plausibility because of growing rumors and media revelations about Campbell's Economic Development Board Chairman, Dick Greer, who was exposed as having a long-term friendship with both Ron Cobb and Gov. Campbell himself.

In the end, it came out that not only did Greer refer clients to Ron Cobb and suggest large fees, but that Greer and Cobb used cocaine together, for which Cobb got immunity from prosecution and Greer was eventually convicted of felony cocaine possession after the 1990 election had passed. However, at the time that Mitchell made the charges just before the election, Mitchell and the media did not know anything solid about the Greer drug scandal which would come out after Campbell was safely re-elected.

Judge Issues Gag Order

As the first trial in the Lost Trust prosecutions neared on October 15, 1990, the federal judge over the case ordered a gag on the media to minimize prejudice against the defendants.

Both judges, Falcon Hawkins and Charles Simon, issued gag orders to stop prejudicial information about the defendants from being published.

McMaster Blames Theodore on Ethics Reform

Lt. Governor candidate, Henry McMaster, released an ad attacking incumbent, Nick Theodore, for failing to take the lead in ethics reform.

The ad, released in early October, blamed Theodore for doing little to clean up the corruption at the State House and for not proposing rigorous ethics reform proposals.

Campbell Rejects Democratic Corruption Allegations

Reacting to Sen. Theo Mitchell's charges that the Carroll Campbell administration was vitiated by corruption, especially in its economic development office, Campbell, in mid-October, lashed out at the allegations and condemned them as false.

Branding the charges as "atrocious" and "irresponsible," Campbell told the public that the Mitchell charges were only "desperation comments fueled by the presence of an also ran." The "also ran" label was directed to Sen. Ernest Passailague who lost the Democratic primary election for governor.

The issue in the exchange was the use of the special highway economic development account which was controlled by a committee chaired by Dick Greer, who was also the chairman of Campbell's re-election campaign and the State Economic Development Board.

Appeals Court Hears Gag Order

The 4th Circuit Court of Appeals acted with unusual speed on October 11, 1990, to hear an appeal challenging the media gag order issued by two federal judges in the Lost Trust cases.

The appeal raised the question as to how much information the media would be allowed to publish as more indictments and more evidence became available.

Faced with the inflammatory television ads of 30 seconds launched by the McMaster campaign for Lt. Governor, the federal judge involved in the Lost Trust criminal trials considered issuing a gag order to stop the ads from showing.

The ads which linked bribed black legislators to Lt. Theodore were criticized as not only racially prejudiced and unduly provocative, but also as perhaps creating public opinion hostile to the defendants, thereby prejudicing their chances for a fair trial in the Lost Trust cases.

The judge who had considered gagging the McMaster television ad shortly decided to abandon the idea. The court announced on October 12, 1990, that no gag order would be issued.

Rep. Moss Pleads to Cocaine Charge

Former Rep. Donna A. Moss, just resigned from the House, pleaded guilty to possession of cocaine on October 12, 1990, although the FBI did not, in fact, actually catch her using powder cocaine. There were no videotapes documenting Moss's use of the illegal drugs, as was the case with those charged with bribery. Moss was not caught in possession.

U.S. Attorney Bart Daniel said that multiple witnesses alleged that Moss had used cocaine on or before April 19, 1989.

NAACP Seeks Racial Bias Probe

Alleging that the Lost Trust FBI sting was directed at black officials, the NAACP demanded that an investigation be held to determine if the large number of blacks caught in the first three months of the sting were selected as targets because of color. The NAACP demand for an investigation was announced October 13, 1990, and published by the media in publications including *The State*.

Rogers Leads Judicial Screening

With growing clouds of suspicion looming over his head, Rep. Jack I. Rogers (D-Marlboro) went ahead and conducted a meeting of the Judicial Screening Committee, charged with determining which candidates for state judicial positions met legal standards for the position.

CHAPTER FOURTEEN

THE TRIAL OF REP. LUTHER TAYLOR

Jury Drawn in Taylor Trial

The jury in the first Lost Trust case to go to trial, the Luther Taylor case, was drawn beginning October 15, 1990, in federal court in Columbia. Taylor, the first of ten indicted in the scandal, appeared at the court house as the selection of jurors began to face five counts of bribery and one of criminal conspiracy.

The judge presiding over the Luther Taylor trial closed the jury selection process to the public view on October 16, 1990. Judge Falcon Hawkins was concerned that a public selection process would prejudice the rights of Luther Taylor to a fair trial.

Fourth Circuit Removes Gag Order

On October 16, 1990, just as the Luther Taylor trial was starting, the 4th Circuit Court of Appeals ruled in favor of the appeals lodged by the media challenging the gag orders issued in the Luther Taylor case. The court held that the public had a right to know what was going on in the trial of the Taylor matter.

Taylor Attacks Witnesses for Drug Crimes

On October 17, 1990, as the Taylor case was beginning, the defense attacked the character of prosecution witnesses against him. Rep. Taylor's lawyers ripped both lobbyist Ron Cobb and Rep. Bob Kohn for drug use, undermining their testimony that they bribed Taylor to vote for the betting bill. In fact, of course, both Cobb and Kohn had known histories of drug abuse at the time of the sting.

Cobb Testifies Against Taylor

The chief prosecution witness against Luther Taylor was lobbyist turned sting agent, Ron Cobb. Cobb led off the prosecution's testimonial evidence by saying that Taylor had a price to be bribed in his repeated acts of extortion and conspiracy.

The Cobb testimony in the first hours of the Taylor trial quickly raised questions about Cobb's own credibility. Suspicions about Cobb's previous payoffs of Sen. Jack Lindsay, his old mentor and friend, made Cobb a less than sterling source of testimony.

Kohn: Legislators Sought Payoffs

Called as a major prosecution witness against Rep. Taylor, disgraced former Rep. Robert Kohn told the court in his testimony on October 20, 1990, that legislators in the South Carolina State House were not the innocent victims of temptation by corrupt lobbyists, but that they eagerly sought payoffs in exchange for political favors.

Kohn told the court that he cooperated with Luther Taylor to bribe House members. Kohn said that he sent Taylor to see Ron Cobb as part of the sting operation and that Taylor told Kohn a few days later that "he could do very good business with him."

U.S. Attorney Bart Daniel asked Kohn if the money given out by Cobb was intended to be a campaign contribution, but Kohn replied, "No. No, sir. I was taking bribes."

Kohn said that he enlisted members of the defunct "Fat and Ugly Caucus" to recruit legislators to back the betting bill. "I talked to Luther and lobbyists. I said, 'We can make some money. We need to see if we can find some fish,' meaning people who would do something they ordinarily wouldn't. I talked to Luther about landing the fish; the opportunity to make money was just too overwhelming for a lot of us." Stressing the close concerted action of the two to promote bribery, Kohn added that he talked every day with Taylor about the opportunity to make some bucks, legal or illegal.

Kohn Testimony in Taylor Trial Paints Sordid Picture

Kohn told the judge and jury that he and Taylor knew they could make a lot of money working with Ron Cobb. He said that the former members of the disbanded "Fat and Ugly Caucus" were easy targets for bribery as they were "not exactly the most honorable group."

In view of the fact that the FBI front, the Alpha Group, pushing the betting bill appeared to have unlimited funds, the decision was made to offer bribes of up to $1,000 to persons known to have little if any integrity, that is, to those "people who had enough larceny in their blood that it wasn't a problem for them."

Kohn testified that the Town House Hotel was a place where crooked deals were cut with legislators who "came to do deals, legitimate and illegitimate," while playing poker on Tuesday nights during the legislative session. Kohn told the court about lobbyists paying bar tabs and even paying for legislators' trips to New York. "You never had to pay any bills," adding that "Even a person who is methodically honest makes money in the Legislature. But you can make a lot more, depending on how you play the system. Make up excuses for junkets.... And just take the lobbyist's credit card with you. So you make money."

Kohn told the court in the Taylor trial that he was once offered $20,000 in cash to help kill a bill involving an amusement company. Kohn said that he got a member of the House Judiciary Committee to kill the bill but the company welshed on the payoff afterward.

Kohn also said that while he served in the House from Charleston County, he was involved in a scheme to pay a black man to run for the Republican nomination in the First District of South Carolina to get out the white vote in an election involving Rep. Arthur Ravenel.

Kohn also admitted that he had cut a deal with the prosecution to testify and cooperate in the Lost Trust cases. Facing a possible sentence of 20 years and a fine of $50,000, Kohn said that, "I think I made a pretty good deal, but I don't know. I have no guarantee. All I know for sure is that if I lie on the stand, I go to jail."

The Issue of Corrupt Intent Raised at Trial

The defense of lack of criminal intent was raised by attorney Joel Collins as a major argument in the Luther Taylor trial when it began in mid-October, 1990, in Columbia. Collins pointed out that Rep. Taylor had been a long-time supporter of horse race betting and the bill to legalize such betting was well before Taylor took any money from Cobb.

This issue had been discussed with Common Cause/South Carolina Executive Director John Crangle, who requested a meeting held in September, 1990, at Collins' law office in Columbia at which Crangle expressed his concerns that Cobb's money to Taylor was not clearly a bribe because it had not changed Taylor's long-standing position to public actions in any way related to the betting bill. Crangle volunteered to testify on condition that Collins issue a subpoena requiring Crangle's appearance at the Taylor trial when it started on Friday, October 18, 1990. Collins issued the subpoena and Crangle appeared at the Court House on that date, but was not called.

Collins made the argument that Taylor had not done anything for Cobb's cash that Taylor was not already committed to doing. There was no quid pro quo—no money exchanged for favors. This argument did not persuade the jury. The video evidence of Taylor taking the money and the audio recording of Cobb and Taylor talking like they were doing corrupt business was enough to convict.

The argument was also made in later defense cases without success, except perhaps in the Tim Wilkes acquittal, when attorney Gedney Howe stressed the point that Wilkes had supported the horse racing bill long before he took any money from Cobb. Howe also made the argument that Wilkes regarded the money handed to him by Cobb as a campaign contribution rather than a bribe taken to pay Wilkes to vote for the racing bill.

Taylor Case to Jury

All evidence having been presented and jury instructions given by the trial judge, the Luther Taylor case was sent to the jury in Columbia on October 23, 1990, on five counts of bribery and one count of criminal conspiracy.

The jury did not reach a quick verdict, however.

The same day as the Taylor case went to the jury, the prosecution said that Sen. Jack Lindsay, a major suspect in State House corruption, had not been given immunity from prosecution by the Federal government.

On October 25, 1990, the jury returned a verdict of guilty against Luther Taylor on all five counts of bribery and one count of conspiracy.

Taylor Guilty Verdict Explained

The FBI sting videotapes of Rep. Luther Taylor taking large handouts of cash from sting lobbyist Ron Cobb was too much for the jury to resist. What doubts existed in the bribery case against Taylor were erased by the grainy tapes and audio of the transaction of a sleazy and very unctuous lobbyist bribing a black politician who was routinely folding cash into his pocket and gratuitously making brazenly self-incriminating remarks to Cobb.

Jurors told the media that the videotapes were a decisive factor in their decision to convict on the charge that Taylor took $4,300 in bribes to vote for the betting bill. The tapes caught Taylor taking the money from an undercover sting agent and saying in thanks to Cobb, "Bless you, my man."

However, the jury struggled and nearly acquitted on the criminal conspiracy charge, but in the end, found the sleazy taped scenes too stark a proof of criminal intent and collusion with Cobb sufficient to warrant conspiracy.

After Taylor's conviction on October 25, 1990, some of the jurors told the media why they voted to convict on all six counts of public corruption. Juror Kimberly Resta, a Clemson University student, commented that "The tapes were damaging. You could listen to them and watch them, and you couldn't overlook what he said and what he did."

At first the jury did not believe the testimony of lobbyist Ron Cobb and former legislator Bob Kohn, who said Taylor was taking bribes. But the jury did not believe Taylor's statement that all the money he took was a campaign contribution. And, in the end, it was the prosecution evidence that convinced jurors that Taylor took the money as a bribe, not as a contribution. Resta remarked, "Luther Taylor never once mentioned (on tape) that the money was [a] contribution. Luther Taylor was a willing participant."

Evidence in the trial indicated that Taylor not only accepted a bribe of $2,500, but also took bribes of $500 each for every other legislator he recruited to take bribes from Cobb on the betting bill. The jury convicted Taylor for "doing business the old fashioned way," as Taylor himself said of his dealings.

CHAPTER FIFTEEN

AFTERMATH OF TAYLOR CONVICTION

Taylor Conviction Spurs Comments

The jury verdict against Rep. Luther Taylor (D-Richland) provoked a variety of comments after it was handed down on October 25, 1990. Some commentators viewed the conviction with favor while others deplored the court's decision.

The Chairman of the Legislative Black Caucus, Sen. Herbert Fielding (D-Charleston), predicted that the conviction would have a negative "chilling effect" on subsequent defendants and their cases. On the other hand, attorney I.S. Leevy Johnson, who represented three Lost Trust defendants from the Black Caucus, believed that the conviction would have no impact on his clients. Representing Reps. Ken Bailey (D-Orangeburg), James Faber (D-Richland), and Frank McBride (D-Richland), Johnson claimed the situation of Taylor was different from that of his clients. Johnson noted that his clients had not even been indicted and he hoped that they would not be.

However, Sen. Rick Lee (R-Spartanburg), who had already pleaded guilty, said the Taylor defense showed that the 1975 Ethics Act did not clearly distinguish campaign contributions from bribes. Lee predicted that it would be necessary for ethics reformers to clearly draw the line between campaign contributions and bribes. Lee also argued for a ban on lobbyists' donations saying: "I think the best way is to outlaw contributions from lobbyists altogether, and at the same time put a limitation on campaign spending."

Speaker Bob Sheheen (D-Kershaw) reacted to the jury verdict against Luther Taylor by saying that the Taylor verdict did not add much to the previous five guilty pleas filed by legislators, noting that, "We're operating under a cloud, and those of us who are going to remain in the House" would have to act to restore confidence.

Sen. Fielding expressed great sorrow, remarking that, "I've known Rep. Taylor for about 10 years and during that whole time, with him and others in this, I've only known them as honorable people." But Fielding said he still felt that black legislators were being picked on. Sen. Kay Patterson (D-Richland) also claimed that the number of blacks singled out for prosecution was disproportionate to their numbers in the General Assembly.

On the other hand, Gov. Carroll Campbell argued that the conviction of Taylor was step in cleaning up the State House, asserting that, "Today's verdict indicates that the system is working to purge itself and will continue to do so." The Democratic candidate for governor, Sen. Theo Mitchell (D-Greenville), did not say that he thought racial discrimination was at work in the Lost Trust cases, concluding, "I just don't have the facts on that."

Big Money From McAlloy to Governor

In all of the Lost Trust cases taken to trial, the clear centrality of so-called campaign contributions which were thinly disguised bribes made the question of money in state politics a major focus of the sting and media examination of the causes of the corruption.

The fact that campaign contributions were unlimited and were being handed out by big money special interests, most commonly large corporations, and that the bulk of such payments went to incumbents was well illustrated by the media exposure of the fact that McAlloy Corporation, a large steel fabricator in the Charleston area, had given $60,000 to the re-election campaign chest of Gov. Carroll Campbell in 1990.

Although a legal payment, the huge amount in 1990 dollars had a shocking impact on the public and became a major factor in the effort made in 1991 to draft a new ethics bill which would get control over the runaway use of large sums to buy votes, legislation, and elections in South Carolina. Democrats bristled at the $60,000 as evidence of the sweetheart relationship of Campbell and big donors to obtain favors at the State House.

B.J. Gordon Asks for Separate Trial

Rep. B.J. Gordon, who had been indicted along with two other legislators, asked for a separate trial on charges of bribery under the Hobbs Act. Gordon argued that his trial along with others would be "prejudiced by spillover of the evidence" against the other co-defendants in the case, who were Blanding and Fant.

Gordon moved the court on October 26, 1990, to order that Gordon not be tried together with any other Lost Trust defendants as the prosecution wanted to do for efficiency rather than have multiple trials of individual defendants, all of whom were charged with substantially the same crimes.

Gov. Carroll Campbell's Ties to Scandal Raised

With rumors swirling about Gov. Carroll Campbell's economic development chairman and old friend, Dick Greer, Campbell was a target for Democratic questions about his own entanglement with Lost Trust.

Campbell needed to distance himself from any taint of corruption spreading from the growing list of indictments of State House politicians in the weeks before Campbell stood for re-election on November 6, 1990. Fortunately for Campbell, it was not until after the governor was re-elected that his henchmen, Dick Greer and David Hawkins, were indicted and convicted on charges to which they both entered guilty pleas.

Sen. Hollings Predicts More Indictments

Sen. Fritz Hollings announced that the FBI investigation of State House corruption would produce as many as 15 more indictments. Making his remarks on October 29, 1990, Hollings said that U.S. Attorney Bart Daniel told him that the federal grand jury would hand down more indictments in two batches of 5 defendants each in November and again in December of 1990. Hollings said that Daniel had indicated that another 5 indictments might come in January, 1991. Hollings said that he did not know whether any more charges would be filed after January.

Hollings told the media at a news conference on October 29, 1990, that Lost Trust had attracted attention in Washington and "It's an embarrassment. I'm hearing it everywhere I go.... They always ask me, 'How many are they going to indict?'"

In addition to his expectation of more indictments, Hollings said of the prosecutions, "I hope they'll clean it entirely out and get on, because General Assembly government has been a shining light heretofore in your state and mine." Hollings said that South Carolina legislators, of which he was once a state senator, "always brag about their service."

New Powers of State Grand Jury Proposed

Following the conviction of Luther Taylor and capitalizing on the massive publicity and growing public outrage provoked by Lost Trust, Gov. Carroll Campbell and Attorney General Travis Medlock launched a campaign to expand the powers of the State Grand Jury to include public corruption. The two began by spending $25,000 on advertising for the proposal and then pooled their money to fly around the state, stopping at major cities to advocate the State Grand Jury as a new weapon to discover, stop, and deter bribery, kickbacks, and other abuses of public office.

House Candidates Want New Ethics Laws

Common Cause/South Carolina conducted and published a new survey of House candidates standing for election on November 6, 1990, which showed that the great majority of them favored new ethics laws. The survey, designed and circulated by Common Cause/South Carolina, was reported on November 3rd, just before the election. The survey was designed by John Crangle, the Executive Director of Common Cause/South Carolina.

A total of 103 candidates running with opposition in 1990 were asked to respond to the survey and 87 did. Eighty three (83) of the 87 said they approved at least six of ten proposed reforms listed on the survey. Seventy one (71) House candidates without opposition were not surveyed.

Support for the ten reform proposals was reported as follows:

98% favored more disclosure of business and financial interests;

91% favored making the State Ethics Commission responsible for enforcing campaign finance and lobbying activities;

88% favored a ban on campaign fund-raising during the legislative session;

81% favored a limit of $250 on campaign contributions from a single source;

91% favored a total ban on cash donations above $49;

86% favored a total ban on lobbyists giving anything of value to legislators or other government officials;

91% favored requiring lobbyists to disclose in detail their compensation for lobbying;

55% favored a tax on lobbyists' spending to pay for administration of campaign finance and ethics laws.

The only proposal receiving less than majority support was a proposal for partial public financing of campaign contributions. Sixty seven (67) percent said they opposed such financing.

A total of 14 candidates favored 100% of the proposals.

Among candidates rumored to be under investigation in the Lost Trust probe, there was a split in opinions. Rep. Kenneth Bailey (D-Orangeburg) favored all proposed reforms. Speaker Pro Tem Jack I. Rogers (D-Marlboro) supported only 50% of the measures on the survey. Both would later be convicted of public corruption in Lost Trust.

Greer Again Denied Drug Use

On the eve of the November 6, 1990, election in which Gov. Carroll Campbell stood for re-election against a flailing opponent, Campbell's Economic Development Board Chairman Dick Greer again denied rumors of drug use. The rumors had been vigorously circulating since the Lost Trust scandal became public in mid-July, 1990.

Greer's protests of innocence were obviously designed to shield Campbell from any guilt by association, even though he appeared in no danger of losing the election. Long after Campbell had been safely re-elected, Greer would, in fact, be indicted and convicted of drug abuse.

Editorial Urges Strengthening State Grand Jury

The State, in an editorial on November 4th, just before the 1990 general election, urged voters to approve a proposed constitutional referendum amendment to expand the State Grand Jury's powers to include public corruption investigation and prosecution.

The State Grand Jury already had jurisdiction over such subjects as obscenity, drug dealing and environmental violations. The need for the amendment was obvious given the number of indictments and convictions which had proliferated in only a little over three months since Lost

Trust became public. The fact that Lost Trust was a federal prosecution of corrupt state officials who had been left alone by state law enforcement, including the State Grand Jury, suggested that state law enforcement was lax and ineffective in addressing corruption by powerful state officials such as legislators and executive branch officers.

House Ethics Panel Fails

On November 4, 1990, *The State* pointed out the need to abolish the legislative ethics committees in the wake of Lost Trust. It was clear Lost Trust badly discredited the idea of legislative ethics committees in South Carolina because they had failed to catch and punish the most outrageous and rampant forms of corruption including outright bribery and shakedowns.

The 1975 Ethics Act had authorized that the House and the Senate each have their separate ethics committees to monitor and, if necessary, investigate and discipline member of each chamber. But the committees had been shown by Lost Trust to be utter frauds and failures. Not only had criminal acts been perpetrated under their noses, but three former House Ethics Committee members—Reps. Danny Winstead, Donna Moss, and Larry Blanding—had been charged with either bribery or cocaine possession.

The idea that the legislature could monitor and regulate itself was the premise on which the legislative ethics committees were founded. The problem was that the premise was manifestly false. The House, in particular, heavily populated with low-income, often self-employed, underemployed, or unemployed members, was little more than a House of hustlers and con-men. Such down-at-the-heels persons were easy prey to big money lobbyists and fixers who spread around a few dollars to buy votes.

Primary to Replace Taylor Announced

The Richland County Democratic executive committee met on November 3, 1990, and decided to hold a primary election to replace Rep. Luther Taylor who had been convicted on October 25, 1990. Chairman I.S. Leevy Johnson said that the 56 member committee would normally decide on a replacement candidate, but the committee thought it would be better to allow the community to elect the candidate because he would serve a full two year term in the House.

Taylor had been unopposed in the general election and asked to have his name taken off of the ballot after his conviction on conspiracy and extortion charges.

District 77 included the northern portion of Richland County. The primary was set for December 4, 1990. Five Democratic candidates were considering a run for the nomination, including Richland County councilman John L. Scott, along with Prof. Andrew Chisholm of the University of South Carolina Criminal Justice faculty.

The Task of Ethics Reform Defined

On November 4, 1990, *The State* ran articles on the issue of the consequences of major criminal scandals in state governments, particularly recent corruption scandals in California, Tennessee, and West Virginia.

Comments from officials and experts in the three states indicated that the public is often apathetic and ignorant about such scandals. In Tennessee in 1984, a House member was re-elected to his seat while in prison, and in 1990 he was later caught up in a federal public corruption case.

Mike Cody, the former Attorney General of Tennessee, observed that his efforts to promote major ethics reforms had failed because "When you've got an issue that's about good government, there's no constituency other than the newspapers that really brings pressure on legislators." The public did not press for reform. Cody noted, "I don't think legislators hear from people back home about ethics like they would hear about taxes."

Even so, Tennessee eventually passed ethics legislation after 45 state officials, lobbyists, and bingo operators had been caught giving or taking bribes. Even so, one legislator still admitted he did not like the ethics reforms but had to vote for them because of the scandal.

The State declared the obvious about South Carolina after it was hit by Lost Trust, arguing the state desperately needed reform to clean up its scandal-plagued government. But the editorial deplored the apathy of the people of the state in the face of the scandal.

The State referred to recent corruption scandals including "Shrimpscam" in California and "Operation Rocky Top" in Tennessee, noting that only five of a total of 34 ethics reform proposals were adopted in Tennessee and those that were adopted were, in fact, weak. In West Virginia, people were more interested in the University of West Virginia football team than in cleaning up a corrupt state government, including a state governor sent to prison.

The State pointed out the need for more citizen activism, noting that John Gardner, the founding chairman of Common Cause, had stressed the need for citizen pressure for ethics reforms, arguing that government corruption was based on a "web of influence woven by special interests and the accommodation of politicians to the influence." Gardner said government could not reform itself without citizen pressure.

Miles Made Ethics the Issue in Campaign

Republican challenger Jim Miles of Greenville made ethics the key issue in his successful campaign against Secretary of State John Campbell, a 12 year veteran.

The race for Secretary of State was normally boring and insignificant, but in 1990 Miles used the public attention and anger over Lost Trust to hammer on Campbell as a cause of the scandal because of his lax oversight of lobbyists at the State House.

Miles convinced the State Ethics Commission to declare that it was unethical for Campbell to continue his old practice of soliciting and accepting campaign contributions from the very same lobbyists he was supposed to register and take disclosure reports from each year.

The race was also a mismatch in age in that Miles was 49 years old and Campbell was 77.

McMaster Made Ethics an Issue in Lt. Gov.'s Race

Challenger Henry McMaster made ethics an issue in his primary campaign for the Republican nomination as Lt. Governor of South Carolina, criticizing his opponent Sen. Sherry Martschink for taking gifts while in the Senate. McMaster's Democratic opponent, Lt. Governor Nick Theodore, had made ethics reform a major issue in his first term in office and had even convened a committee to study and propose various ethics reforms.

Early in the campaign, McMaster talked about abolishing parole, instituting the death penalty for drug kingpins, and stopping hazardous waste shipments into South Carolina. In the end, his focus was largely on ethics reform.

S.C. Voters Lack Outrage

Prof. Blease Graham of the University of South Carolina pointed to the lack of outrage in South Carolina voters over ethics crimes of the state's politicians exposed in Lost Trust. Noting that "the traditional political culture" of South Carolina valued stability over competition, Graham pointed to the difference between South Carolina and progressive states, saying, "We'd have a tremendous outrage in a state like Wisconsin or Minnesota, a moralistic political culture, where those people would be seen as disgraceful and dishonest."

Going into the 1990 general elections, a total of 13 of the 15 House members implicated in the Lost Trust scandal had no opposition. Graham asserted that in states like Wisconsin and Minnesota, there would be strong opposition to those perceived as corrupt. But in South Carolina, incumbents had little or no opposition in spite of the scandal.

Cobb Blames Defense Lawyers

Ron Cobb, master of public bribery and cocaine abuse, adopted a high moral tone after the Luther Taylor trial at which he testified for the first time. Cobb accused defense lawyers of low-life tactics. Cobb told the media that he was appalled because the defense lawyers were using his estranged wife to impugn his testimony as a prosecution witness.

Cobb was upset with Joel Collins who used Cobb's wife's testimony to discredit Cobb. Cobb complained that defense counsel hurt his family. Cobb's wife did provide testimony in the Luther Taylor trial indicating her husband was dishonest and had forged her name on a power of attorney. She also told that Cobb was hiding the immunity agreements he had with the U.S. Attorney and the South Carolina Attorney General.

It also came out that Mrs. Cobb had been involved in perhaps shooting herself in a failed suicide attempt. She went to a North Carolina rehabilitation facility, but claimed that her husband did not pay her medical bills.

Cobb defended his work as a sting agent for the FBI, saying, "I'm proud of what we've done in the public corruption [probe], because instead of being a legislative system, it was a deal-making system."

Blacks Protest Sting

Black demonstrators marched from the U.S. District Courthouse in downtown Columbia to the State House on November 11, 1990, to protest the FBI sting as racially motivated. Multiple speakers told the 150 demonstrators rallied at the State House that their "March and Rally for Equal Justice" was complaining about the black legislators who were being prosecuted in Lost Trust.

It was alleged that, "what is happening at the courthouse—where black legislators are being indicted in greater proportion than white legislators—is just another example of...racism."

"There is a new form of lynching that is taking place, and that new form of lynching is taking place under the guise of the criminal justice system," alleged Adell Adams, president of the Columbia branch of the NAACP. "This lynching is being done with criminal records and computers," Adams said.

The prosecutions of the black legislators in Lost Trust was a symptom of the racism on which the United States and South Carolina was built, according to the speakers at the State House rally.

The rally was the first such rally to protest the Lost Trust probe and prosecutions. Two of the chief suspects in the probe attended the rally—Reps. Frank McBride and James Faber. Neither had been indicted at the time, but would be indicted and convicted later.

Protest Alleges Racial Bias

One of the issues raised by the speakers at the protest rally against Lost Trust was the fact that eight of the 18 legislators known to be targets of the probe were black and the General Assembly only had 20 black members. Sen. Kay Patterson (D-Richland) told the protestors that, "I'm tired of seeing that out of 18 legislators targeted, eight of them was black.... How can you target 43 percent when we only make up 12 percent.... Now if you can't figure that out, then your folks should have kept you at home and sent the mule to school.... And don't let Bart Daniel make a fool out of you."

Daniel had denied charges that the Lost Trust probe was racially motivated, but NAACP attorney John Roy Harper said that, "When this country was formed, we were considered three-fifths of a person. And quite frankly, in dealing with the so-called justice system in America, I get the considered feeling that we're still three-fifths of a person in the legal system."

Attorney I.S. Leevy Johnson, representing McBride and Faber as well as Rep. Ken Bailey (D-Orangeburg), complained that while the Lost Trust probe was important, other black officials were being targeted by white prosecutors in the state and nation.

Criminals Burglarize Taylor's House

Burglars struck the home of recently convicted Rep. Luther Taylor (D-Richland) on November 12,1990, just three weeks after he was convicted of corruption in the Lost Trust scandal.

Located on Sarah Matthews Road in Columbia, the house was entered by burglars during the night. The burglary included the theft of a $3,000 Rolex watch, a $1,000 watch, $800 in coins, $500 in cash, and other items. The Richland County Sheriff's Department investigated the break-in.

Taylor Complains of Pressure to Lie

Former Rep. Luther Taylor (D-Richland) complained that prosecutors were pressuring him to lie about other black lawmakers by threatening to indict Taylor for additional charges and impose longer prison time. Taylor claimed that the prosecution wanted him to lie under oath to blame black legislators indicted in Lost Trust.

Taylor told the media, "The government is pressing me to change my version of events leading to my indictment and to lie on my peers." He told *The State* that, "They are attempting to get me to say that I knew that Rob Cobb was bribing me as well as my peers."

Op Ed on Racial Bias in Sentencing

Rev. J. Arthur Holmes raised the question in an op ed in *The State* on December 19, 1990, of whether the black felons in Operation Lost Trust cases were treated more harshly than the white. He pointed to the light sentence of white Sen. Rick Lee (R-Spartanburg) to a halfway house for six months while black Rep. Luther Taylor (D-Richland) got six and a half years.

Rev. Holmes, President of the Greater Columbia Interdenominational Ministerial Alliance, a group of some 30 ministers in the black churches of Columbia, pastored Bethel AME Church.

Taking into account the fact that Lee cooperated with the probe but Taylor did not, Holmes wrote that Lee was not required to begin his sentence until after the holidays of the year 1990, but Taylor was taken immediately to jail after his sentencing. Holmes asked, "Why, then, was Mr.

Taylor immediately incarcerated in this season when we emphasize caring and compassion?" Holmes suggested that race was a factor.

Admitting that Operation Lost Trust was "a sad comment on our society.... We find it to be more so because of the number of black elected officials either indicted or implicated." Even so, he hoped that the treatment of the black defendants would be fair to "guard against any suggestions or hint of inequity."

New Charges Expected in 1991

The U.S. Attorney was expected to announce a new round of indictments in early January, 1991, after the holidays. Meanwhile, the trials of Reps. Larry Blanding, Ennis Fant, and B.J. Gordon were set for January 22, 1991. The delay in further indictments was thought due to negotiations between the government and suspects not yet indicted.

At the end of 1990, only about half of the suspects in Operation Lost Trust had been indicted. And U.S. Attorney Bart Daniel promised more charges, noting that suspects and defendants had cooperated and given information against others suspected of corruption and drug crimes.

The sting grand jury was continuing to deliberate, but had not issued any indictments since September 21, 1990, as of late December. If indictments of legislators came in 1991, it could remove more of them for the new 1991 session.

Interview
I.S. Leevy Johnson, Attorney at Law

By Dr. Robert J. Moore
December 3, 2014
Columbia, S.C.

I.S. Leevy Johnson

I.S. Leevy Johnson represented two Operation Lost Trust defendants who pled—Rep. James Faber (D-Richland) and Rep. Frank McBride (D-Richland). Mr. Johnson is a graduate of Benedict College and the University of South Carolina School of Law. He was one of the first three African-Americans elected to the South Carolina General Assembly since the end of Reconstruction, becoming a member of the South Carolina House of Representatives in 1970. He is a member of the law firm of Johnson, Toal, and Battiste in Columbia, S.C.

Johnson was the lawyer for Reps James Faber and Frank McBride, defending against charges that they had accepted bribes from Ron Cobb in the FBI Lost Trust sting operation. Both men pleaded guilty. Johnson's recollection is that he treated these clients as he does all defendants in criminal cases. He collected discovery evidence from the prosecutor, advised the men of the strength or weakness of the case against them, advised them of their constitutional right to a trail no matter the strength of the case, and explained to them the prosecutor's recommendation on sentencing to the judge, if they pleaded guilty. The men in this case decided to take the guilty plea.

Both men were sentenced to one year in prison, three years of probation, and 200 hours of community service. Johnson felt the sentences were far too harsh compared to some white defendants who pleaded guilty and were sentenced to no jail time, but to probation and fines. He was particularly upset about McBride. The prosecutor recommended only probation because of his cooperation with the prosecutors. But the judge handed down the harsh sentence anyway.

Summary of Interview with I.S. Leevy Johnson

Was this racial discrimination? Johnson said the real racial discrimination came in with the targeting of more black legislators to offer money for their voting for a bill which they had previously indicated they were going to vote for. He had no way of knowing whether the pari-mutuel betting bill was chosen because most black legislators had committed themselves to vote for the bill. Ron Cobb, who, by the way, was "the scum of the earth," had sought out black legislators disproportionately as targets for receiving money and being caught in the sting. I.S. had no way of knowing whether the FBI was directing Cobb to target particular legislators. But Cobb preyed upon those legislators who were most vulnerable.

This brings up, Johnson said, "the stink of politics" in which money is involved in every successful political effort. When you drive by the State House, there is a "For Sale" sign in front of it. You walk into the lobby and it is filled with lobbyists who are "buying outcome." Ninety-nine percent of lobbyists represent special business interests; one percent represent the masses. That being the case, the people have very little chance to get things done that are beneficial to them. The system in America has always been rigged in favor of the haves as opposed to the have-nots.

Johnson did not observe direct corrupt actions when he served in the legislature, but he did recognize that many lawyer-legislators were retained by large corporations and tended to act in the corporation's benefit. It was abuse of power. It didn't pass the "stink test." But it was legal at the time.

Maybe he didn't see corruption directly because of his reputation. He remembers during the Lost Trust episode going to the State House and seeing a friend who was a deputy sergeant-at-arms. Johnson told him he was so glad he was not in the legislature now. The guard said: "I.S., you would not have had anything to worry about. They knew who to approach." That was one of his greatest complements. I.S. stuck his chest and walked into the lobby and saw Senator Kay Patterson. He told him what the man had said. Kay quickly said: "They wouldn't have offered you a bribe because you ain't worth a shit!" He didn't think they would get their money's worth.

When you compare the income of many white legislators with black legislators, there is a wide disparity. Those who have the means tend to buy their way into power. If those without means achieve some power, they look around and say why can't I have some of those means. They might be tempted to sell that power for money. Yet Johnson had no reason to believe that some of those caught in the Lost Trust sting had abused their power before.

Concerning the question of whether Johnson considered appealing his clients' convictions after the 1991 Supreme Court decision to require that the prosecution prove a quid pro quo in a bribery case, he said he did not remember the timing, but his clients might have already served their one year in prison by then.

Did the favors that lobbyists gave to legislators, food, drink, trips, etc., influence the way they voted? Yes. All political activities are built on relationships. The favors helped build those relationships. One of the goals of the lobbyist is to build good relationships with those in decision making positions. That's part of the process. They seek to influence the outcome of legislation. That's where I.S. had a problem. Big business can buy results, whereas the "people in the streets don't have the voice that the people in the suites do."

He would not label the practice corruption, because at the time it was perfectly legal. It was condoned by those in office and was not being protested by the citizens. Cobb crossed the line, but I.S. would not say that all legislators that accepted gifts were corrupt. Recently, much money has flowed into the state from unknown sources. It is simply buying outcomes.

In 1991 there were some protests by those who thought that black legislators were being unjustly singled out because of their race. Did you think some indictments were based on racism? "I don't remember the specifics, but I think historically in the criminal justice system in America that it has been tainted with racism, that the disparities in the identity of the people who were prosecuted, the types of prosecutions that are made, the way people of color are treated in the criminal justice system, and the outcome of their cases is a blatant example of injustice.... I thought that certain white legislators got more favorable sentences compared to my clients. One that sticks out in my mind is Frank McBride and I think if you look at the transcript it will reveal that Judge Hawkins and I engaged in a heated exchange regarding the imposition of the sentence."

When asked if black legislators were discredited by the Lost Trust scandal, Johnson replied, "I do not think that black legislators have ever been accorded the proper respect for their noble contributions during or after Lost Trust. Some of the best minds that have ever been over there have been African-American legislators. And you might apply some of the conventional or traditional ways of measuring what they have achieved. One of the most important things, in my opinion, that black legislators have done for the people of South Carolina is to prevent bad laws. They have been in a position to expose legislation that was unfavorable to the people of South Carolina and they have stood as impediment to legislation that was disadvantageous to the people. So their lack of respect is derived from the lack of respect that African-Americans experience every day."

Did the passage of the ethics act in 1991 have a positive effect on politics in SC? "It was at best a mediocre or very weak effort. Until you have legislation that controls money that flows to elected officials, it won't be successful. You have got to have laws that control every penny that a legislator receives." PACs are blatant examples of the problem. We have to require contributors to reveal who they are and prevent multiple corporate labels under one ownership from trying to influence what goes on in SC, for example in education.

The problem with making changes in the system is that the very people who are receiving the goodies are the ones that have to vote to take away the goodies. There is not enough outrage in the public to force legislators to make the reforms necessary. So many people have become disenchanted with what is going on so they don't vote. So the people elected do not represent the masses.

The Lost Trust episode had a "profound impact on black elected officials." It reinforced their sense that there was a double standard and that black officials elsewhere, Atlanta, New York, Chicago, etc., were being investigated more than whites. Lost Trust hit home. The positive impact was that officials realized that they had to really be careful "because a lot of wolves come in sheep's clothing." Since Lost Trust, most of the officials prosecuted for corruption have been white. Many of them suffered from "arrogant invincibility." They don't think they can be caught. Jack Lindsay comes to mind. But he was never caught. Sen. Tom Smith said at Lindsay's death he would love to have seen Lindsay defend himself against Lost Trust type charges. That would have been so entertaining. Johnson said, "Jack Lindsay danced by some different music."

Johnson's overall appraisal of Lost Trust was that it was unfortunate. It tainted a lot of innocent people. Many thought that all black officials must be involved in similar activities. Many had lived exemplary lives. But Lost Trust has not led to profound changes. Some way must be found to stop the flow of money to elected officials. And most of the money is used on behalf of the haves, not the have-nots. The "For Sale" sign must be removed from the State House. Every bill that is passed in the legislature results in economic benefit to someone. Many officials are there to get some financial benefit for the special interests they represent. When the budget bill comes up, "the fight is about my slice of the pie."

The reforms in the wake of Lost Trust "did not go far enough." The current situation does not inspire confidence in the system because the impression is so widespread that the officials have been bought. Blacks are "consistently excluded rather than included" in the results of what goes on in South Carolina. "It's so unfortunate."

CHAPTER SIXTEEN

1990—STATE ELECTIONS AND ETHICS REFORM

1990 Election Returns

Gov. Carroll Campbell won easy re-election on November 6, 1990, in spite of the fact that two of his close associates were being investigated by criminal authorities at the time of the election. Both of them, former Campbell staffer David Hawkins and State Development Board Chairman, Dick Greer, would later be indicted and convicted. But none of that rubbed off on Campbell in the election.

On the other hand, Lt. Gov. Nick Theodore, who had stressed ethics reform in his campaign, won re-election. Republican Jim Miles, who had hammered incumbent John Campbell for failing to control the lobbyists, was able to oust Campbell in a close vote for Secretary of State. Campbell had sent thank you notes to lobbyists just before the election, expressing gratitude for the campaign donations given to him by lobbyists. Campbell's tone-deaf thank-you notes did not become public before the election, but they certainly seemed to confirm Miles' campaign argument that Campbell was, in fact, taking money from the same lobbyists he was supposed to be regulating and explained the fact that the lobbyists were out of control. Campbell's conflict of interest and his failure to regulate lobbyists became the only real and deciding issue.

Sheheen Re-elected

Speaker of the House Bob Sheheen (D-Kershaw) rolled through the November 6th election in spite of the scandal in the House which had caused ninety percent of the indictments filed at the time. Sheheen was never linked to the corruption except that it came out that he had taken several actions to stop corrupt and abusive behavior by House members of the "Fat and Ugly Caucus" who had been shaking down lobbyists. Sheheen had also exposed and ended the escort service run by Rep. Ennis Fant out of his House office on the State House grounds.

Of course, Sheheen's record of aggressively exposing and suppressing abuse of office and corruption in the House prior to the election proved a major asset in his re-election. After his return to office, Sheheen continued to promote ethics reform as Speaker of the House and was a major factor in the design and passage of the 1991 Ethics Act.

House Elections Return Incumbents

Voters removed only three incumbent House members in the November 6, 1990, general elections despite the seeming public discontent with the widespread corruption revealed by Operation Lost Trust, which had removed six House members as of the date of the elections. Voters seemed to feel that their legislator was satisfactory even if many others in the House were not.

The number of House members removed in Lost Trust was greater than the number ousted by voters on November 6, 1990. Of the 124 House members in office in January, 1990, before Lost Trust broke, a total of 106 would return after the 1990 general elections. Three incumbents lost, six were forced out by Lost Trust, six retired, and one left to become a circuit court judge (Rep. Tee Ferguson). Two lost in primaries.

House District 77 Election Replaces Taylor

The election to replace convicted House member Luther Taylor (D-Richland) was slated for December 4, 1990. Voters said they wanted to elect a person of integrity who could also bring state funding to District 77 as Taylor had.

One resident of the district, Jim Mullis of Blythewood, remarked that, "I think people want a change. They're looking for more integrity in those that represent them. But let me say, we never had a more responsive representative than Luther Taylor."

Richland County Republican Chairman, Scott Elliott, said that District 77 was ripe for Republican capture, remarking that, "If there ever is a reason to motivate Republicans to get to the polls, it might be that the incumbent Democrat was turned out under these circumstances."

The election pitted Republican Mary Fitzpatrick, a political novice, against Democrat John Scott, a Richland County Councilman. Fitzpatrick, a native of California, argued that "we need to get the old 'citizen legislator' mentality back." She said she would push for fiscal responsibility and ethics reform, including limiting spending on campaigns. But Scott had a regular income which contrasted with Luther Taylor who had no steady employment and had seemed to live off of politics while in office.

Richland County Councilman John Scott won election to District 77 in the House on December 4, 1990, replacing expelled corruptionist Luther Taylor.

Scott received 1,137 votes against 688 for Mary Fitzpatrick, a novice homemaker candidate, who blamed her defeat on apathy in spite of Lost Trust.

In another election on the same day, Rep. Carole Wells (R-Spartanburg) won the Republican primary to replace expelled bribe-taker Sen. Rick Lee (R-Spartanburg).

Scandal Provokes Reform

History showed that public scandals frequently triggered demand for ethics and governmental reforms, *The State* pointed out in its November 4, 1990, edition. Surveying three states recently hit by corruption scandals, *The State* found that Tennessee, California, and West Virginia had reacted to such scandals by passing some reform laws.

In 1989 and 1990 in Tennessee, new laws were passed to compel lobbyists to disclose their spending on legislators and were banned from paying for hotel rooms for legislators. Lobbyists were banned from loaning their credit cards to legislators and giving them credit. Legislators were also required to report their campaign receipts and expenses to a new state agency.

In California, new laws were passed in 1989 which limited the gifts to legislators to $250 and also banned fees paid to legislators for making speeches. In addition, legislators could not lobby until they had been out of the General Assembly for one year. Legislators were required to attend an ethics class once every two years.

In West Virginia in 1989, a new State Ethics Commission was created and new disclosure laws were passed. Lobbyists were required to report all expenditures of $25 or more on officials and a gift ban was imposed. However, lobbyists were still allowed to pay travel and meal expenses for legislators.

Miles Confronts Lobbyists

Newly elected Secretary of State, Jim Miles, served notice of lobbyists at the State House that he would enforce the laws governing lobbyists upon taking office on January 9, 1991. Miles had campaigned almost exclusively against incumbent, John Campbell, on the grounds that Campbell had failed to enforce the provisions of the 1975 Ethics Act which required lobbyists in South Carolina to register and disclose their activities to the Secretary of State.

Miles warned lobbyists on November 24, 1990, that he would make them comply with the law and that, even before taking office, he was already reviewing lobbyists' disclosure forms and contemplating revisions in such documents. Miles indicated that he would not allow persons to lobby who failed to follow the lobbying law and that he would turn them over to the Attorney General for violations.

In the future, Miles said he would insist that lobbyists complete all questions on the registration forms, including the employers and the subject of the lobbying activity. Lobbyists would be required to report their expenses, including gifts, gratuities, and campaign contributions to public officials. Miles explained that, "the reason and purpose for having a lobbyist disclosure form is to see which legislators are being influenced." Therefore, all legislators contacted by lobbyists were to be reported on the disclosure forms as well as places and activities related to the contacts.

Sheheen Pushes Ethics Reform

Speaker Bob Sheheen (D-Kershaw) moved aggressively in late November, 1990, to push ethics reform in the House at the new session set to start in January, 1991. Sheheen sent ideas for new House rules as proposed reforms to a select list of twenty members, which reforms would deal with the problems exposed by Lost Trust.

Sheheen called for a "no-cup-of-coffee" rule similar to that in Wisconsin, which would ban lobbyists' gifts to legislators, a central abuse exposed in Lost Trust. The proposed ban on lobbyists' gratuities was a frontal attack on the corrupt culture of the State House which made it so easy for the FBI to bribe public officials in South Carolina.

The House had an organizational meeting set for December 4, 1990, at which Sheheen wanted to move his reform proposals. Sheheen made the proposals strict to counter his expectation that the House would try to weaken them.

Of course, new House rules could not control the behavior of other branches and levels of government in South Carolina. But it was a good start and put pressure on the Senate to be aggressive about reform in the 1991 session.

Ethics Reform Bills Flood Legislature

By late November, 1990, more than 100 ethics reform bills had been pre-filed in the Senate in anticipation of the 1991 session when legislators would get their first chance after Lost Trust broke to try to clean up the corrupt culture of the State House.

Sen. Marshall Williams (D-Orangeburg), the powerful President Pro Tem and chairman of the Senate Judiciary Committee, led the way in the Senate as Speaker Bob Sheheen led the way in the House in the closing days of 1990. Williams sponsored a bill which was very aggressive and proposed a total ban on lobbyists' spending on legislators similar to Sheheen's proposed "no-cup-of-coffee" rule in the House. Williams also proposed strict campaign finance reform laws and more extensive disclosure requirements.

Williams dramatically said of his ethics bill, that the bill "in one fell swoop, moves us from the unenviable position of having a vague and incomplete system of campaign, lobbyist and ethics regulation to the lofty position of being unparalleled in the country in our system of public accountability."

At the same time, the House was preparing for its organizational session at which the House Rules Committee was expected to take action on lobbyists and on financial disclosure by both lobbyists and legislators. Speaker Sheheen said he wanted to have the House adopt new ethics rules in December so that it could move forward immediately at the opening of the 1991 session with passing a statute on ethics reform that "will cover everybody." Sheheen wanted to strengthen the House Ethics Committee and impose drastic reforms to limit cash campaign contributions, ban corporate contributions, and stop fund-raising during the legislative session.

GOP Seeks Office of President Pro Tem of House

Sensing the impending indictment of Speaker Pro Tem Jack I. Rogers (D-Marlboro), the Republicans in the House put forward challenger Rep. Howell Clyborne (R-Greenville). The election was set for December 4, 1990.

Noting that Speaker Bob Sheheen had proposed new ethics rules for the House, Republicans argued that the new rules would seem cosmetic if Rogers was again elected while under a cloud of suspicion. Rogers was the first sting suspect to face a contested election although he had not been indicted at the time of the election held as part of the House organizational meeting for the new 1991 session.

Rogers had a dubious past, having been a member of the abusive "Fat and Ugly Caucus" which preyed on lobbyists at the State House in the 1980s. Rogers also led two failed attempts to pass the betting bill in the 1990 session at the instigation of Rob Cobb. Rogers was elected as Speaker Pro Tem when the incumbent Speaker Sterling Anderson was indicted for tax evasion and suspended from the House prior to his conviction.

Sheheen Pushes Ethics Reforms

House Speaker Bob Sheheen (D-Kershaw) put forward a sweeping ethics reform package in early December, 1990, which proposed a complete ban on lobbyists' favors, gifts, and gratuities to legislators.

The plan was so drastic that it surprised Common Cause/South Carolina chairman, Eldon D. Wedlock, Jr., who worried that Sheheen's reforms might be impossible to pass and kill off all reform in the 1991 session of the General Assembly. Wedlock also worried that Sheheen's proposal envisioned House rule changes to be made at the organizational session of the House set for December 4, 1990, in Columbia, whereas the state really needed statutory reforms applying to not only the House, but the whole of state government.

However, Rep. Tim Rogers (D-Richland), a steady ally of Common Cause/South Carolina, praised Sheheen's leadership saying that he thought Sheheen was "trying to get the House committed on the principles of those reforms so that when statutory questions came up, we will have committed ourselves and it will be more difficult to have those stronger reforms watered down."

Rep. Larry Martin (R-Pickens) also commented that once Sheheen put out reform proposals, "It's going to be very difficult for any House member to get up and give the appearance you're against reform." But Martin did have questions about how much power the House had to clean up ethics problems with its own rules and whether rule changes would weaken efforts to enact ethics reforms into statutes.

Sheheen States Ethics Reform Package

In announcing his agenda of ethics reforms prior to the organizational meeting of the House on December 4, 1990, Sheheen explained that he wanted immediate action to impose new restrictions on lobbyists' interactions with House members and that he thought House rule changes would provide the fastest way of stopping lobbyists' abuses. Sheheen said that the only real opposition to new ethics rules limiting lobbyists' gratuities would come from "the people who believe their access to the General Assembly and members of the House is tied to money and the expenditure of money."

Sheheen put forward three proposals in his ethics reform package:

(1) increased disclosures of lobbyists' spending and activities;
(2) limits on when and where legislators could receive campaign contributions;
(3) a total ban on lobbyists' gifts and gratuities to state officials.

Ways and Means chairman, Billy Boan, (D-Lancaster) supported Sheheen's demand for urgent action, saying, "I think we are in a position that we have to do something, and I think we need to do something right away."

Sheheen proposed to have the House pass new ethics rules even if the Senate did not take similar action. Even though Senate leaders were known to favor more drastic reforms than those proposed by Sheheen, Rep. Harriet Keyserling (D-Beaufort) argued that, "I saw it that this would be an inspiration to the Senate; that they would not want to be seen as not being willing to do what the House would do."

Poll Backs Sheheen's Ethics Proposals

Just before the House met in its two day organizational session on December 4, 1990, *The State* reported a telephone poll from callers which endorsed Speaker Bob Sheheen's ethics reform proposals, especially the "no-cup-up-coffee" ruling. By a margin of 10 to 1, callers told *The State* that they supported the total ban on lobbyists giving gifts and handouts to legislators. The poll was not scientific but found 1,298 for the ban and 112 opposed.

One supporter of the gift ban remarked that, "I think when they accept things like that, it is actually bribes, and I should think it would be against the law." But one caller opined that, "In my opinion, there should be no lobbyists at all at the State House."

Sheheen's proposal could be enacted in House rules first at the organizational session and then perhaps framed as a statute and later enacted into law by both the House and Senate upon approval by the governor. Sheheen also proposed a ban on large cash donations and campaign contributions by lobbyists while the House was in session. Finally Sheheen proposed more disclosure of lobbyists' spending.

Sheheen's Ethics Reforms Discussed in House

On December 4, 1990, the House met in its organizational meeting to elect its speaker again and to discuss Speaker Bob Sheheen's strong ethics reform proposals. The House also re-elected Speaker Pro Tem Jack I. Rogers by a vote of 77-36 even though Rogers was widely suspected to be under federal investigation for corruption. The vote was along party lines and the Democratic majority of 78 to 42 Republicans picked Rogers.

Sheheen's proposed new "no-cup-of-coffee" rule provoked criticism in the House from the likes of Thomas Road (D-Bamberg), who complained that, "It seems to me you're trying to punish us for doing state business" because under the new rule, he could not go to lunch with a lobbyist who paid the bill. Sheheen retorted that, "No, it says to me state business doesn't depend on someone giving you food."

Sheheen also urged the House to adopt not only a ban on lobbyists' gifts to House members, but also a ban on campaign contributions from corporations and labor unions (similar to federal laws) and a ban on cash donations of more than $50. In addition to more disclosure, Sheheen proposed a new rule that the full House would determine if a member violated the law and could impose a fine of $1,000 and imprisonment until the end of the legislative session. Even so, Republican David Wright indicated that his party would put forward more extensive laws in the future.

House Adopts Strong Ethics Rules

The organizational meeting of the House concluded on December 5, 1990, by passing a new House rule mandating extensive disclosure which required House members to report when they accept legal fees and payments of $1,000 from companies and organizations that employ lobbyists. The new rule passed by vote of 114-0. Republicans had pushed the rule.

The House stayed until 10 p.m. to conclude its efforts to adopt new ethics rules for the new session. Speaker Bob Sheheen remarked, "I'm really encouraged that the House has staked out a really firm stance on ethics reform and campaign reform."

However, some Republicans, including House Minority Leader Terry Haskins (R-Greenville), said that the ethics changes should be made by statute rather than by new rules.

Even so, the House adopted new rules which took effect immediately on passage, including a total ban on lobbyists' gratuities to House members, except to certain groups, and a ban on cash contributions over $50. The new rules required lobbyists to register with the House Ethics Committee and banned honoraria paid to House members.

The House rejected proposals to ban campaign contributions from corporations, banks, and unions, and political action committees.

New House Ethics Rules Criticized

Republicans complained that Speaker Bob Sheheen's ethics reform proposals were not enough. Minority Leader Terry Haskins ridiculed the "no-cup-of-coffee" rule saying, "Coffee and hot dogs is nothing.... Legal fees and retainers are where the abuses have been over the years."

Even so, some legislators grumbled about the ban on free handouts from lobbyists. Rep. Mike Baxley (D-Darlington) complained, "What is wrong with an individual who happens to be a lobbyist sitting down with a legislator over a cup of coffee that he might have paid for." Late in the day, after the "no-cup-of-coffee" rule had been adopted, there was an effort to repeal the rule. Opponents proposed that lobbyists be allowed to spend $25 on meals for legislators, but reform proponents fought off two attacks on the "no-cup-of-coffee" rule.

Rep. David Wilkins (R-Greenville) said it was inconsistent to ban lobbyists from giving free meals to individual legislators, but then allow lobbyists to give free meals to a group of legislators.

The House elected two new chairmen to replace convicted chairmen. And the House elected Rep. Wes Hayes as chairman of House Ethics to replace Pat Harris (D-Anderson), who did not want to continue as chair. Labor, Commerce and Industry Committee replaced its chairman, Robert Brown (D-Marion), and Medical Affairs Committee replaced Donna Moss (D-Cherokee), both of whom had been removed by Lost Trust.

Lobbyists Protest Ethics Reform

Lobbyists at the State House predicted doom if the ethics reforms directed at them were enacted by the House. Blair Rice, Jr., vice president of the South Carolina Textile Manufacturer's Association, warned legislators as the House met on December 4 and 5, 1990, that any votes to limit lobbyists would be viewed with a jaundiced eye by business interests and "the business community will definitely factor this into any future considerations." Blair and other textile industry advocates stood in the lobby of the State House while the House discussed ethics reforms. Business was using scare tactics to block reformers from limiting their use of gratuities to control legislators.

Rice warned that the South Carolina Business & Industry Political Education Committee was watching the voting on ethics issues and would regard the process as "an excellent litmus test as to who's pro-business."

At the same time, lobbyists worked the State House and told House members and journalists about the evil consequences of the ethics reforms being debated in the House. In addition, the South Carolina Chamber of Commerce warned that Speaker Sheheen's ethics proposals were dangerous and "the economic climate of South Carolina will be severely damaged," according to Chamber president Thomas Gregory.

Editorial Calls For Senate Ethics Act

On December 7, 1990, *The State* published an editorial urging the South Carolina Senate to move forward on ethics reform after the House adopted new ethics rules in its organizational session.

Noting that the House had mandated disclosure of legal fees and all payments over $1,000, *The State* recited Gov. Carroll Campbell's view that the payoffs revealed by the Lost Trust probe were small amounts compared to the large legal fees paid to lawyer-legislators to influence legislation.

Citing the complaining of lobbyists about the new House rules as too restrictive, *The State* vainly wrote that it had doubts about the "no-cup-of-coffee" rule, saying the paper questioned "the reasonableness of a restriction that prevents a lobbyist from buying an individual legislator a cup of coffee or a Coke."

Noting Speaker Sheheen's sense of urgency about moving reforms fast, *The State* wrote that the new House rules were passed in haste and "should be refined and broadened to apply to senators and other state officials."

The editors praised the new reforms saying, "The House has taken the all-important first step to restore the image of an institution badly tainted.... The ball is now in the Senate's court."

Senate Prepares Ethics Bill

The Senate Ethics Committee Chairman, Ed Saleeby (D-Darlington), announced on December 5, 1990, that the Senate would take action on ethics reform in the 1991 session of the General Assembly and that a reform package could pass unless legislators disagreed over who would get credit for the reforms. On the same day that the House adopted drastic new ethics rules banning lobbyist handouts, the Senate felt compelled to declare its intentions as well.

Saleeby mailed out letters on December 5, 1990, announcing that the Ethics Committee would hold public hearings on December 20, 1990, on a bill that Saleeby and Sen. Marshall Williams (D-Orangeburg) had pre-filed (S.315). Sen. Glenn McConnell (R-Charleston) was a co-sponsor of the bill and a member of the hearing committee. McConnell frankly stated that the Senate wanted to take action lest it look bad in comparison with the House and its new ethics rules. He further said, "If the Senate fails to act, in light of what the House had done, it'll be like a sitting duck on a hunting pond. Everybody's going to be shooting at it."

Sen. Ed Saleeby (D-Darlington) had been criticized in the 1990 session for trying to weaken ethics legislation and that criticism came from the House. But now, Saleeby said that the new House rules would not dictate to the Senate what it would do about ethics reform in 1991, claiming that, "Our bill is so much more massive than what the House did." He said that the House enacted its new ethics rules without a public hearing, but the Senate bill was more extensive and required a hearing.

Speaker Bob Sheheen had intentionally moved fast in the House to enact reforms in order to pressure the Senate. The Senate reform bill was pre-filed about the same time as the Speaker circulated his reform proposals limiting lobbyists' gratuities and compelling more disclosure.

In fact, the Senate reform bill advanced new and substantial reform elements including limits on campaign contributions, restrictions on the use of campaign funds, more disclosure requirements, and bans on lawyer-legislators practicing before some boards and commissions.

Sen. Marshall Williams expressed confidence that the Senate would pass an ethics reform bill in the 1991 session.

Attorney General Advocates State Grand Jury

Travis Medlock, Attorney General of South Carolina, took advantage of the first convictions in Lost Trust to publish and op ed promoting the expansion of the authority of the State Grand Jury to include public corruption. Medlock spurned the proposed constitutional amendments which tried to limit the authority of the State Grand Jury to obscenity and drugs. The amendments had been rejected by the voters in the November 6, 1990, elections by a huge margin.

Medlock said that the "voters had agreed that the State of South Carolina needs to direct this extremely effective crime-fighting weapon at public corruption and bribery cases."

Medlock said that he would send legislation to the General Assembly in 1991 proposing to expand the jurisdiction of the State Grand Jury to include cases of bribery and corruption. He said it was time for the state to take decisive action to "guarantee the fundamental integrity of our system of government."

CHAPTER SEVENTEEN

CRIMINAL PROSECUTIONS CONTINUE

The Lost Trust cases which began with five defendants' indictments on August 24, 1990, continued with more indictments, pleas, trials, appeals, and finally retrials until 1999.

The first cycle of pleas and trials ended in November, 1991, with the conviction of Sen. Bud Long (D-Horry) for public corruption. Thereafter, the tangled process of filing pleas and motions attacking the convictions at trial followed with considerable successes in that some convictions were set aside on appeal and retrials were ordered in five cases. Later, Judge Hawkins dismissed all charges against the remaining five defendants in 1997 only to have the charges reinstated in 1998 by the 4th Circuit and ordered for retrial, a process which finally came to an end in 1999 with two convictions on retrial of Larry Blanding (D-Orangeburg) and Paul Derrick (R-Lexington), plus the Long guilty plea.

Limehouse Taped Conversation at Issue

Rep. Thomas Limehouse (R-Dorchester) tried but failed to suppress an audiotape which the federal prosecutors wanted to use against him. Limehouse, who was charged with corruption and witness tampering, was recorded as telling FBI sting agent Ron Cobb that he should tell persons that Cobb had paid off to tell the same story. Limehouse said to Cobb that Limehouse told the FBI that he took $1,000 from Cobb and urged Cobb to tell the FBI the same amount.

Limehouse's attorney, Andy Savage, sought to suppress the tape on the grounds that it was partly inaudible.

Limehouse faced charges of conspiracy, taking a bribe of $2,000, and tampering with federal witness Ron Cobb.

Judge Falcon Hawkins also rejected a bill of particulars sought by Savage which would have limited the prosecution's use of evidence in the case.

Three Trials Delayed

The trials of three House members were delayed by Judge Charles Simons on November 19, 1990, until January 14, 1991. The three legislators affected by the postponement were Reps. Larry Blanding (D-Sumter), Ennis Fant (D-Greenville), and B.J. Gordon (D-Williamsburg).

Judge Simons based the postponements on the fact that Fant's attorney, B.O. Thomason, had pneumonia. The decision to delay was made at a hearing at which defense lawyers pressed the prosecution for more details about the crimes of star witness Ron Cobb. Attorney Lionel Lofton, representing Gordon, wanted more information to use to discredit Cobb's testimony by confronting him with all of his crimes. Lofton also demanded to know the names of persons crossed out on government documents provided to the defense.

The government claimed the names were stricken to protect persons still under investigation but not indicted in the probe, but Lofton said he had a right to "know dates, times, places and people, and the government cannot hide behind this ongoing investigation." Lofton demanded to know the identity of a person who was an intermediary in a bribe of $10,000 paid to Rep. Jack I. Rogers (D-Marlboro).

Lofton argued on behalf of Rep. Gordon that the prosecution should release the names in the sealed documents which he claimed listed the names of two lobbyists, a highway commissioner, a member of the State Development Board, a circuit judge, and a former member of Gov. Carroll Campbell's staff. Lofton complained that he should receive all of the names and not just some of them.

Judge Charles Simons ruled that Lofton could not have the names requested in his motions. Simons also denied defense motions by Fant and Gordon to be tried separately rather than together along with Rep. Larry Blanding in a single trial of all three at the same time. Simons saw no reason not to try all three together.

Lost Trust as Sting Operation

William E. Rone, Jr., wrote a column in *The State* on November, 25, 1990, in which he explored the use of sting operations by law enforcement and the problem of entrapment. He related the issues to Lost Trust.

Rone pointed out that some sting operations had lured suspects into committing crimes in cases where they otherwise would not have committed the crimes. The article focused on two cases in addition to Lost Trust which had come to public attention at the same time; all of which involved sting operations.

Letter to Editor Blames Black Protest

Responding to the black protest against the FBI sting, a writer to *The State* on November 26, 1990, complained that the protest had no arguments in support of its complaints. The writer also objected of the black protesters, "The NAACP and the black legislative caucus have the audacity to now argue for quotas, not only in the workplace, but in the judicial system, too. Shouldn't guilt have something to do with this?" The writer was Henry Martin of Columbia.

The letter further complained that, "I don't believe the majority of voting citizens in South Carolina will take this kind of protest seriously. If this crowd wants respect, join a 'rainbow coalition' demanding honest statesmanship."

Martin wrote that Sen. Kay Patterson, a protester at the State House rally complaining that Operation Lost Trust was a racist plot, should look at the question of whether the black legislators implicated in the probe had actually violated the law. "Obviously, a person who breaks the law is not 'a black' or 'a white', but is a 'lawbreaker'." The race of those public officers tangled in corruption was not material as to the question of their criminal actions.

Taylor's Conviction Upheld

On November 26, 1990, U.S. District Court Judge Falcon Hawkins rejected a challenge to the conviction of Luther Taylor on the grounds that the evidence was more than sufficient to prove guilt of taking bribes from Ron Cobb. Hawkins approved the conviction of Taylor on six counts of violating the Hobbs Act by taking five bribes and conspiring to solicit bribes in support of his vote for the pari-mutuel betting bill.

Taylor's attorney, Joel Collins, asked Hawkins to dismiss the charges or order a new trial for Taylor. Collins alleged that a recent hair sample taken from the sting agent and witness, Ron Cobb, tested positive for cocaine and that the jury at Taylor's trial was entitled to know that Cobb, a witness against Taylor, tested positive. The hair test could show that Cobb had used cocaine within six months of the Taylor trial.

Collins also complained that his cross-examination of Cobb and Cobb's wife was too limited. Further, much of the questioning of Cobb and his wife was conducted while the jury was out of the room.

Rep. Moss Sentenced

Rep. Donna Moss (D-Cherokee) pleaded guilty to possession of cocaine and was sentenced to three years of supervised probation and a fine of $2,500. Sentence was imposed on December 5, 1990.

Moss had been detected using cocaine during the 1989 session of the General Assembly. She was the only female legislator charged. She agreed to help the FBI by revealing more about drug abuse at the State House. Federal authorities said that Moss had provided substantial information about drug use which could lead to more indictments of officials. In addition, Moss was expected to testify in trials.

Bart Daniel, U.S. Attorney, asked the court for leniency for Moss. Daniel said that Moss began to cooperate with the probe as soon as she learned that her drug use was known by federal authorities. Her cooperation kept her out of prison.

Lobbyist Brown Dies

Lobbyist James M. Brown, V, who had been convicted of drug violations and who had been called as a prosecution witness at the Luther Taylor trial in mid-October, 1990, died on November 29, 1990, at St. Francis Hospital in Charleston. He was only thirty years old.

Stanley Feldman, Brown's attorney, told the media that Brown had died from pulmonary fibrosis, a disease in which scar tissue formed around the lungs. His condition had deteriorated rapidly after the Taylor trial. Feldman said that Brown was not a major figure in corruption.

Brown had served as the lobbyist for the South Carolina Credit Union League since 1988. The League also employed Ron Cobb as a contract lobbyist. Brown was indicted in September, 1990, for marijuana possession and agreed to serve as a government witness; he told the FBI about persons involved in drug activities, including legislators, lobbyists, and other government officials. Brown testified after Cobb in the Luther Taylor trial and was set to testify later in the Limehouse trial.

Brown had appeared at the U.S. Courthouse in Columbia late October, 1990, because he had been called as a witness in the Taylor prosecution. He did not have to testify on that day, but stood in the hallway outside the courtroom and talked with other persons, including John Crangle, Executive Director of Common Cause/South Carolina, who did not know Brown was dying. Luther Taylor himself had come into the hallway.

Brown surprised Crangle with his candid self-incriminating statements out of Taylor's presence about how Taylor had pressured him to buy him a ticket along with another person, a woman, so that Taylor could travel to Mexico, particularly Cancun, Mexico. Brown also told anecdotes about other similar situations.

Lee and Taylor Sentencings Set

Federal prosecutors told the court that former Sen. Rick Lee (R-Spartanburg) should be given a lenient sentence because he had helped the investigation in the Lost Trust cases. In a motion filed November 30, 1990, U.S. Attorney Bart Daniel advocated a more favorable disposition of his case. The motion read, "Lee was the first target of the Operation Lost Trust investigation to sign a plea agreement...and has been one of the most eager and willing individuals to cooperate with the United States and provide information not only about Operation Lost Trust...but other new matters that are currently under investigation." The motion predicted further indictments in which Lee would be a witness.

Lee's sentencing was set for December 4, 1990. He had pleaded guilty on September 10, 1990, to taking bribes, including $2,000 from Ron Cobb on the betting bill which failed to pass.

Daniel's recommendations of an easy sentence for Lee contrasted with Daniel's efforts to get a harsher sentence for Luther Taylor (D-Richland), who was convicted on all six counts of bribery and conspiracy on October 5, 1990, and was also set for sentencing on December 13, 1990. In a motion of November 23, 1990, Daniel alleged that Taylor's crimes were so bad as to warrant a harsh penalty. Daniel wrote, "Luther Langford Taylor agreed not only to sell his own office, but to recruit others to do the same." The motion blamed Taylor's actions as part of "pervasive corruption" in the General Assembly. But the motion denied Taylor's allegation that he was targeted because he was black. The motion contended that so many blacks were caught because "the government did not choose the targets of this investigation, Luther Taylor did."

Having been one of the first legislators indicted, Sen. Rick Lee received a mild sentence of only 6 months in a halfway house in return for his agreement to help the FBI probe of corruption at the State House. Lee pleaded guilty to bribery in voting for the betting bill. Lee was the second defendant convicted in Lost Trust cases.

Lee agreed to cooperate within only two hours of being confronted by the FBI and promised to tell what he knew about the scandal. His sentence was set to start in mid-January, 1991.

Lee's lenient sentence supported by the prosecution contrasted with the harsh six and a half year sentence given to Luther Taylor (D-Richland), who took the case to trial and was convicted on six counts of corruption. Judge Falcon Hawkins sentenced both defendants and explained the differences in sentences on the grounds that Lee had cooperated and was "doing all he could to right the wrong", whereas Taylor's unrepentant actions were "deplorable and brought shame on elected officials and everyone in this state." Hawkins said he agreed with U.S. Attorney Bart Daniel's recommendation that Hawkins give a sentence in excess of the federal sentencing guidelines, but did not have the authority to do so. But Hawkins alleged that Taylor had "total, absolute, unwavering lack of remorse."

Bart Daniel told the court in the Taylor sentencing that Taylor lied on the witness stand and then falsely alleged that the prosecution was making him testify against other defendants or suspects in the General Assembly. Daniel said that the federal sentencing guidelines did not include penalties for those who recruited people to commit crimes as Taylor did. Daniel alleged that Taylor talked brazenly about bribery with lobbyist Ron Cobb.

But Judge Hawkins did not impose an enhanced sentence on Taylor, as requested by Daniel, for criticizing the government and speaking his mind to the media.

The crimes of Sen. Rick Lee and Rep. Luther Taylor were different in that Lee took two payments amounting in total to $3,000 as a bribe from Cobb, but Taylor took even more payments in total of $4,300 from Cobb. And Lee cooperated and Taylor did not.

Lee's sentence included not only six months in a halfway house, but five years of probation, 400 hours of community service, and repayment of the bribe of $3,000 in installments. Taylor got not only six and a half years in prison, but also three years probation and 200 hours of community service. Hawkins did not impose a fine on either Lee or Taylor, saying they had no money.

The attorney for Lee was Michael Spears of Spartanburg, who urged Judge Hawkins not to impose a harsh sentence on Lee, who was white, in order to avoid possible criticism that the judge hit African-American Taylor with a harsher and unfair sentence. Taylor's attorney, Joel Collins said to the court, "This in not a case for throwing the book at Luther Taylor."

Taylor Faces Santee-Cooper Corruption Probe

Even as Luther Taylor was entering the Richland County Detention Center on December 3, 1990, after being sentenced to six and a half years in federal prison for corruption, the U.S. Attorney Bart Daniel indicated that an investigation showed that Taylor had taken payments from Santee-Cooper, a state owned electric utility company.

Taylor was set to appear before the federal grand jury on December 12, 1990, to testify about his role in contracts to sell coal to Santee-Cooper. Taylor's attorney, Joel Collins, indicated the chance that Taylor could be indicted in connection with a probe of the company.

Furthermore, Taylor was under subpoena to testify before the mid-January, 1991, trial of former Rep. Ennis Fant (D-Greenville), a fellow member of the Legislative Black Caucus as well as of Larry Blanding (D-Sumter), and B.J. Gordon (D-Williamsburg).

Judge Falcon Hawkins denied bail to Taylor after his sentencing while his case was on appeal to the 4th Circuit. The appeal raised the question of whether the pari-mutuel betting bill affected interstate commerce which was the jurisdictional basis of the Hobbs Act, the federal anti-bribery law.

Sentencing Disparities Raise Issues

The State editorialized on December 6, 1990, on the question of whether the lenient sentence imposed on Rick Lee and the harsh sentence imposed on Luther Taylor was evidence of racial bias in view of the fact that both were convicted of bribery, although Taylor took $4,300 and Lee took $3,000 in bribes.

The State asked if "It's true that Luther Taylor was far more culpable that Rick Lee. But how much more?" *The State* noted that Lee would not be separated from his family and his job, but Taylor was headed for prison and was in the Richland County jail.

The State further took note of the fact that "Some lawmakers, including Mr. Taylor, have charged that they were singled out because they are black. Of the 18 targeted in the drug and bribery investigation, eight were black."

The editorial concluded by arguing, "Unless there are other mitigating circumstances that have not yet come to light, we believe Mr. Lee should also have been made to serve some hard time."

Prosecutors Try to Limit Evidence Against Cobb

On December 5, 1990, federal prosecutors filed motions and documents in Columbia and Charleston to persuade the court to exclude evidence about Ron Cobb's use of drugs and marital problems from two sting trials which were about to begin. Cobb was reported to have flunked drug tests while an FBI sting agent and Cobb's wife was prepared to testify that he was dishonest and had forged her name on a bogus power of attorney.

The trials at which Rob Cobb was expected to testify included those of Ennis Fant (D-Greenville), Larry Blanding (D-Sumter), and B.J. Gordon (D-Williamsburg), which were all set for trial as of January 13, 1991, and of Thomas Limehouse (R-Summerville) set for trial in mid-December, 1990, in Charleston federal court.

Fant, Blanding, and Gordon were all members of the Black Caucus and were elected without opposition while under indictment in November, 1990.

The government argued that any evidence of Cobb's drug abuse should be treated by the court as irrelevant to his standing as a witness because "there is no logical inference that individuals who use drugs are liars." Prosecutors asked to suppress evidence of Cobb's marital problems "to avoid the risk that the jury will evaluate Cobb on the basis of something other than his credibility."

Limehouse Pleads Guilty

Former Rep. Thomas Limehouse (R-Summerville) entered a guilty plea in U.S. District Court in Charleston on December 7, 1990, admitting to conspiracy to commit extortion and obstruction of justice. Prosecutors dropped a bribery charge as part of the pleas agreement. The maximum penalties included up to 30 years in prison and a fine of $500,000. The plea ended two days of negotiations between the defense and the government, including a motion made by Limehouse's attorney, Andy Savage, to postpone the trial. When Judge Falcon Hawkins scheduled a hearing on the motion, a deal was reached a few minutes before the hearing and Limehouse waived his right to a trial.

The pleas involved the loss of Limehouse's license to practice law. Daniel said that the plea agreement had been put on the table by the government not long after the indictment was published. Limehouse entered a not guilty plea on October 5, 1990, and told the media, "I am not guilty." But on December 7, 1990, he told the media that he trusted Judge Hawkins to impose a fair sentence.

Daniel told reporters that those who pleaded guilty and cooperated got more lenient sentences. At the hearing, prosecutors showed two video clips of both Limehouse and Cobb cutting a deal on the betting bill. One videotape showed Limehouse and Rob Cobb in Cobb's office in the AT&T Building on January 25, 1990, in which Limehouse said he would promote the betting bill in return for "a couple of suits and five or six shirts." Cobb responded that he would pay $1,600 for the cost of the clothing. Limehouse then told Cobb that his help was crucial to passing the betting bill and said, "This is an issue I'll throw myself on the sword for."

The second videotape of May 17, 1990, Limehouse went to Cobb's suite at the Town House Motel to meet Cobb who said, "Let me give you a little present", and then handed Limehouse $2,000 in one hundred dollar bills. Cobb then said, "Now when we come out of subcommittee...we'll be strokin' again." And Limehouse responded, "I think we can vote that...through in a hurry next year."

Prosecutors also played an audiotape in which Limehouse called Cobb on July 19, 1990, and told Cobb that he had been interviewed by the FBI that day. He also asked Cobb to lie about the money paid, and Limehouse told Cobb that he had told the FBI that the amount was only $1,000. He urged Cobb to tell authorities the amount was only $1,000, not the actual amount of the $2,000 paid.

Limehouse had served in the House since 1984 and served on the Labor, Commerce and Industry Committee which had dealt with the betting bill.

Sting Sentences Less Than Maximum

The sentences imposed on those convicted in Lost Trust cases in the first pleas and the only trial were far less than the maximums provided by statute. The trial conviction of Luther Taylor (D-Richland) resulted in a sentence of six and a half years in prison and no fine, whereas the maximum was 120 years on the six counts of the verdict.

Sen. Rick Lee (R-Spartanburg) faced 20 years in prison and a fine of $250,000, but Lee only got six months in a halfway house and probation. He was also allowed to work in his family furniture business. He had taken a bribe of $3,000, but cooperated with the probe and pleaded guilty.

Former Rep. Donna Moss (D-Cherokee) pleaded guilty to cocaine possession during the 1989 legislative session and was fined $2,500 and placed on three years supervised probation with random drug tests and possible mandatory treatment for drug abuse. She faced a maximum of one year in prison and a $100,000 fine. Moss had cooperated with the prosecution.

The seemingly lenient sentences were based on the federal sentencing guidelines and the facts of the cases. All three defendants convicted to that point had been first time offenders.

CHAPTER EIGHTEEN

ETHICS REFORM HEATS UP

Ethics Bill Proposals Proliferate

Lt. Gov. Nick Theodore's ad hoc ethics committee approved its ethics reform package on December 13, 1990, in spite of disagreements among the members. Rep. Candy Waites (D-Richland), a volunteer member of the committee, said that the resistance to reforms among members of the committee "probably is indicative of what we're going to face."

The Theodore committee advocated some reforms beyond those of the new House rules pushed by Speaker Sheheen and proposals by Sen. Marshall Williams (D-Orangeburg). The Theodore bill would have to be introduced in time for the 1991 session of the General Assembly.

The Theodore bill proposed to limit campaign contributions to $1,000 from individuals and $5,000 from PACs and also advocated a ban on conversion of campaign funds to personal use. The bill advocated that the State Ethics Commission be empowered to investigate legislators and to report findings to the Senate and House with recommendations for disposition. The committee bill would also ban legislators from representing a client before state boards, committees, and commissions.

Finally, the Theodore bill proposed a ban on legislators taking more than $100 per year from lobbyists and also required disclosure of the sources of income of all legislators.

Fake Ethics Reforms Proposed

The struggle to clean up the General Assembly was, of course, triggered by the huge and growing scandal first revealed in mid-July, 1990. Politicians from Gov. Campbell on down felt that something had to be done to get control over renegade officials.

Holding an organizational meeting prior to the new session on December 16, 1990, those legislators who had survived the indictments and 1990 elections gathered in Columbia to make amends and get serious about comprehensive ethics reform.

The House proposed new rules to address some of the most glaring abuses which had been exposed, especially the ways in which lobbyists used free liquor, free food, free trips and gifts of cash, goods, and services to buy access and votes at the State House.

But legislators were reluctant to give up the payoffs and perquisites of public office to which some of them were addicted. When the House proposed a phoney "no-cup-of-coffee" rule to ban lobbyists from giving handouts and freebies to legislators, it only banned handouts to single legislators, not to groups of them. A lobbyist could not go to dinner and drinks with only one, but could go to dinner and drinks with a group of legislators, and the lobbyist could pay the entire cost for the group.

A reform which allowed lobbyists to take an entire county House delegation to dinner and drinks would, in fact, allow eight House members to be hosted individually by a lobbyist because they were in one-member counties. In a dozen cases of two House member counties, the lobbyist could take out two at a time.

Furthermore, there was no limit on what could be given by lobbyists—free trips as well as free drinks and food were allowed. In addition, lobbyists could host all members of a subcommittee and committee.

Such an ethics rule change was a transparent fraud, said Common Cause Director, John Crangle, "It's kind of ironic the House would start its efforts toward reform by perpetrating a fraud on the public." Crangle further dismissed the House's proposed new rules as "too timid, too halting."

The real need was to stop the corrupt practices of lobbyists completely which were the same practices which had set the stage for the bribery of Lost Trust. Common Cause proposed a flat ban on lobbyists from giving anything to legislators. Crangle said of the House, "They should have gone for a flat prohibition: liquor, food, trips. There's no justification for it. These people are already on a per diem. This is food stamps and welfare."

Pols Fight for Freebies

Taking handouts from lobbyists was a way of life for many legislators at the State House. They deeply resented any substantial proposals to stop the corruption and dependence.

Speaker Bob Sheheen, reflecting the traditional entrenched culture of parasitical politics rooted in the House, tried to make the new rule changes look good and ridicule a total ban on lobbyist freebies urged by Common Cause as unrealistic and excessive: "I'm sure they're not perfect, and there won't be any perfect rules even if Mr. Crangle adopted them." Sheheen thought it was not corrupting to legalize a paid lobbyist and clients to provide free food to legislators.

Even so, a few House members spoke out for real reforms. Rep. Joe Wilder (D-Barnwell) said he would not go on a one-on-one freebie with a lobbyist as it "would be circumventing the rules." Rep. Tim Wilkes (D-Fairfield) agreed as did Rep. Larry Gentry (D-Saluda) and Rep. Tom Rhoad (D-Bamberg).

On the other hand, Rep. Jenning McAbee (D-McCormick) said he would take handouts from lobbyists, saying, "If Jerry Beasley (lobbyist for the SC Textile Manufacturers) wants to take me to lunch and talk...yeah, I'm going to go." Beasley had the largest budget for entertaining legislators of all the lobbyists and was particularly hostile to any limitations on lobbyists' dealings with legislators.

Miles Redefines Lobbyists

New Secretary of State, Jim Miles, on December 16, 1990, moved to redefine the meaning of the term lobbyist in the 1975 Ethics Act to include legislators who pushed the interests of their clients in the State House. He proposed to require that such persons register and disclose with his office pursuant to the 1975 Ethics Act.

However, Senate Ethics Chairman Ed Saleeby (D-Hartsville) indicated that Miles might be going too far and threatened legislation to take control of lobbyists from the Secretary of State. Saleeby had been a major factor in successful efforts to block lobbying reform in the 1990 session. Saleeby also opposed a House proposal to move regulation of lobbyists to the State Ethics Commission.

But Miles said that he agreed with Gov. Campbell's theory that lawyer-legislators presented a major problem of conflicting interests. Miles said that he thought the 1975 Ethics Act could be read to construe lawyer-legislators as lobbyists, thereby triggering registration requirements. Miles, a lawyer, said that he thought the problem was common to many lawyer-legislators. Miles said he could turn the names of non-compliant legislators over to the Attorney General for enforcement.

Miles cited state law which defined a lobbyist as a person employed by another "to influence in any matter the act or vote of any member of the General Assembly," with six exceptions. Miles wondered if legislators could be lobbyists.

Miles gave an example of a person employed by an insurance company who, as a legislator, was presented with a bill affecting the insurance industry. Miles said, "Now, one could argue that at that point in time, that triggers the obligation for that legislator to go over to the Secretary of State's office and register and disclose on that issue. That's what I think that law means." Miles said his transition team was working to determine who should register under the law.

Sen Joe Wilson (R-Lexington) defended Miles' theory. A member of the transition team, Wilson said that it, "is a logical approach and one that should be looked into." But Wilson was isolated on the issue. Rep. Terry Haskins (R-Greenville) remarked that, "He's gone way too far with the interpretation." Speaker Bob Sheheen (D-Kershaw) said, "I think he's way out in left field." And Rep. David Beasley (D-Darlington) remarked that, "To say they ought to be registered as lobbyists is ludicrous at best."

Gov. Campbell's Surplus Funds Show a Problem

On December 18, 1990, *The State* reported after his election that Gov. Carroll Campbell came out of the 1990 election with seventy percent of the vote and a huge surplus of campaign funds. His funds were a symptom of the problem of excessive fund-raising and the uses of such surplus for non-campaign purposes. Campbell had $500,000 left.

Under current law, Campbell had almost unlimited discretion to spend the excess money. He could even use it to fund a campaign for the U.S. Senate if he wanted or he could pocket the money himself as personal and private money.

Campbell made it a practice to attend Republican events and to give away presents and he could use the surplus funds to pay such expenditures. He did not need the money to pay for his second inauguration events as it was self-financed.

Campbell had received as much as $60,000 from a single source in 1990 and that came from Macalloy, Inc. of Charleston. He also got $20,000 from a Spartanburg restaurant owner.

House Rules Committee Wavers on Recent Reforms

The House Rules Committee rejected a proposal to ban lawyer-legislators from practicing before boards and commissions. The committee also weakened campaign finance disclosure rules in late December, 1990. The House had just approved the rule changes in early December. But the committee did approve a Republican proposal to ban lobbyists and office-seekers from the House chamber.

The committee wanted to remove the requirement that candidates report not only the name and address of the contributors, but also the employers' names of all contributors. Terry Haskins protested that the name of employers was needed to expose employers who were giving donations through their employees.

The committee also shelved a proposal to require the filing of campaign disclosure reports 10 days before the election rather than quarterly.

Officials Speak Out for Ethics Reform

Lt. Gov. Nick Theodore, who had made ethics reform a major plank in his re-election platform in the November 6, 1990, general elections, soon thereafter testified in favor of the ethics reform bill saying at a legislative hearing, "We both recognize that the general ethics mind-set of public officials has for too long been too loose."

Sen. Theo Mitchell (D-Greenville), defeated for governor the previous month, worried that proposed limits on lawyer-legislators practicing before boards and commissions would harm his law practice, but Theodore said, "That would eliminate influence peddling" based on recommendations from an ethics reform committee Theodore had formed in the fall.

Newly elected Secretary of State Jim Miles, not yet in office, urged the subcommittee to keep jurisdiction over lobbyists under his office and to clarify his authority. Miles said, "I intend to require complete and itemized reporting, and I do intend to audit, and I plan to do so until I'm told to do otherwise."

Lobbyists Say Reform Will Kill S.C. Economy

At a Senate subcommittee hearing on December 20, 1990, the anger and self-pity of the lobbyists was full-blown. The issue was the reform proposal to ban lobbyists handouts to legislators. The subcommittee chair was Sen. Ed Saleeby (D-Darlington), who was a co-sponsor of the Williams-Saleeby Ethics Reform bill introduced by the Senate's most senior members to ban all lobbyists' handouts including free meals and free trips. The bill had been introduced in response to the growing scandal and outrage triggered by Lost Trust shortly after the scandal broke in mid-July, 1990.

Confronted by lobbyists' outrage over the ban, Saleeby retreated saying, "I think it is a little too restrictive on industry." He had previously conceded it might be too restrictive on legislators as well.

Priscilla Sims of CSX tried to depict the ban on lobbyists' freebies as an attack on basic democratic freedoms, saying, "No dictatorship in a banana republic could be as restrictive as some things in the bill."

Even worse, Doug Kingsmore, president of the S.C. Textile Manufacturers Association, the king of corporate welfare for politicians, warned grimly, "Unless reason prevails in this matter of ethics reform, South Carolina can just about kiss economic expansion goodbye." In Kingsmore's mind, the whole future of South Carolina rested in a cocktail glass.

Reform of lobbying threatened to wreck the state's economy, lobbyists told the December 20, 1990, subcommittee hearing, alleging that the "no-cup-of-coffee" rule was a threat to their lucrative careers and the future of economic development in South Carolina.

Doug Kingsmore blasted Common Cause/South Carolina for it's advocacy of ethics and lobbying reform even before 1990 and Lost Trust, saying that Common Cause should spend it's time and money fighting Japanese influence on American politics instead of dealing with "issues like Supreme Court nominees."

Following testimony by Common Cause Executive Director John Crangle in favor of a total ban on all free handouts to legislators, Kingsmore detailed the recent history of Common Cause of Washington, D.C., at the national level before denouncing Common Cause/South Carolina, "because they are the driving force behind this issue and the only group who spoke out last year for broad reforms."

Sen. Kay Patterson (D-Richland), a black Democrat known to take his share of free handouts and free trips to Hilton Head and a bitter critic of the FBI sting as a racist plot, baited Crangle in the hearing, "I ask you, do you think that I'm on the take? Do you think I've been bribed?"

Support Builds for Real Ethics Reform

Major political leaders stepped forward at a critical time to demand real, rather than fake, ethics reform. Ignoring phoney complaints of economic damage by big money lobbyists and their clients, such as Jerry Beasley and the S.C. Textile Manufacturers, who failed to provide any evidence for their protests against limits and ban on lobbyists' handouts, Lt. Gov. Nick Theodore and Sen. Joe Wilson as well as Rep. Terry Haskins retorted that the time for drastic ethics reform had come.

Theodore stated at the Senate subcommittee hearing: "In order to be successful with meaningful ethics reform, we'll have to have citizen support.... We require citizen support to pass strong legislative proposals. I also believe enough of the public can be motivated."

Sen. Wilson predicted that public demand for reform would force legislators to act, saying, "When we actually get the General Assembly back in session, we can start getting the House and Senate members on record. Then we can really make progress." In the next session of the General Assembly, the 1991 Ethics Act was passed into law as Wilson predicted.

Rep. Haskins testified: "I think the public, on the whole, looked at the 'no coffee' rule and thought, 'There you go, you're really cleaning up'." Haskins ridiculed the proposed loophole in the bill which would have allowed the continued practice of lobbyists' freebies to committees and caucuses.

Fight for Ethics Reform Heats Up

"Despite a bribery scandal, legislators pushing ethics reform might find their task difficult, if the beginning of the debate this month is any indication," wrote *Associated Press* journalist Gary Karr in late December, 1990, adding that in the earliest debates on new ethics reform rules in the House, "It seemed the main thing on the House's mind was who could take them to lunch." It was obvious that the newly elected House returned in November, 1990, would struggle over any efforts to make real reforms of the way lobbyists did business with House members.

The proposed new House ethics rules, debated for two days in the organizational session of the House, held the month following a House election, would provoke a fight over ethics reform. Whereas legislators voiced support for ethics reform in the abstract, they often bridled at specific reforms which would stop them from living off the lobbyists and campaign donors. Legislator-lawyers rebelled against proposed limits on their practice before state boards and commissions, a major source of income for some of them.

Lobbyists Fight Lobbying Reforms

In addition to legislators, the main opponents of reform of the old and discredited 1975 Ethics Act were State House lobbyists. Both legislators and lobbyists had profited for years from the corrupt relationship created by lobbyists' gifts of free food, free liquor, free trips, and free cash with no limitations on source and amounts.

Lobbyists, of course, had run wild under the lobbyist-friendly jurisdiction of Secretary of State, John Campbell, who had been taking unlimited campaign contributions and perhaps other gratuities from the very lobbyists he was supposed to register. In fact, of course, he did nothing to enforce the registration and disclosure laws under which lobbyists were supposed to file disclosure reports indicating who they were, how much they were paid, and how much they spent. As a result, untold numbers of lobbyists did not register, and even those who did often failed to report their actual income and expenditures.

In this lax regime, the lobbyists of big money interest groups at the State House often had very large expense accounts and even larger big shot complexes. Jerry Beasley, lobbyist for the S.C. Textile Manufacturers was the worst case of the problem—he had the largest expense account of all the lobbyists and loved to grab checks and take legislators on trips and golf outings. And he deeply resented and connived against anyone who tried to reform the lobbying system to limit the amounts and uses of money.

Support Builds for Reform

Rep. Terry Haskins predicted that in the 1991 session, a bill would be passed to raise ethical standards because of the political reality of Lost Trust that would continue to shock legislators into ethical conduct and ethical reforms. Haskins concluded: "it's seeing fellow members sentenced to prison, that's going to make a difference."

"It was anticipated," said Common Cause/South Carolina Executive Director, John Crangle, of the angry opposition of some legislators and lobbyists to reform proposals, especially limits or bans on handouts to legislators and bans on personal use of campaign funds for non-campaign purposes. "It would change the way business is done over there [at] the State House. There's tremendous resistance to that," Crangle said of the drastic provisions in the Senate ethics reform bill proposed by Sens. Williams and Saleeby and designed to stop lobbyists' handouts.

Rep. Terry Haskins, the House Republican leader, predicted, "Individual aspects of ethics reform will run into very, very hard sledding." Legislators would try to block the reforms that would restrict them, but "Everybody wants to clean up the ethics of everybody else. You get 170 different theories of what ethics is or should be."

Survey Shows 1991 Major Issues at State House

The State newspaper collected responses from 130 legislators on the major issues facing the 1991 session of the General Assembly. Published on December 30, 1990, the survey showed that there was very strong support for a few ethics reform proposals being discussed by the media and politicians in the wake of the Lost Trust scandal.

Of some 23 reform proposals surveyed, only 8 provoked strongly positive responses from the total of 36 senators and 119 representatives who replied to the survey. The findings from legislators were similar to a poll conducted November 29 to December 11, 1990, by the Institute of Public Policy at the University of South Carolina which measured citizen opinion.

Of the major types of issues surveyed, ethics came in fourth and education came in first. However, 79% of legislators considered corruption in state government one of the most important issues at the time. 85% of legislators strongly supported banning conversion of campaign funds to personal use, and a similar percentage favored lobbyists' disclosure of expenses of $100 or more per day on public officials.

65% of legislators supported the state taking control of primary elections, and 81% favored a ban on cash campaign donations.

The survey showed support for campaign finance reforms to counteract the problems exposed in Lost Trust, but only 14% of legislators surveyed supported public financing of elections. However, 51% of legislators favored limits on the size of campaign contributions. 61% of citizens favored a limit of $500 on donations.

64% of legislators favored a requirement that lawyer-legislators report the names of clients they represented before state agencies, but only 47% favored a ban on lawyer-legislators practicing before state agencies.

As to lobbyists giving handouts to legislators, only 60% of legislators favored a ban on legislators taking gifts and free meals from lobbyists and others who did business with state government. Roughly 33% of legislators opposed a ban on lobbyists' handouts. But the public had a very different view as ordinary citizens supported a ban on lobbyists' gifts and largesse to legislators by 66%.

Legislators had reluctant reactions to enforcement proposals and less than 33% of legislators favored allowing agencies which governed ethics to initiate complaints without a formal complaint being filed.

S.C. House Imposes New Rules

The *1991 South Carolina Legislative Manual*, 72nd edition, for the First Session Commencing January 8, 1991, published the new Rules of the House, beginning on page 213, which had been adopted on December 5, 1990. They marked a drastic change. And even more new rules were adopted on January 15, 1991, January 23, 1991, and January 31, 1991, by the House.

Rule 11 of the new Rules of the House of Representatives attacked the problem of out-of-control lobbyists and abusive and corrupting lobbying of House members. The entirety of Rule 11 was new and adopted on December 5, 1990.

Rule 11.2 set up registration and disclosure requirements for all lobbyists which was in addition to the feckless lobbying provisions of the 1975 Ethics Act which had been generally ignored by lobbyists and even the Secretary of State who was supposed to enforce it.

Rule 11.3 required lobbyists to file reports with the House Ethics Committee detailing their income and expenses, including sources, amounts, and specific expenditures.

Rule 11.4 required state agencies to report with the House Ethics Committee detailing their lobbying activity including efforts to influence legislation, expenses, and personnel used in lobbying.

Rule 11.5 granted the House Ethics Committee substantial powers to require disclosure and to effect enforcement of the Rules, including authority to fine violators and gather evidence.

Rule 11.6 imposed on the House Ethics Committee specific duties as to the collection of information, receipt of complaints, and preparation and publication of reports.

Rule 11.7 imposed substantive regulations on lobbyists which banned lobbyists from being employed based on a contingent fee which varied depending on the success or failure of the lobbying activities at the House of Representatives, including matters relating to legislation, administration, or other contingency.

Rule 11.8 imposed penalties on lobbyists for violation of the Rules of the House and for failure to comply fully with disclosure requirements, including penalties of being held in contempt of the House. Furthermore, the rule barred lobbyists for violations of S.C. Code Title 2, Chapter 17, Title 8, Chapter 13 and the bar on lobbying the House was for a total of three years.

Rule 11.9 penalized the willful filing of a complaint with the House Ethics Committee without just cause, or with malice. The punishment was to be imposed by the Committee.

Rule 12 adopted as a new rule on December 5, 1990, attacked the outrageous practices of lobbyists giving unlimited gifts and handouts to House members as exposed by Lost Trust in lurid detail. Under the caption of "Acceptance of Compensation", Rule 12 attempted to stop not only naked bribery, but also the more subtle ways in which special interests had tried and succeeded in buying access and influence at the State House.

Rule 12.2 banned the taking or solicitation of "anything of value" by a House member if the member had reason to believe the thing was given because of "the official's or employee's office or position." The rule also banned the use of office to obtain personal business and financial opportunities for the member. The rule also imposed punishment by the House on anyone who tried to offer or give a thing of value to an official because of his office.

Rule 12.2 (C) somewhat eroded the corruption practices of lobbyists giving things of value to legislators, except that it allowed lobbyists to still give campaign contributions to legislators and it allowed legislators to attend hosted group functions for the whole House, committees, or county delegations, but only if the value of the food and drinks did not exceed $25 per legislator.

Rule 12.3 banned cash campaign contributions over $50 and limited all donations to legislative candidates for House from lobbyists and their employers to $250 for any given campaign.

Rule 12.4 required candidates for the House to keep a record of all funds received and expended and of all contributors of campaign funds.

Rule 12.6 banned the acceptance of campaign funds on the State House complex, including the State House, Gressette Senate Building, and the Blatt House Building, and on any other state-owned property.

Rule 12.7 stuck a stake in the heart of the most corrupt practice of them all which was the ability of candidates under the 1975 Ethics Act to convert campaign funds to personal use. The new rule said, "A candidate for or member of the House of Representatives shall not use campaign funds for personal use."

Rule 12.8 banned the receipt of monetary honoraria by members of the House for speaking before public or private groups, other than for actual expenses.

Editorial—1990 Year of the Scandal

As the sordid events of 1990 came to an end before New Years, *The State* took time to review the list of scandals which had plagued the State of South Carolina, noting that corruption had been exposed at both state and local governments.

The spreading scandals put SLED to the test to such an extent that retired SLED agents had been called back to probe all of the corruption and abuses. And the federal authorities were struggling to get on top of the Lost Trust scandal which was claiming more and more corrupt legislators and drug violators at the State House.

The State noted that as the year 1990 came to an end, a total of ten legislators and one lobbyist had been indicted in the Lost Trust scandal for bribery or drug violations. At that point, seven defendants had pleaded guilty, one had been convicted at trial, and three were scheduled for trial in January, 1991.

The State's year-ending summary of public investigation and prosecutions counted two dozen instances of public corruption in addition to Lost Trust.

CHAPTER NINETEEN

1991—THE YEAR OF TRIALS AND REFORMS

The year 1991 was the year in which both the Operation Lost Trust prosecutions and the ethics reform movements in the State House came to a head. Before the end of 1991 all of the defendants in the Lost Trust cases either pleaded guilty, were acquitted, or were convicted at trial. 1991 also was the year in which the United States Supreme Court handed down on May 25 the decision in *McCormick v. U.S.* (500 U.S. 257 [1991]) which held that the government had to prove a quid pro quo in that a defendant in a Hobbs Act prosecution for public corruption and bribery took official action in return for a bribe. Finally, 1991 was the year in which the South Carolina General Assembly wrote, debated, and passed the Ethics Act of 1991 which Governor Carroll Campbell signed after passage.

Although the guilty pleas entered in 1990 and 1991 were final and not reversed, the convictions obtained in 1990 and 1991 in the Operation Lost Trust trials were appealed and most of them reversed and ordered for new trials based on the finding that the prosecution had not proved a quid pro quo of official action taken in return for a bribe as required by *McCormick v. U.S.* This series of successful appeals began a series of retrials of Lost Trust defendants that continued until 1999.

The 1991 Ethics Act took effect on January 1, 1992, and revolutionized the campaign finance, conflict of interest, and lobbying laws of South Carolina for at least a generation. The Act reduced the corrupt influence of big money lobbyists and donors at the State House.

Lindsay Gets Lung Transplant

Dying Sen. Jack Lindsay (D-Marlboro) underwent an 8 hour operation to replace his diseased lung at the North Carolina Memorial Hospital in Chapel Hill, North Carolina on January 1, 1991. At age 63, Lindsay was the oldest patient ever to have received the transplant of a lung at the hospital. At the time the survival rate for such transplants was seventy percent. Lindsay's general health was poor as he had been worn down over the years by heavy drinking and smoking and he was on an oxygen tank at the time.

Lindsay was also facing almost certain criminal prosecution for public corruption because of his acceptance of money from lobbyists in connection with legislation.

Lindsay lived only a few days after the operation and died on January 11, 1991.

S.C. Campaign Laws Invite Corruption

The State published an extensive article on January 3, 1991, showing that the meaningless campaign finance laws in the 1975 Ethics Act allowed candidates to use the money they took from donors for any purpose, including personal use, and that this made graft not only possible but almost inevitable. In fact, it was hard to distinguish bribery from permissible donations if, in fact, there was any real difference found in the law itself.

Several of the earliest indictments in Lost Trust were of Sen. Rick Lee (R-Spartanburg) and Rep. Luther Taylor (D-Richland), both of whom claimed on indictment that the money they took from FBI sting agent Ron Cobb was only a campaign donation. Lee pleaded guilty and Taylor lost at trial on bribery charges. But to many observers, the real scandal was the 1975 Ethics Act itself, which allowed the most outrageous campaign practices by which campaign money and personal money were stuffed in the same pocket with little, if any, distinction in law.

The worst provisions of the 1975 Ethics Act included the facts that: (1) cash contributions could be given by any source and in any amounts; (2) corporations, banks, and labor unions could give out their treasures in unlimited amounts; and (3) uses of so-called campaign money were unlimited, allowing the use of campaign funds for personal use.

Corruption Promoted By 1975 Ethics Act

Because campaign money could be used for any possible purpose, elected officials often bought things for themselves or for friends or gave the money to charities. John Crangle of Common Cause/South Carolina, who had been denouncing the 1975 Ethics Act as a pious fraud well before Operation Lost Trust broke, pointed out that, "In reality, there's no distinction between campaign money and personal money; you can convert it to personal use."

Lost Trust put a shot of adrenalin into the issue of abuse of campaign money when the new General Assembly convened on January 8, 1991, for its second session. It was almost inevitable that some new restrictions on the raising and uses of political money would be passed into law.

The politicians knew they had to do something. After they had campaigned for re-election in the fall of 1990, House members had all been exposed to voter indignation over the growing number of legislators being indicted and convicted, starting in late August, 1990, with the first conviction at trial of Rep. Luther Taylor (D-Richland) on October 25, 1990, just days before the November, 1990, general elections.

A survey conducted by *The State* just before the Legislature reconvened found that 85% of legislators who responded thought that the use of campaign funds for personal use should be banned. The same percentage thought that lobbyists should be required to report all expenditures of $100 or more on any public official.

Ethics Reforms for 1991 Proposed

The need to stop cash campaign contributions was obvious since all of the corrupt payments made by Rone Cobb to bribe legislators had been in cash and the videotapes shown at trials had Cobb handing $100 bills to the grasping hands of criminal politicians.

But some legislators thought the ban on cash would hamper fund-raising from poor people. Even so, John Crangle of Common Cause/South Carolina called for a total ban on cash, but said that his group might agree to allow small amounts of cash, if documented. But Crangle warned, "It's too easy to convert the money to personal use without some kind of paper trail."

The reform proposal of Senate leaders Marshall Williams (D-Orangeburg) and Ed Saleeby (D-Darlington) suggested that campaign contributions should be limited by amounts, but that the amounts should vary depending on the importance of the office. They suggested a limit of $1,000 for governor, $500 for Senate candidates, and $250 for House races. The Williams-Saleeby plan would also limit repayment of self-loans to $25,000 to stop wealthy candidates from self-financing and then, if elected, pressuring the interests for money to repay the loans.

Common Cause Reform Proposals Published

In addition to strict bans on cash campaign donations, Common Cause/South Carolina advocated the limitation of campaign payments to $250 per person and per political action committee. Common Cause also recommended the same total prohibition on corporate, union, and bank donations as in federal law.

But the ban on donations from powerful economic groups provoked stiff opposition as it had when the House voted down such a ban in its December 5, 1990, organization meeting. Jerry Beasley of the S.C. Textile Manufacturers Association opposed limits on how much businesses could donate out of their own treasuries but said that limits on donations from political action committees were tolerable.

But John Crangle argued that big money corporations could skew the political process and that stockholders should not have their money donated by management from corporate resources, arguing that, "A corporation is supposed to use its resources to run its business, not to influence the political process."

The Williams-Saleeby proposal and Common Cause agreed that partial public financing was a good idea. The scheme was imitative of the federal system of funding presidential elections. Common Cause proposed to raise the money to provide public funding with a 10% tax on all campaign contributions.

Common Cause Proposals Opposed

The advocacy of public financing ran into opposition from the Speaker of the House, Bob Sheheen, who predicted that such a bill could not pass, saying, "It's not going to happen. We are a resource-poor state. We don't have enough money to do what we need to do now."

But Common Cause disagreed with Sheheen's analysis, arguing that the state would lose tax revenue because special interests could buy candidates and elections and buy unjust tax breaks for themselves or use their campaign donations to push spending programs for the narrow benefit of the same special interests. Crangle said that it was very hard to explain the merits of public financing and to convince citizens of the need for it.

New Indictments Published

U.S. Attorney Bart Daniel and the FBI announced a news conference on January 3, 1991, for the following day which stirred speculation on whether any or all of the nine remaining unindicted legislators known as federal targets would be indicted. The two most likely suspects were both from Marlboro County and were Democrats Sen. Jack Lindsay and House Speaker Pro Tem Jack I. Rogers.

Rogers was the floor leader for the pari-mutuel betting bill which became the sting bill of the FBI and Ron Cobb. Lindsay had just had a lung transplant on January 1, 1991, and would die in ten days. Both Lt. Gov. Nick Theodore, president of the Senate, and Speaker Bob Sheheen told the media that they had no advance notice if any of their lawmakers would be indicted.

Among those known as targets who had not yet been indicted were Sen. Bud Long (D-Horry), Rep. Paul Derrick (R-Lexington), Rep. Ken Bailey (D-Orangeburg), Rep. Jim Faber (D-Richland), Rep. Frank McBride (D-Richland), Rep. Tim Wilkes (D-Fairfield), and Judge Tee Ferguson of Greenville.

Rogers Indicted

The long-awaited indictment of Rep. Jack I. Rogers (D-Marlboro) came on January 4, 1991, for extortion and racketeering on ten counts. The indictment was announced by a news conference called by the U.S. Attorney and FBI. The charges were the most severe of all those lodged to that point in the Lost Trust prosecutions.

By House Rule 3.12, Rogers was automatically suspended from the House and submitted his resignation as Speaker Pro Tem. The criminal charges demanded that Rogers pay $53,000 including his legislative pay for three years and, in addition, forfeit the profits of a continuing criminal enterprise pursuant to RICO.

The indictment alleged that Rogers had taken $23,000 in bribes to influence legislation related to three subjects: (1) capital gains tax reductions; (2) hazardous waste disposal; and (3) pari-mutuel betting. Furthermore, the indictment alleged that Rogers tried to tamper with two or three witnesses who were not named.

State Highway Commission member, Wade Ronald "Ronnie" Crow, was also implicated for paying Rogers $1,000 to influence his support of the betting bill. The payment came in a bag delivered by Crow from Ron Cobb.

The RICO charges alone carried twenty years and a fine of $250,000. All of the charges against Rogers exposed him to a total of 180 years in prison in addition to the fine. He was charged with one count of racketeering for taking a total of $23,800 in bribes by extortion plus seven counts of violating the Hobbs Act, three of which were for taking bribes on the betting bill; he also faced two counts of witness tampering.

Rogers Indictment Rocks House

The indictment of Speaker Pro Tem Jack I. Rogers on January 4, 1991, for corruption and racketeering immediately removed him as a member of the House by automatic suspension. His quick resignation as Speaker Pro Tem forced the House as it entered its 1991 session to elect a replacement after just having re-elected Rogers at its organizational session on December 5, 1990.

Rogers had campaigned for election as Speaker Pro Tem by saying that he was not in trouble with the FBI, but after his indictment few members expressed surprise. Speaker Bob Sheheen held a news conference to state the obvious saying that if Rogers was convicted it would then show that he had deceived the House. Rep. James Johnson (D-Laurens) who wanted to replace Rogers complained that, "some of us have been misled. He assured me personally that he didn't feel like he was in any trouble."

House Minority Leader Terry Haskins (R-Greenville) said that the indictment threw the House into "serious disarray" and Rep. David Wilkins (R-Greenville) said that, "This just sinks further into the pits." Republicans blamed Speaker Sheheen and House Democrats for backing Rogers re-election when they knew he was under investigation. Sheheen said that he had asked U.S. Attorney Bart Daniel about the matter in December but had been told nothing. Rep. David Beasley (D-Darlington) said that Rogers had reassured him that he was not in trouble.

Editorial on Roger's Indictment

The State published an editorial on January 5, 1991, the day after the indictment of Rep. Jack I. Rogers, addressing the "leadership gap" that had been created by Roger's automatic suspension from the House.

Noting that *The State* had praised Rogers for his support of education bills, the paper admitted that it had been "duped." Noting that Rogers and Wade Ronald Crow had both held positions of public trust and were attorneys before their indictments, *The State* deplored what it suspected as dishonesty by Rogers when he told the House that he had done nothing wrong. *The State* praised Speaker Bob Sheheen for pushing for ethics reform.

The State wrote, "Did Mr. Rogers know that his own indictment was already in the works? We suspect that he did. And for that reason, whether guilty or innocent, he should have stepped down and allowed another to undertake that important leadership role."

Marlboro County—Origins of Corruption

Rural Marlboro County, South Carolina, produced three of the suspects in the Operation Lost Trust FBI sting. Two of them—Jack I. Rogers and Ronnie Crow—were indicted and convicted. The third, Sen. Jack Lindsay, died in January, 1991, while Rogers and Crow were indicted for corruption. Had he lived, Lindsay would have met a similar fate as he had a plea agreement with the U.S. Attorney.

Rogers and Crow were both attorneys living in Bennettsville who had both contested its only House seat in 1976 with Crow emerging as the winner. But in 1980, Crow decided not to run again and Rogers took his place. Then in 1988, Rogers nominated Crow for the South Carolina Highway Commission and Crow was selected.

Both Rogers and Crow were interested in and owned horses and both of them backed a pari-mutuel betting scheme to bring horse and dog racing to South Carolina.

As a House member, Rogers did not hesitate to challenge the leadership and became a leader in the notorious "Fat and Ugly Caucus" which extorted free meals, liquor, and trips from lobbyists. But he later was selected to the Judicial Screening Committee in 1988 to pick candidates for the judiciary.

When Rogers was indicted, one fellow legislator said, "It blows my mind. Why in the hell would anyone that's that bright and that capable and has the ability to be one of the most successful lawyers in the state sell his office for a paltry sum?"

Rogers Charged With Racketeering

The 10 count indictment of Rogers, involving racketeering, would prove to be the most serious of all the charges lodged against any of the eventual 28 defendants caught in the Lost Trust scandal.

Rogers had been in the House from the town of Bennettsville for 14 years and for an undefined period before his indictment he had been corrupt. Starting with the small fry legislators who took a few hundred dollars in cash for their votes, the probe had moved toward the worst villains at the State House, especially Rogers. The number of indictments kept piling up revealing the General Assembly and its lobbyists as rampantly corrupt.

Announcing Rogers' indictment, Bart Daniel warned of more in the future, adding to those already charged and pointing to others who had had their campaign records seized in mid-July, 1990, when the Lost Trust scandal broke.

Like the others, Rogers took money from Ron Cobb over the betting bill, but unlike the others, he had also extorted money in many ways, demanding money from a lobbyist, Ken Kinard, hired by Laidlaw Environmental Services. And he had demanded money from a person pushing a tax break on capital gains in 1988.

Rogers Pleads Not Guilty

Deposed House Speaker Pro Tem, Jack I. Rogers, pleaded not guilty to multiple federal charges on January 16, 1991, including racketeering under the RICO statute. Rogers thus became only the second public official in the history of the State of South Carolina to be charged with RICO crimes. The first had been Sen. John Long (D-Union) who had been convicted in 1980 of selling government jobs. Long's appeal had failed.

The charges facing Rogers carried a maximum total penalty of 180 years in prison and $2.5 million in fines based on his ten count indictment.

"Ronnie" Crow Indicted

On January 4, 1991, the federal grand jury also indicted state highway commissioner, Wade "Ronnie" Ronald Crow, on charges of aiding and abetting in extortion in connection with the pari-mutuel betting bill. He faced twenty years in prison and a fine of $250,000.

The charges were based on Crow's alleged delivery of a bag containing $1,000 in cash to Rogers which had been sent to Rogers by Ron Cobb as a bribe. Crow claimed that he did not know what was in the bag.

Crow had an interest in horses used for racing. He owned horses and was a former president of the South Carolina Thoroughbred Association which backed betting on horse races and dog races as well.

Lost Trust Looks at Waste Industry

In addition to the pari-mutuel betting bill and the capital gains tax break legislation, federal authorities found evidence of corruption in legislative activities related to the waste industry at the State House. And like the capital gains bill, the waste legislation was not the product of an FBI sting operation related to the pari-mutuel betting.

But the indictment of Jack I. Rogers on January 4, 1991, indicated that he had taken corrupt payments of $13,500 to support waste bills related to the Laidlaw Company's trash business. Laidlaw was in a series of legislative battles against environmental groups that wanted to curtail Laidlaw's waste management activities in South Carolina. In 1990, environmentalists were able to pass legislation reducing the amount of waste that could be buried in South Carolina every year. Rogers supported bills favored by Laidlaw.

When Rogers was indicted and Laidlaw was noted in the charges, environmentalists said that they had thought that in the FBI videotapes from Lost Trust there would be evidence linked to Laidlaw. Rep. Joe McElveen (D-Sumter) even went so far as to say that he was not surprised at the exposure of bribery and said that he had long suspected that lobbyists were buying legislation at the State House, but said that the general suspicion was not that cash was being used to buy legislators, but rather, "golf balls, means, or entertainment." McElveen said that he had long observed the waste lobbyists spent freely, especially the hazardous waste lobbyists.

Politicians Living Off Politics

Rep. Jack I. Rogers (D-Marlboro), as the Speaker Pro Tem of the House as well as an attorney, certainly used his position to get legal work and took a retainer fee of $1,000 per year from the Marlboro Electric Cooperative, and in 1989 Rogers was the primary sponsor of a bill in the House to make it virtually impossible to break up electric cooperatives; furthermore, he regularly supported the cooperatives in legislative matters.

The electric coops hired both House Speaker Bob Sheheen (D-Kershaw) and Sen. Jack Lindsay (D-Marlboro). Lindsay not only supported coopperative legislation but also represented the cooperatives before the South Carolina Tax Commission.

Lindsay also represented Hitachi Data Systems before the State Procurement Review Panel in its contracting with Clemson University. At the time, Lindsay had great influence in the appropriation process which determined how much state money was given to Clemson.

Legislative Conflicts of Interest Exposed

The problem of part-time legislators trying to make a living while also serving in the General Assembly presented perplexing and chronic conflict of interest issues, especially for lawyer-legislators who not only proposed and voted on bills, but also appeared before state boards and commissions and before magistrates and judges that they helped to elect. But the problem of conflicts was also presented by legislator-consultants hired by special interests having business before the General Assembly. And businessmen who had goods and services to sell to governments at the state and local levels also had leverage if they were legislators.

Gov. Carroll Campbell made a major issue of lawyer-legislators practicing before state agencies and some other Republican and Democratic legislators picked up on the issue. A few legislators pushed a bill in the House to force disclosure of income of $1,000 or more earned from lobbyists and their clients.

Some proposed a radical cure for the problem by banning practice by legislators before state agencies or banning voting on bills in which the legislator had a financial interest. *The State* conducted a survey prior to the 1991 session which showed that 64% of legislators favored mandatory disclosure by lawyer-legislators of clients represented before agencies. But only 47% favored a flat ban on such practice. And only 44% favored mandatory disclosure of all income by legislators.

Sen. David Thomas (R-Greenville) worried about the impact of legal fees on lawyer-legislators whose clients might have business before the Legislature, remarking, "It's, in a sense, open season to give undue influence to certain influential members of the Legislature, and when you're talking about megabucks that could come in, a $10,000 retainer, that's obviously not a campaign contribution, that's income coming in." Then Thomas asked, "What is the difference between that and a bribe? I fail to see the distinction."

Rep. David Beasley (D-Darlington) said that disclosure of outside income was critical, arguing, "That is the most important provision in the ethics reform package, because that is really telling the people what's going on between a legislator and a lobbyist." Beasley said the concern about free meals given by lobbyists to legislators was trivial in comparison with the influence of financial relationships between special interests and legislators, saying, "But that's beans. You get down to the crux of serious concerns when big bucks are passing in what may appear to be a legitimate business relationship, when, in fact, it may not be." Of course, Beasley was right. In fact, many legislators were taking money anywhere they could get it.

Another example of a part-time legislator-lawyer making money off of state business was Sen. Mike Mullinax (D-Anderson) who, as an attorney, earned a legal fee of $2,500 for helping Anderson County by approving the County's grant application which obtained $250,000 of state funding.

Sen. John Land (D-Clarendon) reported earning much of his income as an attorney by representing clients before the S.C. Workers' Compensation Commission. Land chaired the Workers' Compensation Study Committee which proposed the terms of the workers' compensation laws of South Carolina.

Lawyers were not the only legislators who found themselves in positions of power which matched their own economic and financial activities. Three of the 10 legislators on the Joint Insurance Study Committee—Reps. Billy Boan, Bob Kohn, and Bob McClellan—were insurance businessmen.

At the time of Lost Trust, the law did not require legislators to disclose their business relationships unless they thought it created a conflict of interest. However, the House at its organizational meeting in December, 1990, passed a new rule requiring its members to disclose all sources of income of $1,000 or more. And a number of legislators told the media that such disclosure would have a beneficial effect.

Legislators in Income Dilemma

The problem of legislators leveraging their office to make money was very real and Rep. Wes Hayes (D-York) pointed out that, "You have lawyers that can parlay this into certain clients that they can get from being a legislator or maybe certain favoritism from judges or certain boards and commissions." The problem with legislators earning money in addition to their very limited legislative salary and per diems was, Hayes said, "I think you've got to also look at the fact that the General Assembly is a part-time job." Hayes worried that limits on the earning of legislators from private sources might "end up running out good, qualified people from being willing and able to serve."

However, John Crangle of Common Cause/South Carolina was less concerned about restricting outside income and said that new law should be passed to ban retainer payments to lawyers unless they actually performed legal services to justify the payments. On the other hand, Speaker Bob Sheheen seemed to feel that the problem of limiting private income was difficult and "I suppose no matter what we pass there'll always be some questions."

In the end the 1991 Ethics Act banned lawyer-legislators from taking retainers from clients unless services were actually provided commensurate with the amount of retainer.

Letter to Editor Blasts State Government

F.T. Connolly of Columbia published a letter in *The State* on January 7, 1991, ripping South Carolina's political class for self-serving behavior and an ethical double standard. Connolly started by ridiculing Gov. Carroll Campbell, writing, "It seems as though Governor Campbell is saying 'ethics' really only apply to the lesser privileged in our society." Connolly pointed to a trip recently taken by Campbell and other state officials to Europe for which they did not pay and charged that "we have people representing us scrambling to take advantage of free trips to Europe and any other perks they can get and don't seem to realize this is a conflict of interest and very unethical."

Connolly further opined that, "This good ol' boy system extends into our state Legislature and such corruption abounds that our Legislature is a laughing stock of the nation because of the unethical conduct of many of its members." He pointed also to the favored treatment given to a federal agent in the Lost Trust investigation by the South Carolina Highway Patrol which fixed a drunk driving case and said, "the average person is fed up with the dual standards of justice and the good ol' boy system."

The letter concluded by saying, "All the public wants is good honest leadership which we can take pride in and help restore our confidence in state government."

New Session Looks to Ethics Reform

Clark Surratt published an article in *The State* on January 8, 1991, that looked at fixing the problems exposed and even caused by the Lost Trust indictments and convictions. Those removed by the scandal would have to be replaced, starting with Jack I. Rogers as Speaker Pro Tem, but ethics laws had to be completely revised after the U.S. Attorney had exposed the fact that South Carolina really had no substantive ethics laws.

Five candidates were positioned to take Rogers' job, including Reps. David Beasley (D-Darlington), Tom Huff (R-Aiken), John Felder (D-Calhoun), James W. Johnson, Jr., (D-Laurens), and Howell Clyborne (R-Greenville). Clyborne had tried and failed to defeat Rogers in the election held by the House in December, 1990.

Surratt listed the most serious ethical problems facing the General Assembly and predicted remedial legislation in the new session, including a ban or at least disclosure of lobbyists' gratuities, detailed disclosure of campaign money, limitations on donations from certain sources, a ban on conversion of campaign funds to personal use, a prohibition of campaign donations from lobbyists during the session, a ban on cash donations, and more disclosure of economic interests as well as strict enforcement of ethics and campaign finance laws.

New Session Convenes

The 109th General Assembly gathered for its first session on January 8, 1991, and was shrouded by a cloud of ethical smoke from the burning careers of crooked legislators incinerated by federal authorities for the previous four months. Another body had just been thrown on the pyre on January 4th, just before the session started, in the person of the Speaker Pro Tem, Jack I. Rogers.

When the new session of the Legislature convened, lobbyists and legislators were anxious over what the exploding Lost Trust scandal would do to the culture of chummy relationships which had flourished at the State House for years based on the easy flow of money, free liquor, and free trips from lobbyists to politicians.

Seventeen year veteran of the lobbying wars, Pat Watson of the South Carolina Auto Dealers Association, told reporter Clark Surratt of *The State* that he came to the State House lobby to find the answer to that question, saying, "I feel like it's my first day at school, even though I've been here for 17 years."

First Day of New Session

As the 109th General Assembly convened at noon on Tuesday, January 8, 1991, the lobbyists collected in the State House between the Senate and House chambers only to see another lobbyist come up and join the gaggle who was known to be a suspect and perhaps and FBI informant in the Lost Trust scandal—Ken Kinard. The media has already revealed that Kinard had relationships with both Rep. Jack I. Rogers who had just been criminally charged and Sen. Jack Lindsay who was widely believed to be the next on the U.S. Attorney's list.

The session was the first since the adjournment of June, 1990, and the first for the new members of the House who had just been elected in November. But it was a strange, even weird setting, as it was the first session since the indictments of legislators started in August, 1990. And 15 minutes before the noon start there were only a handful of lobbyists scattered around the lobby whereas in previous years, the lobby would have been full of them, shaking hands, gossiping, and schmoozing.

One lobbyist said that others did not want to show up for fear of facing news reporters from print and television media asking questions at a time when the fact that lobbyists had been buying legislators for years had just been exposed. But Ken Kinard was brazen enough to show up, certain to attract attention after it had come out that he gave Jack I. Rogers $6,000 on behalf of GSX Chemical Services (which had recently been renamed Laidlaw Environmental Services).

Kinard in Limbo

Even so, Kinard came to the Capitol having lost only one client from the previous year. Strangely, he still represented the South Carolina Trial Lawyers Association although there was a serious question as to whether Kinard himself might be charged. Kinard's attorney, Dick Harpootlian of Columbia, explained to the media that Kinard's lobbying clients were satisfied, saying, "All the clients had concerns and all those concerns have been resolved." He said that Kinard had reassured the clients that Kinard was the victim of the expanding probe at the State House.

Harpootlian Represents Kinard

Lobbyist Ken Kinard, a suspect in Operation Lost Trust, retained Columbia attorney Dick Harpootlian only to find Harpootlian elected at the Solicitor of the 5th Circuit of Richland and Kershaw counties. Kinard was suspected of making an extortionate payment to Rep. Jack I. Rogers of $13,500 to promote the interests of Kinard's client, GSX Chemical Services.

Harpootlian announced that he would continue to serve as Kinard's attorney even after he was sworn in as Solicitor on January 9, 1991. Harpootlian also announced that he would continue his work for client Will Close, a wealthy businessman from the family that owned Springs Mills. Close was charged with possession of cocaine with intent to distribute.

Harpootlian said the other 78 cases he had pending would be referred to other attorneys.

The chairman of the Richland County Republican Party, Scott Elliott, criticized Harpootlian's decision saying that he should not handle private cases while in public office.

Lindsay on Deathbed

As the new session of the Senate convened, the lung replacement surgery of Sen. Jack Lindsay (D-Marlboro) at a hospital at the University of North Carolina in Chapel Hill failed to save Lindsay's life. His condition deteriorated quickly and by January 8, 1991, it looked like he would not survive.

As he lay dying, the federal prosecutors refrained from indicting him although it was well known that he had been in contact with them before the surgery and was likely to be charged. Authorities had said that he would be treated the same as other suspects in Lost Trust, all of whom were ultimately charged or agreed to immunity deals in return for cooperation.

The Lindsay case was abnormal, not only because its subject was dying, but also because the best witness against Lindsay, Ron Cobb, had made a deal with prosecutors that Cobb would not have to testify against Lindsay because of his friendship with him, even though Cobb had told the federal investigators that he had paid Lindsay $10,000 as a so-called campaign contribution which Lindsay failed to disclose on his campaign finance report.

In the end, the idiopathic pulmonary fibrosis which had afflicted the long-time smoker and drinker was not cured by the lung replacement and he died without being indicted on January 11, 1991.

Greer Resigns From Board

Gov. Carroll Campbell's old buddy from Greenville had tried to beat back rumors and media stories that he was the target of the FBI probe which had caught so many legislators and lobbyists from August, 1990, onward. As the pressure built up and after Campbell had been safely re-elected in November, 1990, it was time for Greer to go. On January 9, 1991, he submitted his resignation as Chairman of the South Carolina Development Board, but did not admit any wrongdoing. Greer set a formal announcement of his decision for the following day.

The State reported that Greer had actually submitted his resignation in mid-December, 1990, although there was some information that he did not deliver his resignation letter to Campbell until his inauguration.

The Greenville News had published reports in November, 1990, that Greer was under investigation for drug use. And it was well known that Greer was close to Ron Cobb and had referred

Greenville businessmen to Cobb for lobbying services and also recommended Cobb as a lobbyist for Nucor Steel Company.

Greer had repeatedly denied that he ever used drugs and alleged that *The Greenville News* was trying to hurt Campbell's re-election. And when he resigned, he put a spin on the story to the effect that the chairman's job took too much time and effort. But he would soon be indicted on drug charges and would plead guilty.

Campbell's Inaugural Address

Fresh from a landslide re-election victory over a weak opponent, Gov. Carroll Campbell delivered his inaugural address on January 9, 1991, and emphasized his agenda for reform of state government, stressing governmental restructuring more than ethics reform.

He took time to praise Democrats for their effort to reform the State's ethics laws, noting the work of Speaker Bob Sheheen, Lt. Gov. Nick Theodore, Sen. Marshall Williams, and lauding Rep. David Wilkins, a Republican from Greenville.

Miles Cracks Down on Lobbyists

Fresh from a victory over incumbent Secretary of State, John Campbell, in which his only real issue had been lobbying regulation, new Secretary of State, Jim Miles, served notice as soon as he was sworn in on January 9, 1991, that he was going to take on the lobbyists and make them obey the Ethics Act for the first time since it was enacted in 1975. He soon found that most of them did not want to fight and gave up.

Defeated Secretary of State, John Campbell, had made a mockery of his job of registering and recording lobbyists' disclosure documents as required by the 1975 Ethics Act. He had basically filed whatever came into his office without checking disclosure forms to see if they reported the expenses and incomes of lobbyists as mandated by the Act. He did not even bother to look at the question of whether all persons who were actually lobbying state government were filing their disclosure forms at all.

In fact, many of the lobbyists at the State House and throughout state and local government were not filing and reporting at all. And even those who did file often listed few, if any, expenses and revenues. In some cases, lobbyists filed disclosures in which they did not even report the lobbyists' registration fee of $10.00 they were supposes to pay to file their forms.

Miles Hits Lobbyists

Jim Miles lost no time going after the lobbyists. On January 9, 1991, Miles showed up at the Secretary of State's office, moved into the Secretary of State's desk, and started calling for all the lobbyists' reports to be brought to him for his review. By the end of the day on January 9, 1991, he was already going through a pile of 300 lobbyists' reports which were only one page long.

Miles announced to the *Associated Press*, "These lobbyists are going to do what's required of the law. They don't have a choice...because the law's clear." Miles was an attorney, unlike his predecessor, John Campbell, and he was much younger than Campbell and full of energy in taking his new job, unlike the elderly Campbell who had languished in office for three terms.

Miles warned the lobbyists, some of whom had bitterly denounced him while he was a candidate and after he was elected and had accused him of being a demagogue and an enemy of business. Miles said that if any lobbyists did not file their disclosures and do it right they would be finished, saying, "If they don't do it, they're out of business. So the lobbying problem is solved, for all practical purposes."

His first day in office, Jim Miles sent out letters from the Secretary of State's office to a number of persons saying that they had not complied with the lobbying requirements of the 1975 Ethics Act. He demanded that they provide more details about their spending.

Miles told the media that he would refer any lobbyists who failed to comply with the lobbying law to the Attorney General of South Carolina for action. The law did, in fact, provide criminal penalties of a $500 fine and 60 days in jail as well as a two year ban on lobbying work.

Sen Lindsay Dies

At the State House while the net was closing in on him in late 1990 and the first few days of January, 1991, some old hand lobbyist said to John Crangle that Sen. Jack Lindsay would never be caught in Operation Lost Trust in spite of his longtime reputation as a shady operator. When he died on January 11, 1991, the same lobbyist told Crangle, "See, I told you so. Jack was too smart for them. They never got him."

Lindsay had served in the General Assembly for 38 years and he passed just three days after the new session began on January 8, 1991. Sen. Horace Smith (D-Spartanburg) remarked that Lindsay was one of the last rural barons in the state and was "one of the last vestiges of that particular part of our government." Smith had served with Lindsay for most of his term and like Lindsay, would end his career in 1991 but unlike Lindsay, would not die but would soon be indicted and convicted for fraud.

Lindsay had a reputation for both a rakish personal life of wine, women, and smoking but also of being the most brilliant mind in the General Assembly and the most dominant and convincing orator and politician.

He had served in the Marine Corps during World War II and had suffered personal tragedies when his son died in an accident as a child and his wife was shot in a kidnap attempt in 1971.

Editorial on Jack Lindsay

On January 12, 1991, *The State* published an editorial the day after Sen. Jack Lindsay's death captioned, "John C. Lindsay: Epitaph for a roué." The editorial mixed admiration for his talents with opprobrium for his antics in the Senate.

Admitting Lindsay's abilities as "a gifted orator with a mesmerizing ability to browbeat or beguile as the mood or issue suited," *The State* dismissed him as "an engaging rake." The paper recited the suspicious news about Lindsay which had come out in the Lost Trust cases and the prospect that he might be indicted in the scandal.

Noting his 38 years in the General Assembly, the editors depicted Lindsay as "the consummate insider, recognized by colleagues, clients, and constituents for his canny capacity for getting things done."

But in the end, *The State* wrote, "it is regrettable that he utilized his power so cavalierly and conducted his personal life with such flamboyant disregard for propriety and accepted convention. He was a notorious gambler and womanizer...a colorful character and wheeler-dealer."

Lindsay Funeral

Sen. Jack Lindsay's funeral was held in his hometown of Bennettsville, South Carolina. He was 63 years old. Some 500 mourners attended. Among them were Gov. Carroll Campbell, Lt. Gov. Nick Theodore, Attorney General Travis Medlock, Supreme Court Justice Jean Toal and Justice David Harwell.

Legislators present included Sens. Marshall Williams, James Waddell and most of the Senate as well as Speaker Bob Sheheen. Convicted corruptionists former Reps. Robert Brown and Danny Winstead joined the congregation as did recently indicted Rep. Jack I. Rogers and future governor David Beasley.

U.S. Rep. Floyd Spence of Lexington joined the assemblage.

Wilkins Reports Free Trip

Rep. David Wilkins (R-Greenville) belatedly updated his 1989 disclosure report in early January, 1991, to detail a trip he took in late 1989 with recently indicted House Speaker Pro Tem Jack I. Rogers to New York at the expense of GSX Chemical Services and the South Carolina Trial Lawyers Association. Wilkins explained that he took his wife along on the three day trip in the company of lobbyist Ken Kinard and his wife. Kinard's wife had worked as administrative assistant to Rep. Rogers until she resigned in December, 1990, at the time Rogers was indicted for public corruption. However, Rogers did not report the 1989 trip to New York on his disclosure form in April, 1990.

Kinard had just recently told the federal investigation that Rogers extorted $5,000 from Kinard, a portion of his lobbying fee, for his involvement in the 1988 legislation to cut the capital gains tax rate.

The Trial Lawyers Association told the media that there was nothing wrong about the trip to New York. The airline fare for both Wilkins and his wife was paid by the Trial Lawyers.

Lobbyists Register

Groups that had been lobbying for years without registering and reporting with the Secretary of State as required by law, by mid-January, 1991, began to comply after a new Secretary, Jim Miles, announced his policy of aggressive enforcement. It was obvious that the interest groups that hired lobbyists and the lobbyists themselves did not want to challenge Secretary of State Miles' demands that all lobbyists file appropriate registrations and reports with his office in accordance with Miles' interpretation of the 1975 Ethics Act then in effect.

As Miles had made his promise to enforce the Act and bring lobbyists under control, the main issue in his campaign to unseat incumbent Secretary of State John Campbell, the special interests and lobbyists knew that Miles had to compel them to follow the law and would do so.

Luther Taylor Sent to Prison

Former Rep. Luther Taylor (D-Richland) was sent to the federal prison in Atlanta, Georgia, in mid-January, 1991, to serve the six and a half year term imposed on him after his conviction for public corruption in October, 1990.

Cobb Paid to Push Tax Cut

The media found out more about the infamous capital gains tax fix, reporting the information in mid-January, 1991. The story was that businessmen T. Walter Brashier and Thomas Roe hired lobbyist Rob Cobb to get a tax cut bill passed in the State House in 1988. The fee paid was $87,500.

Cobb, in turn, got Jack I. Rogers to help with the bill and Rogers took $5,000 of the lobbying fee as an alleged bribe from Cobb. There was no evidence that the clients knew of the bribe until it was exposed by the federal indictment of Rogers.

Rogers Pleads Not Guilty

As expected, former House Speaker Pro Tem Jack I. Rogers appeared on January 17, 1991, before federal magistrate Charles Gambrell and entered a not guilty plea to 10 counts of extortion, racketeering, and witness tampering. He was 53 years old and a member of the South Carolina Bar. He was given an unsecured bond of $25,000.

The 10 counts carried maximum punishments of a total of 180 years in prison and fines of up to $2.5 million. As he was charged with federal racketeering under the RICO law, he also faced forfeiture of his legislative salary. U.S. Attorney Bart Daniel told the media that the RICO charge was by far the most serious.

At the time of his indictment, Rogers was the eleventh official charged in the Lost Trust prosecutions and the thirteenth of all those charged to that point.

At the time of the bond hearing no trial had been set. Later, Judge Falcon Hawkins scheduled the trial. As the Iraq War had just started, the proceedings were brief and distracted by talk of the war between the magistrate and the attorneys.

Crow Pleads Not Guilty

South Carolina Highway Commissioner and lawyer, Wade Ronald Crow, appeared at the same hearing as Jack I. Rogers and pleaded not guilty to aiding and abetting a $1,000 bribe to Rogers to secure his support on the pari-mutuel betting bill.

Crow faced twenty years in prison and a fine of $250,000.

Crow and Rogers lived in the same area of South Carolina and both were owners of horses and were favorable to the idea of a betting bill and horse racing.

Kinard Denies Conflict of Interest

Lobbyist Ken Kinard, already under a cloud for his alleged payment of $5,000 to Rep. Jack I. Rogers, denied in mid-January, 1991, that he had had a conflict of interest in lobbying for a state agency which gave Willamette Industries $3.9 million at a time when Kinard was also a lobbyist for Willamette Industries.

Kinard denied that he had anything to do with the grant while he was lobbying for the state agency, the Coordinating Council for Economic Development, when it was granted the money to Willamette.

Kinard was paid $28,000 to lobby for the Council from early January, 1987, to June 30, 1990. He was paid $10,200 per year to work for Willamette from early 1989 until mid-January, 1991, at a time when Kinard's affiliation with Rogers had become public.

Willamette was given state incentives in a grant to build road, bridge, and rail infrastructure in Marlboro County and Kinard, Rep. Jack I. Rogers, and Sen. Jack Lindsay worked to push for state assistance which helped to land a new $325 million paper mill constructed by Willamette in Marlboro County.

In early January, 1991, the rumor was that Kinard had paid Rogers $18,500 in extorted funds in return for Rogers support for GSX (which had recently changed its name to Laidlaw Environmental Services) and also in return for Rogers' help in securing a retroactive capital gains tax break for 21 people worth $8.6 million.

Surprisingly, in spite of all the rumors about Kinard, he still had major lobbying clients as the 1991 session started, including the S.C. Trial Lawyers Association, Seagram Co., Pfizer Pharmaceutical Co., the Institute of Recycling Industries, and the state chapter of Real Estate Appraisers.

Kinard Rolls Over on Rogers

In mid-January, 1991, it became know that lobbyist Ken Kinard had cut a deal with the U.S. Attorney's office to avoid prosecution on a charge that he paid some $18,500 to Rep. Jack I. Rogers based on Roger's demand that he be paid for his help on waste disposal and tax cut legislation for Kinard's clients. The deal was that Kinard would provide evidence to investigators and prosecutors in their probe of Roger's alleged corruption.

The State reported that in the summer of 1990 Kinard had agreed to help the government and that, perhaps, Kinard's wife, Gail, might also be asked to help the prosecution as she was Roger's top assistant for four years leading up to Roger's indictment. The Kinards and Rogers were perceived as close friends in addition to being political allies in legislative activities at the State House. Some lobbyists told *The State* that one of Kinard's major assets as a lobbyist was his close relationship with Rogers. One lobbyist told the paper that, "That was pretty common knowledge: If Ken was for something, Jack was for it." In fact, some sources compared the relationship of Kinard and Rogers to that of Ron Cobb and Sen. Jack Lindsay.

Some observers wondered whether the rumored $18,500 was actually extorted from Kinard by Rogers or whether it was a bribe offered by Kinard. If it was an offered bribe, the charges could have been aiding and abetting extortion.

Kinard had come to the State House in 1978 to work as a scheduler for Gov. Dick Riley. Later he worked as a budget analyst for the Richland County Department of Social Services.

Lobbyist Kinard Not Charged

Ken Kinard, lobbyist for multiple clients including Laidlaw and the S.C. Trial Lawyers Association, escaped prosecution in the Lost Trust scandal, even though he allegedly paid some $18,500 to Jack I. Rogers on demand.

Prosecutors promised Kinard immunity in return for his information on corruption in state government. This immunity was given from both state and federal charges by Attorney General Medlock and U.S. Attorney Daniel.

Prominent Columbia criminal attorney and newly-elected 5th Circuit Solicitor for Richland and Kershaw counties, Dick Harpootlian, represented Kinard in cutting a deal with the U.S. Attorney's office. Harpootlian told the media that the deal provided that neither federal nor state authorities would prosecute Ken and Gail Kinard for their dealings with Rogers. South Carolina Attorney General Travis Medlock said that he had relinquished all of his jurisdiction in the Operation Lost Trust scandal to federal authorities.

Harpootlian explained that, "There's never been any allegation they (the Kinards) committed any crime, so, in fact, what I am doing is representing two witnesses who will testify on behalf of the government." In return, Harpootlian said his clients "have been guaranteed by federal authorities, speaking also for state authorities, that there will be no prosecution."

Kinards Get Immunity

The fact that both the federal and state prosecutors gave lobbyist Ken Kinard and his wife, Gail, immunity from prosecution in their dealings with Rep. Jack I. Rogers was more favorable than the deal given to Ron Cobb. Cobb had only been given federal immunity in return for cooperation.

The other factor which was unusual in the Kinard case was that Harpootlian had just been elected in November, 1990, to the new office of 5th Circuit Solicitor and was transitioning out of his private practice in Columbia. Harpootlian explained that he had some 80 clients and cases in his private practice and that the South Carolina Attorney General had agreed to handle the prosecution of all of Harpootlian's criminal clients for which he had conflicts.

South Carolina Attorney General Travis Medlock gave Harpootlian permission to continue to represent Ken Kinard, Gail Kinard, and one other client even after Harpootlian had been elected as solicitor. And Harpootlian said that Daniel and Medlock had agreed not to prosecute Ken and Gail Kinard even though Medlock told the media that he could do so if he wanted.

Sen. Smith Indicted But Does Not Resign

South Carolina did not have a law in place disqualifying officials on indictment. Sen. Horace C. Smith (D-Spartanburg) refused to resign his seat on indictment on January 23, 1991, in federal court for mail fraud and criminal conspiracy. He faced five years and a $250,000 fine, if convicted.

The indictment stemmed from the sale of $16 million of bonds which were issued by Skylyn Hall Retirement Home in Spartanburg, South Carolina, for which Sen. Smith served as attorney. The FBI alleged the bond sale was vitalized by fraud. And the federal grand jury found that the promoters of the bond sale lied about it and that Smith knew this.

Some 2,000 people in the United States lost money in the bond sale, including 132 investors in South Carolina who allegedly lost $1.5 million according to court records.

At the time of his indictment, Smith had served in the South Carolina Senate for a total of 23 years. He was named on only one count of the 21 count indictment.

The indictment followed a civil law suit for $70 million which was settled in the spring of 1990.

Sen. Smith Does Not Resign

Indicted Sen. Horace Smith, who had been indicted for mail fraud and criminal conspiracy on January 23, 1991, announced that he would not resign from the South Carolina Senate. The announcement came the following day.

Sen. Smith's decision to stay in the Senate presented both a substantive and a public relations problem for the other 45 senators in a body already scorched by the previous indictment of Sen. Rick Lee (R-Spartanburg) for corruption and the suspicion that Sen. Bud Long (D-Horry) would also be charged.

The substantive problem was that the Senate did not have a rule in place to deal with indicted or convicted members with felony liability. The House did have its Rule 3.12 which mandated suspension on indictment and expulsion on conviction of felony. The Senate rule was that there was no mandatory suspension on indictment but only on conviction of a felony or crime against the voting laws. It was then up to the discretion of the Senate as to whether to vote to expel the senator.

Senate Works on Ethics Bill

The Senate took up the ethics reform issue on January 23, 1991, as the new session began. A Senate Judiciary subcommittee focused on the question of what behavior should be prohibited as unethical and corrupt by new ethics legislation being considered.

Sen. Glenn McConnell (R-Charleston) took the position that the proposed rules of conduct should address the use of favors and things of value to buy the official actions of such persons as state legislators.

Sen. Kay Patterson (D-Richland), an avowed cynic about ethics reform bills and a severe critic of Operation Lost Trust as a racist plot, tried to mock efforts to formulate a stricter and more effective ethics bill.

At the same time, three Judiciary subcommittees were considering separate portions of the ethics reform bill, including legislators' ethics, campaign finance reform and regulation of lobbyists.

Letter to Editor Urges Ethics Reform

Charles Von Herrman of Columbia wrote *The State* on January 24, 1991, that, "Some members of the business community are complaining that the proposed ethics reform measures will hamper their access to S.C. lawmakers. I should hope so! That's part of the reason for reform, to prevent special interests from unduly influencing lawmakers with favors, bribes, etc." Von Herrman wanted to level the playing field for everybody.

He also blasted insiders by saying, "lawyer-legislators who represent clients before state boards, courts, etc., have a clear conflict of interest between their responsibility to the public and their responsibility and inclination to serve their clients."

Dismissing the argument that lawyer-legislators needed to make a living outside of their part-time salary and expenses, Von Herrman noted, "No one held a gun on them to run for office" and added, "If the income from their practice is that important to them, it merely proves their conflict of interest."

House Ethics Committee Approves Reform Bill

Chaired by Rep. Wes Hayes (D-York), the new House Ethics Committee just put in place in the 1991 session, approved a draft of an ethics reform bill which would require disclosure of all retainers, fees, and related payments paid to legislators by all companies that hired lobbyists to influence state government.

The bill also proposed to limit the amounts of campaign contributions and ban the mixing of personal and campaign funds, and the bill banned handouts and gratuities given to state officials by lobbyists and also banned payments to officials for making speeches.

Rep. Hayes said of the 30 page ethics reform bill that, "It's going to make major changes in the way we do business." He pointed to the bill as it was the first new reform bill which any legislative panel had approved since Operation Lost Trust was exposed in mid-July, 1990. Hayes predicted the bill would be sent from his Ethics Committee to the House Judiciary committed to be blended with other reform bills in progress.

The Ethics Committee bill proposed that campaign contributions be limited to $5,000 per calendar year for statewide candidates and $1,000 for all other candidates, including legislative and local. It proposed placing jurisdiction over lobbyists with the State Ethics Commission, removing authority from the Secretary of State.

Legislature in Public Relations Nightmare

As the number of indictments and guilty pleas piled up in the fall of 1990 and in the first weeks of 1991, the additional new January 23rd indictment of long-serving Sen. Horace Smith (D-

Spartanburg) for mail fraud and conspiracy was one more bad dream added to the 11 indictments already on file.

Senator Marshall Williams (D-Orangeburg), who had served in the Senate for 45 years at that point, told *The State* reporter Cindi Ross Scoppe the day after Smith's indictment: "everything now comes at a bad time." Surveying the political debris field in which the old stone Confederate era State House sat, Williams decried the disaster and said, "We got ethics questions, and lobbying questions and other kinds of questions. I've been here 45 years and we got more things going on now than we ever have."

Senators were unsure what should be done about fellow senators who had been indicted. Lt. Gov. Nick Theodore, president of the Senate, at first said when the indictments started to pile up that any senator indicted should step down. But after the charges filed against Sen. Horace Smith, he thought the Senate needed various options. And Chairwoman of the Rules Committee, Sen. Nell Smith, said that she thought those charged should take voluntary suspension, but did not know if she would propose new rules.

Miles Forces Beasley Disclosure

Newly elected Secretary of State, Jim Miles, hit the ground running in his first month in office in January, 1991, by demanding that all lobbyists register and file disclosure reports with his office in accord with a law which had not been enforced by his predecessor in office during the previous 12 years.

Miles soon found that most lobbyists chose to comply, but a few fought back, led by S.C. Textile Manufacturers Association lobbyist, Jerry Beasley, the check-grabbing and most aggressive proponent and practitioner of big money wining and dining of legislators in the State House's pay-to-play culture.

Beasley defied Miles, saying his rights were at stake. Beasley's defiance of Mile's demand that all lobbyists file and report their lobbying activities and spending triggered a short, but high-profile battle in which Miles forced Beasley to comply with the demands of the Secretary of State that the lobbying disclosure portions of the 1975 Ethics Act be followed by all lobbyists in South Carolina.

David Beasley Elected Speaker Pro Tem

With the indictment of Jack I. Rogers, the House, on January 25th, elected a new speaker to replace Rogers. David Beasley, who would later become governor in 1995, took the job.

Sting Weakens Lobbyists

In an editorial, *The State* argued that the Lost Trust scandal had weakened the influence of lobbyists at the State House in 1991 and diminished their ability to block bills such as one to ban video poker. *The State* made opposition to video poker one of the main issues in the 1990s.

Sen. Horace Smith Takes Leave

Reacting to his indictment on January 23, 1991, for mail fraud and conspiracy, Sen. Horace Smith (D-Spartanburg) asked for and received a voluntary suspension from his seat from Sen. Marshall Williams (D-Orangeburg), President Pro Tem of the Senate.

At the time, Smith was the fifth most senior senator and chaired the Corrections and Penology Committee. He faced five years in prison and a fine of $250,000 on conviction.

The suspension entitled Smith to reinstatement and back pay if his indictment did not result in a conviction.

The suspension set off a game of musical chairs in the Senate as the next most senior senators could move to other chairmanships in Smith's absence.

Gov. Campbell Promotes Ethics in State of State Speech

In his annual State of the State speech on January 30, 1991, Gov. Carroll Campbell advocated ethics reform and campaign disclosure reforms for legislative action in the 1991 session.

Campbell's proposals were far from aggressive and were not remotely close to what was actually needed, given the magnitude of corruption in the state. Campbell called for a new ethics commission, new ethics standards, more campaign finance disclosure, and full disclosure of financial interests of government officials.

Given the Lost Trust scandal, which was producing more and more criminal defendants and more and more evidence of the rot caused by campaign money and lobbyists' use of money to buy legislators, the need for drastic action was glaringly apparent. The continuing corruption probes at the Highway Department, Santee-Cooper, and Department of Social Services also threatened more scandalous revelations.

Fortunately, the General Assembly's leadership realized that Campbell's emphasis on disclosure without addressing the out-of-control use of big money campaign donations and handouts by special interests to control legislation and elections was far less than what was actually needed. The regulatory proposals of Speaker Bob Sheheen and Sens. Williams and Saleeby showed a much more realistic approach to stop lobbyists and special interests from bribing politicians with gratuities and large campaign contributions.

On January 31, 1991, *The State* published an editorial lauding Gov. Carroll Campbell's annual State of the State address the night before, especially for his stress on the need for major reforms of the structure of state government and his points about the need for new ethics rules.

Gov. Campbell blamed the structure of state government as plagued by duplication and waste of public funds. He urged major restructuring of the tangled departments and agencies.

Campbell praised the draft ethics reform bill, the Government Accountability Act of 1991, as remedy for the corruption and abuses exposed by Operation Lost Trust. He emphasized the need for new disclosure laws, remarking that, "The bottom line to meaningful reform is openness.... There should be full public disclosure of campaign contributions well in advance of elections.

But the governor also advocated new restrictions, limits, and prohibitions beyond mere disclosure. He said, "There should be strict rules to limit cash contributions." As to lobbyists and their abuses, Campbell argued, "We must have reasonable rules governing lobbyists, including full disclosure of expenses."

Campbell bit the bullet with regard to the sensitive issue of jurisdiction over legislators when he stated that the House and Senate ethics committees should be abolished and a new State Ethics Commission should be given authority over investigations of both the executive and legislative branches.

Gov. Campbell concluded by warning, "Change can be dangerous. More dangerous is business as usual."

CHAPTER TWENTY

FEBRUARY, 1991—ENFORCEMENT AND REFORM MOVE FORWARD

February, 1991, marked the start of a very intensified period of prosecutorial actions, administrative enforcement, and ethics reform activity by federal and state government which lasted throughout the year. On the one hand, the U.S. Attorney promoted the indictments of a host of legislators, lobbyists, and government officials which resulted in a long string of convictions. On the other hand, Secretary of State Jim Miles cracked down on the lobbyists. Further, the General Assembly moved aggressively to write and pass a drastic new ethics bill and concluded the task on September 23, 1991. Finally, Gov. Campbell signed the bill on October 1, 1991.

Of course, the revelation of more and more indictments and the action of Jim Miles in cowing the lobbyists broke down opposition to ethics reform among the special interests and lobbyists. At the same time the indictment of more and more legislators and lobbyists in early 1991 further enraged the public and drive legislators to take quicker and more drastic action to pass ethics reform than would have otherwise been the case.

Six More Indicted in Scandal

On February 20, 1991, six more indictments were handed down. On the same day that three more House members were announced as indicted for public corruption, the prosecutors also revealed an additional batch of three lobbyists as defendants.

Martin G. Rohling, lobbyist for Household International, Inc., was charged with possession of cocaine. Rohling had taken Reps. Paul Derrick (R-Lexington) and Thomas Limehouse (R-Charleston) on a golf trip to California. All three were indicted in the scandal.

James Randall "Randy" Lee was the lobbyist for the S.C. Health Care Association and was charged with possession of marijuana. Lee was known to play poker along with other lobbyists and legislators at the Town House Hotel.

The third lobbyist charged was also implicated in illegal drugs. Thomas E. Collins, lobbyist for Hitachi Data Systems, was charged with two counts of possession of cocaine in 1987 and 1988 and one count of possession with intent to distribute. Collins was known as a crony of Ron Cobb and had a dubious reputation in State House circles.

The three legislators were Reps. James Faber (D-Richland), Frank McBride (D-Richland), and Paul Derrick (R-Lexington). All three were charged with taking money from Ron Cobb in relation to the betting bill.

Lost Trust Scandal Welcomed

In a letter to the editor of *The State* on February 1, 1991, the organization Citizens Asking for a Safe Environment congratulated U.S. Attorney Bart Daniel, his staff, and the FBI for their work in Operation Lost Trust.

Citizens said it had lobbied for years at the State House for environmental protection issues and had seen first hand the unhealthy and unethical "love" relationship between lobbyists and legislators in which lobbyists told their legislative stooges what to do even while the House or Senate were in session.

Miles' Campaign Strategy Reviewed

On February 3, 1991, *The State* published an article which reviewed the successful campaign strategy of new Secretary of State Jim Miles in unseating incumbent John Campbell after three listless terms.

The article pointed out that Miles had made hay out of Campbell's incestuous dealings with lobbyists he was supposed to register and monitor, clearly showing that Campbell was taking campaign contributions from the lobbyists at the same time he was supposed to oversee their registration and reporting with his office. Miles showed lobbyists were not registering and complying with the requirements of the 1975 Ethics Act.

At the same time, Miles outspent Campbell in the election of 1990 by a factor of two to one. Miles also appealed to the State Ethics Commission and got the Commission to order Campbell to stop taking campaign donations from the same lobbyists he was supposed to register and oversee. Republican Miles spent a total of $350,000 while Campbell spent $143,000, his funding sources cut off when the lobbyists were stopped by the State Ethics Commission from donating to Campbell before the campaign was over.

Miles Discusses Strategy

In early February, 1991, Jim Miles addressed the question of his strategy of defeating incumbent John Campbell in 1990. Miles talked about the problem of financing his campaign against Campbell who had been taking money from the lobbyists he regulated.

Miles used $234,000 of his own personal funds as the bulk of the $350,000 that he spent beating Campbell. Most of the money was spent on television ads focusing on the lobbyists and their all-too-friendly relations over the years with Campbell.

Asked whether he used his own money to buy the election, Miles responded by saying, "That raises a good point. This whole thing of campaign finance law needs revamping." Miles said that he favored a plan to limit campaign contributions so that a candidate could use only $25,000 of his own money and all individual contributions would be limited to only $1,000.

In discussing the 1990 election, Miles said that Campbell might have had unlimited donations from the lobbyists if Miles had not convinced the State Ethics Commission to stop Campbell from raising money from the lobbyists he regulated. "We cut off his oxygen," Miles remarked.

Miles said that he decided to run for Secretary of State while he was a Greenville County Councilman when Gov. Carroll Campbell talked to Greenville Republicans about running for statewide offices.

Miles Takes Office of Secretary of State

"This ethics thing is serious," Miles told Staff Writer Levona Page of *The State* a few days after he took office. Having used effective attack ads against his incumbent opponent John Campbell, denouncing his failure to discipline out-of-control lobbyists running amok at the State House in the glare of Operation Lost Trust prosecutions, Miles was ready to deal with the lobbyists in decisive and confrontational terms.

"I don't think there's any question that there's a lot of people down there in Columbia saying, 'We don't have to pay any attention to what Jim Miles is saying—We run this state and have always run it, and who is this guy,'" Miles remarked a few days into his new term.

Miles said that he knew the lobbyists felt that they had been really running state government "for generations." Miles said that, in fact, the lobbyists "They've got the power. I'm not deluding myself. I perfectly understand that. Odds are, I'm going to be one of the shortest-lived politicians in the history of the state." (In fact, Miles would be re-elected twice.)

But some political insiders felt that Miles had his eye on running for governor after Carroll Campbell had to leave office at the end of his term in 1995. But Miles denied that he had ambitions to run for governor, at least at that time. (Miles would later run for governor.)

Editorial Blasts Senate Backsliding

On February 3, 1991, *The State* ripped a South Carolina Senate committee for reversing its position on the previous week in banning lobbyists handouts to legislators and then deciding in the next week to again allow such corrupting gratuities. *The State* also denounced the House for flip-flopping on its December, 1990, ban on lobbyists gifts.

The editorial accused both the Senate and the House of thumbing their noses at an outraged public at a time when 11 legislators had been indicted for bribery and drugs. Certainly, the love of free food, free liquor, and free trips as well as cash gifts of money had addicted many officials who had lived in a culture at the State House of parasitical dependency on special interest largesse and bribery.

"State lawmakers who earlier had OK'd the practice of accepting free meals from lobbyists reversed themselves last week and OK'd it again," *The State* wrote indignantly, adding, "They thumbed their noses at an electorate fed up with scandals and corruption."

Noting that the House had acted at the urging of Speaker Bob Sheheen to stop all meals, gifts, and anything of value from the lobbyists, *The State* wrote, "Last week, the House backed off. In a 54-53 vote, representatives rescinded its own rule and decided influence peddlers could wine and dine them after all, up to 25 bucks a throw."

Rep. Candy Waites (D-Richland) blasted the House for changing its total ban on lobbyists' gratuities to a lower standard of allowing lobbyists to give legislators meals for free of a value of not more than $25. Waites said, "What are we going to do next week?"

The State also blamed the Senate which had a subcommittee working on an omnibus ethics reform bill for first adopting a total ban on lobbyists' gifts to officials and then accepting a provision which would allow meals to be given up to $25.

The State denounced the flip-flopping of both the House and Senate on the issue of banning lobbyists' freebies, alleging that, "The actions of both chambers did nothing t re-establish public trust that's at an all-time low."

By contrast, *The State* praised the leadership of Sen. Glenn McConnell who "supported a complete ban on freebies from lobbyists after listening to his constituents." McConnell explained, "The perception I get, at least from the comments back home...is that the atmosphere has got to be adjusted. It's the free lunch that leads to the free trip to the golf course; the free trip to the golf course leads to the weekend away, and the weekend away that leads to the trip out of state." McConnell concluded, the gratuities culture created practices that "become so informal until it can seduce the members into going the wrong way."

The State's editorial of February 3, 1991, further pointed out that Sen. Glenn McConnell's observation that lobbyists' gratuities to officials desensitized them to the dangers of corruption over a period of time was, in fact, true. The editorial said, "Senator McConnell's colleagues should take heed. The 'no-cup-of-coffee' rule is no panacea, but it should be one piece of an overall ethics reform package."

The newspaper also pointed out Gov. Carroll Campbell's complaint that lawyer-legislators were taking and hiding big retainer fees from clients seeking to influence legislation.

The editors concluded by writing, "Operation Lost Trust had proved the need for tougher regulation of lobbyists, legislators and campaign financing."

Legislative Rules Differences Criticized

The State on February 4, 1991, published an essay in which it pointed out the differences in the rules of the House from those of the Senate in that the House imposed suspension on indictment and expulsion on conviction of a felony by Rule 3.12, whereas the Senate did not have mandatory suspension rules on indictment and only provided for expulsion on conviction of a felony.

The fact that senators could hold their seats and participate in the legislative functions while under indictment seemed to demand a remedy. As it stood, only if an indicted senator volunteered to take a suspension could he be excluded from official activities prior to conviction and expulsion by a vote of the Senate. Even conviction of a felony by itself did not trigger automatic expulsion which required a vote by a majority of senators.

Legislators' Pay Detailed

The Associated Press published an article in *The State* on February 4, 1991, which provided in detail the amounts of money that legislators received in pay and reimbursements.

The article started with the $10,000 per year salary paid to each legislator. Then it pointed out that recently convicted corruptionist, former Sen. Rick Lee (R-Spartanburg) had also taken $21,000 in expense money reimbursements in 1990, the same year he was indicted. Lee was joined by another eleven legislators who took $20,000 or more in 1990 expense payments.

Whereas House Speaker Bob Sheheen (D-Kershaw) only got $6,902 in expenses, Rep. Toney L. Farr (D-Union) took $43,401, even though he was only a low-ranking legislator. He was also a paid consultant to the S.C. Employment Security Commission.

For an average session of 23 weeks from January to June of each year, legislators normally received a minimum of $9,425 for expenses.

Corruptionists Replaced

The voids by the indictment and resignation of Speaker Pro Tem Jack I. Rogers and the death of Sen. Jack Lindsay left two seats vacant in Marlboro County. Doug Jennings was elected to replace Rogers and former Sen. Gene Carmichael announced for the Lindsay vacancy.

Carmichael, himself, had a dubious history, having been convicted in a massive vote-buying conspiracy in his previous term in office and sent to prison. Carmichael would later be elected in spite of his sordid past.

House Freebies in Limbo

The waffling of the House on whether to allow freebies from lobbyists entangled members in a conflict between House Rule 11.10, which they had just passed in their organizational session in December, 1990, and their efforts in early 1991 to allow House members to take limited free meals from lobbyists under a newer rule.

House Ethics Committee Chairman Wes Hayes (D-York) admitted that the two rules needed to be reviewed but that changing a House rule required a super-majority vote. Speaker Bob Sheheen, a harsh critic of the legislative tendency to leech off of the lobbyists, wanted to keep the new no-cup-of-coffee rule and seemed amused by the fallibility of those who wanted handouts from lobbyists, observing, "They've still got a problem."

Ethics Bills Move

In early February, 1991, both the Senate and House were slowly moving forward on ethics reform. The Senate was working on bills to address the abusive relationships of lobbyists and officials and the problem of conflicts of interest between official duties and private business and financial interests. The House was also set to discuss statutory ethics reform in addition to the new House rules designed to control lobbyists' handouts.

House Minority Leader Terry Haskins (R-Greenville) explained that now the House was dealing with "a very critical stage in the development of ethics legislation," that is passing new laws, whereas in December, the House had passed new rules just for the House, mostly designed to show and "demonstrate to the public that we are ethical people and we are going to get tough on ourselves." Haskins predicted what would be written in the next few weeks would be what would eventually be passed into law.

Ethics Bill—Weak or Strong?

Early in 1991, it was not clear whether the ethics reform bills working their way through the Senate and House would be real or cosmetic. The Senate was leaning toward a mere disclosure bill, but the House seemed to want to crack down on lobbyists' freebies, campaign finance abuses, and conflicts of interest.

Common Cause/South Carolina Executive Director John Crangle argued in the subcommittees and in the media that a bill which contained only disclosure requirements and no more would be a fraud and a betrayal of the public interest. Crangle expressed disappointment in the Senate subcommittee and its focus only on disclosure and he blamed the House for backing down on its new rule banning lobbyists' freebies. He said that unless the leadership of the House and Senate got tough and the public demanded real reform, then nothing would be accomplished in the 1991 session.

Speaker Bob Sheheen (D-Kershaw) said that he was hopeful, but that it was unclear to him whether the final bill would rely only on disclosure or whether it would include real bans and restrictions on abusive dealings with lobbyists, campaign finance excesses, and conflicts of interest.

House and Senate Split on Ethics Reform

Since the new session began in early 1991, the House and Senate were divided over what reform philosophy would be followed in drafting a new ethics reform bill. This division would continue into the summer of 1991 when the conference committee on the ethics reform bill finally hashed out the bill that was passed on September 23, 1991.

The Senate view was that a reform philosophy of requiring extensive disclosure of money spent by lobbyists on officials and of legislators' work before state boards and commissions would be sufficient. Such a philosophy would leave untouched the abusive practices of lobbyists giving unlimited freebies to officials. Sen. Majority Leader Isadore Lourie (D-Richland) remarked, "I think everybody's reached fundamental agreement about lobbyist regulation and legislators' disclosure. Full and complete disclosure by legislators." Lourie sat on the subcommittee working on the ethics bill and appeared to be satisfied with the mere disclosure requirements rather than the bans.

House wants Tougher Ethics Reform

The soft Senate approach to ethics reform which claimed that new disclosure laws would cure the ethical candor at the State House did not sell with many House members who had seen 13% of their colleagues and leaders go down in Lost Trust indictments and convictions.

Perhaps the difference in approach was due to the fact that only one back-bench senator had been convicted by early 1991, whereas the House had lost its newly elected Speaker Pro Tem, Jack I. Rogers, to a multi-count racketeering indictment for corruption on waste management, tax, and betting bills. Perhaps the House members who had gone through elections in 1990, whereas the Senate had not, had been forced to face the wrath of the voters and had heard plenty during their campaigns for re-election.

In any case, the House wanted to put the clamps on the lobbyists and end business as usual at the State House. House Judiciary Committee Chairman, David Wilkins, correctly predicted that the final ethics reform bill would rely on both disclosure and restrictions, noting that, "Those two philosophies run throughout the legislation, and I think the final comprehensive bill will be some combination of both."

Corruption in Arizona Legislature Exposed

In early February, 1991, just as the South Carolina General Assembly was getting serious about passing major ethics reforms to control state officials and lobbyists, the Phoenix, Arizona, police department revealed a sting operation which caught seven state legislators and seven lobbyists in bribery and money laundering.

The Arizona sting operation was based on legislative proposals to legalize gambling in the state. The sting not only exposed a pay-to-play political culture in Arizona state government, but also exposed serious conflicts of interests affecting state officials.

The well-publicized scandal in Arizona seemed to emphasize the national problem of corruption in state governments, especially among legislators and lobbyists. The scandal certainly did not hurt the efforts of reformers who were pushing for drastic ethics reforms in both South Carolina and Arizona.

Ethics Reform Bill Moves Forward

Decimated by the falling ranks of indicted House colleagues, most recently the Speaker Pro Tem Jack I. Rogers, the House faced a growing public demand and intense media pressure to take serious measures to stop the corruption. February 6, 1991, was the day on which the House Judiciary Committee set a hearing on the draft ethics reform bill which dealt with lobbying reform, campaign disclosure, and new ethics rules.

The hearing included a poll on the question of both lobbyists' freebies and disclosure issues.

Lobbyists Freebies Detailed

In response to the demand letters sent out in January, 1991, by new Secretary of State Jim Miles just after he deposed his conflicted and inert predecessor, John Campbell, the lobbyists were sending in disclosure forms with real and detailed information about the extent to which the lobbyists had infiltrated state government and cultivated symbiotic relationships with key legislators.

The South Carolina Coin Operators Association which lobbied for the big money video poker industry gave Rep. John Tucker (D-Anderson) $212 for tickets to the ACC Basketball Tournament according to its first filing under the Miles regime.

Lobbyist Carolyn Matthews, a contract lobbyist with multiple clients, paid $97 for tickets to the Charlotte Hornets NBA game for Reps. Sam Foster and John Hayes, both York County Democrats. Matthews also gave a pass in 1990 to the Masters Golf Tournament to a constituent of Sen. Ed Saleeby (D-Darlington).

The S.C. Trial Lawyers Association gave $126 to the re-election campaign of Rep. Billy Keesley (D-Edgefield).

Miles was working with a list of lobbyists which started alphabetically of which he was demanding more details and sending out letters of notice with deadlines stated for compliance. Most of the lobbyists contacted chose to comply as required by Miles.

Miles Demands More Lobbyists' Disclosure

Combing through newly filed lobbyists' disclosure forms for 1990 coming into his office, freshman Secretary of State Jim Miles found lots of evidence of lobbyists giving legislators free tickets to professional sporting events, free trips, and free campaign fund-raising events. But he was still not satisfied.

Miles demanded that lobbyists give him more details. He said that it was no longer acceptable for lobbyists to report aggregate amounts spent on entertainment as they had done on their 1990 disclosure reports when John Campbell was in office and taking campaign contributions from lobbyists.

Even so, what had showed up in early 1991 gave Miles plenty of interesting examples of officials living off the lobbyists like parasites on an elephant. For example, Michelin Tire Corp. gave Rep. Paul Derrick (R-Lexington) car tires worth $307 before Derrick was convicted of bribery in Lost Trust later in 1991. Michelin also reported that its lobbyist hosted Reps. Howell Clyborne (R-Greenville) and David Wilkins (R-Greenville) at the Clay Court Tennis Championship at Kiawah Island at a cost of $1,166.

Miles Presses S.C. Textile Manufacturers

Although most lobbyists and their clients quickly and quietly complied with the new demands of Secretary of State Jim Miles for more detailed disclosure filings, the South Carolina Textile Manufacturers Association took a defiant position, Its president, Harold Kingsmore, wrote back to Miles that the Association's lobbyist should not be told by Miles to report more details about his lobbying and spending because the lobbyist, Jerry Beasley, had already filed what the previous Secretary of State, John Campbell, as required under Campbell's interpretation and application of the 1975 Ethics Act's disclosure provisions.

Jay Bender, an attorney for the South Carolina Press Association, wrote back to Miles that more disclosure on his part would violate the attorney-client privilege. This was an anomalous position in that the Press Association had long advocated more disclosure of public matters. Then the Association directed Bender to reply and he wrote Miles that he had, in fact, spent nothing entertaining legislators.

Bender had previously questioned Miles' authority to compel disclosure of expenses by lobbyists, but Miles insisted he had such powers and threatened to refer any non-compliant lobbyists and their clients to the Attorney General for enforcement action.

Speaker Sheheen Target of Critics

The South Carolina Policy Council criticized Speaker Bob Sheheen, just re-elected to his position, over the embattled and embarrassed House, for taking legal fees from the cooperative electrical associations in South Carolina.

On the other hand, *The State* newspaper published a picture on February 6, 1991, of Sheheen with a sign around his neck reading, "I don't do lunch", perhaps pointing to the fact that Sheheen had disbanded the predatory "Fat and Ugly Caucus" which had been shaking down lobbyists for years for free food, free drinks, and other gratuities. Sheheen was also at the center of a growing debate about the issue of whether the new reform bill being put together as the scandal worsened would ban lobbyists' handouts.

Irate Citizens Demand Reform

If the members of the General Assembly came to Columbia for the 1991 session thinking they could get away with passing a fake ethics bill because nobody was watching, they soon found out that, in fact, they were under a microscope.

Sen. Kay Patterson (D-Richland), a chronic cynic about ethics reform efforts, dismissed the whole ethics controversy as one in which there was no real public interest. Patterson had long taken the position that Operation Lost Trust was a white man's scheme to persecute blacks in the legislature.

But some citizens resented Patterson's rhetoric and racial spin on the Lost Trust scandal and made it known by coming to the State House on February 6, 1991, to tell legislators that they wanted a real reform bill and that the people of South Carolina were, in fact, fed up with corruption, inside games, and money-grubbing of politicians.

Ervin Dargan came from Darlington to tell members at the House hearing on ethics reform that, "Most people I know are disgusted." He wanted term limits. Roy Coffee came from Anderson to the State House to talk to legislators for the first time in his life, stating that prior to Lost Trust, "I just hadn't been that mad before." Coffee wanted limits on campaign donations. Janice Timms, a self-described voter and housewife, said that ordinary people were being drowned out by the paid lobbyists in Columbia.

Janice Timms told the House public hearing on the ethics reform bill, that although she was just a housewife and ordinary citizen, she was very concerned, adding, "I'm worried that lobbyists may have your ear because of the meals, the gifts and the trips. I'm really embarrassed by the sting." She also objected to the use of campaign funds for non-campaign purposes, contrary to the subcommittee's view.

Also testifying before the House hearing on the ethics bill was Secretary of State Jim Miles, who argued that his office should retain jurisdiction over lobbyists. But Alice Shorter of the State Ethics Commission said that jurisdiction over lobbyists should be placed with the Commission.

The South Carolina Chamber of Commerce sent Ken Oilschlager to tell the subcommittee that the Chamber did not object to new law which would limit campaign contributions, but said that businesses and corporations should still be allowed to donate.

Subcommittee chairman Wes Hayes (D-York) said he was very impressed by the citizens who took the time to come and tell the subcommittee what they thought, commenting, "They spoke volumes about what the people are thinking out there.... We've got to restore public confidence."

Arizona Sting Shows Bribery

In 1991, the undercover sting operation conducted by the Phoenix City Police Department and the Maricopa County prosecutors office continued to expose state legislators taking payoffs from undercover agents. The sting was revealed just at the time the state legislature was preparing to cut funding for law enforcement in Arizona. Defense attorneys for accused legislators alleged retaliation by local law enforcement.

The Arizona sting was similar to Operation Lost Trust in South Carolina except that the FBI, not local law enforcement, did the sting operation in South Carolina.

In both Arizona and South Carolina, legislators were caught taking payoffs to vote for a betting bill and the bribes were captured on videotapes. One senator was recorded as saying when he took a bribe of $15,000 in cash, "How do you launder this much?" But unlike South Carolina where no women were caught taking bribes (Rep. Donna Moss was charged with cocaine and pleaded), one Arizona corruptionist was a woman, Senate majority whip, Carolyn Walker. One Arizona House member said, "My favorite line is, 'What's in it for me?'"

Arizona had been hit in 1988 with the impeachment of its governor and also two of its U.S. Senators were tangled in the Keating Five scandal going on in Congress at the same time as Operation Lost Trust.

The Arizona bribery sting operation was called "Desert Shame." It used large amounts of money to bribe legislators and may have had some impact on the elections if the money was used to finance campaigns of those who took the bribes. This provoked a call by the Arizona Civil Liberties Union for an investigation to see if the police sting was violating voters' rights Two of those later indicted for corruption were elected by narrow margins.

Desert Shame took a heavy toll on public officials and the political class. Seven legislators, one justice of the peace, a former director of the Arizona Democratic Party, a former jail guard, and five others who were either lobbyists or activists were indicted for conspiracy to bribe and launder money. The same 15 indicted were charged with civil racketeering and some had already had their property seized by the government.

The indictment alleged that the seven legislators had taken bribes of more than $100,000 in cash from an undercover police sting informant posing as a consultant to the casino gambling interests who sought to legalize casinos in Arizona.

Prosecutors said that both of the candidates for governor, Republican Fife Symington and Democrat Terry Goddard, took money from the informant. Both were running in the primary elections set for February 26, 1991, and both promised to return the money, saying they had no reason to believe the money was tainted.

Both candidates had issues. Symington had been accused by U.S. Sen. Howard Metzenbaum (D-Ohio) of violating federal conflict of interest laws in arranging a large loan for himself from a savings and loan association that was seized by the government on February 17, 1989. Goddard had issues about how he got a loan on favorable terms.

In addition, both Arizona U.S. Senators were entangled in problems related to their taking contributions from Charles Keating and his role in saving and loan failures in the southwest, a set of transactions known as the "Keating Five."

Senate Panel Backs Gift Ban

Sen. Tom Pope (D-Newberry) dropped the bomb at a Senate Committee hearing on February 12, 1991, in moving proposed legislation to totally ban all gift-giving by lobbyists to public officials. The motion passed 11-6.

The Senate ethics reform bill then included a ban on all free handouts to legislators as well as a limit on campaign contributions. Both provisions were direct drastic attacks on the culture of corruption at the State House which had spawned Lost Trust.

The Senate, in fact, was in a public shoot-out to show who was the toughest enemy of corruption with the House, which was unwilling to bite the bullet and back real reforms. The House, where by far the most legislators caught in the scandal were found, first passed and then rescinded a "no-cup-of-coffee" rule, which would have banned freebies.

Sen. Glenn McConnell (R-Charleston) took a line of argument that resonated with the Senate when he ridiculed the weak House ethics bill and contrasted it unfavorably with the Senate's bold frontal assault on corruption in banning all handouts to legislators. A common prejudice among senators was that the House was populated by immature and foolish bottom-feeders and small-time hustlers.

The South Carolina Senate suddenly reversed itself in a committee meeting on February 12, 1991, and decided to totally ban lobbyists' handouts to legislators and other public officials. The previous week the Senate Judiciary Committee had backed away from a proposal by Senate leaders to impose a flat ban on lobbyists' gratuities to officials.

The previous week the Senate decided instead to go back to a previous proposal which would allow lobbyists to spend $25 per day on officials up to a total of $200 per year per person and would also allow a lobbyist to pay up to $300 per year for a trip for a legislator.

On February 12, Sen. Thomas Pope (D-Newberry) said that he wanted to return to a consensus view in the Senate in 1990 formulated immediately after the Lost Trust scandal broke to impose a total ban on lobbyists' handouts. The new plan passed the committee by a vote of 11-6.

The committee also approved new campaign finance reform proposals and prepared to deal with the conflict of interest problem, a contentious issue in and of itself. The committee approved a limit of $500 per election per source on contributions to candidates for statewide office and a limit of $250 per election per source for donations to candidates seeking legislative and local offices. The previous week the committee had agreed to higher limits of 2,000 and $1,000 respectively.

Senate Proposes Campaign Finance Bill

Reacting to the exposure of large amounts of political money being handed out on videotape by crooked lobbyist Ron Cobb to grasping legislators, the Senate on February 12, 1991, moved in its Judiciary Committee to crack down on big money donors by limiting donations to only $500 for statewide candidates and $250 for all others. The lower limits were supported by a group of Democrats and Republicans who felt that money was out of control at the State House and that citizens back home knew it.

One of the suspects in the Lost Trust probe who would eventually be convicted of bribery was also a proponent of new strict limits on campaign donations. Sen. Bud Long (D-Horry) said to the committee that he "wanted to get the government back into the hands of the little people." And Sen. Glenn McConnell (R-Charleston) told the committee that senators were listening to the demands of their constituents for reform, remarking that, "I think what the committee did today was to send a message that we hear what they want and that we're responding. I hope that it will meet with that kind of reception now on the floor of the Senate."

The Senate's action to strictly limit campaign contributions and ban handouts contradicted the criticism from the House that the Senate was weak on reform in its previous position of allowing such handouts. The Senate also was aware that the House had just weakened its newly adopted rules banning lobbyists from buying meals for legislators. Sen. Glenn McConnell derided the House ethics reform bill as narrow and weak.

Dick Greer's Drugs Exposed

The widely expected exposure of Dick Greer was announced on February 12, 1991. He had been fingered by an FBI informant in the Lost Trust probe.

Greer had been named by federal authorities in federal court when three defendants in the probe demanded that informant and prosecution witness Ron Cobb reveal if he had any drug dealings with Greer, who had not yet been indicted.

Gov. Carroll Campbell, a friend and political ally of Greer for many years, said that the Dick Greer described in court was not the same person he had known for many years and had appointed to Chairman of the Development Board and chairman of his re-election campaign.

Greer had repeatedly denied using drugs or being involved in any crimes, although he was known to be a poker player at the Town House Hotel with politicians in games which sometimes involved large sums of money.

FBI documents showed that Ron Cobb had told the FBI on May 1, 1989, nearly two years before, that he used cocaine with Greer and had procured cocaine for Greer. At the time of the FBI interview, Cobb was making a deal to avoid prosecution in return for cooperation in the sting.

The exposure of the fact that Rob Cobb had told the FBI he knew of Greer's cocaine issues was forced by the lawyers for Rep. Ennis Fant (D-Greenville), Rep. Larry Blanding (D-Sumter), and Rep. B.J. Gordon (D-Williamsburg) who were all under indictment for corruption and expected to be denounced by Rob Cobb as prosecution witness.

The FBI 302 form produced in court on February 12, 1991, recited that Ron Cobb had told the FBI on May 1, 1989, that he and Greer and Cobb's girlfriend had used cocaine on a trip to Charleston in May, 1988. The document also said that Greer and Cobb had been involved in using, buying and distributing cocaine. The auto in which they traveled to Charleston was identified as a Cadillac loaned to them by Tom Collins, a lobbyist for National Advanced Systems who was later indicted on drug charges.

While Lionel Lofton, attorney for the three House members, was demanding the exposure of the documents related to Greer and others who were not named, the fundamental issue was full disclosure to the defendants of all prosecution evidence related to their cases. But to Gov. Campbell the problem was his political ties with political ally Greer, and the governor denied that anything Greer had done was a reflection on Campbell and his office. Democratic leaders Sen. Isadore Lourie (D-Richland) and Sen. Ernest Passailague (D-Charleston) told the media that the charges came as no surprise.

Cobb Detailed Drug Trip with Greer

Ron Cobb finally told the public in *The State* newspaper the details of a trip that he said he took to Charleston with Dick Greer in 1988 in which they both snorted cocaine. But Greer told WYFF-TV in Greenville that the allegations were false, saying that Cobb had no credibility.

Gov. Carroll Campbell appeared to stick up for Greer and told the media on February 13, 1991, that his family and the family of Greer had been friends for many years and that he was "disturbed and saddened by what was said about Dick Greer." The governor added, "I think it's unfortunate that those type things surfaced the way they did and without any chance of refutation." But as to the merits of the allegations about Greer, the governor refused to comment. Campbell would not respond to an inquiry from the media as to whether he had ever talked to Greer about the drug issue, but the governor's office only admitted that Campbell and Greer had met for about an hour on February 12, 1991.

Bartender Caught in Sting

Al Frakes, the bartender at Beau's bar and restaurant in the Carolina Hotel across Assembly Street from the State House, was busted by the Richland County Sheriff's Department on May 25, 1989, for dealing drugs. Then on January 19, 1990, Frakes was arrested at Beau's for cocaine possession.

Frakes knew who was using drugs and he rolled over on them in return for a lenient deal from law enforcement.

In fact, Ron Cobb had told the FBI on May 1, 1989, that he had bought cocaine from Frakes, setting the stage for Frakes' demise.

Beau's bar was a favorite hangout of lobbyists and legislators and their ilk, especially on Tuesday and Wednesday evenings while the Legislature was in session from January to June of each year. Special interests and their lobbyists set up open bar tabs at Beau's for all legislators and paid for all the food and drinks that legislators used at the establishment.

Senate Waffles on Ethics Enforcement

The issue of who would enforce ethics laws, especially new and much stricter ethics standards, provoked fear in some senators. They liked the old and ineffective system of internal legislative ethics committees made up of fellow senators rather than less friendly outsiders.

As a result, proposals to transfer jurisdiction over ethics enforcement to the State Ethics Commission in cases involving legislators was seen as a threat and met widespread and ultimately fatal opposition from the senators.

The Senate Judiciary Committee rejected a proposal to shift jurisdiction over legislators to the State Ethics Commission and spurned a plan to give the Commission the power to start investigations on its own motion of legislators even without the filing of a citizen's complaint.

Sen. Joe Wilson (R-Lexington) told the senators that citizens, in fact, were afraid to file complaints for fear of retaliation and that the burden of proving such complaints was placed on the complainant, although many complainants were without sufficient legal knowledge to prove their complaints in a hearing.

Judge Orders Revelations on Greer

The judge in the Lost Trust trial ordered the prosecution to reveal more information on Dick Greer's reported use of cocaine while handling Gov. Campbell's campaigns and acting as Chairman of the S.C. Economic Development Board. The order was the result of a demand by attorneys for three defendant legislators in the sting.

The judge also ordered the disclosure of all other officials who took bribes from informant Ron Cobb.

The reason why the judge ordered the release of drug evidence from the prosecution to the defense attorneys was that the defendants were entitled to know of admissible evidence of drug use if a witness was under the influence of drugs when he witnessed an event or when he was testifying in a legal proceeding.

Cobb Pressured to Disclose Prior Bribes

Prosecutors were faced with the fact that, due to the trial court's order, they had to reluctantly disclose some facts about Ron Cobb that they might have preferred to keep secret. Cobb had to tell the identities of all persons he bribed before he went undercover for the FBI and he had to reveal if he was under the influence of drugs when he witnessed events about which he testified in court and, further, if he was under the influence when he was actually giving testimony.

In ordering the discovery of the prosecution evidence requested, the court made the information available to the media and the public.

Attorney General Forces Lobbyists' Disclosure

The request of Secretary Jim Miles, who demanded that lobbyists register and disclose to the 1975 Ethics Act, were met with defiance by some big money lobbyists. Attorney General Travis Medlock backed Miles and decisively took enforcement action. Medlock ordered recalcitrant, check-grabbing, big shot lobbyist, Jerry Beasley, of the S.C. Textile Manufacturers, to stop his refusals to comply and Medlock directed Beasley to register and disclose as demanded by Miles.

Beasley initially refused to provide detailed expenditure disclosures and reported only a lump sum amount of $99,000. It was well known, in fact, that Beasley had a big expense account and liked to buy food, drinks, and golf trips for politicians. He was also the most belligerent lobbyist in fighting new ethics proposals as well as the most defiant of lobbyists who did not want to comply with existing law. He seemed to feel that as lobbyist for SCTM he was above the law.

The S.C. Textile Manufacturers in the end backed down when hit by Medlock's order and agreed to comply with the registration and disclosure provisions of the 1975 Ethics Act. At the same time the Textile Manufacturers Association continued their fight to block new and stricter ethics reform proposals then being considered by the House and Senate.

Suspect Legislators in Limbo

Seven legislators still in their seats in the 1991 session were known to be FBI targets in Lost Trust. Ten other legislators had already been indicted in 1990 and Rep. Luther Taylor (D-Richland) had been convicted on multiple counts in October of the year.

Although the general elections of 1990 had presented voters with a chance to remove those legislators suspected in the scandal, they were all re-elected. This happened in part because the sting had not been announced until mid-July, a month after the primary elections had been held and those who would later be fingered by the FBI had neither primary nor general opposition in gerrymandered districts with little, if any, electoral competition even in normal elections.

Even so, fellow legislators noted that while they were under a cloud of suspicion, those known as targets still kept coming to the sessions and committee meetings of the session. But they all were viewed in an unfavorable light. Rep. David Wright (R-Lexington) remarked, "They're all very aware of what the news media is doing, the pictures that have been taken, the videotaping in the chamber. It's almost like you're guilty by association. I don't know that that's fair." Rep. Lenoir Sturkie (D-Lexington) remarked, "You can't allow a person to be tried and found guilty through the media." Rep. Will McCain (R-Orangeburg) said, "Obviously, they're uncomfortable.... They seem to be somber about the whole thing."

Life Changes for Tainted Legislators

On February 18, 1991, *The State* published an article focusing on the legislators who had been implicated in the Lost Trust investigation. Those in focus had not yet been indicted but were likely suspects as they were reported in the media as targets of the probe.

Rep. Tim Wilkes (D-Fairfield) was an example of a person whose life had been blown off course by the FBI's sting operation. Before he was fingered as a likely prospect for indictment, Wilkes had been a macho and flamboyant figure who had even gone surfboarding on the rising tides churned up by Hurricane Hugo in 1989. But after he came under a cloud of suspicion he changed. "Tim Wilkes, total difference," said new Speaker Pro Tem David Beasley (D-Darlington), adding, "He's quieter. He's less outspoken, less vocal."

Wilkes was one of a total of seven known to be FBI targets since the late summer of 1990 who had not yet been indicted as of the middle of February, 1991. The others in limbo at the time were Reps. Ken Bailey (D-Orangeburg), Paul Derrick (R-Lexington), Jim Faber (D-Richland) and Frank McBride (D-Richland). The sixth was actually a former legislator in the House, Judge Tee Ferguson, elected to the circuit bench in April, 1990, while under secret investigation by the FBI.

And Sen. Bud Long (D-Horry) rounded out that list. All would soon be charged starting February 20, 1991.

Senators Flip-Flop on Real Reforms

The Senate Judiciary Committee was the continuing scene of major battles over new ethics reforms being proposed. Those who wanted a wholesale cleanup wrangled with those who hated to give up the easy ways of the past.

The Committee on February 5, 1991, had taken an original reform bill crafted by Sen. Williams and Sen. Saleeby which banned all free handouts to public officials from lobbyists seeking favors, but on the same day, the Committee had amended the bill to again allow lobbyists to give meals of $25 or less and free trips as well. This was clearly a step back from a clean sweep reform bill.

Then on February 12, 1991, a second committee meeting was hit by angry public testimony demanding the "no-cup-of-coffee" rule, a complete ban on freebies. The committee again changed directions and adopted the "no-cup-of-coffee" rule once more. It was obvious that the public outcry had a beneficial effect on the politicians and was coercing them to adopt distasteful reforms which cramped their life styles as public officials.

In addition to citizen testimony at House and Senate ethics reform hearings, some citizens went so far as to buy advertising demanding serious reforms.

The Sumter Item on February 17, 1991, published a full page ad paid for by citizens demanding action. Signed by 78 Sumter County citizens, the ad, paid by voluntary donations raised by Bill Britton, castigated House efforts to rescind the "no-cup-of-coffee" rule and demanded a flat ban on freebies.

Among the prominent citizens signing the public letter in *The Sumter Item* were the Chairman of the Board of National Bank of South Carolina, Marvin Trapp, two former mayors, the former chair of the Sumter City Council, and the Mayor of the town of Pinewood, S.C.

Lobbyists Buy Influence at State House

Lobbyists try to create a sense of obligation in politicians in order to control them, said *The State* in a February 20, 1991, editorial. Noting the similarity of the Lost Trust sting to the Arizona sting, the editors wrote that seven legislators and eleven others were charged in Arizona.

In both cases, an apathetic public allowed gross abuses and corruption to go on far too long.

Senate Struggles with Reforms

A Senate committee on February 19, 1991, finally agreed to amendments in their ethics reform bill to require legislators to disclose the income received for representation before state agencies. At the same time, the committee rejected Gov. Campbell's proposals to ban lawyer-legislators from appearing before state agencies.

In addition, the bill included a mandatory one year delay before former legislators could begin to work as lobbyists. This was designed to slow the revolving door whereby in the past legislators would leave the General Assembly and immediately hire on as lobbyists at the State House.

Sen. Kay Patterson (D-Richland), a politician who had made a career out of windy rhetoric, often racially inflammatory, and living off of politics, argued strenuously against any ban on lobbyists' gifts to public officials, but without success. Patterson, who had no job in real life, especially liked the fawning of white lobbyists who wanted favors.

Three Lobbyists Indicted for Drugs

Three more persons were indicted on February 20, 1991, by the federal grand jury in Columbia and the U.S. Attorney's office identified them to the public.

All three of them were lobbyists charged with drug crimes.

Martin G. Rohling, a lobbyist for Household International, Inc., was charged with possession of cocaine. Rohling also took Rep. Paul Derrick to Pebble Beach, California. Derrick was later convicted of corruption.

James Randall Lee, a lobbyist for the South Carolina Health Care Association, was charged with possession of marijuana. Lee was known to play poker at the Town House Hotel.

Thomas E. Collins, lobbyist for Hitachi Data Systems, was charged with two counts of possession of cocaine dating from 1987 and 1988 and also with possession with intent to distribute. Collins was known to be a hanger-on with Ron Cobb and was regarded as a suspicious character.

Three More House Members Indicted

Three more legislators, all from the Midlands of South Carolina, were indicted on February 20, 1991, in Columbia. This piled the body count up to 14 since August, 1990. The three were all House members.

Paul Wayne Derrick (R-Lexington), was charged with conspiring to extort a bribe on the betting bill and for taking $1,000 cash bribe on the bill.

Frank Earl McBride (D-Richland), was charged with conspiracy to violate the Hobbs Act as was James Faber (D-Richland).

With the addition of McBride and Faber, the total number of Black Caucus legislators indicted was six out of a total caucus membership of twenty.

Letters Demand Reform

The State published a letter on February 21, 1991, by Robert J. Moore demanding ethics reforms and especially a total ban on lobbyists' gratuities.

Moore was a member of the State Governing Board of Common Cause/South Carolina which had been demanding ethics reform at the State House even before the sting broke in the media. He was also a history professor at Columbia College.

Moore pointed to the public outcry over Lost Trust and condemned the House vote to allow lobbyists to give freebies to public officials. He demanded a total prohibition of all gratuities by lobbyists.

Nancy Means of Columbia also published a letter the same day demanding that lobbyists be stopped from handing out gratuities to officials.

Cobb Busted Again for Drugs

Ron Cobb had agreed with the prosecution that he would clean up his act and cooperate as a condition of immunity, but he could not behave himself. The U.S. Attorney charged Cobb with possession of cocaine on February 21, 1991, alleging that Cobb had possessed cocaine twice on February 22, 1990, shortly after his first apprehension for drugs.

The charge revealed that Cobb had cocaine while he was serving as a sting agent and also as a witness in Lost Trust. Cobb's use of drugs in violation of his agreement with federal authorities made him even more dubious as a prosecution witness at trial allowing defense lawyers to attack his character and credibility even more than before.

At the time he was indicted for cocaine on February 21, 1991, Ron Cobb's deal with the prosecution came out. It was revealed that the prosecution agreed that Cobb would not have to testify against Sen. Jack Lindsay and further agreed to give Cobb immunity on his original cocaine crimes.

Cobb also claimed at the time that a total of 50 defendants would be charged and that the indictments and prosecutions would continue until 1994. As it turned out, a total of 28 defendants were actually charged and the final indictments came in the summer of 1991. It is unclear on what basis, if any, Cobb predicted the 50 indictments, but perhaps he knew that the government could indict that many defendants based on the evidence which Cobb may have known about when he made the predictions.

Fight in Senate Over Lobbyists' Cash

The fight to crush the corrupt influence of big money lobbyists who gave free gifts and large campaign donations heated up in the Senate in late February, 1991, in committee meetings.

A vote to allow the continuation of lobbyists' campaign donations to legislators split. Voting to allow the money were Sens. James Bryan, Isadore Lourie, John Matthews, Tom Moore, Kay Patterson, and Ed Saleeby—all Democrats.

Voting to ban lobbyists' money were Sens. John Courson, Thomas Pope, Glenn McConnell, Samuel Stilwell, and Joe Wilson—all Republicans, except for Sen. Pope.

Sen. McConnell warned that so-called campaign contributions could, in fact, be nothing more than disguised bribes. McConnell had also expressed his concerns about the corrupting effects of lobbyists giving free meals, drinks, gifts, and trips to public officials.

Another issue faced by the meeting was whether to limit the amount of campaign donations. The bill being considered proposed limits of $1,000 on donations from a single donor for candidates seeking statewide office, and $500 for legislative candidates.

The bill defined three election cycles on which the limits would apply—primary, run-off primary, and general.

The bill also imposed a total ban on lobbyists gifts to officials—the "no-cup-of-coffee" rule.

Fant Pleads Guilty

Another House member stopped protesting his innocence and pleaded guilty to bribery on February 22, 1991, right after three more House members were charged. Rep. Ennis Fant (D-Greenville) admitted he sold his vote for $1,300; charges of extortion were dropped as part of a plea deal. Represented by attorney Tommy Thomason, Fant said he took a bribe of $1,000 on February 15, 1990, in Cobb's office at the AT&T Building in downtown Columbia and took a second bribe of $300 on May 19, 1990.

Fant was the first black defendant to plead guilty while eight white legislators had already pleaded. Soon after Fant entered his guilty plea, other black House members would also plead guilty, including Frank McBride and James Faber, Richland County Democrats. By the time Fant entered his plea it had become obvious from the Luther Taylor trial that chances of acquittal at trial were dubious at best and a pleas with cooperation would elicit more leniency from the prosecution and court.

Blanding and Gordon Go to Trial

On February 24, 1991, the jury pool was assembled for the trials of Rep. Larry Blanding (D-Sumter) and Rep. B.J. Gordon (D-Williamsburg) who were tried jointly on similar corruption charges.

Blanding was charged with taking bribes of $1,000 on May 8, 1990, and $300 on the same date. Gordon was charged with taking a bribe of $1,000 on May 8, 1990.

The jury pool included a total of 88 called.

The selection of the jury in the trials of Blanding and Gordon was conducted behind closed doors in the interest of preventing outside influence and prejudice to the rights of the defendants. Closing the doors to the courtroom provoked adverse reactions from the media.

Citizens' Ad Demands Reform

Citizens bought an ad in the *Hartsville News and Press*, local newspaper in the hometown of Sen. Ed Saleeby (D-Darlington), and demanded that Sen. Saleeby, the original sponsor along with Sen. Marshall Williams (D-Orangeburg) of the Senate ethics bill, vote for a ban on lobbyists' campaign donations to legislators.

Signed by 60 citizens, the ad read, "We the people of South Carolina do care about ethics reform.... We will be watching."

Saleeby had flip-flopped on the issue of banning lobbyists' use of money to buy votes and influence at the State House, originally proposing the "no-cup-of-coffee" rule and then opposing it. He had also recently showed his support for continued lobbyists' campaign donations to legislators.

CHAPTER TWENTY ONE

PROSECUTIONS AND ETHICS REFORMS GAIN MOMENTUM

Gordon-Blanding Trials Disputed

Starting on February 28 1991, in U.S. District Court in Columbia, S.C., the opening phases of the trials of Rep. B.J. Gordon (D-Williamsburg) and Rep. Larry Blanding (D-Sumter) were marked by disputes. First, Judge Falcon Hawkins made a dubious ruling that the courtroom should be closed to the public and the media while the jury was selected. Then there was a dispute over testimony given to the grand jury.

Attorney Jay Bender, representing the South Carolina Press Association and other media, argued that the courtroom should not be closed for jury selection. The media took the position that open courtrooms were an essential part of the traditions of American justice and involved the First Amendment.

Then attorney Lionel Lofton, for Gordon, attacked the testimony given by prosecution witness Ron Cobb to the grand jury, alleging that Cobb's testimony was perjury. Lofton further argued that the prosecution was engaging in misconduct by using Cobb's testimony without revealing to the court the lies that Cobb had told. Then Lofton moved to dismiss all charges against Gordon on grounds of Cobb's dishonest testimony and prosecutorial misconduct.

Judge Hawkins did not grant the motion for dismissal in favor of Gordon.

Cobb Confesses at Gordon Trial

Ron Cobb appeared at the outset of the B.J. Gordon trial in Columbia and admitted that he agreed to cooperate with the FBI to avoid prison.

Cobb told about his bribery to fix the tax break for Greenville businessmen who hired him to lobby. Cobb said he also bribed recently deceased Sen. Jack Lindsay, giving him $10,000. He admitted he also gave $10,000 to recently deceased Rep. Tom Mangum (D-Lancaster), Chairman of House Ways and Means, to fix a bill to regulate gas prices in 1985 and 1986.

Cobb told the court that corruption was standard practice at the State House, calling it "a way of doing business in state government for along time." Cobb said he had bribed many legislators before. He said the sting was based on bribery. He also said he had given drugs to legislators and their friends to buy votes.

FBI agent Mike Clemens told the court that Cobb had used cocaine six times while an FBI sting agent, and the FBI had paid Cobb $60,000 for his work in the sting.

Cobb also told the court that the FBI sting was designed to target legislators that Cobb had bribed before the sting began and to bribe them again, but this time on television. Cobb mentioned the names of past accomplices and said specifically that he had previously dealt with Rep. Luther Taylor (D-Richland) and Rep. Bob Kohn (R-Charleston) in corrupt transactions.

Lobbyist Lee Testifies Against Blanding

Lobbyist Randy Lee told the court that he had paid a $137 hotel bill of Larry Blanding. Lee also paid for Blanding's $1,000 of meals at Griff's, a private club, in three legislative sessions. None of this was recorded on Blanding's disclosure forms at the House Ethics Committee, even though Blanding had demanded that Lee pay the bills.

Randy Lee was later convicted of a cocaine crime on guilty plea.

Randy Lee is not to be confused with Sen. Rick Lee (R-Spartanburg) who was one of the first defendants to plead guilty to selling his vote to Ron Cobb.

Taylor Turns State's Evidence

Convicted in October, 1990, former House member Luther Taylor returned from prison as a prosecution witness and took the stand in the trials of Larry Blanding and B.J. Gordon on March 5, 1991, in federal court in Columbia, testifying that he had recruited legislators to take bribes from Ron Cobb. Admitting he knew he had been bribed, Taylor joined another Lost Trust criminal, former legislator Robert Kohn, in telling the court that they had helped lure colleagues into the FBI sting over the betting bill.

Kohn said he targeted fellow House members that he had done corrupt business with in the past and further said that some bills were introduced as a scam. By this, Kohn meant that bills were introduced to do things which special interests were sure to either favor or oppose. This was done not because the sponsors really wanted to pass the bills, but because the sponsors could then ask special interests, especially businesses that wanted or opposed the bills, for money to push or stop the bills. Lobbyists would be involved who would recruit clients from affected parties. Whether the bills passed or not, both legislators and lobbyists had been able to shake down and profit off of the scheme.

Gordon and Blanding Trial

After closing the courtroom again and hearing a motion to dismiss which was denied on March 6, 1991, the trial of B.J. Gordon and Larry Blanding resumed the next day. Judge Falcon Hawkins denied dismissal saying the evidence produced in the trial was enough to convict.

Defense motions to sever the trial of Gordon from that of Blanding and motions to exclude Ron Cobb's testimony were also made and taken under advisement.

Senate Debates Ethics Reform Bill

Even as the Gordon and Blanding trials for bribery were just starting and Rep. Paul Derrick was being arraigned at the federal courthouse at the northern end of Assembly Street in downtown Columbia, the Senate was starting to debate the ethics reform bill at the southern end of Assembly Street in downtown Columbia.

With some sixty amendments pending, the Senate voted to limit fund-raising during the legislative session.

Sen. Glenn McConnell, an emerging Republican leader in the Senate, demanded action by the Senate and an end to stalling and vacillating which had affected the progress of the bill in committee.

Paul Derrick and Tom Collins Face Charges

On March 6, 1991, as the Gordon and Blanding trials were just starting, Rep. Paul Derrick (R-Lexington) was charged on grounds that he took a $1,000 bribe to vote for the betting bill and also on two counts of extortion.

At the same time, star prosecution witness, Ron Cobb, was arraigned and admitted he used cocaine, contrary to his deal with the U.S. Attorney to stay clean and cooperate in return for immunity for his other crimes. As a result, the immunity deal with Cobb was voided.

Meanwhile, Tom Collins, salesman for Hitachi in the computer deal then under scrutiny by law enforcement, was arraigned in Greenville on cocaine charges on March 7, 1991.

Lobbyist Guy Rohling Pleads Guilty

On March 7, 1991, lobbyist Guy Rohling of Raleigh, N.C., appeared at the federal courthouse in Columbia to plead guilty to one count of using cocaine at a party on Hilton Head Island in April, 1988. Rohling was one of five lobbyists charged with narcotics crimes in the Operation Lost Trust prosecutions.

Rohling, a lobbyist for Household International, had been cooperating with the investigation since January, 1991, according to statements made by U.S. Attorney Bart Daniel, who explained that, "He has provided substantial information on drug use among legislators and other elected and appointed public officials."

Rohling faced a maximum sentence of one year in prison and a fine of $100,000, although his cooperation with the government made it likely that his sentence would be lenient.

Judge Falcon Hawkins indicated a personal security bond of only $10,000 allowing Rohling to not pay any money unless he failed to appear in court when scheduled.

Daniel announced that more indictments were expected, venturing that, "We are proceeding in an orderly and systematic manner. We are not rushing anything." Even so, Daniel indicated that the future indictments would likely end soon, saying, "At the same time, this will not go on forever."

Gordon and Blanding Convicted

The trials of former state representatives Larry Blanding and B.J. Gordon went quick as the production of evidence and the deliberations of the jury ended with verdicts of guilty of bribery on March 8, 1991.

Gordon was found to have taken $1,000 and Blanding a total of $1,300 to vote for the horse racing betting bill.

Prosecutor Bart Daniel told the media that the videotape evidence shown to the judge and jury was very strong and persuasive as to the guilty intentions and actions of the two who were convicted.

Daniel also said that the convictions at trial would probably persuade other defendants awaiting trials or indictment to plead guilty soon to avoid a harsh sentence at the end of a trial resulting in conviction.

The jury took only 90 minutes to convict and neither Gordon nor Blanding put up a defense in the trial.

Amazingly, B.J. Gordon had been re-elected to a seat he had held for 16 years in November, 1990, while under criminal indictment.

Candidates Jump at Chance to Replace Faber and McBride

The ink was still drying on the guilty pleas of Richland County Democrats James Faber and Frank McBride when well-known candidates in early March, 1990, declared to run for their vacated seats.

Prominent lower Richland County Baptist minister, Joe Neal, announced for Faber's vacated seat in House District 70 where Faber had defeated a Neal challenge in the June, 1990, Democratic primary election just a few months earlier.

In District 74, where McBride had betrayed the trust of his constituents, longtime Benedict College educator and Richland County School District One Board member, Dr. Alma Byrd, declared as a Democrat. She was joined by Columbia attorney Thomas Mosley. Other possible candidates rumored to be considering the special election for District 74 were Columbia attorney Jerry Screen and auto repair shop owner, Leon Howard. Others rumored to run were Richland County politicians Bernice Scott and Levola Taylor.

I.S. Leevy Johnson, the attorney who had handled the guilty pleas of both Faber and McBride, was serving as the Richland County Democratic Chairman.

All of the candidates and Johnson were African-American as were both Faber and McBride.

Gordon and Blanding Attack Convictions

Convicted on March 8, 1991, along with Larry Blanding for taking bribe money on the betting bill, B.J. Gordon charged in motions on March 11, 1991, that the jury was tainted. Filed by attorney Lionel Lofton, the motions sought an acquittal or new trial order from Judge Falcon Hawkins who had held the trial.

Attorney Danny Martin for Larry Blanding also moved for acquittal and retrial.

Faber and McBride Plead

Advised by their attorney, I.S. Leevy Johnson of Columbia, Reps. James Faber and Frank McBride pleaded guilty to conspiracy to violate the Hobbs Act—one count, on March 1, 1991.

The two had been told by Johnson that the prosecution had a "solid case," but Johnson was in hopes of avoiding a prison sentence in the cases.

They both admitted to taking money from Ron Cobb, but their cases did not appear to be as aggravated as that of Luther Taylor, who was convicted on six felony counts at trial. Johnson hoped that the single count charges against Faber and McBride along with their guilty pleas and agreements to cooperate with the prosecution would cause the court not to sentence the two former legislators to incarceration.

Gov. Campbell Opposes Public Finance

Gov. Carroll Campbell, an advocate of mere disclosure as the panacea for corruption at the State House, spurned a proposal pushed by Sen. Isadore Lourie (D-Richland) to create a tax checkoff of two dollars on state tax returns whereby taxpayers could send money to a public financing fund. The proposal, modeled on the federal tax checkoff for presidential campaigns established after the Nixon scandals of 1972-1974, was advocated by John Crangle of Common Cause/South Carolina.

Sen. Lourie argued that the public finance plan would allow "little people" to provide money to counter the huge amounts being donated by special interests, especially big corporations and political action committees which had come to dominate state elections in South Carolina in the years before the sting.

Campbell said he would veto any public financing bill. He also said that he opposed limits on donations to political parties as well.

Campbell's opposition to any real reforms of the campaign finance system of South Carolina was consistent with his lack of leadership and resistance to major changes in the corrupt political culture of the state which had flourished during his tenure as governor from 1987 onward. Before Lost Trust, Campbell seemed oblivious to the rottenness of public officials in state government, including two of his most trusted appointees, David Hawkins and Dick Greer.

Campbell's Restructuring Bill

Gov. Carroll Campbell sought to use the scandal to get his government restructuring proposals passed. The proposals would greatly increase the governor's control of state government, but they would do nothing to clean up the corrupt practices of the lobbyists and legislators and the out-of-control campaign finance system of South Carolina.

Sen. John Land (D-Clarendon) ridiculed the scheme, pointing to Campbell's selection of Dick Greer as evidence that Campbell could not handle the duties he already had.

Senate Ethics Bill Set for Debate

March 5, 1991, was set by the Senate for a debate on the draft Senate ethics bill which had originally been sponsored by senior senators Marshall Williams and Ed Saleeby.

The bill going into debate included the much fought over "no-cup-of-coffee" rule, limits on the amounts of campaign contributions, and a ban on conversion of campaign funds to personal use. All of these reforms were designed to counter the corrupting influence of lobbyists' and special interest money at the State House.

The Senate bill was, of course, less than what was needed. It failed to restructure the failed House and Senate ethics committees; it did not require a client of a lobbyist to disclose; and the bill did not require the disclosure of clients represented before agencies. The bill did not give the State Ethics Commission original jurisdiction over legislators. Neither did the bill require identification cards or fee payments of lobbyists.

Sen. Horace Smith Pleads to Conspiracy

In a scandal unrelated to Lost Trust, another legislator, Sen. Horace Smith (D-Spartanburg), pleaded guilty to conspiracy in a fraud case involving the Skylyn Hall Retirement Center.

Sen. Smith was an attorney who got tangled up in a prosecution related to some securities issued in conjunction with the Retirement Center. He was in no way implicated in any of the criminal activities in the Lost Trust cases. Even so, Smith's guilty plea added to the public perception that the General Assembly was plagued by corruption and abuses.

Lobbyist Rohling Pleads to Cocaine

Caught up in the Lost Trust scandal as an accidental catch in the bribery fishing expedition of the FBI, lobbyist Martin Guy Rohling of Raleigh, N.C., pleaded guilty on March 7, 1991, to using cocaine at Hilton Head, S.C., in 1988. He joined a total of five lobbyists charged with cocaine in the fallout of the probe. The fact that Daniel was dragging out the process of indicting, prosecuting, and convicting so many defendants implicated in criminal behaviors at the State House tried the patience of the citizenry and facilitated reform legislation.

At the time of the plea by Rohling, U.S. Attorney Bart Daniel announced to the media that he expected more indictments in the Lost Trust scandal.

Holderman Scandal Widens

The media probe of the financial doings and dealings of President James Holderman of USC found out that he had taken a consulting fee of $17,000 from the McNair Law Firm in Columbia.

The growing evidence of abuse of Holderman's abuse of his position as president of the largest university in South Carolina made it appear that public corruption and dishonesty was rampant, infecting not only the executive, legislative, and judicial branches of state government but also public employees, businessmen, lobbyists, and others involved in some way with state government.

Senate Votes to Exclude Selves from Boards

The ethics reform bill then under debate in the Senate opened the door to floor amendments dealing with almost any issue even remotely related to ethics.

Realizing a chance to strike at the long-standing abuse of legislators putting themselves on state boards and commissions instead of ordinary citizens, Sens. Mike Rose (R-Dorchester) and Sherry Martschink (R-Charleston) took a proposal to ban legislators from most boards and commissions to a successful vote in the Senate on March 12, 1991, which prevailed 24-12.

The ban had been proposed initially by Gov. Carroll Campbell but was opposed by Democratic senators Theo Mitchell (D-Greenville), Don Holland (D-Kershaw), and John Martin (D-Fairfield).

Senate Votes to Stop Conflicts

By a vote of 30-1, the Senate voted to ban legislators from representing clients before state agencies.

The proposal would also ban state and local officials from selling goods and services to local governments.

Opposition from the House was expected as the House ethics bill only proposed disclosure of such transactions.

Senate Ethics Debate

In the debate over the ethics reform bill, the Senate on March 14, 1991, killed an amendment to ban lawyer-legislators from voting in elections for judges. The amendment was in accord with Gov. Campbell's well-known dislike for lawyer-legislators and their roles in state government.

The Senate did approve an amendment to require legislators and local officials to file economic interest disclosure on their incomes as to sources and amounts.

The Senate also took up major campaign finance reform amendments to limit campaign contributions to $500 from a single source for statewide candidates and $250 per source for legislators. A total ban on personal use of campaign funds was also considered.

Greer's Help for Cobb Exposed

The close ties between Dick Greer and Ron Cobb were further revealed on March 13, 1991, when it became known that Dick Greer had recommended Cobb to the Nucor Steel Corporation as a lobbyist and had suggested that Nucor pay Cobb $100,000 to lobby for the company in an electrical rate dispute.

It further became known that Greer had referred Greenville businessman Tom Roe to Cobb to lobby for a tax break of $8.6 million with the South Carolina General Assembly. Of course, Cobb did become the lobbyist for Roe and other Greenville businessmen seeking the tax break.

Gordon Moves for Retrial

On March 13, 1991, a hearing was set to be held on April 10, 1991, on a motion by Rep. B.J. Gordon for a new trial after his conviction for public corruption. Gordon alleged that the jury was contaminated and that his conviction was therefore invalid.

The State Urges Quick Action

In an editorial of March 14, 1991, *The State* urged the U.S. Attorney to speed up the process of indicting and trying those implicated in bribery and drugs in the Lost Trust scandal.

The State bemoaned the fact that it had taken since July, 1990, to charge 14 legislators and four lobbyists plus one salesman and that it might take another three years to get to the remaining 50 or so original suspects. The longer the process, the longer the name of the state was dragged through the mud.

The editorial ignored the fact that the protracted process of indicting, taking pleas, trying cases, and imposing sentences had the beneficial effect of repeatedly providing new evidence of the corruption in South Carolina state government and of the need to pass laws to establish new ethics principles and new enforcement practices. The constant drumbeat of indictments from August, 1990, until September, 1991, drove the General Assembly to eventually adopt more drastic ethics reform measures than it otherwise would have.

The State also did not consider the prosecutorial value of dragging out the process of indictments and trials in addition to taking guilty pleas in that the continuous naming of new defendants and convicted corruptionists put intense pressure on corrupt officials and lobbyists to come forward and give evidence and even admit their guilt. Defendants were further discouraged from going to trial and were more willing to plead guilty.

Dick Greer to Plead Guilty

After denying any wrongdoing since the summer of 1990, Gov. Campbell's old friend and campaign advisor announced his plan to plead guilty to cocaine possession on March 13, 1991. Charleston attorney, Gedney Howe, advised Greer in the matter.

Campbell said that Greer was still his friend, regardless of his criminal actions and false statements abut his innocence.

It came out that Greer had recommended that Nucor, a steel company in the coastal part of the state, hire lobbyist Ron Cobb for a fee of $100,000 to help in an electric rate dispute. It was also revealed that Greer had urged Greenville businessman, Tom Roe, to hire Cobb to obtain an $8.6 million tax break from the General Assembly which Cobb later accomplished by bribery.

On March 16, 1991, it was reported that Greer had passed a drug test in November, 1990, after he was asked by Gov. Campbell about drug rumors. Greer clipped a lock of his hair and sent it to a lab.

Ethics Reform Bill Fight

Controversy over the ethics reform bill in the Legislature continued and even worsened in the spring of 1991. Some said the bill was too strict. Critics said the bill was being sabotaged with drastic restrictions which would kill it in the end.

The Senate was working on one ethics reform package and the House was struggling to produce its own set of proposals. Sen. David Thomas (R-Greenville) commented that the task of producing a good ethics reform bill "is serious." Thomas favored a comprehensive plan even if it included some drastic ideas.

Among the most controversial issues being debated in the Senate were proposals to bar legislators from serving on boards and commissions and other proposals to stop or limit lawyer-legislators from practice before boards and commissions. Another area of controversy was the matter of income disclosure by legislators to force the revelations of conflicts of interest.

House Wants Weak Bill

House Judiciary Committee Chairman, David Wilkins (R-Greenville), warned that the House would not approve an overly strict ethics reform bill from the Senate. He said his committee bill stressed disclosure, not limitations on conduct. But Sen. David Thomas (R-Greenville) said that, in fact, there was good support for a tough bill in the House.

In addition, critics said the Senate ethics bill was too weak because it did not bar lawyer-legislators from taking retainers, a scheme which allowed lobbyists and special interest groups to pay lawyer-legislators for doing no legal work at all, thereby buying their vote with fake legal fees. Some legislators had, in fact, become lobbyists.

Critics also noted that the reform bill did not provide for outside enforcement of ethics rules but relied on inside legislative ethics committees of cronies. The bill did not stop lawyer-legislators from electing judges, giving them a courtroom advantage. Sen. John Land admitted that, "I can practice before a judge who I have a lot of influence over."

In the end, the bill would end up in conference committee to write the final draft after all the posturing was over, predicted veteran senator James Waddell (D-Beaufort), Chairman of Senate Finance, who noted that was common practice in budget bills. "This bill will be written in conference. In my opinion, I don't think you'd recognize it when they're done."

Ethics Reform Bill in Senate—Too Strong

Criticism of the Senate ethics bill on the grounds that it was too restrictive and unreasonable mounted in mid-March, 1991.

Sen. David Thomas, a reformer, admitted that, "it may simply have gone past the point of reasonable." Sen. John Land (D-Clarendon) felt that posturing and rhetoric was the order of the day but that a weaker bill would finally be approved: "We're dancing right now, and fencing, before we really get down to doing something that is practical and logical." Land regarded many of the amendments as insincere schemes to make sponsors look good even while they hoped the amendments would fail and "they hope and pray the responsible members will not vote for." Land predicted that on third reading of the bill, it would be made more practical.

However, Sen. Hugh Leatherman (D-Florence) said that he anticipated that in the end, a number of tough provisions would survive. Something would go to the House which had some teeth to it.

Yet some senators, Land among them, believed that it was possible that the Senate would pass an overly restrictive bill which would be designed to provoke House defeat. The danger that the senators would be caught in a situation in which their bluff was called by the House was real. One lobbyist said, "That's like playing Russian roulette with one bullet missing."

Ethics Reform Bill in Senate on Roller Coaster

The Senate debate over the ethics bill was marked by vacillation over whether to include strict or lenient standards for public officials. Strong amendments would be passed only to be watered down later.

The major issues fought over included four amendments which went to a floor vote. Senators voted 24-12 to ban legislators from serving on boards and commissions. The vote was not on party lines with Republicans and Democrats lining up on both sides.

The next vote taken the following day was 30-1 to bar legislators from practicing before boards and commissions. The vote also included a ban on state officials selling goods and services to government agencies. Eleven abstained in the vote.

The following day the vote was 30-7 against a provision to ban lawyer-legislators from electing judges. Voting for the ban were senators Martschink, McConnell, Peeler, Smith, Thomas, and Wilson.

The next day the vote was 20-13 to force disclosure of all income by elected and appointed officials and many government employees.

The State Warns of Overkill

In a March 17, 1991, editorial, *The State* asked if the Senate ethics reform amendments were "realistic actions or overkill?"

On the one hand, *The State* supported the ban on lawyer-legislators appearing before state boards and commissions, but thought that law partners of lawyer-legislators should be allowed to do so.

The State also claimed the proposed ban on government employees and officials from doing business with state or local government "goes beyond reasonable reform" and perhaps might be a sabotage restriction to kill the bill. But *The State* put faith in disclosure, arguing that, "Full disclosure is at the core of meaningful reform. Fortunately, there seems to be a consensus in both the House and Senate" on the need for more disclosure, especially of lawyer-legislators appearing before boards and commissions. Full disclosure of incomes from entities having business before the General Assembly must be required.

There was a danger that if the bill did not provide for reforms that were "reasonable and attainable...the legislation will fall of its own weight," the editors warned.

Senate Wavers on Reform

The week of March 14th, 1991, had been an Olympics contest to see who could throw out the most drastic reform amendments. The week of March 21 began with regrets and retreats.

Sen. Thomas Moore (D-Aiken) said the bill, in fact, was an "open game" and subject to major changes. Moore had met with Gov. Campbell and the Democratic caucus to figure out what to do, noting that the process would end in "a certain level of compromise in some area."

Some senators hoped that the governor and senate leaders would cover their retreat by proposing compromises to water down limitations on legislators doing business with local and state government and on income disclosure, said Sen. Ernest Passailague (D-Charleston) who felt a public statement was needed from leadership to promote compromise.

The meeting on ethics reform was attended by Sen. Tom Moore along with Sen. Sam Stilwell (R-Greenville) and Sen. Marshall Williams (D-Orangeburg) but reached no agreement. One senator reported that in the meeting, Gov. Campbell had indicated he would provide cover but that restrictive campaign finance reforms must be weakened.

Campbell strongly objected to a proposed ban on the use of campaign funds raised to run for one office being used to run for another office. Campbell had $500,000 in his campaign account that he wanted to be available to run for another office. He also objected to a ban on government employees accepting things of value as a threat to economic development.

Tee Ferguson Indicted

Circuit Court Judge, Tee Ferguson of Greenville, was indicted on March 21, 1991, on one count of conspiracy and two counts of extortion. Recently elected to the bench in April, 1990, Ferguson was charged with crimes committed in his House service prior to becoming a judge.

Ferguson became the seventh black charged in the scandal, half of the 14 total indicted at that point. The indictment of Ferguson brought the total number of persons indicted in Lost Trust to 22.

Ferguson was immediately suspended from his circuit court seat on the bench by Chief Justice George Gregory and without pay.

At the same time, it was reported that Jack I. Rogers might plead guilty, joining the growing list of those convicted in the scandal. Evidence in his court file indicated a plea date of March 8, 1991, had been set.

Proposal to Ban Running for Judgeship by Sitting Legislators

The old practice of incumbent legislators getting elected as judges was attacked in an amendment to ban the practice. The major problem with incumbent legislators running the state court bench was that they had an unfair advantage over non-legislators seeking the same positions and that inferior quality legislators were elected as judges as a result. The fact that sitting legislators could and did vote for themselves aggravated the issue in the minds of critics.

Ex-legislators Favored in Judicial Selection

The hyper-politicized character of the South Carolina judiciary was apparent by the composition of the South Carolina Supreme Court. All five of the justices on the court were former members of the State Legislature in 1990 and 1991.

All circuit court judges in South Carolina were selected by the vote of the 170 member General Assembly. As the House had 124 members and the Senate only 46, the power of the House to control the outcome was obvious.

At the time, the law allowed sitting legislators to run for judicial office and even to vote for themselves in the elections, which did happen, in fact. Therefore, sitting legislators had an unfair and often decisive advantage over non-legislative candidates and commonly won their election races.

The fact that Judge Tee Ferguson, one of the defendants in Operation Lost Trust and a former House member, illustrated the results of the election system's institutional bias in favor of legislators. Ferguson very clearly won his election on the circuit court bench because he was a sitting House member when he was elected and was supported by fellow House members in a deal to elect him in large part because he was black and not because he had a record of public service or ethical conduct.

Holderman Indicted

The Richland County Grand Jury indicted USC president, Jim Holderman, on March 22, 1991, on counts of using his government position to obtain financial gains and of receiving compensation beyond that provided by law.

Weak House Bill Moves On

Stressing disclosure, the House Constitutional Law Subcommittee continued work on a superficial bill based on the theory that mere disclosure of financial matters and conflicts of interest would be enough to cure the rampant corruption and special interest control at the State House.

The committee, chaired by Wes Hayes (D-York), worked on a bill to require more disclosure by lawyer-legislators of their income.

The House bill did have a substantial provision to ban gift-giving from lobbyists to legislators and other state officials.

Even so, John Crangle of Common Cause/South Carolina criticized the House bill saying it was "watered down" and allowed for too many free handouts such as trips paid by lobbyists for public officials. Furthermore, the proposed contribution limits in the bill were too high as the bill allowed individuals to donate $1,000 and political action committees to donate $5,000 to candidates.

The House bill proposed to ban the conversion of political contributions to personal use and the commingling of personal and campaign funds. The bill prohibited gifts of means and other items of value from lobbyists. Donations from lobbyists were also banned.

The Senate draft bill was more strict in stopping legislators from doing business with government and in practicing before boards.

Rival Ethics Bill at Issue

In late March, 1991, the House and Senate were working on their own versions of draft ethics bills, although the Senate bill was already being debated while the House bill was still in the Judiciary Committee.

The major differences at that time were related to campaign funds and lobbyist's gratuities. The Senate bill was much more aggressive than that of the House. The Senate proposed contribution limits of only $500 for statewide races and $250 for legislative and local candidates. The House bill would allow individuals to donate $2,000 to any race and political action committees could donate up to $5,000.

The Senate bill proposed to limit the use of campaign funds to the campaign for which the money was explicitly raised and not for any other. The House bill would allow the use of such funds for any campaign including that of another candidate aside from the person who raised the money in the first place.

The Senate bill proposed to ban all gifts to officials from any sources, but the House would only ban gifts from lobbyists.

The Senate would ban lawyer-legislators from appearing before boards and commissions, but the House bill would only require disclosure of such representation. The House would ban legislators from taking retainers, but the Senate would allow it. The House would also require legislators to resign before running for judgeships, but the Senate would not require resignation.

House Judiciary Backs "No-Cup-of-Coffee" Rule

The House Judiciary Committee on March 26, 1991, voted to retain the proposed "no-cup-of-coffee" provision in the ethics bill which had been drafted. Rep. Joe McElveen (D-Sumter) commented that the provision was "the basic building block of reform." However, Rep. Terry Haskins (R-Greenville), thought the ban on lobbyists' gratuities went too far, noting that those indicted had not been charged with eating handouts from lobbyists. But Rep. Irene Rudnick's (D-Aiken) amendment to allow lobbyists to spend up to $25 per day on meals for lobbyists failed by vote of 12-8.

House Considers Ethics Jurisdiction Over Lobbyists

The House Judiciary Committee met on March 26, 1991, and narrowly voted to transfer jurisdiction over lobbyists to the State Ethics Commission, removing it from the Secretary of State. Critics had pointed out that the previous Secretary of State had not only been lax in his duties toward lobbyists but had, in fact, taken campaign donations from them.

The new Secretary of State, Jim Miles, argued that his office should retain jurisdiction, saying that "the voters spoke on this issue." But Rep. Irene Rudnick (D-Aiken) argued that a politician should not supervise the lobbyists.

Senate Wrestles With Ethics Reform Bill

Democratic senators met for several hours on March 26, 1991, to try to work out a compromise ethics reform bill, but Sen. Tom Moore (D-Aiken) reported that "There was no consensus reached or any compromises."

The key issues which troubled the Senate included proposals to ban lawyer-legislators from practicing before boards and commissions and another proposal to ban public officials from doing business with the state. The Senate struggled over proposed campaign contribution limits in the draft bill of $500 per election for statewide candidates and $250 for legislators and local candidates. The bill also proposed to limit contributions to political action committees and political parties to $2,000 per year from a single source.

Another provision was that which required officials to make complete financial disclosures, and idea not welcomed by some legislators who did not want to be forced to disclose their personal, business, or professional financial circumstances and dealings to the general public.

Fant Tussles at Church

As if he was not in enough trouble after being rebuked by the House Ethics Committee for running an escort service out of his House office and after being indicted by the grand jury and convicted for bribery, the turbulent cleric, Rep. Ennis Fant (D-Greenville), was reported by the Anderson County Sheriff's Department to have been involved in a scuffle at his church during a meeting of congregation members.

The incident happened in Fant's church where he was pastor, the Pleasant View Baptist Church in Anderson County. The complaining witness who filed an incident report, Angela R. Bennett, claimed that Rev. Fant slapped her face. But Fant filed a conflicting report alleging that Ms. Bennett cursed him, jumped on his back, knocked him down, tore his shirt, and knocked off his glasses.

At the time of the incident, Fant was awaiting sentencing after pleading guilty to bribery in violation of the Hobbs Act on February 22, 1991.

Carmichael vs. Lindsay in Dillon County

Conflicted former Sen. Gene Carmichael (D-Dillon) faced off in the Democratic run-off primary election to replace the recently deceased and suspected corruptionist, Sen. Jack I. Lindsay (D-Dillon). The late senator's son, Chuck Lindsay, opposed Carmichael.

Carmichael had served 18 months of a ten year prison sentence in federal detention for vote-buying and then returned to his home in 1984.

But in the spring of 1991, Carmichael felt that he had been sufficiently rehabilitated to run for the Senate again to fill Lindsay's seat.

Senate Passes Weakened Ethics Bill

The Senate passed a bill on the evening of March 27, 1991, and sent it to the House after an attempt to pass a major weakening amendment failed by vote of 21-22. The Senate did pass smaller amendments which dropped the ban on lawyer-legislators appearing before state boards and commissions, but did require them to report the clients and fees from such work. Another amendment allowed state and local elected and appointed officials to do business with government agencies.

The "no-cup-of-coffee" rule was not weakened by an amendment to allow legislators to take meals from non-lobbyists of a value of not more than $25. The ban on lobbyists' freebies remained.

The Senate bill required public officials to report business dealings with government agencies and lobbyists. The bill also barred legislators from serving on boards and commissions. The bill imposed a one year waiting period for legislators and the governor after leaving office before they could become lobbyists.

Sales of goods of a value of $200 or more to lobbyists would be reportable if made by officials. Lobbyists were also required to file detailed reports on their income, expenses, and the money they spend on individuals to influence legislation. The Secretary of State was also empowered to audit lobbyists' reports.

The campaign finance provisions of the bill included a ban on use of campaign funds for non-campaign purposes and banned use of surplus funds to run for a different office. Contribution limits were set at $500 from a source to a candidate for statewide office and $250 for General Assembly and local offices. Cash contributions were limited to $25.

Sen. John Land (D-Clarendon) fought for disclosure rather than prohibitions, saying, "We won the war before it was all over." But the question was who was "we", the politicians or the people.

Sen. Glenn McConnell (R-Charleston) ridiculed the effort saying, "This whole think is taking the meat out of the soup and making it consommé."

Senate Ethics Bill Criticized

The ethics reform bill passed by the Senate on March 28, 1991, provoked criticism for both being too strong and being too weak. Gov. Carroll Campbell derided the bill on both grounds, saying that, "I am not happy with the Senate ethics bill because in many ways, it is too weak in some places and unrealistically prohibitive in others." Campbell ripped the bill on the grounds that "it would weaken political parties, protect incumbents and could not claim to have resolved the ethics problem." Campbell regarded the bill passed by the Democratic controlled Senate as an attack on not only the South Carolina Republican Party but also on Campbell himself, a potential future congressional candidate.

Campbell went on to point out that the House ethics bill which had been passed on March 27, 1991, was "a far preferable piece of legislation." Campbell blamed the Senate bill for failing to require full disclosures of legislators' income, assets, and dealing which might disclose financial conflicts of interest. Campbell was particularly upset with the failure of the bill to confront the problem of lawyer-legislators practicing before state boards and commissions.

Campbell charged that the Senate bill placed "unrealistic limits on campaign contributions" by limiting them to only $500 for statewide races and $250 for legislative candidates. He also alleged that the bill would weaken political parties by limiting contributions to them to only $2,000. Campbell also disliked the ban on the use of funds to run for a different office other than the one for which the funds were first solicited.

Senate Ethics Bill Passed in Controversy

Democratic Senators Vern Smith (D-Greenville), Frank Gilbert (D-Florence) and Ernie Passailague (D-Charleston) alleged that some senators had tried to pressure them and others to substitute a new and weak ethics bill for the strong bill that the Senate eventually did pass on March 28,1991.

The provisions at issue included a proposed ban on lawyer-legislators working for clients before boards and commissions which many lawyer-legislators opposed. A ban on state and local officials doing business with state government was also opposed. Finally the financial disclosure provisions were disliked by those who wanted to keep their finances secret. In the end, the weakening amendments failed in the Senate by a vote of 21-22.

Several senators ventilated their anger at what they called "lawyer-bashing." Still others proposed amendments to punish or at least burden their political critics.

Gordon Alleges Jury Taint

Claiming that jurors were intimidated in the courtroom when they saw people pointing at them and talking at the same time, B.J. Gordon's lawyer said that the jury sent a note to the judge the next morning. In talks with Judge Falcon Hawkins on March 6, 1991, the defense lawyer raised the issue of jury taint, according to transcripts released on March 30, 1991.

A hearing was set for April 11, 1991. The defense was expected to allege that five jurors might have been affected. Judge Hawkins did, in fact, clear the courtroom after the issue was raised at trial.

Three white males were in the courtroom. Gordon said that he knew the men and that Sen. Yancey McGill (D-Williamsburg) was one of them and that he had talked with McGill.

The Judge refused to declare a mistrial and concluded that there were no sinister actions. He told the jury that the men they were worried about were legislators, too, and known to Gordon.

Hawkins also said in a transcript that he was concerned about the complaints of the media and appeals filed in the 4th Circuit against his closing of the courtroom in the Gordon trial.

CHAPTER TWENTY TWO

APRIL, 1991—CONVICTIONS AND ETHICS REFORMS BREAK THROUGH

As the number of new indictments of legislators, government officials, and lobbyists piled up, the prosecutors also piled up guilty pleas and jury convictions of corruptionists and drug users among the political classes and lobbyists as well. This growing mass of evidence of public corruption in South Carolina drove public demand for ethics reforms and encouraged legislators to pass badly needed new laws to control political money and the lobbyists.

The prosecutors orchestrated background music and drama for the ethics reformers at the State House by stretching out the process of indictments, trials, pleas and jury trials over more than a year from August 24, 1990, and until the last trial of Sen. Bud Long in November, 1991. The more the scandal expanded and grew, the more the reformers were encouraged and justified in demanding reform. And the more that the prosecutors accused and convicted politicians and lobbyists, the more that the opposition to reform disintegrated among the politicians, special interests, and lobbyists. By the spring of 1991, it appeared that early opponents of reform had been completely routed and resistance to reform outside the State House and most opposition to reform inside the State House had been largely neutralized.

Gordon Sues for Seat

Expelled former Rep. B.J. Gordon (D-Williamsburg), in late March, 1991, sued to recover his old seat. Filed in U.S. District Court in Columbia, the same forum that had convicted him of extortion and conspiracy, the Gordon suit challenged House Rule 3.12 which provided for automatic suspension on indictment without a vote of the House. The suit claimed that the removal violated the South Carolina Constitution which required two-thirds vote of the House to remove and said that a member cannot be removed twice for the same cause. The suit also alleged that Rule 3.12 had not been pre-cleared by the U.S. Department of Justice in accord with the 1965 Voting Rights Act and was therefore invalid.

The plaintiffs asked for relief, including a declaration that the suspension and removal violated the constitutional rights of the voters in House District 101 and requested an order from the court stopping Sheheen from enforcing Rule 3.12 until and unless it received pre-clearance. The suit sought Gordon's reinstatement.

Matthew Perry, the first black federal judge in South Carolina history, was assigned to the case. He refused to grant a motion for a temporary restraining order stopping the election of Gordon's replacement in House District 101 in Williamsburg County.

Just convicted of extortion and conspiracy, disgraced ex-representative B.J. Gordon filed a federal lawsuit to recover his House seat in Williamsburg County.

Joined by several voters of the county, Gordon alleged that the 25,000 residents of his district had been illegally deprived of representation when Speaker Robert Sheheen had again suspended Gordon even after his re-election while indicted in November, 1990.

Gordon had represented rural Williamsburg County for some twenty years when he was indicted and suspended from office in September, 1990. He planned to appeal his suspension pursuant to House rules, arguing that the House rules had not been pre-cleared by the U.S. Department of Justice as required by the 1975 Voting Rights Act. The matter would be considered by a three judge panel. Gordon planned to ask the panel to issue an injunction against the holding of an election to replace Gordon. Sheheen was a defendant in the case.

House Suspensions at Issue

"If there's anything...that has helped us to maintain a steady rudder," said Speaker Sheheen, "it's that we've been able to remove these people from the process" as they were indicted and convicted. Sheheen's comments pointed to the fact that the House had taken action not required by the South Carolina Constitution nor by the South Carolina Code to expel members charged and convicted of felonies using a Rule of the House, not constitutional or statutory law.

B.J. Gordon (D-Williamsburg) had been one of those indicted members suspended automatically from the House under the House Rules. He filed a lawsuit on March 30, 1991, challenging Rule 3.12 that automatically suspended him on indictment which was followed by expulsion on conviction of felony extortion and conspiracy. Gordon contended that the federal court should overturn the rule of automatic expulsion and force the House to seat him again. Gordon also argued that it would also be illegal to elect a replacement for him.

Sheheen explained Rule 3.12 providing for, on indictment, the automatic suspension and expulsion on conviction rule by saying it was designed to protect the House, noting that "everybody adopted the attitude that the institution is more important than the individual," but that Gordon's lawsuit "adopts the other attitude."

Arguing for the lawsuit, Gordon's attorney, Helen T. McFadden of Williamsburg County, claimed that the right to representation of the people of the district had been violated. The suit joined Gordon and seven residents of his district (House District 101) in complaining that they "had no voice in the House." The suit named defendants Sheheen, the House, and state election administrators.

House Backs Weak Reform Bill

Whereas the Senate spent several months framing an ethics reform bill, the House pulled their bill together in only three days. Judiciary Chairman David Wilkins urged, "You take a reasonable approach and a responsible position, and I don't think the House is going to be intimidated into passing irresponsible legislation." House Minority leader Terry Haskins (R-Greenville), noting the Senate's ethics battles, said that "one-upmanship is not the best way to draft a comprehensive ethics package."

Majority leader Joe McElveen (D-Sumter) noted that Speaker Sheheen and Chairman Wilkins were well-respected and would moderate conflicts, but even so, there were differences. McElveen had fought earlier for stricter limits on campaign contributions but without success and indicated an intention to take the matter to the floor.

The House bill set limits on contributions of $2,000 from individuals and $5,000 from corporations. McElveen said, "My perception is that money is too big a part of the process." Whereas the House bill would still allow lobbyists to wine and dine legislators, real reformers wanted to stop this practice. McElveen said, "No-cup-of-coffee is one end of that. Campaign contributions is the other."

Rep. Tim Rogers (D-Richland) said he expected "a number of efforts to amend the bill on the floor to reflect strengthening amendments which failed in Judiciary." Rogers did not expect that the House bill would move without controversy, noting, "I don't think there's that kind of consensus in the House."

Republicans Fight Contribution Limits in House

David Wilkins (R-Greenville) denied any deal to weaken reforms but said he was trying to keep Republicans together in the House to prevent the Judiciary's ethics bill from being broken up. "We obviously were aware that we needed to keep the bill intact or it would unravel on the floor, as in the Senate," Wilkins said at the end of seven hour of floor debates.

Speaker Bob Sheheen (D-Kershaw) led the vote to remove any proposed regulation of the judiciary in the bill which passed 57-41. The bill had proposed to allow the State Ethics Commission to deal with complaints against judges.

House Reform Bill—The Illusion of Unity

Rep. Tim Rogers disparaged the ease with which a weak ethics bill passed the House Judiciary Committee, saying it was the result of a fragile coalition of those who did not want tougher campaign finance limitations and those opposed to more limitations on lawyer-legislators. However, Rogers warned that on the floor, members would "be very reluctant to see some sort of backroom deal and everybody gets something."

Rogers and others objected to the failure of the House bill to stop the big donations by single donors and the failure to stop lawyer-legislators from using public office to make money in their law practices before state boards and commissions.

When the debate started in the last week in March, 1991, the House voted to kill provisions to lower campaign contribution limits and to restrict lawyer-legislators. The House wanted to let lawyer-legislators appear before state boards and commissions and to vote on their budgets and appoint board members. The House voted to allow contributions of $2,000 from individuals and $5,000 from corporations and political action committees. (The Senate limits were only $250 for legislative candidates and $500 for statewide candidates.)

Tim Rogers accused Judiciary Chair David Wilkins (R-Greenville) and the Republican Party of forming an unholy alliance to block real reform and to protect special interests and Republicans who stood to benefit from high contribution limits.

House Ethics Reform Bill Summary

The ethics reform bill sent by House Judiciary committee to the floor included the following as of late March, 1991:

1. Allowed the State Ethics Commission to investigate legislators, but reversed disci plinary authority to the Legislature.
2. Required lawyer-legislators to report their income from practicing before boards and commissions.
3. Banned giving anything of value from lobbyists and their employers to legislators except for meals paid by lobbyist for groups of legislators.
4. Allowed legislators to accept meals and gifts from non-lobbyists, but would make recipients report all gifts over $25.
5. Let State Ethics Commission regulate lobbyists.
6. Banned use of campaign funds for anything but campaign costs and for donations to another candidate's campaign.
7. Limited campaign contributions to $2,000 per source to legislative candidates and $5,000 for business donations.
8. Banned cash contributions above $100.
9. Provided for automatic suspension for indicted legislators.
10. Provided for automatic expulsion for legislators convicted of felonies.
11. Banned legislators from taking retainers from lobbyists and their employers.

House Bill Includes Some Reforms

After rigorous debates in the House, several reforms were eliminated. By vote of 67-37, the ban on lawyer-legislators practicing before boards and commissions was taken out of the bill. Provisions to regulate judges were also cut out by vote of 57-41.

Surviving the cuts were the following reforms:

1. Require all public officials to disclose all business that they did with government agencies and lobbyists and lobbyists' employers and clients.
2. Banned lobbyists' donations to legislators including a ban on campaign contributions. (Would allow lobbyists to host meals for groups of legislators.)
3. Banned cash contributions of more than $100.
4. Banned retainers paid by lobbyists and their employers to legislators.

Senate Fragments Over Ethics Reform Bill

Wrangling over the terms of the ethics reform bill being debated on the Senate floor showed a fragmentation of Senate leadership. Some leaders backed strong reforms and others opposed.

To force a retreat from some stiff reforms, the Senate imposed a limit of only six minutes on debate over each amendment. This tended to check the efforts of some younger senators favoring tough reforms who had been the most able debaters in the struggle.

The battle provoked some senators to accuse others of bullying tactics, such as a threat to call in a loan on one antagonistic senator.

Sen. Ernest Passailague (D-Charleston), one of the younger set, observed, "What you saw in this legislation, just as important as the legislation itself, was the disintegration of the old guard.... They had to pull out all the stops, bullying tactics."

The elbowing and gouging in the Senate caused House leaders to try to prevent a similar conflict in the House. Speaker Robert Sheheen (D-Kershaw) pointed to the "spectacle in the Senate" which he believed would convince the House to "act responsibly." House leaders pledged to stick together. The House bill was, of course, much weaker, relying more on disclosure than prohibitions and limitations related to lobbying and campaign finance.

Senate Ethics Bill Provisions Summary

The Senate ethics reform bill at the end of March, 1991, included a number of reforms not found in the House ethics bill. The reforms peculiar to the Senate were:

1. Required lawyer-legislators to report the names of clients and their income from practicing before state boards and commissions.
2. Required that public officials and their families and businesses disclose all goods and services of $200 sold to lobbyists.
3. Banned legislators from accepting anything from lobbyists and their employers.

4. Allowed legislators to accept meals up to $25 from non-lobbyists.
5. Allowed Secretary of State to audit lobbyists' reports.
6. Banned candidates for public office from using campaign funds for non-campaign purposes.
7. Banned campaign funds raised for one office to be used to campaign for a different office.
8. Limited campaign contributions to $500 for statewide office and $250 for legisla tive office.
9. Banned cash donations of more than $25.
10. Retained regulation of legislators within the House and Senate ethics committees.

Senate and House Bills Agree on Reform

As of the end of March, 1991, after weeks of work and many disputes over ethics reform proposals, the House and Senate bills finally agreed on some major reform provisions.

The agreed upon reforms were:

1. Banned legislators from serving on most boards and commissions.
2. Compelled public officials to disclose all business they did with government agencies, lobbyists, and lobbyists' employers.
3. Forced lobbyists to file detailed reports about their income and expenses and on whom they spent money in trying to influence legislation.
4. Banned lobbyists' campaign donations to legislators.

Even so, there were still major differences between the House and Senate bills on such issues as campaign contribution limits, oversight jurisdiction of lobbyists and legislators, and the sources of legal fees paid to lawyer-legislators, particularly from lobbyists. These disputes were eventually worked out by a conference committee which finished its work during the summer of 1991.

Editorial Evaluates Ethics Bills

The State pointed to issues not addressed by the draft ethics reform bills in the General Assembly, noting good points and missing elements. "Further changes are needed before a final ethics package is adopted," the editors contended on April 2, 1991.

Pointing to the issue of lawyer-legislators practicing before state boards and commissions, the editors said that if the practice was not banned, at least Gov. Carroll Campbell's demand to require full disclosure should be in the final bill. The Senate version still allowed lawyer-legislators to take legal fees from lobbyists, whereas the House bill banned the practice.

As to campaign finance reforms, *The State* observed that the Senate bill capped contributions at $500 for statewide and $250 for legislative races. The House bill had limits of $2,000 for individuals and $5,000 for corporations. *The State* suggested $2,000 and $1,000 limits for statewide and legislative races, respectively. (The 1991 Ethics Act eventually would set the limits at $3,500 for statewide and $1,000 for legislative races with no difference for individuals and corporations.)

As to oversight of lobbyists, the House would transfer oversight to the State Ethics Commission while the Senate would leave it with the Secretary of State. While commending new Secretary of State Jim Miles for cracking down on lobbyists in contrast with his feckless predecessor, John Campbell, *The State* agreed with Rep. Joe McElveen (D-Sumter) that the Ethics Commission would be the better agency to monitor lobbyists.

The State editorial of April 2, 1991, noted that the draft House ethics reform bill proposed to codify the automatic suspension of indicted legislators and the automatic expulsion of convicted. The House had such a rule (Rule 3.12); the Senate did not.

The bills would ban legislators from serving on most state boards and commissions, would limit cash contributions to campaigns, and would require lobbyists to report and disclose income and expenses.

However, the bills failed to force officials to disclose their incomes and conflicts of interest.

The State predicted the final bill would be hashed out in conference committee and would necessitate compromise even while public interest groups and citizens could have a role of influencing the final product. *The State* stressed the need for real reform "in a state whose government has been besmirched by scandal."

House Ethics Bill Gets Weaker

While the Senate was concluding a three week ordeal of debate over its ethics reform bill in which drastic reforms were proposed and opposed, David Wilkins (R-Greenville), Chairman of the House Judiciary Committee, opened the House floor debate with a 30 minute summary of the bill presented by the House Judiciary Committee. Wilkins opined, "The way we go about the task of reform is just as important as the reform itself." He warned about a "frenzy of political posturing and grandstanding" in the House.

Speaker Bob Sheheen said the bill was good and widely accepted, but Rep. Candy Waites (D-Richland) proposed most of the 43 amendments discussed in the floor debate on April 2, 1991, and felt frustrated at the end of the day, saying, "I was really disappointed."

Without recorded votes, the House rejected a proposal to stop lawyer-legislators from appearing before state boards and commissions. (The Senate had done the same the previous week.)

The House turned down a proposal to make legislators resign their seats before running for judicial office. (House Judiciary had removed the resignation requirement the previous week.)

The House also rejected a proposal to limit all campaign contributions to $1,000, but adopted limits of $2,000 on individual and $5,000 on corporate donations. It also rejected a limit of $5,000 on party and caucus donations and set $25,000 instead as the limit.

House Bill Watered Down Campaign Limits

In their debate starting April 2, 1991, the House rejected amendments to impose lower campaign contribution limits. Reps. Candy Waites and Tim Rogers (both Democrats from Columbia) opposed allowing political parties to give $25,000 to candidates, arguing it was an invitation to lobbyists to give to parties if banned from donating directly to candidates. Rogers orated in opposition to Chairman Wilkins, alleging that, "We've heard a lot of high-sounding rhetoric...unless we adopt the amendment, we are tilting the scales of fairness in the state toward one political party, and I ain't going to tell who they are", an obvious allusion to the Republican Party, "the ones with bucks." Rogers predicted that high limits would help to tilt elections to Republican candidates in the future.

But Rep. Wes Hayes (D-York), who would shortly become a Republican, defended high limits of $5,000 and $100,000 for party donations for candidates seeking statewide offices, claiming that, "The reason you have parties is to get good candidates and support them."

Tee Ferguson Pleads Not Guilty

Suspended 7th Circuit Court Judge Tee Ferguson of Greenville pleaded not guilty to bribery and drug charges on April 5, 1991, before U.S. Magistrate Henry Herlong. He was released on $10,000 bond. Ferguson had been suspended by Chief Justice George Gregory on his indictment on March 21, 1991.

Ferguson's tenure on the bench was brief after his swearing in on May 28, 1990, serving less than a year before his indictment and suspension by the S.C. Supreme Court.

Court Denies Pay to Ferguson

As of April 5, 1991, the suspended status of Judge Tee Ferguson came up and the South Carolina Supreme Court decided to continue the suspension from office of Judge Tee Ferguson imposed on him in late 1990 even before his indictment for corruption which came on March 21, 1991. Originally suspended with pay when it became known that he was under investigation by the U.S. Attorney, the indictment presented the Court with a novel issue since no other judge of state court in recent memory had been charged with felony corruption.

Even though the corruption was alleged to have happened before Ferguson became a judge and while he was in the House, the Court had no choice but to suspend him as his integrity had been badly compromised by the charges which were eventually proved.

Lacking constitutional or statutory authority to suspend judges, the Supreme Court relied on its inherent powers to protect itself and the public and the administration of justice. The Court also held that Ferguson would not get paid because he was not working.

Ferguson was charged with taking a bribe of $3,000 from lobbyist Ron Cobb to support the betting bill. The indictment stated that the FBI had videotaped a payment while Ferguson was asking Cobb for money to buy a Mercedes Benz car.

The Court gave Ferguson an opportunity to argue for the continuation of his pay, but did not find it convincing.

Drug Testing for Legislators Proposed

The House passed an amendment by 92-10 to require drug testing of all legislators on a random basis. The proposal set forward a scheme to have the Speaker and President Pro Tem order drug tests for 10 representatives and four senators each year.

Rep. Grady Brown (D-Lee) argued that, "at a time when the House and Senate have been under scrutiny for drug use," the measure was needed.

Gov. Campbell Takes No Drug Test

Even while telling his aides to be drug tested, Gov. Carroll Campbell did not take a drug test himself. Three times during his first term (1986-1991), Campbell required his staffers and political operatives to take the tests. Conducted in 1987, 1989, and 1990, the tests came back negative.

Democrats criticized Campbell for not taking a drug test himself in view of the fact that his close friend and political advisor, Dick Greer, had been indicted for cocaine. As Greer was not a state employee, he was not required to take the test which the governor mandated for his paid staff.

In the 1986 campaign for governor, Campbell made drug testing an issue and promised to drug test his aides. He also challenged his Democratic opponent, Nick Theodore, to take the test—both did and both passed.

Judicial Screening Reforms Proposed

Stung by the indictment of Tee Ferguson in March, 1991, after he had been elected to the 7th Circuit Court bench in May, 1990, the Senate proposed a new judicial screening system be set up as part of the ethics reform process.

The State in an editorial found some merit in the scheme as it proposed to add four non-legislators to the screening panel including two lawyers and two non-lawyers. Noting that the plan might counter the widely held perception that sitting legislators had an unfair advantage in running for judgeships, *The State* pointed out that, unlike almost all states, South Carolina judges of the state courts were elected by the General Assembly.

However, the Senate screening bill did not embrace a recent proposal by the South Carolina Bar to have an 18 member merit selection commission which would submit up to three names for each vacant judicial position.

Sting Indictment Continue

FBI agent John Harley, heading up the Lost Trust probe, told reporters on April 9, 1991, that the pile of federal indictments already presented to the court would be followed by even more indictments based on the amount of evidence the FBI had built up in the Lost Trust cases. Describing the probe as providing "fodder for investigation in years to come," Harley said the criminal charges against 22 defendants soon would be followed by new indictments.

However, Harley predicted that the last of the indictments would be presented by late summer, 1991, saying that the bulk of charges had already been made against known defendants.

The FBI had adopted a policy of focusing on public corruption in recent years in addition to its traditional battles with gangsters and interstate crime. Lost Trust was one of several recent major public corruption cases prosecuted by federal authorities against state government officials, including legislators.

Ethics Bill Vote Challenged As Unethical

Ironically, a Senate vote on ethics reform amendments was attacked by the S.C. Policy Council as a conflict of interest violation of the 1975 Ethics Act. SCPC State PAC President, Hal Eberle, an old World War II bomber pilot, alleged that on March 27, 1991, a Senate vote to strip out an amendment from the draft ethics bill violated a rule prohibiting a legislator from taking action or making a decision which would "affect directly his personal financial interest" without notifying the presiding officer of his conflict of interest.

In a letter to Senate Ethics Chairman Ed Saleeby, (D-Darlington), the Council pointed to Sen. John Land (D-Clarendon), a lawyer, for voting to remove an amendment banning lawyer-legislators from representation before state boards and commissions. Six others did not debate but voted to remove the amendment even though they, like Land, did such work. Land had made $144,000 in 1990 before the S.C. Workers' Compensation Commission.

Saleeby agreed to convene the Ethics Committee but saw no violation himself and acknowledged he also had such practice. Eberle said the SCPC did not file a complaint because it would impose an immediate gag order on the complainant.

Four senators—Saleeby, Land, Isadore Lourie (D-Richland) and Theo Mitchell (D-Greenville) in total earned $367,000 before the S.C. Workers' Compensation Commission in 1990. Sen. Sam Stilwell (R-Greenville) and Sen. Marshall Williams (D-Orangeburg) abstained from voting on a similar amendment, noting "the potential for conflict on this issue."

Drug Defendants Line Up to Plead Guilty

On April 10, 1991, a number of criminals caught up in Lost Trust were slated to plead guilty. Along with Dick Greer on that date, a gaggle of lobbyists were set to join him in pleading to drug violations involving cocaine and marijuana or corruption.

Along with lesser known drug violators, Ron Cobb was charged with two counts of possession of cocaine used by Cobb while serving as an FBI sting agent and contrary to his immunity deal. Cobb was scheduled to enter his plea at 11:00 a.m., following guilty pleas by Randy Lee at 9:30 a.m., Ronnie Wade Crow at 10:00 a.m., and Tom Collins at 10:30 a.m. Then at noon, Greer was lined up to plead.

Lee, lobbyist for the South Carolina Health Care Association, pleaded to possessing cocaine. Crow, former S.C. Highway Commissioner, pleaded to corruption, a violation of the Hobbs Act. Crow was charged with delivering a bribe to Speaker Pro Tem Jack I. Rogers, himself charged with racketeering. Collins admitted possession of cocaine.

The judge who took the pleas, Falcon Hawkins, held a pretrial hearing for corruptionist Rep. Paul Derrick (R-Lexington) at 3:00 p.m. to close out an eventful day of rooting out abuse of office and drugs.

Ferguson Demands Open Trial

Bribery defendant Judge Tee Ferguson on April 9, 1991, asked the court to either drop criminal charges or grant an open and public trial of his case in accord with the U.S. Constitution. Charged with taking a $3,000 bribe and possessing cocaine while in the House, he was also cited for conspiracy to commit extortion and other violations.

The trials of previous defendants had been interrupted by court orders to close proceedings to the public. Judge Falcon Hawkin's closing of some of the Luther Taylor trial in October, 1990, had prompted an appeal to the 4th Circuit which ordered that a hearing was required before closing proceedings. Even so, later trials of Reps. Larry Blanding (D-Sumter) and B.J. Gordon (D-Williamsburg) were closed for much of the time.

Ferguson's attorneys asked not only for an open and public trial, but also for a speedy trial.

Senator Carmichael Returns

Re-elected by the voters of Dillon County where he had been convicted of vote buying in 1980, former Sen. Gene Carmichael on April 10, 1991, prepared to take the seat of Sen. Jack Lindsay who had died in January, 1991, while under agreement to plead to corruption in the Lost Trust scandal.

Carmichael's contaminated record caused Sen. David Thomas (R-Greenville) to object to the return of Carmichael, noting that some senators thought he had disgraced the Senate.

Under the S.C. Constitution, the Senate had the power to determine if Carmichael could return.

The State wrote that when Carmichael was convicted in 1981 of vote-buying, the Senate could not muster the two-thirds vote to expel him. Later both the House and Senate passed rules to clarify when a derelict member could be suspended and expelled. The Senate adopted a softer rule providing for suspension only at conviction and expulsion after a failed appeal. The House rule required suspension on indictment and expulsion on conviction.

S.C. Citizens Have Forgiving View of Corruption

"Sometimes people just get caught up in things, but that doesn't say they are a bad person. You just get caught up in things." Thus spoke Corenia Jackson, 65, while fishing at Lake View, South Carolina, at an old mill pond.

Dressed in a red gingham bonnet, Ms. Jackson said, "All I do is go to church and fish. The rest of it, I let it go."

But even so, she felt sorry for convicted felon former Sen. Gene Carmichael of Dillon County, found guilty of vote buying at the polling booths of Dillon County in 1980. In early 1991, Carmichael was voted back in to replace a dead man, Sen. Jack Lindsay, who was set to plead guilty to vote buying at the State House before he died in January of 1991.

Perhaps the forgiving and passive culture of rural South Carolina was a reason why public corruption was so widespread and widely tolerated.

Quick Verdicts Hit Blanding and Gordon

An alternate juror in the corruption trials of Larry Blanding and B.J. Gordon told the media that, "There was nothing the defense lawyers could do to overcome the impact of those videotapes in my mind." Alternate juror David Nesbitt, who was not used in reaching the verdict, told the media that, based on the evidence, the jury had to convict.

While defense counsel tried to depict the payments of $1,000 to Gordon and $1,300 to Blanding as campaign donations, the jury did not buy any of it. "It just doesn't look like a campaign contribution," said Nesbitt. The jury hit Gordon with one count of extortion and one count of conspiracy to violate the Hobbs Act. Blanding was convicted of conspiracy to violate the Hobbs Act and two counts of extortion. All charges related to the betting bill vote-buying of Ron Cobb.

Medlock Wanted State Grand Jury to Attack Corruption

By mid-April, 1991, Attorney General Travis Medlock thought the Lost Trust scandal and public outrage at the bribery and drug use might be converted into support for giving the State Grand Jury additional power to probe public corruption. The State Grand Jury had the ability to subpoena evidence and probe deeply into crimes such as corruption, election fraud, and other violations.

Medlock told the Senate Judiciary Committee at a hearing that the time had come to give the State Grand Jury powers that the county grand jury system lacked, including subpoena power, grants of immunity, recording of testimony, and jurisdiction over intercounty crimes.

In November, 1990, Medlock had fought a proposed constitutional amendment to reduce the State Grand Jury's powers to only drug and pornography cases. Medlock traveled over the state both campaigning for re-election and in opposition to the proposed amendment. In the election, the voters voted against the amendment and for Medlock.

Deputy Attorney General Cameron Currie testified that, "The state had no investigative grand jury." She complained that county grand juries did not record testimony, could not grant immunity, and could not subpoena evidence. SLED also could not take reliable statements from witnesses.

Medlock also said a state grand jury could take evidence from federal probes and use them for state prosecutions as well. He closed by advocating "an operating state grand jury with public corruption jurisdiction." Estimated cost of the added powers was about $500,000 per annum.

House and Senate Bills Propose Citizen Prosecution

The Senate ethics reform bill proposed that the Senate and House ethics committees would handle complaints against legislators. The bill also required that a citizen who filed a complaint prosecute the complaint to a conclusion, either by arguing the case himself or by hiring an attorney to pursue the complaint for him. If the ethics committee found the complaint was malicious, it could prosecute the complainant according to the bill's provisions.

Both Rep. Tim Rogers (D-Richland) and State Ethics Commission Director Gary Baker felt that the private prosecution requirements were defective and Baker predicted they would discourage citizens from filing complaints because they did not have the resources.

But Sen. John Land (D-Clarendon) disagreed, saying, "I think it's our responsibility for us to judge ourselves just as it is at the national level." Land added, "I would not be willing to turn my political future over to some appointed commission or something like that." Land said that a decade earlier legislators saddled the burden on the complainant because "we wanted to make it as hard as we could for a citizen to bring a frivolous complaint."

Sen. Land Stresses Campaign Finance Reform

Dismissing a score of zero points given to him on a survey conducted by the S.C. Policy Council on their issues, Sen. John Land (D-Clarendon) said that the real problem with ethics in state government and politics was abusive campaign finance activities.

The SCPC survey rated legislators based in their votes on specific bills, but, Land said, only one of the questions on the survey related to campaign finance reform. Much of it related to the issue of lawyer-legislators practicing before state boards and commissions.

Land said the real problem was political money, of which the SCPC political action committee was a significant source. Land said, "Whatever abuse is out there, and a lot of it is subtle, it goes back to campaign contributions."

Weak Enforcement In Reform Bill Criticized

"The thrust of the debate has not been on the enforcement mechanism," observed Sen. Glenn McConnell (R-Charleston), noting that the focus had been "either on prohibitions or disclosure." McConnell urged a reconsideration of the draft ethics bill and stressed the inclusion of strong enforcement of whatever was passed.

Rep. Tim Rogers (D-Richland) worried that he, too, wanted more enforcement to force compliance with new reforms, and he demanded a stronger bill. Rogers also said he feared that the rare opportunity created by the Lost Trust scandal might be squandered without passing real reforms. "This year had been a real window of opportunity, and whatever we get done this year might be all we get done." Reflecting on his experience in the House since the time when the 1975 Ethics Act was passed, Rogers explained that the State Ethics Commission had pointed out failing in the 1975 Act, but the Legislature did nothing.

It was more obvious that the enforcement activities of legislative ethics committees since the 1975 Ethics Act was enacted had been minimal. The Senate Ethics Committee had met only once in the period of 1987 to 1991 and the House Ethics Committee's only action was to close down an escort service run by Rep. Ennis Fant (D-Greenville) out of his House office at a time when three of the committee's members faced federal indictments, as did Fant.

Lobbyists' Fees Pile Up

As lobbyists were central players in the Operation Lost Trust scandal and lobbyist Ron Cobb was the center of the bribery sting handing out bribes at the State House, *The State* looked into the fees being paid to lobbyists to influence policy-making and administrative matters and published its findings on April 19, 1991.

The highest paid lobbyist was Hubert "Ed" Yarborough, who in the 1990 legislative session took in $205, 050. Next was Russ Mellette, who got $181,934 and was followed by Thomas Mulikin with $162,832. Robert Kneece, Sr., took $134,250 and Dwight Drake, $117,500. Then came Ken Kinard at $90,700 and James Fields with $82,060. Numbers 8 to 10 in receipts were Kathy Randall's $80,050, and then Ron Cobb's $78,660, and Ernie Nunnery with $73,958.

The clients who spent the most on lobbying were the South Carolina Education Association at $228,179, Laidlaw Environmental Services' $190,660, the South Carolina Textile Manufacturers at $125,619 and the S.C. Tourism Council at $102,768. Others were the S.C. Chamber of Commerce at $97,130, the S.C. Medical Association's $74,627, and SCANA at $71,124.

The biggest spenders on free food, drinks, and entertainment were Russell Munn, $22,442, Charlie Rountree, $21,456, Dan Jones at $11,820 and Pat Watson who spent $9,928.

State Agency Lobbying Hit

Senators denounced the lobbying activities of leaders of the State Highway Department against a restructuring bill affecting the Department. This raised another question about lobbying at the State House in addition to the issue of lobbyists handing out cash bribes and free food and trips to legislators and other officials.

The presence of Bob McClellan and others from the Department in the balcony of the Senate provoked Sen. Hugh Leatherman (D-Florence) to say, "Under no circumstances should they be in here lobbying for keeping the department as it is, and it really offends me when I look up in the balcony and see them up there."

McClellan, a former Chairman of House Ways and Means, wanted to delay a bill which would restructure the department until the next year after an analysis of the agency had been completed. But Leatherman said of people in the balcony, "I see a paid state employee, the director, up there. He ought to be over there running the department instead of sitting in the balcony trying to influence us."

The conflict pointed to the problem of the use of government funds and personnel to lobby the General Assembly to try to influence public policy. Commissioner Bob Harrell of Charleston described the effort saying, "I don't think it's a lobbying effort as much as it is an effort to try to be helpful and try to show support where we feel that it's appropriate."

Ethics Bill Needs Teeth

In an editorial of April 19, 1991, *The State* derided the ethics reform bills being kicked back and forth in the House and Senate for their weak enforcement schemes. In addition to the failure of the bill to deal with lawyer-legislators practicing before boards and commissions and a loophole allowing lobbyists and corporations to give huge amounts to candidates via political parties, *The State* found the Senate proposal for legislative ethics committees to handle complaints against legislators was designed to fail.

The House proposed to let the State Ethics Commission handle all initial complaints against all officials as less incestuous, but *The State* said, "citizens would have a tough time filing complaints under either bill. Both required the complaining party, not the ethics panel, to prosecute the case, necessitating in most complaints that the citizen hire a lawyer and investigator, a costly and dangerous process.

Further, if a complaint did not prevail, the House bill provided a misdemeanor charge and a fine of $1,000 while the Senate bill provided for criminal conviction and a fine of $2,000 and up to two years in prison, all such penalties being imposed on the complaining witness.

Noting Sen. John Land's concession that the Senate bill "wanted to make it as hard as we could for a citizen to make a frivolous complaint," the editors pointed to Rep. Tim Rogers' analysis in the House that, "This renders the entire enforcement process extremely ineffective.... What we end up with is a self-enforcing process where disclosure is the only sanction."

Editorial Wants Ethics Commission Enforcement

Ridiculing the proposals in the House and Senate bills to use legislative ethics committees to enforce citizens' ethics complainants and to initiate and prosecute cases against legislators, *The State* on April 19, 1991, argued that a better plan would be to give jurisdiction over the investigation of all such complaints to the State Ethics Commission.

Noting the comment by Rep. Tim Rogers (D-Richland) that self-enforcement by legislative ethics committees was doomed to malfunction, *The State* stressed, "After all, no matter how tough the final ethics reform bill is, it will be worthless if it can't be strictly enforced."

The State contended that the regulation of lobbyists and the control of campaign contributions were the most substantive problems needing attention, but "the enforcement of the ethics rules is just as great a problem, even though most lawmakers aren't talking about it."

Citizens could not reasonably be expected and relied upon to investigate violations in order to frame and file complaints. And citizens should not be expected to prosecute cases themselves to a successful result.

Lost Trust Prosecutors Win Honors

Assistant U.S. attorneys John W. McIntosh, Dale L. DuTremble, and John M. Barton received special commendation awards from U.S. Attorney General Dick Thornburgh for their work in the Lost Trust prosecutions. The three went to Washington to receive awards on April 19, 1991, in the Great Hall of the Main Justice Building.

At that point, a total of 13 legislators and one former legislator (Tee Ferguson) had been indicted for corruption and another legislator and seven others had been charged with drugs, a total of 21 with another 7 defendants later indicted.

Taylor Denied Bail

Appealing his conviction for conspiracy and extortion, former Rep. Luther Taylor asked to get out of prison on a six and a half year sentence. On April 19, 1991, Judge Falcon Hawkins denied bail, saying he lost jurisdiction when the appeal was filed.

Hawkins said in his order that although he did not think Taylor was a flight risk, the judge thought he was dangerous, noting that Taylor was overheard to say that if he "could find Ron Cobb he would kill that son of a bitch." The order noted that when first brought in for questioning by the FBI on July 17, 1990, Taylor had a concealed gun. Hawkins noted that Taylor's wife filed for divorce on grounds of physical cruelty.

Hawkins also found that the appeal was unlikely to succeed. The appeal was based on allegations that new evidence showed that prosecution witness Ron Cobb had used drugs while an FBI sting agent and that Cobb had paid Sen. Lindsay, which Cobb denied at Taylor's trial. Since then, Cobb had admitted paying Lindsay for his help, even though he denied the money was a bribe.

Officials File Disclosures

Disclosure forms filed in April, 1991, showed little about legislators' finances as many reported nothing on their official disclosure documents. Such non-reporting had been standard practice for years.

But the ethics bills then struggling in the Senate and House gave a chance to force disclosure, said Rep. Wes Hayes (D-York). Yet the bills were weak even on disclosure. Gary Baker, Executive Director of the State Ethics Commission, said two problems needed reform. First, the bills should require disclosure of all business interests and real estate holdings of officials and their families. "Those are the kinds of issues where your conflicts arise" and mandatory disclosure "puts the public on notice of potential areas of conflict."

Noting the debates and discussions by legislators about the problem of lawyer-legislators practicing before boards and commissions, Rep. Hayes, newly elected Chair of the House Ethics Committee, said it was an issue that could not be denied.

The bills did require disclosure of gifts and services given by lobbyists to officials. But under extant law, officeholders had to report only business done with public agencies and local governments. Thus, Sen. Hugh Leatherman (D-Florence) reported he sold $1.2 million of cement to the S.C. Highway Department.

However, those who benefited from a new law or regulation that fostered profits or tax breaks for businesses in which officials had an interest need not be disclosed. Baker recommended disclosure of all such interests of a value of $10,000 or more.

Financial Interests Need More Disclosure

As the ethics reform bills were being hashed out in the General Assembly, the question of how much financial disclosure by officials was needed. Under the 1975 Ethics Act and actual practice, officials reported almost nothing about their potential conflicts of interest and their personal finances.

Gary Baker, Executive Director of the State Ethics Commission, pointed out that in Congress, the disclosure required was minimal and did not reveal conflicts of interest caused by property holding and official duties. State officials had the same problem and the new ethics bills were a good place to cure the problem.

However, the reform bills under discussion left it to officials to decide what property, financial, and business interests presented conflicts of interest and what to disclose. John Crangle, Executive Director of Common Cause/South Carolina, remarked that such discretion was dubious at best, observing, "Given the level of sensitivity by the General Assembly, I'm sure they would err on the side of non-disclosure." Baker recommended full disclosure, not only by legislators, but also by all constitutional officers, agency directors, chief financial officers, and local governmental officeholders.

At that point in the debate, it seemed unlikely that aggressive financial disclosure would be written into any ethics reform bill.

Ethics Conflicts in Voting on Ethics

A coalition of citizens' groups alleged early in April, 1991, that some six senators had a conflict of interest in voting on ethics reform bills then in process. The groups asked the Senate Ethics Committee for an opinion and its chairman, Ed Saleeby, referred the matter to Attorney General Travis Medlock. Sen. Mike Rose (R-Dorchester) wrote Medlock saying, "I think we have to resolve this issue."

The issue was that six lawyer-legislators in the Senate voted for allowing persons like themselves to continue appearing before boards and commissions. State law prohibited voting by an official on issues that would "substantially affect directly his personal financial interest." The procedure was to write a statement reporting the conflict to the presiding officer, but none of the six wrote to Lt. Gov. Nick Theodore, the presiding officer of the Senate.

Sen. Rose warned that Medlock should act to prevent those who would benefit from allowing such representation from voting on the bill, saying the fate of the matter "is going to be determined by people who have conflicts of interest."

Those involved in the alleged conflicts were Sens. John Land, Isadore Lourie, Theo Mitchell, and Ed Saleeby, all four of whom had earned money before the Workers' Compensation Commission. Two others, Sens. Sam Stilwell and Marshall Williams, had not done so, but declared a conflict of interest and at first abstained, but then later voted against the ban.

State-Run Primaries Bill Set to Pass

A major reform of the election system in South Carolina was passed by the Senate and went to the House in mid-April, 1991. A bill to take away control of the administration of party primaries from parties and place it in the hands of the State Election Commission was set to pass.

The bill, which had been sponsored by Rep. Luther Taylor, recently sent to prison for bribery, was designed to break down a scheme set up in Jim Crow days to keep blacks from voting in primary elections. The General Assembly had taken away control of the primaries from the state in the 1940s after the U.S. Supreme Court ruled that states could not deny blacks the right to vote in party primaries.

Proponents argued that even if the government was corrupt, the elections should not be. "To us, the integrity of the voting process and the opportunity for citizens to vote are the most basic functions that a democratic government should perform," said John Crangle of Common Cause/South Carolina, adding, "We have just had so many irregularities over the years in regard to primaries."

Supporters of the bill included the Election Commission, Common Cause, and the S.C. Republican Party. Sen. Don Holland (D-Kershaw) sponsored the bill. However, Sen. Glenn McConnell objected on grounds of cost to the taxpayers, although he admitted, "State-run primaries are a nice thing to have.... [It] ensures that all the polls are going to open."

Senate Ethics Showdown Looms

"If we have a blood bath, maybe we'll just have it. There is no reason that the majority of the Senate can't prevail on legislation such as ethics," said Marshall Williams of the debate set for April 24, 1991, on the ethics reform bill which had been fought over since January.

Both the House and Senate had passed ethics reform bills already, but they were not the same. The Senate then set debate on the House bill for that date, planning to revise the Senate bill and send it back to the House in anticipation of a conference committee settling the matter in the end.

Sen. Hugh Leatherman (D-Florence) intended to propose a ban on lawyer-legislators practicing before boards and commissions, a ban which had been approved and later rejected by vote of 22-20. Glenn McConnell hoped to move some of the reforms in what he called "the ethics struggle." McConnell wanted to tighten financial disclosure rules. But he and Sen. Jim Bryan (D-Laurens), an attorney, both thought the lawyer-legislator ban was not going to happen. McConnell also wanted to clarify provisions relating to legislators taking retainers from lobbyists and their employers. Sen. Ernie Passailague (D-Charleston) also proposed an amendment on financial conflicts.

House Dodges Another Ethics Fight

Rather than go through another contentious debate over its ethics reform bill, the House decided in late April to turn its bill over to the conference committee. The big issues, of course, were lawyer-legislators and income disclosure.

House Majority Leader, Joe McElveen (D-Sumter), pointed out that his fight to toughen the bill had been frustrated and that he was ready to try the conference committee. But David Wilkins, House Judiciary Chair, thought the bill was strong enough and anything more would be too restrictive.

Bills banning lobbyists' gifts and meals to legislators and limiting the size of campaign contributions were still pending. But a two-thirds vote would be required to make any changes and that was not likely at the time.

Trial Publicity at Issue in Ferguson Case

Defense attorneys in the Tee Ferguson case complained of media leaks and prejudicial news stories in the matter. And Judge Falcon Hawkins puzzled over what to do.

On the one hand, Hawkins told lawyers at a hearing on April 29, 1991, in the Tee Ferguson case, that he might call on reporters to tell the court where they were getting information published in *The State* and *The Spartanburg Herald-Journal*, but Judge Hawkins admitted, "If I had every newspaper article that's come out since this Operation Lost Trust...broke out, they'd cover this desk, and I guess it's a newspaper reporter's dream."

Another publicity issue was whether the prosecution had revealed videotapes to the S.C. Supreme Court on the decision to suspend Judge Ferguson without pay until resolution. Defense attorneys demanded to know who had seen the videotapes. Hawkins was considering a motion to suppress the tapes at trial, but it seemed unlikely at that point that the judge would actually suppress such tapes.

Racial Bias in Sting Alleged

On April 29, 1991, defense attorneys Hemphill Pride III and John Hardaway fought it out with prosecutors in the Tee Ferguson drug and corruption case. Ferguson's team alleged that federal agents had tipped off white legislators about the State House sting while targeting blacks and giving some of them drugs and drinks. Ferguson's attorneys tried to get the judge to remove Assistant U.S. Attorney John Barton from the case for allegedly saying in newspaper articles that the defense claims could not be proved in court.

Barton called for sanctions on Pride and Hardaway for making "frivolous, bald-faced allegations," adding "this kind of trash shouldn't be allowed in court," and urging Judge Falcon Hawkins to dismiss the claims without a hearing. But Pride said that his claims were based on "Judge Ferguson's exercising his constitutional rights," adding that Pride had a witness ready to say that agents acted improperly in the probe.

The judge demanded proof and said he saw no evidence of racial targeting. He demanded that the defense provide the facts that day.

The hearing hashed out a total of 27 motions in getting ready for trial set for May 28, 1991, at which only the conspiracy and bribery charges would be heard. The drug charges of conspiracy and possession of cocaine would be set for trial later in accord with a motion to have two trials held separately for corruption and for drugs.

Senate Passes Ethics Reform Bill

On April 24, 1991, the S.C. Senate finally voted to try to restore public confidence in state government. The ethics reform bill imposed drastic limits on campaign contributions and cut out freebies from lobbyists to legislators, but it was not enough for some reformers.

Sen. David Thomas (R-Greenville) voted against the bill on the grounds that although it had many new features to suppress corruption, the bill was incomplete and a lost opportunity for real reform. He said, "It's just that this is a window of opportunity for South Carolina in ethics, when we could have not just had a decent piece of legislation—we could have had an outstanding piece of legislation." Thomas really wanted, he said, "a bill that the rest of the nation would have emulated."

Even so, a number of senators were proud of their work. Senate veteran Verne Smith (D-Greenville) lauded the bill, "I think we have passed probably the strongest ethics bill in the United States as far as I know." The bill was not perfect and disappointed some, but Smith opined, "I really believe the public interest will be served by what we've done here."

The bill banned lobbyists gifts and meals to legislators and capped campaign contributions at $250 to legislators from a single source and banned all contributions from lobbyists. Cash contributions were limited to $25 to stop cash bribes from being handed out masked as campaign contributions as happened on a massive basis in the sting.

Senate Ethics Bill Disappoints Some Critics

Passed by a large majority vote, the Senate ethics reform bill was widely praised in the Senate, but some thought more was needed. The bill did not do enough to stop elected officials from using their office for personal gain according to critics of the bill.

The Senate voted 34-1 to prohibit lawyer-legislators from representing clients before state boards and commissions in cases where lawyer-legislators voted on the membership and budgets of such boards and commissions. Senators agreed to stop legislators from selling goods and services to state agencies if they voted on those same agencies budgets.

By a vote 24-18, the Senate voted to ban lawyer-legislators from taking retainer payments from lobbyists and their employers.

However, by a vote of 3-19, the Senate rejected a ban on lawyer-legislators appearing before state boards and commissions. No vote was taken to ban lawyer-legislators from appearing before judges they voted on for state court offices such as circuit courts and appellate courts.

Election Returning Felon A Fraud

The election to replace Sen. Jack Lindsay (D-Marlboro) who had died in January, 1991, before he could be indicted for corruption was tainted by fraud, but in the end, Gene Carmichael, who had been convicted of vote-buying in 1980 in Dillon County, defeated Lindsay's son, Chuck. The election held in Dillon County featured the usual irregularities as far more votes were recorded than voters who actually entered the polling places.

In the 1980 federal vote-buying scandal, some 30 people were sent to prison in a scheme to buy absentee votes for $5 each in the Dillon County Democratic primary. Somebody contested the results and so an investigation was launched by the FBI and SLED.

But in the 1991 special primary to replace Lindsay, nobody protested the election irregularities though there were multiple violations. In addition to the mismatch between the number of the votes counted and the smaller number of voters who actually appeared at the polls, the ballots were counted in secret, no voting booths were provided, and a poll manager left the site for a time to pick up selected voters favoring one candidate.

At the time, primary elections were conducted privately by political parties without state or local government personnel at the polling places and in Dillon County, the poll workers were not trained by the parties and did not know the election laws. The S.C. Election Commission, Common Cause/South Carolina, and the S.C. Republican Party had been pushing for a state takeover of primaries and Sen. Donald Holland (D-Kershaw) had sponsored a bill to do so, but the bill was pending.

Judge Softens Secrecy Actions

Under strong media pressure to open up the courtroom to the press and stop keeping so much secret about the trials, Judge Falcon Hawkins decided to release some evidence in the case of indicted Rep. Paul Derrick (R-Lexington). The judge gave reporters the transcript of a conversation recorded between FBI sting agent former Rep. Robert Kohn (R-Charleston) and Derrick on the topic of the 1990 budget bill and its provision to legalize payoffs for video poker.

The transcripts had many words blacked out, probably as profanities, including a reference to Gov. Carroll Campbell's opposition to a video poker bill.

Governor Throws Ethics Party

To celebrate the passage of the House ethics reform bill on April 24, 1991, Gov. Carroll Campbell threw a party at state expense at the Governor's Mansion. Free liquor and caviar were handed out to representatives in attendance, provoking criticism in the Senate.

The Senate ethics reform bill, however, would ban such use of state resources and one critic, Sen. Ernie Passailague (D-Charleston), complained that it was offensive to "have any state official throwing a party at state expense serving liquor and caviar to thank people for taking a position." Passailague predicted he would not be invited to such events in the future.

CHAPTER TWENTY THREE

MAY, 1991—ROGERS, DERRICK, FERGUSON, AND COLLINS CONVICTED
AND
ETHICS REFORM CONTINUES PROGRESS

The guilty plea of House Speaker Pro Tem Jack I. Rogers and the trial convictions of Rep. Paul Derrick and Judge Tee Ferguson littered the bodies of more crooks on the grounds of the South Carolina State House in early 1991. These new carcasses gave off such an odor of corruption that the people of South Carolina and their legislators had to sanitize the rotten political system which had produced the carnage.

Thus, as more legislators were found guilty, the reformers in the House and Senate, with only slight encouragement from Gov. Carroll Campbell, kept hammering the ethics reform bill into final form. Even so, by the end of the 1991 session the first week in June, the ethics bill was still not completed due to differences between the House and Senate and also between Republicans and Democrats.

So much had been written into the draft ethics reform bills of the House and Senate that an expectation had been created in the media and among the public that a bill would somehow still pass in 1991 even if a special session of the General Assembly had to be called by Gov. Campbell. In the end, this is exactly what happened and the bill was finally passed on September 23, 1991, and signed shortly after by the governor on October 1.

Derrick Trial Moves Forward

In spite of defense counsel's efforts to delay the bribery trial of suspended Rep. Paul Derrick (R-Lexington), Judge Falcon Hawkins ordered the trial to go forward in U.S. District Court in Columbia. Derrick was charged with conspiracy and extortion in the Lost Trust sting. The trial was set to start on May 1, 1991.

Derrick's attorneys based their request for a delay on a new group of audio and videotapes which had been delivered to them April 30, just before the trial was set to begin.

But Hawkins directed that the jury selection process be carried out and on May 1, 1991, a total of six jurors were selected from a group of 17 interviewed.

Derrick's lawyer, Vinton Lide, a former federal prosecutor, complained that, "We relied on the government saying they had given us everything and now, at the 11th hour, we found out they haven't." He also worried that more new prosecution evidence might be brought into the trial, saying, "it makes us wonder what in the world is out there yet that we don't know about."

A side issue in the Derrick trial was the court's decision to close the jury selection process to the public. Attorney Jay Bender of the South Carolina Press Association filed a motion in the U.S.

4th Circuit Court of Appeals asking the court to decide if the jury selection should be closed and alleging the public had a right under the U.S. Constitution to attend the jury selection.

Derrick's Trial Begins

When questioned by the FBI in 1990, Derrick at first told the FBI that he had not taken any cash or gifts from lobbyists, but the next day filed an amendment to his campaign disclosure forms listing a $1,000 cash gift from Cobb as a campaign contribution.

U.S. Attorney Bart Daniel in his opening statement told the jury that "public trust in the case of Paul Derrick became a public trough." Daniel said that the prosecution would show that Derrick "willfully, knowingly, and intentionally joined that conspiracy, banded together with that partnership in crime."

The indictment alleged that Cobb talked to Derrick on May 2, 1990, about the betting bill. Daniel said that a videotape of the meeting would show that Derrick asked Cobb for a set of Japanese golf clubs, "the best money can buy." But then on May 29, 1990, Derrick changed his mind and agreed to take the cash because he had won a set of golf clubs in the meantime and did not need more golf clubs.

Daniel denied that Derrick was entrapped and said he acted on his own motion, adding, "God gave us all free will." Daniel emphasized that "There is no evidence that this money was pushed on Paul Derrick or shoved into his pocket."

It came out early in the presentation of evidence that Ron Cobb had shown the prosecution a *South Carolina Legislative Manual* which listed all of the 170 legislators and many other public officials, including judges, executive officers, and federal legislators. Cobb had marked with checks the names of some 70 legislators as persons known to be shady. Judge Hawkins joked with defense counsel Lide that, "I hope they don't have my name or yours in that manual."

In opening statements, Derrick's lawyer, Vinton Lide, admitted that "Sting operations are very important. I have no problem with that being a tool that law enforcement uses. But it is a very powerful and dangerous endeavor that could be abused and misused." Lide then added, "The government induced this crime," alleging that Derrick was the victim of an FBI scheme to entrap him in a crime which, if proved, could have defeated the prosecution's case and acquitted Derrick.

FBI agent Mike Clemens told the court that taping machines in Cobb's office at the AT&T Building and Town House Hotel had been bugged with hidden cameras and microphones and that a microwave transmitter relayed the signals to the nearby Senate Plaza two blocks from the State House where the FBI had an apartment rented on the 19th floor to control and monitor the equipment and watch the payoffs.

Clemens said that he had operated the equipment on June 6, 1990, when Cobb gave money to Derrick and observed the transaction on television while in the Senate Plaza building apartment. The transaction was taped as evidence.

"Cobb: Capitol for Sale"

The State ran a headline on May 4, 1991, which read, "Cobb: Capitol for Sale." The story alleged that corrupt lobbyist and FBI sting agent Ron Cobb had told federal authorities that he could bribe 70 members of the South Carolina General Assembly. It was based on testimony given by Cobb on May 3, 1991, in the Paul Derrick corruption trial in Columbia.

Cobb told the court that he had "done business" with the corrupt group of 70 or knew someone else who had done business with them. Cobb said defendant Paul Derrick was one of the first he wanted to mention to the court. Derrick had allegedly opposed the pari-mutuel betting bill until he took $1,000 from Cobb to vote for the bill.

FBI agent Mike Clemens told the court from the witness stand that Cobb had been known to the FBI since 1987 as a cocaine user and dealer and that Cobb had purchased cocaine from undercover agents for $20,000 when he was caught in the sting. Both Cobb and Kohn were called as prosecution witnesses in the Derrick trial and in other trials as well. Kohn had pleaded to conspiracy but had not yet been sentenced.

Clemens also said that Rep. Luther Taylor (D-Richland) was picked out in the probe as he was known to be a heavy cocaine user. Taylor was one of the 70 legislators marked on a list by Cobb as prone to take payoffs at the State House.

Derrick Trial Details His Corruption

The prosecution promised to show another videotape in which Cobb and Derrick discussed their plan to move the betting bill in 1991 after it stalled in the 1990 session. At the time, Derrick commented to suggest he expected another bribe in the future, saying, "I'm sure I'll have another birthday again next year."

Prosecution presented the picture of Rep. Derrick as a man eager to take whatever lobbyists gave to him. The prosecution also presented former Rep. Robert Brown (D-Marion) who had been convicted in Lost Trust. Brown told the court that Derrick and Brown along with two other House members attended a convention of the American Legislative Exchange Council in California in 1989, but avoided the educational meetings and seminars, instead opting to play golf instead. Then on the way home from the convention, the legislators took a side trip to Las Vegas which was paid for by a lobbyist. Brown also said that Derrick had taken another trip to Las Vegas on a different date paid for by Ron Cobb.

Brown admitted on the stand that he could have been charged with taking two bribes from Cobb but was not, although he pleaded guilty to one count of extortion. Brown explained that he had taken money from Cobb because "he offered it to me." Brown also said that Derrick often took favors from lobbyists.

Derrick was facing a maximum of 40 years and $500,000 fine.

Kohn Brands Derrick as Crook

Rep. Bob Kohn (R-Charleston), who had become an FBI undercover operative, hit Derrick hard. Kohn testified that he told Derrick that Cobb would pay $1,000 to vote for the betting bill and $500 for a "walk" on the bill, that is, not vote at all on the bill. One tape showed Derrick had been told that Cobb had a "package" for him and Derrick said, "That's grand. Thank you."

A tape showed that Derrick talked about hiding cash payoffs on ethics disclosure forms and said that he was thinking about listing the uses of the money he took as for postage or in-kind contributions. Derrick also talked about covering for himself and Cobb to prevent detection.

Bob Kohn took the stand and said that he and Derrick discussed taking money from Cobb and Derrick on June 6, 1990, said that he would report the money as stamps for his newsletter. Then Kohn met Derrick at the Town House Hotel bar before Derrick left the bar to go to room 574 in the hotel which was Cobb's room. Kohn then called Cobb in the room to alert him that Derrick was coming to his room. Kohn also told FBI agent Mike Clemens by phone to activate the recording devices in Cobb's room to capture the conversation and actions of Cobb and Derrick in exchanging the corrupt money.

Kohn said that he had no doubts that Derrick was selling his vote to Cobb because members of the "Fat and Ugly Caucus," to which Derrick belonged, had a habit of taking payoffs. Kohn also said that he approached Derrick to take a bribe and thought him an easy mark because of his past abuses.

Clemens told the court that some 15 payments were made after April 25, 1990, but did not disclose all recipients of the money.

Derrick Trial Paints Sordid Picture

Robert Kohn was fully exposed in the trial of Rep. Paul Derrick as a corrupt and addicted former state legislator. Kohn admitted in court as a prosecution witness that he was formerly addicted to both alcohol and cocaine and other substances as well. He did tell the court that he had given up those substances at the time of his testimony in the trial.

Kohn painted a deplorable picture of the General Assembly and said that many officials were addicted to cocaine just as he was. He also described how the "Fat and Ugly Caucus" was formed to exploit lobbyists for personal profit using the shakedown and the bribe. Kohn said the motto of the Caucus was, "What's the use of having a little power if you don't abuse it?" He also said that the Caucus was looking for "fish" who would pay them off to support or defeat a bill in the Legislature.

Kohn said that the Caucus was started to force lobbyists into paying the lunch bills of House members in the group which could run as high as $1,000. Kohn said that Derrick was one of the most predatory Caucus members notorious for "bleeding" lobbyists. Kohn also said that

Derrick had taken so many favors from lobbyists that he was sometimes conflicted by his competing benefactors demanding that he vote for and against the same bill.

Derrick Defense

The defense strategy in the Derrick trial was to argue that Derrick was entrapped into taking money from Ron Cobb. The defense also planned to argue that Derrick was not the original nor main target of the sting, but was added to the list as a token white defendant to balance the large number of blacks caught in the early phases of the sting. The defense would also argue that the probe was careless and run by a rookie FBI agent. In addition, the defense would show that Cobb and Kohn were both cocaine users and were lawless and dishonest.

Kohn was an easy target to discredit as a prosecution witness because of his many crimes and Derrick's attorney, Vinton Lide, denounced Kohn as a "corrupt individual" who would do anything to get money by any means, including scams. FBI agent Clemens had admitted that when Kohn agreed to help the sting, Kohn's criminal behavior as a sting agent would seem natural to him and would not appear abnormal. He was a "corrupt legislator" who took money from the FBI to recruit targets for Ron Cobb to pay off with bribes that the prosecution admitted to the court.

Lawyers for Paul Derrick presented a new defense to his corruption charges on May 6, 1991, arguing that Ron Cobb gave Derrick cash to set him up for the FBI because Cobb had an old grudge against Derrick. The lawyers asked the judge to show a videotape indicating that Cobb was angry because he thought that Derrick had tried to victimize him. They further alleged that Cobb tried to sting Derrick although Derrick had never taken a payoff from Cobb before, whereas the FBI had told Cobb to only target those he had bribed before the sting began.

The tape was one of several made before the sting which the prosecution objected to as not relevant. The judge did not immediately resolve the controversy over the defense tapes.

Cobb's Testimony

Cobb took the stand on May 6, 1991, to explain the prosecution's tapes of Derrick which were hard to understand due to poor quality. Cobb wore a recording device on April 3, 1990, during a meeting with Derrick at which Cobb told Derrick that he wanted Derrick to "look favorably" on the betting bill and said that he had out-of-state backers for the bill who "got the juice." Derrick then replied, "I can always use a little juice." Cobb explained that both men knew that juice meant money. In another recording of April 17, 1990, Cobb told Derrick that his backers were "heavy hitters."

Cobb's testimony on May 6, 1991, included comments about the April 17, 1990, recording in which Cobb told Derrick, "This is a situation where I can do something for you. Something significant." In a recording of April 24, 1990, Derrick told Cobb that he has "seen the light." In a tape of April 25, 1990, made in the lobby of the State House, Cobb told Derrick clearly he would be rewarded to vote for the betting bill, adding, "I want to do something for you.... I can do something for you."

In a tape of May 2, 1990, Derrick told Cobb he wanted a set of golf clubs and the two talked about where a set of Daiwa clubs might be purchased. In a May 5, 1990, recording, they again talked about the golf clubs. Cobb testified that, "Our deal was that he would help me and I would find him some clubs." Then in another recording of May 29, 1990, the jury heard that Derrick would accept cash instead and would get the clubs himself if Cobb gave him the money.

The money was not actually shown on the tape of June 6, 1990, in which Cobb was supposedly paying a total of ten $100 bills to Derrick at the Town House Hotel, and the tape did not show Cobb on film, and the hand over of the money was not actually shown because Cobb was below camera level on a chair or couch. Even so, the tape recorded the remarks of the two and that Derrick said he planned to report the money on his ethics disclosure forms as "maybe $200 in stamps."

Cobb told the jury in his May 6, 1991, testimony that he gave Derrick $1,000 in cash at the Town House on June 6, 1990. "He took the money and grinned, and he put it in his pocket."

Kohn Testifies Against Derrick

The same day former Rep. Bob Kohn also testified against Derrick and was subjected to harsh cross-examination until Derrick's attorney, Vinton Lide, suddenly ended the process. Lide had tried and failed to secure admission for defense transcripts which were very different from the prosecution transcripts of the tapes which had been given to the jury.

The defense was not able to show that Kohn changed his story that Derrick had initially resisted any payoff tendered to him. Prosecutor Bart Daniel also elicited testimony from Kohn that he did not assist Derrick in taking the money from Cobb and did not provide any transportation for Derrick to the Town House to take the money from Cobb on June 6, 1990.

Kohn Implicates Hopkins in Drugs

While testifying against Rep. Paul Derrick on May 6, 1991, former Rep. Bob Kohn told the court that Ron Cobb and Clemson University computer administrator, John Hopkins, had talked about buying a half kilogram of cocaine for $12,000 in the spring of 1989. Cobb had also worked with Hopkins on two different computer purchase deals made by Clemson University. Kohn said that he himself was unwilling to join the cocaine buy because he knew that Hopkins planned to distribute the cocaine on the Clemson campus whereas Kohn only wanted to buy cocaine for himself and his friends and did not want to distribute it. Kohn said that he worried about giving the cocaine to students because of its harmful properties, adding, "It's a powerful drug. It dominates your life."

Kohn told the court that Cobb and Hopkins frequently talked about buying and selling cocaine and that they were seeking an East Coast dealer from which to buy drugs. "This was a constant topic of conversation between Cobb and Hopkins, that they were going to buy a lot of cocaine."

Cobb and Hopkins had worked on computer deals when Cobb represented Hitachi Data Systems which sold Clemson a mainframe computer for $2.8 million in 1986 and another computer for $2.3 million in 1990. Hopkins was working for Clemson as Director of Marketing and Customer Support in Clemson's division of computing and information technology. Of course, Cobb did not become an FBI sting informant until he was caught in a drug deal in April, 1989.

Randy Lee Testifies vs. Derrick

On May 6, 1991, lobbyist Randy Lee testified in the Paul Derrick trial that Derrick routinely accepted expensive gifts and trips and sometimes asked for them. Lee, a lobbyist for the South Carolina Health Care Association, had been charged with marijuana violations as part of the Lost Trust prosecutions and had turned into a federal witness.

Lee told the court that he had purchased a custom made set of clothing for Derrick at the cost of $800 to $1,000 and had also paid all expenses for Derrick on a trip to Las Vegas along with a companion who was not his wife. Derrick's lawyers tried to prevent the name of the companion from being revealed in court. But Bart Daniel told the judge while the jury was out of the room that the prosecution had more lobbyists who would also testify that they paid for trips for Derrick and his companion because Derrick was a member of the House. Derrick's attorney had previously objected to evidence about Derrick's trips to California and Las Vegas.

Lee had turned into an FBI sting agent after being caught with drugs and had secretly recorded conversations with Derrick. Lee told the court that even prior to Lee's apprehension on drug charges, Ron Cobb had approached Lee and asked him to contact Derrick based on Lee's relationship to Derrick. Lee said that Derrick asked him if Cobb had as much money as rumored to pay off people to vote for the betting bill.

Lee told the court that he knew that Derrick wanted an expensive set of Japanese golf clubs, but later learned that Derrick had obtained such clubs and told Cobb that fact. Cobb then replied to Lee, "Don't worry about Rep. Derrick. I've already taken care of him."

Lee also said that he talked with Derrick after Lost Trust became public on July 18, 1990, and that Derrick had called Lee to tell him that Cobb was under FBI investigation. Derrick asked Lee to try to find out if Cobb was actually under investigation and, if so, to get Cobb's advice as to what to say if asked about the money he had taken from Cobb. Lee also said that he understood that the $1,000 given by Cobb to Derrick "had not been reported and was not going to be reported." The next day, Derrick called Lee to say that the FBI had contacted him that same day. They both assumed that it was Cobb who was in trouble.

Derrick then returned the custom-made clothes Lee had given to him. Lee told the court, "It did not seem to be a good time for lobbyists and legislators to be exchanging anything worth $800 to $1,000."

At the time, the law prohibited unlimited gifts and cash to be given to public officials by lobbyists and anybody else. If the clothing was given to Derrick as a gift, it would have been illegal.

Indicted lobbyist, Randy Lee, helped the prosecution to help himself and Lee depicted Derrick as a parasite who always wanted something for free from lobbyists. Lee said that when he was with Derrick, the legislator always wanted Lee to pay for everything, whether it was for golf balls or airplane tickets and hotel rooms.

Lee did not say that Derrick ever sold his vote, and he knew of no such bribery involving Derrick, which he admitted on cross-examination. He also said that Derrick bought him gifts, including golf equipment and sunglasses, and that the two were friends.

Cobb Testifies Against Derrick

Ron Cobb took the witness stand again in the Derrick trial on May 7, 1991, and underwent cross-examination for much of the day from Vinton Lide. Lide tried to show that the tapes made by the FBI might have been improperly transcribed and also incorrectly interpreted. Some new tapes were presented as evidence that Derrick actually thought that Cobb was giving him a birthday present and that Derrick did not realize that Cobb was trying to get him to take money to vote for the betting bills.

Cobb denied that he tried to bribe Derrick by trickery and that he was motivated by a grudge against Derrick to try to catch him. Cobb denied that he was mad at Derrick because Derrick, as chairman of the House, Labor, Commerce, and Industry Committee, had not taken action on an auto sale bill that Cobb was pushing and that Cobb lost a client over the failure to secure passage of the bill. Cobb admitted he might have said he would retaliate, but later realized that he would need Derrick's help on other issues.

Lide also pointed out to Cobb that his career as a lobbyist was ended when it became known that he was implicated in the Operation Lost Trust sting operation. His payments from the prosecution was all he had left.

The trial was also different than previous trials in that the judge did not close the courtroom to the media and public at various times, even allowing open court when allegations of perjury were raised about prosecution witness Bob Kohn. Several times, Judge Falcon Hawkins asked the media about questions of whether certain evidence should be released to the public and whether some proceedings should be kept open to the public.

Limehouse Testifies Against Derrick

The prosecution brought in former Rep. Tom Limehouse (R-Charleston) as a witness against Paul Derrick on May 8, 1991. Limehouse had already pleaded guilty to extortion and witness tampering in the Lost Trust scandal. He had taken $2,000 to vote for the betting bill.

Limehouse testified that Derrick had tried to disguise $1,000 that Cobb gave him as a campaign contribution and had only decided to report the money on July 18, 1990, after the FBI interviewed Derrick on the first day the probe went public. Limehouse said in court, "Derrick told me that he told the agent that he couldn't recall any contributions. Paul was obviously trying to decide whether to acknowledge the cash contributions he received." Then Limehouse said that Derrick admitted to him that "he did one wrong thing and got caught."

Limehouse told the court that Derrick took the $1,000 and tried to report it as a donation of stamps for his re-election campaign. Limehouse also said that Derrick did not support the betting bill in 1989, but changed to supporting it when Cobb gave him the money. If true, this would constitute bribery quid pro quo.

But finally, after the FBI interviewed Derrick on July 18, 1990, he then deposited the $1,000 into his campaign account according to his bank records. He also told two FBI agents on that date that he did not know of anyone who took cash payoffs from lobbyists. He denied that he took any money for his vote.

Last Witnesses in Derrick Trial

May 8, 1991, was the final day of the Paul Derrick trial and the last witnesses took the stand against Derrick. Several lobbyist told the court that they had paid for golf outings for the defendant in Columbia and Lexington and had also paid for his expenses on trips to Las Vegas and Monterrey, California.

Derrick's lawyers, Vinton Lide and Jim Lengel, moved for a mistrial at the end of the trial on the grounds that Bob Kohn, a prosecution witness, had said he lied in the trial while he was at the Sheraton Hotel swimming pool and that he was overheard by a couple who reported it. However, an FBI agent assigned to check out the story reported to the court that the couple who told the story had been drinking. And Judge Hawkins told the lawyers that the story could be a scam by Derrick's friends. The mistrial was not granted.

Derrick's Defense Asks Court for Entrapment Instruction

Defense lawyers for Paul Derrick asked Judge Falcon Hawkins to direct the jury to consider that Derrick was, in fact, coerced into taking $1,000 from Cobb and that it was not a crime. This defense was an entrapment defense which held that the defendant was provoked to do something he would not otherwise have done and which, if voluntary, would be a crime. Without the instruction from the court, the jurors could ignore the entrapment defense presented to them by Derrick.

Derrick's entrapment defense was the first one presented in the long string of Lost Trust cases. Judge Hawkins dismissed jurors late on May 9, 1991, to consider the defense motion on the entrapment instruction. Earlier in the day, Derrick had taken the stand for over three hours in his defense.

The judge told Vinton Lide and Jim Lengel that the Derrick testimony did not show entrapment, saying, "I'm telling you, it's an awfully, awfully weak entrapment case." Hawkins said the evidence did not show that Derrick was tricked into taking $1,000 from Cobb. Noting that Derrick had gone to Cobb's room at the behest of Bob Kohn and that Derrick commonly went to the Town House Hotel for drinks, Hawkins said, "If Mr. Derrick went there to get a present, he's got problems."

Lengel told the judge that Derrick "had no intent or predisposition to sell his vote... Had Kohn not gone to him, Paul Derrick never would have gone to see Ron Cobb." But prosecutor Sherry Lydon said that Derrick did not have to be convinced and went to Cobb to get $1,000 to support the betting bill.

Derrick Case Goes to Jury

On May 10, 1991, the fate of suspended Rep. Paul Derrick (R-Lexington) went to the jury after seven days of a trial in which they heard testimony and videotapes and also reviewed disclosure documents. Jurors had to decide if he took a $1,000 bribe from Cobb.

Judge Falcon Hawkins instructed the jury while Derrick waited nervously at the defense table. Hawkins had decided on the same day that he would yield to Derrick's motion for an entrapment defense instruction and directed the jury accordingly. Before the jury came in, Hawkins told Vinton Lide and Jim Lengel that, "I have given great thought to the defendant's defense of entrapment. I think it is powerful weak. Nevertheless, I am going to charge it to the jury."

Hawkins doubted the defense strategy pointing out that Derrick planned to hide the $1,000 by claiming it was a campaign contribution to buy stamps.

Even so, Lide and Lengel tried to heap the blame on Kohn and Cobb, remarking, "The problem here is we had some evil, and it wasn't created by Paul Derrick. Nowhere is this case are you going to find that he agreed to vote for the pari-mutuel betting bill in exchange for money." They impugned the motives of Cobb and Kohn, alleging Cobb wanted revenge on Derrick for not supporting a bill before Cobb stung Derrick.

Jury Convicts Derrick

On May 11, 1991, the jury in the Paul Derrick bribery and conspiracy trial returned a verdict of guilty that the $1,000 sting agent Rob Cobb gave to Rep. Paul Derrick was a bribe. The verdict came after only two hours of deliberation and at the end of a trial which lasted more than a week. He was convicted on both counts.

Shaken by the verdict, Derrick, a middle-aged optometrist from Lexington, refused to comment to the media after the trial.

Based on his conviction for bribery under the Hobbs Act, Derrick faced a total of 40 years maximum and a fine of $500,000 according to U.S. Attorney Bart Daniel. The sentencing was set for a later date three months after the conviction and after federal probation officials could prepare a report on the Derrick case. Daniel told the media, "I feel sure he will be serving jail time. A public official who uses his public office to violate the public's trust must spend time in jail."

Derrick's conviction added another legislator to the pile of those who had either pleaded guilty or gone to trial and lost. More convictions would come later along with more indictments. A total of 8 had pleaded and four had lost at trial at that point in the middle of May, 1991.

Comments on Derrick Trial

Juror John Breitling of Blythewood, South Carolina, told the media right after the conviction on May 11, 1991, that, "Unfortunately, it was a pretty clear-cut case. The evidence was overwhelming. I feel sorry for Mr. Derrick and his family."

In spite of the conviction, Breitling said that he had not lost faith in the Legislature, saying, "There are honest and reputable legislators, and obviously ones who are not, as we are finding out."

John McIntosh, Assistant U.S. Attorney, told the media after Derrick's conviction that the videotapes of Derrick taking ten $100 bills from Cobb and sticking the money in his pocket showed there was no coercion of Derrick to take the money, contrary to the entrapment defense argued by Lide and Lengel for Derrick.

Juror John Breitling agreed that the videotape was a major factor, saying, "The videotape was certainly important."

McIntosh said that Derrick knew the $1,000 from Cobb was a payoff for supporting the betting bill. Rep. Kohn had told Cobb in the lobby of the Town House Hotel that Ron Cobb would pay $500 if Derrick would abstain from voting on the betting bill and $1,000 if he would vote for it. Kohn had told Derrick that Cobb had a package for him. Then Derrick went to the fifth floor of the Town House to Cobb's hotel room and took the $1,000 in cash on the secret videotape. The evidence was clear that Derrick took a bribe in McIntosh's view.

Ron Cobb's List Revealed

Ron Cobb checked off the names of some 71 legislators in his *1989 S.C. Legislative Manual* which listed all members of the S.C. General Assembly, including their party, districts, offices, and biographies. The list included 24 senators, roughly half of the 46 total senators in the chamber. Forty-seven of 124 representatives were also listed.

Among those checked off were a number caught up in Lost Trust and one convicted of felony fraud in an unrelated case. Those checked off by Cobb included the following who were indicted later in 1990 and 1991:

Representatives Indicted (12)

Larry Blanding
Robert Brown
Paul Derrick
Tee Ferguson
B.J. Gordon
Robert Kohn
Tom Limehouse
Frank McBride
Donna Moss
Jack I. Rogers
Luther Taylor
Danny Winstead

Senators Indicted (3)

Rick Lee
J.M. "Bud" Long
Horace Smith (Fraud—Not Lost Trust)

Plea Agreements Pending (1)
Jack Lindsay
(Died under investigation; not indicted.)

Cobb's List Included Legislators Not Indicted

Ron Cobb's check-off list of legislators in the 1989 edition of the *S.C. Legislative Manual* included a large number of officials who were not indicted in Lost Trust. Only two of the 24 senators checked off by Cobb were charged in Lost Trust—Rick Lee and Bud Long. Horace Smith was charged in an unrelated fraud crime. Sen. Jack Lindsay was also checked off by Cobb but died before he was indicted while under a plea agreement. Twelve of a total of 47 House members were charged who were checked off by Ron Cobb.

A total of 16 House members were indicted of whom only 12 were checked. Those not checked included Tim Wilkes, James Faber, Ennis Fant, and Ken Bailey; all were later indicted. Wilkes was acquitted at trial.

In addition, of course, none of the lobbyist caught in the scandal were listed in the *Manual*.

Twenty-two of the 24 senators checked off by Cobb in the *Manual* were not charged in Operation Lost Trust. Among those checked off by Cobb but not indicted in Lost Trust were Sens. Bryan, Fielding, Holland, Land, Leatherman, Lindsay (died before indictment), Lourie, McGill, McLeod, Mitchell, Moore, Mullinax, Patterson, Peeler, Saleeby, Setzler, Horace Smith (indicted in a separate fraud), Verne Smith, Thomas, Waddell, Williams, and Wilson.

Cobb's List Provokes Controversy

Ron Cobb's release during the Paul Derrick trial of a list of legislators he checked off in the *1989 South Carolina Legislative Manual* provoked hostile reactions from those listed and even from Gov. Carroll Campbell who was not listed. The release of Cobb's list on May 8, 1991, included 71 legislators' names who Cobb said might be bribed. Cobb explained the list as his effort to show the FBI after he was caught in the 1989 drug sting that he could help the prosecution identify corrupt officials if Cobb was granted immunity himself for his own drug dealing and bribery.

Although Cobb was not allowed in open court to tell the list of names, the judge allowed reporters to see it anyhow. The *Manual* had been introduced into evidence by Derrick's attorneys who were trying to show the absurdity of Cobb's statements, according to Vinton Lide. Lide dismissed the idea of targeting 70 legislators as "ludicrous."

The legislators whose names appeared on Cobb's list but who had not been indicted, lashed out at Cobb as dishonest and not credible in their statements given to the media. Unlisted Sen. John Courson (R-Richland) ridiculed Cobb's list saying, "When accusations are made by a convicted felon indicting half the members of the General Assembly without any proof, and to report it as truth, to me, is unconscionable." Sen. David Thomas (R-Greenville), whose name was on the list, expressed outrage, spurning Cobb's list as "absolutely outrageous. That is sickening and disgusting."

Several legislators listed by Cobb acknowledged that they had, in fact, been approached by Cobb but said they rejected him or the other sting agent used by the FBI, Rep. Bob Kohn (R-Charleston). Rep. Marion Carnell (D-Greenville) said that "Kohn approached me about supporting the betting bill, and I told him there was no way I could go along." Then he added, "Maybe that's why I was on there." Rep. Alex Harvin (D-Clarendon) reported, "I was approached by Bob Kohn seven times, and I declined seven times."

Rep. David Beasley (D-Darlington), the new House Speaker Pro Tem after Jack I. Rogers' removal from the House, theorized that, "Maybe he was trying to get back at some of us trying to clean things up," a theory that would also apply to Speaker Sheheen who thought the lobbyists were out of control before the sting.

Sen. Theo Mitchell (D-Greenville) claimed during his 1990 campaign for governor that he had been offered a bribe by Ron Cobb but had rejected it. Mitchell was, of course, one of those listed and checked off by Cobb in the *1989 S.C. Legislative Manual*.

Cobb's List Provokes Continued Indignation

The release of the list of 71 legislators marked off by Ron Cobb provoked anger for several days after Judge Falcon Hawkins made it public on May 8, 1991, toward the end of the Paul Derrick trial.

Sen. Phil Leventis (D-Sumter) excoriated the release saying, "This is probably one of the low points in this state, to have honorable people charged by innuendo and have no opportunity to defend themselves." Leventis and 11 other senators held a news conference to denounce the list on May 9, 1991. Sen. Sherry Martschink (R-Charleston) charged that, "Someone had been robbed of their good name. We're not up here defending guilty people, but rather...good people who have been caught in a situation that is not a guilty situation. A situation of being used by someone who's been referred to as a sleaze bag."

Sen. Doug Hinds (D-Georgetown) remarked, "I think that all right thinking individuals should be offended by this." Sen. Alex McMacauley (D-Oconee) pointed out that "a very small group of people have been charged. A single group." And Sen Mike Rose (R-Dorchester) asserted that he would "stake my life that some of the people on that list are not corrupt."

Also on May 9, 1991, Sen. Theo Mitchell (D-Greenville) said on the Senate floor that he wanted the federal authorities to release a tape showing that he rejected a bribe offered to Mitchell from Cobb.

Cobb's listing of 71 legislators he told the FBI he thought were vulnerable to possible bribes included a total of 12 names of officials eventually convicted of corruption or drugs or both. On the other hand, the names of 5 legislators who were convicted in the scandal were not found on the list. Another 59 names were listed of legislators who were never convicted in the prosecutions associated with Lost Trust.

Many of the names of those on the list who were never charged by the government were those of prominent legislators, including committee chairmen as well as the Speaker of the House Bob Sheheen and the President Pro Tem of the Senate, Marshall Williams, who also chaired the Senate Judiciary Committee. Sheheen had actually been trying to promote some reforms in the House to curb lobbyists' abuses and the uses of gratuities. Williams said of Cobb, "I didn't even know the bastard." House Judiciary Committee Chair David Wilkins (R-Greenville) remarked, "It's a desperate attempt to name the leadership of the House in order to try to get the FBI to help him with his cocaine case." And Sen. Ed Saleeby (D-Darlington), Chair of Senate Ethics, impugned Cobb and said, "I wouldn't be surprised at anyone who abuses cocaine as much as he did using a lot of names to get a lighter sentence. He never asked me to support that bill or discussed with me any contributions or gave me any contributions."

The State Editorial Justifies Publishing Cobb's List

The publication of Ron Cobb's list of 71 legislators he though susceptible to bribery provoked such an outcry from named officials who protested their innocence that *The State* felt compelled to explain the fact that the newspaper had published the entire list of names in its edition of May 9, 1991.

In an editorial of May 11, 1991, *The State* wrote that it published the list because it came out as evidence in the Paul Derrick corruption trial. "We printed it, but we didn't print its implication as 'truth'. Fact is, we find it deplorable, a maligning of individuals we believe to be innocent of wrongdoing." *The State* went on to say that the list was "evidence introduced in court, evidence of a gossipy nature whose circulation moves quickly from the courthouse to the State House to the bars."

Worrying that if the list were not published to its readers, the inevitable rumors would be worse than the truth, the editors wrote, "rumor stretches and becomes more damaging than the simple truth of an imaginatively concocted list." Pointing to Sen. John Courson (R-Richland), a resident of Columbia, as an example of a "respected legislator" whose name was not on the list, the editorial closed with a blast at Cobb dismissing the "list as malodorous foreplay by Rob Cobb, and he is the party who is further diminished by it."

Cobb's List Explained by Cobb

Ron Cobb revisited the list of 71 legislators he had marked as vulnerable to corruption. In an interview with the *Greenville News*, Cobb said that the marked *1989 S.C. Legislative Manual* which had been published by the Court in the Derrick trial was not intended to indicate that all of the 71 persons named were corrupt. Cobb told the *News* in mid-May, 1991, that, "I was in no way trying to say that everybody in the General Assembly had their hands out or that I bribed everybody in the General Assembly because it wasn't a fact."

Cobb explained that he had marked the names of legislators at the request of the FBI because they had had him list the "people I had done business with, or given campaign contributions to, knew took trips and gifts and things of that nature." Cobb said that many of those listed had taken campaign donations from him.

Prosecutor Bart Daniel said, in explaining after the Derrick trial had ended, that the list was not used by the Lost Trust probe to target legislators.

Cobb said of the matter, "I don't regret any of my involvement in Operation Lost Trust. I do regret the list was taken out of context by a lot of the press in trying to create something that just wasn't there and causing a lot of people undue embarrassment that didn't deserve it."

Rogers Pleads to Racketeering

Disgraced House Speaker Pro Tem Jack I. Rogers entered a guilty plea on May 8, 1991, to one count federal racketeering crimes. This was the most serious violation of criminal law filed in any of the Lost Trust cases to that point and, as it turned out, in all of the cases made against a total of 28 defendants. As U.S. Attorney Bart Daniel stated at the time, "It is the most serious violation in this investigation, and he [Rogers] pleaded guilty to the most serious charge in the indictment."

The allegation of facts included that Rogers demanded and got $6,000 from lobbyist Ken Kinard because Rogers helped Kinard get a lobbying job with a waste disposal firm paying him $36,000 annually in 1988 and until 1990.

The racketeering charge carried a sentence of a maximum of 20 years and $250,000 fine.

However, Rogers was not compelled to plead to nine criminal charges and to taking bribes to vote on capital gains tax bills and a pari-mutuel betting bill. A total of nine counts were dismissed in accord with the plea agreement. He did admit, "All of the elements of intent were there."

Attorney Thomas Simpson handled the plea for Rogers who had earlier been represented by Rep. Tim Rogers (D-Richland).

Rogers declined the chance to hear the indictment read at his open court plea entrance. Sentencing was not set until a later date.

Rogers' Plea Deal

In return for leniency, Jack I. Rogers pled to racketeering and promised to cooperate with the prosecution in the scandal probe and resulting prosecutions. Daniel agreed to recommend a lighter sentence in return for full cooperation. The nine dismissed charges would still be weighed in the sentencing.

Rogers' Plea Deal Explained

The guilty plea of former Speaker Pro Tem Jack I. Rogers (D-Marlboro) on May 8, 1991, was based on different evidence than most of the Lost Trust cases. The government had no videotapes of Rogers taking money from anybody and relied on testimonial evidence which could have been presented at trial had Rogers not decided to plead guilty and cooperate with the prosecution.

Prosecutor John Barton told the court that the government had made a deal with Rogers in part because they had no taped evidence to prove Rogers took money, but only one videotape made in January, 1990, in which Rogers visited Cobb's hotel room at the Town House Hotel and said that he would support the betting bill. At that meeting, Ron Cobb told Rogers that he represented an interest in the betting bill which was "very flush" with money for legislators. Cobb also said on the tape that he was willing to pay Rogers more money than Cobb had paid Rogers before to pass the capital gains tax break bill benefiting the Greenville businessmen a few months before in 1988.

The major charges against Rogers in the indictment alleged that he took $13,500 from a lobbyist for GSX Chemical Services in 1988, 1989, and 1990. The company handled waste disposal in two locations in the state. Another count said that Rogers took $5,000 from an unnamed lobbyist for help on the tax cut bill in 1988. Another charge alleged Rogers took three bribes of $3,500 in total to support the betting bill late in the 1990 session.

Editorial on Rogers' Conviction Blames Rogers

In response to the guilty plea on racketeering charges filed in court on May 8, 1991, *The State* published an editorial on May 11, 1991, ridiculing the dishonesty of Jack I. Rogers in protesting his love of the House of Representatives while at the same time disgracing it by taking multiple payoffs as a member.

The editorial quoted the statement that Rogers had made on December 4, 1990, on his re-election as Speaker Pro Tem which said, "I love this institution and I promise you that I will never do anything that I believe will do harm.... I don't believe I have done anything wrong, and I thank you for your confidence in me."

The State then quoted Roger's statement of May 8, 1991, on entry of his guilty plea when he refused to hear the indictment counts read in his case. Rogers said, "I would rather not hear it again, your honor."

CHAPTER TWENTY FOUR

JUDGE FERGUSON GOES TO TRIAL

Judge Tee Ferguson went to trial on May 28, 1991, on one of the two major charges against him, that of bribery. The other charge of cocaine use was withheld for a separate trial which was never held because Ferguson later elected to plead guilty to drug violations.

The bribery trial proved to be an unusually contentious litigation because Ferguson's lawyers chose to fight over both jury selection and the trial on the merits. The defendant alleged that the court was complicit in tolerating racial bias against Ferguson as an African-American in both the jury selection process and the trial itself. Ferguson claimed that he had been singled out because he was black and subjected to unfair treatment by the FBI and the U.S. Attorney's Office. He said he was targeted in the sting by the government because he was a black man who had attained the high position of state court judge after having served as a state legislator.

The jury found little merit in Ferguson's claim that he was the victim of racial discrimination and, further, found no merit in his defense that he had not taken a bribe. The prosecution successfully presented evidence that Ferguson was a cynical and dishonest public official who tried to use his office as a legislator to take a bribe. The jury convicted Ferguson of public corruption under the Hobbs Act as charged.

Ferguson was represented by attorneys Hemphill Pride, III, John Hardaway, and Donnell Jennings.

Ferguson Sought Jury From Columbia

Lawyers for Judge Tee Ferguson asked the court May 8, 1991, to limit the pool of jurors called in the case to those living in the Columbia area to increase the chances of selecting more black jurors. Columbia was the county seat of Richland County, an entity which had a population almost half black in contrast with some other counties in South Carolina which had very large white majorities.

The normal procedure for selecting juries in U.S. District Court was to use a statewide system of drawing the jurors in the pool which would include jurors from the three regions around Columbia, Charleston and Greenville counties.

Ferguson's attorneys told Judge Falcon Hawkins that a jury with more blacks would be more fair to their client who was black. But the U.S. Attorney's office countered by telling the court that the statewide pool provides a better cross-section of the population and limiting the pool for racial purposes was racist.

Hawkins did not immediately rule on the motion to limit the jury pool. The trial was slated to start on May 28, 1991, only on the corruption charges against Ferguson. The drug charges had not at that time been slated for trial in a separate and later litigation.

Ferguson Alleges Racial Targeting

Suspended Circuit Judge Tee Ferguson on May 10, 1991, alleged that, as a black man, he was being treated worse than white suspects in the Lost Trust cases. He said of his indictments on drug and corruption charges that other lobbyists and state officials who were white were being ignored by the prosecutors.

In a seven page motion filed in federal court, Ferguson's lawyers claimed that blacks including himself were targeted in the sting and that the charges against him should be dismissed. He pointed to "unconstitutional targeting of black legislators." The motion went on to assert "the government was aware in 1989 that white legislators, a lobbying firm, a lobbyist and an ex-member of the governor's staff not heretofore targeted or indicted had been engaged in corruption and drug dealings related to the General Assembly."

The motion referenced Dick Greer by name who had been the chair of the State Development Board under Gov. Carroll Campbell. The motion claimed that Greer had been directly involved in the tax break legislation of 1989 which was tainted with corruption involving Sen. Jack Lindsay and Rep. Jack I. Rogers.

Ferguson Alleges More Corruption

The Ferguson motion to dismiss his charges promised to reveal the names of other suspects in the scandal but to do so in private with Judge Hawkins. The motion also mentioned, but did not name, two senators and one representative who were implicated in the 1989 sting of Ron Cobb for drug dealing but noted that they were not charged. The motion further asserted that "a prominent lobbying firm and a lobbyist...operated as intermediaries between other lobbyists and legislators to be bribed" and that "an ex-member of the governor's staff...was involved in a vote buying scam."

The motion blamed Sen. Jack Lindsay as "a prime example of a legislator known to the government to be involved in corruption but...not targeted or indicted. However, federal authorities had told the media that Lindsay would have been indicted had he not died in January, 1991.

The motion filed by the defense team of Hemphill Pride, III, and Donnell Jennings mentioned that the persons who stood to benefit from the tax break bill had paid Ron Cobb an amount of $75,000 to move the bill and that he had paid a senator to help. It was further alleged that "Richard Greer was the intermediary between the individual paying money for the rollback and Cobb."

The motion claimed that when the tax break bill was opposed in 1988 by some Republican senators, the senator who had been paid by Cobb to move the bill "contacted Greer, who in turn contacted the governor's office." The tax break was furtively slipped into the 1988 state budget bill.

There was evidence that the allegations in the motion had some basis in fact. Greer had told *The State* not long before the motion was filed that he had, in fact, recommended Cobb to a person seeking to hire a lobbyist to move the tax break bill. Furthermore, an indicted lobbyist had told the federal grand jury that he was in the room when Greer witnessed a conversation between Cobb and Lindsay in which they discussed splitting a bribe of $150,000 to move the tax break bill. And at the time of the motion, Greer had already pleaded guilty to cocaine charges.

Gov. Campbell's office denied that the governor had any involvement in the tax break bill, and *The State* had investigated the matter and found that few, if any, senators, aside from Sen. Jack Lindsay and Sen. James Waddell, knew about the secret tax break bill in the 1988 budget.

The motion also alleged that Dick Greer's brother-in-law, Hunter Howard, had addressed the Senate Finance Committee about the matter and had "misled the committee into believing the rollback would have a statewide impact, when in fact, only 20 to 23 persons would benefit." Howard responded to the allegations in the motion by saying that he never talked to senators about the tax rollback.

In fact, some 21 taxpayers stood to gain an $8.6 million tax break while some 60,000 taxpayers stood to receive a tax cut of $22.4 million from the state of South Carolina under the secretly inserted tax break clauses of the 1988 state budget bill.

Ferguson Trial Begins

The trial of Judge Tee Ferguson for corruption began on May 28, 1991. The case was the first of the Lost Trust cases to go to trial after the U.S. Supreme Court ruled in *McCormick v. U.S.* (1991) on May 23, 1991, that it was essential for the prosecution to prove a quid pro quo in bribery cases under the Hobbs Act, which presented a more difficult task for the prosecution than previous cases.

Ferguson complained that the indictment charges were a "classic case of racial bias" and said that the government plied him with alcohol to set him up for the sting by Ron Cobb.

The date set for the start of Ferguson's trial, May 28, 1991, was exactly one year after Ferguson had been sworn in as a circuit court judge on May 28, 1990.

Ferguson's efforts to limit the jury pool to the Columbia area had been rejected by the court. His efforts to get charges dropped on grounds of racial bias because eight of the defendants charged in Lost Trust were black while only 21 blacks sat in the Legislature had not succeeded. In pretrial, the two sides had fought over the question of whether jury selection would be open or closed, with the defendant demanding an open process. Judge Falcon Hawkins ruled that the selection be closed and it was not open to the press and public.

Ferguson Trial: Battle Over Jury Selection

Judge Ferguson moved in pretrial to have the entire trial process open to the public, including jury selection. But Judge Hawkins wanted to close the jury selection.

In the week of May 21, 1990, the issue of whether the selection of jurors would be held in secret was appealed by the South Carolina Press Association and by five newspapers by the 4th Circuit Court of Appeals.

A special panel of the 4th Circuit ruled that the question of whether a selection of jurors could be held in secret compromised a defendant's constitutional right to a fair trial under the Sixth Amendment to the U.S. Constitution. The panel did not issue an immediate ruling. But federal prosecutors revealed that Hawkins planned to open the jury selection.

Jury Selected in Ferguson Trial

The selection of jurors in the Ferguson trial proved a tortured process. Ferguson tried and failed to limit the jury pool to the Columbia area. The pool of prospective jurors called had 47 members. Of the 29 who qualified as jurors, only 7 were black. One of them, Myrtle Glascoe, director of the Afro-American history museum at the College of Charleston, was excused because she required a special diet and sanitized housing which would cost too much, Judge Hawkins ruled. She had also said that she was depressed to be in a position which she thought part of a historical trend to place blacks in positions of power and then remove them.

The total of 47 people were questioned and 18 were excused. Some six of those excused said they had already formed opinions. One person was excused because she had read that Ferguson was also charged with cocaine and the defense was afraid she would tell others if placed on the jury. Lawyers were also asking if prospective jurors would ignore tapes which they could not understand.

Jury Selection in Ferguson Case in Turmoil

The selection of jurors in the Tee Ferguson case proved to be very contentious. Judge Falcon Hawkins, on May 31, 1991, told the lawyers in the case that in the selection matter, "the process is being abused; this court is being abused, and I don't know if the government or Judge Ferguson is being abused." His remarks came on the final day of selection.

Hawkins told Ferguson's attorney, Hemphill Pride, III, the defense teams demand for an open jury selection process was designed to put on "a charge."

Meanwhile a jury pool of 47 waited in a nearby courtroom. Pride alleged to the judge that the prosecution had struck half of the blacks available from the pool, and he demanded that the judge require the prosecution to explain its strikes, asserting that there were racially motivated factors in the strikes.

The prosecution explained the reasons for some of the strikes. Pride then said that Ferguson felt that "he's not getting a fair deal from the U.S. Attorney's office in terms of the manner in which they have racially struck the jury." Then prosecutor John Barton asked the judge to compel the defense to explain their 13 strikes of whites in the jury pool. When Pride refused to say in open court what the reasons for the strikes were, he claimed attorney-client privilege, but the judge required Pride to explain in open court what he had done.

Ferguson Trial Charges Stated

Ferguson faced only the corruption charges against him in his first trial. (The drug charges of cocaine possession and conspiracy were separated and set for a second trial at a later date.) The specific charges in the first trial starting on May 28, 1991, were criminal conspiracy and extortion relating to $3,000 taken by Ferguson from lobbyist sting-agent Ron Cobb on the betting bill while Ferguson was in the House and shortly before he was elected to the circuit court bench in April, 1990.

The corruption charges were based on the alleged bribery transaction of March 21, 1990, when Ferguson took the money from Cobb, a crime which carried a very severe set of penalties of up to 60 years in prison and fines up to $750,000. (The charges of cocaine possession on five counts and one count of conspiracy to possess cocaine carried a total of six years in prison and fines of up to $650,000.)

At the time of his trial, Judge Ferguson was only 40 years old and had previously served in the House of Representatives since 1983 as a Democrat from Spartanburg. He was one of 21 black legislators in the 1990 session. A graduate of the University of South Carolina School of Law, he had been sworn in as circuit court judge on May 28, 1990, only to be relieved of his judicial duties just three months later at his own request when he learned that he was being investigated for corruption by the FBI.

Ferguson Trial: Wrangling Worsens

The role of the videotapes of alleged bribery was a major issue in the Ferguson case, perhaps more so than in prior cases in Lost Trust. The tapes were grainy and the audio was very poor quality and hard to understand. The question for the prosecution was whether the jury would find the visual portion sufficiently persuasive even if the audio was difficult. On the other hand, the prosecution normally provided transcripts. As the tapes included some obscenities, the jury was warned and one woman asked to be excused as she thought that vulgar words would affect her opinion.

Defense attorneys probed the persons called to try to find evidence or racial bias. They were asked about memberships in clubs and organizations that practiced racial discrimination. Did they believe that blacks were crime prone? Did they think public officials should be held to a higher standard than others?

In screening the jurors, the number of those called was a total of 47, but only 15 would eventually be chosen. Defense attorneys had 13 peremptory challenges and prosecution had 9.

In the end, a third of the government's strikes were used to eliminate blacks from the jury, but the defense used all of its strikes to remove whites from the jury. When asked by the judge for the reasons behind the strikes, defense attorney Donnell G. Jennings told the judge in private what they were. Among the reasons given were that some of those removed had bias that Ferguson was guilty, others were related to law enforcement people, and still others might be racially biased. One person, a medical student, was rejected because he seemed too intelligent and might dominate the jury. Another was not selected because she had a Christian dislike for vulgar words.

The final jury drawn included 11 whites, three blacks, and one Asian-American. All three alternates were white.

Ferguson asked the court to hold jury selection in public whereas four other defendants asked for closed door selection.

The screening process revealed only 9 of 58 prospective jurors who indicated that pretrial publicity would affect them. One Anderson man told the court that he thought that Ferguson is "probably guilty like the others." An Orangeburg student referred to the defendant as one of a group "no better than common criminals." A Saluda farmer told the judge, "I feel that he is guilty." A Spartanburg insurance agent said he had read too much about Ferguson and that "it would be hard for me to be fair." A Columbia secretary said she could not swear that she was impartial. A Summerville truck driver said, "How could he be on videotape and not be guilty?"

Jurors Finally Seated in Ferguson Trial

After the battle to select a jury was finished, those who made the final 15 included the following: a food service worker who was 49 years old, female, and white; a 40 year old white female who was a respiratory therapist; a white 65 year old man who was a cabinetmaker; a 55 year old textile worker who was white; an Asian female, 37, forklift driver; an electrical engineer, 29, who was white; a black man, 73, a retired postal worker; a 60 year old white male engineer; a 31 year old factory worker who was black; a white shift manager, 49; a 59 year old woman seamstress who was black; and a white 31 year old utility superintendent. The alternates were all white, including a 36 year old trainman, a 41 year old farmer, and a 53 year old unemployed man.

Of the 15 jurors, one had a grade school education, six finished high school, five went to college, and three went to trade school. All jurors came from various parts of the state of South Carolina, including many small towns, but no large cities such as Columbia, Greenville, Charleston, or Spartanburg.

Pulling the jury took four long days; perhaps, Judge Hawkins thought, because the process was done in open courtroom rather than behind closed doors. No jurors answered a long questionnaire as had been done in previous Lost Trust trials. But the fact that 47 persons were called before final selection made the process more time-consuming, whereas, in previous trials, jurors knew at the outset if they would be chosen or released. Even so, racial bias in jury selection was a likely basis for appeal of any conviction.

U.S. Supreme Court Hurts Prosecutions

A West Virginia case decided by the U.S. Supreme Court on May 23, 1991, in the midst of Lost Trust, shifted the playing field in favor of defendants. In *McCormick v. U.S.* (500 U.S. 257 (1991)), a case involving state Rep. Robert L. McCormick of West Virginia, the Court found that the Hobbs Act (18 USC § 1951) required that the prosecution prove a quid pro quo between the public official and the party tendering a bribe in order to convict.

The court ruled 6-3 that a campaign contribution could be a bribe under the Hobbs Act, but an exchange of official action for the money must be proved. The opinion read, "Political contributions are vulnerable...but only if the payments are made in return for an explicit promise or undertaking by the official to perform or not perform an official act. In such situations, the official asserts that his official conduct will be controlled by the terms of the promise or undertaking."

The State, in an editorial on June 4, 1991, worried that the *McCormick* precedent could make future convictions under the Hobbs Act harder to get, a regrettable decision the editors thought.

Ferguson Trial Halted

The illness of Ferguson's attorney, Hemphill Pride, III, stopped the Ferguson trial on June 5, 1991. Pride collapsed in his Columbia office on that date and was taken to Baptist Medical Center. Pride's associate, Donnell Jennings, described the problem as a cardiac disorder causing a loss of blood flow to the brain.

The defense was expected to begin its presentation of evidence on that same day, including testimonial evidence. The prosecution had listed a total of 15 witnesses and 13 tapes, all of which were focused on Ferguson's alleged efforts to sell his vote to get money to buy a Mercedes Benz. The tapes also suggested that Ferguson intended to sell his judicial office in the future.

The defense had moved to reduce charges on June 5, 1991, but Judge Hawkins had denied the motion, refusing to drop conspiracy charges. He did say he would consider whether Ferguson had been charged with too many crimes. John Hardaway, associated with Pride, argued on that date that prosecutors had asked the grand jury for separate charges for each cash payment taken by Ferguson from Cobb. Hardaway argued that one crime had been made to look like two separate crimes: "He is being tried twice for the same crime."

Ferguson faced charges for conspiring to violate the Hobbs Act and for two counts of extorting bribes. The grand jury said that he had taken two payments from Cobb of $2,000 and $1,000 on the betting bill.

Ferguson Moves to Reduce Three Charges to One

In a hearing on June 5, 1991, Ferguson's attorney, John Hardaway, tried to not only get two charges of bribery consolidated into one charge, but he also sought to have the conspiracy charge to violate the Hobbs Act consolidated into the bribery charge under the Hobbs Act. Under federal law, a conspiracy required two persons to agree to commit a crime, but one of the two could not be a federal agent.

However, Judge Hawkins ruled that, in fact, Ferguson knew that other legislators were also involved in taking money from Cobb to back the betting bill and that the other legislators, not federal sting agent Ron Cobb, were the second parties to the conspiracy.

Ferguson Defense Attacked Before Jury

Going back to their key witness, Dale DuTremble had to recognize that Ron Cobb was a pretty sorry prosecution witness who was not easy to believe. He said, "Those of you who believe that Ron Cobb is a no-good, dope-dealing scumbag, ask yourself, if you believe he is a no-good, lying rascal, what is this man doing so close to him, going up to his room, slapping him on the back, embracing him, calling him a home boy." In fact, Ferguson was dishonest like Cobb.

DuTremble stated that the meeting in which Ferguson told Cobb he would help on the betting bill for no money happened only twenty days before Ferguson went to the judicial screening committee hearing at which his candidacy for the bench was at issue. But after Ferguson cleared the screening process and was approved as a candidate for election and sent to the General Assembly for a vote, then Ferguson returned to his old corrupt ways.

DuTremble also cast doubt on a defense witness who said that Ferguson returned $1,000 to Cobb on his own motion to avoid the appearance of impropriety. But convicted House member, Luther Taylor, had testified in the Ferguson case as a prosecution witness that he had warned Ferguson on May 9, 1990, that Cobb was under investigation and that Ferguson then felt an urgent need to return the money in the $1,000 payment to Cobb that same day.

However, two defense witnesses said that they were in the same room with Taylor and Ferguson and heard no warning given by Taylor. Furthermore, in defense, Attorney Larry Smith told the court that he was with Ferguson on the night of May 9, 1990, and that Ferguson was worried about whether the money from Cobb was improper and had returned it to Cobb.

Ferguson Defense Argument Rips Prosecution

Pride went on to tell the jury, "If the government wanted to be fair, they would have given you tapes you could hear. Don't tell me a state judge can be convicted on the testimony of a drug dealer and an addict and a bunch of film you can't even hear." Pride also attacked Cobb's motives in testifying, stressing the fact that Cobb stood to be paid a bonus by the prosecution for his help in the case and had a financial motive to help convict Ferguson.

The defense attorney, John Hardaway, blasted Cobb, saying of Cobb that Cobb had said, "'Home Boy, I'm going to help you,' and help him he did." Hardaway also tried to defuse the vulgarity of Ferguson's comments in the tapes, arguing that what they had seen and heard "may not be pretty, may not be nice, but it's not against the law."

Hardaway also pointed out that the prosecution had not shown that the money that Cobb gave to Ferguson resulted in any specific official action by Ferguson in return, that is, there was no required quid pro quo which the Supreme Court had held an essential element in the crime of bribery under the Hobbs Act in the May 23, 1991, *McCormick* case. And Hardaway cited a meeting in which Ferguson told Cobb that he would help out with the betting bill as a favor to his friend, Ron Cobb, and asked for nothing in return.

But in his final remarks, prosecutor Dale DuTremble quoted from 13 tapes in which Ferguson had told Cobb that he wanted money to buy a Mercedes car so he "'could ride out of the State House in style.'" Ferguson sold his office to get that money, DuTremble said.

Ferguson Arguments Close

The federal charges, filed on March 21, 1991, against Judge Ferguson, went to the jury on June 6, 1991, and included some, but not all of the charges in the original indictment. The original indictment charged three counts of violating the Hobbs Act, one count of conspiracy to possess cocaine, and five counts of cocaine possession.

The evidence showed in videotapes that Ferguson took money from Cobb, including $2,000 on March 29, 1990. Prosecutor Dale DuTremble told the jury that, "Those tapes show Mr. Ferguson accepting a bribe. Those tapes show Mr. Ferguson was selling his office." DuTremble pointed out that Ferguson said that when he came up for screening as a candidate for election as a judge, then Ferguson changed his conduct to avoid detection, an admission of guilt. The prosecution also stressed that Ferguson talked about promoting the betting bill after he took money from Cobb. This was a "quid pro quo, something for something," the prosecution alleged.

The defense attorneys pointed out that Ferguson had backed the betting bill before he took any money from Cobb. They pointed to a tape in which, on February 7, 1990, Ferguson had told Cobb that he did not need any money in exchange for his support of the betting bill. John Hardaway told the jury, "The question in this case is...whether this man entered into an implicit agreement to do something, whether it was a quid pro quo, something for something. If you find such explicit agreement does not exist, you must find him not guilty."

Ferguson's defense attorneys were prohibited by Judge Hawkins from raising racial discrimination issues in the case. After they had protested racial discrimination in the jury selection process, Judge Hawkins said that he would not allow the racial discrimination issue to be raised at trial. This prevented the defense from arguing that Ferguson was targeted by the FBI because he was black.

In closing arguments to the jury, attorney Pride urged the jury to listen to the tapes which were difficult to understand. He also said that the prosecution wanted to put up tapes showing Ferguson making sexual remarks. Pride admitted that both Ferguson and himself were embarrassed by the remarks, saying Ferguson "never wanted anyone to hear him in that light." The tapes did not show Ferguson in a good light as a defendant and on the same tapes, Ferguson said that some legislators might be criminally charged for their involvement with Cobb.

In jury selection, the defense had chosen jurors who said they would not rely on somebody's interpretation of conversations on tape that they could not themselves understand.

In closing, Pride did not mention race in the case, but reminded the jurors that they promised to give equal justice to all. He also pointed out that Ferguson had struggled in his earlier life to become somebody of stature and that his fate should not be placed in the hands of a drug dealer and cocaine user like Ron Cobb who served as the prosecution witness in the case.

Ferguson Case Turns on Cobb

Ferguson's defense attorneys repeated their attacks on Ron Cobb, the chief prosecution witness and sting agent, pointing out that he agreed to work for the FBI as a sting agent because he was caught with cocaine and that after agreeing to work for the FBI, Cobb again used cocaine six times contrary to the agreement. Impugning Cobb's veracity, Hardaway said, "Is this the kind of man you are going to trust? Is this the kind of man you put your faith in?"

The prosecution tried to rehabilitate Cobb, noting that Cobb and Ferguson were friends, and said that Cobb could still be believed: "Even if you believe Cobb is such a no-good, lying rascal...why is (Ferguson) so close to Cobb? It's just like they say, ladies and gentlemen, 'birds of a feather flock together'." DuTremble conceded, "You might not like Ron Cobb and I don't blame you."

The defense also put up four witnesses and two of them said that Ferguson had admitted he took money from Cobb but intended to return it. Ferguson did not take the stand, and the defense rested its case. After the jury left the room Ferguson told the court that he wanted to testify but his attorneys advised against it.

Judge Ferguson Convicted

On June 7, 1991, the federal jury convicted Judge Tee Ferguson of taking bribes while in the House. Jury deliberations began in the later part of the previous day and concluded on the following morning. It took three hours and one minute to reach a verdict of guilty on bribery to vote on the betting bill. (The court did not deal with six cocaine charges against Ferguson which was set for a separate trial in federal court on five counts of cocaine possession and one count of conspiracy to possess cocaine.)

The jury convicted Ferguson on two counts of violating the Hobbs Act and also one count of conspiring to violate the Hobbs Act. The possible sentence in the Hobbs Act violations amounted to a maximum of 66 years in prison and a fine of $1.3 million.

At the time of his conviction, Judge Ferguson was the fifth defendant to go to trial and be convicted, following Rep. Paul Derrick (R-Lexington), Rep. Luther Taylor (D-Richland), Rep. Larry Blanding (D-Sumter) and Rep. B.J. Gordon (D-Williamsburg). Five defendants still had pending cases. Seventeen had pleaded guilty. One more would be indicted.

Sentencing of Ferguson was delayed for a month or more during which a pre-sentencing report was prepared for the court. Of course, the likely sentence for a first-time offender would be much less than the maximum permitted by the Hobbs Act.

Ferguson Conviction in Review

The conviction of Judge Ferguson for crimes he committed before he became a judge while he was in the House representing Spartanburg would surely result in his leaving the bench. At the time, Ferguson had only been suspended by South Carolina Supreme Court Justice, George Gregory, based on the Court's assertion of its inherent powers although there was, in fact, no constitutional or statutory authority for the removal.

The jury pondered the evidence and the law for some two hours before asking the judge to let them review the prosecution evidence, particularly the 13 videotapes and audiotapes of Ferguson taking $3,000 from Ron Cobb which the government alleged was a bribe.

After the verdict was presented to the court, the prosecution told the media that not only had Ferguson "abused his office, but we showed evidence that he planned to continue abusing his office when he became a judge," according to Assistant U.S. Attorney John Barton, adding, "I am happy on behalf of the people of South Carolina that we eliminated that possibility."

The Ferguson case evidence showed that the defendant was not approached by Ron Cobb offering a bribe on the betting bill. In Ferguson's case, he approached Cobb and asked for money to buy a Mercedes in return for Ferguson's promise to help move the betting bill in the House.

Ferguson predicted he would be convicted saying, "the government did a good job of setting me up."

Jurors in Ferguson Case Comment

After convicting Judge Tee Ferguson of three counts related to the Hobbs Act, the jurors in the case responded to media questions. They indicated the stress of the ordeal and disagreements within the jury.

Charles D. Brooks, 73, of Barnwell, South Carolina, said that he held out against the 11 other jurors who wanted to convict Ferguson. A retired postal worker, Brooks remarked, "I held out by myself. I thought the FBI set him up, but then we looked at the tapes again. I watched what he did and I listened to what he said, and I had to change my vote." Admitting some doubts, Brooks added, "Maybe they set him up, but he didn't have to do wrong. Being a man of his caliber, he should have known better. And the way I see it, it was just nickels and dimes. Nothing but nickels and dimes." When the jury was polled after the verdict, Brooks told the court that he agreed with the guilty verdict.

Brooks commented on the fact that he was black along with two other blacks on the 12 person jury which included 9 white citizens. Ferguson's attorneys had made a major issue at jury selection about racial bias in the process against black persons called from the jury pool. "We were outnumbered. No doubt about that," Brooks said, but then added that he could not be intimidated and did not, in fact, feel under pressure to vote for conviction. He did not cave into white pressure, "I'm not that kind of man."

Juror Charles Brooks spoke as a black man on the majority white jury, but said that in trying the black defendant, Tee Ferguson, "I can't say that race had nothing to do with what we all thought and felt. But what we did was right."

Juror Walter H. Lavender, a 65 year-old retired cabinetmaker from Hanahan, South Carolina, and who served as foreman of the jury, told the media that the jury thought that a legislator and judge should behave better than Ferguson had and that public officials ought to be honest. Lavender observed that the people caught up in Lost Trust destroyed not only themselves, but also public trust in public officials.

Juror James M. Hanna, aged 60 of Seneca, South Carolina, told reporters that he hoped the verdict would send a message. Hanna, a head of engineering services at Clemson University remarked, "I hope that we 12 coming to a meeting of the minds...did our duty to rid ourselves of some of what obviously is less than honest legislators." Hanna said the jury was not surprised that

Ferguson did not take the witness stand in the trial and they did not hold it against him. Even if he did testify, Hanna surmised, "I don't think it would have helped. The tapes were good enough."

Editorial on Ferguson Conviction

The State published an editorial on June 8, 1991, the day after Judge Tee Ferguson's conviction for public corruption, saying that although Ferguson "is just another loser in the vote-selling scandal...Ferguson, who was convicted Friday, is different in one important aspect. He had been elected to the circuit court bench." And as a judge, if he had not been caught for his bribery as a legislator, he "might have remained on the take as a circuit judge."

The State complained that the "system operates to elect legislators as state judges. In the case of Mr. Ferguson, a legislative screening panel quickly approved him, notwithstanding testimony about his lack of judicial temperament."

The editorial then cast doubts on the selection process and suggested, "An objective, merit-selection process might have eliminated him from consideration." A better process might have elected a non-legislator better qualified for the bench than Ferguson.

Ferguson Faces Judicial Discipline

Upon his conviction, Judge Tee Ferguson faced multiple problems with his judicial position. Already suspended without pay by the South Carolina Supreme Court, he also faced action by the Judicial Standards Commission which considered misconduct by judges and which made recommendations for actions against judges upon finding of misconduct in office.

Chairman of the Commission, Judge John Hamilton Smith, announced in response to the Ferguson conviction that, "it strains the bounds of credibility to deny that our commission would get involved when a judge is convicted," even as Smith noted the Commission acted in secrecy. Smith added that Ferguson would be "suspended from the South Carolina Bar, not because he is a judge under a cloud, but because he is a lawyer."

Barbara Henson, assistant to the Board of Commissioners on Grievances and Discipline, further went on to explain the Commission's normal procedures in dealing with such cases as Ferguson, saying, "The standard course of action when an attorney is convicted is that once we get the certificate of conviction, he will be suspended." Henson said that once Ferguson was sentenced then he would be suspended, "It is not contingent on whatever happens to him as a judge. It's because he is an attorney, and it is automatic."

Ferguson Faces Impeachment as Judge

Given his status as a suspended judge since his indictment, the conviction of Tee Ferguson on June 7, 1991, was bound to force the issue of his removal from the bench. As the South Carolina Supreme Court had no explicit authority to suspend Ferguson under the South Carolina Constitution and Code, the future status of Ferguson was not clear upon his conviction.

The South Carolina Supreme Court might have alleged that it had inherent powers to permanently remove Ferguson as a circuit court judge following its previous assertion of inherent power to suspend Ferguson absent specific legal authority. This would be, therefore, a second phase of the Court making the law rather than relying on statutory or constitutional authority.

However, the South Carolina Constitution provided for impeachment of state court judges. In the meantime, Chief Justice George Gregory announced on June 7, 1991, that he had determined that Ferguson would remain in suspended status without pay. But there was, of course, no precedent in the history of South Carolina for such a situation.

House Judiciary Committee Chairman, David Wilkins (R-Greenville), presided over the committee which had constitutional power to charge judges with impeachable offenses and refer them to the full House for action. Wilkins said on Ferguson's conviction, "I don't believe that someone who had been convicted should be a member of the judiciary, and I am satisfied the House will take appropriate action."

Ferguson Considering Resignation

Suspended Circuit Court Judge Tee Ferguson was facing sentencing on his recent conviction on corruption in May of 1991 which raised the question of how much longer he would remain on the bench. His salary had been suspended by the South Carolina Supreme Court, and after being convicted of a felony, he would certainly face a coerced resignation or else impeachment by the General Assembly pursuant to the South Carolina Constitution. He was also facing a trial on drug charges in the near future.

In his hometown of Spartanburg, he was pondering what to do and told the media on May 19, 1991, that "I'm trying to make an informed decision and proceed cautiously, not waive any rights, and do what is best for me at this time." He said he was not trying to embarrass the judiciary or legislature by continuing to hold on to his judgeship. He faced up to 60 years on his conviction at trial on extortion and conspiracy.

House Judiciary Chair David Wilkins (R-Greenville) surveyed the scandalous posture of a convicted corrupt judge still on the bench and said, "I would hope that Mr. Ferguson would resign, but if he doesn't, I don't think the General Assembly is going to allow a convicted felon to remain on the judiciary any longer than is necessary." Wilkins added that the House might hold a short session to impeach Ferguson if necessary.

Ferguson's Judgeship a Bargaining Chip

Convicted Circuit Court Judge Tee Ferguson refused to resign after being convicted of corruption, although he had been suspended on March 21, 1991, by the S.C. Supreme Court. The question was whether he intended to offer his resignation as part of a plea deal to cut his sentence.

Some lawyers speculated that he might try to sue to ask the U.S. Supreme Court to order that his salary back to March 21st be returned to him as back pay. Speaker Bob Sheheen, a lawyer from Camden, South Carolina, speculated that Ferguson hoped his conviction would be overturned and he would then still have his judicial office.

Ferguson had been convicted on June 7, 1991, of conspiracy and extortion in taking two cash payments of $3,000 in total from Ron Cobb.

The judge still faced charges of conspiracy to possess cocaine and five counts of possession of cocaine.

Speculation was that Ferguson might offer his resignation in return for a reduction in his drug sentence, if he pleaded guilty. He might also have been hoping that Judge Falcon Hawkins would reduce his drug sentence and allow it to run concurrently with his corruption sentence.

Some lawyers believed that Ferguson had made his plight worse when he took his weak case to trial and lost. One Spartanburg attorney said, "You start with a bad situation, but how much worse can you make it?"

CHAPTER TWENTY FIVE

ETHICS REFORM IN PROGRESS

The 1991 legislative session approached its end in May and early June, but progress on drafting and passing an ethics reform bill was halting and it appeared that no bill would actually be passed before the session came to its final day of June 6th. Bills had been framed and passed by both the House and Senate but they differed on such important issues as campaign contribution limits and permissible uses of campaign funds. Furthermore, the argument over whether jurisdiction to enforce the ethics act as to lobbyists should be conferred on the State Ethics Commission or the Secretary of State remained unresolved. In addition, the question of jurisdiction to enforce ethics laws as to legislators remained in contention as the House preferred giving the authority to the State Ethics Commission while the Senate preferred letting legislative ethics committees deal with legislators.

Even though the prospect was that no ethics bill would be passed before the end of the session, there remained the possibility that Gov. Campbell would call a special session of the Legislature if he could agree to the right terms with the leadership of the House and Senate over the provisions of the final conference bill should it be passed. In the end, Campbell did call a special session which passed the bill later signed into law on September 23, 1991 and which became known as the 1991 Ethics Act.

Wrangling Over Lobbyist Regulation Bill

The General Assembly took up the controversial issue of regulating lobbyists in the 1991 session in a much more intense context than in 1990 before the Operation Lost Trust scandal broke after the 1990 session ended. In 1990, the session had failed to resolve disputes over a lobbying reform bill, one of which was the question of whether lobbyists should continue to register and report to the Secretary of State or should be assigned to the State Ethics Commission instead. But, of course, in 1990 the issue was not as compelling as it was after the Lost Trust exposé of Ron Cobb's massive vote-buying in previous years which began on July 18, 1990.

House members argued that the Commission was less political than the Secretary of State who was elected by all of the voters of South Carolina. Senators thought that this same electoral factor would promote better enforcement by the Secretary of State even though the previous Secretary had failed for twelve years under John Campbell to require lobbyists' reporting or the accuracy of reports that were actually filed. Jim Miles had ousted Campbell in the November, 1990, election and, in fact, he was much more aggressive about enforcing the regulation of lobbyists as enforcement had, in fact, been his only campaign issue.

Regulation of Lobbyists

The conference committee on ethics reform had been wrangling over the jurisdictional issue because the House wanted to shift control of lobbyists to the State Ethics Commission but the Senate wanted it to continue with the Secretary of State. The split was 3-3 along chamber lines.

Rep. David Wilkins, a House conferee, remarked on May 8, 1991, that, "I don't see any compromise on it," but he thought it would be resolved in the end. Sen. Sam Stilwell (R-Greenville) on the other side, argued "The Senate thought that it would be best having a person with that responsibility who is directly responsible to the voters of the state."

All of the conferees praised the new Secretary of State Jim Miles who had taken office in January, 1991, and had moved very aggressively against lobbyists and their employers who did not want to follow the lobbying provisions in the 1975 Ethics Act. (The Act was weak, of course, imposing no limits at all on lobbyists' gratuities and campaign donations to legislators.) Rep. Wilkins admitted that the militant actions of Miles lent credence to the Senate position that the Secretary of State should continue to have jurisdiction over lobbyists even though the House preferred jurisdiction in the Commission.

New Ethics Code for State Employees

Given the growing public outrage at the proliferating indictments and convictions for corruption and other crimes, it was to be expected that Gov. Carroll Campbell would take some action in the executive branch to improve the ethics of its staffers, employees, and officials. And, in fact, Campbell did appoint a committee to write a set of principles as a "first step in renewing a sense of ethical responsibility throughout state government."

The principles adopted by the committee were taken from the Boy Scout manual and included integrity, respect for others, honesty, fairness, and accountability.

The principles in the new ethics code were first applied to the 1,300 employees of the South Carolina Budget and Control Board, which adopted the Code on May 14, 1991. They would then be extended to all of the 65,000 state employees.

"It's a bold statement in that it challenges each public employee to live up to the high standards of public service, and live them every day," said Mike LeFever who was a member of the committee that put the code principles together.

Larry Ellis, Executive Director of the State Employees Association, thought the new code was timely, "In view of what's going on, it's very good at times to publicly state something such as this, which I think simply confirms the way state employees act every day." Ellis said that employees were discouraged by the Lost Trust scandal and its revelations.

Ethics Reform Inches Forward

The ethics bill conference committee met some six times, but only at about half of the meetings had serious compromises been proposed. No votes had been taken as of May 25, 1991 as the session came within two weeks of its end. At that time, the differences which separated the conferees were substantial enough to provoke doubts about the future of the bill.

Even so, two of the conferees were tied up in the wrangling over a contemporary reapportionment bill which was set for debate on another bill in both the House and Senate on May 20, 1991, and which had produced a time-consuming distraction from the ethics bill.

But ethics conference chair, Sen. Tom Moore (D-Aiken), said that the committee had, in fact, made progress and that both sides in the tug-of-war over the House and Senate ethics bills understood the provisions of the bills. Admitting that as to "perceived progress that you can see and read about the next day, obviously there hadn't been anything you can read about." But in spite of the lack of apparent progress, Moore concluded "that through the education process, progress is being made."

Conferee Rep. David Wilkins (R-Greenville) also offered reassurance to the public, saying that the work of the committee was slow and difficult because "this is probably the most detailed, comprehensive...piece of legislation we've passed in years." In the end, Wilkins predicted, "It'll all fall into place." And in the end, both Moore and Wilkins were proved correct.

Ethics Reform Bill Bogged Down

As the 1991 session of the General Assembly neared its end on June 6th, the ethics reform bill seemed bogged down over disputes between the House and Senate over what should be included in the bill. Since the session convened in mid-January, the indictments and convictions had piled up. Those state officials who survived tried to tell the public they were not like those caught in the Lost Trust scandal, but that was not an easy sell as the whole State House had been sullied by the crooked legislators, executive officials, and lobbyists caught by the FBI since the summer of 1990.

The House did not seem to show as much anxiety late in the 1991 session as they might have given the fact that some 13% of House members had been indicted since August, 1990. In fact, those left behind had followed the leadership of Speaker Bob Sheheen and had adopted already in December, 1990, in their organization meetings after the fall elections, a new set of House Rules which cracked down on the taking of handouts from lobbyists and provided for removal of criminous legislators.

Even so, Speaker Sheheen evinced optimism and said that, "I think we'll have an ethics bill, but if we don't we don't, we're not in any trouble because the House had already spoken on the issue." The Speaker added, "The House members at least will be governed by those (new House) rules even if the Senate doesn't pass anything."

"I feel we must do something this year, and there are some very good choices between the two bills that can be made. But I think the people of Sumter are feeling like this is going by the wayside," said Rep. Joe McElveen (D-Sumter), the House Democratic leader in the 1991 session. He had been one of the most powerful legislators who had pushed the most aggressively for drastic reforms in the state's lax ethics laws.

Sen. David Thomas (R-Greenville), who had also fought hard to make major changes in ethics laws, despaired, admitting, "There's a good chance we are not going to get to the ethics bill before January" of 1992.

Meanwhile, the conference committee labored assiduously on the bill under the chairmanship of Sen. Tom Moore (D-Aiken). The public and legislative interest in the bill was intense, said committee member Rep. Candy Waites (D-Richland), remarking that "Numbers of House members are coming up to me and saying, 'What's going on with the ethics bill? What's going on with the ethics bill? What's going on with the ethics bill?' And I'm saying nothing is happening. And they are saying to me...nobody wants to go home without an ethics bill."

House and Senate Ethics Bills Compared

As the 1991 session in late May neared its end, the House and Senate had both drafted ethics bills but they were not the same in important respects. Both bills proposed to impose strict limits on lobbyists' gratuities given to state officials. Both bills proposed to limit campaign funding as to amounts, sources, and uses. And both bills proposed enforcement schemes.

The major differences related to political money and enforcement. The Senate favored lower campaign donation limits of $500 per source per candidate for each election cycle. The House wanted a limit on donations from a source to a single candidate to be $5,000 per cycle, and the House bill would allow political parties to donate up to $100,000 to each candidate.

The House bill would have the State Ethics Commission investigate violations of all state ethics laws by all officials, but the Senate would have House and Senate legislative ethics committees investigate and penalize legislators, leaving all other state and local officials to the jurisdiction of the State Ethics Commission.

Letter to Editor on Corruption

On May 27, 1991, The State published a letter from R.M. Sullivan of St. Matthews, South Carolina, which stated, "We have seen enough corruption to last ours and our children's life-time. The legal system does work...even when our senators and representatives are the target."

Mr. Sullivan pointed out that as to understanding the abuses of office plaguing South Carolina at the time, "the people of South Carolina can handle" the problem and "It does not take lobbyists, lawyers, and legislators to see or seek out public corruption...with the groundwork the U.S. attorney's office has laid."

He believed that the public was tired of corruption and "We want people to represent us who are more concerned with the progression and problems of South Carolina and not with who is the highest bidder for their vote."

Sullivan concluded by expressing both shock and resolve at the Lost Trust scandal, saying "Corruption of this magnitude is new to our state and not very pleasant, but it is something that has to be dealt with."

Conference Committee Works on Ethics Bill

On May 29, 1991, the House-Senate conference committee wrangling over the ethics reform bill reached a tentative compromise on the contentious issue of which entity should be used to investigate complaints against legislators. The conferees agreed that the Senate plan to have the legislative ethics committee probe complaints against legislators would be accepted instead of the House proposal for jurisdiction to be assigned to the State Ethics Commission.

The committee had not met for the previous two weeks as the session-ending days had been filled with other business. But the meeting May 29th was highly productive with the conferees, chaired by Sen. Tom Moore, reaching compromises on 54 of the 85 major differences in the terms of the bill.

The committee agreed to exclude a House provision in the bill which would have required random drug testing and to exclude a Senate provision banning legislators from having sex with lobbyists.

As the conference committee on the ethics reform bill remained a work-in-progress in the final days of the 1991 session, the conflicts among conferees over whether enforcement and campaign finance provisions would be relaxed or strict worried conferee Candy Waites (D-Richland). She felt it important to have the State Ethics Commission investigate legislators but she did not regard the meeting of May 29th as finalizing anything.

However, John Crangle, Executive Director of Common Cause/South Carolina, warned that self-policing by legislators could lead to "lax enforcement" that had plagued the old House and Senate ethics committees for years ever since the 1975 Ethics Act created such committees. Crangle said that some mechanism of outside investigation was "certainly something that needs to be included in any serious bill." Even so, he acknowledged that the legislative ethics committees had been more active since the revelations of Lost Trust began in mid-July, 1990.

Conferee David Wilkins admitted that he was willing to compromise in favor of investigations by the legislative ethics committees because he realized the Senate would not agree to investigation by the State Ethics Commission.

House conferees insisted on a provision that authorized the legislative ethics committees to start investigations on their own motion without waiting for somebody to file a complaint. The bill also allowed the State Ethics Commission to start probes on its own.

The campaign finance provisions of the draft bills provoked 31 disagreements among the conferees and they decided to delay 15 of the disputed provisions for later deliberations. A major point of conflict was the fact that the Senate bill proposed to limit donations to candidates to only $500 from a single source while the House bill wanted the limit much higher at $5,000 per source. The Senate also wanted to ban the use of campaign funds raised to run for one office in a race for a different office.

Chairman Sen. Tom Moore observed, "I think, obviously, where we categorized them as major-ticket items, it will require a great deal of discussions and bending on everybody's part. But we'll have a bill."

The ethics bill conference committee meeting of May 29, 1991, caused conferee David Wilkins to yield on the Senate bill's provision retaining jurisdiction over lobbyists with the Secretary of State. The House bill on ethics reform in the 1990 session had stalled in the Senate because it proposed to transfer control of lobbyists to the State Ethics Commission.

The conferees postponed the decision on limiting lobbyists' and their clients' gifts and meals and cash handouts to officials, but it was clear in the light of the abuses exposed by Lost Trust and the media that strict limits on such transactions would probably be imposed by any ethics reform bill which would be passed.

Democrats Blast Gov. Campbell on High Campaign Limits

Gov. Carroll Campbell had fought hard against proposals to include low campaign contribution limits in the ethics bill, especially the low figures of $250 for legislators and $500 for statewide candidates written into the Senate reform bill passed in 1991.

S.C. Democratic State Chairman, Albert McAlister, blasted Campbell for insisting on higher contribution limits in the bill, saying big money limits would gut the bill. (Of course, Gov. Campbell had taken a $60,000 campaign contribution from McAlloy, Inc., a Charleston steel corporation, in his 1990 re-election campaign.)

Campbell had taken a position for limits of $5,000 on political action committees and $100,000 on political parties. Ridiculing Gov. Campbell, McAlister opined, "If this is his idea of ethics reform, he'll probably hire Jim Holderman as his next fund-raiser." McAlister demanded that Campbell call for lower limits. (Holderman had been charged for his criminal conduct while president of the University of South Carolina in the same time period.)

McAlister also raised a question indirectly as to whether Campbell was tainted by Lost Trust and said, "It seems that ethics reform is hitting too close to home for Carroll Campbell." In fact, the chairman said, big money politics was the top ethical problem in South Carolina. He also noted that two of the governor's henchmen, Dick Greer and David Hawkins, were ensnared in the probe for cocaine and witness tampering respectively.

Money Limits at Issue

Higher campaign contributions limits favored by Gov. Campbell were also supported by half of the House Democrats, even while Chairman McAlister blamed Campbell for the higher numbers.

Tucker Eskew, spokesman for Campbell, said that the governor opposed the Senate proposal to ban the use of funds raised for one office to be used later to run for another office and that Campbell opposed limits of $500 supported by the Senate was well. Eskew said, "He views that measure and the unreasonably low contribution limits as blatant incumbent protection that are designed by the Democratic Party incapable of maintaining long-term majority status without a stacked deck."

The rumor was that Campbell would veto the bill if limits were low and that rumor worried the conference committee meeting on May 30, 1991, causing some conferees to say that their efforts might all be in vain. Eskew noted that Campbell had made clear, from the time the Senate adopted low limits, that he opposed them. But Eskew did not clarify the standard that would be used to determine whether a veto would be imposed on the bill.

Ethics Reform Bill in Dispute

As the 1991 session came to an end on June 6th, the major disputes were both partisan and inter-chamber. The Republicans in the House did not oppose the proposed ban on lobbyists' campaign donations, but wanted to allow those who hired lobbyists to donate. The Senate, controlled by Democrats, wanted to ban both lobbyists and their employers from making donations.

The conference on the bill agreed that candidates could use surplus funds left over from a run for one office to run for a different office. They also agreed that the bill should ban candidates from donating money from their campaign account to another person's campaign account.

But the conferees were still split on the contribution limits. The House conferees wanted adamantly to impose higher limits of $5,000 for statewide candidates and $2,000 for all others, such as candidates for the legislature. The Senate conferees rigidly wanted the limits set at $500 for statewide and $250 for all others.

Then Senate conferees, on May 30, 1991, proposed a compromise of $3,000 for statewide and $1,000 for others, but the House rejected it. And the House said it still wanted to let parties give $100,000 to statewide candidates and $5,000 to others, but the Senate wanted the limits on party donations set at $500 for statewide and $250 for others. The deadlock remained unbroken.

Senator Moore joked of the two different proposals, saying of the House scheme, "yours are extravagant," and of the Senate proposal, it might be "unreasonable." It seemed like the dispute over amounts would persist.

Ethics Reform Bill at End of Session

As the General Assembly neared adjournment on June 6, 1991, the ethics reform bill which had been in formulation since January was still not finished. As the deadline neared, House Judiciary Chairman David Wilkins (R-Greenville) proposed that the contentious campaign finance reform section of the bill be dropped and only the remaining ethics reform proposals be considered. The Democrats and Republicans had episodically been fighting over the issue of amount limits on donations in the last weeks of the session.

Sen. Tom Moore (D-Aiken), who chaired the conference committee working on the reform bill, ridiculed Wilkins' idea, saying, "That would be analogous to Moses, when he went on Mount Sinai, God saying, 'Here are the 10 Commandments. Do your best to keep nine of them.'" And Sen. Sam Stilwell (R-Greenville) recognized the centrality of the campaign finance reform problem could not be ignored, saying of the proposed reforms, "If we don't do it now, will we ever do it?"

Rep. Wilkins said that he was afraid that if the reform bill was held over until the next session, the political pressure would be less as the Lost Trust scandal faded from public attention. Wilkins said, "If the choice is we get 90 percent of the bill or get nothing, I'd want to get 90 percent."

The end of the session came more abruptly than expected because there was a general expectation that the session would be extended, but the Senate was unhappy about a reapportionment bill and announced that the Senate would let the session end at 5 p.m. of June 6.

Session Ends Without Ethics Bill Passage

The adjournment of the General Assembly on June 6, 1991, left the draft ethics bill in the conference committee without having been voted on by the House and Senate. If no vote was taken before the end of the year, the bill would have died in December, 1991, and would have required reintroduction in the House in the new 1992 session. The General Assembly declined to extend the session to deal with the ethics bill. That left the bill in jeopardy unless Gov. Campbell called a special session to pass it.

The session ended with the Republicans feeling that they had gained power and could control the agenda of the General Assembly, said House Republican leader Terry Haskins (R-Greenville), even though they did not hold a majority in the Senate or the House.

But Gov. Campbell expressed disappointment that the session had ended without passing bills on ethics, reapportionment, state-run primary elections, and bonds. Campbell indicated he might consider calling a special session, but only if there is an agreement to limit the length and agenda of the session.

1991 Session Ends

The disgraced S.C. General Assembly came to the end of its 1991 regular annual session on June 6. During the session, the indictments of corrupt legislators had piled up, lobbyists had been implicated, and executive branch and state employees had been ensnared in Lost Trust and its fallout.

Two of the most powerful officials had been removed—Sen. Jack Lindsay by death and Speaker Pro Tem Jack I. Rogers by conviction of racketeering corruption. Ten percent of the Legislature was charged in the scandal with bribery, conspiracy, obstruction, racketeering, and drug crimes.

The shock of so many scandals in the State House hit senior legislators especially hard and the internal conflict in state government had ruined efforts to pass legislation. The most senior legislator, Sen. Marshall Williams (D-Orangeburg), President Pro Tem of the Senate and Chairman of Senate Judiciary, complained of partisan paralysis and the inflexible positions taken by Gov. Carroll Campbell, opining, "the governor is saying, its going to be my way or no way."

The Operation Lost Trust scandal had a tendency to paralyze the General Assembly session in 1991 as the indictments and convictions continued to pile up during the late winter and spring of the year. By the end of the session on June 6, a total of 15 members would be indicted a few months later.

Speaker Bob Sheheen (D-Kershaw) observed, "I do think that the apprehension that was in the air as a result of the continuing indictments every 30 to 46 days caused everybody to be very careful about what they did and how they did it."

The death of Sen. Jack Lindsay in January, 1991, just as the session began, triggered a competition to replace him as the leader of the Senate and the dominant figure in the Senate Finance Committee. Among those maneuvering toward the leadership position was Sen. Glenn McConnell (R-Charleston) who provoked Sen. David Thomas (R-Greenville) to remark that McConnell had become a reincarnation of Jack Lindsay, joking that, "All he needs is a cigarette hanging out of his mouth and a gruff voice, and you wouldn't be able to tell them apart."

Special Session or Not?

The question of whether to call a special session of the General Assembly to complete its unfinished 1991 agenda provoked disagreement. Some felt that a special session was needed to clean up the unfinished business of ethics reform which had become more and more an acute issue as the indictments and convictions proliferated. But an issue was whether the cost of the special session would be worth it.

In an editorial, *The State*, on June 9, 1991, wrote, "after five months of wind-bagging, legislators failed to pass ethics legislation or reapportionment plans." Noting the cost of a special session would be $50,000 per day, *The State* warned that any special session should not allow an unlimited amount of time if a special session was called by Gov. Campbell.

Noting the wrangling over the campaign finance provisions in the draft ethics bill, *The State* predicted, "a House-Senate conference committee will continue to try to iron out those differences.... There is no question that a strong ethics bill is needed." Admitting the House and Senate had passed new rules to regulate ethical conduct, the editors observed that such rules were easy to change at will by each chamber, and therefore could not be relied upon as a permanent standard of ethics.

But the question was, "Do they deserve a $50,000 one-day session to get off the hook?" Gov. Campbell had to decide that issue and his answer ultimately was yes.

Democrats Blame Gov. Campbell on Ethics

On June 11, 1991, Democrats blamed Gov. Carroll Campbell for his failure to get the ethics reform bill passed in the session ended on June 6th. State Democratic Chairman, Albert McAlister, charged that Campbell stalled the bill to protect his "campaign honey pot" from new restrictions so he could perhaps use leftover funds to run for Congress.

Campbell had said soon after the session ended that he might call a special session to pass ethics reform and reapportionment bills. His office blamed Senate Democrats for wanting to drag the 1991 session beyond its normal adjournment.

Democrats alleged that Campbell had blocked passage of the ethics reform bill which had low campaign contribution limits because he wanted much higher limits. McAlister alleged, "More than any politician in South Carolina's history, Carroll Campbell had prospered from the free-wheeling spirit of our campaign laws," adding that, "Big money has been very good to Carroll Campbell, and Carroll Campbell has been very good to big money."

McAlister listed 400 contributions of $1,000 or more to Campbell in the 1990 election campaign and one for $60,000 from McAlloy Corp. He also pointed out that donors of $27,000 and another of $21,000 were appointed to state positions at the Research Authority and Development Board.

Campbell Calls Short Special Session

Gov. Carroll Campbell announced on June 12, 1991, that he would call a limited special session of the General Assembly to complete unfinished business left behind when adjournment was effected at 5:00 p.m. on June 6, 1991. The Governor said that the session would be limited to voting on the ethics reform bill and the reapportionment bill which were badly needed, provided the conference committee on the ethics reform bill and the House Judiciary Committee could both agree on an ethics bill and a reapportionment bill and present it to the special session for votes.

Lt. Gov. Nick Theodore remarked that the ethics reform bill was the most urgent of the two bills, saying, "The citizens aren't as concerned about reapportionment as they are about ethics reform, so I think as far as I'm concerned, the premier part of this agreement would be the Legislature having one more opportunity to deal with ethics reform, and therefore should not be ignored." Theodore would preside over the Senate in special session, if called.

Campbell included his proposal for a limited special session in letters he sent to Speaker Bob Sheheen (D-Kershaw) and Senate President Pro Tem Marshall Williams (D-Orangeburg). Campbell said that if the House and Senate could agree on reapportionment by June 26, 1991, then he would call the special session for a two week period to pass ethics reform, reapportionment, and other bills. However, if they could not agree on reapportionment, then he would only call a one day special session to vote on the ethics reform bill.

In response to Gov. Campbell's letters of June 12, 1991, Sen. Tom Moore (D-Aiken), chairman of the conference committee on the ethics reform bill, said that the committee would meet as often as necessary to complete its work on the bill. Sen. Williams said that he would call a meeting of Senate leaders within a few days in the week of June 16th to decide what the Senate would do in response to Campbell's proposal for a limited special session, predicting, "I think that everything can be worked out if everybody works for the good of the church."

The major distraction was the reapportionment bill. Sen. Williams thought a special session on the bill would be of no use unless the House and the governor would agree to the Senate reapportionment plan. Speaker Bob Sheheen said that he had recommended to Campbell that he call the special session to focus on the ethics bill and that reapportionment be postponed until a later date, saying of the reapportionment bill, "I really do not think any agreement was going to be reached."

The reapportionment fight had caused the adjournment without final action on the bill. Campbell had said he would veto the proposed Senate plan which wanted to combine reapportionment schemes for the House, Senate, and congressional district into one bill. If the General Assembly could not fix the problem, then the federal courts would likely do so.

Ethics Panel Finalized Bill

The House-Senate conference committee working to find a compromise solution to ethics reform made progress in the middle of June, 1991, in anticipation of the special session Gov. Carroll Campbell had expressed an interest in calling if a bill was agreed upon.

Conference met on June 13, 1991, and agreed to compromise on campaign contribution limits but did not finalize the amounts. Rep. David Wilkins (R-Greenville) said that, "I don't think there's any question that we all feel under the gun to make some movement, and I think everyone is making a good-faith effort.... I think we've come a long way." Chairman Sen. Tom Moore (D-Aiken) agreed that progress was being made and a recent meeting had been productive.

The conferees were well aware that Campbell had said he would call a special session on ethics reform if the committee would agree on a bill by June 26, 1991. Otherwise, ethics reform would have to wait until the following year. The biggest bone of contention still was the issue of how much campaign donations should be limited in amount. Another issue was how much the uses of political money should be limited.

When the conference committee met in the week of June 10, 1991, the House Ethics Committee Chairman, Wes Hayes (D-York), suggested limiting contributions to statewide candidates to $3,500 and to $1,500 to candidates for legislative and local offices. He also proposed limits on political party donations to statewide candidates to $50,000 and to all others, $10,000. Hayes further proposed to ban the transfer of campaign funds from one candidate's account to another candidate's account. Finally, Hayes also proposed that candidates not be allowed to use money raised to run for one office to run for another office starting in 1993.

However, the votes on Hayes' proposals were split. Rep. Wilkins and Sen. Sam Stilwell (R-Greenville) voted yes, but Sen Tom Moore and Sen. McKinley Washington (D-Charleston) as well as Rep. Candy Waites (D-Richland) opposed.

Sen. Stilwell then cleverly sensed exactly the right compromise number and proposed limits of $3,500 for statewide candidates and $1,000 for legislative and local. Waites and Stilwell voted for this, but the other four opposed. The question remained unsettled.

Even so, the proposals were much closer together than those presented to the committee by the House and Senate. The House had proposed donation limits of $5,000 on statewide and $2,000 on legislative and local candidates. The Senate had proposed only $500 for statewide and $250 for others. But in the end, the Stilwell compromise was passed into law as part of the 1991 Ethics Act.

Reformers Urge Conferees on Ethics Bill

Lt. Gov. Nick Theodore and Common Cause/South Carolina Executive Director called a news conference while the conference committee was deliberating on and debating the ethics reform bills passes by the House and Senate and trying to find a compromise.

Theodore said that after a year of scandals and shame, the legislators had reached a crossroad and must act: "We can take the high road and pass meaningful, significant legislation, or we can stay on the same road that has led some members of the General Assembly to the penitentiary."

In addition to the issue of the limits and uses of campaign funds, the conferees had to decide whether the Secretary of State would continue to regulate lobbyists or the State Ethics Commission would be assigned the task.

Editorial Burns Campbell on Ethics Reform

The State published an editorial on June 18, 1991, asking the rhetorical question, "Where's the Governor on ethics reform bill?" *The State* opined, "If ever there was a need for leadership from Governor Campbell, it's now." The newspaper pointed out that the ethics reform bill was tangled up in the conference committee over issues relating to campaign finance reforms.

"It's time for the Governor and his minions to stop insisting on the whole hog," a clear reference to Campbell's advocacy of higher contribution limits in contrast to the Democratic Senate's bill to limit donations to only $500 per donor for statewide candidates and $250 for all other candidates.

The House bill proposed that individuals could donate $2,000 and corporations could donate $5,000 to candidates, and political parties could donate $100,000 to statewide candidates and $25,000 to all other candidates such as legislators. But Candy Waites (D-Richland) revealed that she had polled House members and that a majority actually favored lower limits than those in the House bill.

Waites, following Sen. Stilwell's lead, proposed limiting contributions of both individuals and corporations to the same amounts, that is $3,500 per source to statewide candidates and $1,000 to local and legislative. (This was exactly the amounts actually adopted, passed, and signed by Gov. Campbell.)

The State's editorial faulted both Gov. Campbell and Rep. David Wilkins, one of the conferees, for thinking of their own interests in advocating higher contribution limits. Campbell had a reputation as a strong fund-raiser and Wilkins was believed to be planning to run to replace Campbell on his term-limited mandatory leaving of office in January, 1995. Both were holding out for higher limits in the conference committee negotiations at the time of the editorial. Both Campbell and Wilkins had great power and seemingly were intimidating some committee members who were willing to accept lower limits but opposed higher limits.

The editorial concluded with a call for action, "Statesmanship is needed at the top. With a green light from the Governor, House conferees will fall into line post-haste and approve the lower contribution limits." The editors then added, "Mr. Campbell claims that an inability to pass an ethics reform bill was the biggest failure of the 1991 Legislature. If so, all he has to do it put aside partisanship and support a reasonable cap on campaign financing. Then, the ethics reform is a done deal."

Ethics Bill Finished

The six person House-Senate conference committee finally came to an agreement on the ethics reform bill and reported it out on June 18, 1991, the same day as *The State* had written an editorial calling for action by Gov. Campbell and the committee membership. The bill proposed strict bans on lobbyists' handouts to officials and for the first time in the history of South Carolina, new limits on campaign contributions which were also remarkably low, much lover than Gov. Campbell had been holding out for.

House Judiciary Committee Chairman, David Wilkins, a member of the conference committee, told the media, "The message is that we are serious about having an ethical playing field for governmental and political business in South Carolina, and the days of the environment that brought on the sting are ended forever in South Carolina."

Chairman of the Conference Committee, Sen. Tom Moore, said the bill reported out of his committee addressed the same problems as those exposed by the scandal and, he added, "I think that speaks clearly and loudly to citizens in South Carolina that we have addressed that problem."

However, the governor's office did not say that Campbell would call a special session just because the bill was finished. He had to mull it over and decide later.

The ethics reform bill presented to Campbell was not what Campbell had hoped for. He was concerned about such issues as funding limits which would hurt political parties, large loopholes in campaign contribution limits, and a failure to address the issue of lawyer-legislators practicing before state boards and commissions.

However, John Crangle, Executive Director of Common Cause/South Carolina, who had been lobbying for ethics reform since 1988, remarked that the bill "looks pretty good" even though he had been complaining for some time that the bill was too watered down and weak. Crangle added, "It's certainly a lot better than what we have now.... I think they've got the freebies under pretty good control."

The bill was a frontal assault on the very same problems exposed by the sting, especially the ways in which lobbyist Ron Cobb exploited the lax terms in state laws which allowed him to hand out large and unlimited amounts of personal cash bribes to legislators under the guise of giving them campaign donations. The bill inflicted a flat ban on lobbyists giving officials anything of value whether in cash, food, drinks, hotel rooms, or trips. Employers of lobbyists could host large groups for free meals, such as county legislative delegations and could also provide lodging and meals for legislators who they invited to speak to a group. All such transactions would be subject to mandatory disclosure by both donors and donees.

In addition, the conference bill also was directed at conflicts of interest, especially hidden conflicts, and required officials to disclose all business they did with government, lobbyists, and lobbyists' employers. The bill also barred lawyer-legislators from voting on the budgets of state agencies before which they practiced law.

The draft ethics bill from the conference committee banned lobbyists from giving campaign donations to legislators. Cash contributions were banned with trivial exceptions which allowed a maximum of $500 in total donations from a church collection for statewide candidates and $250 for legislative candidates. Gov. Campbell objected to the church collection exception but it was pushed into the bill by black legislators who raised money in churches. Campbell regarded it as a loophole.

The conference bill finally settled on contribution limits of $3,500 for statewide and $1,000 for legislative and local candidates from any single source for each election cycle. A primary election, an if-needed run-off primary, and a general election were each seen as a separate election cycle, allowing candidates to take the maximum amount for each cycle in which they ran, up to three times the maximum for any candidate running in three elections. The bill also limited party donations to candidates to $50,000 for statewide candidates and $5,000 for legislative and local candidates. Such limits were remarkably low given the original Republican demands for much higher limits on political money.

<u>Ethics Bill Self-Policing of Legislators</u>

The enforcement provisions of the ethics bill reported out by the conference committee failed to deal with the enforcement problem effectively and would prove to be problematic for decades into the future. The basic conflict between the House bill which proposed enforcement of the ethics law by the State Ethics Commission and the Senate, which proposed enforcement by separate House and Senate ethics committees was settled in favor of the Senate bill. This meant that all complaints against legislators could not be taken to the State Ethics Commission even though all complaints against statewide and local officials would be taken to the Commission.

This self-enforcement of the law by each chamber crated huge conflicts of interest which caused legislators in following years too often to ignore enforcement and gloss over violations by members. The root problem was that legislators were afraid to complain against fellow legislators, especially fellow party members and powerful legislators such as committee chairs and the Speaker in the House and also leadership of the Senate. A related problem was that, in their own self-interest, the bill was framed by legislators to ban the publication of complaints against officials unless the committee or the Ethics Commission chose to release it to the public.

Ethics Bill Gets Tougher

The six person conference committee working on the House and Senate ethics reform bills passed before the 1991 session adjourned made unexpected progress in constructing a bill much stronger than had been expected. There were several major reasons.

First, the committee consisted of six legislators, three Republicans and three Democrats, who were themselves officials of exceptionally high integrity and ability and who were intensely serious about cleaning up the mess at the State House which, by association, made everybody in the General Assembly suspect and discredited. Second, the Legislature was only one year from the coming elections in 1992 which would include all House members and all Senators. No incumbent intending to run for re-election wanted to go into the election year and face the prospect of being challenged in the primary and general elections by a candidate who could attack them for not being sufficiently aggressive on ethics reform. Third, the constant drumbeat of shocking and disgusting revelations of more and more indictments and convictions of public officials, especially of 18 legislators, which had begun in the summer of 1990 continued into the fall of 1991 even while the conference committee was hashing out the ethics bill. This kept the corruption issue before the media and the public as the grand jury, trial courts, and prosecutors kept hammering the voters in what seemed like an unending chronicle of legislators and officials being indicted, tried, pled guilty, convicted, and sentenced for bribery, conspiracy, and drug crimes by the federal government which state law and feckless state government officials, including the General Assembly, had done nothing to prohibit, prevent, expose or stop.

Tough Ethics Bill Finalized and Presented

The day after the conference committee finalized the ethics bill, Rep. Candy Y. Waites, one of the six conferees on the ethics bill, said on June 19, 1991, that she was amazed by the willingness of the conferees to take deficient House and Senate bills and add much stricter limitations on the traditionally permissive State House practices involving campaign finance and lobbying. In the pre-Lost Trust 1990 session, Waites had tried and failed to arouse some interest in reform proposals, she reflected, but the membership wanted no reforms. As to even the most basic ethics reforms, Waites said, in the old days the "membership was just saying, 'We don't want it, we don't need it, leave it alone, we don't want to talk about it'."

But by the summer of 1991, the attitude had dramatically changed after the scandal had raged for nearly one year. Waites observed, "Now most if not all of those things are included, plus much, much more. The thought of limiting contributions—you didn't even talk about it." As to abusive lobbyists and their handouts, Waites said, "The thought that you didn't receive a gift from a lobbyist was just unheard of."

Looking over the content of the ethics reform bill as the conference committee came to the end of its work, Waites said, "It's much stronger than what I thought we'd be able to pass."

Ethics Bill Attacks Lost Trust Abuses

The draft ethics reform bill being finalized by the conference was a direct attack on the very same abuses that Ron Cobb had perpetrated in Lost Trust. Whereas Cobb had given unlimited cash campaign contributions which were really bribes, the bill would ban cash contributions and also ban lobbyists' contributions completely. Whereas, in the past, legislators had taken money bribes from Cobb and put the money in their pockets, the bill banned the use of campaign money for personal uses.

Although there was considerable opposition, the real reforms during the construction of the bill directly tried to attack the root causes of corruption rather than use cosmetic trickery to only deal with the symptoms of corruption.

Advocates or real reform saw a once-in-a-lifetime chance to change the corrupt culture of the State House. Even though the limits on the amount of campaign contributions were deemed to high by Common Cause/South Carolina, the group realized that the proposed limits were much better than the unlimited cash handouts of the past.

The bill dealt with conflicts of interest in a serious way. Although Gov. Campbell thought the conflict issue was not cured by the draft bill, it did require legislators to report their financial dealings with lobbyists and state agencies, including lawyer-legislators' dealings with state boards and commissions, a key concern of Gov. Campbell.

South Carolina Bill Limits Cash

Although the bill did not ban cash donations to candidates completely, the bill did set a limit on cash donations of $25 per source and only in certain circumstances. Some 23 states permitted but limited cash contributions. Even so, the amount of cash that could be given at any one fund-raising event was limited to $500 for statewide and $250 for all other candidates.

The ban on large cash contributions from a single donor was a precision strike on the use of cash bribes postured as so-called campaign contributions. Cash donations created no paper trail and could easily be converted into personal uses by officials taking the money from bribe-givers. Of course, large cash bribes could still be illegally given, but they could no longer be disguised as campaign contributions by the donor and donee.

South Carolina Ethics Bill in National Perspective

The Council of State Governments noted that states which passed an ethics reform bill after a major corruption scandal commonly referred to their new laws as among the toughest in the nation. The question was, how did South Carolina's bill compare, in fact, to other states?

But the Council on Governmental Ethics Laws did say that the South Carolina bill would be among the most rigorous in the nation. In addition to a total ban on lobbyists' gifts and contributions to politicians, the bill had strict caps on campaign donations. Only five states—Alabama, Alaska, California, Mississippi, and Vermont—had limits on campaign donations of $1,000 or less to candidates for legislative and local office. Only two states had limits below the South Carolina limit of $3,500 on donations to constitutional office candidates; they were Hawaii and Rhode Island.

The limits on donations from political parties to candidates were limited by the South Carolina bill to $50,000. Whereas 14 states had lower limits, and Montana had limits of $300 on party money to candidates, Michigan only had a limit of party donations of $750,000 per candidate.

The Josephson Institute on Ethics, a Marina Del Ray, California, group, listed 10 elements of ethics laws of which the South Carolina bill met 7. The chief failings of the South Carolina bill were that the bill failed to protect whistle-blowers and failed to deal with legislative obstructionism.

The problem always remained that certain parties would try to use legal loopholes to engage in corrupt acts, the Council on State Government noted. This would prove to be true in South Carolina from 1992 forward.

S.C. Ethics Bill Compared to S.C. Law

The ethics bill in the conference committee in its final form in late June, 1991, made drastic changes in the ways in which lobbying, campaign finance, and conflicts of interest were regarded in South Carolina. A comparison of the proposed new law and the old law showed great differences.

Ethics Bill (1991 Ethics Act)	Existing Law (1975 Ethics Act)
Lobbyists banned from spending money on legislators	No limits on lobbyist spending on public officials
Detailed lobbyists' disclosure required	No real lobbyists' disclosure required
Total ban on lobbyists' campaign donations to legislators	Lobbyists can donate anything; no limits

Campaign contributions limited Only specified uses of money allowed	No limits on sources, amounts, or uses of campaign funds
Cash contributions limited to $25 each	No limits on cash contributions, any amounts, sources, and uses of money permitted
Campaign contributions limited to campaign and office uses	No limits on uses of campaign funds for any purposes
Legislators must report business with lobbyists	Reporting laws ignored
Lawyer-legislators must report on representing clients before state agencies	No reporting required
Lawyer-legislators may not vote on budgets or bills affecting agencies they appear before	No limits on voting
Legislators police selves by committee	Legislators police selves by committee
State Ethics Commission polices constitutional officers and local government officials	State Ethics Commission polices all non-legislator officials

Ethics Bill Not Perfect

The ethics reform bill which came out of the conference committee and was later signed into law did not complete the task of cleaning up South Carolina politics and government even though it made great progress.

Gary Baker, director of the State Ethics Commission, pointed out that the conflicts of interest problem was not adequately cured in that legislators would not have to disclose that they represented a client who stood to gain from legislation and budget provisos which they sponsored. Baker also pointed out the lack of independent investigation and enforcement which still allowed legislators to police themselves. Even so, Baker said the bill "puts us in the forefront of what's going on across the nation."

The South Carolina bill also allowed clients of lobbyists to give campaign donations to legislators as well as limited free meals, whereas Wisconsin banned lobbyists' employers' gratuities to legislators. Furthermore, South Carolina continued to allow legislators to raise campaign funds during legislative session whereas Florida, Georgia, Wisconsin, and Texas banned in-session fund-raising.

South Carolina did join Oregon and Maryland in banning lobbyists' donations to legislators.

Ethics Debate Neglects State Grand Jury Idea

Throughout the 1991 legislative session, the General Assembly wrangled over the drafting of the ethics reform bill and squabbled with Gov. Campbell over such issues as contribution limits on donors. At the same time, Attorney General Travis Medlock fought a less visible battle to strengthen the investigative and enforcement resources of his office in battling corruption and abuse of office. Along with Robert Stewart, Chief of the State Law Enforcement Division (SLED), Medlock campaigned steadily from January to June, 1991, to extend the powers of the state grand jury to include authority to investigate and prosecute public corruption cases. Gov. Campbell applauded the effort.

The state grand jury system had other types of jurisdictions such as drugs but not the power to probe corruption. However, in 1988, the voters of the state had approved a constitutional referendum amendment which would grant new powers to the state grand jury to attack corruption. The new powers included the authority to subpoena witnesses, grant immunity, record testimony, and look into cases crossing county lines within the state.

However, the amendment required legislative ratification to take effect under the South Carolina Constitution's three step amendment process. In the 1991 session, the focus had been on ethics reform against a backdrop of more and more indictments and convictions of legislators, executive employees, and lobbyists which continued during the entire session. Even so, the amendment had not been ratified. Medlock complained, "No one can deny we need it," pointing to the growing parade of scandals.

Campbell Reviews Ethics Bill

Gov. Carroll Campbell said on June 25, 1991, that he would review the ethics bill presented by the conference committee when it was finished before he decided to call a special session of the General Assembly to vote on the bill. He indicated that he had no reason to object to the bill as it stood at that time.

However, Campbell said he would not allow such a special session to consider an unrelated bill to move primary elections from the control of political parties to the administration of the state.

Campbell said of the ethics bill which came out of the session in June that, "I just want to make sure that what's in it is what everybody said was in it." As he spoke, the conference committee chaired by Sen. Tom Moore (D-Aiken) continued to work on the 100 page ethics bill throughout the day and into the evening.

When the 1991 session ended without passing a final ethics reform bill, many felt that the most important problem faced by the state after all of the corruption and drug scandals had not been addressed. Campbell then promised to call a special session if the conference committee could present a reasonable bill to him. However, it sounded for the first time that Campbell would only call the special session if he liked the bill and wanted it passed. Campbell said it would not be fair to the Legislature to call a special session for a bill which he might find objectionable and veto.

Campbell Questions Contribution Caps

In considering the ethics reform bill then being prepared by the conference committee, Campbell said on June 25, 1991, that one of his main concerns with the draft bill being hashed out by the committee was the inclusion of low caps on campaign contributions of $3,500 for statewide candidates and $1,000 for all other candidates such as legislators, but that he could accept them at the level if in the final bill

Campbell announced his plan to meet with House Speaker Bob Sheheen (D-Kershaw) and Sen. Marshall Williams (D-Orangeburg), President Pro Tem of the Senate, to discuss the terms for calling a special session. The governor said that he wanted to review the ethics bill coming out of the conference committee and said that he wanted to agree on it, adding, "I want to take their bill." But some legislators worried that Campbell would insist on a bill meeting his standards without compromise.

Action Council Bemoans Lack of Ethics Bill

The S.C. Christian Action Council wrote to *The State* bemoaning the failure of the General Assembly to pass an ethics reform bill before it adjourned on June 26, 1991.

The Council said that it lobbied for new ethics rules early in the session. But, nothing was passed. "it appears that the various interest groups in state government stalemated each other...and the real interests of South Carolina are being ignored."

Council Executive, Minister L. Wayne Bryant, wrote that it was time for action. Urging the conference committee, Gov. Campbell, and the House and Senate to move forward, Bryant said, "We think it is time for state government to work under strict ethical standards. We think it is time for government to divest itself of partisan interest and serve the people."

CHAPTER TWENTY SIX

MORE CRIMINALS FACE THE MUSIC

In the early summer of 1991, the Lost Trust prosecutions were moving forward on multiple fronts as new indictments were being presented and older charges were being disposed of by the court systems. At the same time, the controversy over the legitimacy of the Lost Trust sting operation and the work of the prosecutors and the courts was being debated in public, in court and in the media. In addition, multiple events came to public attention that indicated a number of problems and issues related in some way to Lost Trust and public corruption.

At the same time, the conference committee on the ethics reform bill was concluding its work on a compromise bill, which it finally agreed upon on June 18, 1991, and sent to Gov. Campbell for his approval in the expectation that he would call a special session of the General Assembly perhaps in the early fall of the year, which he eventually did.

And while the prosecutions moved on and the ethics reform bill came out of the conference committee, the task of cleaning up behind the Lost Trust prosecutions continued and new elections were held to replace those legislators who had been convicted of corruption and drug crimes.

Sen. Horace Smith Resigns

Sen. Horace Smith (D-Greenville) decided to spare the South Carolina Senate the agony of deciding to remove him by resigning after pleading guilty to a felony not involving his public office. He was convicted of federal charges of conspiracy to defraud in conjunction with the securities of a nursing home in Spartanburg.

As the Senate had no automatic expulsion rules similar to House Rule 3.12 which mandated removal on indictment, the Senate would have to debate the question of removing Smith on conviction. This same issue had proven difficult in the previous case of Sen. Gene Carmichael of Dillon and Marlboro counties who had been convicted of federal charges of vote buying a decade earlier.

Smith first asked to be suspended after his indictment and then four months later, on May 30, 1991, he resigned after entering his plea. Smith had held his Senate seat for 25 years.

Lt. Gov. Nick Theodore, the President of the Senate, praised Smith's resignation, saying, "You couldn't ask more from a senator."

Sen. Marshall Williams, Senate President Pro Tem, read Smith's letter to the Senate which said, "Although I firmly believe that the Senate...would see fit not to expel me, I refuse to place my colleagues in that position and force the Senate to endure such an experience." In fact, the issue was already agonizing the Senate.

The removal of a senator according to Senate Rule required the Senate Ethics Committee to vote to recommend expulsion on conviction of a felony, but also required a two-thirds vote of the Senate, a difficult task.

Editorial on Sheheen

The State published an editorial on May 31, 1991, which took the side of Speaker Bob Sheheen for enforcing House Rule 3.12 which ordered that indicted House members be automatically suspended and that those convicted of felonies should be automatically expelled. Sheheen had invoked the rule to remove all those indicted who had not resigned their seats before removal.

The State was responding to Rep. B.J. Gordon's federal lawsuit challenging his removal on indictment and conviction from the House as violative of the 1965 Voting Rights Act. Gordon argued that his removal deprived the 25,000 residents of his House District in Williamsburg County of their right to representation in violation of the Act because House Rule 3.12 had been implemented without getting pre-clearance from the U.S. Justice Department.

The State supported Sheheen who had filed a brief in the Gordon case asserting that the suit was asking that the Voting Rights Act be extended into an area which "it has never been previously understood to govern." *The State* pointed to the "constitutional right of a representative body to judge its members and, under appropriate circumstances, to suspend or expel them."

The editorial pointed to the need to remove those charged with serious crimes, quoting Sheheen's view that, "Can you think what would happen if we had people who were convicted sitting in the House?"

Lobbyist Collins Pleads Guilty

Tom Collins pleaded guilty to possession of cocaine in federal court on May 30, 1991. He had been the lobbyist and sales agent of Hitachi Data Systems which had sold computers to state agencies in previous years. He faced up to three years in prison and a fine up to $300,000.

Collins explained that the pressure of his work caused him to turn to cocaine addiction which had resulted in his indictment in the Lost Trust probe of drugs and corruption in state government.

Collins had agreed to plead guilty and to cooperate with the probe. He was allowed to plead guilty to three misdemeanor counts of cocaine possession instead of the original charge of possession with intent to distribute cocaine, a much more serious felony crime on which he had faced 41 years in prison and a fine of $2.1 million.

FBI agent Tommy David testified in court at the hearing that Collins had used cocaine with legislators, lobbyists, and other state government employees. The FBI targeted Collins because he had the potential to influence legislators.

The grand jury indicted Collins for possessing cocaine on April 1, 1987, and for both possessing and distribution of cocaine on November 5 and 6, 1987, and also between July 18 and July 31, 1988. At those times, Collins was in the company of other lobbyists who later pleaded guilty and also Dick Greer, Chairman of State Economic Development agency. The venues of the offenses were hotels in Columbia, Charleston, and Greenville.

Tom Collins' plea on May 30, 1991, was accepted by Judge Falcon Hawkins, but he delayed sentencing until a later date during which a report by probation officers would be prepared to assist the court in imposing penalties.

Collins became the most recent of six lobbyists charged in Lost Trust. All of them but one had been charged with drugs and all of them would eventually plead guilty. Four of the 17 legislators convicted in the scandal were also charged with drug offenses as of the date of Collins' guilty plea.

Sting Defendants Proclaim Innocence

Not guilty pleas were entered on June 6, 1991, by Rep. Kenneth Bailey (D-Orangeburg) and Rep. Tim Wilkes (D-Fairfield), both under suspension by the S.C. House of Representatives pursuant to House Rule 3.12. Both denied the charges of conspiracy and extortion for taking money from Ron Cobb to vote for the betting bill. Bailey faced 40 years in prison and a fine of $500,000 for accepting $500 from Cobb to vote for the betting bill. Wilkes took two payments in total of $1,500 from Cobb for the betting bill.

James V. Hopkins of Clemson University pleaded not guilty to charges of one count of possession of cocaine. He was a 40 year old administrator of computer services at the University.

David O. Hawkins also pleaded not guilty to charges of obstruction of justice for alleged witness tampering. He had served in the House from Spartanburg County as a Republican and had also served as an aide to Gov. Carroll Campbell in the State House.

Both Hopkins and Hawkins had been discovered during the course of the Lost Trust probe into drug dealing and public corruption centering on Ron Cobb and the betting bill he was promoting. Hopkins had been involved in the purchase of computer equipment for Clemson University in his position of administrator in charge of marketing and customer support. The FBI was interested in the role of cocaine in the purchase of millions of dollars of computer equipment from Hitachi Corporation which involved state legislators. Even after his indictment by a federal grand jury on cocaine charges, Clemson allowed Hopkins to continue his employment, only restricting his work to Clemson employers and not any others. A Clemson spokeswoman, Cathy Sams, said the University was waiting to see what would happen to Hopkins after he was indicted on May 23, 1991.

In the case of David O. Hawkins, age 45, the grand jury found in their indictment of May 23, 1991, that Hawkins had approached former Rep. Robert Kohn on May 1, 1990, and asked Kohn to refuse to tell law enforcement what he knew about possible criminal activity. At the time, Kohn was not cooperating with the FBI in the sting but would soon become a sting agent after he was caught in corruption himself. Hawkins faced a possible sentence of up to 10 years in prison and a fine of up to $250,000 for his alleged witness tampering and obstruction of the FBI probe.

As of the indictments of Bailey and Wilkes, a total of 26 defendants had been charged in Lost Trust cases of which 16 House members and one senator were charged. Sen. Bud Long (D-Horry) would soon be charged and tried in November, 1991, on bribery charges.

Little Pleads Not Guilty

Spartanburg businessman, David D. Little, III, appeared on June 7, 1991, in U.S. District Court in Charleston and pleaded not guilty to one count of cocaine possession dating from May, 1990. Little's charges stemmed from the Lost Trust probe into public corruption in state government. David D. Little, III, owned a nursing home management company.

U.S. Magistrate, Robert S. Carr, granted Little a personal recognizance bond of $25,000 and therefore no payment was required of Little. The judge also set June 27, 1991, as the date for filing motions in the case.

Four others indicted on May 23, 1991, were also allowed to be released on bond of $10,000 after pleading not guilty to drug and bribery charges on June 6, 1991.

Lobbyists Get New Disclosure Forms

Newly elected Secretary of State, Jim Miles, sent out new disclosure report forms to the 300 lobbyists working at the State House in 1991 on behalf of some 500 clients. Miles' major campaign issue had been that he would force lobbyists to register and disclose their activities according to the law and Miles had taken office in January, 1991, with the announced intention of doing what he promised.

Miles new-style forms included four pages asking lobbyists to report all food, gifts, entertainment, expenses, and campaign contributions which they had provided to legislators between June 20, 1990, and June 6, 1991, the end of the 1991 session of the Legislature.

Miles' office announced that the new forms would be sent out by June 13, 1991, and that the return date was set at July 6, 1991.

The new forms designed by Miles and Bob Knight, Deputy Secretary of State, had four pages, whereas the previous Secretary of State, John Campbell, who had lost on the lobbyist issue, had sent out only a one page form. Miles had defeated Campbell in November, 1990, on the basis of the fact that Campbell had not done much of anything about lobbyists and had not insisted that they file, report, and disclose basic information about their activities.

In view of the fact that the House in early 1991 had responded to the sting scandal by passing new harsh rules to ban house members from accepting gifts and meals from lobbyists with few exceptions and the Senate had passed even stricter rules, not even allowing exceptions, new Secretary of State Miles mused that his new reports would probably not find evidence of much old-style wining and dining in the 1991 session. Even so, he planned to include a list of lobbyists' expenditures on each individual legislator.

Grand Jury Looks At Tax Break

The federal grand jury examining Lost Trust corruption moved to widen its probe by deciding to look into the special capital gains tax break bill which slid through the Legislature in the rigged 1989 state budget. The bill gave 21 persons a tax break which saved them $8.6 million in state taxes.

The bill had provoked criticism and the criminal prosecution. One of the chief beneficiaries of the bill, Greenville businessman, Tom Roe, had revealed that he refused to pay crooked lobbyist Ron Cobb a bribe to push the bill and had testified to the same before the grand jury in late May or early June of 1991. And former House Speaker Pro Tem, Jack I. Rogers, had been convicted on racketeering and Sen. Jack Lindsay wisely died before his indictment in relation to the tax break bill.

Roe's testimony raised the question of whether more persons would be indicted at a time when U.S. Attorney Bart Daniel was saying that the sting probe was nearing its end. It came out that Ron Cobb had told the grand jury that Lindsay had paid off another senator in his efforts to move the tax break bill. And Rogers had pleaded guilty to racketeering and agreed with the prosecution to tell what he knew about the bill.

Roe did know the names of other businessmen who had paid Ron Cobb to push the tax break bill. Prosecutors thanked Roe for his information in revealing cases in which persons refused to pay bribes to Cobb on demand.

Roe had previously told *The State* in August, 1990, that Roe and Greenville businessman Walter Brashier had been hit with higher tax bills when the law on capital gains was changed in 1987. They therefore went to State Development Board Chairman Dick Greer for help and Greer, an old friend and political ally of Gov. Carroll Campbell, suggested that the businessmen hire Greer's cocaine buddy, Ron Cobb, to move legislation providing tax relief in the matter. Tom Roe then paid $25,000 to Cobb for help.

Cobb, in turn, went to Sen. Jack Lindsay, his friend and so-called mentor, and got Lindsay to slip a tax break proviso into the 1989 state budget. The proviso was put in by Lindsay while Sen. James Waddell (D-Beaufort) was chair of the Senate Finance Committee. The seemingly invisible proviso was moved without debate and passed the Senate and the conference committee with no trouble. (Waddell later denied that he had been paid off in the matter.)

Cobb then went back to Roe and demanded $80,000 because Cobb said some people had to be taken care of, according to Roe. Roe refused to pay the money. Former lobbyist, Randy Lee, who pleaded guilty to drug crimes in Lost Trust, said that he was present in a room when Lee and Dick Greer saw and heard Lindsay and Cobb talking about splitting a $150,000 bribe to get the tax break bill passed into law.

As passed, the tax break bill provided a break of some $22.4 million for about 60,000 people with about a third of the amount going as a tax break to Tom Roe and his 20 other businessmen. Later Lindsay and Waddell tried to take the tax bill away for persons who had made capital gains by selling stock and Roe was one such person. The Senate then decided to keep the part of the proviso which would benefit stock sellers. Roe ended up with half of his expected tax break in 1991 but the other half slated for 1992 was eliminated.

Medlock Takes Lawyers' Donations

South Carolina Attorney General, Travis Medlock, was running for re-election and was raising money for the campaign in 1991. Medlock was taking campaign donations from lawyers, including those who had been employed as outside contract lawyers by the state government. This raised the question of whether the Attorney General, who often employed outside counsel in state civil cases, was acting in a conflicted role in seeking donations from the same lawyers he hired to do work for the Attorney General's office.

Medlock asked the State Ethics Commission in May, 1991, to consider the issue and render an opinion. The Commission wrote an advisory opinion published on June 14, 1991, stating that donations from lawyers to the Attorney General was permissible under the 1975 Ethics Act, a piece of legislation which had been exposed as a fake in the Operation Lost Trust scandal.

Even prior to Medlock's two terms in office, it had been common for lawyers to donate hundreds of thousands of dollars to the campaigns of South Carolina's Attorneys General, much of the money coming from law firms, frequently large law firms.

In Medlock's case, some of the donor lawyers were also lobbyists and subject to possible prosecution by the Attorney General for misconduct and violations of the law as lobbyists and as lawyers. Thus they were in a vulnerable position and did not want to antagonize the Attorney General.

The opinion rendered by the Commission only addressed the question of whether the Attorney General could take donations from lawyers and did not address the issue of whether he could take money from lobbyists, too. Medlock told the media on June 14, 1991, that he thought that there was no question under state law that he could also take donations from lobbyists and therefore he did not ask the Commission for an opinion on the question of lobbyists' donations.

However, in 1990, the Commission had ruled in a case related to Secretary of State John Campbell, who had taken large amounts from the same lobbyists whose reports his office was supposed to collect and store, that he could not take donations from lobbyists. It was also deemed unethical for the state treasurer to take donations from bankers regulated by the treasurer's office.

Gary Baker, executive director of the Commission, said the rulings on the Secretary of State was based on a state law prohibiting a public official from taking more than $10 for any reason from a person or business the official regulated. However, Medlock denied that he regulated lobbyists or any other types of persons. In a letter dated May 13, 1990, Medlock wrote the Commission in seeking an advisory opinion and he said, "To my knowledge, the Office of Attorney General has not been deemed regulatory in any of its many functions as far as the ethics laws are concerned."

Medlock also asked the Commission to determine if there was a conflict of interest for the Attorney General to take donations from private attorneys hired by the state. The Commission responded that the hiring of "associate counsel" was hired on an arms length basis and there was no conflict.

Medlock told the media that he was not influenced by contributions from any sources and that, "Acceptance of contributions from attorneys, or anyone else for that matter, has never affected, nor will it, my performance of duties and no one has suggested otherwise."

Probe of Legislators in Florida

At the same time as Lost Trust was in its final phase of indictments, trials, and convictions, the State of Florida, in late May, 1991, charged ten of its legislators with taking illegal gifts and trips from lobbyists, including gratuities such as football games and quail hunts in Georgia. The scandal in the Florida Legislature was quite similar to that in South Carolina where lobbyists' unlimited gifts were being handed out to legislators, except that in Florida, such gratuities from lobbyists were illegal, whereas in South Carolina, such transactions were legal until the Ethics Act was passed later in 1991 and took effect the following year.

In Florida, the Speaker of the House of Representatives, T.K. Wetherell, and the Chairman of the Senate Appropriations Committee, Winston "Bud" Gardner, were among those charged. A senator who was a candidate for the office of Senate President, Sen. Pat Thomas, was also charged.

The Florida Attorney General's office announced that some thirty other legislators would be charged in the following weeks.

Hawkins Pleads Guilty

David O. Hawkins entered a guilty plea to one count of obstruction of justice for warning former Rep. Robert Kohn (R-Charleston) that the FBI was investigating corruption in Lost Trust. Hawkins had been a Republican House member from Spartanburg and an aide to Gov. Campbell serving as Director of Legislative Affairs. He faced a future sentencing of 10 years and a fine of $250,000 maximum.

Hawkins filed his plea on June 19, 1991, the day after the conference committee reported out the new ethics reform bill. At the time of his plea, he had retired due to mental illness after taking a leave of absence from Campbell's office in September, 1990.

In his legislative career, he was a leader and mastermind of the infamous "Fat and Ugly Caucus" which used to pressure lobbyists to give them free meals and gratuities in the 1980s until it was disbanded by Speaker Bob Sheheen about 1988. As it turned out, 11 of the 14 legislators convicted in the sting by mid-June, 1991, had been past members of the Caucus.

Hawkins' crime was telling Kohn about the Richland Solicitor's probe of Ron Cobb. Kohn, in turn, told other legislators who were spooked to avoid the sting when Cobb's bribes were offered to them. Kohn thus alerted those who might have taken bribes.

As was later revealed, 5th Circuit Solicitor Jim Anders had told Hawkins about an investigation Anders was conducting of Ron Cobb, and, of course, Hawkins spread the word to others. In fact, Anders did not know about the FBI sting operation even though it was in Columbia where he lived and worked and was in progress when Anders unwittingly warned Hawkins of the Anders probe.

Sentencing Dates Set for Sting Criminals

On June 21, 1991, the dates for sentencing convicted Development Board Chairman Dick Greer and former Rep. Ennis Fant (D-Greenville) were set.

Fant pleaded on February 22, 1991, to conspiracy to sell his vote on the betting bill. Sentencing was set for Fant on July 30, 1991. He faced a maximum sentence of 20 years and a fine of $250,000.

Greer pleaded guilty to drugs on April 10, 1991. His sentencing was then set for July 30, 1991, on possession of cocaine. Greer faced one year and $100,000 fine.

Sentencing for former Rep. James Faber (D-Richland) was set for July 31, 1991. He had pleaded guilty on March 1, 1991, to conspiracy to sell his vote. Faber faced the same sentencing maximums as Fant.

North Carolina-based lobbyist, Guy Rohling, was set for sentencing on July 12, 1991. He pleaded guilty to possession of cocaine on March 7, 1991, and faced a sentence of one year in prison and a fine of $100,000. His sentencing was set for Charleston.

B.J. Gordon Moves for New Trial

Convicted Rep. B.J. Gordon (D-Williamsburg) filed a motion for a new trial and acquittal on his bribery conviction on June 21, 1991. The motion was based on the new U.S. Supreme Court decision, *McCormick v. U.S.* (1991), in a bribery case similar to the Gordon case.

Gordon's attorney, Lionel Lofton, moved on the grounds that the prosecution failed to meet the new standards set by the *McCormick* Court requiring that the prosecution must show a definite promise was made to perform an official act in exchange for a money payment.

Gordon was convicted at trial on March 8, 1991, of conspiracy and selling his vote. He faced a maximum of 40 years in prison and fines of $500,000 on the two convictions.

Defendants Move to Overturn Convictions

Attorneys for former Rep. B.J. Gordon (D-Williamsburg) and former Rep. Larry Blanding (D-Sumter) both moved to overturn their convictions on bribery charges in late June, 1991, before Judge Falcon Hawkins.

Based on a new U.S. Supreme Court decision, *McCormick v. U.S.*, (500 U.S. 257 (1991), the attorneys asserted that both convictions failed to prove all elements of the Hobbs Act crime of bribery. The new decision required a clear showing that the defendant agreed and promised to take an official act in return for a consideration of value, such as money. The new ruling was based on a case in which a West Virginia legislator was convicted of bribery under the Hobbs Act and then had his conviction overturned for failure of the prosecution to prove a quid pro quo between McCormick and an alleged briber.

In the Gordon case, FBI informant Ron Cobb testified that he gave Gordon $1,000 in cash as a campaign contribution but did not know for a fact that Gordon intended to take the money as a bribe in return for his official action in the future. However, convicted corruptionist Luther Taylor testified that, in fact, Gordon was not for sale.

Gordon's lawyer, Lionel Lofton, told the court in Charleston that there was insufficient evidence to convict Gordon, saying, "Where is the evidence of a quid pro quo? It does not exist." Lofton added, "The only evidence in this case is that Mr. Gordon's vote was note for sale."

Assistant U.S. Attorney John Barton retorted that Luther Taylor's testimony was not credible, arguing that even though Taylor said Gordon was not for sale, "Mr. Taylor, even as he sits in prison today, does not maintain he had done anything wrong."

Larry Blanding was wrongfully convicted and his conviction should be overturned, Danny Martin, Blanding's attorney, told Judge Falcon Hawkins in Charleston on June 25, 1991. Martin said that there was no evidence in the tapes that Blanding agreed to do anything for the money given to him by Ron Cobb. "Even if he had gone to Ron Cobb's office a thousand times and received millions of dollars...if he did and said nothing more than is on the transcript," there was no evidence of a quid pro quo by which Blanding promised to take an official action in return for Cobb's money.

Assistant U.S. Attorney John Barton disagreed with Martin's theory and said that sufficient evidence and testimony showed that Blanding was offered $500 but then wanted $1,000 as a bribe from Ron Cobb.

Prosecutors Request Sentence Reduction for Taylor

Claiming "unusual circumstances," Assistant U.S. Attorney Dale DuTremble asked the federal court to reduce the 6½ year sentence of Luther Taylor on June 29, 1991. Seven months earlier, the prosecution had asked the court to sentence Taylor to more time than specified in the federal sentencing guidelines.

The reason for the request to cut the sentence was that Taylor had since "directly assisted the government in obtaining the convictions of three corrupt legislators" when Taylor testified against them at trial. The three defendants were former Reps. B.J. Gordon, Larry Blanding, and Tee Ferguson.

At the time, Taylor was one of only two defendants who had been sentenced in the scandal, although a total of 27 had been charged. The other was former Sen. Rick Lee who also helped the prosecution and received only probation, not prison time. Taylor's help, according to DuTremble was "at least equal to, and in several instances greater than, others who have agreed to cooperate."

DuTremble said that while Taylor was then serving his sentence in a Florida federal prison, his sentence should be cut "even if its only a couple of months, he ought to get some credit." Taylor had originally refused to cooperate.

Campbell Called to Return Donation

The South Carolina Democratic Party called on Gov. Carroll Campbell to return a $60,000 donation from McAlloy Corp. after the business was fined $55,000 for 15 air quality violations in early June, 1991, by the South Carolina Department of Health and Environmental Control. The government agency had originally planned to impose an even more severe fine on McAlloy but the amount was eventually negotiated and imposed. The violations were based on the releases of emissions from McAlloy's North Charleston facility.

Campbell had taken the $60,000 from McAlloy in his 1990 re-election campaign, but the Executive Director of the South Carolina Democratic Party, Betsy Durant, called upon the governor to return the full amount saying of Campbell, "He's been talking about ethics legislation, and big money is the problem in this state. He needs to give it back."

During the 1990 campaign, Campbell had been criticized for the McAlloy emissions but had said they were not that serious. Even so, the Democrats thought the money was contaminated and should be returned. Sen. Herbert Fielding (D-Charleston) observed, "The amazing thing is the closeness between the $55,000 (fine) and the $60,000 contribution."

The governor's office rejected the call to return the $60,000 and ridiculed the credibility of the Democrats in demanding the return of the money.

Noting the perception that Campbell had somehow tried to protect McAlloy from the S.C. Department of Health and Environmental Control (DHEC), Rep. Joe McElveen (D-Sumter) observed, "He can correct that misconception by giving the money back." McElveen said there was some public suspicion that the Governor intervened for McAlloy. Robert Barber (D-Charleston) called upon Campbell to act immediately, "Governor, cough up the tainted money."

Critic Knocks Use of Church to Collect Political Money

Luther R. Jackson, Sr., of Dillon, South Carolina, wrote *The State* on June 29, 1991, to criticize a new portion of the draft ethics bill which would allow the collection of campaign donations in churches. "God's house is no place to let politicians to collect money for their own coffers.... It is certainly unethical in my opinion to raise money in churches for political use."

Jackson also disliked the bill because, "It favors its members in some ways, even though it is better than nothing and would show a little effort not to repeat a most terrible thing like the recent 'sting' that has tarnished South Carolina's good name." He especially deplored the provision of the bill to allow in-house ethics enforcement, saying, "Reprimanding themselves is still 'good ol' boy' politics. Will any meaningful action be taken, especially for long entrenched, powerful members?"

Noting that Gov. Campbell did not like the bill very much, Black said of the bill, "If it isn't revised I hope he vetoes it."

Racial Targeting Alleged

A large, predominantly black Baptist group executive board alleged on May 8, 1991, that blacks had been unfairly targeted by the Lost Trust sting. Meeting in Greenville, South Carolina, in its 114th annual session, the Educational and Missionary Convention of South Carolina complained that too many blacks were caught up in the sting.

The Convention had a membership of 450,000. The Past President of the Convention, Rev. S.C. Cureton, said that the statement reflected the concerns of members of the Convention which included some 1,800 churches. Cureton also said that, "We would hope that the government and those in charge would take a second look at what has happened. It appears that every time a black seems to be moving up the ladder, something takes place to undermine his influence." Cureton found the fact that seven of 15 legislators charged at the time were black men was out of proportion and that few blacks held office in the state.

The Convention's reaction to the number of blacks caught in the scandal reflected a common ambivalence among blacks in South Carolina at the time. Cureton felt that some of the persons caught in the sting came from difficult environments and from underprivileged backgrounds and perhaps needed money worse than whites. On the other hand, the minister said that in the future, blacks needed to seek out better quality candidates "who would not allow $5 or $5,000 to mislead and misguide them." The Convention statement also said that all such crimes should be punished and urged black leaders to condemn violations by public officials.

CHAPTER TWENTY SEVEN

ELECTIONS REPLACE CRIMINAL LEGISLATORS

As the criminal convictions of state legislators expelled House members and forced the resignation of Sen. Rick Lee (R-Spartanburg), it was necessary to hold special elections to replace those ousted in the Lost Trust scandal. These special elections moved forward in 1991 as voters picked new legislators who all campaigned on clean government platforms and stressed their own integrity.

House Special Elections Held

Special elections to replace House members expelled on conviction of bribery moved forward in Richland County in early May, 1991. But the scandal had hurt the electorate, said Richland County Democratic Chairman I.S. Leevy Johnson, observing, "All this sting stuff has chilled people and made them indifferent." But candidate Levola Taylor said that there was interest in the races and remarked, "There's no voter apathy here." Candidate Nathaniel Roberson also commented that there was no drop off in interest in comparison with the race he ran for the House in 1986. But House candidate Rev. Joe Neal noted, "A lot of people are disenchanted, and some others are outraged."

The issue of honesty was, of course, a major factor in the special elections to replace those removed for corruption. Neal said he was stressing the integrity issue in his campaign. The disgraced former Rep. James Faber was active behind the scenes in backing Levola Taylor. But Taylor denied that Faber had any official role in her efforts, protesting that "He doesn't have anything to do with my campaign." But she added, "if he wants to support me, that's fine."

Seven Candidates Seek McBride's Seat

The expulsion of Rep. Frank McBride from House seat 70 opened the door to seven black candidates and no whites to run for the district in North Columbia which McBride had held for six years. The election was set for June 25, 1991.

The candidates included Dr. Alma Byrd, a Richland One School Board member and faculty member at Benedict College, and three lawyers—Mary Myers Montgomery, Thomas Mosley, and Jerry Screen. Activist Redfern, II, department store salesman, Alvin Jefferson, and chronic candidate Alvin Portee rounded out the field.

House District 74 Runoff—Byrd vs. Screen

The scramble to replace deposed felon Rep. Frank McBride in House District 74 in Columbia ended up in a Democratic runoff election pitting two black candidates to take over for the ousted black legislator. There was no Republican candidate.

The two were well known figures. Dr. Alma Byrd, a Richland County District One School Board member, and Jerry Screen, a local attorney, had no trouble with voter identification, but Byrd was perhaps better known as a public official and had led the field in votes in the first primary election.

However, the two candidates caused some sparks. Screen opened his statement at a Democratic election forum on May 19, 1991, by saying of Byrd, "Any difference between my opponent and I is our zeal and intellectual ability." Byrd, who called herself a "senior citizen" even though she was not retired and continued on the teaching faculty in foreign languages at Benedict College said, "You won't hear me address my opponent in any way."

Byrd was regarded in the heavily African-American District 74 as a known factor who, if not spectacular, as a public official would not take any bribes like McBride had. Franchot Brown, a Columbia black attorney, said of Byrd, "We can trust her downtown." But local activist Kevin Gray said Byrd was a status quo person and Screen would be likely to shake things up.

Dr. Byrd Wins District 74 Race

Dr. Alma Byrd ran over attorney Jerry Screen by a vote of 892 to 557 in District 74 House race on May 21, 1991, to replace expelled bribe-taker Frank McBride. Byrd was the better known candidate in the black district and she held public office on the local school board when elected. Seventy-six percent of the district was black population.

Her defeated opponent, Jerry Screen, chalked up his loss to the work of the "old-line" Democratic establishment. "Black people stayed home and let a handful of white voters on the other side of the district decide who their representative would be. Screen claimed that low-income blacks stayed home in the runoff primary allowing the decision to be made by middle class whites and blacks who Screen called "old-line status quo Democrats." Screen also alleged that Byrd cut a deal with McBride to get his support.

Byrd and McBride were both employed by Benedict College at the time of McBride's conviction on March 1, 1991, when he resigned. He had held the seat since 1984. Byrd denied making any deals with McBride for his support. It was also the case that Jerry Screen's wife was the secretary to Dr. Marshall C. Grigsby, the President of Benedict College. Coincidentally, Common Cause/South Carolina Executive Director, a prominent advocate of ethics reform at the State House, was a professor of history at Benedict College as well.

Justice Department Warns Against House Expulsions

The U.S. Department of Justice took the Speaker of the South Carolina House to task for moving to suspend indicted members and to expel those convicted in Lost Trust. Speaker Bob Sheheen had been relying on House Rule 3.12 to remove those charged and convicted in Lost Trust.

But the Justice Department warned the Speaker that expulsion violated the 1965 Voting Rights Act because House Rule 3.12 had been put into effect without obtaining pre-clearance from the Justice Department as required by the Act.

Rep. B.J. Gordon (D-Williamsburg) had filed suit in federal court attacking the rule as violative of the Act after he was convicted of corruption on March 8, 1991. Gordon's suit claimed that the 25,000 citizens in Gordon's House District 101 would be deprived of their right to representation if he was removed from the House.

In the lawsuit, a federal judge refused to halt the special elections in District 101 set for May 29, 1991, in the primary and for July 9, 1991, in the general election.

The Justice Department said in a brief filed May 17, 1991, that a special three judge panel could halt the elections and restore Gordon's seat under the Act. However, Justice said that the judges could order an expedited request for approval of House Rule 3.12 by Justice, which, if granted, could remedy the problem. The three judge panel included district judges Joe Anderson, Matthew Perry, and William Wilkins, a U.S. Circuit Court of Appeals judge.

Ex-Felon Carmichael Elected to Senate

Disgraced former state senator Gene Carmichael cast a new cloud on the State House when Dillon and Marlboro County's voters elected Carmichael again to the Senate by a vote of 4,433 to 2,031 on May 14, 1991. Carmichael had been convicted in a massive vote-buying scandal a decade earlier and had served time in federal prison.

The election was also abnormal in another way in that it was a special election to fill the senate seat vacated by the death of Sen. Jack Lindsay, one of the top suspects in the Lost Trust bribery scandal. Furthermore, Carmichael had defeated Jack Lindsay's son, Chuck Lindsay, in the Democratic primary, but in the special general election, Lindsay still received 1, 367 write-in votes, all but 52 of them from his home county of Marlboro.

In the Senate, however, several senators indicated an intention to force a vote on the question of whether Carmichael would actually be allowed to take his place. But the general view was that the Senate would accept the decision of the voters and, as Sen. Donald Holland (D-Kershaw) said of the matter, "I will vote to seat Mr. Carmichael. Because you're not depriving him of anything. You're depriving the people he represents.

The election of Gene Carmichael was not a welcome event for a state Senate already embarrassed by the bribery conviction of former Sen. Rick Lee (R-Spartanburg) and the impending indictment and eventual conviction of Sen. Bud Long (D-Horry). Therefore, Sen. John Courson (R-Richland) wrote to the Attorney General, Travis Medlock, and asked whether a convicted felon could take the seat.

The Senate had the power under the S.C. Constitution to remove a senator convicted of a crime while serving. Even so, Sen. John Land (D-Clarendon) a supporter of Carmichael, said that provision allowed Carmichael to take the office if the Senate decided to admit Carmichael.

The Senate did admit Carmichael without serious problems and he took his seat on May 21, 1991, returning to the Senate chamber for the first time since 1982 when he had been forced out. Even so, some senators worried that Carmichael's return would aggravate the bad reputation of the State House made even worse by continuing Lost Trust indictments and convictions which had been going on from August, 1990, to the time of Carmichael's return and would continue until 1999.

Federal Court Halts Expulsions from House

A federal judge ruled that Speaker Bob Sheheen as of May 29, 1991, could not use Rule 3.12 to suspend House members upon their indictment as he had been doing. The judge found that the rule had not been pre-cleared and approved by the U.S. Department of Justice prior to its implementation.

Rule 3.12 provided that a House member would automatically be suspended upon indictment and expelled on conviction of a felony. Based on that rule, the House had been removing members charged in the Lost Trust cases, including a number of black representatives.

The court found that the 1965 Voting Rights Act required the pre-clearance to protect black voting rights against historical racial discrimination. South Carolina was one of a number of southern states to which the Act applied. However, the court found no evidence that the rule had, in fact, been applied unfairly against blacks in the scandal. Nor did the court find that the rule had any illegal intent.

At the time, the Sumter County June 4, 1991, special runoff primary election continued to replace Rep. Larry Blanding who had been removed in Operation Lost Trust upon conviction along with three others convicted. But federal judges enjoined the holding of any special elections to replace any others ejected under the rule.

Former Rep. B.J. Gordon (D-Williamsburg) had filed a suit challenging his ejection from the House under Rule 3.12 alleging it violated the 1965 Voting Rights Act's pre-clearance requirement. He asked that the court order his reinstatement in the House.

The court did not order reinstatement but it enjoined any more ejections under Rule 3.12. The court chose to await the final decision on whether pre-clearance had been violated.

Sheheen argued that the Act was intended to protect the rights of voters and not to protect officials charged with crimes. The court relied on a regulation of the U.S. Attorney's office that restricted change affecting the ability of people to remain holders of elective offices and practices affecting voting.

Sheheen protested that he did not want to set a precedent for submitting all proposed House rules to the Justice Department for pre-clearance in the future. Sheheen was uncertain as to what he would do, but thought it a major issue which could affect many offices.

The House adopted Rule 3.12 in 1982 because the Senate had been unable to expel a member, Sen. Gene Carmichael, for conviction of vote-buying. The Senate had no automatic expulsion rule at the time.

Candidates File for Rep. Derrick's Vacant Seat

The indictment and conviction of Rep. Paul Derrick (R-Lexington) for public corruption triggered the filing of four Republicans and one Democrat for vacant seat 69 in the House. The primary election was set for July 23, 1991, and the general election was set for September 10, 1991. Derrick had been convicted by a federal jury of taking a $1,000 bribe from lobbyist Ron Cobb in the Lost Trust sting.

Two candidates for the seat in House District 69 stressed the need for ethics reform. Republican Lexington County Councilman Paul Peters and South Carolina Republican Party Committeeman Lou Mintz both said stronger ethics laws were needed to stop public corruption. Two other Republican candidates, retired Clemson University Extension Service Agent Bill Riser and Attorney Bill Oswald both agreed in announcing their candidacies. Riser said, "The whole point of public service is to help people. Unfortunately, some politicians are only interested in helping themselves."

Democratic candidate, J. Stephen McCormick, worried that, "There has been so much bad government in so many different forms. I would hope the people of District 69 are fed up with the good ol' boys running the show."

Urban League Urges Blacks to Hold Officials Accountable

The fact that eight of the defendants in Operation Lost Trust were black House members provoked the Columbia Urban League to write and release a report June 17, 1991, which demanded that black people in South Carolina hold black officials to a higher standard of accountability than in the past. Written by black political science professor, Rick Hill, of South Carolina State, the report concluded: "No longer can any black community accept unresponsive representation simply because that representation is black. Black voters must make it clear that they will hold black political authorities accountable for their actions."

The report by Prof. Hill was part of the Urban League's annual study entitled "The State of Black South Carolina." Hill, the chairman of the political science and history departments at South Carolina State, said that blacks should reject any excuses from black politicians that their convictions for public corruption were racially motivated. Hill said that the convictions of so many black legislators had reduced the influence of the black community's voice in the General Assembly on such issues as reapportionment.

Hill argued that as blacks generally suffered from poor health care, poverty, and poor housing, they could not afford to have politicians abuse their trust. He also said that economic insecurity might have made black officials more vulnerable to corruption.

Professor Hill's provocative remarks about black officials' failures to perform ethically and effectively triggered some controversy among prominent blacks in Columbia. Rep. Joe E. Brown (D-Richland) took issue with the idea that black officials should be held to a special code of conduct, remarking, "Why must there be this racial distinction in ethics?" Brown added, "Corruption is an individual thing, not a race-based thing." Brown was a colleague of Rep. James Faber, Rep. Frank McBride and Rep. Luther Taylor in the Richland County House delegation before they were suspended and then expelled on conviction of corruption.

Richland County Councilwoman Bernice Scott also took exception to the notion of a special type of accountability standards for black officials of which she was one. Scott said, "As far as I'm concerned, there are only two issues in the forefront—right and wrong. Race shouldn't even be a factor in a question of ethics, though, unfortunately, it is often made to be one." Scott also noted that the bigger problem was corruption by both white and black officials in South Carolina, observing, "Politicians, both black and white, seem to have forgotten that they are servants of the people and are not in office to serve themselves."

Urban League President, James McLawhorn, Jr., said the annual report of the League had played a significant role in identifying reforms important to blacks in South Carolina.

Pointing to the problem of black officials lacking income and being tempted by corrupt money, Hill said that black officials "need to have real jobs making real money to fight their vulnerability to bribes and tokens." Hill noted that, in many cases, black officials had no other sources of income except public office.

But Nelson Rivers, Executive Director of the South Carolina branch of the NAACP, said that gainful employment was not enough and Rivers opined: "Just because you can prove you are gainfully employed doesn't mean you're more ethical."

Hill's report in the Urban League's annual study recommended that public officials must be prohibited by law from taking anything of monetary value from lobbyists, corporations or individuals for the purpose of selling official votes and actions. He also said that all campaign donations over $100 should be made public. And he added that officials should be required to provide proof of gainful employment if they held part-time public offices.

Editorial Endorses Urban League Plea for Higher Standards

The State picked up on the report prepared by Professor Ricky Hill of South Carolina State for the Columbia Urban League, arguing that some black politicians of the State of South Carolina had shown more interest in lining their pockets than in helping the black community. The Hill report criticized black part-time officials who tried to make a living off of public office by using it for personal gain. Instead, he said that all such part-time officials should have a real job as a condition of holding office.

Even though the Hill proposal seemed a bit farfetched, he brought out the issue of small-time hustlers in the General Assembly, city councils, and county councils. Living off of politics invited abuse of office and corruption.

On June 22, 1991, *The State* wrote: "so many who have been given a place of honor have succumbed to graft. Blacks can't ignore racial implications or set aside suspicions when a disproportionate number of their elected officials are charged." Admitting that "racism exists," *The State* said blacks caught in corruption should not be allowed to dodge personal responsibility by pleas that they were victims of racial discrimination. "When blacks abuse their trust (as did the seven former legislators convicted in the State House sting) the response should be condemnation" for the damage inflicted on the black community."

The State's editorial clearly affirmed, "There is a need for blacks, tired of being sold down the river by 'friends' of whatever hue, to speak loudly to the problem." Praising the Urban League's report pointing to black corruption as a scandal and insult, *The State* wrote, "Elected black officials carry a heavier load. They represent, unofficially, far more than the hopes of minorities inside narrow electoral districts. And when seven fall, and entire racial group feels the pain."

Candidate Replacements Win Three House Seats

The special elections held on June 25, 1991, to replace black Democratic expelled House members were won easily by black Democratic candidates who brushed aside opponents in Richland County and Greenville. Richland District One School Board member, Levola Taylor, a black Democrat, took District 70 in lower Richland County by a vote of 1,173 to 40 for Republican Scott Wartham. She replace Jim Faber who had plead to bribery.

Dr. Alma Byrd, a black Democrat and professor at Benedict College, took District 74 by a large margin. Dr. Byrd had also served on the Richland One School Board. She replaced Frank McBride who had pled guilty to bribery.

In Greenville County, Fletcher Smith won District 23 by a margin of 67 to 41. The black Democrat Smith replaced Ennis Fant who was convicted of corruption in office.

CHAPTER TWENTY EIGHT

PROSECUTIONS AND REFORMS MOVE FORWARD

In July, 1991, the trial of Judge Tee Ferguson of Greenville, South Carolina began and ended with a conviction for public corruption as did that of Rep. Danny Winstead (R-Charleston). By the time of the Winstead and Ferguson trials, most of the defendants in the Lost Trust prosecutions had been convicted, mostly by plea agreement, but a handful by jury trials.

The conference committee created to compromise the House and Senate ethics bills, chaired by Sen. Tom Moore (D-Aiken), made good progress and presented its final report on July 18, 1991, in which it set forward a remarkably aggressive reform plan to regulate campaign finance, lobbying activities, conflicts of interest, and public disclosure by campaign donors, candidates, elected officials, lobbyists, and political organizations.

Gov. Carroll Campbell called a special session for September 23, 1991, at the State House and a new ethics reform bill was passed on that date and signed on October 1 to take effect on January 1, 1992. And that is what happened.

Winstead Sentenced

Former Rep. Danny Winstead came up for sentencing in Charleston on July 3, 1991, before Judge Falcon Hawkins and got 2½ years in prison for selling his vote on the betting bill, which he had believed was connected to the Mafia, and for witness tampering. In addition, he got three years of supervised release and a fine of $25,000.

The sentence was quite stiff, but a factor was that Winstead, while pleading guilty, had not been very helpful and cooperative with the government. It took eight interviews with federal agents since Winstead was "never fully truthful and forthright with them," Assistant U.S. Attorney John Barton told the Court.

On hearing the harsh sentence "his jaw dropped," wrote Margaret O'Shea in *The State*, "He lowered his head a moment. When he raised it, his eyes were moist and his mouth set a firm, grim line. Behind him, his wife of 24 years sobbed.... His mother cried quietly."

Hawkins delayed the start of Winstead's sentence service to September 3, 1991. Winstead's wife told the judge that Winstead was "the best husband anyone could ever have" and said that he had never done anything to make her ashamed until that time.

Of the 15 legislators convicted to that point on July 3, 1991, Danny Winstead was only the fourth to be sentenced. His sentence would prove to be less than some and more than others when the process was finally ended.

Although the prosecution asked for some leniency in imposing sentence, Assistant U.S. Attorney John Barton said that Winstead would have been a helpful witness in the trial of former

Rep. Tom Limehouse if Limehouse had not entered a guilty plea. Even so, Barton told Judge Falcon Hawkins the problem with Winstead was that he was "reluctant and misleading" and refused to name the person who told Winstead to lie to the FBI even though the person was said to be a law enforcement friend of Winstead. (Bart Daniel did reveal that the person was a SLED agent named Ron Cook, but no federal charges had been filed at that point. Winstead's attorney, John Weaver, said that, in fact, Cook had only told Winstead that he did not have to talk to the FBI.)

The prosecution had a tape of Winstead telling former Rep. Robert Kohn that a law enforcement friend had advised Winstead to deny any wrongdoing and said, "Let it roll and deny everything." Kohn, in fact, was acting as an undercover aide of the government at the time he talked with Winstead.

S.C. House Expulsion Rule Approved by U.S. Justice Department

The policy of the S.C. House rule 3.12 of suspending members automatically on indictment and expelling them for conviction of felony was approved by the U.S. Justice Department on July 3, 1991. Former Rep. B.J. Gordon, convicted on March 8, 1991, of corruption, had challenged the law in an attempt to retain his seat.

The rule had been adopted in 1982 by the House in reaction to the problem in the S.C. Senate caused when Sen. Gene Carmichael (D-Dillon) was prosecuted and convicted of vote buying but continued to hold his Senate seat.

In his lawsuit, Gordon alleged that the rights of his constituents would be violated if they were stripped of representation by his removal. He further said the new rule had been adopted without prior approval from the U.S. Justice Department in violation of the 1965 Voting Rights Act which required pre-clearance in the State of South Carolina.

A three judge panel did not reinstate Gordon but had told the House not to use the rule until approved by the Department of Justice. Speaker Bob Sheheen defended Rule 3.12 saying that the rule had no racial discriminatory intent but was "meant to protect the institution. That institution doesn't belong to us. It belongs to the people of South Carolina."

Expulsion Rule at Issue

As of July 7, 1991, House Rule 3.12 had been used repeatedly. In fact, House Rule 3.12 had been used to suspend 14 House members by Speaker Bob Sheheen when they were indicted, but only B.J. Gordon challenged the rule. Five representatives were also expelled under the rule upon conviction, including Gordon. The others who pleaded guilty resigned.

Sheheen said the rule had prevented the House from malfunctioning if those indicted and convicted had been allowed to continue to remain in the House while business was being transacted.

The U.S. Justice Department's letter of July 3, 1991, to the S.C. Attorney General, Travis Medlock, stated that the department reserved the right to reexamine the matter if any further information came to its attention, according to Gerald W. Jones, Chief of the Justice Department's voting section. But at that point, the Rule would be allowed to continue in effect.

In the controversy raised by B.J. Gordon's lawsuit filed by Helen McFadden, Sheheen had argued that Rule 3.12 was designed to protect the rights of voters, not of officials accused of crimes. But the three judge panel relied on a regulation of the U.S. Attorney's office which held that any change affecting the ability of people to "remain holders of elective office" was the standard.

Sheheen seemed to be in a belligerent mood about "that invasion of federalism" and talked about a challenge to take the issue to the U.S. Supreme Court as to whether the Legislature was required to obtain Department of Justice approval of all of its rules.

Gordon Suit Heard on July 8, 1991

B.J. Gordon's lawsuit to keep his seat in House District 104 was set for hearing on July 8, 1991. The suit sought to stop the holding of an election to replace Gordon who had been expelled from the House on conviction for corruption in federal court.

Gordon had held the seat for 18 years and he contended that his expulsion violated state law. He named Williamsburg County Election Commission Chairman, Ernest Reeves, who was ordered by 2nd Circuit judge-at-large, Duane Shuler, to show cause why the election should not be delayed or postponed. However, Reeves said, "As far as the election is concerned, we are proceeding with it.... I don't have authority to stop it. The judge would have to postpone or delay the election."

The election for the open seat pitted Republican Steven D. Grady against Democrat Ken Kennedy. Grady made ethics an issue in the campaign, saying that voters wanted to elect a legislator "they don't have to worry about what they're doing in an unethical manner." Grady was a counselor-in-charge at the S.C. Department of Youth Services in Williamsburg County and Kennedy was a six-year member of the Williamsburg County Council and a businessman from Greeleyville. Kennedy said that he intended to lead "by setting an example for the citizens of the county to follow. I feel as if I have set an example on County Council." He owned a hardware supply, car sales company, and a plumbing company in Greeleyville.

Convicted Lawyers Ripped From Law Practice

The failure of the S.C. Supreme Court to suspend or disbar three lawyers convicted in Lost Trust drew the ire of critics who expressed dismay that the three were still practicing law in South

Carolina. However, public perception that felony conviction always led to lifetime disbarment was not true.

Pointing to disgraced House Speaker Pro Tem Jack I. Rogers, convicted of racketeering, bribery and extortion, and to Rep. Thomas Limehouse as well as former Highway Commissioner, Ronnie Crow, critics knocked the Court for allowing felons to hold positions as officers of the court.

Prior to 1988, disbarment in South Carolina was permanent, but in that year, the rule was changed to allow for readmission. After that date, several were readmitted prior to Lost Trust.

Jack I. Rogers continued to practice law after his conviction for racketeering and corruption. When he appeared at the Marlboro County Courthouse in his hometown, a juror complained, "You've got criminals representing criminals."

Dan Byrd, Chairman of the State Board of Commissioners on Grievances and Discipline, explained that the policy in South Carolina was to allow such practice by convicted felons until the Supreme Court acted to suspend or to disbar. But Jim Grego, President of Citizens Against Violent Crimes, bluntly stated, "The fact that Jack Rogers is practicing law is an absolute travesty."

Grego was especially critical of Jack I. Rogers' role as chairman of the judicial screening committee, but Chief Justice George Gregory refused to comment on the matter. However, Professor Robbie Wilcox of the University of South Carolina School of Law, said that the state followed the American Bar Association model on lawyer discipline, although he did not know whether the state's policy that held conviction only began at sentencing was widespread in the nation.

Rogers had pleaded guilty on May 8, 1991, but no sentencing date was set for some months and therefore he was allowed to continue to practice, even while facing a possible sentence of up to 20 years for his crimes. Rogers said that he had told the Supreme Court that he would make no appearances in court even while he was closing down his practice, but said he was still practicing office law such as real estate transactions.

Convicted highway commissioner, Ronnie Crow, hoped to keep his law license in view of the fact that his crime was not so serious. But Tom Limehouse, who pleaded on December 7, 1990, to conspiracy and obstruction of justice had closed his practice by December 31, 1990, knowing the charges were very grave.

Professional Licenses in Jeopardy

In addition to the three lawyers convicted in Lost Trust by July, 1991, other professionals faced loss of their licenses. Robert Brown, former chairman of Labor, Commerce, and Industry, pleaded to corruption on September 4, 1990, and had his real estate license revoked on October 16, 1990, and also lost his insurance agent's license on October 23, 1990.

Former representative, Ennis Fant, lost his real estate license on May 23, 1991, after pleading guilty on February 22, 1991. He also faced a hearing by the S.C. Department of Insurance on

July 24, 1991, at which his license was to be suspended or revoked. Former representative Larry Blanding failed to renew his real estate license after his conviction on March 8, 1991, of bribery. Former representative Paul Derrick faced loss of his license as an optometrist after conviction on May 11, 1991, of selling his vote. All of the three faced sentencing at the time.

B.J. Gordon and Blanding Replaced

The election to replace expelled House member B.J. Gordon on July 9, 1991, in District 101 went to Ken Kennedy, a black Greeleyville businessman and member of the Williamsburg County Council.

A circuit court judge strictly refused to stop the election in spite of Gordon's lawsuit to reclaim his seat on grounds that he was illegally expelled pursuant to House Rule 3.12.

In Sumter County, an election was held July 9, 1991, to replace disgraced former representative Larry Blanding in District 66 after Blanding had been convicted of corruption in the sting. Ralph Canty, another black Democrat, won the seat.

Hopkins Pleads Guilty to Cocaine

Clemson University administrator, James V. Hopkins, who had been a key informant in the Lost Trust probe, pleaded guilty to cocaine possession on July 10, 1991. Hopkins tipped off the FBI to Ron Cobb's drug dealings which led to Cobb's arrest and eventual decision to help the FBI catch corrupt officials.

Taylor Seeks Tape in Appeal

Luther Taylor's attorney, Joel Collins, wanted to use the videotape of Luther Taylor's nemesis, Ron Cobb, in support of Taylor's appeal to the 4th Circuit Court of Appeals in Richmond, Virginia. The tape at issue showed FBI sting agent Cobb buying $500 of illegal drugs from former Charleston Rep. Robert Kohn in December, 1989.

Taylor was appealing his conviction at trial of corruption and conspiracy, including selling his vote for a $4,500 bribe. Taylor was doing over six years in federal prison in Florida in mid-July, 1991, at the time the tape was requested by Collins.

The U.S. Attorney's staff told the court and its Chief Judge Falcon Hawkins that all evidence against Taylor had been turned over to the defense attorneys, except information affecting the investigation.

Martin Guy Rohling Sentenced

North Carolina lobbyist, Martin Guy Rohling, was sentenced to three years probation and a fine of $1,000 by U.S. District Judge Falcon Hawkins at a proceeding in Charleston on July 12, 1991. Rohling entered a guilty plea in March, 1991, to one count of cocaine possession.

Rohling of Raleigh, North Carolina, was ordered to perform 100 hours of community service and pay probation costs. He could have been given four months and $2,500 fine.

The drug charge was based on an incident on April 15, 1988, at a party in a hotel in Hilton Head Island, S.C., which was attended by other lobbyists and legislators.

The U.S. Attorney Bart Daniel said Rohling had helped the prosecution, "He was one of the key witnesses which led directly to Rep. Tom Limehouse pleading guilty." Limehouse had pleaded to bribery and obstruction in 1990.

At the time of Rohling's plea, a total of 27 had been indicted on corruption or drug related charges, including 17 legislators. Twenty had pleaded guilty, five had been convicted at trial, and two awaited trial in the autumn of 1991.

Rohling apologized to the court, saying, "I deeply regret what happened, and the embarrassment and pain this has brought to my family."

Rohling's attorney was Ralph Hoisington, who admitted, "He got involved and he made mistakes."

Robert Brown Gets No Jail Time

Former Marion County House member, Robert Brown, was sentenced by U.S. District Judge Charles Simon on his guilty plea to bribery on July 15, 1991. As he had cooperated with the prosecution, Brown got only 6 months in a halfway house, 200 hours of community service and 5 years probation.

Brown had been the first legislator to plead guilty. He faced up to 20 years in prison and a fine of $250,000. (The second to plead was former Sen. Rick Lee who had been given 6 months in a halfway house and a $3,000 fine.)

Brown had resigned from the House on August 23, 1990, and was indicted the next day on charges he took $2,000 to support the betting bill. He entered a guilty plea on September 4, 1990, on one count violation of the Hobbs Act for bribery.

He turned state's evidence and testified for the government in the trials of Luther Taylor, B.J. Gordon, and Larry Blanding, as well as Paul Derrick and Judge Tee Ferguson.

The evidence in the case against Brown was a videotape made on April 14, 1990, aboard a cabin cruiser boat at Hilton Head Island, S.C. called "the "Tally Ho" while it was moored during the Heritage Gold Classic on the island. The tape showed sting agent Ron Cobb giving Brown $2,000 in cash.

Ethics Reform Bill Grinds On

The "Conference from Hell" continued its tortured journey during the summer of 1991 after the General Assembly had on June 6 adjourned. The descriptive term was given to the conference committee by Rep. Candy Y. Waites (D-Richland), one of three House conferees along with Rep. David Wilkins and Wes Hayes who doggedly met with Senators Tom Moore, Samuel Stilwell, and McKinley Washington in the Senate office building.

By late June, 1991, the conference committee, ably chaired by Sen. Moore, had reached an understanding on the major features of the ethics bill running to some 150 pages. After that the deliberations were about lesser issues.

At a meeting on July 16, 1991, Rep. David Wilkins had suggested that the preamble of the bill be shortened to stress its focus on reforming ethics, lobbying, and campaign finance, all areas exposed by the Lost Trust scandal. However, when Wilkins complained that the bill put too much stress on campaign finance reform, Chairman Moore retorted that the Senate though that campaign finance was the most important reform in the bill.

Gov. Carroll Campbell said he would decide whether to call a special session to pass the ethics bill based on his assessment of the contents of the bill. Campbell raised questions about a provision requiring elected state officials to get the approval of the governor before traveling out of state at the expense of a lobbyist principal.

Toll of Casualties One Year After

On July 18, 1991, the one year anniversary of the public revelation of the FBI sting Operation Broken Trust a/k/a Operation Lost Trust, the casualty toll of those convicted of corruption and drugs had piled up a total of 27 indicted. The toll included 17 legislators, 5 lobbyists, a highway commission lobbyist, a former state official, a college administrator, a former aide to Gov. Campbell, and one judge (charged for crimes while a legislator).

The List of Convicted Legislators as of July 18, 1991

Jack I. Rogers..Pleaded to racketeering. Awaiting sentence.
Robert Kohn..Pleaded to corruption. Awaiting sentence.
Luther Taylor..Convicted of corruption. Expelled from the House. Sentenced 6 1/2 years in prison.
Ennis Fant..Pleaded guilty to corruption. Awaiting sentence.
Frank McBride..Pleaded guilty to corruption. Awaiting sentence.
B.J. Gordon..Convicted of corruption. Expelled. Awaiting sentence.
Larry Blanding..Convicted of corruption. Awaiting sentence.

Paul Derrick..Convicted of corruption. Expelled. Awaiting sentence.
Jim Faber ....Pleaded guilty to corruption. Awaiting sentence. Resigned.
Danny Winstead..................................Pleaded guilty to corruption and obstruction. Sentenced to 2 1/2 years in prison, 3 years probation, $25,000 fine. Resigned.
Robert Brown..Pleaded guilty to corruption. Sentenced to 6 months halfway house and 200 hours of community service. Resigned.
Rick Lee...Pleaded guilty to corruption. Sentenced to 6 months in halfway house, 5 years probation, and $3,000 restitution. Resigned.
Tee Ferguson..Convicted of corruption. Awaiting sentence.
Donna Moss..Pleaded guilty to cocaine possession. Sentenced to 3 years probation and a fine of $2,500. Resigned.
Tom Limehouse....Pleaded guilty to tampering and corruption. Awaiting sentence. Resigned.

Legislators Charged and Awaiting Trial as of July 18, 1991

Tim Wilkes...Suspended from House. Entered not guilty on June 6, 1991. Awaiting trial. (Acquitted September 25, 1991.)
Ken Bailey........................Suspended from House. Pleaded not guilty to bribery on June 6, 1991. Awaiting trial. (Convicted August 27, 1991.)

Not Charged as of July 18, 1991

Sen. Bud Long (D-Horry)..................Would be charged August 20 with bribery and conspiracy. (Convicted of bribery on November 23, 1991. Conspiracy charge dismissed.)

Executives Convicted as of July 18, 1991

David Hawkins............................Former aide to Gov. Campbell. Pleaded guilty to obstruction on June 19, 1991. Awaiting sentence.
Dick Greer...................................Former Chair, S.C. Economic Development Board. Pleaded guilty on April 10, 1991, to cocaine possession. Awaiting sentence.
James Hopkins............................Ex-Clemson University administrator. Pleaded guilty to cocaine possession on July 10, 1991. Awaiting sentence.

Lobbyists Convicted as of July 18, 1991

James Brown, V..............Lobbyist. Pleaded guilty to marijuana possession on October 3, 1990. Died of lung disease on November 29, 1990, prior to sentencing.

Martin Guy Rohling...............Lobbyist. Pleaded guilty to cocaine possession on March 7, 1991. Sentenced July 12, 1991.

Ronnie Crow...Lobbyist and ex-highway commissioner. Pleaded guilty to ~~cocaine possession~~. Awaiting sentence.

Thomas Collins.....................................Lobbyist. Pleaded to cocaine possession on May 30, 1990. Awaiting sentence.

Randy Lee............................Lobbyist. Pleaded guilty to marijuana possession on April 10, 1991. Awaiting sentence.

Others Convicted as of July 18, 1991

David Little, III....................Spartanburg businessman. Pleaded guilty to cocaine possession on June 18, 1991. Awaiting sentence.

Rep. Landford Asks For Lobbyists' Donations

In spite of all the furor over lobbyists giving handouts of free food, free drinks, free trips, and free cash, tone-deaf Rep. Steven Landford (R-Greenville) of Woodruff was asking lobbyists to give him money for his campaign at the same time that both the House and Senate had cracked down on lobbyists giveaways.

Running for vacant Senate seat 13, Landford faced an August 13, 1991, primary in which four other candidates sought the Republican nomination. The two major issues in the struggle were ethics reform and auto insurance reform. But even while Landford sought donations from the lobbyists, the other four candidates all said they would not take any lobbyists' money at all and no PAC money either.

Landford protested weakly, "I've not done anything wrong.... I'm operating under the bounds of the laws of South Carolina." He tried to distract attention from himself onto lawyer-legislators by saying he wanted to stop clients from donating to lawyer-legislators interested in pending legislation. Landford protested that "If a lawyer-legislator or lawyer seeking public office accepts a $20,000 retainer fee from a utility or a PAC, it's all right, but it's not all right for me to accept a 55 cent cup of coffee from a lobbyist."

But at the time when the conference committee on the ethics reform bill was finishing a provision banning lobbyists gifts and campaign donations, Landford's chief opponent, Ty Courtney, and the eventual winner of the seat on October 13th, would say, "I'm surprised that he did that, I really am." And another candidate, retired businessman Frank Dillard, opined, "If something looks like a skunk, it's usually a skunk."

CHAPTER TWENTY NINE

ETHICS REFORM BILL FINALIZED

As the summer dragged on, the draft ethics bill reported by the Conference Committee on July 18, 1991, was reviewed by the House and Senate and forwarded to Gov. Carroll Campbell for his consideration. The Senate directed that any differences with the governor on the bill be negotiated which proved easy as Campbell did not demand any significant changes in the bill.

Conferees Finish Ethics Bill

On the anniversary of the FBI's sudden revelation of Lost Trust as of July 18, 1990, the Senate-House conference committee on the ethics reform bill finished its work on July 18, 1991. After protracted ordeals, the ethics reform bill which had been in the drafting stage since the fall of 1990 was finally ready.

"I think this certainly is an answer...to take care of 'business as usual' in government," said Sen. Tom Moore (D-Aiken), chairman of the conference committee which had aggressively rewritten the bill. Since late April, 1991, by taking differing ethics reform bills passed by the House and Senate in the spring, the committee had been splicing together a bill.

The committee had "free conference" powers which gave it unusually wide latitude to add and subtract elements of the two House and Senate bills, even creating new elements if it saw fit.

The committee voted its final approval of the bill at 6:35 p.m. on Thursday, July 18, 1991, almost exactly to the hour, a year after the first culprits in Lost Trust were confronted by the FBI for their misdeeds. "That is very ironic," Sen. Moore mused, when told of the fact, but, he said, "It was not planned that way. That is hopefully a positive reaction to that."

Ethics Reform Conference Report Would Limit Donations

The conference committee report of July 18, 1991, put a stop to many of the worst evils in South Carolina government such as lobbyists' gifts and campaign donations to statewide candidates and to legislators and the use of cash as so-called campaign donations which often were really bribes.

One chronic problem was not adequately addressed but it was partially remedied by the bill—private campaign contributions to candidates for state and local offices. Rather than go to a public finance scheme, which was out of the question with almost all legislators and especially with Gov. Carroll Campbell, the bill put a limit for the first time on the amount of money that donors could give to a candidate or a political party.

This effort to limit the size of donations pitted the Democrats led by Sen. Tom Moore against Republicans such as Rep. David Wilkins, and even more so, Campbell. Moore wanted low donation limits of $250 as first proposed by the bill which passed the Democratically controlled Senate. Wilkins wanted much higher contribution limits as envisioned by the House and Campbell.

In part, the interest in limiting the size of donations was a result of Lost Trust, but more so, it seems, a reaction to the fact that incumbent Gov. Carroll Campbell had been a master of peeling big money special interests for huge sums in his 1990 re-election campaign against a self-destructive Democratic opponent, Sen. Theo Mitchell. In that campaign, Campbell had pulled a $60,000 donation out of McAlloy Corp., a major metal processor in the low country.

Campaign Money Limited

The conference bill capped campaign donations to individual candidates at the amount of $3,500 per donor per election cycle for statewide office, such as Governor or Attorney General. The limit for all other candidates such as legislators and local was $1,000 per donor per election cycle.

An election cycle was defined as a campaign for primary election, a run-off primary, or a general election. A candidate for governor, for example, could take a total of $7,000 if he only ran in a primary and won it and then ran in a general election. If there was no primary, the total amount was limited to only $3,500 for the general election. If a candidate had a primary, run-off primary, and a general election, he could take a total of $10,500 from a single donor.

These limits were no doubt an improvement, but they were high. The bill as passed out by conference and as finally passed and signed by Gov. Campbell in the fall of 1991 allowed corporations, political action committees, partnerships, trade associations, lobbyists' principals, and unspecified other entities to donate money to candidates. It proved to be the case in subsequent years that special interests would evade contribution limits by almost unlimited creative schemes and stratagems, especially through the use of political action committees which could be proliferated in unlimited numbers by the same money source, such as a rich person or big money special interest group.

Major Reforms in Conference Bill

The chief reform in the bill approved by the conference committee on July 18, 1991, was that it banned lobbyists' free gifts of food, drinks, travel, cash, and also campaign donations to elected officials. However, the bill still allowed lobbyists' principals (i.e., employers of lobbyists) to give free food to groups of legislators and to give limited campaign donations to candidates. The bill had many compromise provisions over issues which divided Democrats in the Senate and Republicans in the House.

The other provisions of the bill were:

(1) limited the amounts of campaign contributions to individual candidates to $3,500 for statewide and $1,000 for all legislative and local offices.
(2) compelled disclosure filings by legislators of all business they did with government agencies, lobbyists, and lobbyists' employers.
(3) barred all lawyer-legislators from voting on legislation that affected state agencies before which they practiced law.
(4) allowed legislators to police own members using a House Ethics Committee and a Senate Ethics Committee. All other employees and those of the executive branch, but not the Judiciary, were under jurisdiction of the State Ethics Commission.
(5) banned personal use of campaign funds by candidates.
(6) imposed both civil and criminal penalties for violation of the Ethics Act.

Conference Bill in Perspective

House Judiciary Committee Chairman, David Wilkins (R-Greenville), noting the ethics reform bill conference report was approved by conferees on the fist anniversary of Lost Trust, observed that the timing was "very appropriate." Realizing the political significance of the achievement, Wilkins knew that "This is the first step in getting this tragedy behind us and regaining public confidence.... We'll take the second step when we come back and pass it."

Wilkins believed that it would take several weeks for Gov. Campbell and legislators to go over the bill before Campbell would call a special one or two day session to vote on the bill. Campbell had telegraphed that he would call such a brief session. The bill was set to take effect on January 1, 1992, if passed.

The conference committee had come to a general agreement by mid-June, 1991, on the major reform provision in the bill and then spent the next month perfecting the document. Although some members of the committee wanted a tougher bill, both Wilkins and Sen. Moore thought the bill approved on July 18, 1991, would pass both houses. There was no question that it was a drastic improvement over the worthless 1975 Ethics Act which had no meaningful limits on campaign finance, political money, or lobbyists handouts to politicians. Even its feeble disclosure terms had been ignored by feckless Secretary of State John Campbell and the lobbyists.

Conference Ethics Reform Bill Attacks Corruption

Even a casual reading of the ethics reform bill passed out of the conference committee on July 18, 1991, shows that it obviously was designed to attack the major forms of corruption exposed by Operation Lost Trust, especially the crisis caused by unregulated political money and out-of-control lobbyists at the State House. But the bill also addressed problems such as non-disclosure and conflicts of interest facing public officials.

The bill made a direct frontal assault on the inherently corrupt practice of lobbyists giving officials at state and local levels of government in South Carolina unlimited handouts and campaign money by flatly banning all handouts and campaign contributions by lobbyists to officials and outlawing the use of campaign funds, especially cash, for personal use. These outrageous abuses, all legal under the fake 1975 Ethics Act, were the major means used by arch-corruptionist Ron Cobb to buy politicians and legislation for years in state government.

The lines separating campaign funds and personal money were clarified to counter the defense put up by some of the corrupt legislators at trial that the bribes they took from Cobb were really campaign donations that they legally converted to personal use as permitted by the 1975 Act. Cash contributions were banned, too, as cash had been the medium used by Cobb in paying his bribes.

DOJ Review of Ethics Reform Bill

The ethics reform bill presented to the Legislature in mid-summer of 1991 had to pass pre-clearance from the U.S. Department of Justice before it could take effect. This pre-clearance was a requirement of the 1965 Voting Rights Act which imposed on states with a history of racial discrimination in their elections a pre-clearance provision for all legislation affecting voting and elections in any way.

Rep. David Wilkins, Chairman of House Judiciary Committee, wisely suggested that pre-clearance be requested of the Justice Department as a precaution to assure its compliance with the Voting Rights Act. He had experience with the problem because House Rule 3.12 had not been pre-cleared before it was used to suspend and to expel House members charged with corruption and later convicted, and ousted Rep. B.J. Gordon had filed suit attacking Rule 3.12 because it was not cleared before it was used to throw him out.

Speaker Bob Sheheen predicted no issue from DOJ, reasoning that, "If they're going to say 'certainly' about kicking out a convict, they're going to say 'certainly' about this." Sheheen was proved right.

Sen. Stilwell Opines on Pre-Clearance

Sen. Samuel Stilwell (R-Greenville) said of the ethics bill produced by the conference committee he sat on that he was not worried and he did not think the ethics bill they had crafted should be sent to the U.S. Department of Justice for pre-clearance but he recognized the issue. "Oh, I don't like it," he said, "I think that in the total context it's unnecessary, and yet South Carolina just happens to be one of those states that still has such a national reputation—although certainly undeserved—that we do have to pre-clear everything with the Justice Department." Stilwell then added, "We have to get the OK of Big Brother."

Wilkins correctly expected no problem in getting clearance from the Justice Department of the ethics reform bill, noting, "I just see it as a procedural step we have to go through, and I don't think it should or will delay implementation of the bill."

However, South Carolina had had a plan rejected by DOJ to require all probate judges to have college degrees on the grounds that fewer blacks than whites had college degrees in the state. Of course, a DOJ objection to the ethics bill was remotely possible based on the 1965 Voting Rights Act.

Costs of Ethics Reform Conference Committee

The extra meetings of the ethics reform bill conference committee, chaired by Sen. Tom Moore, lasted from the end of the legislative session on June 6, 1991, until the final bill was reported on July 18, 1991. A total of 12 meetings were held during that six week period.

Six legislators on the committee and also the professional committee staff invested a great deal of time in the crafting of the bill. The travel costs of mileage and expense allowances totaled $5,997.97 as of the date of the report. In the end, that would be cheap as committee member Sen. Samuel Stilwell (R-Greenville) sagely observed, "If we finally get a bill, yes, it was worth it."

Rep. Candy Waites (D-Richland) ironically said of the committee on which she was seated, "I guess you can compare it with what the sting cost," an amount not known to the public at the time, but a cost she knew would be huge not only in dollars, but in damage to the reputation of state government and South Carolina as a whole.

Rep. Waites went on to say that the time, effort, and cost was fully justified by the results, "Now we have this very comprehensive legislation that should help us not have the kind of problems we've had in the past. I don't think you can put a price tag on this."

The costs of the ethics reform bill conference committee included payments to each member of $39 per day in "per diem" reimbursement plus another $79 per day in "subsistence" payments for every meeting of the committee. In addition, each member received travel expense funds at the state rate of 25.5 cents per mile for their trips to and back from Columbia based on the distance between their home and the State House.

Lobbyists Report Spending on Legislators

Finally giving in to the demands of new Secretary of State Jim Miles, lobbyists, many for the first time in their careers, began to file the reports required by the 1975 Ethics Act which had almost universally been ignored or defied for over sixteen years. At Miles' insistence and backed by Attorney General Travis Medlock's recent announcement of his intention to enforce the lobbyists' disclosure laws which Miles had been elected to enforce, the lobbyists, 526 of them in all, in early July, 1991, began to report their 1991 session spending on legislators The amount of spending on the 46 Senate members and 124 House members averaged $4,806 per member.

Lobbyists reported representing 300 companies and that they spent a total of $5,312,063 to lobby the 170 legislators in the period from June 20, 1990, to June 6, 1991. But most of the money went to lobbyists' salaries and fees while $816,984 went to handouts to legislators, including gifts, free food, free drinks, entertainment, campaign donations and other gratuities including free trips.

However, the disclosure filings revealed that since the start of the year 1991, the amount of spending by lobbyists on legislators had greatly decelerated, most likely because of the massive negative publicity in the media about the ways in which the lobbyists had been using money to buy access and influence, and even legislators' votes at the State House.

The July, 1991, lobbyists' filings with Secretary Miles' office, the first even remotely accurate reporting of lobbyists' spending and actions, showed the drastic impact of a daring new House rule enacted and effective at the start of the 1991 session of the General Assembly on lobbyists' handouts to legislators. The rule, called in popular jargon, "the no-cup-of-coffee" rule, banned lobbyists from giving House members free meals, free drinks, free golf outings, and receptions for legislators sponsored by lobbyists.

The Senate, however, did not adopt a similar ban by rule until June, 1991, after the session was nearly finished. And the House rule still allowed lobbyists to give handouts to large groups such as a legislative committee, caucus, delegation, or the entire chamber of the House, all 124 of them if they wanted to attend.

Love of Freebies Dies Hard

Even as the scandal showed the corruption of the political class by lobbyist Ron Cobb using cash and drugs, the new House rule set in December, 1990, adopting the "no-cup-of-coffee" rule was still too lax. And big money lobbyists and their clients continued to hand out freebies to the legislators during the 1991 session at the State House.

The South Carolina Education Association, an organization of public school teachers, was among the most recalcitrant sources of largesse at the Capitol. Every week from January 16 to

May 8, 1991, the SCEA sponsored different kinds of free events for the politicians in state government.

The first such act of kindness was an SCEA-sponsored reception for the General Assembly at a cost of $8,468. Then came luncheons for the county legislative delegations, including all House and Senate members from each of the state's 46 counties, at a cost of $11,792.

Even so, the media storm and public outrage over the antics of the lobbyists and legislators plus the House's new "no-cup-of-coffee" rule did seem to curtail spending quite dramatically. Whereas the spending of lobbyists on freebies to legislators in 1990 had cost $452,088, the spending in the first half of 1991 dropped to $227,192, roughly half.

Lobbyists' Freebies Bared

As new Secretary of State Jim Miles, starting in January, 1991, when he took office for the first time, demanded that lobbyists name all legislators they spent money on and all issues discussed, most lobbyists finally complied with the law for a change in reporting their activities during the 1991 session of the General Assembly.

Gwyn Voss of the Carolina Power and Light Co. reported that she spent $1,540 on lawmakers to promote "general good will," explaining that this meant CP&L was trying to "build good relationships and exchange information. It is not to influence specific legislation."

Walter Brown of Norfolk & Southern Railroad reported spending $1,355 for entertaining legislators and playing golf with them on 15 outings from June 25, 1990, to November 29, 1990, but he indicated that no legislative business was discussed at the outings

Bobby Horton of SCANA ran up "public relations" expenses of $2,290 in dealings with legislators. Johnny Gregory of Sunbelt Coca Cola spent $903 on expenses for various entertainments and free food on legislators for "good will" by which he meant, he said, "maintains some presence, I guess.... It's all moot now."

"Everyone took a look at their activities at the State House," said Dan Jones, a spokesman for Laidlaw Environmental Services which cut its spending of free food, free drinks, and other freebies from $45,936 in 1990 to just $4,680 in the 1991 session, some 90% in all.

In 1990, the south Carolina Chamber of Commerce spent a total of $27,948 on free entertainment, free food, and the like on legislators, but in the 1991 session cut down to only $395. The Chamber's chief lobbyist, big-spending Russell Munn, lavished in 1990 a total of $22,442 in free handouts on legislators, but in 1991 he spent only $154. Munn explained, "The sting changed the climate at the State House and threw the lobbying rules into chaos.... Many of the legislators and lobbyists also were just unaware of what was right to do. Many of us did nothing."

Lobbyists' Freebies Will Not End

The generosity of the lobbyists just would not quit, even as the indictments and convictions for bribery kept piling up. Ree Mallison of the S.C. Hospital Association bought lunch on the House floor for a House Ways and Means sub-committee on March 11, 1991. "They didn't ask me to do it. I just did it." The Chairman of the House Ethics Committee, Pat Harris (D-Anderson), was one of those at the table.

Edwin Johnson, II, of W.R. Grace and Co., spent $284 on a hunting trip to Hutchinson Island for Sen. Tom Pope (D-Newberry) and his 14 year-old son in October where the Popes stayed two nights.

On August 4, 1990, Walter Brown, lobbyist for Norfolk Southern, paid $200 for Sen. John Martin (D-Fairfield) to go golfing at the R.J. Reynolds Golf Tournament in Nashville, Tennessee, where the National Conference of State Legislatures was meeting. Martin's usual partner in golf was Randy Lee, a lobbyist convicted on April 10, 1991, in the drug indictments of Lost Trust. However, Martin made it his practice to pay for his own golf fees, meals, and drinks. Martin and Lee played golf on March 6 and 20, April 23, and May 1 and 15 of 1990.

The fight to stop lobbyists' free handouts to legislators had a few belligerent and recalcitrant enemies, none more so than Sen. Kay Patterson (D-Richland) and Jerry Beasley, the lobbyist for the S.C. Textile Manufacturers. Both publicly denounced the ban on freebies.

In spite of growing public hostility to such giveaways, lobbyist Bill DeLoach took Patterson to lunch seven times during the 1991 session at the S&S Cafeteria at a cost of $131.37. Beasley paid $487.83 for a reception for Sen Ed Saleeby at the Lamar Country Club on July 18, 1990, the day the FBI seized the records of all House members in Columbia. Charlie Rountree of Laidlaw chipped in $800 for the golf outing, dinner, and reception and Steve Smith of S.C. League of Savings, a veteran lobbyist, threw in $58.50 while Gwyn Voss of Carolina Power and Light put up $800 for "general good will" at Saleeby Day.

Even reform leaders such as Lt. Gov. Nick Theodore, who had formed an ethics committee in response to the scandal, could not resist a free trip to New York as part of a legislative leaders' program at which Philip Morris' lobbyist, Leslie H. Turner, III, tossed in $250 for theater tickets, $150 for a dinner at LeCirque, and $52 for tickets to an NFL game of the Giants against the Vikings at the Meadowlands.

The lobbyists reports filed in July, 1991, showed a total of nearly a quarter million dollars of gifts to legislators, some of them a bit ridiculous. Lloyd Hendricks of the S.C. Bankers Association spent $101.92 on popcorn for legislators. The S.C. Trial Lawyers commissioned a portrait of Rep. Jack I. Rogers, Chairman of the Judicial Screening Committee, at a cost of $1,710, but decided not to give the portrait after Rogers was indicted for bribery, witness tampering, and racketeering in May. The gift was for "consumer legislation." Nola Armstrong of the Association said of Rogers, "He was considered to be an exemplary legislator." But the picture remained in the Association office and, said Armstrong, "There are absolutely no plans to give it to him," perhaps because he was no longer in the House but in prison.

Carolina General Contractors gave notebooks on March 12, 1991, at a legislative reception at a cost of $2,000, but Sens. Glenn McConnell and Mike Rose returned the notebooks.

Critics Scorn Continued Lobbyists' Freebies

In the filing of lobbyists' reports in July, 1991, which for the first time forced lobbyists to tell the truth about their spending on free handouts to legislators, the lobbyists' disclosures showed that they had cut such spending in half since 1990 but still spent nearly a quarter of a million dollars on gratuities. Deputy Secretary of State, Bob Knight, answered a reporter's query by saying, ironically, "It certainly raises the question of how much good will costs in Columbia." In fact, his boss, Jim Miles, had finally forced the lobbyists to show what it cost to buy influence at the State House in Columbia.

John Crangle of Common Cause/South Carolina also voiced his doubts about the continued refusal of some lobbyists to stop giving things to legislators, saying that what lobbyists reported on their filings with the Secretary of State's office as 'good will' "probably means buying favors, buttering a guy up." But even he reported that Common Cause had spent a total of $99 on award certificates given to legislative leaders in the fight for drastic ethics reform legislation. Among those getting the awards were Sen. Ernest Passailague (D-Charleston), Rep. Candy Waites (D-Richland), Rep. Tim Rogers (D-Richland), and Lt. Gov. Nick Theodore. Other award recipients were Sen. Glenn McConnell, Sen. Mike Rose (R-Dorchester), Sen. Sherry Martschink (R-Charleston), Sen. John Matthews (D-Orangeburg), Sen. David Thomas (R-Greenville) Rep. Joe McElveen (D-Sumter), and Sen. Sam Stilwell (R-Greenville).

Drug Testing Officials at Issue

The number of lobbyists and legislators caught up in cocaine and marijuana crimes in Lost Trust provoked an outcry for drug testing of government officials

Secretary of State Jim Miles agreed to join the governor and Attorney General in having their staff employees randomly drug tested. Miles said on July 26, 1991, that he and his senior staff would test several times per year and announce the results to the media, noting that if "I was looking to the performance of Jim Miles as my elected official, then I'd want to know that he's abiding by the laws and that he's not addicted to drugs." In view of the Lost Trust scandal, Miles said, "It's the right thing to do in this day and time."

Other agencies having drug testing programs were the S.C. Highway Patrol, the Alcoholic Beverage Control Commission, SLED, the office of the Attorney General and the Office of the Governor. Gov. Campbell said he had ordered drug testing in 1987 when he came into office for personnel in the Governor's Office.

Judge Ferguson Case "Appalling"

Bart Daniel, the U.S. Attorney, told the Columbia Rotary Club on July 19, 1991, that he regarded the case against Judge Tee Ferguson as the "most appalling of all" the scandals. It was bad enough that Ferguson took payoffs while he was a state representative, but he also indicated an intention to take bribes when he became a judge. Daniel said Ferguson told corrupt lobbyist Ron Cobb that, "When I'm a judge, I'll really be able to help you."

The evidence in the Ferguson prosecution showed that he had taken bribes from Cobb while in the House before he was elected to the circuit court bench near the end of the 1990 legislative session. At the time of Daniel's speech, Ferguson had recently been convicted at trial on three counts of extortion but had not yet sentenced for his crimes. Ferguson still had not resigned his judgeship even after conviction.

Daniel also said that the evidence in the scandal "made me sick." He was surprised that even when defendants came to his office to view videotapes of them taking bribes they "still didn't believe they had done anything wrong." The shocking denials of guilt, "That's what's really appalling and makes you sick to your stomach."

The State Likes Ethics Bill

In an editorial on the ethics bill on July 31, 1991, *The State* found that, "Overall, it's a good bill that tightens regulation of public officials, lobbyists, and campaign financing."

Noting that the ethics bill stressed public disclosure for officials, the newspaper pointed out that officials would be required to report their practices before boards and commissions, their conflicts of interest, and their campaign contributions.

The editorial approved the caps on the amount of campaign contributions of $3,500 per source to statewide office candidates and $1,000 for legislative and local officials. *The State* praised limits on political party donations set at $50,000 to statewide candidates and $5,000 to all others. Cash contributions were capped at $25. Regulations on the use of such funds were deemed good.

The State also liked the new provisions barring legislators from lobbying after they left the General Assembly for at least one year. And the strict limitations on the lobbyists and their employers were also an improvement, including the "no-cup-of-coffee" rule barring lobbyists from giving officials anything of value and new limits on lobbyists' employers gifts to no more than $25 per day per official and a total maximum of such handouts to $200 per year.

Even so, the editors opposed the calling of a special session of the General Assembly to vote on the ethics reform bill, saying, "That's costly and unnecessary. It may even be unconstitutional." *The State* thought that only under "extraordinary occasions" did the S.C. Constitution allow the governor to call a special session.

Ethics Reform Bill Sent to Governor for Comment

Finished by the conference committee on July 18, 1991, the anniversary of the public revelation of Operation Lost Trust, the bill then was sent to Gov. Campbell's office for review and consideration. This raised two questions; (1) would the governor find the bill satisfactory, and (2) if so, would he be willing to call a special session of the General Assembly to vote on the bill. If he did not like the bill or wanted changes, he could leave it to the next session of the legislature to hash out the differences, but even if he did like the bill, he could still wait until January, 1992, when the next session convened to take up the conference bill and debate and vote on it.

Reviewing the prospects of the conference bill, *The State* in an editorial on July 31, 1991, wrote that the bill had many good features but that the consideration and final vote on the bill could wait until the new year, arguing, "A better plan would be to wait until next year, unless agreement can be reached on a truly extraordinary problem—reapportionment." However, if both issues could be resolved, *The State* concluded, "then it will be time for a short special session to pass both reapportionment and ethics legislation."

Special Session Uncertain

Two weeks after the conference committee finished its ethics reform bill and sent it to Gov. Carroll Campbell, he still had not decided whether to call a special session of the General Assembly to vote on the bill.

Campbell's spokesman told the *Columbia Associated Press* that the Governor's Office received the bill on August 1, 1991, and that the governor had not yet decided what to do as the conference committee members had signed it on the same date that it was sent to the governor for review.

As a final bill was not ready when the General Assembly adjourned on June 6, 1991, the bill could not be voted on unless Campbell called for a special session. But conferee Sen. McKinley Washington (D-Charleston) urged Campbell to call a special session saying that as one of the conferees who signed off on the bill, "We need to pass this bill. We spent a whole lot of time in this committee putting what we think is a pretty decent bill together." Sen. Washington felt some urgency for action on the bill so it could take effect sooner rather than later. "To wait until January, you push the effect of the bill back a year or two. Not only that, I doubt seriously whether or not, if you wait until January, that you would get a bill before the end of the session next year."

Survey: Lawmakers and Journalists Disagree on Ethics

A recent survey by the Josephson Institute of Ethics, a California research institution focused on public ethics and corruption, published a survey of state legislators and their staff in the United States and found that they thought that they had high standards of public ethics. One of the major issues under examination was the influence of campaign contributions on public officials.

The survey also showed that journalists covering state government and state capital buildings tended to hold legislators to higher standards of ethics than the legislators themselves did. Therefore, legislators often think of journalists as too critical and unfair.

The Josephson survey instruments were answered by a total of 225 legislators and their staffs and also by 112 journalists around the nation.

One specific question presented a fact pattern in which a legislator dealt with and represented clients before the state tax commission. Among legislators and their staffs, 31 percent thought it would be improper and 25 percent thought such representation would be questionable. Forty percent thought such work would not be improper. However, journalists had a much more critical view and thought in only 25 percent of the responses that such legal representation would be proper.

On the other questions on the survey, journalists also had stricter views and were more inclined to suspect ethical violations.

Medlock Takes Contributions

Attorney General Travis Medlock denied that he had sent legal business of the state to law firms donating to his election campaign. Evidence showed that half of the top ten law firms which did the most state-contracted work did not give to Medlock's campaign in the 1990 election year.

Law firm Nexen, Pruet, Pollard, and Jacobs, which did the most legal business with the state government, gave only $250 to Medlock in that year. But records showed that most of the $177,000 raised by Medlock came from law firms and lawyers.

Medlock pointed out that "many who have contributed large sums do little or no work for the state." And, in fact, the decision to hire lawyers to represent the state was done by Medlock's executive assistant, Nathan Kaminski, and by the state agencies involved in the cases rather than Medlock himself.

In the fiscal year concluded on June 30, 1991, the total legal fees paid by state and local government in South Carolina were $6.9 million.

CHAPTER THIRTY

ETHICS BILL PASSED AND SIGNED

As the conferees had maintained close communications with both the House and Senate as well as Gov. Campbell's office, the final conference ethics reform reflected a consensus by the major parties. There was little chance, therefore, that there would be significant opposition to the bill in the General Assembly, and it was expected that Gov. Campbell would approve the bill in due course.

Gov. Campbell complied with widespread opinion in the Legislature and in the public mind that the conference bill was satisfactory and should be enacted into law. Campbell accordingly called a special session of the General Assembly at the State House to be held on September 23, 1991. The bill was passed by massive margins on that date and signed into law on October 1, 1991, by Campbell as the 1991 Ethics Act set to take effect as of January 1, 1992.

Campbell Finds Ethics Bill OK

Aside from some "specific questions," Gov. Campbell said to the media and a meeting of the Columbia Sertoma Club on August 5, 1991, that "Most everything in the bill's OK." However, as the bill was "a big, thick bill" it took time to consider it and he did not predict when he would decide on the question of calling a special session of the Legislature.

Although individual parts of the bill by themselves might not cause him to decide against the bill, Campbell said, "They're not bill killers necessarily, but they could be if you take them altogether."

Campbell's major concern was really not ethics reform itself, but restructuring of state government, a cause he had been advocating along with *The State* newspaper for some time. He complained of "bureaucratic lethargy and inertia" and said creating a cabinet system of state government which gave the governor more power would save millions of dollars each year. He deplored the competition of state agencies for appropriations at taxpayer expense "to run their own little part of government with no coordination whatsoever."

He called upon the citizenry to focus on the problem of disorganized government saying, "That is what is eating at this state, and that is what is causing a lot of our problems." He said it was necessary to "save our state from this system that has consolidated power in the hands of a group of unelected state officials who answer to no one and are accountable to no one."

Gov. Campbell Has Questions About Ethics Bill

Gov. Carroll Campbell, a consistent critic of campaign finance reforms, raised serious doubts about the ethics reform bill presented by the House-Senate conference committee. Campbell had been an adversary of low campaign contribution limits and other restrictions on the use of campaign funds.

One question he raised after going over the bill for almost three weeks was why the bill defined election cycles as lasting for only two years when some offices—such as state Senate and all constitutional officers—served four year terms. "It kind of works in favor of an incumbent—pretty strong, as a matter of fact," the governor said on August 5, 1991. He claimed that the provision he worried about allowed a senator to collect maximum campaign donations twice but an opponent only once during a campaign.

Campbell also raised an issue about provisions that required organizations which rated legislators to file detailed disclosure reports even more detailed than those required of legislators.

In addition to the question of whether Campbell would find the bill sufficiently satisfactory to cause him to call a special session of the General Assembly which had done out of session in early June, there was the issue of whether Campbell would sign or veto the bill.

Special Session Up in the Air

While Gov. Carroll Campbell read over and pondered the conference bill on ethics reform for nearly a month after getting it on July 18, 1991, some legislators raised the question of whether Campbell should even call a special session to vote on the bill some time in the remainder of the year. Some legislators thought the bill could wait until the 1992 session of the Legislature met in January.

Sen. Joe Wilson (R-Lexington), a strong proponent of strict ethics reforms, opined that the bill should be delayed until the next year arguing, "I think it's an unnecessary expense to the state." Wilson noted that the conference committee improved the bill but that the bill still failed to regulate the practice of lawyer-legislators before state boards and commissions. Also, the bill did not require income disclosure by legislators to a sufficient degree.

Wilson reasoned that more pressure would be on legislators in the next session of the General Assembly because it was an election year in which all House and Senate members would be up for voters' review. "I like the media glare of an election year so the voters are very familiar with how each legislator has voted."

Senators Discuss Ethics Deal with Governor

Senators set a meeting for Thursday, August 22, 1991, to discuss a proposal to vote on an ethics reform bill later in the year that would meet Gov. Carroll Campbell's terms for calling a special session to pass the bill.

Sen. Marshall Williams, President Pro Tem of the Senate, said he called an informal caucus to discuss Campbell's proposal to make nine changes in the draft's 151 page ethics reform bill. Just before the meeting, Williams said, "The governor has laid down certain things that he thinks is wrong. It's a little unusual, but he's our governor."

In a letter of August 14, 1991, Campbell wrote to Williams and Speaker Bob Sheheen that he would call a special session if the bill was changed as he requested. In the letter, Campbell also said that he would allow other items to be dealt with at the special session, including a bond bill, a state-run primary elections bill, and vetoes, provided the session was limited to only one day and not more.

Campbell's points in criticizing the bill and demanding changes included his view that the bill gave unfair advantage to officials such as senators and statewide officers who held four year terms because the bill limited campaign contributions based on two year election cycles, allowing such senators and officers to raise double the money permitted by the contribution caps. He also disliked the provision which allowed an additional amount of campaign money to be raised for those candidates having a primary election. In addition, he claimed that disclosure requirements on groups chilled free speech.

Conference Committee Makes Final Touch-Ups on Ethics Bill

The six person conference committee set a meeting for the afternoon of August 22, 1991, to make adjustments on the draft bill in response to Gov. Campbell's suggestions and opposition to legislative self-policing provisions advocated by the Senate.

House conferees surely would go along with the suggestions, said House Ethics Committee Chairman Wes Hayes (D-York). Sen. Tom Moore (D-Aiken) said the Senate would be willing to negotiate. Hayes said that Campbell's remarks were similar to the House positions on the bill. Moore said the self-policing was based on constitutional principles that an executive branch agency, the State Ethics Commission, would not have power over the legislators. Furthermore, the Legislature could not police non-members.

David Wilkins (R-Greenville), Chair of House Judiciary, said that the announcement of the federal prosecutor's last indictments and the end of the Lost Trust probe and grand jury actions presented the right time to pass the ethics reform bill. And Rep. Hayes said that it was good that the culprits had been caught, otherwise they "might have continued to poison the system had they not been caught."

Senate Caucus Defers to Campbell

Gathered in an unusual caucus on August 22, 1991, in Columbia, and rocked on August 20 by a second indictment of another of their members, Sen. Bud Long (D-Horry), the Senate voted 28-2 to instruct the three senators on the conference committee to work out any differences with Gov. Campbell so as to finalize the ethics reform bill. The meeting lasted 95 minutes.

Senate leaders predicted they would have the votes to pass the ethics bill by supermajority.

Two black senators, Herbert U. Fielding (D-Charleston) and Frank Gilbert (D-Florence), abstained after complaining that the governor limited the topics to be considered by the special session. Sen. Kay Patterson (D-Richland) also complained that the governor was going to call him back and then "tell me what to do."

But Sen. Tom Pope (D-Newberry) said the Senate was in a weak position against Campbell, "When we adjourned without a bill, all the bargaining chips are in his corner.... We need an ethics bill bad enough. I say accept every word here."

Senators felt the issues raised by Campbell were minor and could be worked out with slight revisions of the bill.

Senate Votes for Ethics Bill

Even while the Senate voted for the ethics reform bill, two senators rejected the bill. Sen. Joe Wilson (R-Lexington) and Sen. Ryan Shealy (R-Lexington) both voted against the bill on the grounds that it was too weak.

This provoked an outburst of kidding from the Democrats. Sen. Isadore Lourie (D-Richland) hooted out "Senator Wilson's against ethics," and Sen. Kay Patterson (D-Richland), a foe of ethics reform and a friend of kindly lobbyists, cried out, "Look at who's the good ol' boy now." Patterson then pointed out the fact that he and Sen. Theo Mitchell (D-Greenville), who had been badly trounced by Carroll Campbell the previous year, had voted for the bill whereas Wilson and Shealy were against it, all for the benefit of the pro-reform conservative S.C. Policy Council President, Hal Eberle, in the gallery to rate senators on their vote. Patterson predicted that by the Policy Council's rating standards, "Joe Wilson and Ryan Shealy get a zero.... Kay Patterson and Theo Mitchell get 100 each."

Sting Ends and Reform Next

The announcement by U.S. Attorney Bart Daniel that the indictment of Sen. Bud Long on August 20, 1991, would be the last in Operation Lost Trust came at a time when the final touches were being made to the draft ethics bill by the House-Senate conference committee. The time for a drastic overhaul of South Carolina's ethics laws had clearly come.

Daniel called upon the media to go forward and "fully comment" on the investigation, obviously hoping that journalists would aggressively make the case that the rot in state government must be torn out.

Gov. Campbell still complained that the 151 page draft ethics reform bill provided too much protection for incumbents and said the "overriding concern I have is equal protection under the law." The governor objected to provisions which allowed self-policing by incumbent legislators while challengers would police challengers, but he thought it would be even worse if legislative ethics committees policed challengers, too. "The people that administer the law ought not to be the people who are governed by it."

Campbell said that his criticisms of unfairness in the bill were enough to "destroy the public confidence in the Legislature itself. They are not great enough in my opinion to gut the bill."

Legislators Make Some Concessions to Gov. Campbell

Under pressure to convince Gov. Campbell to call a special session of the General Assembly to pass the ethics bill finalized by the conference committee, legislative negotiators agreed to make some concessions to Campbell and to modify several terms of the conference bill. By late August, 1991, legislative leaders indicated a willingness to address most of the nine criticisms Campbell had directed at the bill.

However, legislators refused to agree with Campbell's objection to the provision in the conference bill which would allow the House and Senate to continue to police its own members. Campbell favored the transfer of jurisdiction over legislators accused of wrong-doing to the State Ethics Commission.

But the legislators charged with coping with Campbell's criticisms agreed to amend the bill to meet the governor's other objections. The major concessions included the following: (1) legislators would resign from almost all state boards and commissions effective on January 1, 1992 rather than on January 1, 1993; (2) candidates could raise money to pay off old campaign debts and treat the funds raised as applying to the campaign for which the debt was incurred rather than for future campaign cycles; and (3) candidates for Senate and statewide office would be subject to contribution limits on four year rather than two year cycles.

However, the Senate was adamant about refusing Gov. Campbell's argument that senators should be subject to the jurisdiction of the State Ethics Commission rather than the Senate Ethics Committee made up of senators. Senators took the position that they could not subject themselves to jurisdiction of anybody but senators due to the separation of powers doctrine in the South Carolina Constitution.

Sen. Samuel Stilwell (R-Greenville), a member of the conference committee which finalized the ethics bill, explained the Senate position, arguing that, "I certainly agree with the concept that what you have to file should be identical, that the penalties be the same and that the law be clear." However, Stilwell contended that "you have the problem of separation of powers."

Gov. Campbell argued that the ethics reform bill would be worthless if it was not enforced. The governor was joined by reformers outside and inside government in arguing for independent enforcement by the State Ethics Commission. Critics complained that the legislative ethics committees ignored the misconduct of legislators and did not enforce the weak 1975 Ethics Act. Critics also pointed to the fact that three of the six members of the House Ethics Committee were indicted at the time of Operation Lost Trust by the federal grand jury and all of them were eventually convicted.

The objections of Gov. Campbell to provisions in the conference ethics reform bill continuing to allow legislators to use legislative ethics committees to have jurisdiction over the enforcement of the ethics act were seconded by John Crangle, Executive Director of Common Cause/South Carolina. Crangle said that some senators had told him privately that they were really not concerned bout the separation of powers issue, telling the media, "The fact of the matter is is that legislators on the Senate side do not want the State Ethics Commission to have jurisdiction over them." The truth was, Crangle alleged, that "They want to continue to be the judge and jury of their own conduct. I just think the doctrine of separation of powers is being used as a fairly transparent effort to protect themselves against outside jurisdiction."

House conferee Rep. Candy Waites joined in urging that the State Ethics Commission be given auditing power over lawmakers' disclosure reports lest the reports be ignored. However, conference committee chair, Sen. Tom Moore (D-Aiken) argued that the legislative ethics committees did not need to enforce any new ethics laws, observing, "The public is the watchdog now. The public would continue to be the watchdog."

Special Session for Ethics Bill Expected

Although Gov. Carroll Campbell had remained coy about whether he would call a special session of the General Assembly to deal especially with the ethics reform bill passed out of the conference committee, it did appear by early September that Campbell would make the call.

Campbell had indicated earlier that it depended on whether he could work out differences he had with the bill being prepared by the conference committee. If those differences could be resolved to his satisfaction then he would likely call the Legislature back.

By September 4, 1991, it appeared that the negotiations were going well. Campbell told the media after a speech in Greenville, S.C., "We're about there.... It's a very comprehensive bill and we've got to finish the drafting of it. We're on agreement on everything in it."

The conference committee was set to meet on September 9, 1991, to formally approve the bill.

Campbell reported that he had met with senators on September 3, 1991, and was pleased with the progress of the bill to that point.

Campbell Calls Special Session

On September 9, 1991, Gov. Carroll Campbell made the expected announcement that he would call a special session for two days starting on September 23, 1991. The Legislature was to assemble at 10 a.m. on the first day and to adjourn at 5 p.m. on the following day. The agenda was limited by the governor's announcement and was conditional on the leadership of the House and Senate agreeing to his limits.

The primary purpose of the special session was to pass the ethics bill which had been drafted by the conference committee and approved by both house's members on the committee. The session would also be allowed to vote on a bond bill and perhaps a few other minor matters.

Senate and Governor At Odds on Ethics Special Session

The negotiating between the General Assembly and Governor Carroll Campbell over the issue of if and when and for what he would call a special session of the Legislature dragged on and paralleled the conference committee's deliberations on the ethics bill and the continued trials and sentencing of convicted parties even as new indictments were handed down on Rep. Tim Wilkes and Sen. Bud Long.

The issue that still divided the Senate and the Governor in mid-September, 1991, was whether the special session would be limited to considering only a small agenda. While the House voted to accept Campbell's restricted agenda, the Senate was split. In a poll of senators in the week of September 9th of 1991, a majority of only 24 senators agreed to Campbell's conditions for a special two day session with a limited agenda to include the conference ethics reform bill. However, 8 said no and 7 said they would agree to discuss ethics and a few other matters but did not want the session limited to only two days. Campbell was demanding a two-third Senate vote for his conditions before calling the special session.

Special Session Agenda Up in Air

Gov. Carroll Campbell and Senate President Pro Tem Marshall Williams, in the end, had to work out a deal before Campbell would make his long-delayed call for a special session. Williams had some holdout senators who did not like the governor's proposed restricted agenda and two day session as conditions.

As the Senate split over the topics and time, House Speaker Bob Sheheen told the media, "If 46 senators want to sit there and look foolish...I think the voters will take care of them next year." Indeed, the full Senate was up for election in 1992. Sheheen said on September 16, 1991, that his survey of House members showed that the House would pass the ethics reform bill and go home either at the end of day one or in the morning of day two, that is, September 23 or 24, 1991. Sheheen said that if Campbell called the session he thought that public pressure would demand good judgment.

But Sen. Glenn McConnell (R-Charleston) said the Senate would not be bullied. He said more time was needed to evaluate the 151 page ethics bill and that the Governor's Office had been delaying, arguing that "They have had ample time to sit down with the conferees and get this changed and that changed and now they want the Legislature to just gulp that thing up like a chunk of meat being thrown at a hungry dog." Even McConnell thought the bill was too weak.

Deal Set on Special Session

The Senate would not agree by two-thirds vote to Gov. Carroll Campbell's demands for a special session restricted in time and subject matters, but on September 17, 1991, he decided to call the Legislature in to deal with the ethics reform bill. Campbell's decision was based on a gentlemen's agreement with three Senate leaders, Lt. Gov. Nick Theodore, President Pro Tem of the Senate Marshall Williams, and Sen. Tom Moore, chairman of the ethics reform bill conference committee which had produced a bill.

According to the South Carolina Constitution, the governor had the power to call a special session but not to end it. The House did vote by two-thirds to Campbell's limited time and agenda, but the Senate did not.

Campbell spokesman, Tucker Eskew, said, "I don't think anyone likes to keep anything in the oven too long." Therefore, the governor called legislators into session two hours early on Monday morning, September 23, 1991, to give them more time to review the 151 page ethics reform bill.

The special session would also deal with a $333 million bond bill that contained money for local projects, new prisons, and college construction. Certain appointments and a Greenville school tax would also be on the agenda.

Instead of taking the $250 per day per legislator for the special session, legislators had agreed to not take the money and only accept their per day expenses and travel mileage. Common Cause/South Carolina had suggested that the legislators forego their pay as a way of neutralizing some legislators who offered the cost of the session as a reason for not holding it.

Ethics Reform Bill Finalized

The House-Senate conference committee was still wrangling over the terms of the draft ethics reform bill just two days before the special session of the General Assembly was set to convene on September 23, 1991, at the call of Gov. Carroll Campbell. At that point, the committee had been meeting for five months in the Senate Office Building on the State House grounds.

The bill sent forward by the committee contained a total of 151 pages and would make South Carolina one of the most advanced states in the nation in the field of ethics law, imposing new restrictions on lobbying and campaign finance as well as on conflicts of interest which were much more drastic than the great majority of states. South Carolina would go from having the weakest and most permissive ethics laws to the most restrictive and rigorous.

A number of legislators did not like the tight limits on campaign contributions, but most agreed that some limits were needed in place of the old law which had no limits on the amounts, sources, types, and uses of campaign funds.

Near the end of the process, the biggest issue in dispute was the question of whether some restrictions should be placed on lawyer-legislators who practiced before state boards and commissions and who had often, in the past, taken large retainers from corporate clients without doing any legal work in return, thereby becoming de facto lobbyists in the Legislature.

Loopholes in Ethics Bill

The conference ethics bill which went to the General Assembly in special session on September 23, 1991, failed to address a number of significant issues. In some cases, these failures may have been an oversight, but in too many instances, the reason was an intentional avoidance of sensitive issues, including conflicts of interest.

One of the most volatile issues was that stressed by Gov. Carroll Campbell while the bill was being drafted—the issue of lawyer-legislators practicing before state courts, boards and commissions. Although there were well over a hundred amendment bills offered as the ethics bill was being crafted, the only bill which would have barred lawyer-legislators from voting on state court judges was withdrawn and not debated.

Other problems with the bill included a provision which exempted lobbyists for churches from being defined as lobbyists and from any requirements that they file and disclose with the state.

The enforcement process was kept secret by law according to the bill. Any person filing a complaint with legislative ethics committees and the State Ethics Commission was prohibited from publicizing the fact under pain of criminal sanctions. This protected accused officials while probably violating the free speech, free press, and right to petition clauses of the First Amendment of citizen-complainants.

Ethics Reform Bill Passes

The sudden passage of H. 3743, the bill which became known as the 1991 Ethics Reform Act on September 23, 1991, was possible because such large majorities in both the House and Senate came to the special three day session convinced that the legislation was needed to counteract the Lost Trust scandal which had plagued South Carolina since July 18, 1990.

The vote in the House was unanimous 108-0, including, of course, Speaker Bob Sheheen and House Judiciary Chairman David Wilkins. In addition, representatives not present on that date to vote sent in their views on the bill. Reps. Marion Kinon and M.O. Alexander both wrote for the *House Journal* that they were supportive of the bill and Rep. John B. Williams indicated his support for free conference powers.

On September 23, 1991, the General Assembly moved with amazing speed to pass the ethics bill and to wrap up the three day special session by the late afternoon of the first day. They also passed a bond bill and rejected a bill to have the State Election Commission take over the administration of primary elections which had been bungled and corrupted for years by the parties. The speed of the session was, perhaps, caused by the fact that legislators had agreed, under pressure from Common Cause/South Carolina, to not take their salary of $250 per day which they were entitled to take for each day of the special session. This demand by Common Cause was designed to neutralize the objection raised by some legislators, including Sen. Joe Wilson (R-Lexington), that a special session should not be called because it would cost too much. Common Cause Director, John Crangle, responded to Wilson by saying that the Legislature had embarrassed the people of South Carolina so much with 18 members indicted for corruption that legislators should do penance for their sins by foregoing their pay. This caused Wilson to drop his objection.

Ethics Act Passes the Senate

While the ethics reform bill sailed through the House by vote of 108-0 in just 90 minutes, it took Sen. Tom Moore (D-Aiken) four hours to push the bill through a more hostile Senate. Moore, the chairman of the conference committee, had fought hard for drastic reforms, especially in limiting campaign contributions.

The Senate passed H. 3743 as the 1991 Ethics Act on September 23, 1991, by a vote of 36-6. The vote on the bill was dramatically accelerated by Sen. Nikki Setzler (D-Lexington) who moved that unanimous consent be provided for a grant of Free Conference Powers and that the Report of the Committee of Free Conference be adopted.

A roll call vote was requested. Sen. Setzler moved and with unanimous consent, a roll call vote was dispensed with a vote of 36-6. The Report of the Committee of Free Conference was adopted as reported on September 16, 1991.

Of the six senators voting against the adoption of H. 3734, several filed statements in the *Senate Journal* as of September 23, 1991. Sen. John Martin (D-Fairfield) stated for the record that "I feel that this Bill will chill the right of the public to let their consensus and needs be known to their elected members of the General Assembly." Sen. Glenn McConnell (R-Charleston), Sen. Ernest Passailague (D-Charleston), and Sen. Michael T. Rose (R-Dorchester) recorded statements which complained that "The Senate, in a panic...just stampeded into approving the rewriting of the Bill and its passage without knowing fully what it was doing or what was in the Bill." McConnell, Passailague, and Rose also listed seven specific substantive objections to H. 3734.

Members of the conference committee which had patiently worked out compromises between the House and Senate versions of their reform bills praised fellow legislators for their votes. Rep. Candy Waites (D-Richland) said, "I'm proud of the South Carolina Legislature and I'm proud of the people of South Carolina, because if the people had not spoken out about the need for this kind of legislation, we would not have had it." Fellow conferee Rep. David Wilkins exulted, the bill "takes us from being a 1 on a scale of 1-to-10 to being a 9 or 9½," Speaker Bob Sheheen, reflecting on his long history of advocating real reforms noted, "The House had been ready for 10 years to pass lobbying reform."

But some black legislators withheld their votes. Rep. Maggie Glover (D-Florence) did not vote because she thought the bill would make campaigning more expensive, and Rep. Juanita White (D-Jasper) called the bill "a bunch of garbage." Glover did not think the bill would stop corruption. Perhaps this reflected a view of public office all too common among blacks that public office was a traditional way of financing your lifestyle by living off of deals and lobbyists, a view also clearly demonstrated by all of those, black and white, who went down for corruption in the scandal.

Ethics Act in Perspective

On September 23, 1991, the special session of the Legislature called by Gov. Campbell finally passed the Ethics Act. It was the culmination of a legislative effort which had actually begun long before the revelation of Lost Trust in the mid-summer of 1990.

Speaker Bob Sheheen had long wanted to pass ethics reform bills in previous years but could not muster the support until Lost Trust shocked the House and Senate into action.

The discussion of the ethics reform bill in the House took only 90 minutes and the bill passed by unanimous vote of 108-0. The 36-6 vote in the Senate was almost as overwhelming where the only six votes against the bill protested that it was not tough enough. Within six hours of the start of the session the bill had been passed and sent on to the desk of Gov. Campbell.

Cindi Ross Scoppe had been covering the scandal and the reform effort throughout the previous fourteen months and she entitled her story on the passage of the bill, "The General Assembly abolished business as usual Monday."

Ms. Scoppe wrote further that, "Acting with surprising speed and unanimity, lawmakers in less than six hours finished work on a sweeping ethics reform bill designed to make amends for decades of sins uncovered by the federal investigation into legislative corruption."

Flaws in Ethics Reform Act

The major flaws in the bill which passed with little resistance were that it continued to allow legislators to police themselves. The Senate had resisted the idea of outside enforcement of the act and the House gave up its offer to support the transfer of enforcement to an outside entity such as an independent commission. The bill still allowed some wining and dining of legislators by lobbyists' clients, but it was limited to a small dollar amount. It still allowed the use of campaign funds for so-called "office related expenses," a loophole which invited abusive uses of campaign funds for personal use under the pretext of office expenses.

The bill did limit the amounts and sources of campaign contributions but left the door wide open for big money corporations and political action committees to donate huge amounts of money collectively from various economic interest groups seeking favors for their money. The bill also allowed for the appearance of leadership political action committees whereby key legislators, such as the speaker, committee chairmen, and the like could use their positions to shake down special interests for political donations to their leadership PACs; the money could then be used for almost any purpose including making payments to friends and political cronies and including donations to the campaigns of other politicians.

Benefits of the Ethics Act

The ethics bill which became law was in many of its provisions a direct attack on the evils exposed by the Lost Trust scandal. Even though imperfect, many of the prohibitions and restrictions, did, in fact, countervail the most outrageous abuses.

The bill banned the conversion of campaign funds to personal use which had been the main way in which so-called campaign contributions had been pocketed by corrupt officials who were actually taking bribes. The bill banned cash contributions, the main way in which bribes were handed to all of the targets of the sting.

The bill banned lobbyists from giving anything of value to legislators and statewide officials and attempted to stop the ways in which lobbyists bought legislators with unlimited gifts of free food, free liquor, free trips, and free cash. As the actions of corrupt lobbyist Ron Cobb were at the center of the sting, the restriction of lobbyists and their actions was an absolute necessity.

The bill also attacked the conflict of interest problem, although it had not been completely exposed by the scandal. The bill forced some conflicts into the open by disclosure requirements and banned certain conflicted transactions.

Scope of Ethics Act

The reforms in the Ethics Act were actually more expansive than was necessary to just address the abuses exposed in Lost Trust.

Sen. McKinley Washington (D-Charleston), a member of the conference committee which finalized the bill, commented after its passage on September 23, 1991, that, "I think a lot of folks other than those in the Legislature will probably find that we have gone beyond what the public had been pushing for in applying many provisions to all state and local officials."

The bill also required lawyer-legislators to file and disclose their practices before state agencies, even though the Lost Trust scandals had not clearly shown such practice to be a major source of corruption. Gov. Campbell had made the matter a big issue in commenting about reform and repeatedly complained about the alleged conflicts of interest of lawyer-legislators appearing before state boards, commissions, and courts.

Ethics Act—Application to Local Government

The Ethics Act was, of course, written to address the huge scandal at the State House. But even so, it was written to apply not only to state, but also to local governments and their officials.

The changes affecting local governments were an afterthought, said John Crangle, Executive Director of Common Cause/South Carolina, and that local officials were often part-timers who for years had a dubious history of doing business with local governments; therefore, they might find it difficult to accept the more stringent standards for reporting and disclosing their economic interests. Crangle added, "I think it was sort of an afterthought that they put the business in about local officials, and I think it will be beneficial."

Mike Cone, Director of the South Carolina Association of Counties agreed, saying, "I think we would all have to assume full disclosure a very healthy thing." Mayor Bob Coble of Columbia said some adjustments would be needed but that, "I think we all recognize, as local officials, we'll have to study it and understand it and comply with it." Coble expected the citizens to support the new law, observing that, "I don't think in today's climate the public is going to understand any complaining or moaning."

Howard Duvall, Director of Intergovernmental Affairs of the Municipal Association of South Carolina, summarized the new ethics law as "more a matter of disclosure for local officials than it is a matter of prohibition."

Senate Passes Ethics Bill in One Day

When the Senate took only six hours to discuss and pass the ethics bill and the bond bill while rejecting the bill to transfer primary elections from the political parties to the state, some people rejoiced at the result. A three day special session called by Gov. Carroll Campbell had lasted only one day. It might have been viewed as a breakthrough in a normally arthritic legislative system better at doing nothing than in doing something constructive.

But Cindi Ross Scoppe of *The State* thought the speedy process was a sign of the lack of leadership in the Senate which otherwise might have debated and wrangled over the ethics bill for days and perhaps not even passed it. In an article written just two days after the ethics bill and the bond bill whizzed through the Legislature, Scoppe wrote, "The quick action had little to do with leadership of the body that used to control South Carolina's government." She went on to describe "the Senate that showed up for the special session was a schizophrenic group of 43 independent players.... The leadership vacuum that worsened when Marlboro Sen. Jack Lindsay died in January could be seen...in the Senate's handling of the ethics reform bill."

When the Ethics bill came up for debate, Scoppe argued, "the Senate failed to act as a deliberative body that slowly and carefully considers weighty matters. Less than halfway through an orderly debate, senators panicked." Sen. Nikki Setzler moved to act on the bill by voice vote and Lt. Gov. Nick Theodore quickly moved the bill through the vote and it passed.

The speed of the Senate in passing the ethics bill in less than one day alarmed Sen. Glenn McConnell. He contended that, "There was a stampede in there." He felt that the Senate acted in haste from "fear that people would be cast as being against ethics [which] forced them to just sweep it on through."

The rumor that the House would go home before the Senate finished its work caused anxiety in the Senate which shot them forward to vote on the ethics bill. But Speaker Sheheen said that, in fact, he had no plans to send the House home until the Senate was done. But the rumor that the House was going to leave early caused the legislation to race through the Senate because of rumors, McConnell said.

Mike Burton, Executive Director of the South Carolina Republican Party, commented that whereas Sheheen could move bills fast, the Democratically controlled Senate "is unfortunately left unstructured, and there's not much leadership to point to over there."

President Pro Tem Marshall Williams (D-Orangeburg) did not seem to command attention and control the session, but he was glad the ethics bill passed. Sen. David Thomas (R-Greenville) commented that after the death of Jack Lindsay at the start of the 1991 session, senators were no longer dominated by his leadership and each senator acted on his own. But Sen. John Land (D-Clarendon) said that it was better to slow down the legislative process. He said that Speaker Sheheen was very adept at not proposing and passing bills the Senate wanted and the Senate resorted to trying to create its own bills.

Gov. Campbell Signs Ethics Bill

Gov. Carroll Campbell signed the Ethics Reform Act on October 1, 1991, at a ceremony at which he was surrounded by legislators and the media. Campbell remarked that the legislation was "one of the strictest bills in the country right now" and called for a "shake-out period" when the law would go into practical effect. "I'm not going to criticize any part of the product right now," he added. However, Campbell remarked that, "You know and I know that I would like to go ahead and move ahead with the lawyer-legislator side of the thing, but we fought that battle, and that's it. It'll come up again."

Campbell predicted that the bill would not do much good unless the citizenry was interested in it, observing, "You can have all the laws in the world, and if nobody knows about it, nobody knows what's done, the may not be enforced."

John Crangle, Executive Director of Common Cause/South Carolina, at the time expressed concern that the new law was not strict enough and that it would not by strictly enforced.

Campbell did not comment on the campaign finance reforms in the legislation but did say that the new lobbying regulations "would elevate the status of a lobbyist to the point that they are a professional offering information and ideas to make arguments, instead of drinks and dinner and things like that."

Senate Pay at Issue

The question of whether the senators who attended the special session on September 23, 1991, would be paid was still undecided when the session was held. Whereas the House had voted on a binding resolution to reject their pay for the time they attended the special session, the Senate had not considered the issue.

The amount of pay at issue for senators was a total of $11,180 for all 43 senators who attended. Normally, legislators received $79 per person for each day of session plus mileage.

Senate President Pro Tem Marshall Williams (D-Orangeburg) observed that, "Constitutionally, I don't think we could prevent those who want to take the $260 from getting it.... That's why we didn't do it. We were getting along so well. I don't think any of them will [take the money]."

The House went ahead and approved a resolution limiting members to expense money, as moved by Speaker Bob Sheheen (D-Kershaw). This use of a resolution obviated the need for individual members to sign waivers rejecting their compensation entitlements.

Gov. Carroll Campbell had agreed to call the special session on condition that House and Senate not take their pay. On two instances, the Senate agreed to all of Campbell's conditions. Sen. Glenn McConnell (R-Charleston) joked, "You'd have to be bold as a rat to take that money." Lt. Gov. Nick Theodore added, "For all practical purposes, in my judgment, they've all agreed to waive the extra pay for the special session." Nobody took his pay.

Ethics Act Underfunded

The new Ethics Act of 1991 just passed and signed by Gov. Campbell took effect on January 1, 1992. But the 1991-1992 state budget provided no money to fund the implementation of the Act. Of course, the writers of the budget had not foreseen the passage of the Act and had not funded it.

Even so, the budget being prepared for the fiscal year July 1, 1991, to June 30, 1992 still did not provide enough money to fund the implementation of the Act, proposing only 40 percent of the amount needed according to the Budget and Control Board.

Rep. Candy Waites (D-Richland) pointed out the huge gap saying, "How can we tell the people of South Carolina we passed ethics reform, which we all believe was needed and important; we came back for a special session, and then say, 'Oh, I'm sorry, we're not going to fund this piece of legislation.'"

The State Budget Division estimated it would cost a total of $607,800 to implement the new Ethics Act. Yet the budget proposal prepared by the same division only proposed $235,259.

The State Ethics Commission budget of 1991-1992 did not have the approximate amount of $30,000 to print new disclosure forms. Gary Baker, Director of the Commission, announced his plan to appear before the Budget and Control Board on October 31, 1991, and ask for more money, but only the General Assembly could provide the funds and even then, only after it convened on January 14, 1992.

Money Shortage at State Ethics Commission

The State Ethics Commission reported that it lacked $50,000 it needed and had to obtain special permission from the Budget and Control Board to operate with deficit so it could mail out new forms, hold meetings, investigate complaints, and avoid laying off employees. The crisis came at a bad time as the Commission was gearing up to enforce the new Ethics Act which was set to take effect on January 1, 1992.

Rep. Billy Boan (R-Lancaster), Chairman of the House Budget Committee, said that the General Assembly would probably pass a supplemental appropriation bill in the 1992 session to fund the commission. Gov. Carroll Campbell also commented that more money was needed, saying, "It's kind of stupid to pass an ethics law and then say you can't do it."

The commission's budget had been cut in the 1991-1992 budget year to only about $264,000 as there was no anticipation of the additional work the Commission would be expected to do under the Ethics Act which was passed after the budget was finalized.

Commission Director Gary Baker said the money was needed to avoid cutting staff, which at the time, numbered only six employees. And half of the $50,000 was needed to print new forms mandated by the Act.

Ethics Bill Raises Problems

As soon as the Ethics Act was passed on September 23, 1991, those affected by it began to worry about its rules. To some it was unclear what the bill required and to others it was overkill.

Blair Rice of Blair Mills complained after a panel discussion at the Economic Summit meeting held by the South Carolina Chamber of Commerce that he might be considered a lobbyist for serving on the panel. Some companies worried that the new law would require too many of their employees to register as lobbyists.

Cathy Novinger, SCANA's Vice President for Governmental Affairs, called upon Secretary of State Jim Miles to answer questions about the law. Sen. Sam Stilwell, a conference committee member, predicted that the bill would have to be amended.

CHAPTER THIRTY ONE

LOBBYISTS' DISCLOSURE FORMS FILED

The lobbyists' disclosure reports filed in the summer of 1991 after the session came to an end in June showed the beneficial effects of new Secretary of State's Jim Miles' implementation of a breakthrough policy of strict enforcement of the disclosure requirements of the 1975 Ethics Act which had been ignored under the feckless leadership of Secretary of State John Campbell.

The reports filed at the end of the 1991 session of the General Assembly finally exposed to the people of South Carolina the huge amounts of money which interest groups had spent on lobbying activity in the first half of 1991. Even so, the amounts reported were probably substantially lower for the session than they otherwise would have been since all the negative publicity generated by the exposure of the bribery of lobbyist Ron Cobb most likely caused lobbyists and their employers to cut back their spending drastically, especially on lobbyists' freebies to state legislators.

Jim Miles' campaign strategy of promising to strictly enforce the disclosure provisions of the 1975 Ethics Act had won overwhelming support from the voters. Miles and his assistant, Bob Knight, had gone to extraordinary lengths to fulfill Miles' promise to finally bring the lobbyists under control and force them to disclose what they were doing and how much they were spending.

Lobbyists Cut Spending on Legislators in 1991 Session

Pursuant to new Secretary of State Jim Miles' demands that lobbyists comply with existing laws and file detailed disclosure reports with his office about their spending on gifts and handouts to legislators, the lobbyists' reports started rolling in during the early days of July, 1991.

Miles had changed the old disclosure forms to add a requirement that lobbyists report all gifts. Compliance with the reporting requirements was not complete as some lobbyists only reported their spending since January 1, 1991, whereas the law required reporting for the full twelve months dating back to July 1, 1990.

Even so, the reports showed that they spent only $211,000 on entertainment and gifts in the 1991 session as opposed to a reported total of $615,009 in 1990. Total lobbyists' salaries and activities cost a reported $4,277,000 to influence the General Assembly, or about $25,000 per legislator for the 170 in the House and Senate.

As a result of a showdown in January, 1991, when Miles came into office and demanded more detailed disclosures as promised in his campaign for the office, the lobbyists were forced to comply. The revised disclosure forms Miles created included places for lobbyists to report the legislators and other officials they tried to influence with handouts of food, entertainment, travel, and campaign donations.

Lobbyists Finally Disclose

By July, 1991, Miles had beaten even the most recalcitrant lobbyists into submission and they filed their first real disclosure forms in the 16 years the 1975 Act had been in effect. Five hundred twenty-two lobbyist disclosure forms were filed in Miles' office as of July 9, 1991, providing to the public information kept hidden for years, including income and how much they spent on trips, food, drinks, golf, annual meetings, and other handouts to politicians, especially legislators.

Lobbyist Robert Kneece, Sr., reported a total income of $204,788. Kneece, an attorney, had become a lobbyist after leaving the South Carolina House in 1978. Kneece said he might have over-reported his income but that "people have a right to know it." The McNair Law Firm reported its cash payment for services from clients such as Laidlaw Environmental Services and other waste companies.

Although it was not entirely clear as to what basis should be used to calculate income, lobbyists tried to conform to the guidelines of the Secretary of State. Deputy Secretary of State, Bob Knight, acknowledged that the figures submitted for entertainment, food, and campaign contributions might not be based on uniform standards, but said "A lot of these guys run their operations out of a shoe box." Knight said his office planned to audit the reports and try to determine what was being reported.

The lobbyists' disclosures filed by July 9, 1991, showed that the first half-year total amount of income for 1991 to that point was $5,283,343, up from slightly over $5 million reported for the whole of 1990.

However, it is likely that the gift amounts would have been much larger for 1991 had the House not adopted new rules in December, 1990, upon organization for the new session after the general election, which banned lobbyists from giving House members anything of value, the so-called "no-cup-of-coffee" rule. This cut an estimated $370,000 to $470,000 from entertainment, food, and travel expenses which might otherwise have been spent.

Top Spending Lobbyist Groups

Among the organizations which hired lobbyists in the 1991 session of the General Assembly, the amount of spending varied a great deal. Big money, high-powered groups spent much more than smaller entities. Furthermore, the incomes of lobbyists varied a great deal. The amounts reported to Secretary of State Miles as of July 9, 1991, for the first half of 1991 were:

Top Spending Employers of Lobbyists

Independent Consumer Finance Association..$158,725

S.C. Textile Manufacturing Association............ $135,285
S.C. League of Saving Institution............ $121,125
Laidlaw Environmental Services............ $119,777
S.C. Education Association............ $111,901

Highest Paid Lobbyists

Robert Kneece, Sr............ $204,788
Russell Mellette............ $189,393
Dwight Drake............ $165,100
Thomas Mullikin............ $139,687
Ed Yarborough............ $127,389

CHAPTER THIRTY TWO

AN OVERVIEW: OPERATION LOST TRUST COMES TO AN END

In the summer and fall of 1991, the Operation Lost Trust investigations and original indictments came to an end. U.S. Attorney Bart Daniel announced on August 28, 1991, that there would be no more indictments. And in the remainder of the year, the last defendants would either plead guilty or go to trial for the first time.

The final toll of those convicted included 27 defendants found criminally liable for corruption and for drug crimes related to the Lost Trust sting and probe. One was acquitted by a jury.

Appeals, dismissals, reinstatements of charges, re-indictments, one more guilty plea, and two retrials, a hung jury in one of the retrials, and a second retrial of the Blanding case would follow. In 1997, defendants Luther Taylor and B.J. Gordon would die while awaiting retrials after their convictions had been overturned on appeal. The final three defendants were found guilty—Derrick and Blanding at trial and Long by misdemeanor plea bargain.

The Sting Goes Public—A One Year Retrospective on Lost Trust

The FBI sting operation first called Operation Broken Trust went public on the morning of July 18, 1990. The day before, the FBI had come to Rep. Luther Taylor's house and took him to the Ramada Inn to keep him quiet. About 10:00 p.m. on July 17th, the FBI head of the probe, Fred Verinder and U.S. Attorney Bart Daniel told Gov. Carroll Campbell that the sting was going to be revealed to the public the next day. Daniel told Campbell that "our investigation cut across racial, political, and party lines, and while it was extensive, it wasn't a sign that state government was crumbling."

The morning of July 18th at 7:00 a.m., Daniel and his assistant, Dale DuTremble, met at the FBI control center, and at 10:00 a.m. DuTremble went to the grand jury room to continue his presentation of evidence. Daniel and Verinder flew to Washington, D.C. to tell Sen. Strom Thurmond and Sen. Ernest Hollings that the scandal was about to go public.

Daniel and Verinder then returned to Columbia to learn that all but two of the targets had been contacted. (Rep. Jack I. Rogers was on a trip to Germany and B.J. Gordon could not be located.) FBI agents working in pairs had surprised some suspects between 9:00 a.m. and 11:00 a.m. July 18th and had asked them incriminating questions as to whether they had ever taken cash from a lobbyist, did they know anyone who had, and did they know of any wrong-doing in the General Assembly. Agents had also served subpoenas on legislators.

Daniel returned from Washington to find that FBI agent, Pat Sena, had collected information gathered by interview teams and that posters with the names of the suspects had been placed on the walls of a conference room indicating that all suspects had talked, but some had given false statements to the FBI. This came as something of a surprise as some investigators had anticipated that some suspects would not talk without getting a lawyer first.

Late on July 18th Daniel briefed his staff, breaking the code of secrecy which had, to that point, allowed only five of Daniel's assistant attorneys to know of the sting. They were John Barton, Dale DuTremble, John McIntosh, Sherry Lydon, and Scott Schools.

FBI special agent, Mike Clemens, said at the time that he had worked a year and a half to catch Ron Cobb in a drug probe and then was turned in an entirely new direction when he found out from Cobb about bribery at the State House. For another year, Clemens pursued the corruption sting operation until it went public on July 18th.

All the while, Cheryl Denton, supervisor of the typing pool, had overseen her staff transcribe barely audible videotapes, struggling to understand legislators' southern accents and vulgar language. She was surprised that new tapes kept coming into her office for transcription.

Staff Work Backs Sting

All the while the Operation Lost Trust probe was in progress, both before and after it went public, the professional staff worked to process the paperwork generated by the investigators.

In addition to the typing pool under Denton, FBI agent Tom Brown was responsible for collecting and organizing every document produced by the sting. The prospect of all the evidence that would come in caused Brown to later tell reporters, "I had a sinking feeling about how much paper all those interviews would generate."

Another agent, Mike Morehart, had prepared data packages for the FBI agents who would confront the suspects, including the locations at which the suspects could be found and other administrative data. Morehart said that at the time, he thought, "God, I hope they can find those people with what I gave them."

Meanwhile, agent Mike Clemens was baby-sitting Luther Taylor at the Ramada Inn ever since he was picked up on the afternoon of July 17th to keep him isolated so he would not tip off any suspects. Taylor, by the morning of July 18th, seemed ready to talk to the FBI and cooperate. Clemens also directed agent Bob Johnson to install recording equipment at Taylor's home to collect any calls from other suspects.

Reflecting on Sting—One Year Later

Agent Clemens went to the command center to find out what the suspects had said when interviewed and compared their statements. About 3.00 p.m., his beeper went off and signaled a call from Rob Cobb who had been collecting videotapes of those he had lured into his bugged suites 574-576 at the Town House Hotel and his office in the AT&T Building and the boat the

"Tally Ho." Cobb was worried that word had leaked that he was under investigation and Clemens thought that legislators would avoid Cobb.

Thinking that suspects would most likely contact Robert Kohn, FBI agent Tommy Davis went to meet Kohn and spent the rest of the day with Kohn and at a motel near Kohn's home in Charleston. Recording devices were set up to catch calls coming to Kohn but none came in until the evening of July 18th. Clemens was surprised at the lack of calls, but later came to realize that, "I think that people were skeptical of Kohn because he was so closely associated with Cobb."

Davis and Kohn drove to get lunch. Kohn turned on the radio and they were shocked to hear news bulletins that subpoenas had been served on legislators. Davis had not anticipated that the news would get out so fast. But Kohn was not surprised. He never had expected the legislators to keep quiet about the FBI probe when they found out about it.

Agent Davis, a year afterward, expressed surprise that the citizens of South Carolina had not been more outraged at their politicians. Davis told a reporter in the summer of 1991, "A year ago, I would have expected more change. I would have thought there would be 300 people outside the State House every day demanding reform, insisting that the governor be given more power. I would have expected a sweeping ethics bill. None of that has happened. The people haven't demanded it."

Operation Lost Trust Indictments End

The final indictment handed down in the Lost Trust sting operation and criminal prosecutions in late August, 1991, proved to be that of Sen. Bud Long (D-Horry). At that point, there were only two defendants left to be dealt with—Long and Rep. Tim Wilkes—who would both go to trial in the fall of 1991. However, there were appeals in progress for Luther Taylor, Ennis Fant, B.J. Gordon, and Paul Derrick. And when Sen. Long was finally tried and convicted in late November, 1991, he too would file appeals.

Even though in August the last two trials and the pending appeals were still in progress, the U.S. Attorney Bart Daniel and FBI Special Agent-In-Charge John C. Harley announced in Columbia on August 28, 1991, that no more indictments were to be brought in the scandal. They also said that there would be no spin-off indictments based on the evidence developed in the cases already completed or still pending against Long and Wilkes. Daniel and Harley said that every lead had been followed and had not produced any more evidence that could be used to file more indictments.

The sting and investigative and prosecution procedures had started some 28 months before the public announcement of the end of the indictments. But after more than two years, it was now over, "Nobody connected with this case needs to fear that the other shoe is going to drop at any minute," said Agent Harley.

News Conference Reveals Details of Sting

A 75 minute news conference held in Columbia announced not only the fact that the last indictment in Operation Lost Trust had been made, that of Sen. Bud Long, but that the scandal and probe involved some facts which had already been revealed to the public by federal authorities and some matters which had not yet been publicized.

U.S. Attorney Bart Daniel and the FBI Agent-In-Charge told the media at the press conference on August 28, 1991, considerable new details for the first time which helped to complete the story of the scandal. Other information simply confirmed what was already known.

Daniel said the investigation was driven by corrupt lobbyist Ron Cobb, who had become a paid government informant and sting agent. Cobb relied on his friendships and business relationships with political figures developed over his years as a legislator and lobbyist. Cobb recruited Reps. Robert Kohn and Luther Taylor to help him find legislators who would take bribes from Cobb. Nobody who came to Cobb for bribe money was refused by Cobb. Daniel explained the sting's strategy, "We had an open door policy...when somebody came knocking at that door, we didn't look to see if it was a Republican or a Democrat or a black or a white or a man or a woman. And once we saw who was in the door, we never slammed it shut."

Bart Daniel told the media at his news conference on August 28, 1991, that some of those approached by the FBI sting refused to take bribe money, but their names were not revealed.

The probe found that only two officials took bribe money to fix the capital gains tax cut bill which Ron Cobb pushed through on behalf of 8 Greenville businessmen who had hired him as their lobbyist. Daniel said that Rep. Jack I. Rogers and Sen. Jack Lindsay had taken payoffs to slip the bill through, but that Lindsay died in January, 1991, before he would be indicted as intended. Rogers, of course, was convicted of bribery and racketeering.

The media were also told that officials of GSX (a/k/a Laidlaw Environmental Services) did not know that their lobbyist, Ken Kinard, was coerced into giving part of his lobbying fee to Sen. Lindsay. In addition, in 1985, Lindsay took a bribe from Ron Cobb to help National Advanced Systems, later known at Hitachi Data Systems, win a bid to sell a computer system to Clemson University. However, National Advanced Systems employees did not know their lobbyist, Cobb, had paid the bribe.

Daniel and Hartley told reporters that every legislator who took a bribe was indicted and every bribe that was offered was taken. (Sen. Theo Mitchell (D-Greenville) had claimed that he had been offered and rejected a bribe, making that statement while he was the Democratic candidate for governor in 1990.)

The use of illegal drugs was limited to a small group of legislators. However, among those discovered as drug users, not all of them were indicted—only those deemed to be able to influence legislation were charged.

As the sting and trials were coming to an end, the government had offered Ron Cobb the opportunity to go into the federal witness protection program, but he had not decided in late August, 1991, what he would do.

Cobb had been given immunity on his original drug crimes, but was charged and pleaded guilty to two counts of using drugs in violation of his immunity agreement while he was functioning as a federal witness, but sentencing was delayed while he was still testifying.

Daniel and Hartley revealed that a total of 63 videotapes and 99 audio recordings were made during the sting probe.

The FBI agents, lawyers, and staff who conducted the sting were disappointed at how many public officials took bribes and used drugs.

Operation Lost Trust produced a total of 27 criminal indictments for corruption, obstruction, and drugs. That number included a total of 17 legislators, one ex-legislator and judge, the chairman of the S.C. Department Board, an aide to Gov. Carroll Campbell, six lobbyists, one businessman and one Clemson University administrator.

Daniel said that leaks about the sting proved worrisome. Certain state officials were concerned about the exposure of corruption and drug use among their colleagues and how it might affect their images.

Daniel offered reassurance at the end of the sting when he told reporters, "I can tell you now, without reservation, that the vast majority of our elected officials are men and women of honor who serve the public in the finest sense of the term." He hoped that the public trust could be restored after Lost Trust was completely finished.

South Carolina Did Not Prosecute Related Cases

As Operation Lost Trust went on for so long with 15 months of secret federal stings and investigations and another 17 months of public indictments and non-appellate prosecutions, the question arose in the minds of some citizens of South Carolina as to whether state law enforcement would also take action against those indicted by the federal grand jury. It was a further cause of speculation as to whether the state would also pursue some leads and file charges against persons and suspects who had been discovered by the FBI and federal grand jury but who had not been charged as federal defendants.

South Carolina Attorney General Travis Medlock announced at the time the federal indictments came to an end on August 28, 1991, that his office would not take action on any spin-off evidence the probe had revealed. And the state took no action thereafter related to Lost Trust defendants or evidence.

CHAPTER THIRTY THREE

THE TRIAL OF KEN BAILEY

Rep. Ken Bailey went to trial starting on August 20, 1991, as one of the last three Lost Trust defendants to be processed by the criminal justice system. His trial followed a large number of guilty pleas and lost trials by other state legislators. Bailey's trial would be followed by the acquittal of Rep. Tim Wilkes (D-Fairfield) on September 24, 1991, and the conviction at trial of Sen. Bud Long (D-Horry) on November 23, 1991.

Like the other six House members who elected to go to trial before Bailey went to trial, Bailey would be convicted. But unlike the others who were convicted at trial from the House, Bailey would not successfully appeal his conviction and win a new trial in the years following.

Bailey Confident

Rep. Ken Bailey (D-Orangeburg) expressed confidence he would win as jury selection in his bribery indictment trial got underway on August 20, 1991, in Columbia.

Bailey had been indicted on May 23, 1991, for conspiracy to violate the Hobbs Act and agreeing to sell his vote to FBI informant Ron Cobb for $500 in bribe money. Bailey faced 40 years and $500,000 in fines.

Of the total of 17 legislators indicted in Lost Trust at that point, only five had tried their cases and all had lost and now Bailey would be the sixth to go to trial.

Serving in the House since 1985, Bailey was an educational administrator. He was automatically suspended from the House on indictment by Rule 3.12.

Bailey's attorney, Charles H. Williams of Orangeburg, said the FBI videotapes did not show bribery, arguing, "I don't see how any reasonable person can look at the videotapes and say my client sold his vote." Williams dismissed the evidence, contending that, "When you look at the film, you don't see nothing" as there was no evidence of money being taken by Bailey nor of any discussion of the betting bill between Bailey and Cobb.

Williams ended, "Who would take somebody to trial if they thought they would lose? They'd be a damn fool."

Race Issue Raised in Bailey Case Jury Selection

Rep. Ken Bailey (D-Orangeburg) went on trial on August 21, 1991, on charges of public corruption. However, the picking of the jury got off to a bad start when the defense lawyers alleged that the prosecution was trying to keep blacks off of the jury. Bailey was black.

At the time, six of the 11 jurors drawn were black. The prosecution then accused the defense of trying to exclude whites from the jury.

The judge, Falcon Hawkins, sequestered the jury and accused both sides of playing games.

Bailey Trial—Opening Statements

When Rep. Ken Bailey (D-Orangeburg) went on trial, prosecutors said the charges against Bailey were conspiracy to sell his vote and extortion.

Assistant U.S. Attorney John McIntosh told the jury, "This case is about the betrayal of the public trust that we place in our elected officials." He promised to show a videotape of sting lobbyist Ron Cobb handing Bailey a $500 bribe and another tape made at the State House where Bailey promised to sell his vote as well.

Bailey's attorneys said the money given by Cobb was a campaign donation.

Cobb and several legislators were set to testify.

Opening the prosecution's presentation of evidence against Bailey, former Rep. Bob Kohn (R-Charleston) testified that Rep. Bailey had taken $200 for his help in getting a road paved with state funds in Orangeburg County at the request of a constituent. Kohn admitted that he paid Bailey the bribe money himself. Bailey did not report the money on his campaign disclosure documents. The payment allegedly was made in the same month that FBI sting agent and lobbyist Ron Cobb gave Bailey a cash payment of $500 to support the betting bill.

Bailey was defending charges of extortion and conspiracy to sell his vote, not on any matters related to taking a bribe in the road paving matter, and Bailey's attorneys objected to the evidence and asked the judge to withhold it from the jury.

Bailey's attorneys tried to portray Bailey as naive and not corrupt in his dealings with Cobb. Bailey denied that the $500 he took from Cobb was a bribe, saying that he had supported the betting bill well before he took any money from Cobb. Bailey's attorneys blamed Rep. Frank McBride (D-Richland), another Lost Trust defendant, for pressuring Bailey to take the payment from Cobb. When Bailey voted on April 25, 1990, for the betting bill, the bill failed of passage, but the government argued that bribery drove the attempt to pass the bill, regardless of its failure.

Cobb took the stand and the prosecution presented an audio recording and two tapes made secretly on May 9, 1990, the day Bailey allegedly sold his vote. The audiotape was made in the State House on that date. On the tape, Bailey said he was getting pressure from McBride to support the bill.

The prosecution presented another audiotape made in the State House lobby on which Ron Cobb told Rep. Bailey that the betting bill was in position to be voted on in the House and that Cobb was ready to pay Bailey for his vote. Cobb told Bailey, "It will be $500 now, and if we get something rolling, I'll come back with some more." At a second meeting in Cobb's office later the same day, Cobb gave Bailey another $500 in cash.

Cobb asked Bailey to talk with Sen. John Matthews (D-Orangeburg) and Sen. Kay Patterson (D-Richland) about voting for the betting bill and Bailey said, "I'll be supportive." The meetings with Bailey and Cobb followed a day after Cobb had met with Rep. Frank McBride (D-Richland) to promote the betting bill.

McBride testified on August 23, 1991, that, "I told Bailey that I had received $1,000 cash from Mr. Cobb, and that Rep. (James) Faber had received $1,000 in cash from Mr. Cobb for supporting the pari-mutuel bill." At the time of the testimony, McBride had already pleaded guilty to selling his vote and also testified that Bailey knew that Cobb was paying bribes.

August 24, 1991, was the last day of the trial of Rep. Ken Bailey. The prosecution tried to portray Bailey as a man who was frantically trying to file amended campaign disclosure forms on July 18, 1990, the same day that he suddenly found out that he was under FBI investigation. The new filings were allegedly designed to hide the fact that Bailey had taken bribes from Ron Cobb over the betting bill amounting to $500. The FBI had trouble locating Bailey that day.

The court also admitted testimony from former Rep. Bob Kohn (R-Charleston) that he had paid Bailey $200 on behalf of a client to get a road paved in Orangeburg County. The judge thought it evidence of Bailey's intent. Bailey objected.

Rep. Ken Bailey, under suspension in the House, relied on attorney Charlie Williams who took a defense strategy of putting up no evidence and merely attacking the government's presentations. Bailey did not testify and avoided what would have been a withering cross-examination.

Testimony revealed that Rep. Frank McBride (D-Richland) told Bailey that sting agent Ron Cobb was paying legislators to vote for the betting bill and that Bailey then, on May 9, 1990, asked Cobb for money. McBride testified against Bailey who he called "one of my best friends in the General Assembly." At the time, McBride had pleaded to conspiracy and was awaiting sentencing.

Bailey met Cobb at Cobb's office later on May 9, 1990, where Cobb promised to give Bailey $500 but said he did not have the money at the time but would get it. Cobb then asked the FBI for the money and the authorization to pay the bribe and give it to Bailey at a second meeting in five $100 bills. A camera videotaped the bribe payment and the tape was played repeatedly for the jury. Bailey also promised to try to persuade others to vote for the betting bill. Bailey did not report the $500 on his campaign disclosure forms until July 18, 1991, after he found out the FBI wanted to talk to him.

In fact, the House rejected an attempt by Bailey and others to pass the betting bill, and the bill never passed thereafter.

Even so, the $500 was a bribe and "It was really a pretty simple case," said Assistant U.S. Attorney Scott Schools.

Bailey Convicted of Bribery

The trial of Rep. Ken Bailey (D-Orangeburg) began on August 22 and ended on August 27, 1991, after the jury took only 90 minutes to convict Bailey on extortion and conspiring to extort $500 from sting lobbyist Ron Cobb in return for Bailey's support for the betting bill.

Bailey faced up to 40 years in prison and a fine of $500,000. Guidelines called for a much lower sentence. The sentencing was set for a later date.

A juror, Stephen Saylor, 22, of Lexington, after the trial, told the media that there was no doubt that Bailey sold his vote. "All the evidence was there, and spoke for itself.... We felt for the man, but we had to see justice done."

Bailey offered no defense testimony or documents and his lawyers relied on arguments that Bailey was naive and that the government's witnesses were liars.

Saylor frankly admitted that the witnesses were "real slime" but the jury believed them anyhow.

CHAPTER THIRTY FOUR

JUDGE TEE FERGUSON PLEADS GUILTY TO DRUG CRIMES AND RESIGNS FROM BENCH

Judge Tee Ferguson decided to plead guilty to drug charges involving cocaine and announced his decision on August 16, 1991. Ferguson had been convicted at trial on June 7, 1991, of public corruption dating from his service in the House of Representatives. But even as he faced the fact that he would have two criminal felony convictions, Ferguson did not resign as judge until later.

The plea was entered August 19, 1991. Eventually, Ferguson resigned on August 26, 1991.

Ferguson Borrows to Pay Legal Bills

Financially stressed by his indictment and conviction on vote-selling charges, former Rep. Tee Ferguson (D-Greenville), a suspended Circuit Court judge, reported that he had borrowed money from friends and needed a free transcript of his legal proceedings in order to prepare his appeal.

Magistrate Charles W. Gambrel reported to Judge Falcon Hawkins that Ferguson lacked the money to pay the $5,000 for the transcript. Ferguson had been suspended without pay on March 21, 1991, losing his salary of $86,606 per year. In an affidavit, Ferguson reported that he had no income, little equity in real estate, and bank account of little value. Gambrel reported that a friend had loaned Ferguson $15,000 and Ferguson's wife, Kay, had obtained $23,000 for him from lenders. He also owed $138,000 on property, a car, and taxes.

Ferguson reported that he had paid his attorney, Hemphill Pride, III, in full and planned to pay his new appellate attorney, Gaston Fairey, $15,000 with a refund from the S.C. Retirement System.

At the time of his plea, Ferguson still faced a trial for cocaine possession on five counts and one count of conspiracy to possess cocaine. Without his former source of income as a circuit judge, Ferguson could not pay his attorney.

Ferguson Announces Plea on Drug Charges

Faced with a personal financial crisis and one conviction for corruption, suspended Judge Tee Ferguson announced on August 16, 1991, that he would plead to drug charges in a hearing in Aiken, S.C., before Judge Charles E. Simons of the U.S. District Court on August 26, 1991.

This was a dramatic change of position by Ferguson who had strongly maintained his innocence ever since he was charged in March, 1991, saying, "I'm not about to go to court, any court, and admit to a lie simply out of fear of going to jail." He also had complained that he was a target because he was black and refused to resign his judicial seat even after conviction for selling his vote on June 7, 1991, for $3,000 on the betting bill. Ron Cobb told the court that Ferguson wanted the money to buy a Mercedes-Benz and planned to use his judicial position by selling favors.

The alleged cocaine possessions dated from incidents in 1987, 1988, and 1989.

Ferguson Sentencing Hearing

On August 19, 1991, Tee Ferguson wore his usual bow tie to his sentencing hearing but was hit hard by accusations from Assistant U.S. Attorney John Barton and pressed by sentencing Judge Charles E. Simons to admit his guilt.

After Ferguson's attorney, Gaston Fairey, seemed to deny that Ferguson violated the law and was only present while others used cocaine, Judge Simons told Ferguson bluntly, "You've got to admit to me that you possessed cocaine, period."

Ferguson responded, "Legally speaking...my understanding was that I was in possession."

Simons then accepted the pleas and found him guilty on all charges to which he pled. By pleading, Ferguson dodged a trial set for September 9, 1991.

The evidence did not include videotapes of Ferguson using cocaine, but only of testimony of two dubious figures, former Rep. Robert Kohn (R-Charleston) and lobbyist Ron Cobb, both of whom had admitted drug use themselves, and both had been involved in selling and buying votes by their own admission. Kohn got off on the drug charge after pleading guilty to vote selling and agreeing to help the government. Both Cobb and Kohn would have been highly impeachable witnesses for the government.

Ferguson Pleads to Drugs

The guilty plea on cocaine possession and conspiracy to possess cocaine presented two contrasting views of Ferguson's conduct. His attorney, Gaston Fairey, claimed that, "The charges came about as a result of his being in a room where several people were using cocaine. Mr. Ferguson regrets his poor judgment in dealing with people who use cocaine."

But Ferguson had made no plea bargain with the prosecution and Assistant U.S. Attorney John Barton, who had prosecuted Ferguson in his corruption conviction in June, 1991, called the Ferguson case "the most repulsive we've faced in all of Lost Trust." Barton added, "How such a corrupt drug abuser got elected in the Legislature to begin with is beyond my comprehension." Even worse, Barton observed, "And then to have risen in the esteem of his peers to the point where he got elected circuit judge. It speaks, sadly, many volumes about the way government was conducted in South Carolina." (The General Assembly elected Ferguson to the circuit court bench in April, 1990.)

Ferguson Sentencing Hearing on Drugs

The sentencing hearing of Tee Ferguson after his pleas of guilt and no contest in drug charges revealed that Ron Cobb, Robert Kohn, and Tee Ferguson had all used cocaine together while at the Town House Hotel where Cobb and Kohn lived.

U.S. Attorney Bart Daniel did not identify others who were also present and used drugs, including another lobbyist even though they had all pleaded guilty earlier in the probe.

Ferguson pleaded guilty to conspiracy and possessing cocaine on May 3, 1988, and March 21, 1989. He also pleaded no contest to possession of cocaine on January 26, March 8, and April 26, 1988.

Ferguson Refuses to Resign as Judge

Despite his conviction on August 19, 1991, of six crimes relating to cocaine possession, suspended Circuit judge Tee Ferguson refused to resign his seat. But House Speaker Bob Sheheen warned that the House was ready to act and that an impeachment resolution "has already been drawn and is sitting on my desk."

No date for sentencing on his convictions for vote selling and cocaine was set as of August 19, 1991, and Ferguson was saying he intended to appeal his corruption conviction.

Ferguson Faces Impeachment

Under the rules of the S.C. Supreme Court, the Court could not consider sanctions on Ferguson until after he was sentenced on his criminal charges. And it appeared that he could only be removed from his judicial office by an impeachment proceeding involving charges framed and voted on by the South Carolina House in a bill of impeachment and a trial before the South Carolina Senate.

Even though the process of impeachment would be difficult and time-consuming, legislative leaders started to say openly that the impeaching should be launched unless Ferguson resigned from the bench. Sen. Tom Pope (D-Newberry), chairman of the legislative committee that was charged with screening candidates for election to the judiciary, felt that action was needed. Opining on the Ferguson case, Sen. Pope, an attorney himself, said, "I don't think there's any doubt, because a guilty plea is a different category than somebody having been found guilty by a jury who technically has a right to appeal."

And, as federal prosecutor John Barton pointed out, "It's kind of hard to hold court in federal prison," alluding to the future prison term faced by Ferguson after his sentencing was completed.

Ferguson Pressured to Quit

Suspended circuit judge Tee Ferguson hung on to his seat on the bench in the face of both convictions for corruption and multiple drug charges. But in the House, he had little support and his prospects of getting impeached grew more and more grim. Even black members who had promoted Ferguson's candidacy for the bench suggested that he resign.

Rep. Danny Martin (D-Charleston), an African-American attorney who had been defense counsel in Lost Trust said, "He's pled guilty to a crime, he should not hold the judiciary hostage.... He should go ahead and resign so we can have his replacement in as early as possible." Martin also said that there was no support for Ferguson left in the House.

Speaker Bob Sheheen predicted impeachment for Ferguson if he did not quit. Charges "will be a matter of course," Sheheen said he told Ferguson in June upon his conviction. Since then, articles of impeachment had been prepared.

David Wilkins (R-Greenville), chairman of House Judiciary Committee through which such impeachment articles would have to be processed predicted, "I think it will be a clear vote. Mr. Ferguson can save himself a lot of additional public embarrassment if he goes ahead and resigns."

Facing the prospect of inevitable impeachment and removal, Tee Ferguson saw no hope. No black legislators would stick up for him due to the number and magnitude of the convictions. Sen. McKinley Washington (D-Charleston) warned Ferguson that his failure to resign would hurt the chances of other black candidates for the judiciary in the future. At the time, there were only three black judges, including Ferguson, while the total population of blacks in South Carolina was nearly a third. Washington said, "We don't have many black judges. This is the sad part of this whole scenario. A lot of folks worked hard to get Judge Ferguson elected because we needed more representation in the courts."

James Clyburn, head of the S.C. Human Affairs Commission, said he might contact Ferguson soon to ask him why he had not resigned. But Clyburn did not think Ferguson's actions hurt other blacks, saying, "I am always a bit insulted when the action of any one person is assigned to the group. I know we tend to do that."

Editorial: Ferguson Should Resign

On August 22, 1991, *The State* came out and said what everybody in South Carolina was thinking—Tee Ferguson should resign his seat as circuit court judge.

The criminal convictions just kept piling up and the political pressure on the Legislature was becoming irresistible. Ferguson would either resign or be impeached.

The State wrote: "When will Tee Ferguson come to his moral senses, muster what little character he may still have and resign his circuit judgeship?"

Pointing to Ferguson's guilty pleas on two counts of possession of cocaine and three counts of possession he did not contest, *The State* found his jury conviction for selling his vote the last straw.

Noting that all the S.C. Supreme Court could do was to suspend Ferguson, the newspaper said it was clear impeachment was the final option and action should be taken when the General Assembly went into session in January, 1992.

Ferguson had shown "an arrogant disregard for the laws he solemnly pledged to uphold as a member of the House of Representatives and, later, as a circuit judge" and he should step down, the editors urged.

Ferguson Resigns as Judge

After holding out as long as he could, suspended circuit court judge, Tee Ferguson, finally turned in his resignation from the bench just over a year after being elected by the General Assembly. In a letter of resignation on August 26, 1991, delivered to Chief Justice George Gregory one week after Ferguson pleaded guilty to cocaine possession, the judge stated that he was giving up his fight to stay on the bench.

Ferguson's attorney, Gaston Fairey, said Ferguson had decided after his convictions that he would resign "at the appropriate time." Fairey stated that, as to Ferguson, "It was never his intention to force the state to go into any kind of impeachment proceeding or anything.... That issue was resolved a long time ago in our discussions."

However, it was apparent that the House of Representatives was getting ready to take impeachment action unless Ferguson gave up. Judiciary Committee Chairman David Wilkins (R-Greenville) said that Ferguson had done the right thing for himself and the state. "I think it's important to close a chapter and get this sad episode behind us.... An impeachment process would have been fairly lengthy and would have dragged it out, and would have prolonged the agony this episode had brought us and the embarrassment it has brought."

A bizarre factor in the Judge Ferguson case was that the South Carolina Supreme Court did not have the constitutional or statutory powers to remove Ferguson as a state court judge. Chief Justice George Gregory had suspended Ferguson in March, 1991, soon after his indictment for conspiracy and selling his vote as a legislator, but the Chief Justice could not order removal. Even the suspension had not been based on any explicit provision in state laws and Gregory had claimed he took action based on what he called the inherent powers of the Supreme Court.

Then the conviction of Ferguson on the public corruption charges in early June, 1991, made the crisis even more acute as it appeared that more drastic action was needed to deal with Ferguson and the likely prospect that he would be sentenced to prison. Even so, the Chief Justice and the Court did not act to try to remove Ferguson and the crisis remained unresolved through the summer of 1991. At long last, Ferguson finally turned in his resignation.

CHAPTER THIRTY-FIVE

THE LAST LOST TRUST CASES

In the final months of 1991, the federal courts held the last trials in the Lost Trust series of cases and took the last group of guilty pleas. At the same time, appeals were moving forward to attack the trial convictions of five defendant legislators.

Sentencings were held for Reps. Blanding, Faber, McBride, Limehouse, Fant, and Gordon as well as for Clemson University administrator James Hopkins, III, businessman David Little and finally, Development Chairman Dick Greer.

The last two cases taken to their trials led to the acquittal of Rep. Tim Wilkes (D-Fairfield) on September 25, 1991, and the conviction of Sen. Bud Long (D-Horry) on November 23, 1991, for corruption.

Appeals and motions would overturn the convictions of Reps. Derrick, Blanding, Taylor, and Gordon as well as Sen. Long. Taylor and Gordon died in 1997 before retrial. Blanding and Derrick were convicted on retrial in 1999. And Long pled down in 1999 to the misdemeanor charge of lying to a federal agent.

Greer Pleads—Get No Time

On July 30, 1991, Dick Greer pleaded guilty to cocaine but was not sentenced to any prison time. He admitted cocaine possession and got a sentence of only two months in a halfway house, three years probation, and a fine of $7,700. He was a longtime friend of Gov. Carroll Campbell, a former campaign operative in Campbell's run for governor, and Chairman of the S.C. Economic Development Board.

Greer had agreed to provide damning evidence of criminal acts in the Lost Trust corruption probe. Greer revealed that Sen. Jack Lindsay, who had died in January, 1991, was implicated in public corruption in a major way. This cooperation by Greer warranted leniency, said Assistant U.S. Attorney John Barton.

Barton told the court that Greer would have testified against the late Sen. Jack Lindsay, had he lived, that Lindsay took a bribe to pass a capital gains tax cut. Greer would also have testified that Jack I. Rogers also took a similar bribe, if Rogers had not pleaded to racketeering already. Greer's help showed that only Lindsay and Rogers were to blame and the governor's office was not involved in the tax break.

Even so, Judge Falcon Hawkins hit Greer with a sentence for cocaine possession which included three years probation, two months in a halfway house, 600 hours of community service, and a fine and fees of $7,700.91. Sentence was imposed on July 31, 1991.

When Hawkins announced his original sentence on July 30, 1991, Greer's attorney, Gedney Howe, told the judge, "In the face of the government's motion to depart downward, you've departed upward." Howe then raised the question of whether the judge had the power to exceed the four month ceiling in the sentencing guidelines. But Hawkins shot back, "Six months in a halfway house is a lot different from four months in prison.... I don't suppose you're trying to tell me I ought to give him four months in federal prison instead."

On July 31, 1991, Dick Greer, buddy of bribe-master Ron Cobb, asked Judge Falcon Hawkins to reconsider the sentence that he had imposed on him for drugs on July 30, 1991. Lawyers for Greer and for the prosecution both asked Hawkins to reconsider the three years probation he had imposed on Greer along with six months confinement in a halfway house, 200 hours of community service, and $11,142 in fines. The argument was that Greer had helped the FBI after he was caught in the Operation Lost Trust scandal.

Greer was charged with only one count of possession of cocaine although the records of the court showed other uses as well. Hawkins agreed to review the sentence that was, in fact, lighter than he had contemplated assessing which was five years probation and a fine of $13,000.

Hawkins had cut the sentence down from the five years of probation he intended because he learned that the federal court sentencing guidelines required a lesser penalty. But he did not welcome the request by both sides to go easy on Greer, protesting that, "I don't know why the government chose to prosecute Mr. Greer if they wanted me to just turn him loose and say, 'Go home. You've been a bad boy.'" Then he added, glaring at the prosecution, "You should have known I wouldn't do that."

Asking on review for a more lenient sentence, the lawyers for Dick Greer tried to compare Judge Hawkins' sentence of Greer to the lighter sentence imposed on expelled Donna Moss for using cocaine, but the judge would not hear it. Moss had been given three years probation and a smaller $2,500 fine. Hawkins said that Greer was worse than Moss because he was supposed to represent the State of South Carolina in trying to recruit new business in all parts of the world.

Hawkins said he intended to make an example of corrupt public officials such as Greer and that he knew the public was very interested in what he did to the culprits, observing, "The press is out there, and in the morning everybody is going to know what happened to Dick Greer. People are going to wonder why that judge did what he did."

The federal sentencing guidelines in the Greer case allowed the court to give anything from no time to a four month prison sentence and a fine of $2,500. But because of Greer's cooperation, the U.S. Attorney asked for a downward departure from the guidelines.

Greer helped the FBI to learn that state tax officials were not pressured into lying about the tax break as rumored. "We have conclusively proven that none of that is true," Barton said and that Greer's help cut short the probe and saved time and money.

Both the prosecution and defense lawyers had asked the judge to cut down Greer's original sentence based on Greer's help to the FBI. Judge Hawkins did cut the time on a halfway house from six months to only two months, but increased the mandatory community service from his original sentence of 200 hours to 600 hours instead. Hawkins explained that the focus of the hearing was not on the bribery aspects of Lost Trust but on Greer's drug violations, saying, "Mr. Greer is here on a drug offense, and I am sentencing a drug offender."

Even so, Cobb's corruption and relationship with Greer was overhanging the case. Court records showed that a lobbyist caught in the Lost Trust sting told the FBI that Greer was present in 1988 when Cobb talked about splitting $150,000 with Sen. Lindsay when the capital gains tax cut passed. Then Cobb was caught in his illegal drug dealing and agreed to cooperate with the FBI. Strangely, however, Cobb's deal with the government said Cobb would never have to testify against Lindsay, his longtime friend and mentor.

When caught by the government in December, 1990, for his drug use, Dick Greer told federal authorities that Ron Cobb had told him that Cobb needed "more money to pay off Jack Lindsay and Jack Rogers for their help on capital gains," FBI Agent Tommy Davis told the court at Greer's sentencing hearing. Yet Greer did not reveal the information to authorities for more than a year until after Greer was caught by the FBI.

Greer would not comment to the media after his sentence was imposed in final terms on July 31, 1991. Had Greer gone to the FBI or told the media about his knowledge of corrupt dealings before the November, 1990, general elections in which his friend Carroll Campbell was a candidate, Greer's disclosure might have had an effect on the elections, but probably not much because the Democratic candidate, Sen. Theo Mitchell (D-Greenville), was such an inept opponent of Campbell.

Rep. Ennis Fant Sentenced

Rep. Ennis Fant (D-Greenville) finally gave in to prosecutors, pleading guilty to selling his vote and received a sentence in prison of 20 months and three years supervised probation in U.S. District Court on July 31, 1991. He was sentenced by Judge Falcon Hawkins. The judge also imposed community service of 200 hours on Fant.

When first indicted, Fant, a Baptist minister, had indicated that he would go to trial but then decided to plead guilty and cooperate by testifying against fellow legislators caught in corruption. Fant hoped that this would get him leniency from the court.

Fant's attorneys had said that Fant's violations were similar to Sen. Rick Lee (R-Spartanburg) who had pleaded and got merely six months in a halfway house and five years probation after his cooperation with the government. Fant testified against former House members Larry Blanding and B.J. Gordon who were both convicted of bribery on the betting bill. Fant was also expected at the time of his sentencing to testify against Tee Ferguson who was convicted at trial even though Rep. Fant was not called in the corruption prosecution.

Assistant U.S. Attorney John Barton told the court that Fant was helpful to the case and important in that Fant showed that some lawmakers were warned to report the money Cobb gave them as campaign contributions.

At his sentencing, Ennis Fant brought to court the chairman of the board of deacons in the church Fant pastored and also brought in a fellow minister who had headed the S.C. Baptist Convention. Fant's mother also joined the others asking for leniency.

But Judge Hawkins was not much moved and said, "One of my duties...is to discourage other young men from falling into the same trap as Mr. Fant." The judge also said that in Fant's testimony in the Blanding and Gordon cases, he showed less remorse than at his sentencing hearing and that Fant had not admitted any wrongdoing. Fant said he pleaded guilty and cooperated only to save himself from more punishment.

Although Fant would not comment to the media after the sentencing, Bart Daniel said he had asked for leniency to reward those who had cooperated in contrast with those who had not helped.

Blacks Allege Bias on Fant Sentence

The harsh sentence of twenty months in prison imposed on former Greenville House member Ennis Fant for bribery on the betting bill provoked criticism from blacks who alleged that he was treated worse because he was black compared to white senator Rick Lee who got only six months in a halfway house. Both took bribes on the betting bill and both helped the FBI after their apprehension.

Sen. Theo Mitchell (D-Greenville) claimed, "There is nothing different in these two men and who they are and what they did other than the color of their skin." But Bart Daniel, as prosecutor, said that Lee was more cooperative than Fant. Also, Fant pushed the betting bill more aggressively after taking money than Lee did. Lee took $2,000 and pleaded to bribery on the bill. Fant took only $1,300 but pleaded to conspiracy. Daniel said that Fant was more like white House member Danny Winstead who lied and got 30 months in prison.

But Sen. Mitchell, a lawyer, pointed out that, in fact, Fant did cooperate with authorities and testified against Blanding and Gordon, whereas Winstead did not. "Either the Constitution stands for something or it stands for nothing. It guarantees protection of all."

Rev. J.M. Flemming called on the Greenville community to protest the harsh twenty month sentence imposed on Rep. Ennis Fant, saying the matter was not just the black community's fault. Fant had represented a black district in Greenville.

Flemming said that Greenville community leaders planned to talk with both of South Carolina's U.S. senators—Fritz Hollings and Strom Thurmond—about disparities in the operation of the judicial system and the determination of community leaders to make the system fair to all.

Fant Sentence Criticized as Racist

Criticism of the sentence inflicted on former Rep. Fant (D-Greenville) by the court on July 31, 1991, mounted among blacks on the grounds that Fant was treated more harshly than white Lost Trust defendants. The court gave Fant a total of 20 months in prison on his guilty plea to conspiracy to sell his vote to Ron Cobb. Two white legislators—former Sen. Rick Lee (R-Spartanburg) and former Robert Brown (D-Marion) had both pleaded to corruption and had been given six months in a halfway house.

Sen. Theo Mitchell (D-Greenville), the 1990 Democratic candidate for governor, charged that, "It's appalling that this would happen in the United States of America in the latter part of the 20th century, that such blatant racism had raised its head in such a nasty fashion from a man who is sworn to uphold the law and the Constitution of the United States."

Some two hundred people marched with Fant in Greenville to protest the sentence. Sen. Herbert Fielding (D-Charleston) said people across the state were concerned about the apparent inequity.

Judge Falcon Hawkins who imposed the sentence did not defend himself, but the U.S. Attorney Bart Daniel said Fant had not been very cooperative, whereas Lee and Brown had. Daniel pointed out that uncooperative white defendant, former Rep. Danny Winstead (R-Charleston) was sentenced to 30 months in prison. Even so, Rev. J.M. Flemming, who organized a Greenville protest against the Fant sentence claimed, "What it is doing is pushing the black community back to where we were in the '50s and '60s." And Sen. David Thomas (R-Greenville) worried, "It certainly does give the appearance that there was prejudice...in the judge's mind when he gave such a disparate sentence."

Judge Affirms Convictions of Blanding and Gordon

Spurning a request to reject the convictions of Reps. Larry Blanding (D-Orangeburg) and B.J. Gordon (D-Williamsburg), Judge Hawkins finalized his order. The decision was filed on August 7, 1991, and disposed of the first such request to throw out bribery convictions since the U.S. Supreme Court ruled in *McCormick* in May, 1991, that the Hobbs Act's anti-corruption provisions required a showing of quid pro quo in order to prove bribery.

Hawkins ruled that the evidence in both cases showed a quid pro quo and that the money was given to Blanding and Gordon to buy their vote in return, a criminal transaction under the new *McCormick* standard. However, some of the other Lost Trust cases that had gone to trial and resulted in convictions under the Hobbs Act would be successfully appealed and ordered for new trials based on the *McCormick* case which required a quid pro quo showing.

Ken Bailey Trial to Start

Jury selection for suspended Rep. Ken Bailey (D-Orangeburg) was set to start on August 21, 1991, on charges that he took a bribe of $450 to support the gambling betting bill.

Gordon and Blanding Set for Sentencing

Convicted Reps. Larry Blanding (D-Sumter) and B.J. Gordon (D-Williamsburg) were set for sentencing in Charleston on September 10, 1991.

Little Set for Sentencing

Spartanburg businessman, David D. Little, was set for sentencing on September 11, 1991, in Charleston.

Multiple Sentences Set for September 12, 1991

The date of September 12, 1991, was set for sentencing proceedings in U.S. District Court in Columbia for multiple defendants who had pleaded. Former Rep. James Faber (D-Richland), lobbyist Tom Collins, former highway commissioner Ronnie Crow, and David Hawkins, former aide to Gov. Campbell, were all to be sentenced on that date.

B.J. Gordon Sentencing

In early September, 1991, faced with a possible sentence of 40 years in prison and a $500,000 fine on his conviction for bribery at trial, Rep. B.J. Gordon (D-Williamsburg) appeared calm before going to court to hear the judge's decision.

Interviewed at his hometown of Kingstree, South Carolina, a small farming community on the mainline railroad from New York to Florida, Gordon told the *Associated Press*, "I live by the prayer of serenity, knowing they are things I cannot change."

In March, 1991, the jury had convicted Gordon of taking a bribe of $1,000 to support the betting bill in violation of the Hobbs Act and also of criminal conspiracy, the cumulative penalties amounting to 40 years and the huge fine.

Locals in Kingstree who had known Gordon as a prominent black preacher and politician for years felt a sense of regret that Gordon had gone down. Mayor Jimmy Williams said, "B.J. was involved in everything here. He was certainly a person you could go to if you had a problem or needed help and it's sad that it has come down to him being sentenced to prison.... And all over $1,000, somehow it doesn't seem right."

Prosecution Blames Gordon for Unindicted Crimes

Prosecutors filed a motion asking Judge Falcon Hawkins to consider matters not in the record of B.J. Gordon's trial and conviction. For example, it was alleged that Gordon had made a "personal loan" to himself from public funds he was supposed to use for a center for the retarded which he operated. Gordon also tried to get his 6 year old daughter put on the payroll of the county recreation commission where his wife already worked. The motion said such evidence showed, "Again the defendant is using his position as a public official to improperly reap personal benefit on himself, his family, and his friends."

Adverting to the $1,000 bribe given to Gordon, the government's motion read, "The State of South Carolina has suffered greatly because of the actions of those elected officials, including this defendant, who chose to sell the public's welfare to the highest bidder in Operation Lost Trust."

Gordon's attorney, Lionel Lofton, said the new prosecution allegations were the invention of Gordon's political enemy, George Richardson, county recreation director, who had opposed Gordon twice and lost in elections for Gordon's House seat.

The prosecution's unusual motion asking Judge Hawkins to consider in sentencing Gordon matters for which he had not even been criminally charged, let alone convicted, stated that Gordon's abuses in public office constituted "activity which will otherwise go unpunished that the United States asks the court to condemn."

In fact, Gordon had been the target of previous criminal investigations which had not ended with charges being filed. Some of the probes related to a gasahol business that was subsidized with government funds which resulted in Gordon receiving $50,000 in insurance benefits from the death of an employee, Eddie McClary. Gordon also gave himself interest-free loans from the Gordon Developmental Center and took $12,500 in cash from a state grant that was supposed to be used to pay for a heating unit for the Center. A publicly funded day care center in Hemingway, S.C., under Gordon's auspices for one year, spent $25,000 on expenses unrelated to the day care operations.

Prosecutor Barton said that this sort of activity by Gordon was borderline and even though it did not warrant prosecution, it provided aggravating information which supported the government's motion that Barton said, "cries out for upward departure."

Sentencing Departures Requested by U.S. in Gordon Case

U.S. Attorney Bart Daniel's office asked for departures from federal sentencing guidelines in several of the Lost Trust cases. In some cases, the departures requested were upward asking for more punishment and in others the request was downward asking for lesser punishments.

In the B.J. Gordon case, the government asked Judge Falcon Hawkins to consider Gordon's behavior pattern and actions even in cases where no criminal charges were lodged and punish

Gordon more than indicted by the guidelines. In the cases of former Highway Commissioner Ronnie Crow and former Democratic state representatives Frank McBride and Jim Faber who helped the prosecution, the government recommended lesser penalties than those found in the guidelines. On the other hand, the prosecution asked for more punishment for former representative Paul Derrick, a Lexington Republican. Faber and McBride pleaded to bribery and testified against Ken Bailey.

The reasons stated by the prosecution were, in addition to the alleged dubious history of B.J. Gordon, that Crow had contacted the FBI shortly after subpoenas were served on targets and agreed to cooperate with the probe. Crow also testified before a grand jury and was "one of the first cooperating targets to offer testimony." Prosecutors said that Crow helped to obtain a conviction for racketeering against Jack I. Rogers.

B.J. Gordon Sentence Delayed

U.S. Attorney Bart Daniel and his assistant, John Barton, asked Judge Hawkins to throw the book at convicted corruptionist Rep. B.J. Gordon in a hearing held in federal court in Charleston on September 10, 1991.

Daniel asked that the sentencing guidelines be disregarded as not applying to the great magnitude of Gordon's abuse of office saying, Gordon has "repeatedly and consistently abused his position of authority and influence in Williamsburg County to the detriment of that county and the State of South Carolina, and did so for his personal financial benefit." Prosecutor John Barton told sentencing Judge Hawkins that, "We're saying we have evidence of three decades of abuse by B.J. Gordon, and we're going to offer that evidence to the court."

Judge Hawkins responded by delaying the imposition of sentence from September 10, 1991, when it was expected, until thirty days later to give Gordon's lawyer, Lionel Lofton, time to respond to the government's accusations that Gordon had been a career crooked politician who had intimidated law enforcement into ignoring his abuses.

Judge Falcon Hawkins reacted to the demands by prosecutors Daniel and Barton, that he sentence defendant B.J. Gordon for alleged crimes for which he had not yet been charged, by giving Gordon's attorney 30 additional days to prepare a response before sentence imposition. Hawkins said that a sentence for uncharged crimes would set a new legal precedent.

Lofton called Gordon "a prince of a guy" and ridiculed the smearing of Gordon by Daniel and Barton as "trash" and "totally incredible." Lofton said that he would fight any effort to give Gordon a twenty year sentence when the longest sentence to date was that of six and a half years imposed on Luther Taylor.

The hostile exchange between Lofton and the prosecutors was a second act in a drama featuring legal combat in the trials which convicted Gordon and Rep. Larry Blanding of conspiracy and extortion.

Hawkins said the prosecution papers asking for an upward departure from guidelines in the Gordon case had been filed just a few days before the September 10, 1991, sentencing hearing and more time was needed to consider the matter.

Gordon Sentence Proposal Attacked

The proposal of the U.S. Attorney that convicted corruptionist B.J. Gordon be sentenced to twenty years in prison based not only on the crimes on which he was convicted but also on other unproven allegations of abuse of office was denounced by Gordon's attorney as unconstitutional.

In fact, however, federal judges did have discretion to deviate from federal sentencing guidelines which called for only 41 months of prison time in Gordon's case, if strictly followed. Judges in the early 1990s did follow the guidelines on some 85% of criminal sentences. In 1990, only in three percent of such cases did judges give more time than the guidelines indicated.

Gordon had been the target of repeated criticisms during his 18 year service in the South Carolina House but had never previously been charged for any suspicious situations.

Gordon's attorney, Lionel Lofton, said that, "Nobody else has been treated this way. I don't see where this is fair." The South Carolina Civil Liberties Union also protested and its director, Steve Bates observed, "Punishing people for crimes they have not been convicted of committing is un-American and unconstitutional."

Prosecution's Proposed Sentence Criticized

Legal experts from outside B.J. Gordon's defense team joined Gordon's attorneys in casting doubt on U.S. Attorney Bart Daniel's motion for enhanced sentencing above the 1987 federal guidelines. Prominent criminal attorney, John Delgado, observed, "I'm not saying that B.J. hasn't dodged some bullets before, but if they have anything, don't you think they would have indicted him before."

Kevin Gray, a political activist at *The Black News*, an African-American newspaper in Columbia said, "Whatever you think of B.J. Gordon, to sentence him to crimes he hasn't been convicted of is outrageous, irresponsible, and dangerous."

Some comments noted that the African-American Gordon seemed to be treated more harshly than the white James Holderman sentenced to house arrest in his ocean-side house in Ponte Vedra Beach, Florida. Kevin Gray clearly pointed out the difference and even John Montgomery, Dean of the University of South Carolina School of Law also noted the difference, commenting that, "There's a legitimate fairness question, to say nothing of the fact that one is white and one is black." Dick Harpootlian, who as prosecutor had convicted Holderman, opined that as to the prosecution motion, the "solution isn't to let B.J. Gordon go. It's to yank Holderman back in."

However, Harpootlian did say that the court could, in fact, consider prior bad acts noting, "It does appear that he did over time use his office for personal gain."

Another complication was that upward departures in sentencing were not only rare, but were automatically appealed.

The State Editorial on Gordon Criticizes Prosecution Motion

The State in an editorial of September 13, 1991, the day after his sentencing to prison, spiked Gordon as "a preacher man who hides his halo under a homburg," adding he "is no saint."

The editors pointed out that "His name cropped up in almost every tale of skullduggery that has surfaced in his Pee Dee fiefdom over the past several decades, and that county has had more than its share." Even so, Gordon dodged the law and "for years the Reverend had a Teflon coating. Investigations into his questionable affairs never produced prosecutions."

Questioning the unusual motion of the prosecution to ask the judge to impose more punishment than found in the 1987 federal guidelines, *The State* wrote, "the federal prosecutors...tried to make up for lost time." Even so, the editors found no justification for Hawkins to impose sentence above the guidelines, arguing that while Hawkins had taken the motion under advisement for 30 days before he would sentence Gordon, in the end, the judge should do the right thing. "Judge Falcon Hawkins is faced with a novel situation. But, to us, the solution is simple. The Constitution talks about it. It's called due process. No extra convictions; no extra hard time. Even for B.J. Gordon."

Blanding Sentenced

Former Rep. Larry Blanding (D-Sumter) was sentenced to serve 37 months in prison for his conviction at trial of vote selling. The sentence was imposed in the U.S. District Courthouse in Charleston by Judge Falcon Hawkins on September 10, 1991.

Blanding sat quietly in the courtroom and came forward to accept his sentence which included not only 37 months in prison but also three years of probation and 200 hours of community service. In addition, he was ordered to treatment for alcohol and drug addictions. His sentence was pursuant to a guilty plea on three charges.

His prison sentence was set to begin on October 28, 1991.

Blanding made no comment at trial and no opposition nor protest by Blanding's attorney was made.

Limehouse Gets Prison Time

Former Rep. Tom Limehouse (R-Charleston) went to the U.S. District Courthouse in Charleston to accept sentence on his guilty plea to two counts on September 11, 1991. Judge Falcon Hawkins imposed a sentence of twenty months and a fine of $15,000.

Limehouse chose to make a statement to the court and said, in an emotional voice, that he wanted to "publicly apologize to friends, family and the people." Some three dozen people including family members were present for the proceeding.

Limehouse had pleaded in December, 1990, to conspiracy to accept a bribe on the betting bill and to tampering with a witness. Pursuant to the plea agreement, Limehouse had a third charge dismissed by the government. He faced a total of 33 months in prison and a fine of $75,000 based on federal sentencing guidelines.

Prosecutors urged leniency and a lighter sentence based on Limehouse's full cooperation and his testimony against Rep. Paul Derrick (R-Lexington).

Limehouse's attorney, Andy Savage, told the court that his client was "humbled and humiliated" and that "He didn't play down his involvement. He didn't sugarcoat his involvement." Savage also noted that his client withdrew as a candidate for re-election after his indictment and closed his law practice.

Faber and McBride Get One Year in Prison

Even after pleading guilty and fully cooperating with the prosecution, former House Democrats James Faber and Frank McBride were hit with one year in prison by Judge Falcon Hawkins on their convictions for public corruption. In spite of the leniency pleas of the prosecution, the Judge dashed the hopes of the crowd of supporters who packed the courtroom, and imposed time. Hawkins added three years probation.

The federal guidelines called for a maximum of 33 months in prison and a fine of $60,000 without any consideration of cooperation which could be used to reduce penalties. Sentence was imposed on September 12, 1991.

Defense attorney I.S. Leevy Johnson, an African-American lawyer and a lifelong member of the small black community in Columbia, took off his glasses and wiped his eyes, telling the media that his clients Faber and McBride were also lifelong friends. Johnson then told the court in a shaking voice and backed by amens from teachers, neighbors, and clergymen in the courtroom, "How can your Honor in good conscience allow a man like Rick Lee to come into this court and plead guilty to an offense more serious than these men have committed and give them six months in a halfway house, while these men go to prison."

Controversy Over Faber and McBride Sentences Erupts

The racial differences between Sen. Rick Lee, a white Republican, and Reps. Jim Faber and Frank McBride, black Democrats, were bound to provoke criticism because the lenient sentence of Lee to six months house arrest for bribery and the sentences of Faber and McBride to a year in prison were so much harsher.

When attorney I.S. Leevy Johnson pointed out the fact to Judge Falcon Hawkins at the Faber and McBride sentencing hearing, Hawkins was highly defensive saying, "If there's a disparity, it's because I didn't give Rick Lee a higher sentence." Then he added, "But if I had done that, your clients would have gotten higher sentences, too."

Hawkins went on to say that the Lee sentence was based on a secret hearing that would eventually be disclosed. The judge retorted to Johnson, "I don't mean to call you down in public, but when you talk about Rick Lee, you're talking about something you don't know anything about." Hawkins added, he was tired of being criticized for alleged racial bias and would not hear it anymore.

Hawkins had handed out prison time to others convicted in the scandal and had recently given white Republican Tom Limehouse twenty months in prison. However, whites Rick Lee and Robert Brown (D-Marion) had avoided prison time.

Blacks Complain of Racial Bias in Sentences

Black leaders reacted to the prison sentences imposed on former Richland Democratic state representatives Frank McBride and James Faber by claiming that they were treated more harshly than white legislators already sentenced to non-jail punishments.

Richland County Councilwoman, Bernice Scott, expressed outrage that the federal court had given McBride and Faber prison time when she expected them to be sentenced to a halfway house instead. Scott announced on September 18, 1991, the she and 11 other black Richland officials planned an effort to pressure federal judges to treat black defendants more fairly.

Scott and Sen. Kay Patterson (D-Richland) predicted violence if black legislators continued to be treated worse than whites in the Lost Trust cases. "We're trying to head that off," Scott said, claiming that she was trying to explain the justice community to the black community.

A total of eight black legislators had been charged, including three of the five black legislators of Richland County, all of whom had been sentenced to prison—Luther Taylor, McBride, and Faber. McBride and Faber had cooperated with the prosecution.

Tom Collins Pleads to Drugs

Former Hitachi computer equipment lobbyist, Tom Collins, had pleaded guilty to cocaine possession on May 30, 1991, and came up for sentencing on September 12, 1991, on the same day as James Faber and Frank McBride were sent to prison.

Collins was represented by attorney William Bannister who said that his client was not a major figure in the Lost Trust sting, but "got caught in the very wide net" of the probe."

Judge Falcon Hawkins sentenced Collins to one year in prison, suspended, and two years of probation. In addition, he got 150 hours of community service and was obligated to enroll in treatment for addictions to drugs and alcohol.

Hawkins Gets House Arrest

On September 23, 1991, David Hawkins, 45, former aide to Gov. Carroll Campbell, pleaded to obstruction of justice in Lost Trust and was given six months of house arrest and two years of probation for obstruction of justice. He was indicted for telling Rep. Bob Kohn that the FBI was investigating Ron Cobb at a time when Cobb was working undercover to sting Kohn and others in the probe of State House corruption.

Hawkins had earlier been a member of the South Carolina House where he was the ringleader of the infamous "Fat and Ugly Caucus" which pressured lobbyists for free meals and other gratuities before it was disbanded on the order of Speaker Bob Sheheen in 1987. Eleven of the 14 legislators convicted of corruption in Lost Trust at the time of Hawkins' sentencing were members of the notorious Caucus.

David Little, III, Sentenced

Spartanburg businessman, David D. Little, III, appeared in U.S. District Court and was sentenced to three years probation on October 1, 1991, on charges of possession of cocaine. His crimes were exposed as part of the Lost Trust probe.

Little apologized to Judge Falcon Hawkins before his sentence and said, "I don't know what to say. I'm sorry for the mess and I'm sorry for taking your time."

Little owned a business called Health Management Systems, Inc. which managed nursing homes.

He was facing a maximum sentence of four months in prison.

Commissioner Crow Sentenced

Sentence was imposed on former South Carolina Highway Commissioner, Wade "Ronnie" Crow, on October 3, 1991, for one count aiding and abetting extortion. He admitted he helped former Speaker Pro Tem Jack I. Rogers get a payment from a lobbyist by coercive means.

The Court imposed a sentence of $17,411 and six months in a halfway house for his crimes. The judge rejected probation.

Crow was a lawyer and businessman, age 52, from Bennettsville, S.C., the hometown of Jack I. Rogers and Sen. Jack Lindsay, both entangled in the Lost Trust scandal and its fallout.

Sting Racial Bias Alleged

Marching demonstrators protested an alleged disparity based on race in the sentences imposed on those convicted in Lost Trust. In a gathering in which marchers carried signs reading, "We Shall Overcome" and "Halfway House for Whites, Jailhouse for Blacks," the protest heard Sen. Kay Patterson (D-Richland) complain that blacks were treated unfairly by federal judges.

Patterson told the rally of some 200 in front of the State House that, "We are here because we are tired of the double standards in our judicial system." Patterson went on to complain, "It seems that our judges tell us if you're white, you're right. If you are black, get on back." The remarks provoked a chant of "yes" from the demonstrators.

The march started on the morning of Saturday, October 5, 1991, at the U.S. District Courthouse on Assembly and Richland Streets in downtown Columbia and proceeded a half mile south to the State House grounds.

Richland County Councilwoman, Bernice Scott, opened by saying to the small gathering that, "We're not asking for special favors," but then added, "We just ask for equal justice. And that's not too much to ask for."

As the sting progressed, it indicted more and more black legislators, a total of 8 out of a total of 18 legislators. Forty-four percent (44%) of all legislators indicted were black, but only 12 percent (12%) of the legislators in the 170 member General Assembly were black.

At first blacks seemed to think that Bart Daniel's actions reflected racial bias. The when Judge Falcon Hawkins started jailing blacks, black leaders seemed to feel that the judge was biased as well. Hawkins, in fact, had sentenced to prison three black legislators who had cooperated with the prosecution. They were former Reps. Ennis Fant, Frank McBride, and James Faber. (All three of them attended the rally.) On the other hand, two white legislators who had also cooperated got six months in a halfway house (Sen. Lee and Rep. Brown). Two whites who had cooperated also got prison time, but they were both attorneys (Reps. Kohn and Limehouse).

At the October 5th State House protest claiming racial bias against black defendants, Rev. William M. Bowman told the small crowd that Fant, McBride, and Faber were innocent: "These men didn't do anything wrong. But you know, they had been in office, and they couldn't get them out, and they were going to be chairmen of committees." This amounted to a claim that there was a white man's conspiracy to purge blacks from the State House and keep them out of leadership positions, even though, in fact, the blacks at issue had little seniority in the House and relatively little power to affect policy-making.

Rep. Levola Taylor (D-Richland) told the State House rally that the all black crowd should write their senators in Washington, Strom Thurmond and Fritz Hollings, to complain about the sentences imposed on blacks compared to whites and to ask for an inquiry by Congress. She also promised to continue focusing on the racial disparity of sentencing issues she alleged existed. Rep. Taylor had just been elected to replace Jim Faber after he was expelled from the House on conviction of felony in the scandal.

Another protestor from lower Richland County where Faber had had his district told the rally that, "We just don't see justice at all." Cynthia Brown went on to say, "I don't want to worry about people trying to do me in. I thought this was America. We're not going to go no place. We're going to make it right here."

Limehouse Law License Suspended

On October 29, 1991, The South Carolina Supreme Court temporarily suspended the state law license of convicted corruptionist former Rep. Tom Limehouse who had entered a guilty plea and was sentenced to 20 months in prison and a fine of $15,000. He was set to report to prison in December, 1991, according to his lawyer, Andy Savage.

Limehouse closed his practice in Summerville in December, 1990, after he pleaded guilty to extortion and witness tampering in the Lost Trust scandal.

The suspension was effective until the Board of Commissioners on Grievances and Discipline would evaluate the case and decide on whether to disbar Limehouse and would make a recommendation to the Supreme Court an appropriate action against Limehouse.

Hopkins Sentenced

Former Clemson University administrator, James V. Hopkins, III, was sentenced on November 2, 1991, to three years probation, a fine of $1,000 and 150 hours of community service for possession of cocaine. Hopkins' sentence was reduced because he cooperated with the Lost Trust investigation into drugs and corruption in state government. Judge Falcon Hawkins, who imposed sentence, praised Hopkins for his help into turning his arrest for drugs into public service by helping the probe.

FBI Special Agent Mike Clemens, head of the FBI sting operation, testified that Hopkins helped find evidence in the scandal.

Gordon Opposes Sentence Recommendation

On November 1, 1991, B.J. Gordon's attorney, Lionel Lofton, refuted the prosecution's demand to impose an enhanced sentence on B.J. Gordon for uncharged allegation of abuse of public office as unprecedented in South Carolina. Lofton pointed to a case from the 8th Circuit in which prosecutors made a similar demand that a man charged with one count of theft be given a more severe penalty because he could have been charged with additional crimes but was not. The trial judge refused saying that the government could have charged more crimes if they wanted a greater sentence. The 8th Circuit affirmed.

But prosecutors claimed the additional evidence of abuses was like any other evidence presented in sentencing and they wanted the judge to determine that other abuses had happened even though they were not asking the judge to convict. In fact, federal guidelines did allow consideration of a convict's reputation and character in the sentencing process.

The specific background evidence the prosecution wanted to present was that Gordon had been investigated in 1987 for misuse of public funds put through Gordon's Developmental Center for retarded adults which he operated in his home county.

Gordon denounced the probe saying it was instigated by his political enemies. He also claimed that the funds had not, in fact, been under his control. Lofton said that Gordon did not dispute the allegation because it did not affect the sentence, but prosecutors treated that as an admission.

Gordon Gets Evidence

Judge Falcon Hawkins granted B.J. Gordon's request that he receive from prosecutors all evidence they had in support of their efforts to convince the court to impose harsh penalties on Gordon because of an alleged pattern of abuses even though the abuses had not been criminally charged at the time of the sentencing hearing.

Gordon had been convicted in March, 1991, of conspiracy and extortion in the sting. According to federal sentencing guidelines, the crimes for which Gordon was convicted called for 41 months. But the prosecution claimed more time was justified because Gordon had "repeatedly and consistently abused his position of authority and influence in Williamsburg County...for his personal financial gain."

However, Judge Hawkins cast doubt on the demand that he weigh uncharged allegations and also worried about exposing grand jury information about Gordon, saying that he thought such information should be kept secret, otherwise, if it were opened to everybody, "the grand jury would do just as well to go over to Williams-Brice Stadium and conduct their hearings over the public address system."

Prosecutors explained that they did not want to put Gordon on trial in his home county, Williamsburg, because they thought it would be difficult to convict him there. (In fact, there was no federal courthouse in Williamsburg County.) They also did not want to charge Gordon for fear of revealing the sting too soon as the probe remained unfinished. (In fact, there would be no more indictments in the Lost Trust investigations.)

But since the prosecution, as demanded by John Barton, insisted on trying to include uncharged actions, the judge said he had to release the file on Gordon.

Fant Asks to Stay Out of Jail

Former Rep. Ennis Fant (D-Greenville) on November 20, 1991, asked the court to allow him to delay serving his twenty month sentence in prison until his appeal was decided by the 4th U.S. Circuit Court of Appeals in Richmond, Virginia. Fant had been sentenced on July 30, 1991, and had been on unsecured bond since October, 1990, in conjunction with an indictment and conviction on charges of conspiring to take a bribe of $1,300 to vote for the racing bill.

Fant's sentence had been enhanced because the court was told that he had obstructed justice by reporting the bribe as a legitimate campaign contribution. Fant's attorney, B.O. "Tommy" Thomason argued that the additional penalty should not have been imposed.

In August, 1991, Fant had made a request of the trial court that his sentence be reduced and corrected, but that request had been denied.

Appeal Rules for Closed Jury Selection

4th Circuit Court of Appeals in Richmond, Virginia ruled on October 7, 1991, that the decision of Judge Falcon Hawkins to select jurors behind closed courthouse doors was not a violation of the U.S. Constitution. Hawkins' closed-door proceedings in jury selection was at issue in the cases of black House members Luther Taylor, Larry Blanding, and B.J. Gordon. Hawkins had ruled that closing the selection was permissible when there was a possibility that those called for jury service would lie about their ability to be fair if they had to do so in open court.

Although this might have been viewed as a reasonable way to weed out prospective jurors who were racially biased and had preconceived notions about guilt, the 4th Circuit said judges were limited in their ability to close courtrooms and that Hawkins, himself, had created conditions which virtually mandated the closing of the doors and exclusion of the press.

The Appeals Court faulted Hawkins for not holding a hearing before he promised potential sting jurors confidentiality in the selection process. The hearing should have determined whether he should and could exclude the media from the selection.

Hawkins had, in fact, distributed questionnaires to potential jurors and had promised them that their answers would be confidential. That promise was the basis for the appeal filed on behalf of the South Carolina Press Association and nine of its members attacking the secrecy.

The appeal of the secret jury selection came too late to affect the trials of Luther Taylor, Larry Blanding, and B.J. Gordon, all of whom were convicted before the 4th Circuit ruled.

The appeal also related to the jury selection process for the trial of Rep. Paul Derrick (R-Lexington), but in that case, Judge Hawkins called a hearing on the issue of closing the jury selection and then decided to do so. Derrick was also convicted.

The 4th Circuit found that the Lost Trust cases were so provocative that they warranted special treatment in that they related to indictments for bribery and narcotics. The Court said that the "prosecutions arose out of a 'sting operation' and there are film and videotape recordings of many of the illegal acts." The 4th Circuit also pointed to the racial bias issue, finding that "Certain defendants claim that they are being persecuted in addition to being prosecuted because of their race, and that a disproportionately large number of black legislators have been targeted for prosecution."

In view of the subject and the bias questions, the court needed to examine the prospective jurors for partiality. But the media wanted to know who the jurors were so they would know who to seek out for post-trial interviews about how the jury decided the case.

The 4th Circuit ruling was written by Judge Robert F. Chapman for a unanimous panel. The opinion read: "We agree with the district court that under the very unusual circumstances of these cases, no reasonable alternatives to closure will adequately protect the fair trial rights of the accused." Under the Sixth Amendment, weighing the rights of the defendant against the First Amendment speech and press rights of the media and public, the court found that the defendant's interest was superior to that of the media. Chapman wrote, "The right of the press to access criminal proceedings is presumed, but it is qualified because it must yield to a defendant's Sixth Amendment right to a fair trial."

Attorney Jay Bender, who represented the South Carolina Press Association in the appeal, argued that the sting litigation was of great public interest and the media had a strong interest in observing the jury selection. But the three judge panel held that if the judge held a hearing on the expulsion issue, he could find it necessary to deny the media and the public access in order to protect the defendant's rights. Bender noted that the opinion might be relevant in the trial of Sen. Bud Long which would follow late in 1991.

Sting Cost $1 Million

On September 26, 1991, the government revealed that the cost of Operation Lost Trust sting to date amounted to more than $1 million just to pay for prosecutors and investigators. In addition, more taxpayer money had to be spent to pay for the cost of operating two grand jury probes of 23 grand jurors each as well as court clerks, court reporters, U.S. Marshals, law clerks, judges, probation officers, trial jurors, witnesses, and prison costs. And travel costs and expenses for persons involved had to be paid.

Attorney John McIntosh, who handled the budget of the prosecutor's office, did not know the exact amount and would not even try to guess what it was. However, McIntosh and FBI spokesman, Charlie Shepard of the Columbia office said that the FBI spent some 17,000 to 20,000 hours in the Lost Trust probe which lasted a total of 27 months, and much of that time was used to set up the actual bribery sting centered on Ron Cobb. That much time would cost some $400,000 according to an estimate by the *Spartanburg Herald-Journal* newspaper based on FBI salaries of $50,000 a year for each agent.

In addition, the U.S. Attorney's office spent some 8,800 hours on the Lost Trust scandal since 1989; the total cost estimated by the *Herald-Journal* of staff salaries was some $200,000. And Judge Falcon Hawkins who spent most of his time since July, 1991, on Lost Trust and earned an annual salary of $125,000.

Sting agent Ron Cobb was paid $80,000 and the FBI spent a total of $7,000 to rent an office in the AT&T Building for Cobb which he used to hand out bribe money on a hidden television camera.

Each trial cost some $37,000 and the total number of jury trials would, in the end, be seven for a total of eight legislators—Blanding and Gordon were the only defendants to be tried together from the House and Sen. Bud Long was the only senator to go to trial at the end of 1991. All the rest of the legislators, lobbyists, businessmen and state employees tendered guilty pleas.

The cost of the grand juries was kept secret but it was known that two grand juries of 23 jurors each convened for many days and were paid $79 per day for subsistence and $40 per day per juror for attending the grand jury sessions.

The cost of future appeals and retrials could not be calculated in 1991, but would include litigation continuing until the last three defendants were convicted in 1999. There were no further appeals in Lost Trust cases after 1999.

South Carolina After Lost Trust

One of the big questions as Lost Trust came to an end with the last two trials of Rep. Wilkes and Sen. Long was whether there would ever be such a big scandal again in South Carolina. Speaking on September 26, 1991, U.S. Attorney Bart Daniel thought it unlikely as his staff was already overloaded with criminal cases.

Daniel said that his office was concerned that they clean up the corruption at the State House while they could. "We were really worried that we would go to our graves with a dirty, dirty, secret," Daniel remarked to the Columbia Forum, a group of the Chamber of Commerce, adding, "and it would be business as usual over there [the State House] for another 100 years."

CHAPTER THIRTY SIX

REP. TIM WILKES' TRIAL ENDS IN ACQUITTAL

The trial of Rep. Tim Wilkes began on September 16, 1991, in Columbia in U.S. District Court. Wilkes was represented by one of South Carolina's best criminal lawyers, Gedney Howe of Charleston. The trial proved to be a contest of litigators' skills as well as of the application of the law.

Jurors Seated in Wilkes Trial

Even as the Legislature and Gov. Carroll Campbell haggled over his terms for calling a special session to reform public ethics in South Carolina the second to last Lost Trust defendant, Rep. Tim Wilkes, went to trial.

Nine jurors were seated on September 16, 1991. The rest were to be selected on the following day, including three more plus three alternates.

Wilkes, who was white, was charged with extortion under the Hobbs Act for taking a bribe from Ron Cobb to vote for the betting bill. The prosecution's evidence included videotapes of Cobb giving Wilkes $1,000 in cash on April 19, 1990, and another $500 in cash on May 10, 1990.

Wilkes' defense was expected before trial to be that he took cash as a campaign contribution and not as a bribe. Wilkes was only the seventh of a total of 28 defendants to go to trial. The first six to go to trial were all convicted by juries.

The extortion charges against Rep. Tim Wilkes carried a maximum penalty of 20 years in prison, three years of supervised release, and fine of $250,000.

The jurors seated on the first day included six whites and three blacks. The jurors in the Wilkes trial came from many parts of the state of South Carolina and they had a variety of educational and occupational backgrounds, including high school and college graduates and textile, retail, teaching, and welding jobs.

Some of those who were excused had followed the news stories about Lost Trust, of which there had been an enormous amount in print and on television and radio. Others excused included those employed in law enforcement or related thereto. One women was excused because she felt nervous about passing judgment on a criminal defendant.

Wilkes Trial Begins

Wilkes' lawyer, Gedney Howe, got off to a fast start on the first day of trial of September 17, 1991, when he said in opening that his client was innocent and blamed lobbyist Ron Cobb for giving Wilkes two payments of $1,000 and $500.

Sheri Lydon opened for the government by saying the prosecution would introduce into evidence videotapes showing Wilkes taking a bribe on the betting bill and then other evidence showing Wilkes tried to cover it all up. Lydon told the jury, "You will hear Ron Cobb hire the defendant to help out on the pari-mutuel bill." She then added, "When the time came for the defendant to just say no, he said yes."

Howe appealed for the jurors' sympathy by painting Wilkes as just a poor kid who grew up without a father and worked hard all of his life. Howe claimed that Cobb and the FBI lured Wilkes into the sting. Further, he said that Wilkes had always supported the betting bill and that made it easy for him to say he would support it some more. Saying "Ron's the spider" and referring to the short-statured Wilkes as "Timmy" and "little Timmy," Howe noted Wilkes had only been in the House for two terms and was naïve. Howe also dressed Wilkes in plain clothes unlike his usual flashy dress.

The prosecution planned to call not only Cobb but also convicted former representatives Robert Brown and Bob Kohn. Kohn had introduced Wilkes to Cobb at a party for the betting bill.

Wilkes Defense Strategy

Gedney Howe planned to counter the prosecution's witnesses and videotapes with a list of witnesses from Wilkes' hometown of Winnsboro in Fairfield County, a small farming and forestry community in central South Carolina. Howe also indicated on the opening day of the Wilkes trial that he would bring in campaign experts who advised Wilkes to take the money in cash from Ron Cobb and who helped with his campaign. Howe also said that Wilkes would take the stand and "He'll answer any questions you have in your mind."

There was no question that the Howe strategy for trying the Tim Wilkes case was both shrewd and daring at the same time. By opting for trials Howe threw away a plea deal and risked conviction and a harsh sentence. The effort to paint Wilkes as a sympathetic figure was framed to play on the jury's natural tendency to feel for the underdog kid who came from a tough background, worked hard, and made something of himself in the cruel world as a business professional and legislator. The strategy, however, was also very risky in that it attempted to use a line of argument that had badly failed in the previous trials of Reps. Luther Taylor, Larry Blanding, and Ken Bailey to the effect that the defendant was a well-intentioned person who had committed to vote for the betting bill before he took any money and, further, that the money given by bribemaster Ron Cobb was a campaign donation. Furthermore, Howe's decision to put Wilkes on the witness stand could have become a disaster if it was not persuasive or if demolished on cross-examination by the prosecution. Even so Wilkes and Howe took the chance of a big win or a disastrous loss.

Prosecution Presents in Wilkes Case

Relying on the videotapes of Wilkes taking money from Cobb while Cobb kept up a chatter of incriminating remarks making it look like he was giving money to buy votes, the prosecution seemingly had persuasive evidence of corruption. Cobb was heard to say that it would be "a happy time for us" if the betting bill passed the House. Cobb also said he would provide even more rewards to Wilkes, promising "I'll do at least what I did before... if not more. If that meets with your approval, that is." Wilkes then appears to jump into the trap, responding, "Absolutely."

The tapes also showed that Wilkes seemed very concerned with winning his upcoming June, 1991, primary election in Winnsboro. And as the evidence piled up the government attorneys kept harping on the point that selling a vote and exchanging official action for money was illegal.

When the prosecution put up Ron Cobb and convicted corruptionist former Rep. Bob Kohn, Wilkes' attorney Gedney Howe turned his questions to the legislative and election practices of the South Carolina General Assembly which both Cobb and Kohn knew from long experience at the State House. Howe said little about the money that Cobb gave Wilkes, but appeared to infer that such handouts of money from lobbyists to legislators were an ordinary and a common way of raising campaign funds in the state legislature which was, of course, completely true.

Federal prosecutors closed out with their case against Tim Wilkes with the testimony of Special Agent John Pearson who said that when he interviewed Rep. Tim Wilkes his first response was to deny that he took a cash payment from lobbyist Ron Cobb. But when Pearson showed Wilkes a subpoena for his campaign records then Wilkes asked Pearson to pose his questions again. In response Wilkes next said that he did take money, "but not illegally."

Hidden cameras, in fact, showed Cobb giving Wilkes two cash payments in April and May of 1990 in the amounts of $1,000 and $500 and the prosecution played the tapes to show the jury the money.

Pearson was the last witness to present for the prosecution in support of the charge that Wilkes sold his public office in violation of the Hobbs Act prohibiting bribery.

<u>Tim Wilkes Trial—Defense Witnesses</u>

The defense team of Rep. Wilkes called as witnesses two persons who had worked with Wilkes' campaign. They were Frank Knapp, a political advisor and former Executive Director of Common Cause/South Carolina, and Ben Gregg, a professional public relations and political operative. Both took the stand on September 19, 1991.

Both said that they told Wilkes it was legal to take cash from a lobbyist. But Ben Gregg admitted that it would be illegal to take such money in return for a promise to take official action and "raise some hell" in support of the betting bill. It also seemed problematic that Cobb promised to give Wilkes another $1,000 if the House passed the betting bill.

Advisor Frank Knapp said that Wilkes would never sell his office.

Wilkes Takes Stand

The trial of Rep. Tim Wilkes reached the point on September 20, 1991, where attorney Howe put up Wilkes himself as a witness. On the stand, Wilkes said that he had long backed the pari-mutuel horse betting bill and that he took cash from Ron Cobb but only as a campaign contribution and not as a bribe. Wilkes admitted, however, that he failed to file a disclosure report with the House listing the money received from Cobb in cash payments.

Wilkes spent over four hours on the witness stand trying to become the first Lost Trust defendant among a total of 28 charged to avoid conviction. All previous defendants had either been convicted at trial or more often had pleaded guilty.

"In my heart and my mind, I did nothing wrong," Wilkes told the jury. "I sold nothing to Ron Cobb. He gave me a campaign contribution for which I promised nothing.... I swear to God, if I had it to do over, I would do it the same way."

Wilkes put on a show for the court and when he read from documents he dramatized and waved them to such an extent that his attorney asked him to stop.

Wilkes explained his failure to report the cash money from Cobb by the deadline set by law, saying it was because he did not have the records in his Columbia office when he needed them to complete the report since they were back in his hometown of Winnsboro. He claimed that he asked for more time to file his disclosure report and asked for more forms to be sent to him. But by then the FBI had subpoenaed and taken his campaign records.

Wilkes explained that his response to FBI agent John Pearson was accurate because he thought that Pearson was asking him about taking a bribe from Cobb in cash. Wilkes had said he knew of no lobbyist who gave cash to legislators. He insisted that the money he took from Cobb was not a bribe but a legal campaign donation.

Wilkes relied on transcripts and not videotapes to support his testimony. The prosecution indicated that it would present the videotapes again on September 21, 1991, the next day of the trial.

In Wilkes' testimony of September 20, 1991, defense lead attorney Gedney Howe got Wilkes to tell moving stories about his hard childhood without a father and with an alcoholic mother who died of smoking caused disease. He told about putting himself and his brother through college and how he became an accountant and a state representative.

Wilkes followed other witnesses who testified that Wilkes had supported a betting bill well before he took any money from Cobb which might have been related, in fact, to the betting bill based on videotaped conversations captured by the FBI. Wilkes said Cobb first offered him money at a party held for supporters of the betting bill.

Wilkes explained Cobb's references to money to buy Mercedes Benz and Jaguar cars if the betting bill passed; Wilkes told that jury that he thought that Cobb was talking about how much money Cobb as a lobbyist would get if the bill passed. Wilkes further thought that Cobb wanted to give him money for his campaign so he could defeat his primary opponent, a Baptist minister opposed to the betting bill.

Wilkes claimed that the videotaped interviews showed that Cobb tried to frame the giving and taking of money to make it look corrupt and thereby "to set me up. He was setting me up again." Wilkes said he had qualms about taking cash campaign contributions but his advisors said it was legal under state law, which it was, in fact.

Wilkes Trial—Defense Attacks

Gedney Howe countered the videotapes of Cobb giving money to Wilkes by dismissing Cobb as a con artist who had conned the FBI into not charging him with cocaine dealing and into giving him $4,000 per month to work as the FBI's sting agent.

Howe depicted Cobb as being able to use manipulative and dishonest language to get what he wanted, even saying that if Cobb wanted to con FBI agent Mike Clemens, sitting in the courtroom, out of his suit he could have: "If Cobb wanted to negotiate that off his back, he'd have done that too."

Howe also said that in an alleged conversation in which Cobb offered bribes to vote for the betting bill Wilkes could not have heard the remarks.

Howe brought 11 witnesses in to testify that Wilkes always regarded the betting bill as legislation he favored even before taking Cobb's money and would have voted for the bill regardless of the money. Witnesses also confirmed the view that Wilkes regarded the money as for his campaign and intended to report it.

Attorney Howe took the floor on September 24, 1991, to answer the prosecution's charges that Rep. Tim Wilkes took a bribe. Howe argued that the videotapes of the transaction in which Ron Cobb handed Wilkes cash were narrated by Cobb rather than by Wilkes and that Cobb used clever words to make it look like the money was a bribe when it was not.

Howe pointed out that Wilkes never called the money anything but a campaign contribution and that Wilkes stated that he would use the money for campaign costs. On the other hand, Cobb tried to use loaded and coded words to frame the money as a payoff. Howe pointed to the fact that Rep. Bob Kohn, a crooked politician turned sting agent for the FBI, tried to lure Wilkes to meet with Cobb. Kohn said that Cobb had a campaign contribution to give to Wilkes. Howe said of Cobb's narrative to Wilkes, that "If there was a code, Timmy Wilkes never knew the code."

Howe said that Cobb's use of the word "Peekaboo" was trick language designed to frame Wilkes as a crook, but that it had no real meaning, observing that "The government would tell you that he should have been tipped off because Cobb said 'Peekaboo', and he didn't say: What the hell do you mean, 'Peekaboo.'"

Prosecution Closes Wilkes Case

Assistant U.S. Attorney John Barton tried to discredit Wilkes' testimony with Wilkes' actions, saying that Wilkes tried to make himself look innocent but his actions appeared dishonest. Barton asked why Wilkes had no records of taking cash from Cobb as a campaign donation, saying "If it was an honestly obtained, no-strings-attached campaign contribution, why had a CPA got no records of it?"

Barton pointed out that Wilkes had said that he knew of no lobbyists who gave cash to legislators and that Wilkes had not taken any cash payments himself when, in fact, he had. It was only after the FBI seized Wilkes' campaign records that he tried to report the money to the House Ethics Committee. Wilkes excused his failure to report earlier by saying his campaign records were left behind in Winnsboro while the House Building was located in Columbia.

Barton also pointed out that Wilkes had voted five times on April, 25, 1990, to try to advance the betting bill and get it up for a vote. Barton also said that "If you accepted Tim Wilkes' version of the facts... you are accepting that our government has deteriorated to the point that no matter how important an issue is, our legislators can be expected to do nothing on it until somebody starts handing out money."

Wilkes Acquitted

The jury in the Wilkes case took a little less than three hours to acquit Wilkes of bribery on September 24, 1991. The jurors rejected the prosecution's theory that it did not matter whether Wilkes took money from Cobb to pay for his campaign costs or whether he kept the money for himself -the transaction was a bribe taken in exchange for Wilkes' promise to vote for the betting bill.

The videotapes never caught Wilkes saying that he was taking the money in return for his vote, but showed him saying that he was taking money for his campaign. Even as Cobb said that the $500 he handed to Wilkes could be used personally Wilkes never took the bait, reacting to Cobb's comment that "Maybe you can use that—have some fun with it" by talking about his upcoming rough re-election campaign in November. It was never clear that Wilkes took money for his vote.

However, the prosecution showed a tape in which Wilkes denied knowing of any lobbyists who gave cash campaign contributions and told the FBI that he did not know anything specific about such payments even while he had taken cash from Cobb twice already. Wilkes later told the FBI that he did, in fact, take cash campaign donations but not any illegal payments. The jury appeared to believe Wilkes in the face of the evidence. Wilkes told the court that "To me, a payment means there is an exchange...and I never exchanged anything for a campaign contribution." Wilkes appeared to frame his seemingly dishonest denial that he took money in such a way as to indicate that he had a different interpretation of the meaning of the government's question by explaining that he thought the question was whether he took a bribe which, of course, he denied.

Key factors in Gedney Howe's presentation related to the flaw in the prosecution's evidence because it did not clearly show that Wilkes' taking official actions in reciprocity. There was no clear quid pro quo demonstrated as Wilkes' comments proved ambiguous and elusive and of little use to prove criminal intent.

Among the key factors helping Wilkes' case was the fact that Wilkes always talked about the cash from Cobb as campaign money. Wilkes also called his campaign advisors and asked them if taking cash contributions was legal; they all said it was which was true in South Carolina at the time. Wilkes also spent the money on his campaign and disclosed it after asking about amending his disclosure forms. Wilkes said he misunderstood the FBI questions about taking cash from lobbyists and did not realize that the FBI was talking about cash bribes.

Wilkes further rebutted the prosecution's arguments that he did nothing to promote the betting bill until after taking the money, by saying there was little he could do to advance the bill as he was a weak novice representative with virtually no influence. Wilkes convincingly showed that he had supported the betting bill long before taking money from Cobb and Wilkes' numerous witnesses corroborated that. The jury seemed to accepted Wilkes' explanation that he did nothing before or after taking money from Cobb to promote the betting bill and that there was, in fact, little he could do at any time because as a new member of the House he had accumulated no seniority and had no influence over the legislative process.

After 16 legislators had been convicted in Lost Trust either at trial or plea agreement, Rep. Tim Wilkes (D-Fairfield) was acquitted by a federal jury in Columbia on September 24, 1991. Jurors were simply not convinced beyond a reasonable doubt that the $1,500 in cash given by sting agent Ron Cobb was a bribe to get Wilkes to vote for the betting bill.

At the time of verdict Wilkes was the 27th defendant to be tried or pleaded guilty and he was the first to be exonerated. Only Sen. Bud Long (D-Horry) was left to be disposed of by the courts and he would go to trial later in the year and be convicted of corruption.

Not long afterward Speaker Bob Sheheen lifted the suspension of Wilkes in the House and he was restored to status as a member. Sheheen said that a suspended representative had never been reinstated before.

Barbara McFadden sobbed at the verdict. She had reared Wilkes from childhood after his father had disappeared and his mother lapsed into alcoholism. McFadden said she did not want to see Wilkes go to prison like the rest.

Jurors Explain Acquittal

Jurors told the media after Wilkes acquittal that the evidence was too vague to show crime.

Juror Ed Harrelson told reporters that "We all looked at the evidence and there was nothing concrete.... The government offered a bribe.... I had nothing but praise for the prosecutors.

They did a tremendous job." Harrelson felt that the prosecutors had, in fact, convicted many of actual crimes in the sting, saying "All those people that have been taken out deserved to be taken out. But for Tim, the sting was a set-up." Harrelson accused the prosecution of devious actions, "They baited him and baited him, but they never could get him to bite."

Harrelson said that the jurors were impressed that Wilkes did not waver, noting that "They'd try to talk about Jaguars and Mercedes, and he'd talk about the Hugo debt and how the state needed money to pay it off."

Juror Thomas O. Hill, Jr., blamed the prosecution for unfairness, saying "They looked at everything he did and said so negative and he'd just come back with a positive." Hill added, "What impressed me was he swore to God and that he was telling the truth. He swore on the Bible. I'm a believer myself, and I wouldn't want to go against God."

Hill explained the acquittal by stressing the ambiguity of the evidence. The prosecution videotapes did not prove criminal intent, Hill said, noting that "Never once did anybody say to him, 'We'd like you to vote this way, and here's some money; and Wilkes never got caught saying, 'Hey, man. I'll do it.'"

Jury foreman Bruce Gillespie said that the jurors concluded that the FBI tried to trick Wilkes, but the tapes never proved criminal intent, "We could see him reaching for the money, but he never promised to do anything for it, and he always referred to it as a campaign contribution."

Gillespie also said that as the jury began to deliberate they all headed toward acquittal from the start.

Defense Attorneys' Comment

Defense lawyers who had represented other defendants in Lost Trust told the media that Wilkes benefited by telling others about Cobb's offer of money before he actually took the money. Joel Collins, Luther Taylor's attorney in the first case to go to trial in Lost Trust, said that the evidence in the Wilkes case showed that there were major questions about the prosecution's use of the Hobbs Act which would have to be cleared up by appeals. Collins also said that the Lost Trust cases turned on how Cobb characterized the money in the videotapes when he handed it out. Jack Swerling who represented two defendants in Lost Trust said that each case was unique and would be decided on its merits. He would later take the Bud Long case to trial. Long would be convicted.

Wilkes' Faith in Justice

After his acquittal by a jury on September 24, 1991, as the only Lost Trust defendant to avoid conviction, Rep. Tim Wilkes (D-Fairfield) said at the end of 1991 that his faith in the American system of justice had been restored.

While 16 of his fellow legislators were suffering for their convictions, Wilkes prepared to go back for the new session of the House in mid-January 1992.

Wilkes told the media that the process of indictment and trial was frightening but that the principle of presumption of innocence was a high ideal and that, in fact, in the criminal justice system the presumption appeared rather to be one of guilt.

"I believe I was acquitted because I was innocent," Wilkes said, adding, "But I realized all along how easy it would be to be convicted anyway. When you are No. 27, and the prosecutors are batting 26 and 0, you walk into court presumed guilty."

Even so, in spite of his doubt about his own chances in court, Wilkes said that "… my faith has been restored. Faith in my friends. Faith in the Lord. Faith in the system, although I realize now that there are imperfections in the system that need to be addressed."

Wilkes also said that he continued to support the pari-mutuel betting legislation even though it was the issue which was used by the FBI to sting him.

CHAPTER THIRTY SEVEN

SEN. BUD LONG INDICTED, TRIED AND CONVICTED

Sen. Bud Long (D-Horry) was the second of only two state senators indicted in the Lost Trust prosecutions. The other, Sen. Rick Lee (R-Spartanburg), entered a guilty plea to taking a payment from Ron Cobb to support the betting bill and was the second legislator to plead guilty in the scandal.

Sen. Long had the dubious distinction of being the last of eight defendants to go to trial and he proved to be the last convicted in the first round of trials which ended on November 23, 1991. As it turned out, Long would also be one of the last defendants convicted in the 28 Lost Trust cases when he faced a retrial ordered by the trial court but chose to enter a guilty plea in 1999 to providing false information to a federal investigator in return for the government's agreement to dismiss public corruption charges against Long. In view of the fact that the conviction was based on a plea agreement and charge was only misdemeanor, Long was not incarcerated at any time during the proceedings which extended from 1991 until 1999.

<u>Sen. Bud Long Indicted</u>

On August 20, 1991, a federal grand jury indicted Long on two counts of violating the Hobbs Act for selling his vote on the betting bill. He was the 18th and final person in the General Assembly to be charged.

Long's records had been subpoenaed clear back in July, 1990, along with those of the members of the S.C. House. Ever since that time Long had been haunted by the prospect of his coming indictment and he had tried to reassure his colleagues in the Senate that he had done nothing wrong. He was known to be having protracted financial difficulties including tax problems.

The indictment alleged that Long sold his vote on the betting bill and took $2,800 in cash from Ron Cobb. He protested that he had done nothing wrong and was "shocked, surprised, disappointed" by the indictment.

Long explained his innocence by saying that the money given in 1990 did not influence his vote because "I was for pari-mutuel when I first went to the Senate." Long said that he had backed the idea long before taking any cash and said he had "been the whole time. Nobody would have any reasons to even try to buy me for that, because they knew where my vote was."

Sen. Long contended that for five years before he took any money from Ron Cobb on the pari-mutuel betting bill he had supported the bill. When *The State* newspaper asked legislators in December, 1990, for their priority issues in rank order prior to the 1991 session starting in January Long said he "strongly supported" betting on horse racing.

The indictment, however, said Long needed money and went looking for $2,800 to make a house payment on May 17, 1990, and found FBI sting agent Ron Cobb who said he might get the money if Long could help get the pari-mutuel bill out of committee. Cobb also said he might be able to come up with even more money if Long could get the bill to vote in the Senate and "Long agreed to this arrangement and stated his pleasure with the arrangement," the indictment alleged.

Then Long joined seven other senators in signing the polling document to move the betting bill from the Judiciary Committee to the Senate floor. The bill was put on the Senate calendar on May 23, 1990, near the end of the session where it died.

On May 22, 1990, the indictment said, Cobb met with Long in Cobb's office and gave Long $2,800, the amount Long sought.

But Long said in public on August 20, 1991, after his indictment was handed down on the same day, that Cobb only gave him $300 in the year 1990 and that was at a reception held by Long to raise campaign funds. Newspaper reporters overheard Long say he only took $300.

Bud Long had served 16 years as the 15th Circuit Solicitor for Horry County and he had served as a municipal judge for eight years before being elected to the Senate in 1985.

Long's financial difficulties had plagued him for many years. He had trouble paying his taxes for much of his legal career and he carried the burden of raising seven children. In early 1991 the U.S. Internal Revenue Service imposed garnishment on his wages and expenses and his station wagon was almost sold at auction.

His earlier attempts to develop a subdivision in Conway, S.C., in the 1960s and 1970s nearly threw him into bankruptcy. His service in the Senate cut his time for his law practice and reduced his income by about $30,000, Long said.

The charges against Long included extortion and conspiracy to commit extortion. Long faced a total of 40 years and a fine of $500,000, if convicted.

As the Senate had no rule similar to House Rule 3.12 Long did not know on indictment if he would ask for his own suspension as he would not automatically be suspended as he would be in the House. Sen. Rick Lee, the only other senator caught in the entire Lost Trust debacle, had resigned his Senate seat and pleaded guilty almost immediately after his indictment.

Long, 64, had considered switching parties but was not welcomed in the Republican Party in 1990, two years before Senate elections.

In the Senate he was a champion of local interests and opposed the Beachfront Management Act which would have depopulated the Grand Stand. He tried to slip provisions into the state budget to let Horry County collect extra taxes, but backed down when exposed by the media.

Sen. Long Suspended

On Long's own motion, the South Carolina Senate suspended Long on August 22, 1991, just two days after his indictment.

Long announced his decision to Senate colleagues gathered in Columbia to discuss the ethics reform bill. Long stated, "I just want to say to you that I'm not guilty of the charges therein made and will dedicate my time, energy, and resources to a vigorous and successful defense." Long told the hushed group, "I have chosen to ask the president pro tempore to excuse me from all privileges of membership in the Senate until this matter is concluded. I say to you I'll see you in January." Long then walked out of the Senate chamber.

The President Pro Tem, Sen. Marshall Williams, granted the request without comment. In fact, Sen. Bud Long's career was over.

Long Reacts to Indictment

Sen. J.M. "Bud" Long tried to dismiss the federal indictment against him as just politics after he was charged. "I don't know why anybody would run for public office these days." He did not say who was behind it all.

Long alleged that the political scheme against him "was plotted, planned and schemed to drive me out of the Senate." But Long did not blame the S.C. Republican Party. He did say that federal prosecutors took advantage of the fact that he was short of money to try to bribe him over the betting bill. (At the time of the alleged bribery Long owed $36,085 in back federal and state taxes as of May, 1990.)

Long met Ron Cobb in 1985 when Cobb had just started out as a lobbyist and Long had just entered the General Assembly. Long recommended Cobb as a lobbyist to the Myrtle Beach Chamber of Commerce and the Grand Strand Water and Sewer Authority in 1985 and 1986. Cobb held a fund-raiser for Long.

Long claimed to find inspiration in a quotation from Albert Schweitzer who said, "There's no higher religion than public service. Working for the common good is the greatest creed."

Long Pleads Not Guilty in Sting

On September 4, 1991, Long came to the federal courthouse in Charleston where he had his fingerprints taken, signed documents to secure his bond and entered his plea of not guilty. His attorney was prominent criminal attorney Jack Swerling of Columbia. At the arraignment Swerling told the media, "We're pleading not guilty and we're preparing for trial." Swerling also picked up a brief of evidence which the prosecution intended to use at trial.

Noting that seventeen other legislators had been charged in the scandal, Swerling stated that whatever had happened to all of the previous defendants who had been convicted was not relevant and that "This case is going to be decided on its own merit."

The indictment alleged that Long asked Cobb for the sum of $2,800 in order to make a house payment and that Long had financial problems which led him to take the money from Cobb on May 22, 1990. Cobb delivered the bribe at his office in the AT&T Building in Columbia where he had previously paid other defendants with bribe money.

At his arraignment Long, an attorney and former solicitor of the State of South Carolina who understood the charges, chose not to have the indictment read to him. Afterward he left the courthouse along with his wife, Judy Long, and did not speak to reporters.

Long had told the media in previous comments that he only took $300 from Cobb and that the money was a campaign contribution.

The U.S. Magistrate who held the hearing was Charles Gambrell who allowed Long to be free based on his unsecured $5,000 bond. No trial date was set by Gambrell but he did set motions as of September 24, 1991, only three weeks later.

Dismissal Moved in Long Case

Patrick Hubbard, an attorney for Sen. Bud Long filed a motion to dismiss the indictment of Long for taking an alleged bribe of $2,800 from Ron Cobb. The dismissal motion claimed that the indictment of Long was too vague and the federal government was improperly trying to regulate South Carolina campaign practices. In addition, Hubbard argued that the betting bill on which Long allegedly took a bribe had no chance of passage in the South Carolina Senate and would have no effect on interstate commerce. The Hobbs Act on which Long was charged was based on the commerce clause in the U.S. Constitution.

Hubbard was a law professor at the University of South Carolina School of Law and was assisting Long's primary attorney Jack Swerling.

The motion added that the indictment did not allege that Long took any action in his official capacity as a state senator in return for the money given to him by Ron Cobb. This point of the motion addressed the recent ruling of the U.S. Supreme Court in *McCormick* (May 23, 1991) which required that the prosecution prove that the defendant charged with a Hobbs Act bribery be shown to have taken official action as quid pro quo for the bribe received.

Assistant U.S. Attorney Sherri Lydon told the court that it had already ruled against the issues raised by the motion in previous Lost Trust cases.

Long Trial Starts

On Tuesday, November 12, 1991, the U.S. District Court convened by Judge Falcon Hawkins selected a jury in the trial of Sen. Bud Long.

Attorney Swerling intimated in his questions to prospective jurors that he intended to argue in defense that Long had previously supported the bill for years and that his vote for the bill could therefore not be bought.

The grand jury indictment of Sen. Bud Long on two counts of extortion and conspiracy to commit extortion alleged that he took a bribe of $2,800 from Ron Cobb on May 22, 1990, to vote for the betting bill and that Long, in fact, took action to move the bill forward by voting on May 23, 1990, to poll the bill along with seven other senators and thereby move it out of the Senate Judiciary Committee and to the full Senate. On May 23, 1990, the bill was put on the Senate Calendar where it died at the end of the session as of June 6, 1990.

The trial of Bud Long began on November 12, 1991. Attorney Swerling indicated that the defense argument would be that Long did not take a bribe but did take a legal campaign donation from Ron Cobb. During the second day of jury selection Swerling told the media, "Sen. Long accepted some money from a lobbyist and it's going to be on the pari-mutuel bill. The whole issue is what that money was for." Long contended that he took only $300 and not as a bribe.

Swerling said that he would produce evidence that Sen. Long had backed the betting bill before he took any money from Cobb. He also said that "Bud took some money... You cannot sell control of something you favor."

Swerling clashed with prosecutors over the burden of proof contending that the prosecution was obligated by the *McCormick* (1991) case to prove more than that Long merely promised to do a specific act, such as voting for the betting bill. Swerling said that the prosecution must prove that not only did Long make a promise but that he took an action as a public official to fulfill the promise.

News Reporters Summoned in Long Trial

One of the most bizarre episodes in the Lost Trust trials was the decision of Judge Falcon Hawkins to treat five prominent newspaper reporters as witnesses in the trial of Long. Hawkins ordered the reporters sequestered with other witnesses so they could not hear the progress of the trial before they testified.

The judge's decision made two reporters of the Myrtle Beach *Sun News* unavailable to cover the trial and they were the news staffers who knew the most about Bud Long as Long represented Myrtle Beach and Horry County on coastal South Carolina. Even so the judge went ahead with his plan to isolate the newspaper reporters. He also ordered that one reporter from *The State* and two reporters from *The Post and Courier* be compelled to come to court. This action had been preceded in the trial of Tee Ferguson when a reporter of *The State* was subpoenaed, but was not compelled to testify and in the trial of B.J. Gordon when a Charleston reporter was forced to testify. Press Association attorney Jay Bender worried that this practice would inhibit news reporters in the future.

Hawkins acknowledged the chilling effect of such subpoenas but the controversial judge said there was no exception for reporters in the law and that there was no qualified privilege for reporters in the law of the 4th Circuit, but there was in other circuits.

Prosecution Omits Facts in Indictment

On November 15, 1991, it was revealed that the government had failed to tell the grand jury in seeking an indictment for extortion against Sen. Bud Long that Long had voted to move the betting bill out of committee even before Ron Cobb offered Long $2,800 to vote for the bill. This evidence seemed to indicate that Long had not taken the money to vote for the bill as alleged by the prosecution and as alleged in the indictment handed down by the grand jury. An FBI witness revealed the prosecution blunder.

Even though it was true Long needed money badly to pay a house mortgage payment, he took the money only after he already voted for the betting bill and not because of the money which was given to him later after he voted. This unexpected admission by the government seemed to raise a question about whether the prosecution could still go forward now that it was apparent that the Cobb money which the prosecution alleged to be the cause of Long's vote was actually given after the vote was taken in the Senate. Judge Hawkins admitted that he was shocked by testimony which might indicate that the indictment was flawed from the outset and that the prosecution knew it.

Long's attorney, Jack Swerling, said that there was a recording, in fact, to be presented as defense evidence that clearly showed that Long took action on the betting bill before he took any money from Cobb and even before the offer of money.

On November 16, 1991, Judge Hawkins was confronted with the question of whether the indictment had a serious, even fatal, defect. The issue was the fact that the government had not told the grand jury that Long voted to move the betting bill before he took any money from Ron Cobb and even before Long discussed any money with Cobb in relation to Long's support for the betting bill.

Hawkins said that he was shocked to learn that the prosecution and FBI knew about the defect from the time the indictment was handed down. Hawkins opined, "This is not some kind of little technical thing we're fooling with. It's the heart of the case... somebody or the other had better come up with some sort of explanation for why it is the way it is." Then he added, "Is this a slip-up?"

Jurors were in the courtroom long enough before they were ordered out to realize that the indictment was dubious, but they did not hear Hawkins' penetrating remarks.

The indictment stated that Cobb promised Long more money for future actions than the first amount ($2,800) given to Long but that, in fact, Cobb did not give Long any more money for actions taken by Long after he took the first amount. And the indictment did not charge Long for taking any more money from Cobb.

The FBI memorandum in evidence at the start of the trial did not indicate that the FBI instructions to Cobb were broad enough to authorize Cobb to offer a bribe for general help on the betting bill.

Long Trial—Defense Has Edge

While the jury was out of the courtroom in the early phases of the Bud Long trial spectators commented that the defense seemed to be getting the upper hand after two days of prosecution evidence. Jack Swerling seemed to be turning prosecution witnesses in Long's clear favor in his cross-examinations.

Swerling got government witnesses to admit that Long had a history of supporting lotteries, betting on racing, off-shore gambling and anything else that would promote tourism in his senate district.

When FBI special agent Mike Clemens testified on November 16, 1991, he told the court that after Long told Cobb he needed $2,800 to stop his house from foreclosure, the FBI told Cobb to offer the $2,800 amount for whatever Long could do on the betting bill. Clemens also said that on May 17, 1990, Long told Cobb that Long had already signed a polling document to move the betting bill out of the committee and to the full Senate before he took any money from Cobb.

Even so, Clemens said in spite of the fact that Long had previously voted to move the bill before any money was offered or taken it was still possible for Long to take future actions to promote the bill. In fact, on May 22, 1990, Long took the $2,800 from Cobb after Long had voted.

FBI agent Mike Clemens told the court on November 16, 1991, that the government had paid Ron Cobb some $100,000 for his work in Lost Trust and that Cobb would be recommended for a bonus payment once the trials were ended.

Attorney Swerling commented that Cobb was a shrewd operator who without the assistance of any attorney had convinced the FBI to give him immunity and even return the $20,000 in cash that Cobb had paid an undercover drug agent for cocaine in the sting in which Cobb was first caught. In addition, Cobb cut a deal to be paid monthly for helping to catch corrupt officials to whom Cobb handed out FBI bribe money.

Rick Lee Testifies in Long Trial

Former Sen. Rick Lee who had pleaded guilty in 1990 to taking a $3,000 bribe from Ron Cobb testified in the Bud Long trial on November 16, 1991, that Lee knew the money Lee took was a bribe to help to poll the betting bill out of the Senate Judiciary Committee. Lee also said that he was not surprised to see Sen. Long's name on the polling sheet because Long was well known to strongly support bills such as the betting bill.

Rick Lee's testimony showed that as a senator Lee admitted he took a bribe but Lee certainly did not allege that Long took a bribe on the betting bill. Indeed, Lee's statement that Long had an established record of supporting the betting bill before he took any money from Cobb would suggest that Long was not influenced in any way to vote for the betting bill by the $2,800 he took from Cobb. At best, Lee's testimony was of little value to the prosecution and perhaps more helpful to Long's defense.

Prosecutors Move for Mistrial Rejected

Realizing that their case was looking worse and worse, prosecutors moved on November 16, 1991, for a mistrial, but Judge Hawkins refused to grant it.

Prosecutors told the court that their case had been damaged by misleading claims that government agents had withheld evidence from the grand jury that had charged Sen. Long with conspiracy and extortion. The judge also refused to tell jurors to disregard evidence that the FBI did not tell the grand jury that Long did not offer his vote on the betting bill until after he had actually voted on the bill.

Hawkins had said in court on November 15, 1991, that he was shocked that Long might have been charged for taking a bribe to vote for a bill when he had voted for the bill before he agreed to take the money. But the prosecution said that the grand jury knew from a tape of a Cobb and Long conversation that Long had already voted on the betting bill. And the prosecution said that it made no difference whether Long had voted on the bill before he talked to Cobb.

The prosecution motion for a mistrial read: "The court's comments seemed to indicate that the court believes that the government is trying to prove that the defendant actually voted for the bill in return for the money when the government's case is that he promised to support the bill for money."

Long Trial on Brink of Failure

Ron Cobb admitted in court that he never told Sen. Bud Long that the $2,800 that Cobb gave to Long was for continuing support of the betting bill. The admission came on November 18, 1991, and seemed to throw even more doubt on the prosecution's case which had struggled from the start.

Cobb also admitted that Long had been a strong supporter of the betting bill well before he took $2,800 from Cobb and that there was no need to pay Long to vote for the betting bill. Long would have voted for the betting bill regardless of the money given to Long by Cobb after Long voted for the betting bill. Cobb agreed with a remark made by Long's attorney, Jack Swerling, that paying Long to vote for the betting bill was "'like giving a dog some money to chase a cat'".

In a recorded conversation of May 17, 1990, Cobb and Long talked about the betting bill before Cobb raised the issue of giving $2,800 to Sen. Long. Cobb then added that he could get more money for Long, remarking, "I think I can come up with the $2,800 Monday, and then if we get the damned thing polled out, I know I can come up with another couple thousand."

The prosecution played eight tapes for the jury, one of which showed Cobb giving Long 28 $100 bills while Cobb counted out the money. But attorney Swerling dismissed the tapes as poor quality evidence, observing what they said about bribery was vague, if they said anything about bribery at all.

Cobb Testimony Doubts Long's Guilt

In his second day of testimony on November 19, 1991, Ron Cobb told the court that he had serious doubts about what was done to Sen. Long and that the extortion charges should not have been filed against Long. Cobb told the court, "I have strong concerns about this case. I don't think Sen. Long should be here, and I don't think I should be here testifying against him." Cobb's testimony followed his testimony the previous day that Cobb had not made it clear to Long that the money given to Long was in return for his voting on the betting bill.

Long talked so much on the videotapes about the betting bill that Cobb may not have made it clear that he was offering money to Long to vote for the bill. Cobb told attorney Swerling on cross examination that "Ever since this whole thing started, I have prided myself on telling the truth in this courtroom—sometimes to my own disadvantage—and that's what I did. That's what I said."

Cobb went on to explain, "I did my job as best I could, like the FBI told me. But that's my impression. I have real problems with why the senator is here and why I am here testifying against him." Cobb had grave doubts about whether Long took a bribe.

Cobb's testimony was given in spite of opposition from the prosecution. And the prosecution summoned Bart Daniel from Charleston to do damage repair. Daniel told reporters at that point, "If we lose this one, we'll lose it together."

FBI Testimony v. Long Appears Dubious

The prosecution put up FBI agent Larry Bruns on November 19, 1991, who accused Sen. Long of lying to every question asked of him by Bruns and FBI agent Don Myers when they interviewed Long on July 18, 1990, the day the sting became public and the same day that the FBI was sending teams of agents to interview suspects and sources of information all over South Carolina. However, the FBI did not warn Long at first that he was a target of the probe, but later handed him a subpoena demanding his campaign records.

When Bruns and Myers met with Long they told him that the FBI was conducting a survey about "improprieties" that might have happened during the 1990 legislative session. At that time Long told the FBI that he had never taken cash from a lobbyist and that he never took any amount above $100.

Under cross-examination Bruns denied that the FBI tactics in the interview were deceptive and that Long did not know the probe was about him. Bruns said that it was not a lie to tell Long the FBI was conducting a survey because "a survey can be part of an investigation." And Bruns added, "Everybody knows the FBI conducts investigations." Bruns also explained, "We asked him the questions we needed to ask. They weren't trick questions."

Swerling remarked that that the FBI had used the word "payment" in asking Long if he took any money and that might have confused Long. Bruns also admitted that the other FBI agent, Don Myers, was the same person who wanted to run for solicitor in Long's district in Horry county but could not because of a bill that Long introduced requiring solicitors to be attorneys.

Daniel Saves Long Trial

The appearance of Bart Daniel on November 19th to try to save a collapsing prosecution of Sen. Long gave new energy but it aggravated the battle between warhorse defense attorney Jack Swerling and the prosecution team. Swerling accused Daniel of skirting the rules of the court in trying to salvage the prosecution case. Daniel, in turn, accused the defense of trying to tie his hands.

As the courtroom became more and more a battle ground of shouting lawyers, Judge Hawkins called the room to order, warning "if there is any more shouting, I'll have the marshals take care of it." He also said "There will be no more screaming at me.... I'm not hard of hearing."

Reporters Defy Judge and Go to Jail

Reporters had made it very clear to the court before they were jailed on November 20th that they would not testify in the Bud Long trial and would go to jail if they had to. Even though the prosecution said that Long lied to the media about taking only $300 from Cobb rather than the larger $2,800 amount he eventually admitted to, the reporters refused to take the stand.

S.C. Press Association lawyer Jay Bender stated that the issue was critical and that journalists must be free to gather news without governmental pressures. Bender said of the five reporters who challenged Judge Hawkins' demands that they testify that "each firmly believes that his or her professional obligation to the public as a journalist is to remain in a position where each can freely gather and report news on matters of public interest."

Judge Hawkins said that he realized that there might be a "chilling effect" if he put people in jail under the circumstances but he rejected an effort to quash the subpoenas issued to the reporters to come to court and said that he had to do so since no media privilege existed. He noted, "The only thing worse than going to jail that I know of is going to jail when you don't belong there."

The prosecution fought to force newspaper reporters to testify against Bud Long, saying the testimony was vital to their case, and asked Judge Hawkins to jail the reporters if they would not talk. The confrontation happened on November 20, 1991.

Assistant U.S. Attorney Buddy Bethea called South Carolina Press Association attorney Bender who represented the reporters a "criminal" for opposing the request.

Media advocates alleged that the judge was violating the First Amendment rights of the journalists and injuring the public interest in knowing about the matter. The media argument was that sources would not talk to reporters if they knew they would be exposed in court later on. Bender explained, "The reasons we have the First Amendment is to allow reporters to go out and gather information of public importance without having to be compelled to testify against their sources." Bender added, if sources knew they would be revealed "you won't have stories asking state senators about their involvement in Lost Trust."

Prosecutors repeatedly demanded that the four reporters from *The State*, *The Sun News*, and *The Post and Courier* take the stand and talk about the stories published in which Sen. Long had said that he had only taken a $300 campaign contribution from Ron Cobb. The issue appeared to be novel in South Carolina.

However, in federal courts of appeals the judges seemed to have some sympathy for the journalists, according to Floyd Abrahams, a media attorney, who added, "When the (reporters) are not eyewitnesses, that some serious effort should be made to obtain the information elsewhere first, and that the information be of great significance."

Jane Kirtley of the Reporters' Committee for Freedom of the Press said that federal courts used three criteria in deciding whether to compel testimony from reporters: (1) the evidence must be relevant; (2) it must be essential to the case; (3) it must not be obtainable from other sources. Her opinion was that the facts of the Long case did not satisfy the criteria.

Paul McMasters, with the Society of Professional Journalists, opined that the prosecutors in the Long case were on a "fishing expedition." That meant that they were trying to find out new information which might have been discovered by the agents and the grand jury.

South Carolina did not have a shield law to protect journalists against compelled testimony, although 28 other states did. Rep David Wilkins (R-Greenville), Chairman of House Judiciary Committee, told the media that the Long case would provoke interest and should raise the question of whether the state needed a shield law too. Fifth Circuit Solicitor Dick Harpootlian said he felt such a law was needed.

Gil Thelen, executive editor *The State* newspaper, stated that the demand to force reporters' testimony meant that "democracy will be threatened."

The executive committee of the S.C. Press Association issued a statement which claimed that the integrity of reporters would be compromised if they were forced to testify in the trial, asserting, "Reporters are not policemen.... Surely they cannot find out anything in interviews with Sen. Long that law enforcement officers cannot find out themselves."

At the time of the Long trial the U.S. Court of Appeals for the 4th Circuit had not ruled on the question of whether reporters had a qualified privilege which would allow them to decline to testify. U.S. Supreme Court rulings on the question were not clear. And state courts in Texas and Florida had sent reporters to jail for refusing to testify in court cases.

Jane Kirtley remarked that federal courts had ruled that reporters could be compelled to testify, although Ms. Kirtley knew of no instance in which reporters had been jailed.

Four Reporters Held in Contempt

Upon the request of the prosecution that the reporters who refused to testify in the Long case be held in contempt and put in jail, trial judge Falcon Hawkins did just that on November 20, 1991, when he held four reporters in contempt and put them in detention for five hours while the trial was in progress that day. The four included Myrtle Beach *Sun Times* reporter Andrew Shain, Charleston *Post and Courier* reporters Schuyler Kropf and Sid Gaulden, and *The State* reporter Cindi Ross Scoppe. They were advised by S.C. Press Association attorney Jay Bender in the matter. Lisa Greene of *The Sun News* and Barry Myers of SCETV Radio were subpoenaed but not called and jailed.

The reporters had previously said that they would risk going to jail rather than to take the witness stand under compulsion and testify as to what they knew about the Bud Long case.

The State Editorial Rips Jailing of Reporters

In reaction to the jailing of four reporters found in contempt by Judge Falcon Hawkins for failing to testify in the Long trial, *The State* published an editorial on November 21, 1991, in which the editors argued First Amendment issues in the matter, citing two centuries of press freedom based on the Bill of Rights of 1791.

The editorial recognized that the stories published were public property, but said that "the notes and the reporters' recollections... were protected by the First Amendment, which gave them a qualified privilege against compelled testimony."

Noting the efforts of S.C. Press Association attorney Jay Bender to move the judge to quash the subpoenas to the reporters, *The State* pointed to the judge's admission that his actions might have a chilling effect on the media.

The U.S. Supreme Court had ruled that compelling media testimony was an extreme measure which might be used only when the evidence could not be obtained by any other means. U.S. Attorney Bart Daniel had made that claim in the Long case. But *The State* argued that Daniel had not proved that only the reporters had the information the prosecution needed in the case.

The editorial concluded, "There ought to be an easier way to protect the news-gathering function from damage without causing individuals to face the coercion of incarceration. That way, of course, is to establish a qualified privilege, in cases like this, either through legislative or judicial process."

Reporters Released from Jail

After sitting in federal custody for five hours at the U.S. District Court House in Columbia, Judge Falcon Hawkins ordered the reporters he had jailed for contempt to be released from custody late on November 21, 1991. Pursuant to the court's order federal authorities released Cindi Ross Scoppe of *The State*, Andrew Shain of *The Sun News*, and Sid Gaulden and Schuyler Kropf of *The Post and Courier*. The four had persistently refused to testify at the trial of Sen. Bud Long since its start on November 16, 1991.

Their attorney, Jay Bender, told the court that the reporters would have no admissible evidence to present if they were to testify because "They would have been asked to say what Bud Long said to them... And that's hearsay, that's inadmissible..." Bender praised the four who went to jail for their "great dedication to the First Amendment," noting that they "stood up to the government."

Judge Hawkins' contempt order was being appealed at the time of the release but no ruling was expected for some time.

Gil Thielen, executive editor of *The State*, opined that "There was never any reason established for those reporters to testify, yet they were put through a number of days of hell because of the government's insistence on a wrong-headed course."

The four reporters held in contempt were kept in the magistrate's courtroom on November 20, 1991, and then were released for the night while Judge Hawkins pondered his contempt order. Yet the next morning Hawkins sent the four to holding cells in the basement of the courthouse after they again refused to testify in the trial of Long continuing on that day.

At the second detention the reporters were treated more like criminal suspects than on the first day in the courtroom. U.S. marshals took fingerprints, mug shots and denied them any visitors except their attorney, Jay Bender.

The trial judge again demanded that the four testify about a statement that Long had made to them that he only took $300 from Cobb and not the amount of $2,800 indicated by the videotape of Cobb giving Long the larger amount in cash. The amount of only $300 was reported in the media.

While Attorney Bender stated that the compulsion of testimony would have a chilling effect on journalists and discourage news sources from telling reporters what they knew, the Executive Editor of the *Post and Courier*, Larry Tarleton, disclosed that "We're getting more subpoenas" and he added, "The disturbing thing is, they're coming from prosecutors and not the defense. I don't know why prosecutors feel reporters have to investigate and do their work for them...." And

Sue Deans, editor of *The Sun News*, defended her reporter Andy Shain and the others, arguing "This is not a situation where we saw anyone commit a crime and refused to testify."

Long Trial Limps to End

The prosecution portrayed Long as eager to grab money and in financial distress needing fast money. On May 1, 1990, Rep. Robert Kohn, who became a government sting agent two weeks later, told Long that Ron Cobb had a "fish" willing to pay to get help on the betting bill. Then on May 10, 1990, Long told Cobb, "What have you got going? I'm hungry." Then on the same day that members of the Senate Judiciary Committee were polled about the betting bill, Long, a member of the committee, asked Cobb for help with his mortgage payments. At the time Long said that the betting bill would be good for Horry County, his district, but also would benefit Long's finances, said prosecutor Alred Bethea. And prosecutor Sherri Lydon said that Long agreed to help move the betting bill after Cobb promised more money for Long.

As the trial came to its final moments on November 21, 1991, Judge Hawkins seemed to find the prosecution's case quite flimsy, observing that "The best y'all can come up with is a 'fish' and a fellow saying 'What have you got going on.'" Then Hawkins cast even more ridicule on the prosecution by commenting, "He's got this friend, a lobbyist, that seems to have money coming out of his ears, and he needs $2,800. They're about to take his house... He doesn't say, 'I'm willing to do anything you say to do so I can help you get that fish to give us more money.'"

Long Trial Looks Bad for Prosecution

On November 21, 1991, the defense moved the court to acquit. Attorneys Jack Swerling and his associate, Tommy Brittain, said that even Ron Cobb had admitted on the stand that he believed that Long did not think of the money Cobb gave him as a bribe. The defense also said that the money from Cobb to Long was sought by Long who thought that Cobb was his friend and would help him avoid foreclosure on his house. The defense tried to frame the money as a loan, though Long has said it was a campaign contribution.

The defense said that Long never promised to do anything specific for the Cobb money and that even though Cobb tried to make the money seem like a payment to Long to vote in the future for the betting bill, in fact, Long had already voted on the bill before he took any money from Cobb.

Defense said that Long could not in law conspire with Cobb to commit extortion because Cobb was, in law, a government agent and Long could not conspire with former Rep. Robert Kohn who had also become a government agent on May 15, 1990. As to Kohn, the defense said that Kohn only talked with Long once about the betting bill and all Long said was that he would "scope it out." In addition, although Kohn had told the grand jury in 50 pages of testimony about many corrupt persons, Kohn never once mentioned Long because, Kohn said, "I didn't know he'd done anything wrong."

Long Trial—Witness Kept Out

The prosecution in the Long Trial never was allowed to bring a witness to the stand who would have told the court that Sen. Bud Long charged him $2,500 to make a telephone call when the man needed a legislator to intercede for him. The witness wanted to testify against Long and waited in vain in the hallway of the U.S. Court House in Columbia while the Long trial was going on. The man was George Stover.

When prosecutors told Judge Hawkins they wanted to use Stover's story in the bribery case the Judge refused and told the prosecution that it could indict Long in the future on an additional charge based on Stover's statement.

U.S. Attorney Bart Daniel pleaded with Hawkins to let Stover testify, saying "We have had five witnesses refuse to testify...and now the court is refusing to let our strongest witness take the stand. We believe our case has been gutted.... I don't believe we are being given a fair shot."

Stover would have said to the jury that he came to Myrtle Beach after the hurricane to deal with insurance claims from Hurricane Hugo in 1989 and had hired a lawyer, but the lawyer could not get through to the South Carolina Insurance Commission. Stover then asked Sen. Long to help Stover get the Insurance Commission to assist Stover with his claims. Stover said he told Long he wanted a legislator's help but Long, an attorney, charged him a legal fee of $2,500 instead of handling the matter free of charge. Swerling said it was a legitimate fee.

Long Case Goes to Jury

As the presentation of evidence and the closing arguments in the Bud Long case came to an end, the prosecution appeared to be in trouble. The Court had rejected five witnesses, including four news reporters and their news stories as witnesses for the government. The testimony of Ron Cobb had failed as Cobb said that he did not think that Long knew he was taking a bribe or intended to take a bribe. The videotapes and audiotapes were perhaps some evidence but not conclusive.

Judge Falcon Hawkins declared that he would ponder until the next day whether he should acquit Long on the extortion count and would then announce his final decision on November 23, 1991.

Prosecution Thought Long Case Was Weak

It came out in the final first round trial of operation Lost Trust cases that the prosecution's strategy was to put the strongest cases up for trial first and to hold the weakest cases until last. The case against Senator Bud Long was considered to be very weak on the evidence and therefore the indictment of Long was last and was delayed until August 20, 1991, and his trial was scheduled to be the last as well.

The anxiety of prosecutors about the Long case caused them to contact Washington on October 31, 1991, for permission to subpoena reporters to provide more evidence since the evidence then available was so dubious. The memo indicated the fact that "the order in which these cases were indicted was determined by our evaluation of the strength of the evidence we had," wrote Alred "Buddy" Bethea, Assistant U.S. Attorney, in his contact with the Justice Department.

Bethea went on to point out that Tim Wilkes had made no statement to the press and had been acquitted. Perhaps the lack of statements to the press was a critical missing element in the prosecution's evidence. And Wilkes, according to Bethea, "convinced the jury that he believed the money paid to him by the government's undercover informant was a campaign contribution. Bethea then added that Long's attorney, Jack Swerling, "indicated that the testimony of these reporters may make the difference in the case."

Judge Dismisses Conspiracy Charge

Judge Falcon Hawkins acquitted on the conspiracy to commit extortion charge in the two count indictment of Sen. Bud Long on November 22, 1991, but let the count of extortion stand and go to the jury. Hawkins found the evidence of conspiracy too weak to be considered by the jurors but found sufficient evidence of extortion to warrant a verdict.

Swerling Attacks Government Case

Long's attorney, Jack Swerling, then moved for a mistrial on the remaining charge, arguing that the weak evidence for conspiracy presented to the jury might have created a bias in favor of conviction on the remaining extortion indictment. Hawkins refused the motion telling Swerling, "I don't blame you for trying...but you can stretch these things only so far."

Prosecutor Sheri Lydon stated in closing argument that Long has sold his vote, alleging that "Cobb determined what would happen to that bill, because he had bought himself a senator."

Swerling retorted that the sting had taken unfair advantage of Long's financial problems and need for money in tempting him with Cobb's money, alleging that "A man in need was taken advantage of. They twisted and turned the truth to make it look like Bud Long was committing a crime." It was not illegal in South Carolina for candidates to take a cash campaign donation and Swerling said the prosecution had not proved that Long took a bribe.

Swerling also argued that Long was not trying to hide the fact that he took money from Cobb in 1990 because Long did not have to report the money as a campaign contribution until he ran again for the Senate in 1992 according to South Carolina's campaign finance disclosure laws. Perhaps the laws of the state were too weak on timely reporting of such donations Swerling said, but it was not the business of the federal government to try to impose new reporting timelines on states for such money.

Swerling explained that, in fact, Sen. Long did have serious financial problems and needed money to make a house payment and that Long asked Cobb for the money. Swerling told the jury Long went to Cobb as a friend and said to Cobb, "They're going to foreclose my house." Swerling then said the truth was that Long "said he needed $2,800. The method of payment was chosen by the FBI. Bud Long never asked for cash. He asked in the middle of the Senate with people standing around." Long's defense seemed to be inconsistently arguing that the $2,800 given by Cobb to Long was both a personal loan and a campaign contribution.

Swerling added that "Everything Bud Long did was out in the open. Everything Ron Cobb did was behind closed doors." Swerling then pointed to the fact that Long had been an elected public official for some two decades as a solicitor and senator and argued that there was no evidence of previous corruption, asserting, "If Bud Long was going to violate the public trust, he would have done it before May 22, 1990." The prosecution never presented any testimony or other evidence of prior wrongdoing, Swerling asserted, but they would have if it was known, claiming "With all the resources of the U.S. government, if it ever happened, they'd have it."

The prosecution's case was weakened further, Swerling argued, when Ron Cobb, their major witness against Long, told the court that he did not think the extortion charges against Long were justified because Cobb felt that Long believed the money he took was not a bribe.

The prosecution's case was further denied possible evidence when news reporters refused to testify when the government wanted to call them to report that Long had told the media that he only took $300 from Cobb, not nine times that amount as alleged. (The four reporters who had been called by the court were kept in custody by Hawkins while the trial was in progress because they would not testify. Once the prosecution rested its case the demand on the reporters ended and the court released them from custody.) The jury never saw the newspaper articles which the four reporters had written about the Long case.

Another blow to the government was that it did not present the witness who would have told the court that Sen. Long had charged him $2,500 for a public service which perhaps should have been provided by Long for free.

Swerling impugned the government's case and alleged that it was a shambles and needed no rebuttal. Swerling had offered no witnesses for Long, not even Long, avoiding a harsh cross-examination which surely would have damaged Long's image before the jury. The prosecution witnesses had functioned as defense witnesses.

Long Trial—Closing Arguments

The prosecution's case going to the jury was required by *McCormick* to show not only that Long took money from Cobb but that Long agreed to take official action as consideration for the money. Even if the jury found the money handed by Cobb to Long was not a campaign contribution but a gift or a loan the prosecution still had to show that Long promised to take or took official action in return for the money. Extortion case law required a quid pro quo, not just the movement of money from Cobb to Long. At a minimum it was necessary to show that Long made a promise of official action in return for the money or actually took action as a senator in return for the money in order to meet the *McCormick* standard.

Prosecutor Sheri Lydon told the jury in closing about the videotapes of Long taking money from Cobb including audio recordings in which Long promised to "pump up" other senators to get help on moving the betting bill out of committee. She said that Long even asked Cobb if the senator should try to get the betting bill set for special order which would give it priority and speed the bill to vote. Lydon asked, "Why else does he mention the bill as he gets the money?" Lydon further remarked about Long taking the 28 hundred dollar bills while talking about the betting bill and the advantages of betting on horses and dogs in Long's senate district of Myrtle Beach and its surroundings.

The audiotaped remarks of Cobb and Long were clearly suspicious. The jury heard Cobb tell Long on May 17, 1990, that "I think I can come up with the $2,800 Monday, and then if we can get the damned thing polled out, I know I can come up with another couple thousands." Long then jumped into the trap and said, "That'd be great."

But Long had also referred to the Cobb money as "a contribution" so Lydon tried to reframe the matter as a bribe, telling jurors that the defense was trying to make too much out of the remark, and saying "They're basing this entire full-of-baloney story on that one statement.... He got a contribution for his own billfold."

Lydon also said that even if Long needed money for his house payment "it was wrong to hit up a lobbyist for money." She further rebutted the defense efforts to create sympathy for Long, saying that Long had been treated fairly by the government and that 'The government pulled the covers off this scam and exposed it, pure and simple."

Swerling's closing praised the prosecution for exposing corruption in South Carolina's government but said the prosecution had gone too far and "it's time to close the door, turn out the lights and go home....That should have been done before this case came to court."

In final remarks Sherri Lydon rejected the defense theory that the government's case fell apart, retorting that Swerling "says our case had evaporated...The tapes are still here. The lies to the FBI are still here. Of course, Mr. Swerling told you that. He is a criminal defense lawyer. You wouldn't expect him to tell you that the government had proved its case beyond a reasonable doubt." She then spurned the notion that the prosecution had gone on too long and gone too far, rebuking Swerling because "He wants us to turn out the lights and stop.... We won't stop looking for public corruption until public officials stop engaging in corruption."

In reaction to Lydon's effort to discredit his presentation, Swerling jumped to his feet and interrupted the closing argument, a rare action in such trials, and denigrated the prosecution's closing be saying "I've never heard a prosecutor say somebody was innocent either."

Videotapes Hurt Long

Judge Hawkins admitted a videotape into evidence which was made on May 17, 1990, which the judge believed contained evidence the jury could reasonably use to convict Long. In the tape Cobb keeps talking about getting money for the betting bill and Long seems to respond. When Cobb said that he could get the $2,800 Long needed to make his overdue house payments while also talking about the betting bill and the need for Long to take action on the bill, Long stepped into the trap and said, "Then I'm going to be in a damned sweat on Monday now, if I ain't got somewhere to turn," referring to the deadline for foreclosure on his property. Cobb then told Long that he thought he could get the $2,800 by Monday and Long said. "That'd be great."

Jurors were swayed by the prosecution's videotapes shown to them indicating Long's eagerness to take money from Cobb, especially the tape made in Cobb's office in the AT&T Building on May 22, 1990, when Long said to Cobb "You done good, my friend." And Cobb responded, "Senator, you done good yesterday." Mentioning that he is referring to the betting bill, Cobb said to Long, "You've got to help me some more now" to which Long responded, "Well, you know I'm for that." Then Cobb counted out $2,800 in $100 bills and handed them to Long and said, "I hope that $2,800 helps my senator." Long then expressed his appreciation, "Thank you, my friend, you know it will.... I've got to support the bill any way I can. For me, it's going to do an outstanding job in Horry, No. 1. It'll help us not only from the standpoint of being a tourism attraction and bringing people in, but it will also give a market for people and jobs."

Long then kept talking about the economic benefits of a horse racing and betting bill for his district, even mentioning that it would increase the market for farm products such as hay and feed. But Cobb turned the talk back to the money, trying to incriminate Long, saying to the senator, "if we can make money together, we'll make money."

Cobb then pressed Long for more help on the bill, again referred to more money from the interests behind the betting bill, and said "I can go back to these folks and get some more money, cause they got money." The dialogue on the tape does not clearly show a quid pro quo of Cobb offering a bribe for Long's help and Long's acceptance of the bribe by making a promise to act or by acting. The evidence on the tapes was less than conclusive.

Long Convicted of Extortion

The trial of Sen. Bud Long ended on Saturday, November 23, 1991, with a conviction on one count of extortion but acquitted on one count of conspiracy to commit extortion under the Hobbs Act. The trial jury took only one hour and 45 minutes to conclude that Long was guilty.

Jurors later said that the videotape of Cobb giving Sen. Long 28 hundred dollar bills was convincing. Donna Mercer, the jury forewoman from Simpsonville, said "It was the acceptance of the money with him talking all the time about the pari-mutuel bill." Along with other jurors, Ms. Mercer concluded, "he looked like he pretty much knew what was going on."

Jurors told reporters they were convinced by the videotapes that Long was guilty of extortion even though Judge Falcon Hawkins acquitted Long on the conspiracy to commit extortion indictment for lack of evidence.

The scene in the courtroom was dramatic when the verdict was read. Long's wife, Judy, wept, and Long's seven children seemed stunned by the finding of guilty. Long's mother seemed focused on her son. After the jury left the courtroom the family embraced in tears and thanked supporters who had come to the courtroom for the verdict.

Defense lawyers Tommy Brittain and Jack Swerling explained the guilty verdict by saying that the fact that publicity that so many defendants in Lost Trust had been found guilty seemed to give momentum favoring a guilty verdict because so many people in South Carolina thought that there was massive corruption at the State House. A reflective Swerling observed, "The public attitude is that there was corruption at the State House. Twenty-seven people were convicted because of it. The momentum of Operation Lost Trust was in the prosecution's favor, and it worked against Bud Long."

Brittain thought that jurors would pay great attention to the evidence showing that Cobb had a "fish" ready to pay for help on the betting bill and that Long knew that Cobb would pay for help. Long stepped into the trap when he asked Cobb what Cobb was looking for and then Long told Cobb, "I'm hungry. I'm looking for a deal."

Another factor which helped the prosecution was that it was able to present evidence in support of the charge of conspiracy to commit extortion even though the conspiracy charge was acquitted by the judge. The evidence of conspiracy still may have tainted the jury on the remaining extortion charge.

Defense attorneys indicated an intention to ask for post-trial relief and for the judge to set aside the guilty verdict on the grounds that the evidence was too weak.

Scoppe Explains Jail Choice

Cindi Ross Scoppe, one of the four reporters jailed by Judge Hawkins, wrote an op ed in the Insight/Opinion section of *The State* on November 24, 1991, explaining why she and her other three colleagues chose to defy the court and take a contempt citation and detention on two consecutive days in the Bud Long trial.

As a young staff writer for *The State*, Scoppe wrote, "I have been a reporter for seven years, but my mother didn't understand why I would disobey a federal judge and risk going to jail rather than testify about an interview I did with a state senator accused of selling his vote."

Scoppe went on to say that one of the most important unwritten rules in journalism is: "Don't let anything interfere with your ability to tell the public the truth about its government." She went on to explain, "The biggest, and perhaps the most difficult, part of our job is getting people who know what's really going on in the government to trust us." She pointed out that people in government preferred to keep their business secret. Even so, she argued, "But, our job is to find out what they're doing—how they're spending tax money, what they're doing with the power you have entrusted to them."

She warned that journalists would not be trusted by those who know important information about government and politics unless they know reporters "won't become an agent for government prosecutors, turning what they have told us freely against them."

<u>Long Seat in Limbo</u>

The conviction of Sen. Bud Long on November 23, 1991, opened the question of whether the Senate seat Long still held would remain open until the next general elections in November of 1992 because Long had only taken a voluntary suspension from the Senate when he was indicted and was not subject to automatic expulsion on conviction of felony. This was unlike the House which by Rule 3.12 required automatic expulsion on conviction of felony and which had been used many times against those representatives who pleaded guilty or were convicted at trial in Lost Trust cases.

Long's status was similar to that of Judge Tee Ferguson in that in neither case was automatic expulsion imposed on either of them on conviction of felony because no law or rule of the Senate or Supreme Court rule required expulsion. They had to resign to end their service and if they did not they continued in office for term. If Long's seat in District 33 was vacant the Lt. Governor could call a special election for 11 Tuesdays after the vacancy began.

The Ethics Act of 1991 dealt with this anomaly by providing in 8-13-560 that expulsion from office for a felony was automatic for any state or local official on conviction. But the Act did not take effect for another month as of on January 1, 1992, even though it had been as of October 1, 1991, passed and signed at the time of Long's conviction.

As the law stood at the time of the conviction of Sen. Long, the Senate could not take action to remove him until after he had exhausted his appellate rights without relief from his conviction.

However, once the new Ethics Act of 1991 took effect then Long would arguably have been expelled as of January 1, 1992, unless the trial or appellate courts provided relief from his conviction before that date.

The legislative delegation from Horry County, including all House and Senate members representing any part of the county, refused to pressure Long from office when they met on December 11, 1991, and did not even put the issue of Long's future on their agenda. The delegation's new chairman told the media after the meeting that the matter of Long's future would be left up to him and that the delegation intended not to consider the matter for the foreseeable future.

Senate Clerk Frank Caggiano explained that the Senate could not consider expelling Sen. Long until his appeals from conviction for extortion had been exhausted without success. Long's term expired in November of 1992, a year after his conviction. Referring to the question of whether the delegation should try to demand that Long resign the Chairman of the delegation, Rep. Tom Keegan, a Republican, told the media after the meeting that "I don't think that's appropriate for the delegation to do.... I think Senator Long has the concerns of the county at heart...and that will weigh very heavily on any decision he makes."

Editorial Knocks Long's Status in Senate

The fact that the South Carolina Senate had no automatic suspension and expulsion rules for indicted and convicted senators provoked *The State* to editorialize against the "gross inequity that exists between the Senate and the House in their rules governing members indicted on criminal charges." *The State* felt the automatic provisions in the House Rule 3.12 raised a serious question in comparison with the Senate's lack of a similar rule.

The Senate had a set of rules governing such cases but they were more lenient than those of the House. The Senate's rule was that a senator could only be suspended at the time of conviction and that expulsion was not possible until all appeals had failed. Even then expulsion was not automatic and could only be affected if the Senate voted by majority to expel the member.

The State said the disparity in the rules was exposed glaringly by the Lost Trust prosecutions in which fifteen house members and two senators had been convicted, one of whom, Sen. Rick Lee, resigned without a fight. The convicted House members were also expelled on conviction but *The State* complained Long was still allowed to hold his Senate seat in spite of his conviction of a felony under federal law.

CHAPTER THIRTY EIGHT

1992—SENTENCES AND APPEALS

Those who had pleaded guilty or been convicted at trial in 1991 had not all been sentenced that same year and some remained to be sentenced in the following year.

Among those sentenced in 1992 was Rep. Ennis Fant (D-Greenville) who was given 20 months on January 3rd. The others followed shortly thereafter.

Ironically, the new so-called 1991 Ethics Act went into effect on January 1, 1992, and was designed to counteract the many failings of the 1975 Ethics Act. The new 1991 Ethics Act came as a shock to those acculturated in an era when lobbyists' handouts to legislators and bribery had run rampant at the State House.

Appeals were filed in cases during 1992 based largely on the new *McCormick* case of 1991 which required that a quid pro quo be proved to convict defendants of bribery under the Hobbs Act.

Fant Ordered to Prison

Former state Rep. Ennis Fant (D-Greenville) was ordered to prison by Judge Falcon Hawkins even though Fant had filed an appeal from his conviction for corruption. Hawkins ordered Fant to start serving his sentence beginning on January 20, 1992. Hawkins had given Fant a two week delay in starting his sentence.

Fant's attorney, B.O. Thomason, told the media that Fant would be sent to a minimum security prison at Seymour Johnson Correctional Institution in Goldsboro, N.C.

Fant's appeal to the Fourth Circuit Court of Appeals contended that the sentence imposed on Fant was unfair in comparison with other defendants. The judge asserted that the lower level of cooperation of Fant as compared with other defendants justified the harsher sentence imposed on Fant. The judge said there was no abuse of discretion on his part.

Jack Rogers Sentenced

On January 8, 1992, U.S. District Judge Falcon Hawkins sentenced former Speaker Pro Tem Jack I. Rogers to 46 months in federal prison on conviction of racketeering for his role in Lost Trust bribery and prior corruption. Sentence was to begin in March, 1992.

The U.S. Attorney said that racketeering was one of the most serious federal crimes. Rogers was found to have peddled his influence and demanded that lobbyists pay him a percentage of their compensation for lobbying state government. In addition to 46 months in prison, Rogers faced three years of probation and 300 hours of community services.

The federal government was seeking to seize Rogers' assets equal to the bribes he took plus his salary as a legislator, an amount of $53,000 in total. The South Carolina Supreme Court was also expected to begin proceedings to revoke Rogers' law license.

Rogers had been indicted on ten counts but was allowed to plead to one count of racketeering, a crime carrying a maximum sentence of 20 years in prison. The sentencing guidelines provided for 46 months in prison. Rogers asked for a downward departure based on the fact that Rogers had testified for the government in the Tee Ferguson case, but Judge Hawkins said Rogers' help was minimal and his crime was very serious. The judge found that Rogers had tried to hide his bribes and encouraged two witnesses to lie.

Ron Cobb Sentenced

The government's chief sting agent and witness was set for sentencing on January 9, 1992 at a hearing in Charleston. A sentence of probation was expected. Cobb was charged with cocaine violations.

Assistant U.S. Attorney Sherri Lydon filed a request for leniency in favor of Cobb, stating that "Aside from his continued use of drugs, Cobb followed FBI instructions to the letter." Lydon said that Cobb's work in the sting was invaluable. She said that allegations of corruption in state government had circulated for years but it was only when Cobb served as an FBI sting agent that the corruption was finally exposed.

Cobb worked for the FBI for over two years. At one point Cobb's tape recorder went off while he was having dinner with two suspect legislators; but Cobb was quickly able to deceive the suspects with a scheme whereby the FBI was able to contrive a device that looked like Cobb's tape recorder but was really a garage door opener. The door opener was shown to the suspects to convince them that they what had seen at dinner was not a tape recorder but a door opener.

With Cobb's help a total of 28 defendants had been charged. Cobb testified in all of the cases tried in 1990 and 1991.

The sentencing hearing of Ron Cobb on January 9, 1992, painted a picture of Cobb as a drug and alcohol-abuser who helped the FBI to pull off the biggest public corruption sting and prosecution in South Carolina history.

The court sentenced Cobb to six months in a halfway house for using cocaine while he worked undercover for the FBI. Cobb had pleaded guilty in April, 1991, to two counts of cocaine possession. Cobb also got two years' probation and 200 hours of community service in addition to time in a halfway house.

Judge Falcon Hawkins heard impassioned pleas for leniency from the government related to Cobb's role in the sting. Normally, FBI sting agents got counseling and help to assist them in their work but Cobb got no such advisement. FBI agent Mike Clemens blamed himself for not providing Cobb more help.

Prosecuting attorney Dale DuTremble said that Cobb had said to him many times, "If you'll just take the shackles off of me, I'll bring you three-fourths of the Legislature." DuTremble said that Cobb expressed remorse for using drugs. The U.S. Attorney said Cobb had lived in protective custody since the sting became public and Cobb had received threats.

Cobb seemed to take pride in his work as an FBI agent and told the court, "I am firmly convinced it will have a lasting impact on the way government business is done, not only in this state, but, I suspect, some others."

State Editorial on Ron Cobb

The State published an editorial on January 12, 1992, on the role of Ron Cobb in South Carolina politics. The editors described Cobb as "the key to exposing State House corruption in Operation Lost Trust, but he was no hero."

The State noted that Cobb was forced into being an FBI sting agent because he was caught in a sting operation himself while making a drug deal. Before then, he had been a sleazy influence-peddler offering lawmakers money and drugs for political favors.

The editorial brushed aside the praise lavished on Cobb by prosecutors and the FBI in Cobb's sentencing hearing and wrote "Judge Hawkins rightly refused to let Mr. Cobb off scot free," noting that the Judge pointed out that Cobb was "not here because of what he did in Operation Lost Trust. He's here because he had cocaine."

Randy Lee Sentenced

On January 13, 1992, James Randal Lee, a lobbyist caught with possession of marijuana, was sentenced in federal court to three years' probation, a fine of $2,500 and 150 hours of community service. Lee lobbied for S.C. Health Care Association. His attorney was Mike Spears.

Federal prosecutors told the court that Lee had helped to convict at least half of the 28 defendants indicted in Lost Trust. Lee testified in the trials of five legislators. Lee had volunteered to assist the probe as soon as it was made public because he knew that he was implicated for using drugs with legislators and lobbyists. Lee told the media that he regarded Lost Trust as a chance to break out of the corruption and drugs in which he had become entangled at the State House.

Federal agents told the court that they relied on Lee's memory of the workings of state government as well as of drug abuse and corruption at the State House and its surroundings. Lee wore a body recorder and allowed FBI agents to wire his car to make tapes of legislators and lobbyists who used drugs and were implicated in corruption, prosecutor John Barton told the judge.

Lee testified in corruption cases directed against Rep. B.J. Gordon (D-Williamsburg), Rep. Larry Blanding (D-Sumter), Rep. Paul Derrick (R-Lexington), Rep. Ken Bailey (D-Orangeburg), and Judge Tee Ferguson.

Prosecutor Barton said that Lee also collected evidence against Dick Greer, Judge Ferguson, Rep. Jack I. Rogers (D-Marlboro), Rep. Robert Brown (D-Marion), Rep. Donna Moss (D-Cherokee), Rep. Tom Limehouse (R-Dorchester), and Rep. Robert Kohn (R-Charleston). Lee also obtained evidence of drugs and bribery involving other lobbyists.

S.C. Legislature Meets for New Session

The new session of the South Carolina General Assembly met on January 14, 1992, at the State House in Columbia. Rep. Tim Wilkes (D-Fairfield) returned to the House, the only defendant in Lost Trust to be acquitted. On the other hand, Sen. Bud Long did not appear in the Senate as he was still under suspension and had been convicted at trial in late November, 1991.

The Senate could have expelled Long but took no immediate action to do so on the first day of the session. Long requested a delay from the Senate on the issue until January 22,1992, when a federal judge was set to decide Long's request to set aside the conviction.

The State House lobby held an abnormally small number of lobbyists and others for the first day of the session. It so happened that at the same time the U.S. Department of Justice had given pre-clearance approval to the 1991 Ethics Act as required by the 1965 Voting Rights Act.

Ex-Rep. Paul Derrick Gets 34 Months in Prison

On January 21, 1992, Judge Falcon Hawkins sentenced former Rep. Paul Derrick to 34 months in prison for taking a $1,000 bribe. Derrick denied his guilt on conspiracy and extortion.

Videotapes at trial showed Derrick taking cash from Ron Cobb. But Derrick told the court that he had not voted based on a payoff.

Judge Hawkins observed, "If Operation Lost Trust has not already had an effect on lobbyists and legislators, I don't know what will." Noting that Derrick had no previous problems with the law, Hawkins mused, "It is particularly difficult for me to imagine how you got into this predicament."

The convictions on conspiracy and extortion carried separate sentences which the judge ordered served concurrently.

Prior to the imposition of sentence Derrick's attorney Jim Lengel argued that Derrick had never been charged with bribery but the government focused on bribery at trial. Derrick was not charged with obstruction but he got more time because he tried to deceive the FBI and told them he took no cash money from Ron Cobb, but later that day deposited the money in the bank and told the House Ethics Committee it was a cash campaign donation. However, Hawkins ruled that falsifying a bank deposit was obstruction of justice and penalized Derrick for it.

Hawkins followed the sentencing guidelines which prescribed 33 to 41 months in prison and a fine of up to $75,000. Prosecutors had asked for more time on the grounds that Derrick intended to take a bribe in the next session of the Legislature from Ron Cobb to promote the betting bill.

Sen. Long Asks for Reversal of Conviction

On January 22, 1992, Tommy Brittain, attorney for Sen. Bud Long, appeared in federal court in Charleston and asked the court to overturn the conviction of Long on extortion charges. Brittain argued that at trial the court had allowed evidence on a conspiracy charge to be presented before dismissing the conspiracy charge and that the evidence affected the jury when it decided to convict Long of extortion under the Hobbs Act.

Brittain argued that the conspiracy evidence should have been excluded and was prejudicial to Long and may have caused his conviction. The remedy for admission of highly prejudicial evidence in such a case included the reversal of conviction and award of a new trial.

Bart Daniel Resigns

U.S. Attorney Bart Daniel announced on January 2, 1992, that he would resign and return to private practice as of March 8, 1992. Attorney Dick Harpootlian, Fifth Circuit Solicitor, complemented Daniel saying "He has had a tremendous impact on the politics of this state." Attorney I.S. Leevy Johnson praised him, saying "Bart was a tremendous prosecutor."

Sen. Strom Thurmond (R-S.C.) asked President George H.W. Bush to nominate John S. Simmons to replace Daniel. Simmons had prosecuted Orangeburg County Corner Paul Simmons on drug charges and had also convicted Camden developer E. Michael Sheheen for fraud, embezzlement, and enticing 50 people to invest in a bogus company.

Robert Kohn Gets 15 Months

Ex-Rep. Robert Kohn (R-Charleston) was sentenced to 15 months on January 22, 1992, for conspiring to buy votes at the State House. Prosecutors asked for a more lenient sentence for Kohn on grounds that he cooperated with the FBI and worked undercover to catch crooked legislators involved in drugs and corruption.

The prosecution asked the court for leniency for Kohn on the basis of the fact that he wore tape recorders and allowed himself to be videotaped while plotting bribery and snorting cocaine with politicians. The prosecution claimed that Kohn had a major role in gathering evidence for the indictment of all 28 defendants charged in Lost Trust. Bart Daniel went so far as to say that the government would have aborted the sting operation without Kohn's continued help. Kohn told a sad story of how Operation Lost Trust hurt his family and ruined his life. In fact, he had been a dubious official for years. Judge Falcon Hawkins pointed out that Kohn had helped to create corruption at the State House before he tried to clean it up. The judge could have given 30 to 37 months under federal guidelines but gave him 15 months, plus two years' probation, and 200 hours of community service.

Gov. Campbell's State of State Address

On January 28, 1992, Gov. Carroll Campbell delivered his State of the State Address in the House Chamber in Columbia. Campbell focused on the need to reorganize government administration. He asked for a constitutional amendment proposal to allow voters to approve a new cabinet form of government.

Letter to Editor Protests Paying Cobb

Katherine Donovan, MD, of Charleston, S.C., published a letter to the editor of *The State* on February 2, 1992, in which she complained about the fact that the prosecution in the Lost Trust cases paid Ron Cobb for his work as a sting agent and witness. Dr. Donovan alleged that the government paid Cobb "$300,000 or more, for his part in the Lost Trust sting operation."

Donavan asked, "Am I the only one in South Carolina who is appalled that our federal government paid Ron Cobb—a self-professed gambler, womanizer, and cocaine user…." She went on to write, "In these dark days of recession and trillion-dollar deficits, is it reasonable or fair to pay an exorbitant sum like that to a man who already abused his position of power when 'serving' in Columbia?"

Donavan concluded, "Isn't it enough that he was not fined $100,000 and not sent to jail for his various crimes without having honest, hard-working taxpayers now line his pockets with a 'bonus'?"

Senate Passes Bill to Give State Grand Jury Anti-Corruption Power

The South Carolina Senate voted on February 25, 1992, to give the State Grand Jury new authority to investigate public-corruption cases in South Carolina.

However, the Senate voted 25-11 to limit jurisdiction to cases of public corruption which crossed county lines only. This would prevent the State Grand Jury from probing corruption located only in one county.

Attorney General Medlock and nearly every law enforcement group in South Carolina stated their intention to support the bill to fight crime.

Faber Fined for Deal

Former Rep. James Faber (D-Richland) was fined by Circuit Court Judge Costa Pleicones on March 2, 1992, for failing to report a business dealing he had with the Town of Eastover, South Carolina, while he was in the House. The court fined Faber $500 for failure to disclose the profit he made in selling a backhoe to Eastover in 1988. The judge could have imposed 90 days in jail and a fine of $1,000.

In March, 1991, Faber had pleaded guilty to taking a bribe of $1,000 from Ron Cobb to vote for the betting bill and was serving a one year sentence in the federal prison in Goldsboro, N.C., when he was convicted of the backhoe-sale violation.

Faber had been indicted in the summer of 1991 for omissions about the backhoe sale in the financial disclosure forms he was required to file with the House Ethics Committee which were supposed to report his dealing with state or local governments. SLED investigated the matter in preparation for the indictment.

The sale of the backhoe was made on January 13, 1988, to Eastover for the amount of $28,345. Faber had paid $22,000 for the backhoe. The funds to buy the backhoe came from funds amounting to $100,000 that Faber had inserted in the 1986 state budget for the use of Eastover. Some $3,000 was also spent from the appropriation to buy supplies from Eastover Lumber Co. which was owned by Faber.

Suspended Long in Limbo

In mid-March, 1992, Sen. Bud Long was still suspended, officially, in the Senate, and his seat was vacant after his conviction for selling his vote in late November, 1991. The result was that the citizens of Horry County had no senator on active status representing them in the Senate. The absence of Long from the body was a grim reminder of the damage caused by Lost Trust.

Judge Orders New Trial for Sen. Long

On March 26, 1992, Judge Falcon Hawkins ordered a new trial for Sen. Bud Long on the grounds that the court's "oversight" denied Long a fair trial. Hawkins admitted that he should have told the jury in his instructions that they were to ignore secretly taped remarks that Long might be willing to accept a bribe.

The comments about Long's possible acceptance of a bribe were related to evidence introduced in the trial by the government in support of the indictment of Long for criminal conspiracy. However, the court ruled against the conspiracy. Hawkins either should have instructed the jury to disregard the evidence, or perhaps, more wisely, should have declared a mistrial and should have ordered a new trial before sending the case to the jury for a verdict.

Sen. Long reported that he received calls of support after the court ordered a new trial on the indictment for taking an alleged bribe of $2,800 from Ron Cobb. But Republican officials called on Long to resign. New U.S. Attorney John Simmons said on March 27, 1992, immediately after the court ordered the new trial, that the government would have to decide to appeal the order, go to a new trial, or dismiss the remaining charges.

General Assembly Empowers State Grand Jury

On April 8, 1992, the South Carolina General Assembly passed a bill which granted to the State Grand Jury the power to investigate public corruption in state and local governments. The bill resolved a controversy as to whether the authority to probe public corruption should be limited to only cases of multi-county corruption by deciding that the State Grand Jury could probe both corruption in only one county or in more than one county.

Gov. Carroll Campbell had supported the bill which was being pushed by Attorney General Travis Medlock. The bill was especially timely in that the Lost Trust scandal had been exposed and prosecuted by federal authorities without any state law enforcement participation which raised questions about whether state authorities were unwilling or unable to deal with state and local bribery and abuse of public office.

Medlock remarked that the bill had to pass in 1992 in order to exploit the public indignation over Operation Lost Trust. Medlock and SLED Chief Robert Stewart persuaded opponents in the House to drop their opposition to an early form of the bill which included the expansion of the authority of the State Grand Jury to deal with one county as well as multi-county corruption.

Medlock praised the bill saying "We have the strongest grand jury investigative unit in America." His only concern was whether there was enough funding to support the expanded powers of the State Grand Jury and whether there were too few prosecutors to do the work in the future.

Prosecutors Drop Efforts to Increase Sentence of B.J. Gordon

Fearing that they might expose secret grand jury testimony and investigative information, the U.S. Attorney's office on April 7, 1992, dropped their motion to try convince the court to increase the amount of prison time to which B.J. Gordon was sentenced.

Assistant U.S. Attorney John Barton filed a motion in which the government withdrew its request for more time for Gordon and sought to speed up the sentencing for Gordon.

Gordon's attorney Lionel Lofton expressed surprise at the government's actions in the case. The prosecution was trying to convince the judge to impose more time on Gordon based on uncharged and unconvicted allegations that Gordon had been involved in prior unindicted crimes related to the use of state grant money. The use of evidence of past conduct was admissible, in fact, under federal sentencing guidelines.

In November the court ordered the government to turn over files of investigation materials, grand jury testimony, and other information related to a 1987 probe of activities at a Developmental Center for Retarded Adults run by Gordon in Williamsburg County. Gordon was not formally charged in that matter. However, the government did not produce all of the evidence ordered. Lionel Lofton then moved to force production on March 30, 1992, and the government responded by withdrawing its motion for sentence enhancement.

Opposition to Ethics Restriction

The provisions in the 1991 Ethics Act provoked criticism from some legislators who disliked the ban on lobbyists giving free meals and drinks to legislators. The law only allowed free meals and drinks for legislative groups but only if they were formed on the basis of political party, gender, or race.

Some legislators missed the good old days when lobbyists could wine and dine legislators as much as they liked. But on April 13, 1992, Speaker Bob Sheheen beat back a House rebellion seeking to restore the old culture of lobbyists giving free meals and drinks to legislators. The vote to repeal the ban on freebies from lobbyists was defeated in the House by a margin of 38-47. But then on April 14, 1992, a motion to reconsider the bill was passed 78-30. The Black Caucus had voted against the repeal of the ban on the first vote but shifted in favor of the repeal in the second vote.

The State published an editorial on April 14, 1992, urging indignant action by the citizenry, saying "Now's the time for South Carolinians to raise Cain with their representatives. If citizens protest loudly enough, they can derail this back peddling before it hits the House floor for a vote."

Prosecution Moves to Stop New Trial for Long

The government announced on April 15, 1992, that it would move to have Judge Falcon Hawkins reconsider his decision to order a new trial for Sen. Bud Long and to overturn Long's conviction on November 23, 1991, for taking a bribe. Assistant U.S. Attorney Buddy Bethea announced the motion would be filed in a week.

The government's brief, filed on April 8, 1992, argued that "the evidence does not weigh heavily against the verdict" and further that "any errors which might have been committed were harmless errors which cannot support granting a new trial."

If Hawkins ruled to reinstate charges against Long then Long could appeal to the Fourth Circuit U.S. Court of Appeals in Richmond, Va. Long faced up to 20 years in prison and a fine of $250,000.

The government could also appeal if Hawkins insisted on granting a new trial or dismiss all charges against Gordon and thereby avoid having to prosecute Gordon again in a new trial.

Ken Bailey Gets 27 Months

Ex-Rep. Ken Bailey (D-Orangeburg) was sentenced to 27 months in prison on April 23, 1992, for selling his vote. He had been convicted at trial in August 1991, on charges of conspiracy and extortion. The jury convicted Bailey of taking a bribe of $500 from Ron Cobb to vote for the betting bill.

The court gave Bailey 90 days to prepare for prison. He asked to be sent to the federal prison in Goldsboro, N.C., where his friends caught up in Lost Trust were also serving time. Bailey also remarked after the sentence was imposed, "Jesus, lead me. It looks like the government wants to feed me."

In addition to his prison term Bailey faced probation for three years and 200 hours of community service.

The federal sentencing guidelines called for prison time of 41 to 51 months. Judge Hawkins tended to side with Bailey against the prosecution claim that Bailey was prone to corruption because he let Rep. Robert Kohn, lure him into taking money to get a road paved in Orangeburg County.

Bailey's attorney, Charles Williams, son of Sen. Marshall Williams (D-Orangeburg), told the court that Bailey was "a little country bumpkin from Orangeburg that got snared up in something." But Hawkins rejected the attempt to trivialize Bailey's role, remarking that the jury thought it serious enough to convict and that there were tapes of Bailey asking Cobb about money for supporting the betting bill.

Ferguson Blames Rae for Conviction

Attorneys for convicted bribe-taker Judge Tee Ferguson told the court on April 24, 1992, that Ferguson was the victim of a racially biased prosecution. Ferguson argued that blacks were deliberately excluded from the trial jury. Ferguson's new attorney, Gaston Fairey, appeared.

The government responded that the trial jury had three black members who voted to convict Ferguson and that even an all-black jury would still have convicted Ferguson on the evidence.

Fairey asked for a new trial and Judge Falcon Hawkins listened to both prosecution and defense and then said he would rule later on the motion for a new trial. Fairey, who had just been hired by Ferguson to handle the appeal, told the court that the prosecution had shown racial bias in questioning juror prospects. Fairey said that only black candidates were asked questions about their political and religious affiliations. Fairey told the court, "The government cared about only one thing, and that was the color of their skin."

Assistant U.S Attorney Scott Schools urged the court to reject the defense argument and speed up the process of sending Ferguson to prison along with others convicted in Lost Trust cases.

Ron Cobb Appears on TV

Ron Cobb came to the steps of the State House in Columbia on April 28, 1992, to appear on CBS' "60 Minutes" and be interviewed by Mike Wallace for a show focusing on Operation Lost Trust.

Cobb's appearance was his first at the State House since the FBI had started to interview legislators about their dealings with Cobb over the betting bill. But Cobb did not go inside the State House when he came for his TV interview. Cobb said of the lobbyists and legislators staring at him that "We're not going to create any more havoc than we already have."

Cobb remarked that he did not miss life at the State House, saying, "Fifteen years of that stuff was about long enough. It wouldn't have been any fun without (Sen. Jack) Lindsay."

Prosecutors Oppose New Trial for Long

Sen. Bud Long's request for a new trial was opposed by the prosecution even after it was granted by trial Judge Falcon Hawkins on March 2, 1992. Prosecutors asked Hawkins to reconsider his grant of a new trial. Hawkins had granted a new trial on the grounds that he allowed the jury to view prejudicial evidence related to a conspiracy charge Hawkins later decided to dismiss. Hawkins feared that the immaterial evidence was improperly used by the jury to convict Long of extortion.

In a 52 page memorandum filed on May 4, 1992, the prosecution informed the court that the government had polled three of the jurors who had voted to convict Long and the jurors said that they did not look at tapes related to the conspiracy charge which had been dismissed while deciding to convict Long of taking $2,800 from Ron Cobb in extortionate payment. The memorandum was supported with affidavits and transcripts.

The government pointed out that the defense did not object to the fact that the tapes at issue were going to the jury before the jury began deliberations, arguing that the defense was admitting the tapes were not inadmissible evidence.

The government argued that the tapes were material evidence and corroborated witness testimony about Long's agreement to support the betting bill and Long's acceptance of the money from Cobb. Technically, the tapes were hearsay admitted under a legal rule allowing hearsay to provide background information to the jury.

Hawkins also refused Long's motion which was to dismiss the corruption charge on the grounds that it was flawed.

Kohn Enters Prison

Forer Rep. Bob Kohn reported to federal prison the last week in May of 1992. He began his 15 month sentence based on his 1990 guilty pleas to conspiracy charges related to the Lost Trust bribery sting.

Kohn entered the Butner Federal Correctional Facility near Durham, North Carolina.

Kohn had served as an FBI sting agent along with Ron Cobb after Kohn was caught by the federal government and decided to cooperate.

House Judiciary Weakens Restrictions on Lobbyists

The House Judiciary Committee voted on May 13, 1992, to allow lobbyists to recommend which legislators should receive campaign donations but retained the prohibition on lobbyists giving donations to candidates for state offices.

Lobbyists had complained that the law prohibited them from telling their employers about the voting records and conduct of legislators and about which of the legislators deserved to be given campaign donations by their employers. Lobbyists wanted to be allowed to report such information to employers. But Chairman David Wilkins (R-Greenville) insisted that lobbyists not be allowed to deliver campaign donations to legislators, saying, "We don't want to open it up...to the question of being a bagman."

New Bribery Trial Ordered for Taylor

The 4th Circuit Court of Appeals ordered a new trial for convicted former Rep. Luther Taylor (D-Richland). The order was issued May 29 and published on June 1, 1992. The court held that the jury was not clear as to what bribery was under federal law and had to guess that Taylor violated the law and took a bribe. The court concluded that Taylor might have been erroneously convicted because of public prejudice since he worked in a notoriously corrupt climate at the State House and not because he took a bribe.

The prosecution responded by telling the media that it planned to take Taylor to his new trial as soon as possible, said new U.S. Attorney John Simmons, noting that the 4th Circuit did find sufficient evidence in Taylor's first trial to warrant conviction when the jury convicted Taylor of taking a $4,300 bribe from Ron Cobb and rendered its verdict in late October, 1990. Taylor had been charged with taking five bribes and conspiring to solicit bribes in return for his support of the betting bill.

The 4th Circuit ruled that a jury in a Hobbs Act corruption case alleging bribery must be told what kinds of payments constitute bribes under the Hobbs Act. The court ruled that "it is clear that the payment must be made in return for an explicit promise or undertaking by the official to perform or not perform an official act. The principle was not adequately set forth in the instructions given to the Taylor jury."

At Taylor's trial Judge Hawkins failed to charge the jury that based on *McCormick v. U.S.* (500 U.S 257 (1991) that a quid pro quo was required because Taylor was convicted in October, 1990, before *McCormick* was decided on May 23, 1991. The 4th Circuit applied the *McCormick* holding retroactively to Taylor's case and thereby found that the government failed to prove a quid pro quo.

Taylor Seeks Release from Prison

At the time the 4th Circuit ordered a new trial for Luther Taylor, he was in prison at the Seymour Johnson Federal Prison Camp in Goldsboro, N.C. serving his sentence of six and a half years.

On June 2, 1992, Taylor left the Prison Camp under guard of U.S. Marshals Service and was taken to the Richland County Detention Center in Columbia, S.C., located a few blocks from the federal courthouse. Taylor intended to ask the federal judge to release him on bond until he could be given a new trial pursuant to the order of a new trial for his case issued by the 4th Circuit. Taylor had been incarcerated since December, 1990.

Taylor Appeal Upsets Other Convictions at Trial

The retroactive application of the ruling of the U.S. Supreme Court in *McCormick v. U.S.* to the Taylor case entitled Taylor to a new trial, but the 4th Circuit's decision also applied not only to Taylor's conviction but to other persons convicted at trial in the Lost Trust prosecutions before May 23, 1991. The failure of the court to instruct the jury on the need to prove a quid pro quo in Hobbs Act bribery cases in the Taylor case was also a failure in other such cases and would trigger multiple appeals and orders for new trials.

McCormick meant that the prosecution had to prove that the defendant in Hobbs Act bribery case had taken a compensation in return for taking an official act, that is, a quid pro quo. Hawkins had failed to instruct the jury in not only the Taylor case but in all other pre-*McCormick* Lost Trust cases that the prosecution had to prove a quid pro quo. Thus the cases taken to trial following Taylor's case and prior to May 23, 1991, were all vitiated by the same instructional failing and doomed to be reversed and ordered for a new trial.

However, the U.S. Supreme Court also held that the prosecution did not have to prove that the defendant asked for a bribe but only that he took a bribe. In a number of the Lost Trust cases the defendants had not asked for a bribe but had been offered one by Ron Cobb. The court ruled that the initiation of the bribery process was not a material factor.

Long Announces Intention Not to Run Again

On June 3, 1992, Sen. Bud Long took time from his preparations for a new trial on bribery charges to announce that he would not run for re-election. Long said that another election campaign would put too much strain on his family.

On that date, the South Carolina Senate allowed Long who had been under voluntary suspension from his Senate seat since late 1990, to address the Senate where Long told his colleagues that he apologized for not being able to help the Senate during a difficult time. But Long said that "I have not resigned because I am not guilty," adding that "Secondly, I have not resigned because I had hoped that my troubles would get resolved by now." The Senate gave Long a standing ovation after his remarks.

The Senate did not take action to expel Long while his appeal was in progress and successfully resulted in an overturn of his conviction and order of retrial. Under the circumstances, Long could have contested his Senate seat in the November, 1992, general elections.

Gordon Asks for New Trial

On June 11, 1992, former Rep. B.J. Gordon made known that he had decided to seek a new trial after the 4th Circuit ordered a new trial for Luther Taylor based on the *McCormick* case. Gordon became the first convicted defendant who had gone to trial and lost and who sought to take advantage of the ruling in the Taylor case by the 4th Circuit.

Hawkins had not instructed the jury to indicate that the government had to prove a quid pro quo in the Gordon case. On the contrary, Hawkins told the jurors that, "There need be no specific quid pro quo to establish extortion under color of official right. That is, the government need not prove that the defendant's promise to do anything in particular in return for the payment of money."

The instructions given by Hawkins in both the Taylor and Gordon cases were correct on the law and precedents in place in the 4th Circuit at the time. But when the 4th Circuit started to apply the new *McCormick* ruling of the U.S. Supreme Court, Hawkins' instructions were retroactively deemed improper and a sufficient reason to order a new trial.

Appeals Triggered by *McCormick* Case

The Taylor ruling also appeared to apply to not only the case of Gordon, but also to Rep. Larry Blanding and Rep. Paul Derrick who also were the victims of improper instructions in trials before *McCormick* was decided in May 1991.

Defense attorneys who lost trials before *McCormick* reacted to the 4th Circuit ruling ordering a new trial for Luther Taylor based on *McCormick* by moving forward with appeals also based on *McCormick*.

But attorney Danny Martin, who represented Larry Blanding, was not thrilled by the order for new trial given to Taylor, saying, "A new trial is nothing but prolonging the agony....I was looking for an acquittal."

On the other hand, Taylor's attorney, Joel Collins of Columbia, raised additional issues with the 4th Circuit including the question of whether it was constitutionally proper for the federal government to interfere with state and local political processes with an undercover sting operation directed toward state legislators and relating to a state legislative activity such as the passage of the betting bill.

Collins raised issues relating to the question of whether the Hobbs Act was affected by the provisions of South Carolina's campaign finance laws in effect prior to 1992. An additional issue was whether the FBI broke its own rules under U.S. Justice Department guidelines which prohibited the government from conducting stings related to bills that "will affect the lives of the citizenry" or would "legalize gambling." The effect of the betting bill on interstate commerce was still another issue since the constitutional basis of the Hobbs Act was the commerce clause in Article I, Section 8 of the United States Constitution.

McCormick Case Disrupts Lost Trust Convictions

The retroactive application of the quid pro quo principle found in the *McCormick* case to the Luther Taylor case began a domino-like effect which quickly resulted in a ruling on June 22, 1992, that the case of Larry Blanding must also be retried because his jury instruction was also defective as the Court failed to instruct on quid pro quo.

The 4th Circuit found sufficient evidence in the trial record in the Blanding case to support conviction, but the conviction could not stand.

The U.S. District Court in Columbia released Luther Taylor on bond, pending a new trial and the same was expected in the Blanding case.

The rulings ordering new trails for Taylor and Blanding made certain that B.J. Gordon would get a new trial too as would Paul Derrick, both of whom having gone to trial with pre-*McCormick* instructions from Hawkins. Former Judge Tee Ferguson had also moved for a new trial on the same grounds, but Assistant U.S. Attorney John Barton argued that the jury instructions in Ferguson's post-*McCormick* trial had been up-dated to follow the *McCormick* precedent and therefore were proper.

Ken Bailey also filed notice of appeal but had not yet stated the grounds of his appeal.

Blanding Freed on Bond

Former Rep. Larry Blanding became the third legislator convicted at trial to win a new trial on appeal. He was released from federal prison on June 29, 1992.

Blanding was released on $25,000 unsecured bond by U.S. Magistrate E. Skipworth Swearingen in Florence, S.C., according to Assistant U.S. Attorney John McIntosh.

Blanding had been convicted by a jury on March 8, 1991, on one count of conspiracy to violate the Hobbs Act and two counts of taking bribes under the Act. He was serving 37 months in prison and facing three years probation and community service of 200 hours. Again, the jury instructions given by Judge Hawkins failed to require a showing of quid pro quo to prove a Hobbs Act violation as the U.S. Supreme Court found necessary in May 1991, in *McCormick*.

Pres. Bush Announces Nomination of Simmons

On June 30, 1992, President George H.W. Bush announced that he would nominate John S. Simmons to become U.S. Attorney in South Carolina. Simmons had been acting as interim after Bart Daniel resigned in March of the same year. Simmons was recommended by Sen. Strom Thurmond.

Judge Reaffirms New Trial for Long

Rejecting the protests of federal prosecutors, Judge Falcon Hawkins reaffirmed his order for a new trial for Sen. Bud Long. Hawkins' order came on July 2, 1992, and reiterated his original order for a new trial issued in March of 1992 which was based on the theory that the court instruction erred.

Hawkins rebuffed prosecution arguments that the tapes related to a later-dismissed conspiracy charge were known to the defense but the defense did not object when the tapes were made available to the jury. The government also asserted that, in fact, the jury did not consider the tapes in making their decision to convict Long of extortion under the Hobbs Act.

In an eight page order Hawkins wrote that, "the government seeks relief based on the defense counsel's inaction or acquiescence." But, he added, "The court sees no difference between the actions of the government and the alleged inaction of counsel for the defense."

Hawkins admitted that he intended to give a more complete warning to the jury about the dismissed conspiracy charge and its evidence but he failed to do so. Hawkins' ruling awarding a new trial was based on his belief that he had failed to tell the jury to completely disregard all evidence introduced by the government in support of the indictment which accused Long of being involved in a conspiracy to extort money from Ron Cobb. As the conspiracy charge had been dismissed by Hawkins, he believed that he should have more effectively told the jury that all evidence submitted in support of the conspiracy charge was immaterial.

Reporters Ask for Shield Law Passage

Reporters who had been jailed by Judge Falcon Hawkins for refusing to testify in the Bud Long case in November, 1991, had their day in court on July 7, 1992, when their attorney, Jay Bender, appeared before the 4th Circuit's three judge panel.

Bender told the court that, "Any time you have a news gathering function impeded, it interferes with the ability to gather news then and in the future." Bender also said that the press would push for a new media shield law to be passed in the South Carolina General Assembly in the near future because the state had no law to shield reporters from compelled testimony about confidential sources and non-published information.

The 4th Circuit, however, said that the information the trial court in the Long case was seeking was not given to the reporters in confidence and the government sought the information for legitimate reasons, not for harassment. However, one judge concurred with the majority but worried that reporters might be "uniquely vulnerable" to subpoenas because they often got information from public figures. He was concerned that the government would be too inclined to rely on reporters for information. The judge was James Harvie Wilkinson, III.

Gil Thielen, executive editor of *The State*, complained that the ruling was less supportive of the media than in some other circuits. And reporters Cindi Scoppe of *The State* and Sid Gaulden of *The Post and Courier* both said they were still of the opinion that they should protect their sources from compelled disclosure by the courts.

Ferguson Sentenced to 33 Months

On August 10, 1992, the saga of former judge Tee Ferguson was interrupted when the court sentenced him to 40 months in prison, the maximum, on drug and corruption charges. Ferguson was the first judge in South Carolina's history to go to prison so far as was known at the time.

Even so, Ferguson still contended that his demise was the result of a racist plot to keep blacks out of the judiciary, and he accused the government of devious schemes against him. Outside the court house where he was sentenced, he refused to make a public apology to the media, saying, "Apologize for what?"

Senior U.S. District Judge Charles E. Simons handed down a seven-month sentence on a guilty plea to six cocaine charges, remarking that Ferguson showed, "one of the most depraved attitudes toward the judicial system I have even seen in my life." Simons was 75 years old. Ferguson had denied he ever had cocaine.

Judge Falcon Hawkins gave Ferguson 33 months on corruption for which he was convicted. The sentencing guidelines would have allowed less time but Hawkins noted evidence that Ferguson "intended to use his judicial office to continue his criminal activity." The FBI had a tape of Ferguson telling Ron Cobb that he planned to sell judicial favors.

Judge Simons read aloud at the Ferguson sentencing on cocaine charges confidential information that said that Ferguson had used cocaine in four legislative sessions with Ron Cobb, Reps. Bob Kohn, Robert Brown, Luther Taylor and Alex Harvin. In addition, he used drugs with lobbyists Randy Lee and James Brown. Robert Brown and Taylor were convicted of corruption, but not drugs. Randy Lee pleaded guilty to marijuana as did James Brown, although neither was charged with cocaine. In the end, Ferguson admitted to Judge Simons his use of the drugs for which the judge imposed seven months.

Judge Falcon Hawkins on July 15, 1992, rejected a motion for a new trial filed by former circuit judge Tee Ferguson. Hawkins stated that the instructions he had given the jury in the Ferguson corruption case were not defective and did include the quid pro quo requirement stated by the U.S. Supreme Court in 1991 in the *McCormick* case because Ferguson went to trial after the *McCormick* case was decided.

Elections Reflect Voter Apathy about Lost Trust

Voters went to the polls to vote in primary elections in which some of the candidates were persons who seemed to be suspicious as a result of the Lost Trust sting and prosecutions. In about half of the cases, the dubious candidates were defeated but in another half the shadowy candidates won their primaries. The primaries were held on August 25, 1992.

Prof. Neal Thigpen of Francis Marion University expressed surprise that some of the dubious candidates did not go down to defeat. Prof. Earl Black of the University of South Carolina remarked that the candidates who were under attack on ethical grounds usually could produce some kind of explanation which gave those who wanted to vote for them an excuse to do so.

In Florence County an attack alleging conflict of interest was directed against Sen. Hugh Leatherman (D-Florence) by challenger Tommy Rogers but Leatherman used extensive newspaper ads accusing Rogers of running a sleazy campaign. Leatherman was reelected.

Rep. Tim Wilkes (D-Fairfield) was not hurt by his bribery charges in Lost Trust. Wilkes beat back challenger Edward Murphy.

On the other hand, Rep. Levola Taylor (D-Richland) who had just taken office was ousted after questions were raised about her appointment of her brother to a position as magistrate. Rev. Joe Neal won the seat.

Sen. Mike Mullinax (D-Anderson) finished second after his record in the Senate was attacked and some questions were raised about his receipt of $150,000 in fees from state grants he obtained for his district. Challenger Bob Waldrep won the seat.

Appeals Court Orders Re-sentencing for Fant

The 4th Circuit Court of Appeals ruled that the sentence which had been imposed on former Rep. Ennis Fant (D-Greenville) was in violation of his plea agreement and therefore that Fant was entitled to a new sentencing process. Fant had agreed to cooperate with the prosecution after he was charged with corruption in the Lost Trust sting operation.

The FBI had used an undercover sting agent to pay Fant and others for their support on the betting bill and after Fant was caught taking a payoff he agreed to plead guilty and assist the government.

The re-sentencing order was released by the 4th Circuit in the Fant case on September 11, 1992. The order did not affect the conviction on corruption charges as the court found no defect in the conviction itself.

Appeals Court Orders Reporters to Testify

The ongoing battle between U.S. District Court Judge Falcon Hawkins and four hard-headed reporters started still another round when the 4th Circuit Court of Appeals in Richmond, Virginia, rejected an appeal by the reporters which had asked that Hawkins' order compelling reporters' testimony be overturned. The Court of Appeals ruled on October 27, 1992, that the four reporters did not have a constitutional right not to disclose their news sources to the trial court in the Sen. Bud Long case which was set for a new trial. Judge Hawkins demanded the four testify in Long's retrial.

The four reporters were Cindi Ross Scoppe of *The State* in Columbia, S.C., Andrew Shain of *The Sun News* in Myrtle Beach, S.C., and Sid Gaulden and Schuyler Kropf of *The Post and Courier* in Charleston, S.C. All four had refused to testify in Long's original trial in November, 1991, and had been jailed twice by Judge Hawkins for contempt of the court directive that they tell the court what Long had said to them about how much he took from Ron Cobb. At trial Long was charged with taking $2,800 from Cobb and convicted on grounds that the money was given as a bribe. There was some evidence that Long had told the reporters that he only took $300 from Cobb as the reporters used that amount of money in their news articles about the Long case.

Attorney Jay Bender of the South Carolina Press Association handled the case for the reporters and indicated an intent to appeal the matter to the full panel of judges at the 4th Circuit as he had done in 1991 at the time of the first Long trial.

Fant's Sentence Cut

The U.S. District Court on November 18, 1992, ordered the release of former Rep. Ennis Fant after he had served only ten months of his sentence for conspiring to solicit a bribe. Fant's original sentence was for 20 months in prison.

The 4th Circuit Court of Appeals overturned the original sentence in September 1992, on grounds that it violated a plea agreement Fant had with the government in which Fant agreed to testify against other Lost Trust defendants. Fant had originally been charged with conspiracy and two counts of bribery in the amount of $1,300.

The plea agreement provided that Fant would tell the government what he knew even if it meant that he would make incriminating statements about himself. Such statements were not to be used to increase the sentence on Fant.

The Court of Appeals ruled that the prosecution, in fact, improperly did use information that Fant had tried to make the bribes look legal to tell the court at sentencing that Fant obstructed justice by trying to make the bribes look legal. The original sentence of 20 months was based in part on the allegation that Fant had obstructed justice even though Fant was not convicted of obstruction. Therefore, the government violated the Fant plea agreement by using evidence against Fant it should not have.

The hearing at which Judge Falcon Hawkins cut Ennis Fant's sentence in half gave Fant the opportunity to tell the public that he was a new man. The Baptist preacher said to the media that he intended to get back into the ministry after his release from prison. He also reported that he had been accepted into a graduate theology program at Duke University with a scholarship of $17,000 for the 1993 academic year. In the meantime he planned to attend classes at Erskine College, Due West, S.C.

Judge Hawkins seemed impressed by Fant's record since his conviction. Hawkins cited letters from the schools and also from prison officials that Fant had done his work in prison well and that he had been a model inmate.

The court cut Fant's sentence to time served as of the hearing date on November 18, 1992, which was ten months. Fant was also put on probation for three years and given 200 hours of community service. No fine was imposed at the original trial nor at re-sentencing.

Long Continues Law Practice While on Appeal

Although Sen. Bud Long had been convicted of corruption in his first trial in November, 1991, he was still able to continue practicing law because his conviction had been overturned after the trial by Judge Falcon Hawkins on grounds that Hawkins later admitted giving the jury defective instructions. Long continued to practice although he had decided not to run for re-election in November, 1992.

As Long awaited the scheduling of his new trial, the U.S. Attorney's office in South Carolina was appealing to the 4th Circuit Court of Appeals in Richmond, Va., trying to get the court to reverse Hawkins' order for a new trial which would allow Long's conviction at trial to stand. The controversy over the Long retrial would drag on until 1999 when Long would plead to a misdemeanor of lying to a federal agent in return for the government agreement to dismiss felony corruption charges.

Sen. Mitchell Gets Video Showing No Bribery

Sen. Theo Mitchell (D-Greenville) finally received the videotapes of an alleged bribe he was offered by Ron Cobb and said he had refused. The tapes were turned over to Mitchell in early December, 1992, more than two years after Mitchell had originally asked to receive them during the time he was a candidate for governor of South Carolina in 1990.

The FBI videotapes showed that Mitchell had told the FBI informant that he would not accept any money for his vote because it would be an illegal transaction. Mitchell had claimed during his 1990 campaign that the offer was made and rejected but he had not been able to obtain and present any evidence that he turned down a bribe.

On December 9, 1992, Mitchell again said that he had refused the bribe and had never taken any money from Ron Cobb.

Mitchell gave a copy of the videotape which he obtained from the U.S. Department of Justice to *The Greenville News* to prove what Mitchell had been saying since 1990 but could not corroborate with videotape evidence.

Mitchell had told Cobb in February, 1990, that he needed "a lot of money" for his campaign for governor in which he was defeated by Gov. Carroll Campbell. But on the videotape Mitchell told Cobb, "OK, well, you know I just know there's so many things going on in regards to politics and that naturally a vote committed on the basis of contributions, I believe, is unethical and illegal." Mitchell did not take any money from Cobb on the tape.

1993 Reform Proposals Up for Legislature

House Speaker Pro Tem David Wilkins said on December 11, 1992, that the new session of the South Carolina General Assembly would begin in January, 1993, and would take up new reform proposals including bills to impose terms limits, ballot initiative, and recall of public officials. Wilkins said that 1993 might be the year in which new legislation would empower citizens with more of a role in state government.

CHAPTER THIRTY NINE

1993—APPEALS AND REFORMS CONTINUE

Winstead Case Reviewed

Judge Robert S. Carr ruled that the U.S. Attorney's Office violated a deal it had with former Rep. Danny Winstead (R-Charleston) that the office would recommend leniency for Winstead at his sentencing for public corruption on the grounds that Winstead had helped the prosecution in Lost Trust. The ruling on January 16, 1993 held that the prosecution did not, in fact, urge leniency at the sentencing of Winstead and that the court imposed a stiff sentence of 30 months in prison in July, 1991. Winstead had helped the prosecution of Rep. Tom Limehouse (R-Dorchester).

Judge Carr found that Winstead was sometimes reluctant to help the prosecution in its probe but was entitled to a recommendation of leniency from the government. Winstead's attorney, Lee Bowers of Estill, South Carolina, said that his client's cooperation was elicited on a promise of cooperation and that Winstead's help warranted leniency.

Winstead had pleaded guilty to bribery and obstruction of justice in July, 1991. The prosecution claimed his help was not honest or complete. At the time Winstead was in prison at a federal camp in Jesup, Ga.

Judge Carr's findings went to trial judge Falcon Hawkins and the government had ten days to respond to the order.

House Limits Access to Floor

The South Carolina House of Representatives passed a rule on January 19, 1993 at the start of its new session to limit access of certain persons to the floor of the House while it was in session.

The new rule banned any former representatives who had been convicted in Lost Trust or of any other crimes and also banned lobbyists and those seeking appointments from the General Assembly. The focus of the new rule was clearly on those House members who had been convicted in Lost Trust.

Rep. Terry Haskins (R-Greenville) remarked that "A member of this House who has committed this type of crime while a member has disgraced this body. For any member of this body who loses that trust, they should not be restored the privileges of the House."

Rep. Preacher Harrelson (D-Colleton) said that those convicted in Lost Trust should be denied access to the House chambers. Harrelson expressed anger that the CBS "60 Minutes" program had interviewed Ron Cobb and Former Rep. Bob Kohn (R-Charleston) who had told the media that legislators were corrupt.

The rule change barred former legislators who were lobbyists from the House floor during sessions. Former legislators seeking jobs appointed or reelected by the General Assembly were also barred from the floor during sessions by the new rule.

The State Editorial Slams "60 Minutes"

The State dismissed the "60 Minutes" program on Lost Trust which was aired in January 1993 as old news. But CBS spokesman Ray Brunet defended the program as presenting the story of the scandal to the whole nation, most of which was not aware of the corruption probe in South Carolina.

The State pointed out that the CBS account only mentioned bribery and no drug charges. *The State* also objected to the fact that the program presented the allegation of former Rep. Bob Kohn (R-Charleston) that the new Ethics Act of 1991 would only force legislators to be more creative in their abuse of office. *The State* argued that a rebuttal defending the Ethics Act was needed to counter Kohn's cynical opinion.

Shield Law Proposed to Protect Press

The issue of news reporters being forced to testify at court hearings had been raised in glaring light when Judge Falcon Hawkins cited four reporters for contempt on two successive days and ordered them jailed for refusing to testify in the trial of Sen. Bud Long in November 1991. The court wanted the reporters to testify that Sen. Long had told them he took only $300 from sting agent Ron Cobb rather than the $2,800 he admitted to authorities and the public at a later date.

The South Carolina Press Association had retained attorney Jay Bender to assist the reporters in the matter and also protested that the reporters had First Amendment rights under the press clause to refuse to testify. Even though the court imposed no further penalties such as a fine and even though the jailings were for only a few hours on the two days, the issue rankled not only the media but also the public and some politicians who took the side of the reporters.

In the new session of the General Assembly convened in January 1993, a bill was introduced to provide a shield of protection in the future to prevent any further compelled testimony of reporters in criminal cases where they had obtained confidential information, except in rare cases in which the information was "material and highly relevant" and vital to the case and could not be obtained from any other source.

Sen. Glen McConnell (R-Charleston) was the chief sponsor of the bill and advocated the shield bill saying that it was necessary to the public because, "it opens up the flow of information —things you would not otherwise have an opportunity to know about.... They talk about a privilege for the press. What we're talking about is a privilege for the public."

The S.C. Press Association made the shield bill a top priority for the 1993 session arguing that sources needed to be protected from exposure otherwise they would not talk to the media and reveal important information of public concern.

However, Sen. Sam Stilwell (R-Greenville) and Sen. James Bryan (D-Laurens) opposed the bill and said it was bad public policy. Stilwell alleged that the bill, "created a bastard privilege" because he claimed, "This lets them (reporters) disclose anything and everything that was said and then keep secret who said it." Stilwell also charged that the bill would result in abusive behavior by journalists saying, "you are encouraging the worst of reporters, not the best of reporters, because they cannot be called to task."

But McConnell responded that the shield bill would not block defamation lawsuits against reporters for publishing false and injurious information.

Senate Proposes Expulsion for Felony

The 1993 session of the new General Assembly could not ignore the embarrassment caused by the refusal of the Senate in 1982 to expel Sen. Gene Carmichael on conviction of vote-buying and the more recent spectacle of suspended Senator Bud Long who had been tried and convicted for extortion while still a member of the Senate. Even after Long's conviction, the Senate had no rules in place to impose automatic expulsion.

The bill introduced in the Senate was given approval by the Senate Rules Committee of February 17, 1993 which would empower the Senate Ethics Committee to recommend expulsion of any Senator who pleaded to or was convicted at trial of a felony. The matter would then be referred to the Senate which would have to vote by two thirds majority to expel.

This would speed up the old Senate process which only allowed expulsion after both conviction and also exhaustion of appeals. The new rule would allow expulsion before appeals had been exhausted, that is, expulsion on conviction.

Senators seemed very concerned about the rights of senators faced with the expulsion on conviction of felony. The situation of Senator Long was perplexing in that Long stayed in the Senate while he was indicted, tried, and even convicted in 1991, but his conviction had been upset in 1992 and a new trial had been ordered as a remedy.

Senator Luke Rankin (D-Horry) who had replaced Long in December, 1992, worried that, "While we certainly want to improve the public perception of our image, we can't ignore the rights of the individual person." And Senator Linda Short (D-Chester) warned that "once you deny someone their constitutional rights, it becomes much easier to do it again."

Senator James Bryan (D-Laurens) took the other side and said that there was a difference between rights and privileges and that, "Serving in the Senate I'm not sure is a right protected by the Constitution." And other members of the Rules Committee asserted that it was more important to make sure that citizens were represented in the Senate than to protect a senator from being removed on conviction of felony. Senator Greg Ryberg (R-Aiken) said, "The rights of the 70,000 to 80,000 constituents in the case of an appeal far outweighed the rights of one individual senator." Sen. Robert Waldrep (D-Anderson) also worried that a seat could be vacant for several years pending an appeal of conviction.

Cobb Op Ed Ridiculed

After allowing Ron Cobb to publish his op ed denouncing the good old boys' culture at the State House, *The State* newspaper published an editorial spoofing Cobb's new self-appointed rule of populist crusader.

On February 24, 1993, *The State* made light of Cobb's efforts to urge the people to reclaim the government and demand reform, saying, "Having Ron Cobb offer advice about government reform—now that's a real knee slapper."

The State went on to laugh at Cobb as "the genuine article" offering those words of wisdom on the opposite page—Ron Cobb, premier performer of Operation Lost Trust and last heard and seen doing a star turn on CBS TV's "60 Minutes.'"

The newspaper added, "When Mr. Cobb says the principal barriers to establishing 'effective and accountable state government are agency heads, special interest groups and other bulwarks of the status quo,' he ain't a woofing.... Recent hearings before House Ways and Means Committee were classic exercises in turf protection.... Ron Cobb is no dope. He knows the territory."

U.S. Attorney Simmons Resigns

Republican U.S. Attorney for South Carolina John S. Simmons resigned effective April 22, 1993, to allow the new President Bill Clinton to pick his successor. Simmons had held the position for one year, taking over from U.S. Attorney Bart Daniel who resigned and was replaced by Simmons in March, 1992. Daniel went into private practice in Charleston, S.C., in the area of maritime law.

Simmons had been recommended by Sen. Strom Thurmond (R-S.C.) and was appointed by President George H.W. Bush. When Simmons took over as U.S. Attorney he found that a number of the cases which Daniel had taken to trial and convicted were being appealed.

Senator Fritz Hollings (D-S.C.) had the authority to nominate a replacement for Simmons and was considering multiple candidates including J.P. Strom, Jr., who was eventually appointed to the position by President Bill Clinton.

FBI Did Not Intrude on State's Rights

The 4th Circuit Court of Appeals ruled that the FBI Lost Trust probe of corruption in South Carolina state government did not violate the rights of the states when the Lost Trust sting operation identified a number of corrupt state legislators. That rule came on March 22, 1993.

The appellate ruling was the result of a lawsuit filed by former Rep. Ken Bailey (D-Orangeburg) who contended that his prosecution for bribery violated the U.S. Constitution. The 4th Circuit held that the U.S. Constitution protected the legitimate activities of state and local governments against federal interference but that the violation of the federal Hobbs Act by corrupt actions was not a legitimate government function of Rep. Bailey.

Bailey took a payoff from FBI sting agent and lobbyist Ron Cobb paid in cash to vote for the pari-mutuel betting bill. Bailey started to serve his 27 months sentence in August, 1992.

The Circuit ruled that, "Operation Lost Trust did not interfere with the legitimate legislative process of the state of South Carolina. It was directed solely at the dishonest acts of some of the members of the state's General Assembly. This is not a violation of the Tenth Amendment." The opinion was written by Judge Robert Chapman for the three judge appellate panel, *Bailey v. U.S.*, 990 F.2d 119 (4th Circuit 1993).

State of Appeals

In early 1993, the future of some of the Lost Trust defendants who had been convicted at trial was still undecided. As of March 23, 1993, several had won new trials – ex-Sen. Bud Long (D-Horry) and ex-Rep. Larry Blanding (D-Sumter). But the appeals of ex-Rep. Paul Derrick (R-Lexington) and of ex-Rep. B.J. Gordon (D-Williamsburg) were still undecided as was that of ex-Rep. Luther Taylor (D-Richland).

Critics Chide Lawyer-Legislators

Critics of the old practice of lawyer-legislators appearing before state boards and commissions also pointed to the ability of senators to earn money from their involvement with state-sanctioned insurance contracts. The career of the late Sen. Jack Lindsay (D-Marlboro) was a prime example of legislators making money out of appearing before state agencies as lawyer-legislators.

The reforms of 1991 only banned the gratuities given by lobbyists to legislators but did not stop lawyer-legislators and others who profited by their work with state government.

House Judiciary Committee Chairman Jim Hodges (D-Lancaster) said the practice of legislators appearing before boards and agencies over which they had influence did not look good, remarking that, "I think it's a problem when a public official appears before a body that he has some influence over, for his personal financial gain." Hodges pointed to the work of the late Sen. Jack

Lindsay who helped his clients get contracts when Lindsay appeared before the state Reinsurance Facility.

Rep. Becky Meacham (R-York) said that lawyer-legislators should be banned from appearing before state boards and agreed with Hodges that the Ethics Act of 1991 should be amended. Joining them in demanding improvements to the Act to deal with the kinds of conflicts of interest exposed by Lindsay's conduct was Sen. Wes Hayes (D-York) and Rep. Herb Kirsh (D-York).

Pete Strom, Jr., Nominated for U.S. Attorney

The new administration of President Bill Clinton nominated Pete Strom, Jr., to replace John Simmons as U.S. Attorney for South Carolina on April 11, 1993. Strom, 33, was the son of the former chief of the State Law Enforcement Division. Strom had also served as an assistant solicitor in the Fifth Circuit in Columbia. He was a 1984 graduate of the University of South Carolina Law School.

While still in law school Strom had challenged incumbent Rep. Tim Rogers (D-Richland) in 1983 but lost the election in the Democratic primary.

Taylor Gets New Trial

The 4th Circuit in Richmond, Va., ruled on May 10, 1993, that Luther Taylor should get a new trial based on erroneously stated instructions provided by Judge Falcon Hawkins to the jury in October, 1990, when Taylor was convicted of corruption. The instructions failed to tell the jury that in order to convict Taylor of bribery he had to promise to do something specific in return for taking money from sting agent Ron Cobb. The court affirmed a ruling made in 1992.

The Taylor holding on appeal also by implication would require that four other convicted legislators be given new trials. In those cases the prosecution on retrial would have to prove that the defendant took action in his official capacity in return for receiving something of value from a party seeking the official action. This was based on new U.S. Supreme Court case law in *McCormick*.

The Circuit held that it was not illegal for officials to take money that would not have been offered to them if they were not public officials. But the court found that Judge Falcon Hawkins' jury instructions had told the jurors that simply taking the money was bribery under the Hobbs Act. In law a quid pro quo act was also needed to prove "extortion under color of official right" under the Hobbs Act.

The jury instructions tainted by Hawkins' error also affected the trials and triggered the appeals of Larry Blanding, B.J. Gordon, Paul Derrick, as well as of Luther Taylor.

Whistle-blower Act Needs Changes

In an editorial of May 11, 1993, *The State* wrote that the South Carolina Whistle-blower Act was weak and needed to be amended with Senate bill proposals then pending at the State House. The paper noted that the Act had been passed in 1988 "to protect state workers while removing the opportunity for an unlimited run on taxpayers."

The law was designed to protect public employees who exposed government waste, fraud, and mismanagement. Yet, *The State* complained that the law had been abused by disgruntled state employees and opportunistic lawyers (who) see it as a gold grab." Agency heads had complained about this.

The State endorsed House amendments to limit the payout of public funds to $250,000 and to place a burden of proof on the employee to prove that his injury was retaliation for his whistle-blowing.

The Senate was proposing amendments which would require law suits under the Act to be non-jury and to limit the awards to reinstatement, lost wages, and a maximum of $15,000 in damages. *The State* endorsed the amendments. But veteran Columbia lawyer Lewis Cromer who had stung state agencies with big jury awards under the Act warned that the amendments would "kill whistle-blowing in South Carolina."

Cromer published an op ed in *The State* on May 17, 1993, criticizing the move in the General Assembly to weaken the South Carolina Whistle-blower Act by lowering the amount of damages a plaintiff could recover in a successful law suit.

Cromer argued that if the law was weakened it would make it harder for state and local government employees to expose corruption where they worked. Cromer pointed out that before the Act was passed in 1988, government agencies prohibited their employees from reporting criminal activities in the agencies. But since 1988, employees had been allowed by the Act to disclose such crime and had, in fact, done so.

Cromer warned that the weakening amendments being considered in the Senate Finance Committee would mean that whistle-blower protection would become a thing of the past and Chinese walls would again rise up to insulate state agency wrongdoing.

Media Shield Law at Issue

Operation Lost Trust helped to focus public attention on the question of whether the media needed a better state shield law to protect the media from coercive judges. On the one hand, South Carolina Press Association attorney Jay Bender argued that the shield law needed to be reinforced in order to protect the media in its mission of ferreting out corruption and abuse of governmental power. But Sen. Larry Richter (R-Charleston) minimized the problem, saying it rarely happened that a reporter was pressed by the court to reveal confidential sources.

The jailing of four reporters in 1991 by Judge Falcon Hawkins dramatized the problem of reporters wanting to keep their sources confidential for fear that future sources might not talk to them. Then the issue came up again when a Horry County newspaper, The Weekly Independent, used confidential sources as a basis for a news story that a grand juror had a conflict of interest in a probe of the county public works department because he worked there.

The proposed new shield law would protect reporters from compelled disclosure of their sources and documents in many, but not all cases. Reporters could still be forced to disclose in cases where they were the only source of information which was vital to the case.

Taylor Appeal Asks Limits on Stings

Appealing to the full bench of the 4th U.S. Circuit Court of Appeals in Richmond, Va., in May, 1993, Luther Taylor's attorney, Joel Collins, asked the court to go beyond granting Taylor a new trial on his 1990 convictions for corruption but also to impose limits on how far the FBI could go in trying to catch suspects in sting operations.

Collins argued that the Lost Trust sting and prosecution of Taylor was an unconstitutional interference with the functions of the South Carolina General Assembly. He also alleged that the pari-mutuel gambling referendum on which the bribery sting was based was not related to interstate commerce and therefore Congress had no power to regulate the referendum. Collins also said that politicians were in jeopardy if the court did not distinguish bribery from legal fund-raising activities. Taylor had claimed that the money he took from Ron Cobb was a campaign donation.

A three judge panel had twice ruled that in Taylor's case his trial jury had been misinstructed by the court that it was illegal for a public official to take money even if he took no official action in return for the money. On appeal, the court ruled that an official could legally take money if he did nothing in return for the money based on *McCormick*.

Taylor Appeal Alleges DOJ Violations

Having been awarded a new trial by the court of appeals on grounds of erroneous jury instruction in his case, former Rep. Luther Taylor asked the appeals court to rule that the federal government had violated its own rules in that money was wrongfully offered by sting agent Ron Cobb to Taylor to influence a bill of statewide application rather than a bill of only local impact as specified in the U.S. Department of Justice manual.

The motions made by Taylor asserted that the U.S. Constitution does not permit any intrusion into a state's legislative process. However, the motions said that the appeals court had erroneously indicated there were no limits on federal intrusion into the state legislative process nor were there any limits on federal intervention in state political fund-raising activities.

The Taylor motions also said that the proposed referendum on pari-mutuel betting contained in the betting bill would only affect South Carolina intrastate commerce and therefore the federal government had no jurisdiction under the interstate commerce clause to regulate such intrastate legislation.

Taylor's attorney, Joel Collins, said that the questions posed in the Taylor appeal "raise weighty, unanswered constitutional issues concerning the operation of an undercover sting-style investigation by federal investigators in a state legislature."

Ethics Act Reconsidered—State Editorial

The 1991 Ethics Act was the result of the exposure of the culture of corruption at the State House and the public demand for drastic action. Since the 1991 Act was passed and took effect the politicians had learned to live with the new regulations imposed on lobbyists, donors, and candidates as well as public officials, *The State* wrote in an editorial on May 31, 1993.

But some of those affected by the 1991 Act did not like its restrictions on the flow of money and gratuities between lobbyists and officials. That raised the question of whether there would be an effort by some legislators to weaken the Act and allow a return to the good old days of massive corruption.

The editorial agreed with the point made by Rep. Candy Waites (D-Richland) that a proposed change in the campaign finance disclosure rules would remove the requirement that campaign donations and expenses be reported to the State Ethics Commission 15 days prior to an election. Waites said that such a change would make it more difficult for voters to find out who was donating and in what amounts because the information would only be available from the candidates' campaign headquarters in 15 days just prior to the elections.

Black Caucus Subject to Criticism

Black political scientist Ricky Hill of South Carolina State University wrote a report for the Columbia Urban League alleging that the Legislative Black Caucus lacked direction and an agenda of issues. He also said Lost Trust had hurt the caucus' clout.

The State wrote an editorial on June 14, 1993, in which it argued that Lost Trust had removed seven legislators from the Black Caucus and replaced them with new ones who did not always agree with senior black legislators. *The State* pointed out inter-caucus disagreement between new Sen. Darrell Jackson (D-Richland) and old Sen. Kay Patterson (D-Richland) over Jackson's bill to make county elections non-partisan.

The State welcomed "Senator Jackson's independence and leadership on this important issue" and further said that some disagreements were beneficial, asserting that "Diversity of thought within any organized body of people is a healthy sign." Sen. Jackson had been elected for the first time in the general election of 1992 to replace Sen. Isadore Lourie who had retired.

Pete Strom Becomes U.S. Attorney

The election of Democrat Bill Clinton as president brought a change in the office of U.S. Attorney in South Carolina with Democrat Pete Strom, Jr., taking the place of his Republican predecessor John S. Simmons who had become U.S. Attorney in March, 1992, and resigned effective April 22, 1993.

One of Strom's first actions was to go to the federal grand jury in the Luther Taylor case and ask for a new indictment with new defendants included. He therefore asked the trial court Judge Falcon Hawkins to delay the re-trial of Taylor which had been scheduled for mid-August, 1993, until the grand jury could act to issue new indictments.

Taylor concurred with the request for a delay in trial as his attorney, Joel Collins, wanted to go to the U.S. Supreme Court and seek dismissal of all charges. Collins contended that the federal government had no right to interfere with the state legislature by criminally charging legislators.

Taylor had won a new trial in 1992 from the appeals court on grounds that his October, 1990, trial had been tainted by faulty pre-*McCormick* jury instructions which did not make it clear that in order to convict Taylor of bribery it was essential for the prosecution to prove that he sold his vote and took official action.

Appeals Pending in 1993

Based on McCormick, former Rep. Larry Blanding (D-Sumter) was given a new trial because the jury instructions in his case failed to make it clear that the prosecution had to prove he sold his vote in order to be convicted on bribery charges. Former Reps. Paul Derrick (R-Lexington) and B.J. Gordon (D-Williamsburg) had filed appeals on the same issue of faulty jury instruction by Judge Hawkins. As of the middle of June, 1993, Gordon had been convicted of corruption but had still not yet been sentenced even though he was tried together in 1991 with Blanding. The appeals court could not consider any appeal from Gordon until he was sentenced.

Paul Derrick's appeal, filed by his attorney Jim Lengel, asked the court to not only invalidate Derrick's conviction at trial but also to dismiss the charge, preventing a new trial, on grounds that Derrick was illegally entrapped by the government and had no prior inclination to commit the crime he was lured into by FBI sting agent Ron Cobb.

The conviction of former Sen. Bud Long (D-Horry) had been thrown out by the trial judge Falcon Hawkins who admitted that he erroneously had admitted evidence of a dismissed conspiracy charge in the case which was immaterial.

Coming in after Daniel's successes in getting convictions in the first round of trials in 1990 and 1991, the new U.S. Attorney Pete Strom Jr., was faced in 1993 with the difficult problem of retrying cases and fighting appeals.

New Trials Ordered

While new U.S. Attorney Pete Strom, Jr., faced the daunting task of handling second trials for Lost Trust defendants, the attorneys for the defense prepared to fight again.

In July, 1993, Bud Long's attorney, Jack Swerling, expressed some hope in the coming second trial because he believed that the public attention to Lost Trust had dropped, saying, "I think for both parties, especially the defense, it's easier to try a case in that kind of climate because you don't have the passion involved."

There was also the issue of whether the government should waste time and money on new trials in view of the fact that all of the accused legislators had left the General Assembly. The possibility that the convicted former legislators would again take bribes for their votes was zero by 1993.

Even so, Pete Strom, Jr., wanted to go ahead with new trials remarking, "I see it as my job to enforce the law." In the end, however, it turned out that the prosecution of the retrials would be handed over by Strom to the Justice Department's own lawyers.

Judge Hawkins Announces Retirement

Chief District Judge Falcon Hawkins, who presided over most of the original Lost Trust trials, notified President Bill Clinton in late July, 1993, that he was retiring as of October 1, 1993. He would then assume senior status which would allow him to handle reduced judicial duties.

Sen. Fritz Hollings (D-S.C.) was the only Democratic senator in South Carolina and therefore would nominate a candidate to replace Hawkins. Several candidates were thought to be likely prospects to be nominated, including former Assistant U.S. Attorney Cameron Curry, who was then heading the grand jury. Curry eventually was appointed by Clinton and confirmed by the U.S. Senate.

Taylor Retrial Delayed

Judge Falcon Hawkins moved to delay the retrial of Luther Taylor on his October, 1990, convictions for corruption. Acting on July 29, 1993, Hawkins postponed the retrial until November 8, 1993, giving Taylor's attorney's time to appeal to the U.S. Supreme Court and the prosecution more time to re-indict Taylor.

Taylor wanted to convince the high court to find Lost Trust unconstitutional and invalidate all counts in the indictment of Taylor on the grounds that the federal government was intruding on the powers and functions of state governments. The prosecution wanted to retry Taylor and merge his retrial with those of Larry Blanding and B.J. Gordon.

Taylor's attorney Joel Collins pointed out that it was difficult, if not impossible, to distinguish a bribe from a campaign contribution and that the U.S. Supreme Court appreciated the fact that "all legislators are raising money all the time. The people who hold fund-raisers for them are people who have an interest in pending legislation."

New Indictments Handed Down in Lost Trust

A federal grand jury handed down new indictments against Lost Trust defendants former Reps. Luther Taylor, Larry Blanding, and B.J. Gordon on August 18, 1993.

The government was seeking a consolidation of the three cases so as to try them at the same time and together in the same courtroom and before the same judge and jury. But defense attorney Lionel Lofton, representing Gordon, objected, saying that the fact that Blanding and Gordon had been previously tried together had caused a "ripple effect." Lofton worried that the addition of Taylor and the trial of all three in the same proceeding would result in "facing a tidal wave effect" in which the guilt of any one defendant would impugn the others.

The U.S. Attorney explained that he wanted to try the three cases together as "it would certainly save a substantial amount of time and money" but would not prejudice the defendants and government.

Taylor's attorney expressed optimism that a second trial for his client would not result in convictions again as the first trial had in October, 1990. Collins told the media, "the new evidence that has come to light since my man went to trial being the first one...adds up to the defendant's having a much better chance." Collins argued that going into the new trials the court was now aware that, "As the Supreme Court noted, every time someone gives a contribution to a politician, there may be subtle ulterior motives, but that's not good enough" for a conviction on grounds of bribery under the *McCormick* precedent requiring a showing of quid pro quo.

Arraignments

B.J. Gordon was arraigned again on September 7, 1993, before U.S. Magistrate Joseph McCrorey in a ten minute hearing at which again he pleaded not guilty to selling his vote to sting agent Ron Cobb as alleged in both the original indictment and the re-indictment. The magistrate allowed Gordon to remain free on an unsecured bond of $25,000 until his retrial was to start on November 8, 1993. Gordon's conviction on conspiracy and selling his vote in 1991 was overturned but he was re-indicted along with Luther Taylor and Larry Blanding in August, 1993. Gordon had never been sentenced.

Taylor and Blanding were arraigned on new indictments on September 8, 1993. New U.S. Attorney Pete Strom, Jr., had re-indicted the three so as to try them together and save money. But Lionel Lofton said he planned to file motions opposing a joint trial of his client Gordon with Taylor and Blanding. Lofton thought that the cases of Taylor and Blanding would prejudice the rights of Gordon to a trial strictly on the facts of the Gordon case and possibly contaminate Gordon's case.

Responding to their re-indictments, former Reps. Luther Taylor and Larry Blanding pleaded not guilty to selling their votes. They were allowed to remain free on bond until November 8, 1993, when their new trial was slated. U.S. Magistrate Joseph McCrorey ordered both men to post unsecured bonds of $25,000, the same as Gordon.

Ferguson Reprimanded by S.C. Supreme Court

The South Carolina Supreme Court finally took disciplinary actions against former judge Tee Ferguson on September 20, 1993, when it reprimanded him for his misconduct. At the time of the reprimand Ferguson had already served one year of the total of 33 months in prison imposed by the federal courts for taking a $3,000 bribe and possessing cocaine.

The court took such a long time, it appeared, because there was no precedent in South Carolina law of any corrupt judge being convicted for such crimes in the state's history. Ferguson seemed without remorse, contending that his prosecution and conviction was a racist plot designed to remove a black judge from the bench.

The Supreme Court agonized over Ferguson's objection that since he had resigned his office as judge on the circuit court, the Court had no jurisdiction over him. In the end, the Court ruled that, "it is not in the public's interest to ignore Ferguson's actions. We must act to close this chapter on the wrongdoing giving rise to this judicial complaint. To do otherwise merely delays the inevitable and leaves the issue open to speculation."

The Court found that Ferguson had violated the Code of Judicial Conduct which said that, "A judge should respect and comply with the law and should conduct himself at all times in a manner that promotes public confidence in the integrity and impartiality of the judiciary." The S.C. Supreme Court cited a taped conversation in which Ferguson told an FBI undercover agent that he would sell judicial favors when he became a judge. Ferguson was elected by the General Assembly to the circuit court bench in April, 1990, and was later convicted of taking bribes and having cocaine prior to becoming a judge. He became the first state court judge to be convicted of a major crime in South Carolina's history.

Cobb Op Ed Published Blasting S.C. Government

The State published another op ed by Ron Cobb in its September 24, 1993, edition in which Cobb reflected on his experiences as a House member, lobbyist, and FBI sting agent in Lost Trust and gave advice as to "the citizens of South Carolina taking back control of their state government."

Cobb wrote that, "As a one-time 'good ole boy', I am fully aware of the difficulty and problems they face in making South Carolina government accountable to the people that pick up the tab for all expenditures—the hardworking taxpayers." Cobb's analysis concluded that the major barriers to creating an accountable state government included: (1) state agency heads who opposed change; (2) special interest groups that had excessive influence over state government; and (3) public officials and bureaucrats who opposed change and who wanted to "use their positions to feather their own nests at taxpayer's expense."

"All these problems are like a thick brick wall." Cobb urged citizens to "[d]emand that your House member and senator commit to making state government accountable to you...and that career politicians who care only about themselves go home!"

Hawkins Deemed Not Biased

In early October, 1993, the Luther Taylor saga continued when U.S. District Court Judge Charles Simons rejected a motion filed by Joel Collins, attorney for Luther Taylor, alleging that trial Judge Falcon Hawkins was biased against Taylor and should be removed from the Taylor case in the future.

The factual basis of the motion was that Hawkins had stated in court that Taylor had shamed South Carolina by his corrupt actions. Simons ruled that Hawkins' comments were the truth and that Hawkins could continue to handle the retrial of Taylor set for November, 1993. "My definite conclusion is that there is absolutely no basis that I see or any basis for a reasonable person to have any doubt or question about Hawkins' impartiality," Simons wrote rejecting Collins' allegation that Hawkins' comments had caused questions about his impartiality.

Assistant U.S. Attorney John Barton had told Simons that Hawkins could only be removed for prejudice if Hawkins' "extra-judicial" actions showed prejudice against Taylor, and Simons agreed with the argument as all of Hawkins remarks criticizing Taylor had been made in his official capacity as trial judge in the case and were not extra-judicial comments.

Simons also noted that the 4th Circuit Court of Appeals had previously rejected efforts to remove Hawkins on grounds of prejudice. Taylor was still set for retrial on November 8, 1993, along with Larry Blanding and B.J. Gordon.

Gordon's Illness—Defendants Ask Postponement

Due to B.J. Gordon's radiation therapy for prostate cancer, Assistant U.S. Attorney John Barton filed a motion on October 15, 1993, asking a postponement of the joint retrials of Gordon, Blanding, and Taylor set for November 8, 1993.

Gordon's attorney, Lionel Lofton, had already filed a motion to allow Gordon to be tried separately and not with Blanding and Taylor, alleging that Gordon would otherwise be tainted by the charges against the other two defendants. At the time Gordon had not yet served any time in prison as he had had his conviction overturned before he could be sentenced.

Lofton told the Court that Gordon had a total of 32 radiation treatments set for the period October 22 to November 30, 1993, for the cancer. Lofton said that Gordon did not concoct the prostate problem to avoid retrial and that he wanted to go to retrial and finish the matter.

Gordon had been the focus of several criminal probes in conjunction with the death of a chemist at Gordon's gasohol plant in Williamsburg County which did not result in a charge and another probe of the personal use of public funds at the Gordon Developmental Center for retarded adults which also ended with no charges. Gordon had been reelected in 1990 while under federal indictment for extortion in Lost Trust.

Black Caucus Faces Issues

The Legislative Black Caucus held a retreat to discuss its role and agenda in state government on October 29, 1993. The Caucus was younger and more diverse as a result of the fact that seven Caucus members were convicted and removed from the General Assembly in Lost Trust prosecutions. Rep. Joe Brown, Chairman of the Caucus, noted that the scandal had cost the Caucus seniority and positions on important committees but that the new black legislators were better educated and more politically experienced on coming into office.

The Caucus was also confronted with a critical research report written at the behest of the Urban League by Prof. Ricky Hill of South Carolina State University. The report alleged that the Caucus was without a programmatic agenda and failed to prioritize the interests of the black population of South Carolina.

In fact, the Caucus admitted that they had only passed four pieces of priority legislation in the 1993 session. Sen. Theo Mitchell (D-Greenville), a member of the Caucus, claimed the Caucus was not dealing with vital problems like creating new jobs and improving education because the Caucus was so often fighting to stop bad proposals such as a Republican bill to reduce property taxes which funded public schools. But novice Sen. Robert Ford (D-Charleston) felt that the Caucus was fixated on futile goals such as removing the Confederate flag from the State House. Yet others held out hope for pulling it down.

Cobb Gets His Real Estate License Back

Ron Cobb was awarded a real estate license on December 15, 1993, returning the license which had been taken from him during his days in the Lost Trust scandal. The real estate commission found that Cobb had paid his dues to society since pleading guilty on cocaine possession charges. The vote to reinstate Cobb's license was 5-2.

Cobb told the media, "All of us stub our toe from time to time—and I nearly knocked the end of mine off—but I've paid the price and learned my lesson." Cobb planned to open a new real estate business in Greenville, S.C.

The decision to reinstate Cobb provoked commissioner Robert Hoes of North Augusta, S.C., to complain, "What bothers me is even if a person has made corrections, what about the gravity of the crime in the first place?" Hoes voted against reinstatement. The real estate commission had some 28,000 members, including brokers, agents, and property managers. The commission had the authority to revoke licenses on conviction of crimes. But one year after completion of sentence a person could petition for reinstatement by the commission.

Cobb had pleaded guilty in 1991 to two counts of simple possession of cocaine and was given two years sentence to probation, a six month term in a halfway house, and 200 hours of community service. Cobb told the Commission that he should be reinstated and given his license because, "I've done everything I was instructed to do."

Commissioner Manning Biggers of York, S.C., asked Cobb whether he could use his experiences to help other real estate people with similar problems in the future. Cobb said he was available to help.

Before becoming a lobbyist and corruptionist at the State House, Cobb had been a broker-in-charge at GBA Properties in Greenville, S.C. At the time he applied for reinstatement, Cobb was working for his family garment business and was also writing a book on Lost Trust which he promised would be "very interesting." Cobb was also watching the outcome of cases which had been ordered for retrial after Cobb had testified in the original trials.

CHAPTER FORTY

1994—IMPACT OF LOST TRUST CONTINUES

The secondary and collateral consequences of Operation Lost Trust continued into the year 1994. In that year the appeals generated by the original convictions at trial were continuing with some success. The allegations of prosecutorial misconduct made by the convicted defendants caused a federal probe which did not result in any findings of misconduct by the U.S. Attorney. But the charges worried Judge Hawkins.

Meanwhile the reformers at the State House were continuing to exploit the Lost Trust scandal to demand new reforms, including the reform of the incestuous judicial selection system used by the General Assembly to pick state court judges one of whom, Tee Ferguson, had been convicted in the Lost Trust prosecutions.

1994 was also the year in which it was possible to evaluate the effectiveness of the 1991 Ethics Act which had been in effect for two years. It appeared that the new provisions of the law relating to the regulation of lobbyists, campaign financing, and conflicts of interest were having some beneficial results.

Derrick Gets New Trial

The 4th Circuit Court of Appeals ruled on February 9, 1994, that former Rep. Paul Derrick (R-Lexington) would be given a new trial. He had been convicted in 1991 of taking a bribe of $1,000 from FBI sting agent and lobbyist Ron Cobb to vote for the betting bill.

A three judge panel of the Circuit ruled that the jury instructions given by trial Judge Falcon Hawkins again failed to state that the prosecution needed to show that Derrick took some action as a public official in return for the $1,000 given by Cobb as required by McCormick.

The Circuit rejected another point of appeal presented by Derrick saying that the audiotapes sent to the jury by the government as evidence of bribery were, in fact, not sufficient evidence of bribery. The appellate court ruled, "Derrick cannot get around his picture, his voice and his actions reflected in the audio and videotapes that were seen and heard by the jury.... The evidence reflects that Derrick was a party to many conversations with his co-conspirators concerning the means of securing passage of the pari-mutuel bill." No retrial date for Derrick was set. The retrials of Luther Taylor, Larry Blanding, and B.J. Gordon were reset for April, 1994.

Taylor Moves Dismissal for Prosecutorial Misconduct

Attorneys for Luther Taylor filed papers in federal court on February 10, 1994, alleging that former US Attorney Bart Daniel violated the law in order to convict Taylor in his October, 1990, trial. Taylor moved to have all charges dismissed on grounds that Daniel "withheld evidence, misrepresented facts and allowed perjured testimony in order to win the precedent setting first trial in a series of cases ironically named 'Operation Lost Trust.'"

Taylor's attorney Joel Collins also filed a motion stating that newly obtained government records showed that the prosecution allowed sting agent Ron Cobb to testify that he never bribed the late Sen. Jack Lindsay when, in fact, he had bribed Lindsay and the prosecution knew it. Asking for dismissal, Taylor argued that if the records had been available to the defense then such records could have been used to impeach Cobb's testimony against Taylor.

Taylor Seeks Evidence on Tax Break Bill

Luther Taylor's attorney, Joel Collins, filed the second of two motions on February 10, 1994, seeking information about the role of Gov. Carroll Campbell and his aides in the capital gains tax break bill which Rep. Jack I. Rogers and Sen. Jack Lindsay helped to pass. The motion asked for all evidence as to whether Campbell was involved in the tax break bill. In addition, the motion asked for any evidence that money was paid to advance the tax break bill by four aides to Gov. Campbell and by three Tax Commission officials.

At the time of Taylor's motions, Rogers had been convicted of corruption and Lindsay had died in January 1991. Gov. Campbell's office had maintained since 1990 that it had no role in the tax break bill and that no evidence of such involvement had been presented since then.

Probe of Prosecutors Asked

Newly appointed U.S. Attorney J.P. "Pete" Strom, Jr., a Democrat, responded to questions raised by defendants in the Lost Trust cases about alleged prosecutorial misconduct by asking on February 16, 1994, that the U.S. Department of Justice launch an investigation of the matter. The requested probe would look at allegations by Luther Taylor in his motions on February 10, 1994, that the government had withheld evidence, misrepresented evidence, and allowed Ron Cobb to lie to the court.

Taylor also raised questions about whether Gov. Campbell was involved in the tax break bill, an issue which Democrats had been talking about since the Lost Trust prosecutions began in August, 1990.

Former U.S. Attorney Bart Daniel, a Republican appointee, denounced all allegations that impugned the integrity of his prosecution as "reckless and irresponsible." Daniel said that a tip about Campbell's alleged role in the tax break bill was provided by lobbyist Randy Lee, who was charged with drug violations, but that Lee said on February 15, 1994, that he was mistaken about Campbell's role in the tax matter. Daniel said that the tip had been checked out by the prosecution and found to be groundless after a special probe by the Assistant U.S. Attorney, John Barton.

Reform of S.C. Judicial Selection Pushed

The conviction of Judge Tee Ferguson for corruption and drug charges provided ammunition for reformers who had long believed that the judicial selection system used in South Carolina was plagued with political cronyism. A long-standing criticism was that the General Assembly which selected judges of circuit and appeals courts too often picked sitting legislators over better qualified non-legislator candidates. Ferguson was a good example as he had been elected while sitting as a member of the House of Representatives and as a result of voting-trading among legislators pushing their favorite candidates.

On February 10, 1994, reformers called a news conference at the State House to demand that the judicial selection system be reformed. Among those taking the lead at the news conference were Lt. Gov. Nick Theodore, Secretary of State Jim Miles, House Ethics Committee Chair Denny Nielson, and Common Cause officials Prof. Ken Gaines and John Crangle.

Lt. Gov. Theodore opened by stating, "An Operation Lost Trust in our judiciary could be waiting to happen. Let's act before it does." Prof. Gaines, a University of South Carolina law professor, argued "it chills most young lawyers or even older lawyers who would aspire to something like that when they see that legislators have the inside track."

The reformers told the media that the General Assembly should pass legislation to create a judicial nominating commission that would screen candidates and then present three qualified candidates from which legislators could select one for the judicial position. Furthermore, no sitting legislators would be eligible as candidates. Resignation would be required before a legislator could file as a candidate.

Reformers pointed out that as of 1994, all five Supreme Court justices and over half of the circuit court judges in South Carolina were former legislators. It clearly appeared that legislators had a material and perhaps unfair advantage in seeking election to the state bench.

However, Speaker Robert Sheheen (D-Kershaw) defended the existing judiciary saying, "I have a never become convinced that the system in South Carolina is severely deficient. I don't know why just because they are in the legislature, they ought to be excluded from being judges."

In December, 1993, *The State* newspaper had conducted a survey in which 80 legislators said that sitting legislators should not be able to run for judicial office and only 56 said they should. House members indicated more support for reform than senators, and House Judiciary Chairman Jim Hodges and subcommittee chair Doug Jennings both supported a ban on sitting legislators running for judicial offices.

Governor Spurns Allegations

Gov. Carroll Campbell again rejected any innuendos to the effect that he was involved in bribery related to the capital gains tax break. Speaking out on February 17, 1994, at a meeting with the editors and reporters of *The State* newspaper in Columbia, Campbell complained that "This is what I've been combating for several years.... This constant little attack."

At the time, Campbell was being mentioned as a possible candidate for President and he was being used as a target by motions filed by Luther Taylor trying to find out if Campbell and his office were tangled up in the tax break bill.

At the same time, another attorney, Paul Perkins, had filed a request under the Freedom of Information Act to get evidence about Campbell's role in the tax break. Perkins was a self-appointed public interest lawyer who had helped unmask the abuses of former University of South Carolina President James Holderman. In addition, Columbia Attorney Joe McCulloch was running for South Carolina Democratic Party chairman and promised to pursue questions about Campbell. McCulloch called on Campbell to release all information related to the matter. Campbell refused to release information from the FBI files open to him saying such FBI files often held false and unfair information. Campbell could have asked the FBI to release its files on him.

In the meeting with the editorial board and news staff of *The State*, Gov. Campbell refused to answer the question of whether he had ever taken a bribe but then said he had not. Campbell pointed to evidence from the sentencing hearing of his old friend Dick Greer, who pleaded guilty to cocaine, at which assistant U.S. Attorney John Barton, a Democrat, told the court that allegations about Campbell had been found to be baseless.

Campbell said that Barton explained that there were, in fact, two separate tax bills moving in the General Assembly. One was the notorious bill involving bribery, but Campbell had no interest in that bill. The other bill was a bill proposing to change the South Carolina tax code related to capital gains and Campbell did, in fact, have an interest in the second bill.

Two defendants in Lost Trust made an issue out of the notorious tax break bill when they came up for sentencing. Sen. Rick Lee (R-Spartanburg), charged with bribery, and lobbyist Randy Lee, charged with drugs, both talked about the tax break bill and Randy Lee even intimated that Gov. Campbell was involved, but in February, 1994, Randy Lee disowned his insinuations against Campbell.

Gordon Alleges Misconduct by Prosecution

Lionel Lofton, attorney for B.J. Gordon, filed a motion on February 22, 1994, alleging prosecutorial misconduct on the grounds that "The government attorneys lied to the defendant, lied to the court...and...they allowed their star witness (Ron Cobb)...to lie." At the time of the motion, Gordon was set for his retrial in April, 1994.

Assistant U.S. Attorney John Barton ridiculed the motion saying "there was no prosecutorial misconduct and that these motions are nothing more than a continuation of an effort to try everyone but the defendants in these cases."

At the time of the Gordon motion, the new U.S. Attorney Pete Strom, Jr., had asked the court to delay the retrial set for April, 1994, and had asked for a Justice Department review of the allegations of misconduct stated in the defense motions.

The Gordon motion pointed to a court hearing of February 28, 1991, in which Barton said that there was no FBI 302 of any statements made by Cobb about a payoff to Sen. Jack Lindsay. Then the defense found a transcript of September 25, 1989, in which Cobb said that he made a "payoff" to Lindsay for his help on the capital gains tax break bill.

Editorial—Campbell Too Sensitive

Based on its meeting with Governor Campbell on February 17, 1994, *The State* wrote an April 10, 1994, editorial in which it criticized Gov. Campbell for being too self-important and vulnerable to criticism saying, "Mr. Campbell is an extraordinarily thin-skinned man for a politician. The general public doesn't know this because Campbell manages his public exposure with an artful care... He stands above the fray."

The editorial painted a picture of Campbell meeting with the editorial board and staff of *The State* on February 17, 1994, and overreacting to questions and expressing anger at reporter Twila Decker who had written about him in a way that he did not like.

The meeting ended when the governor stormed out without the usual handshakes around the table—without even eye contact. In the parking lot, Campbell met Consulting Editor Bill Rone and told Rone that "he was so mad at Decker he wanted to spank her."

Probe of Prosecutors Finds No Violations

The probe of prosecutorial conduct in Lost Trust which had been requested by new U.S. Attorney Pete Strom Jr. came to an end on October 19, 1994, when the U.S. Department of Justice released a letter saying that no evidence of prosecutorial misconduct was found.

However, the Justice Department announced that in the future all of the remaining Lost Trust retrials and appeals would be handled by the Department and the U.S. Attorney for South Carolina would not be involved in the cases. At the time, a total of five retrials were pending from cases in which convictions had been overturned. The five defendants facing retrials were former Sen. Bud Long and former Reps. Taylor, Blanding, Gordon, and Derrick.

Lionel Lofton, the attorney for B.J. Gordon, found the Justice Department probe unsatisfactory, remarking, "I'm extremely disappointed with the letter and the results of this so-called investigation... Our motions are still pending in court, and we intend to present evidence that there was prosecutorial misconduct."

The U.S. Justice Department's investigation of whether federal prosecutors engaged in misconduct in the Lost Trust cases provoked even more criticism from defense counsel who alleged that the probe was superficial and failed to answer specific questions posed by B.J. Gordon's attorney, Lionel Lofton, as well as Luther Taylor's attorney, Joel Collins, in motions filed by the defense in February, 1994.

Lofton's motions included excerpts from a hearing of February 28, 1991, in which he asked prosecutors for evidence that Ron Cobb had ever discussed making a payment to Sen. Jack Lindsay. At the hearing, Assistant U.S. Attorney John Barton said there was no evidence of any such discussions. Lofton asked FBI special agent Mike Clemens about any evidence of any such discussions and Clemens denied knowing of any such evidence.

Later, after the new U.S. Attorney Pete Strom, Jr. took over as the new Clinton appointee, Strom turned over a transcript to defense attorneys dated September 25, 1989, in which Ron Cobb told agent Clemens that he made a payoff to Sen. Lindsay for his support for the capital gains tax break bill.

Hearing on Misconduct Set

On October 20, 1994, after wrestling with Lost Trust since 1990, Judge Falcon Hawkins set a hearing for defense attorneys to present evidence of prosecutorial misconduct in the five remaining cases in the Lost Trust series of prosecutions. Hawkins set the hearings after the U.S. Department of Justice filed a letter, dated October 19, 1994, with the court saying that it had investigated defense allegations of misconduct and found none in the cases of the remaining five the Lost Trust defendants—Gordon, Blanding, Taylor, Derrick, and Long.

Defense attorneys spent much of October 20, 1994, in Hawkins' court room complaining that the Justice Department probe was superficial and alleging that the prosecution lied to Hawkins. The defense made special issue of a document which the prosecution said in the first trials did not exist, but which was later found and which showed that Ron Cobb had paid Sen. Lindsay on the capital gains tax break bill. Lofton told the court, "an agent who prepared the document said they don't exist. They do exist. He lied."

Editorial—Time to End Lost Trust

On October 23, 1994, *The State* published an editorial asserting that it was "time to wrap up Lost Trust." The newspaper which had been assiduously covering this scandal since July, 1990, found the U.S. Justice Department's report that the prosecution had not engaged in misconduct provided sufficient grounds to go forward with the remaining five retrials.

The State called the report not only "good news for him (Bart Daniel) but for the cause of justice." *The State* pointed to the allegations made by the three black defendants (Taylor, Gordon, and Blanding) remaining to be tried in the final five retrial cases which asserted that blacks had been singled out and targeted by the FBI to take bribes. The editors dismissed the allegations of racial discrimination as "A flimsy distraction," noting that a number of white politicians, including Dick Greer, also had been caught by the FBI.

Noting that the FBI had evidence that could have been used to charge Sen. Jack Lindsay, but that the FBI never told Bart Daniel about it, the editors wrote that the evidence never led to an answer as to Lindsay's actions. But in view of the fact that Lindsay was dying for months before he finally passed on January 11, 1991, the paper believed that he would not have lived long enough to go to trial. In the end, *The State* argued the issue was not what Lindsay had done but what the final five—Gordon, Blanding, Taylor, Derrick, and Long—had done.

Defense Asks for Records in Retrials

Attorneys for the final five defendants in Lost Trust moved the trial court on December 16, 1994, to order prosecutors to unlock a metal filing cabinet which the defense believed to contain hidden FBI evidence in Lost Trust. But Justice Department prosecutors, who had replaced the U.S. Attorney's staff on the cases, objected and asked that trial Judge Falcon Hawkins review the documents in private.

The prosecution said that the documents in the file cabinet "are not material to the defendants' preparation" and further claimed that the documents included the names of confidential informants. The defense, in turn, asked for a hearing on the release of the documents.

Judge Hawkins had ruled in 1990 that the prosecution could not withhold any evidence, but since that time, the defense had repeatedly alleged that evidence had been withheld.

Even though the Justice Department had probed alleged misconduct and found none, the FBI itself was conducting a probe in 1994 to see if one of its agents had withheld evidence in the cases. The file cabinet was eventually opened and found to be empty.

Early Results on Lobbying Reform Pondered

The lobbying reform provisions of the 1991 Ethics Act had been in effect since January 1, 1992, in South Carolina. The Associated Press undertook on December 17, 1994, to assess the impact of the new lobbying rules over the period from 1992 to the end of 1994.

The *AP* reported that it appeared that the regulations on lobbying and lobbyists had an effect. Longtime political operative and State House lobbyist Dwight Drake remarked that since Operation Lost Trust legislators had maintained a "healthy skepticism" of lobbyists. Even so, Drake felt that the new system "has been good in many ways for the lobbying business. It requires that we make our case better."

One fact that was perhaps related to lobbying abuses was the growing number of reformist Republicans in the General Assembly and state government in the early 1990s. Perhaps Lost Trust had discredited incumbents and Democrats as so many of them had been caught in Lost Trust. In addition, Republican Secretary of State Jim Miles had made lobbying reform the dominant issue in his successful campaign in 1990 to oust Democrat John Campbell, and once in office, Miles hammered the lobbyists and forced them to comply with the existing 1975 Ethics Act. Miles had also pushed lobbying reform while the 1991 Ethics Act was being written and had enforced the 1991 Ethics Act aggressively.

Republicans Capture House

The Republican Party won its first majority of the House since Reconstruction in November, 1994, and Republican Speaker of the House David Wilkins observed on December 16, 1994, that the old corrupt lobbying and legislative cultures which had existed before Operation Lost Trust had been badly damaged. Wilkins, who had played a major role as Chairman of the House Judiciary Committee and as a member of the conference committee which had written much of the lobbying law in the 1991 Act, observed that since Operation Lost Trust and the enactment of the 1991 Ethics Act, "The days when all you [lobbyists] had to do was have some good times with a couple of legislators are over." Wilkins believed that under the new lobbying system, lobbyists had to reach a larger and broader number of legislators rather than just convince a few legislative leaders by showering with them with gratuities.

CHAPTER FORTY ONE

1995—YEAR OF NEW ISSUES AND LITIGATIONS

Wilkes Sues FBI for Expungement

Rep. Tim Wilkes (D-Fairfield) sued the FBI in early January 1995, alleging that the FBI failed to destroy his file as ordered by the federal judge in his case. Wilkes had been acquitted by the jury in September, 1991, on charges of corruption.

Falcon Hawkins, the trial judge, had ordered Wilkes' file destroyed after the acquittal, but had learned that his file still existed. Hawkins ordered the FBI to appear at a hearing in Charleston on January 18, 1995, to respond to Wilkes' allegations.

The FBI spokesman would not tell the media whether the judge's orders had been violated. But Wilkes told reporters that he did not trust the FBI to follow the court order to destroy his file. Wilkes said that until December, 1993, he had believed that his file was destroyed but then learned that the file still existed when he wrote to the FBI about the matter. He got a letter back from the FBI saying they had the file. Wilkes remarked to the media, "I thought when the jury found me innocent and the judge issued in expungement order, it was done. You can imagine the shock I had when I realized it hadn't been done."

Sen. Mitchell Fights Expulsion from Senate

Imprisoned Sen. Theo Mitchell (D-Greenville) announced on January 16, 1995, that he would oppose Republican efforts to expel him from the South Carolina Senate at the beginning of the 1995 session of the General Assembly. Mitchell, an attorney, was serving a 90-day sentence for failure to report large cash transactions he handled on behalf of a legal client who was later convicted of drug trafficking.

Mitchell alleged that the effort to expel him was based on a "racially biased double standard." Sen. Kay Patterson (D-Richland), always ready to provoke volatile racial antagonism, predicted "a knockdown, drag out fight with blood all over the bar room floor, with all the participants knowing upfront we have only eight or nine votes to keep Senator Mitchell in the Senate."

The Mitchell case contrasted with that of former Sen. Gene Carmichael who have been convicted in 1981 on federal vote buying charges but was not expelled on a close vote in the Senate. Carmichael later resigned as did two other senators who were later found guilty of felonies, including Rick Lee (R-Spartanburg) convicted in 1990 of bribery in Lost Trust and Horace Smith (D-Greenville) also convicted in 1990 in a financial fraud case. Sen. Bud Long (D-Horry) did not resign after his indictment and conviction in Lost Trust but had his conviction reversed and decided not to seek re-election in 1992.

The South Carolina Senate acted quickly to expel Sen. Theo Mitchell after he was convicted of crimes and sentenced to prison. The expulsion took effect on January 18, 1995. The expulsion of Mitchell contrasted with the failure of the Senate to expel Sen. Gene Carmichael who had been convicted on federal voting violations in 1982. However, the fact that Carmichael was white and Mitchell was black raised the question of whether Mitchell was expelled in part due to his race. The vote to expel Mitchell was held in the Senate session on January 16, 1995.

Senate Proposes Lifetime Bar on Office Holding

The South Carolina Senate proposed a constitutional amendment which would impose a lifetime bar on any public official convicted of felony public corruption. The bill containing the amendment was taken to vote on January 25, 1995, in an effort to block those who have been convicted in Lost Trust from running for public office again. The house also was considering a similar bill which would ban felons from office.

Felon Ban Stalled

A bill proposing to ban felons from public office and a bill to impose term limits were both stalled in the Senate in early March, 1995. On March 7, 1995, the Senate voted 21 to 20 to send a bill back to committee which would have imposed a ban on former legislators convicted of bribery from being returned to public office. The bill to ban felons was attached to a term limits bill which provoked strong opposition from Sen. Glenn McConnell (R-Charleston) who opposed the proposed limit of 12 years of service in the General Assembly. Senator Joe Wilson (R-Lexington) bemoaned the way in which the term limits bill was tied to the felon ban bill. Arguing that opponents of term limits would kill the felon bill, Wilson said, "This is important and people need to know there are a large number of convicted felons who will have the opportunity now to run for public office."

Ferguson Set for Release

Former Circuit Judge Tee Ferguson was set for release from federal prison camp in Manchester, Ky., on March 22, 1995, according to an announcement by the U.S. Bureau of Prisons. Ferguson had served a total of 29 months on his sentence of 33 months in the Lost Trust prosecutions. Ferguson had been allowed to go into a halfway house in Greenville, S.C., his hometown, for a time but then was cited for probation violation and returned to the Manchester prison camp in November, 1994. The nature of the violation was not released by federal officials.

Efforts to Improve Judicial Selection Stalled

The Vice Chairman of the General Assembly's judicial screening committee resigned in protest saying that the committee's efforts to devise a better system were stalled. House minority leader Jim Hodges (D-Lancaster) quit the committee saying that it was failing to create a new way of picking judges which would put merit over political deal making. Rep. Tim Rogers (D-Richland) joined Hodges in denouncing the existing judicial selection system calling it "rancid. It makes me sick." Rogers thought the political horse-trading in the most recent round of judicial selection in the Legislature clearly showed the need for reform.

FBI Defends Lost Trust

The director of the FBI defended the FBI's conduct in Lost Trust against the criticisms of defense lawyers who had handled Lost Trust cases. Commenting on March 29, 1995, FBI director Louis J. Freeh told a news conference in Columbia that defense allegations of official misconduct by the FBI had been investigated by the FBI: "We've investigated it fully and made our findings known to both the defense attorneys in the court."

Five Year Retrospective on Lost Trust

The State published an extensive retrospective series of articles on Lost Trust in July, 1995, noting not only what happened in the scandal but the reforms and changes in state government since 1990.

The changes in the ways that politics and government operated since the scandal broke on July 18, 1990, were certainly reasons for hope. The shock of the massive corruption had provoked new ethics laws that banned the old ways in which crooked lobbyists bought politicians with unlimited cash, gifts, trips, and handouts.

Reflecting on the reformation in the culture of State House lobbyists and legislators, John Crangle, Executive Director of Common Cause/South Carolina, observed of the change: "We were on the dark continent of American politics there for a while.... We've become a national model." He was pointing to the many provisions of the 1991 Ethics Act which limited campaign finance and banned all lobbyists' gratuities and campaign donations to officials.

Impact of Lost Trust on the Black Caucus

Reflecting on Lost Trust in 1995, the fact that eight of the total of 20 black legislators in the General Assembly were convicted in Lost Trust whereas only nine of the 150 white legislators were convicted in the scandal provoked divergent reactions in the black community. On the one hand, there were those blacks who saw Lost Trust as a part of a massive conspiracy to eliminate black officials. On the other hand, there were blacks who blamed the black legislators caught in the scandal for betraying their duties and turning to bribery.

Rep. James Faber (D-Richland) had pleaded guilty to bribery in taking money from Ron Cobb to vote for the betting bill, but he also saw himself as a victim of a white conspiracy to get him and blacks, alleging "anytime an African-American man tries to achieve in this state, he can be expected to be investigated, denied access to the economic system and ultimately sent to prison.... That's why they're building more prisons in the state."

But black community organizer Kamau Marcharia of rural Fairfield County put the blame on crooked black politicians, alleging that black legislators have lost touch with their mission in the black community and pointing out "I can see them stuffing money in their pockets—they're actually being bought.... I think basically what happened is they lost touch with their base."

Lost Trust and Black Caucus—Ambiguous Consequences

The impact of Operation Lost Trust on the legislative Black Caucus was that it took out seven black House members—Luther Taylor, James Faber, Frank McBride, Ken Bailey, Larry Blanding, Ennis Fant, and B.J. Gordon. It also took down former House member turned circuit court judge Tee Ferguson. Seven other black representatives and three black senators were not charged in Lost Trust.

Sen. Kay Patterson (D-Richland), who never hesitated to allege racial bias as the explanation for the problems of black officials, called Lost Trust the most serious political blow that blacks had experienced in the 1990s. Remarking in 1995 on the problems facing black officials, Patterson admitted the rise of the South Carolina Republican Party was another direct threat which he called "the second coming of Lost Trust."

In fact, the number of blacks in the General Assembly had actually increased from a total of 20 before Lost Trust in 1990 to a total of 30 black legislators in 1995. But as Rep. Gilda Cobb-Hunter (D-Orangeburg) pointed out in the summer of 1995, "I don't see anyone in terms of elected officials trying to bring reconciliation."

Between 1990 and 1995 the Republican Party had captured a majority in the General Assembly. Cobb-Hunter pointed out that appeals to racial justice and doing the right thing made by blacks had little impact on Republicans. Blacks also pointed to the 1995 expulsion of black Senator Theo Mitchell (D-Greenville) from the Senate upon his imprisonment for federal violations. In the expulsion vote, all six remaining black senators voted against expulsion with only one white joining them.

Cobb's Book Alleges Racial Targeting

Ron Cobb revealed the book he was covertly writing on Lost Trust on April 19, 1995. The book alleged that the prosecution knew that the use of the pari-mutuel betting bill would inevitably lure more black than white legislators to take money from him. The book manuscript was revealed for the first time in federal court when attorneys for appellant convicts Long, Gordon, Taylor, Blanding, and Derrick asked the court to force the prosecution to reveal the book manuscript to defense counsel. Defense attorneys claimed that the manuscript showed the government entrapped their clients and targeted blacks by the use of the betting bill.

In the book manuscript, Cobb responded to a question about whether the FBI knew in advance that the betting bill would likely draw more black supporters of betting to take money to vote for it, by admitting, "Sure they knew it. I knew it. Hell, if I knew it, I know they did.... I'd talk a lot of times. I will make the comment a lot of times that I would have the whole black caucus."

Cobb also said that the FBI targeted Rep. B.J. Gordon (D-Williamsburg) because he had been able to escape prosecution in previous manners investigated by law enforcement. Cobb also said that he had decided to focus on Rep. Paul Derrick (R-Lexington) because he disliked Derrick.

Attorney Lionel Lofton, who represented Rep. B.J. Gordon on appeal, was ordered by the court to be given access to three pages of the 50 page manuscript. Cobb's book dealt with several subjects, including the 1988 capital gains tax break bills which cut taxes $8.6 million for some 21 people. But the court sealed that portion of the book. Defense attorney Joel Collins complained that the prosecution had never tried to find out more about the tax break for fear that Gov. Carroll Campbell might be implicated in the corrupt tax break. Collins argued that Lost Trust was also rigged to protect certain white politicians while at the same time targeting blacks. Collins further said, "There was an elaborate cover-up on the government's investigation into the capital gains proviso as it relates to the governor of South Carolina." Collins also alleged that the FBI interviewed Dick Greer about the Greenville capital gains tax break but that the FBI had refused to release the interview manuscript to defense attorneys. The U.S. Attorney's office's Richard Pilger denied there was such a transcript.

Attorneys for the appellants argued that the Cobb book showed the government was trying to entrap the defendants in the case. Attorneys also said that they needed all the evidence to prepare for the retrials and to move for dismissals on grounds of prosecutorial misconduct.

Status of Defendants' Appeals As of 1995

Of a total of eight Lost Trust defendants who went to trial, seven had been convicted and one was acquitted. The seven who had been convicted at trial filed appeals. Five appeals voided convictions.

In mid-July, 1995, the status of the appeals of the appellants was as follows:

Judge Tee Ferguson (D-Greenville) had been indicted March 21, 1991, and had been convicted by jury of corruption on June 7, 1991. Appeal had been denied. Conviction was post-*McCormick.*

Rep. Ken Bailey (D-Orangeburg) had been indicted May 23, 1991, and convicted of selling his vote for $500. The jury returned its verdict on August 27, 1991. Appeal had been denied. Conviction was post-*McCormick.*

Rep. Paul Derrick (R-Lexington) was indicted on February 20, 1991, and was convicted by jury of extortion and conspiracy on May 11, 1991. New trial ordered as a verdict was pre-*McCormick.*

Rep. Luther Taylor (D-Richland) had been indicted on extortion and conspiracy on August 24, 1990, and have been convicted by jury on both charges on October 25, 1990. New trial ordered. Pre-*McCormick.*

Rep. B.J. Gordon (D-Williamsburg) had been indicted on charges on September 21, 1990, and was convicted by jury on March 8, 1991, of selling his vote for $1000. New trial ordered. Pre-*McCormick*.

Rep. Larry Blanding (D-Sumter) was indicted for extortion and conspiracy on September 21, 1990, and was convicted by jury trial on March 8, 1991. New trial ordered. Pre-*McCormick.*

Sen. Bud Long (D-Horry) was indicted for extortion and conspiracy on August 20, 1991, and was convicted by jury trial on November 23, 1991. New trial ordered by trial judge for erroneous jury instruction allowing admission of evidence to go to jury on dismissed conspiracy charge without correcting instruction.

The Results of Lost Trust—1995 Retrospective

Five years after Lost Trust broke on July 18, 1990, the long-term impact of the scandal and the reform legislation it provoked was becoming more obvious. Cynicism in the first months of the scandal was replaced by growing public confidence in the Legislature's drastic actions to clean up lobbying and campaign-finance in South Carolina.

The ban on lobbyists giving officials anything including campaign donations had taken effect on January 1, 1992, and it had cut the power of lobbyists. Veteran lobbyist Steven Smith remarked in 1995 that if lobbyists did not have good facts and reasons behind their proposals they had no impact, commenting that "They don't mind ignoring lobbyists today."

The power of money over legislators had been considerably reduced by new campaign contribution statutory limits. Special interests could no longer give unlimited donations. Chem-Nuclear gave legislators $20,000 in donations only to find that some of the donees took the money and voted against the company's bill to reopen its Barnwell facility to more radioactive waste dumping.

The South Carolina Chamber of Commerce reacted to the new Ethics Act of 1991 by scaling back its old methods of trying to influence the General Assembly by professional lobbying, campaign donations, and lobbyist handouts and, instead, stressed new grassroots lobbying by its many members who were often not professional lobbyists.

The new ban on lobbyists' handouts in the 1991 Ethics Act put some distance between legislators and lobbyists. In the old days, the relationships of lobbyists and legislators were so close it was difficult to distinguish a bribe from a gift.

In mid-July, 1995, Sen. Glenn McConnell (R-Charleston) recalled the blurred line between bribery and hospitality prior to 1992 by saying that some legislators who did not intend to become corrupt were ensnared by the free lunch that led to a free dinner, then to all night partying and free weekend trips all at the expense of lobbyists. No clear line between social interaction and bribery existed in state law or actual practice before 1992.

Robert Brown (D-Marion) who had been convicted of corruption in the scandal admitted in 1995 that because of all the handouts and socializing "Legislators and lobbyists were friends, and they helped each other out." Six of the 16 members on the House Labor, Commerce, and Industry which Brown chaired went to prison for corruption and Brown himself took a bribe of $2,000 from Ron Cobb to vote for the betting bill.

Strom Removed from Lost Trust

Pete Strom, Jr., replaced John Simmons as the U.S. Attorney for South Carolina in mid-1993 soon after Bill Clinton became president. Upon taking office, Strom confronted defense motions alleging prosecutorial misconduct. Strom then asked the U.S. Justice Department to investigate the matter after attorneys such as Lionel Lofton complained that defense motions for discovery have been rejected by the prosecution on false grounds. The Justice Department's Office of Professional Responsibility conducted the investigation and found nothing.

Strom then recused himself and his office from the prosecution of the remaining defendants and the Justice Department took over, sending in Washington, D.C., lawyers Daniel Butler and Richard Pilger to handle the remaining legal proceedings, including three final retrials until 1999.

Jack I. Rogers Ends Sentence

Even while the final five Lost Trust cases were still under appeal the worst offender in all of the Lost Trust cases got out of jail in July, 1995, when former Rep. Jack I. Rogers served out his racketeering sentence after 34 months of incarceration. Rogers had received the most harsh indictment and conviction.

Rogers had started to serve his sentence at a federal prison in Jesup, Georgia, where he was assigned to clerical work and held there for 17 months. He was later moved to Estill, South Carolina, where he worked in a warehouse and suffered a serious back injury. He spent 15 months helping inmates prepare for the GED and his students had the highest passing rate in the federal prison system. He then moved to a Florence, South Carolina, halfway house near his home but he was denied any furloughs because he was a high-profile inmate. Rogers then moved home and went to work as an airport manager.

On release, Rogers' plan was to take the bar examination and the professional responsibility examination and then apply to the South Carolina Supreme Court for reinstatement as a lawyer.

Sting Convicts Ponder Future in 1995

Former Rep. and Circuit Court Judge Tee Ferguson told the media in 1995 that he had no definite plans for his future after his convictions for cocaine and selling his vote for $3,000 and his service of 33 months in federal prison which allowed his release in 1995.

Former Rep. Robert Brown (D-Marion) reflected on his guilty plea to corruption five years after he entered the plea, saying that he sometimes wished that he had fought the charges but decided not to because of the fear of a conviction at trial and a much harsher sentence. After completing his sentence in 1995, Brown returned to the family insurance and real estate business in Marion County. But Brown admitted, "I'm not without blame, and I've accepted responsibility for what I did wrong." Even so, he denied he ever had criminal intent, saying he took money.... But never with the intent of selling out to any kind of vote or influence or anything like that."

Another convict from Lost Trust, Dick Greer, said in 1995 after completing his drug sentence that he was still interested in politics and government and that "I'm pretty much at peace with myself and the world... I'm still proud of the job we did at the State Development Board when we were there."

Ron Cobb reflected in 1995 on his dubious career in politics and lobbying, saying that after his role as drug dealer and undercover sting agent for the FBI in Lost Trust, he had left lobbying, moved to a townhouse on a golf course in Greenville, South Carolina, and had joined the Greenville First Baptist Church and the Greenville Chamber of Commerce. "Lobbying wasn't real," Cobb told a reporter in the summer of 1995, but said he was still working on a book about his experiences. Cobb said that people had indicated that they approved what he did to expose corruption in state government and politics, noting that "they appreciate what I did. They felt like things had gotten out of hand. That makes me feel good."

Rep. Tim Wilkes (D-Fairfield) was the only defendant acquitted in Lost Trust among the total of 28. Wilkes said that he experienced euphoria on his acquittal in September, 1991, but that it "probably delayed the process of healing." Wilkes still had some "unresolved and very complex things that I will have to deal with."

Former Rep. Robert Kohn (R-Charleston) emerged from the Lost Trust scandal in which he had been caught in corruption and also turned by the FBI into an undercover sting agent without changing much, he said in 1995. Kohn told the media that he, along with Ron Cobb, could have bribed half of the General Assembly had he been given enough time. Kohn described the General Assembly in 1990 as rotted out with corruption, alleging "We were just an absolutely depraved group of people.... You look back now, you say, 'How did we get so stupid'." Kohn's son committed suicide in 1993 after Kohn's conviction.

In the years since the scandal, Kohn delivered lectures on ways to make sting operations more effective. And he still maintained contact with the FBI. Even so, Kohn admitted, "I'm upset with myself that I was as evil and rotten as I was. And I'm really sorry for what I did to the citizens, my friends, and my family. But I don't have one bit of remorse for what I did to the Legislature. They deserved everything I did to them."

Among those he stung, Kohn was still reviled in 1995. Former Rep. Jim Faber (D-Richland), who pleaded to corruption in 1990, denounced both Kohn and Cobb as "the degenerates of society." And Kohn was widely believed to have enjoyed his work as a sting agent once he found out how much leniency his cooperation with the FBI would buy. In fact, he got only seven months incarceration in a federal work camp in North Carolina.

Former Rep. Donna Moss (D-Cherokee), convicted of cocaine on a plea bargain, said that she did not think the Lost Trust prosecutions had done any good, remarking, "I don't think things have changed at all. There still are people taking advantage of the system. Maybe they're just being a little more careful about how they're taking advantage of it." Moss had tried to run for election to the House but she lost the Democratic primary election. She captured 43% of the vote in spite of her criminal conviction.

Former Sen. Rick Lee (R-Spartanburg) reflected on his role in Lost Trust five years after he was convicted by plea and said that he did not think that he had sold his vote on the betting bill. However, he acknowledged that he had borrowed money to run for the Senate and did so only because he thought that he could raise the money from lobbyists once he got elected.

Former Rep. Tom Limehouse (R-Charleston) told *The State* in the summer of 1995 that since he was indicted and convicted of corruption, "I no longer want to be a public figure." Limehouse added, "I did my federal time I was sentenced to, and prior to that, I did my state time for six years in the House."

Felons Think of Return to Office

Five years after Operation Lost Trust hit South Carolina's political class, several of those convicted in the scandal were considering a run for election to public office. State law actually permitted convicted former public officials to make a run for office again even in cases of bribery and public corruption.

As it turned out in the years since Lost Trust, none of the elected officials who were convicted in Lost Trust was ever elected to public office again and the only legislator acquitted in Lost Trust, Rep. Tim Wilkes (D-Fairfield), soon left the house after his exoneration in September, 1991, and never ran again.

Two convicted House members tried and failed to win re-election after they completed their sentences. Former Rep. Donna Moss (D-Cherokee) and former Rep. Ennis Fant (D-Greenville) were rejected by voters in primary elections.

Bill to Ban Felons Fails

Repeated efforts to pass bills banning felons from running for and holding state public offices all failed. As of 1995, the House had passed two bills to ban felons from the General Assembly, but the Senate had rejected them both.

In 1995 a bill to ban felons from office was pushed by Rep. Bubba Cromer (I-Richland) and passed the House, but it was pulled back into subcommittee in the Senate by Chairman Glenn McConnell (R-Charleston). Even so, Sen. K Patterson (D-Richland), a cynic about ethics reform and action against corrupt officials, objected to any ban on felons saying, "If the people in your community want to vote for you, they have that right. I don't think that you and I should try to act like the great white father who knows what's best for people back home."

Poll Rejects Felons for Office

A poll taken by *The State* in late July, 1995, showed 450 respondents opposed to felons being allowed to run for state public office while only 37 favored it. One respondent told the interviewer, "I feel they would do the same thing again. I would not trust them." However, another responded and said that, "defendants in Lost Trust were wrongly convicted in the beginning."

At the time the House had passed new legislation barring felons from holding office, but the Senate had not acted. One respondent said the convicted corruptionists should be hanged while another asserted, "I certainly don't think that these crooks should be allowed to run for office." However, another responded and said that once the sentence was served felons should be allowed to hold public office.

Results of Lost Trust Continues

The limits on campaign contribution amounts and the ban on lobbyists' campaign donations still angered some special interests. Some lobbyists, for example, raised the question of whether the ban on lobbyists' campaign contributions violated the Constitution. But nobody ever filed a lawsuit to challenge the ban on lobbyists' gratuities and campaign donations since it took effect in 1992.

To dodge the ban on the lobbyists' donations, some lobbyists tried the trick of resigning as lobbyists after the session ended and then giving donations before refiling as lobbyists again. (In 1995, the legislature took action and the temporary resignation scheme was stopped by the new law.)

However, by 1995, the reforms had been in effect since 1992, and it was evident that the Ethics Act of 1991 had serious flaws. It allowed legislators to continue to police themselves with the prospect that they would not really do so. Legislators still elected almost all judges before whom lawyer-legislators practiced law. Campaign contribution limits were easy to avoid. Corporations could donate from their treasury and then each corporate employee could donate maximum amounts as individuals and also donate to corporate political action committees. Campaign funds were still being converted to personal use.

Interest groups could still invite officials on trips provided that the officials paid their own way. Some interest groups complained that they could not offer free food to officials.

But Speaker Bob Sheheen (D-Kershaw) defended the strict new limits in the Ethics Act of 1991 as necessary in the context of the terrible scandal of 1990, saying of the public, "They ought to be able to know that the process is fair, the people who participate in the process are honest."

Reflections on Lost Trust from the Perspective of 1995

"If multiple people think because the ethics law was passed that now all the sudden you don't have money influencing legislators, they're mistaken and.... It may not be as prevalent as in the past, but it still is the case."

—Rep. Gilda Cobb Hunter (D-Orangeburg)

"I think a lot of them did look at this as though it was just the way business was done. In the end, it was the right thing to have taken place, to take us out of the business as usual kind of atmosphere."

—Gov. Carroll Campbell (R)

"Lost Trust had nothing to do with restructuring. But they culminated at the same time, resulting in one of the most historical changes in government structure in South Carolina."

—Gov. David Beasley (R)

Joel Collins Continues to Fight for Justice

Joel Collins was by far the most outspoken and aggressive defense attorney still, in 1995, fighting for his client, Rep. Luther Taylor, one of the final five left in the Operation Lost Trust appeals.

As the appeal moved forward in 1995, Collins charged that the prosecution had ignored FBI regulations, withheld evidence, and allowed its star witness, Ron Cobb, to lie on the witness stand.

In October, 1990, when Collins took the first Lost Trust case, Luther Taylor's, to trial, his harsh denunciation of the prosecution seemed excessive; but in the following years, Collins' appeals raised troubling and serious questions about prosecutorial misconduct.

After being paid for his work in the first trial of Rep. Luther Taylor, Collins agreed to handle the impoverished Taylor's appeal on a pro bono basis. Collins was especially angered by way in which he thought the prosecution used perjury and evidence withholding in the Taylor case. In one instance, the key prosecution witness, Ron Cobb, took the witness stand and answered Collins that he had never paid Sen. Jack Lindsay any money when it was an established fact that Cobb had given Lindsay $10,000 for his help on the tax break bill.

Collins was influenced to take the Rep. Taylor case to trial rather than to urge his client to plead guilty because of the fact that Taylor had evidence that he had backed the pari-mutuel betting bill long before he took any money from Cobb.

Collins won a major victory before the U.S. Supreme Court when the Court ruled on behalf of Taylor, Derrick, Blanding, and Gordon that their pre-*McCormick* convictions were in error and that the jury had been wrongly instructed that the money given to the four legislators by Cobb without a quid pro quo was bribery. The Court held on appeal that the mere gift of money to a public official was not a bribe unless the official took official action in return for the money.

Another major achievement by Collins and other defense attorneys came in November, 1993, when Judge Hawkins ordered that the government prosecutors put all of their evidence into one room and allow defense attorneys free range to examine the materials.

Judge Orders Release of Lost Trust Files

On July 27, 1995, Judge Falcon Hawkins responded to motions from attorneys for five former legislators already convicted in the earlier Lost Trust prosecutions by ordering files of those covered by the motion released to the defense in the cases of Reps. Taylor, Blanding, McBride, Derrick, and Sen. Long.

Hawkins' order ruled that the attorneys could review the government's records of how much money the prosecution paid to former House member Robert Kohn (R-Charleston) for his undercover work in setting up sting targets. The attorneys believed that they could find evidence of misconduct by the FBI in the cases of the five defendants who were continuing to appeal their convictions in the corruption trials.

At the hearing on July 27, 1995, Judge Falcon Hawkins reflected a dim view of the prosecution in its failure to release documents to defendants on discovery request. Hawkins ruled that the defense could obtain the documents but that they would not be released to the public. At issue was information about government payments to former Rep. Bob Kohn to serve as an undercover informant to the FBI.

Defense attorney, Joel Collins, representing Rep. Luther Taylor, welcomed Hawkins' order releasing the documents, remarking "This question about whether the government is playing fair has been there from the beginning." But former U.S. Attorney Bart Daniel who had first prosecuted the cases ridiculed the order, saying, "The defense lawyers are just fishing."

Prior to issuing his order, Hawkins examined 12 boxes of documents, including seven from the U.S. Justice department and four boxes from the FBI.

A Justice Department probe found no evidence of prosecutorial misconduct. But an FBI internal investigation found that FBI Agent Mike Clemens used poor judgment and was negligent at times.

In reviewing the evidence, Judge Hawkins found that some of the documents were withheld by the prosecution until after the trials and that some of the evidence might have shown the defendants were not guilty. Prosecutors had withheld 65 tapes but the judge ordered them turned over to the defense as they related to drug activity. The judge thought "that the drug investigation was hand-in-glove with a corruption investigation known as Lost Trust."

Judge Hawkins' comments at the July 27, 1995, hearing indicated a serious concern that the prosecution had withheld evidence from the court and defense. In issuing his order compelling the prosecution to produce documents related to the final defendants, Hawkins remarked, "Although the purpose of this order is not to address the motions to dismiss, government arguments such as this cause the court to look very closely at what was withheld by the government that they may have jeopardized the rights of the defendants."

Hawkins noted that allegations of misconduct went beyond the prosecutors and the FBI and reached the Justice Department. Defense attorneys had argued that a so-called investigation of Lost Trust by the Justice Department was really a whitewash in which key witnesses were not, in fact, interviewed and that the report on the investigation did not summarize all interviews. One question was whether the Justice Department really probed bribes paid to fix the capital gains tax cut in the matter of why Sen. Jack Lindsay was never charged even though Cobb gave Lindsay $10,000.

Appellants Blame Prosecution Abuses

Attorneys for the last five defendants in the Lost Trust prosecutions attacked the government in the U.S. District court in a three day hearing starting on October 17, 1995, arguing that the prosecution had told the defense attorneys in the court that certain documents related to the cases did not exist only to reveal later that such documents did, in fact, exist when the prosecution moved to retry the cases of the five defendants after the original convictions were overturned.

The hearing produced evidence that a potential witness for the defense would have told the court at previous trials of the appellants that he knew about bribes given to Sen. Jack Lindsay, but the federal prosecutors ignored all allegations about Lindsay and the witness was not called to testify.

Defense attorneys blamed Ron Cobb, who the defense had argued on appeal had lied at trial, saying that he did not give a payoff to Sen. Lindsay when the prosecution knew that, in fact, Ron Cobb had paid off Lindsay.

The defense also subpoenaed former U.S. Attorney Bart Daniel to testify at the hearing, but Daniel told the media beforehand that "it's easy for those guys to play Monday-morning quarterback. They cannot, much as they try, rewrite history."

The question of whether Dick Greer was somehow involved in the capital gains tax break was an issue on October 17, 1995, before Judge Hawkins. On May 23, 1991, Assistant U.S. Attorney John Barton had asked Greer if he was aware of any payoffs to legislators on the tax bill of 1988. Greer denied any such knowledge. But just two months later, Bart Daniel told the court at Greer's sentencing for drug crimes that Greer was cooperating with the prosecution in the capital gains tax bill investigation and asked the court to give Greer a more lenient sentence. The point was that Greer could have been of little help to the government in view of the fact that he said he knew nothing about payoffs the government was probing.

The Justice Department told the court that even if the prosecution did not pursue the capital gains tax bill question, that was not sufficient justification to dismiss all charges in Lost Trust which were unrelated to the tax bill.

Even so, Ron Cobb's new book, still in manuscript, alleged that Governor Campbell was, in fact, involved with the tax bill along with Lindsay and some Republican senators but wanted to hide the matter from view as much as possible.

Appellants Demand Dismissals

After the appeals court granted new trials for Reps. Larry Blanding, Paul Derrick, B.J. Gordon, and Luther Taylor as well as Sen. Bud Long, the prosecution and defense wrangled over what the court should do in the five cases.

The defense argued that the new trials were not enough of a remedy for all the misconduct they alleged against the prosecution and instead asked Judge Hawkins for a complete dismissal of all charges against the five defendants in the cases. In preparation for the new trials, defense motions alleged that substantial evidence of prosecutorial misconduct had been found. But the U.S. Department of Justice and the FBI claimed they had investigated allegations of misconduct and found nothing.

The defense subpoenaed Weldon Waites, who was in a federal prison at the time, to testify that Waites knew of the bribery of Jack Lindsay but that the FBI did not want to hear about it in the matter of the capital gains tax break.

The motion hearing raised questions about whether somehow Governor Carroll Campbell was involved in the tax break bill, but he denied it, remarking that, "This had been taken and twisted by some people for their own good, and it's unfair, because when it's being said in a court of law, there's nothing you can do about it."

Prosecution Explains Itself

Reacting to allegations made by defense attorneys for the five defendants awaiting a new trial, former U.S. Attorney Bart Daniel told a news conference outside the U.S. District Courthouse in Columbia on October 20, 1995, that his office did not break the law in its efforts to convict the Lost Trust defendants in the first round of prosecutions in 1990 and 1991.

"To spoil the reputation of the FBI and U.S. Attorney's Office is an outrage," Daniel told the press at the end of three days of motion hearings in which the attorneys for the five defendants presented evidence and made arguments that the prosecution engaged in misconduct in the cases of Taylor, Blanding, Gordon, Derrick, and Long. "The truth of the matter is that all of these attorneys' allegations aren't true."

Motions—1995: Defense Forces Issue of Prosecution Misconduct

Complaints against federal operatives in Lost Trust piled up in the fall of 1995. Defense attorneys lamented the conduct of U.S. Attorney Bart Daniel, Assistant U.S. Attorney John Barton and FBI agent Mike Clemens. All three denied any misconduct. A critical hearing further embarrassed the prosecution on October 28, 1995, by exposing false prosecutor's statements.

On February 28, 1991, a hearing has been held at which defendant Rep. B.J. Gordon, through his attorney, Lionel Lofton, asked the court to compel the prosecution to give certain documents to the defense which included evidence of a discussion in which FBI informant Ron Cobb discussed paying off Sen. Jack Lindsay. Responding to Lofton's request for the evidence of the payoff, Assistant U.S. Attorney John Barton told Judge Falcon Hawkins that, "if he's (Lofton) looking for the secret 302 (FBI interview summary) of Ron Cobb where this is discussed, it does not exist."

At the same 1991 hearing, Lofton questioned FBI special agent Mike Clemens, who also denied any knowledge of the FBI transcript about Cobb giving a payoff to Senator Lindsay. However, by the court hearing of October 28, 1995, the defense attorneys had, in fact, obtained a copy of four different 302 records in which Cobb said that he did pay off Senator Lindsay. Defense attorneys had also obtained an internal document from the government indicating that Cobb paid off Lindsay.

After the prosecution was forced to produce copies of records of FBI 302 documents which the prosecution had told a court hearing on February 28, 1991, did not exist, defense attorney Lionel Lofton told the hearing on October 28, 1995, four and a half years later, that the documents would have helped the defense to impeach Ron Cobb's testimony. In 1991, Cobb had told the trial court under oath that he had not given Sen. Lindsay a payoff when, in fact, he had given such a payoff.

Lofton told the hearing on October 28, 1995, that Cobb defined money he gave to people differently if he liked them or if he disliked them. Cobb characterized money given to a friend like Senator Lindsay as a legal fee, but he would call money given to an enemy a payoff, Lofton alleged.

Lofton also said that conflicting statements have been given in 1991 to the grand jury and to trial Judge Hawkins about what Dick Greer had said about the capital gains tax cut bill. Attorney John Barton at the start had asked before a grand jury hearing if Greer knew about any bribery involving the tax cut bill, and Greer denied any such knowledge. Then Barton persuaded Judge Hawkins a month later in 1991 to reduce Greer's cocaine sentence on the grounds that Greer was cooperating with the prosecution in the capital gains tax bill probe when it appeared that Greer was not really cooperating and was giving dubious testimony.

Defense attorney Lionel Lofton complained to the court hearing of October 28, 1995, that the prosecution said it did not have any documents of Dick Greer's statements about the capital gains tax cut bill even though Greer had told the court the previous week that he had four different conversations with the prosecution about the tax bill. The government had only produced one document and that dealt only with drug matters. The defense argued that there should be some documentation about Greer's statements on the issue of the tax bill.

The defense also complained to Judge Hawkins that the government would not release the tape-recording (tape No. 98) in which FBI informant Bob Kohn talked about an insurance fraud scheme in which Kohn was somehow involved. The defense could have used the tape to impeach Kohn as a prosecution witness. The prosecution also did not release the tape of Kohn snorting cocaine, which the defense could also have used to impeach Kohn at trial.

As the appeals dragged on into late 1995, it did appear that the prosecution had engaged in dubious conduct in Lost Trust, but that the court was not likely to dismiss all charges against Derrick, Long, Taylor, Gordon, and Blanding. Prof. Eldon D. Wedlock, Jr., of the University of South Carolina School of Law and the former state chairman of Common Cause/South Carolina in 1990–1991, told the media that even if the prosecution had engaged in some misconduct, the defendants' alleged corruption had hurt the public interest to an extent that the charges could not be dismissed.

Pete Strom, Jr., Resigns as U.S. Attorney

U.S. Attorney Pete Strong, Jr., turned in his resignation on November 30, 1995, after holding the position since mid-1993 during the later Lost Trust prosecutions, appeals, and retrial orders. An appointee of the Clinton administration following the Republican appointee, John S. Simmons, Strom raised alarm about the tactics of his Republican predecessors and requested that the U.S. Department of Justice investigate their original prosecutions, especially the first round of trials conducted by the U.S. Attorney's office in 1990 and 1991. During the Strom era as U.S. Attorney, the trial judge and appellate courts ordered new trials for five of those convicted at trial and as of the end of Strom's tenure, the trials had not yet been completed. Strom's resignation was to take effect in mid-January, 1996. Strom announced his plan was to return to private practice on January 19, 1996.

Lobbyists Asked for Money

The South Carolina Republican Party sent out letters in late December, 1995, inviting registered lobbyists to fundraising events for legislators in spite of the fact that the 1991 Ethics Act strictly prohibited lobbyists from giving campaign contributions to any candidates for state offices. The prohibition in the Act had been included to stop the excessive and often corrupt use of lobbyists' campaign donations to bribe legislators as exposed by Operation Lost Trust.

The Republican Party explained that the reason for the solicitation sent to lobbyists was that the party had a list of over 100,000 sources of political money and could not afford the time and expense of purging the names of lobbyists from the list.

Lobbyists complained that the Republican Party's communications with lobbyists looked like an attempted return to the days of Operation Lost Trust when legislators often shook down lobbyists for political donations, free trips, free liquor, and even free cash money. By 1995, many, if not most, lobbyists had adjusted to the ban on lobbyists spending to buy access and favors and did not want to return to the old corrupt practices.

CHAPTER FORTY TWO

1996—APPEALS AND MOTIONS FOR DISMISSAL CONTINUE

Five Defendant Dismissal Motions Move Forward

Judge Falcon Hawkins set March 11, 1996, as the day for closing arguments on motions for dismissal on the issue of whether prosecutors engaged in misconduct in the cases of the final five defendants still left in Lost Trust. Hawkins also ordered the FBI and the U.S. Justice Department to release additional documents to defense attorneys in time for the March 11, 1996, hearing on appellants' motions to dismiss on grounds of misconduct.

Defendant attorneys had argued in a three day hearing in late October, 1995, that the prosecution withheld documentary evidence from the court and that the prosecution allowed its star witness, Ron Cobb, to lie to the court in the trials of some of those who had been convicted.

The defendants asking the court to dismiss all charges against them were former Reps. Larry Blanding, Paul Derrick, B.J. Gordon, and Luther Taylor, joined by former Sen. Bud Long. The convictions of all five defendants were overturned because of errors in the original trials in 1990 and 1991 and new trials have been ordered. The new trials were on hold until trial Judge Falcon Hawkins could rule on the motions to dismiss. Hawkins postponed the conclusion of the hearing until he could review evidence in several boxes of documents belonging to the prosecution. Hawkins wanted to make sure that no documents were being withheld that should be delivered to the defense.

Defense Moves Dismissal

On October 3, 1996, defense attorneys began a new massive attack on the federal prosecutors of the Lost Trust cases in a hearing in the U.S. District Court before Judge Falcon Hawkins. Defense counsel alleged that the government lawyers violated ethical canons by concealing evidence, deceiving the court about evidence, and by presenting their star witness Ron Cobb who gave false and misleading testimony in the Lost Trust trials. The attorneys at the hearing represented former Reps. Luther Taylor, Larry Blanding, Paul Derrick, B.J. Gordon, and Sen. Bud Long.

Judge Hawkins had the power to sanction the prosecutors and even to dismiss all charges in the cases of the remaining defendants attacking the prosecution in the hearings. Attorney Joel Collins for Luther Taylor argued that the conduct of Bart Daniel, John Barton, and FBI agent Mike Clemens was so violative of prosecutorial standards that all charges should be dismissed.

At the October 3, 1996, hearing, attorney Collins alleged that new documents obtained by the defense justified dismissal of all charges against his client. Collins said that the prosecutors allowed their chief witness Cobb in the Luther Taylor case and later cases to make false statements in court about his dealings with Sen. Jack Lindsay.

Collins also said that the prosecution changed its practice during the Lost Trust sting operation. At first the FBI and the U.S. Attorney's Office planned to let legislators come asking for bribes but legislators did not ask for bribes. Then in mid-1990 the government adopted a new tactic of soliciting legislators to take money from Ron Cobb. Legislators finally took the bait.

Collins argued that the documents which defense lawyers could not get from the prosecution until after the original trials ended in 1990 and 1991 would have allowed the defense to show that the defendants did not think the money they were given by Cobb was a bribe but rather was a campaign contribution. But the government said that it was immaterial whether the legislators approached Cobb or Cobb approached them because in either case they took the money from Cobb as a bribe.

Daniel also pointed to the fact that the Justice Department and FBI had investigated the question of misconduct and found none.

Judge Falcon Hawkins derided prosecution behavior in the Lost Trust prosecutions on the grounds that prosecutors engaged in a "pattern of discovery abuse" in refusing to release hundreds of documents in the Lost Trust cases to the prejudice of the defendants and appellants. On October 3, 1996, Hawkins' criticism of the prosecution left open the question of whether he would find the abuses so serious as to warrant dismissal for the defendants.

Joel Collins told the court that all charges should be dismissed because of prosecutorial misconduct. Collins warned the judge that unless he dismissed the charges the court would be "giving the Good Housekeeping Seal of Approval to everything that's going on."

Dan Butler, trial lawyer with the U.S. Department of Justice, admitted prosecution mistakes but said they were not intentional. Butler told the court that, "It's not a matter of punishing society's interests...and giving the defendants a windfall." The defendants seeking dismissal on October 3, 1996, were Luther Taylor, B.J. Gordon, Larry Blanding, Paul Derrick, and Bud Long. Hawkins had options, including not only a dismissal of charges, but also filing a grievance against the prosecutors with the South Carolina Supreme Court. Hawkins was clearly upset that he had been told by the prosecution that all documents had been produced only to learn later that hundreds of documents had not been produced and fully disclosed to the court and the defendants.

Felon Candidates Ban on Ballot

The 1996 general elections presented to the voters Amendment 2A which applied to legislative candidates and Amendment 2B which applied to all candidates for public office in South Carolina. The amendments to the South Carolina Constitution proposed to ban anyone convicted of a felony from running for public office for 15 years after completion of the prison sentence and probation. The amendments were directed at the Lost Trust felons. (Adopted as Art. III, §7 of S.C. Constitution; see also Art. VI, §1 of S.C. Constitution.)

The issue of convicted felons running for state office had come up in 1991 when former state senator Gene Carmichael was again elected by Pee Dee area voters as a state senator even after he was convicted of vote-buying in a federal prosecution a decade earlier. The return of Carmichael had provoked controversy in the Senate and some senators voted against allowing him to take his seat.

The amendments had been proposed by Rep. Bubba Cromer (I-Richland) who convinced the General Assembly to approve the proposed amendments and put them on the ballot as referenda items. Sen. Kay Patterson (D-Richland) had objected to the amendments as "paternalism at its worst," arguing that voters should be allowed to elect freely even if they wanted to elect a felon.

The candidacy of Chris Pracht, who was running as a Democrat in Anderson, South Carolina, illustrated the issue in the 1996 elections as he had been convicted of drug violations in 1984. Two candidates who had been convicted in Lost Trust had failed in their efforts to return to the house when voters rejected Ennis Fant of Greenville and Donna Moss of Cherokee. Ironically, a 1981 law banned felons from voting.

Editorial on Judicial Selection

The State printed an editorial October 29, 1996, which argued that the South Carolina judicial selection system should be changed to deny sitting legislators from being elected to state court judgeships. *The State* pointed to the 1995 elections of House members Hicks Harwell and Danny Martin even though a judicial screening panel found them deficient in their knowledge of the law. In addition, the same election returned a candidate for the Supreme Court who was given the lowest score by the South Carolina Bar.

The State proposed that a constitutional amendment be passed by the General Assembly that would create a judicial selection panel to review candidates for judgeships and recommend them for election. *The State* also endorsed the idea that a legislator could not run for a judicial office until out of office for at least one year.

The State said the proposed amendments, "should receive overwhelming approval from every citizen who wants a fair hearing" in the election of November 5, 1996. Under the South Carolina Constitution all constitutional amendments had to be proposed by two-thirds vote of both houses of the Legislature and approved by a majority of voters as a referendum on the ballot at a general election and finally approved a second time by a simple majority of both houses. (The Judicial Merit Selection Commission was adopted in 1997 as Art. V, §27 of S.C. Constitution.)

CHAPTER FORTY THREE

1997—INDICTMENTS DISMISSED AND REINSTATED

In 1997 Judge Hawkins became so indignant at the misconduct of the prosecution that he dismissed all charges against all five final defendants. But in 1999, the Circuit Court of Appeals on appeal by the DOJ prosecution reinstated the charges and set re-trials for convicted defendants former Rep. Paul Derrick, former Rep. Larry Blanding, and former Sen. Bud Long.

In the middle of the appeals, two of the appellants, Rep. Luther Taylor and Rep. B.J. Gordon died. Taylor died on March 23, 1997, of pancreatic cancer in a Columbia hospital. Gordon died on July 12, 1997, of stomach cancer. The estates of Taylor and Gordon sought standing to sue the prosecuting attorneys for violation of their rights but were denied standing by the courts.

Judge Hawkins' Dismissal Order Issued In 1997

Judge Falcon Hawkins' drastic dismissal order of February 28, 1997, justified dismissal as "the only remedy available to these defendants that would be commensurate with the misconduct of the government.... I am of the opinion that the nature and breadth of the misconduct is indicative of the drastic steps the prosecution took to win these cases, and the resultant injustice to the defendants cannot be fully remedied by new trial."

Hawkins denounced the prosecution and alleged that, "over-zealousness and political pressure upon those in positions of authority appeared to be detours that led the government to rush to trial...and to mislead the court to such an extent as to perpetrate a fraud on the court."

Hawkins accused the prosecution of showing unfair treatment to the five defendants pursuing appeals into 1997 and alleged that Dick Greer received special treatment: "When the government found itself in position which forced it to investigate Greer, the situation became even more explosive.... There is no way the court can ignore the inconsistence in and omissions from the record in the matter of Greer and the capital gains tax bill," Hawkins wrote. "The government actions...suggest a total avoidance of pursuing information that might have been adverse to Greer. The record is replete that Greer was heavily involved in payoffs related to the capital gains bill, yet no...(FBI investigative) notes or debriefings of Greer regarding capital gains...can be found, "Hawkins concluded.

Charges Dismissed Against Five

Judge Falcons Hawkins dismissal order of February 28, 1997, cleared five defendants of the following charges:

Larry Blanding (D-Sumter)—convicted on March 8th, 1991, for selling his vote for $1,300. Sentenced to 37 months. Served 8 months. Verdict overturned. Retrial ordered.

Paul Derrick (R-Lexington)—convicted on May 1, 1991, of selling his vote for $1,000. Sentenced to 34 months. Not imprisoned. Verdict overturned. Retrial ordered.

B.J. Gordon (D-Williamsburg)—convicted on March 8, 1991, of selling his vote for $1,000. Conviction was overturned prior to sentencing. Never served any time. Died July 12, 1997, before retrial.

J.M. "Bud" Long (D-Horry)—convicted on November 23, 1991, of selling his vote for $2,800. Trial Judge set aside conviction prior to sentencing. Retrial ordered.

Luther Taylor (D-Richland)—convicted on October 25, 1990, of selling his vote for $4,300. Sentenced to 78 months. Served 18 months. Retrial ordered. Died March 23, 1997, before retrial.

Hawkins Dismissal Order

Hawkins' February 28, 1997, order of dismissal concluded by saying, "the court is of the opinion that the evidence of the government's misconduct from the time this investigation commenced until the present, in its totality, is sufficiently egregious to warrant dismissal of those indictments with prejudice." Hawkins alleged that the prosecution had ignored evidence pointing to criminal conduct by Dick Greer, but also suborned perjury from important witnesses presented in the Lost Trust trials by the government.

Attorneys for the defendants welcomed the dismissal order. Ed Bell, attorney for Rep. Larry Blanding, said, "It's not that these guys got off on a technicality. These guys got off because they were innocent. These cases were dismissed because the government used perjured testimony to convict these people, they targeted them as minorities, and they withheld evidence that would have proved their innocence. And I don't know if there's any more of an outrageous act than that."

In his order dismissing all charges against the five remaining defendants in the Lost Trust prosecutions, Judge Falcon Hawkins ripped the prosecution for what the court believed was devious conduct in the cases. Hawkins seemed to say that the prosecution used unfair and dishonest tactics and also played favorites as to its selection of targets for indictment.

Hawkins said he concluded that, "the nature and breadth of the misconduct is indicative of the drastic steps the prosecution took to win these cases, and that the resultant injustice to these defendants cannot be fully remedied by new trials." Hawkins felt that political pressure on those in charge of the prosecution, "led the government to rush to trial…and to mislead the court to such an extent as to perpetrate a fraud on the court."

Judge Hawkins dismissal order of all charges against the final five Lost Trust defendants ran to some 86 pages and much of the order was a blistering indictment for the prosecution's allegedly abusive tactics. However, Hawkins never came out to say that the defendants were not guilty or that their behavior in office was even legal let alone ethical. He did say that the evidence withheld by the prosecution might have been helpful to the defense and that they were legally entitled to get it on discovery.

Dismissal Order Rips Cobb

Judge Hawkins' order of dismissal pointed to the use of the dubious figure of Ron Cobb as a key agent and prosecution witness in Lost Trust. Although the original goal of the sting was legitimate, the prosecution became more focused on scoring big hits than on playing by the rules. In the end, Hawkins wrote, "Cobb maneuvered himself into the driver's seat position, and the government was a hostage to him. It was apparent that the government knew it had to 'court' Cobb in order for him to work with them effectively. At times, he literally took over the investigation and directed its course."

Hawkins further opined that Cobb lied on the stand and the prosecution knew he was lying. When Luther Taylor alleged at his 1990 trial that he was targeted while the government did not charge Sen. Jack Lindsay, Ron Cobb took the stand to misinform the court that he never bribed Lindsay when, in fact, he had apparently bribed the senator according to evidence later released by the prosecution to the defendant.

Jack Swerling commented on Hawkins', dismissal order of charges by saying that he expected the U.S. Department of Justice to soon reject Hawkins' harsh denunciations of Bart Daniel and his prosecutors for white-washing Dick Greer, predicting "I think they're going to vigorously defend what the whole office did.... They'll take a fallback approach that if there was misconduct, the remedy should not have been dismissal with prejudice." Swerling's prediction proved correct.

Swerling said that Hawkins' opinion was solid and that efforts by the Department of Justice to appeal for reinstatement of charges would fail, remarking "I thought the judge's opinion was well-reasoned. It was done with painstaking research and a lot of soul searching."

Daniel and Greer Knock Dismissal Order

The judge's condemnation of Daniel and accusations against Greer provoked Daniel, several prosecutors, and Dick Greer to file arguments along with the government appeal to reinstate charges against the five appellants dismissed by Hawkins. Gedney Howe, attorney for Dick Greer, alleged that Hawkins' dismissal was a legal error, "assuming everything Judge Hawkins said is true, he acted improperly. They don't have to take on our issues at all."

Daniel, who had helped to plan the sting and who had prosecuted the first Lost Trust cases, reacted defensively to Judge Falcon Hawkins' order of dismissal of all five remaining defendants. Daniel told the media as soon as the order was issued on February 28, 1997, that what he had done was justified and that there was no prosecutorial misconduct. Daniel denied that his office ever intentionally withheld any evidence in the cases. He said that it was "ludicrous" to assert that defense attorneys were denied access to evidence they needed to cross-examine Ron Cobb.

Daniel turned the blame to the defense lawyers, saying that "I think this goes back to when you have no defense, you try to put the prosecutors on trial. Because when the evidence is on trial, it didn't take the juries long to convict any of these people. You've got public officials caught on videotape selling their public office for cash. As they stuffed the cash in their pockets, they talked about selling their votes."

Daniel also denounced the political system of the State House as rotten with corruption, but said that, "fortunately changes have been made, and the way business is done in the General Assembly is changed forever."

Daniel correctly predicted that the appeals court would reverse the order of dismissal and reinstate the charges. However, based on the allegations of prosecutorial misconduct and Hawkins' order, it was possible that the prosecutors might have been subjected to an investigation and sanctions, perhaps even disbarment as lawyers.

Hawkins remarked in his order that, "some of the investigators and lead prosecutors got lost on their way to the lofty goal of weeding out drugs and corruption from the South Carolina State House." Hawkins said that he wrestled with his options and considered something less drastic than dismissal but that dismissal was the only solution "commensurate with the misconduct of the government." Hawkins added that the prosecution had gone to extreme and excessive lengths to gain convictions and that "the resultant injustices to these defendants cannot be fully remedied by new trials."

Hawkins Dismissal Ordered Lauded

Attorney Jack Swerling remarked after the dismissal order was released on February 28, 1997, that Hawkins' decision to dismiss all charges against the five defendants was "probably the most significant criminal decision that's been issued in this state against the federal government. The fact is that around the country, literally you can count on one hand the number of cases that a judge has ever found the conduct so egregious to warrant a dismissal for prosecutorial misconduct."

Swerling's client, Sen. Bud Long, told the media after the dismissal that the order removed a dark spot from his life, but that he did not plan to run again for public office.

Dismissal Order Derides Prosecution

Luther Taylor was convicted in October, 1990, but the tape recording of Ron Cobb and Rep. Bob Kohn talking about the sting strategy to set up legislators was not released by the prosecution until three years later even though defense attorneys were entitled to the tapes immediately as evidence in mitigation. Judge Hawkins wrote in his order that the tapes "certainly must be viewed as exculpatory evidence which could have been used to further the defense...that they considered the monies received from Cobb as campaign contributions."

Larry Blanding's attorney, Ed Bell, said of the sting operation on February 28, 1997, when Hawkins issued his dismissal order that "Larry Blanding advocated the pari-mutuel betting bill seven years before this ever came up. How can anyone buy his vote? He was the original sponsor of this bill."

The tape of the Cobb conversation with Kohn showed that Cobb said that the betting bill "got out of committee with no one doing anything...no money" and that Cobb did not want Kohn to help him trap legislators by making it look too much like the sting agents were actually trying to buy votes for the bill while at the same time making it look like they were trying to buy votes on the videotapes eventually shown to the juries. Even so, Bob Kohn insisted that those charged were, in fact, guilty of bribery, adding "there were no good guys in this whole thing."

Hawkins Suggests Greer Whitewash

Judge Hawkins' dismissal order of February 28, 1997, clearly indicated that Hawkins believed that the prosecution had played favorites and had given Dick Greer a pass probably because he was a friend of Governor Carroll Campbell. The Judge wrote, "when the government found itself in a position which forced it to investigate (Dick) Greer, the situation became even more explosive. There was no way the court can ignore the inconsistencies and omissions from the record in the matter of Greer and the capital gains tax bill." Hawkins concluded that the prosecution chose to ignore evidence that Greer was implicated in the capital gains tax cut bill scheme, including the bribery of legislators with whom Greer had contacts. Hawkins' order read: "The government's actions...suggest a total avoidance of pursuing information that might have been adverse to Greer. The record is replete that Greer was heavily involved in payoffs related to the capital gains tax bill... [yet] no indication that government ever sought to review his financial records can be found."

Judge Hawkins' order of dismissal acknowledged the undeniable fact that the relationships between legislators and lobbyists were clearly corrupt and that the General Assembly had taken serious steps to control such relationships in the future as a way of trying to stop the abuses of the Lost Trust era from continuing after 1991. By 1997, the new Ethics Act of 1991 had been in effect for 5 years with good results. Even so, the attorneys for the five defendants whose charges were dropped by Hawkins order claimed that the dismissals vindicated those innocent clients who had been convicted on perjured testimony, partial evidence, and as racial minorities targeted by the sting.

Reflections on Lost Trust by the Guilty

The dismissal of all charges of the final five defendants in Lost Trust on February 28, 1997, proved to be a brief illusion as the federal government appealed dismissals and later the Court of

Appeals reinstated all charges. But, at first, the dismissal seemed to bring closure to a series of prosecutions which had dragged on for seven years to 1997, but which would, in fact, drag on further until 1999.

Some of those who pleaded guilty reacted to the 1997 dismissals by proclaiming their innocence even though they had pleaded guilty. Ex-Rep. Faber said of his plea to taking a bribe for $1,000 that, "I think anybody who knew us knew we were not guilty." As excuse Faber explained that he pleaded because it was easier and eliminated the risk of going to trial before a jury which did not like politicians. Former Rep. Robert Brown said of defendants, "I think about what they have been through the last seven years." Also Brown denied that he had ever violated the law, arguing that the law in 1990 was unclear as to what legislators could take as gifts. Brown pointed out that even the chairman of the House Ethics Committee took a casual approach to the disclosure requirements of the weak 1975 Ethics Act and ignored it himself.

Tee Ferguson, who had pleaded guilty to cocaine and was convicted at trial of corruption, blamed Cobb's testimony and said in reaction to the dismissals, "Until the general public gets instances in layman's language as to the types of things these people did, I still don't think they will fully appreciate just how perverse this whole affair was.... What the judge has now come to realize, I knew from day one."

Reflections on Lost Trust by the Innocent

Reflecting on his experiences under the out-of-control political and social culture of the State House in 1990, Rep. Bubba Cromer (I-Richland) said that he had served as a young staff attorney for the House Labor, Commerce, and Industry Committee at the time when it was known for its corruption and abuses as the "lobbyist, cash, and influence committee." Cromer said that the outrageous behavior he witnessed provoked him to launch a successful bid for a seat in the House from the Columbia area. In 1997, Cromer said of the year 1990, "What the legislature was doing was abhorrent" and he believed that even the dismissal of charges by Judge Hawkins "will not change public perception, and the legislative perception that we were in a system gone awry that needed massive overhaul." The Ethics Act of 1991 was the cure the General Assembly imposed, Cromer concluded.

But Rep. Tim Wilkes (D-Fairfield) who was the only one to dodge the bullet in Lost Trust in 1997 still blamed the federal government and denounced Ron Cobb as a liar and the federal prosecutors as "self-serving Zealots." Wilkes alleged multiple abuses by the government, including "the fabrication of evidence, the perjury, the withholding of evidence, the lies.... I don't think that any worse possible spin for the General Assembly or the defendant could have been orchestrated than it was in 1990."

Summary of Convictions in Lost Trust (As of March 1, 1997)

Charges—Pleaded Guilty	Number Convicted
Pleaded guilty to cocaine possession	8
Pleaded guilty to selling their vote	7
Pleaded guilty to racketeering	1
Pleaded guilty to extortion	1
Pleaded guilty to obstruction	1
Pleaded guilty to marijuana possession	1
Pleaded guilty to tampering with witness	1
Charges—Jury Verdicts at Trial	
Acquitted of selling vote	1
Convicted of selling votes (5 overturned)	7
Total Defendants Convicted	27
Total Acquitted	1

Note: Some defendants convicted on multiple charges.

Questions Raised About Legitimacy of Lost Trust

In early 1997 questions about the value and justice of the Lost Trust prosecutions were being given increased public scrutiny, especially because of Judge Falcon Hawkins' decision to dismiss all criminal charges for the final five defendants in the Lost Trust series of cases on grounds of prosecutorial abuses.

One of the major issues raised over the six years after the first Lost Trust cases had been filed and taken to trial was the question of whether the courts had been unfair in the imposition of sentence. Whether the court had given some defendants inequitable leniency while imposing excessively harsh penalties on other defendants was an issue which was being hashed out not only in courts, but also in the media and politics.

The issue of disparity in sentencing and especially of racial disparity in sentencing had been articulated from the early months of the prosecutions. I.S. Leevy Johnson had said in court in 1991, when his clients and personal friends Rep. James Faber and Rep. Frank McBride had been sentenced to one year in jail by Judge Falcon Hawkins, that the two black Democrats had been treated much more harshly than the white Republican Sen. Rick Lee who had taken bigger bribes. "How can Your Honor in good conscious allow a man like Rick Lee to come into this court and plead guilty to an offense more serious than these men have admitted and give him six months in a halfway house while these men are going to prison?" Johnson asked Hawkins.

Questions about Racial Bias Raised By Cobb

Since Judge Hawkins had imposed a harsh sentence on Rep. Luther Taylor after his conviction in October, 1990, the judge had been presented with some new and disconcerting information which apparently shocked his conscience and sense of professional ethics. The judge's apparent growing anxiety over prosecution behavior in Lost Trust finally resulted in his decision to dismiss all charges against the last five defendants, all of whom had been granted new trials as of 1997 which were still pending.

One new factor was that Ron Cobb had announced he was still writing in 1997 a book on Lost Trust and his role in the sting and prosecutions which raised major questions about the integrity and fairness of the sting operation. Cobb wrote in his manuscript, which was sealed at the time, that the government knew that the sting operation based on the pari-mutuel betting bill would snare a disproportionate number of black legislators because so many of them were committed to the betting bill.

Cobb wrote, "I would make the comment a lot of times that I could have the whole black caucus. There would be no damned n_________ (niggers). It was kind of funny to them for a while until we got half of them and they said, pull in the reins, but believe me; I could have had most of them."

Questions Raised About Cobb's Control of the Sting

Another issue which drew critical attention was the revelation that the prosecution had given Cobb the authority to pick those he wanted to target with his offers of bribe money and that the government also wanted Rep. B.J. Gordon to be a target because Gordon has frustrated law enforcement investigators for years and they wanted to finally catch him in a successful prosecution. On the other hand, Cobb admitted that he picked Rep. Paul Derrick (R-Lexington) as a sting target because Cobb did not personally like Derrick.

The person of Sen. Jack Lindsay was also a central question related to the conduct of the Lost Trust prosecutions even though Lindsay had died in January, 1991. Judge Hawkins was baffled by the fact that the records available to the court showed that Cobb and Lindsay had a long history of corrupt relations based on bribery but that Cobb absolutely refused to testify against Lindsay. Furthermore, Cobb refused to call his payments to Lindsay bribes even though it was crystal clear that they were bribes.

When defense attorneys asked for FBI records about payments made by Cobb to Lindsay the government said there were no such records. But Hawkins came to know that when Cobb was first arrested in his cocaine sting, Cobb had told the FBI about his corruption; and Cobb had told about how he paid Lindsay and another senator $10,000 to fix a gasoline tax bill. FBI 302 documents reported that Cobb had made at least seven payments to Lindsay and one of them for $10,000 was for the capital gains tax bill.

<u>Prosecution Use of Perjury Raised by Court</u>

Cobb's bank records had not been made available until 1995 at which time it came out that Cobb had written seven checks to Lindsay, two of them were for $10,000 and one was for $20,000.

Defense attorneys thought the evidence of Cobb's payments to Lindsay would be helpful to discredit Cobb as a witness and because of the fact that the money Cobb gave to unindicted Lindsay was much larger than the small sums he gave the legislators indicted for bribery.

Cobb had also said that he sometimes gave legislators money to keep them friendly, not for specific official actions. And Cobb did give money as campaign donations, not just as bribes. These facts would have helped the defense arguments that the legislators were not taking bribes from Cobb. Cobb even admitted on a 302 document that it was sometimes difficult to distinguish a bribe from a campaign donation.

Hawkins wrote that, "Most offensive to the court is that the government sat silent—when it knew that its silence would not only foil the efforts of the defendants to fully develop defenses to which they were entitled, but would misrepresent facts to both the grand jury and the trial jury, and mislead the court to such an extent as to effect its rulings.... As reluctant as this court is to call it such—this silence in several instances constitutes subordination of perjury."

<u>Hawkins' Dismissal Blasts Prosecution</u>

Judge Hawkins reviewed the conduct of the government in Lost Trust and in 1997 concluded, "that some of the investigators and lead prosecutors got lost on their way to the lofty goal of weeding out drugs and corruption at the South Carolina State House." Hawkins remarked that the desire to attack corruption "led the government to rush to trial, especially in the cases of Taylor, Blanding, and Gordon; to withhold volumes of exculpatory evidence; to allow it's primary cooperating witness, Cobb, to take an unusual amount of control of the sting operation; and to go outside of its own regulations to target certain legislators and to mislead this court to such an extent as to perpetrate a fraud upon the court."

<u>Ethical Questions about Prosecutors</u>

The ethical standards of prosecutors were tested by some of the things that Bart Daniel and his subordinates did in Operation Lost Trust. Some critics alleged that Daniel and his staff engaged in abusive and even illegal practices such as withholding evidence and putting on perjured testimony.

The use of cocaine dealer and lobbyist Ron Cobb by the prosecution raised major questions about the integrity of the U.S. Attorney's office in handling Lost Trust. In the trial of Sen. Bud Long, Cobb upset the prosecution by saying that even though he gave Long cash money in 28 $100 bills while being videotaped, Cobb did not say that Long believed he was taking a bribe.

It later became known that the prosecution had been aware before the Long trial that Cobb did not think he had bribed Long but that the defense attorneys were not told in advance about Cobb's opinion. First Assistant U.S. Attorney John McIntosh became so upset over Cobb's opinion and the failure to notify defense counsel of Cobb's opinion that he withdrew from the Long case on ethical grounds.

Luther Taylor Dies

Former Rep. Luther Taylor (D-Richland) died of cancer on March 23, 1997, just three weeks after all charges against him still pending on his retrial were dismissed by Judge Hawkins. His death was announced by his attorney, Joel Collins, who had handled all of the Taylor litigations since his trial in October, 1990. Taylor died at age 47 at the Baptist Medical Center in Columbia after a long bout with pancreatic cancer.

As the charges against Taylor had been dismissed as of the time of his death, it was easier for politicians to take his side. Rep. John Scott (D-Richland) who took Taylor's District 77 seat in the House said, "The system stole this young leader's life from him. That was wrong. He had a lot to give to the community." Sen. Kay Patterson (D-Richland) remarked of Taylor, "He was a person who cared for the little people and he represented them well.... He knew he would be vindicated."

Taylor Planned Civil Suit Against Prosecutors

Shortly before his death on March 23, 1997, former Rep. Luther Taylor was planning a civil lawsuit against the federal prosecutor and the three others involved in the Lost Trust prosecution of Taylor. Taylor's attorneys filed papers related to the lawsuit in late March, 1997, in the U.S. District Court in Charleston.

The papers disclosed that Taylor had cancer. Taylor's attorney, Arthur Aiken, asked the court to allow Taylor to give a videotaped disposition in the case due the gravity of the disease which was diagnosed as "terminal, metastatic pancreatic cancer." The filing asserted that "Taylor expects to be a plaintiff in an action asserting claims for violation of his constitutional and other federally protected rights." Taylor's filing was triggered by the February 28, 1997, decision of Judge Falcon Hawkins to dismiss all charges against Taylor to remedy the allegedly outrageous misconduct of the prosecution in Taylor's case. At the time of the order of dismissal, Taylor had served a total of 18 months in prison before a new trial was ordered and he was released.

Sen. Hollings Intervenes

At the request of defense attorneys in the Lost Trust cases Sen. Fritz Hollings contacted Attorney General Janet Reno in 1994 and asked to arrange a meeting between key defense attorneys and senior officers of the U.S. Department of Justice related to the Lost Trust prosecutions and the issue of alleged prosecutorial misconduct by Daniel and his lawyers. At the 1994 meeting defense attorneys said that a Justice Department probe of allegations of misconduct had failed to conduct a proper investigation and was little more than a whitewash of prosecutors.

In 1997, Hollings defended the call he made to the Justice Department as constituent service and not as an attempt to interfere with the prosecution of a Lost Trust defendants. Hollings had contacted the Attorney General in October 28, 1994, on behalf of Charleston lawyer Lionel Lofton who represented B.J. Gordon. Hollings reported the incident, saying "Lionel said he needed to talk with someone in Justice about the truth, the whitewash. And it was a whitewash."

After receiving a request in February, 1994, to investigate if Lost Trust prosecutors broke the law, the department's Office of Professional Responsibility conducted a probe and filed a report on October 18, 1994, which found no violations.

In reaction to the report of October 18, 1994, attorneys Lionel Lofton for B.J. Glover and Joel Collins for Luther Taylor flew to Washington, D.C., in early November, 1994, to complain that the report was inadequate.

Lofton in 1997 remarked, "We thought they had done a pretty crappy job" and he said that he asked Sen. Fritz Hollings to help him make contacts with the appropriate person at the Justice Department.

Hollings said that when he contacted Janet Reno she did not know about Lost Trust but referred the matter to the Office of Professional Responsibility.

Judge Hawkins was a former partner of Sen. Hollings and had been appointed to the bench by Hollings. Hollings said he worried that the burden of Lost Trust had damaged Hawkins' health. Hollings said that Hawkins admired the ability of Bart Daniel and it was difficult for Hawkins to dismiss the charges on grounds of prosecutorial misconduct.

Prosecutors and Greer File Against Dismissal Order

Reacting to Hawkins' allegations of unprofessional and even unethical conduct against Bart Daniels and some of his prosecutors as well as Hawkins' remarks implicating Greer in the capital gains tax cut bill, Daniel, Greer, and Dale Du Tremble wanted to join the Justice Department's 1997 appeal seeking reinstatement of the five indictments, but the Court of Appeals denied them the opportunity to file as interested parties in the appeal. However, the court allowed them to file friend of the court briefs in support of the government's appeal to resurrect the charges.

Hawkins also denied requests for access to evidence in the court's evidence room which were filed by Greer, Daniel, and Dale Du Tremble because Hawkins concluded that the Court of Appeals ruling denying standing to the three to join the appeal meant they were not interested parties in the appeal. However, Hawkins noted that since grievances had been filed against Daniel and Du Tremble with the South Carolina board charged with attorney discipline and misconduct cases, the lawyers would get access to the evidence to prepare their responses to the grievances filed with a disciplinary board.

Gedney Howe, for Dick Greer, expressed surprise that Hawkins would not grant access to the evidence room to his client and the prosecutors and Howe felt that it handicapped his ability to file an amicus brief for Greer with the appellate court handling the government's appeal to re-instate the criminal charges.

Daniel and Du Tremble Appeal Dismissal Order

On March 28, 1997, Daniel and DuTremble announced a planned motion to the 4th Circuit Court of Appeals to oppose the Hawkins' dismissal order and alleged that it contained, "inaccuracies and misrepresentations." Daniel and Du Tremble said the government's appeal only would address the issue of indictments, not allegations of prosecutorial misconduct.

Daniel and Du Tremble were compelled to file their motion attacking the misconduct allegations because otherwise the allegations, if not contested, would be accepted as fact and could be used against the two prosecutors in any proceedings of the South Carolina Supreme Court's office of the Disciplinary Council. In fact, an ethics complaint with the office had been filed by Joel Collins putting the prosecutors in some jeopardy as members of the South Carolina Bar.

Daniel and Du Tremble also filed a motion on March 28, 1997, which asked Judge Hawkins to authorize the two attorneys to access the evidence room in Columbia which contained thousands of documents related to Lost Trust which they would need to proceed.

S. C. Senate Ready to Probe Tax Cut Law

In April, 1997, the South Carolina Senate prepared to investigate the passage of the capital gains tax break bill of 1988. And lobbyist Ron Cobb prepared to testify about the tax bill as he was implicated in the suspected bribery which moved the bill to passage. The Senate probe started on April 30, 1997.

The issue to be probed was whether the Senate was deceived and bribed into passing a special capital gains tax break in the fiscal year 1987-1988 which benefited 21 people and gave them a tax break of $8.6 million dollars and also gave a tax break of $22.4 million dollars to 60,000 taxpayers. The Senate committee formed to conduct the tax break probe contended that they had the power under the South Carolina Constitution to subpoena anyone. Critics argued that the committee had no such subpoena power and was little more than a witch hunt.

Sen. Tom Moore (D-Aiken) said that, "It's incumbent upon this General Assembly to find out what went wrong and how we can correct it." Moore had proposed the probe to find out how the Senate had been tricked into granting the tax break.

Senate President Pro Tem John Drummond (D-Greenwood) and Senate Judiciary Committee Chair Don Holland (D-Kershaw) were to appoint seven members of the special committee to investigate the tax bill. Some speculated as to whether the committee was not targeted at former Gov. Carroll Campbell. Campbell commented that the probe was driven by partisan politics of Democrats in the Senate.

The creation of the special committee to probe the capital gains tax break was supported not only by Democrats but also some Republicans, including Sen. Glenn McConnell (R-Charleston), a frequent critic of Gov. Carroll Campbell. McConnell denied that the probe had anything to do with partisan politics.

One of the major tasks of the probe would be to look into the question of whether criminal charges should be brought against those who paid fees to Ron Cobb, the lobbyist who pushed the tax bill. The two people who hired Cobb, Tom Roe and Walter Brashier of Greenville, told federal authorities that they did not know the money they paid to Cobb would be used to eventually pay bribes. It was quite possible that Ron Cobb would be called to testify. And it was also possible that the committee would discover some other issues aside from the tax break.

Ron Cobb Speaks Out

Ron Cobb said that he was ready to talk to the special Senate committee created to probe the capital gains tax cut bill of 1988. Cobb told the media on May 1, 1997, that, "I welcome the opportunity to testify; I look forward to it. I have nothing to hide."

Speaking to reporters in a restaurant in Clinton, South Carolina, on May 1, 1997, Cobb said the senators in the probe were people living in glass houses and he wondered about the probe into the bill. Cobb also criticized Judge Falcon Hawkins who had said that Cobb was a drug dealer who took control of the Lost Trust probe. Further, he said that neither Dick Greer nor Gov. Campbell knew anything about bribes given to pass the tax bill to certain legislators. However, Cobb did agree with Hawkins' finding that the prosecution got out of control because of its determination to win convictions. Cobb said of Hawkins, "He's probably right in that a lot of things were probably done by the prosecutors that shouldn't have been done. I think they felt they could do anything they wanted to do to get these convictions."

Ron Cobb told reporters on May 1, 1997, that he resented the fact that Judge Hawkins had said that Cobb lied under oath when he said that he had not bribed Jack Lindsay. Cobb said that an FBI note saying that Cobb admitted bribing Lindsay was wrong. Cobb said the money he gave to

Lindsay was just a legal consulting fee and not a bribe. Cobb said, "If they knew our history of how we have operated together, they would understand why I didn't consider it a bribe."

Cobb said the FBI lured him into a 1989 drug sting operation in order to force him to conduct an undercover bribery sting at the State House. Cobb said that once the sting began the only person Cobb refused to sting was Jack Lindsay. Cobb said he had no control over whom he bribed and that the FBI told Cobb to approach Rep. of Bob Kohn (R-Charleston) and Rep. Luther Taylor (D-Richland) and to offer them bribes and ask them to recruit other legislators to also take bribes. Cobb said that he gave cash money to anybody that showed up seeking money.

Cobb said also that the book he was writing on Lost Trust was unreliable, remarking that the manuscript notes he was using "reflect some facts and a lot of fiction." Cobb said he was trying to spice up the story and sell the publisher, "a novel with fiction, based on fact."

Tax Breaks Scandal Investigation Begins

The Senate probe launched in April, 1997, of the 1988 tax break bill raised some real questions. One of the major questions was how much of a role in passing the bill two of Gov. Campbell's close associates, including Dick Greer, played in view of the fact that Greer had a lot to do with the hiring of Ron Cobb to lobby for the tax cut bill. Another question was whether the U.S. Attorney's Office in Lost Trust was affected by partisan bias in that prosecutors were Republican appointees and Campbell was a Republican and, as a result, did not dig deep in order to avoid implicating Campbell.

Campbell protested of the tax break scandal, "I know full well that I didn't know anything about it until well after the fact." It was also suspected at the time in 1997 that Campbell might decide to challenge U.S. Sen. Fritz Hollings in 1998. Campbell finished his second term as governor in 1995.

The most troubling question was how Dick Greer could be perhaps tainted by the tax break because of his close ties with Ron Cobb and the people seeking the break. And if Greer was implicated how could his close friend Campbell not know? It was known, in fact, that Tom Roe was referred to Ron Cobb for lobbying work on the tax bill by Greer and Roe paid Cobb a fee of $25,000.

Tax Break Scandal Probe Looks at Greer

The Senate probe of the tax break bill had to consider the allegations of lobbyist Randy Lee, who had pleaded guilty to marijuana possession in the early months of Lost Trust, that Lee was present in a room at the Townhouse Hotel in April, 1988, with Ron Cobb and Dick Grier and that they were using cocaine when he first heard about bribery being used to push the tax break bill. Lee claimed that Dick Greer said at the time that a change in the tax law proposed by the bill "would help a lot of the governor's friends."

Lee said he learned that Greer had arranged for Greenville businessmen Tom Roe and Walter Brashier to pay $150,000 dollars to Ron Cobb and Sen. Jack Lindsay if the tax break bill was passed. Lee said he often saw Cobb and Lindsay together plotting to pass the tax bill. Lee also said that he heard Greer tell Cobb that he would talk over the tax break bill with Gov. Campbell.

In 1991 Greer pleaded guilty to cocaine possession but he told the federal grand jury that he did not know about any bribery. However, Greer's attorney, Gedney Howe, said that Cobb tried to enlist Greer to help pass the tax break bill but Greer refused. At the time the South Carolina Economic Development Board which Greer chaired was working on promoting a bill to lower capital gains rates for all.

Tax Break Probe Looks Into Gov. Campbell's Role

However, when the budget bill came up in the Senate, it was decided that the capital gains tax break passed in the budget bill in 1988 was a bad idea. During the 1988 debate Sen. Frank Gilbert (D-Florence) held up a paper which he said was a list of major donors to Gov. Campbell's campaign which included the 21 persons who benefited from the tax break bill of 1988. Nobody asked to see the list. In 1990 Gilbert admitted the list had never existed.

Lobbyist Randy Lee told federal investigators that aides to Gov. Campbell, in fact, met with senators about the tax break. Senators were given answer sheets with information as to how to answer questions about the matter. Sen. Rick Lee (R-Spartanburg), who pled guilty to bribery over the betting bill in 1990, told federal agents about the same meeting.

However, Campbell and his supporters said that Campbell was promoting a different tax break bill which would only lower capital gains tax rates in the future, whereas the 1988 tax break bill pushed by Lindsay and Rogers had retroactive effect. Sen. Joe Wilson (R-Lexington) in late April, 1997, said that he attended every meeting held by Campbell staff and the retroactive tax rollback was never discussed.

Both Randy Lee and Rick Lee wrote Gov. Campbell admitting they had confused the retroactive tax break bill with the prospective tax cut bill. Randy Lee's letter said of Campbell, "I now know that you and your staff did absolutely nothing wrong."

Tax Break Scandal Probe Focuses On Bribery Issues

Cobb told investigators in 1989 that he did not want to bring down Greer. On May 1, 1997, Cobb said he never gave Greer any reason to suspect that Cobb's lobbying was corrupt. Cobb denied Randy Lee's statements about the bribery that Lee alleged on the bill.

Sen. Lindsay went ahead and slipped the tax break provision into the 1988 state budget bill which was very voluminous. The bill sailed through the Senate and went to a conference committee where senators and House members worked out differences in the budget bill. Lindsay then enlisted the help of Speaker Pro Tem Jack I. Rogers (D-Marlboro) and paid $10,000 to Rogers. However, when asked about the alleged corrupt bill in late April, 1997, Rogers refused to talk about it.

The budget bill passed and conferred a special tax break on Roe, Brashier, and 19 other taxpayers, and another 60,000 taxpayers received $13.8 million in tax breaks as well. However, Roe claimed that he did not know about any bribery until after the bill passed when Cobb came to Roe and demanded more money from Roe to pay some persons who Cobb said, "had to be taken care of."

Brashier said in 1995 that his agreement with Cobb provided a contingent fee that Cobb would be paid $12,500 up front to lobby for the tax break and if it passed then Roe was to pay another $62,500. Roe said he did not know the second amount was for a bribe. Roe refused to pay Cobb any more money. In retaliation Sen. Lindsay slipped a provision into the next year's 1989-90 budget taking away the tax break which benefited Roe and others who made their money on capital gains from stock sales. Later the 1991 Ethics Act outlawed such contingent fees. (S.C. Code, 2-17-110(A))

Tax Break Probe in Controversy

Bart Daniel said the tax break bill of 1988 was thoroughly probed by the FBI but nothing criminal was found implicating Gov. Campbell. The information gathered was presented to the grand jury by Bart Daniel but it did not indict. Daniel then presented the records to Attorney General Travis Medlock. Later U.S. Attorney Pete Strom, Jr., sent the matter to the Justice Department. Daniel contended in 1997 that, "the investigation was clean. The investigation was thorough."

Even so, Judge Falcon Hawkins took a dim view of the federal probe of the capital gains tax break bill. The judge was angry that Dick Greer had told the grand jury in 1991 that he knew nothing about bribes related to the tax bill. The FBI told Hawkins that Greer did not learn of the bribes until after the tax bill was passed in the 1988 session when Cobb told Greer he needed more bribe money to pay off Jack Lindsay and Jack Rogers for their help in passing the bill.

Even though the FBI told Judge Hawkins in 1991 that Greer had not violated the law, Hawkins said the court records were, "replete with implications that Greer was heavily involved in the payoffs." Joel Collins, attorney for Rep. Luther Taylor, complained that the FBI had no notes of any interview with Cobb about the capital gains bill. Collins bemoaned gaps in the evidence and asked, "the important thing is what happened. What's the truth?"

Tax Break Probe in Trouble

The Senate probe into the 1988 capital gains tax break bill was in trouble in late May, 1997,. Some senators worried that the probe would set a precedent and others questioned whether the Senate had subpoena powers. Without subpoena power it appeared that the probe would have difficulty getting witnesses to testify about the 1988 tax bill. But Sen. Glenn McConnell argued that the Senate did have subpoena powers; yet he anticipated that some witnesses would file lawsuits to challenge the use of such powers to force them to appear and testify before the committee.

McConnell argued that the South Carolina Constitution and case law supported his theory that the Senate had subpoena powers. McConnell asserted, "Subpoena power is an inherent power." He also asked, "Why wouldn't legislators have it to govern?" But speaker Bob Sheheen responded by saying that the General Assembly had never exercised subpoena powers, "If they have that power inherently, I find it curious that it hasn't been exercised for 200 years."

In fact, the legislature did have subpoena powers based on a 1986 statute, but they were limited to government workers and documents and some special legislative panels. Prof. James Underwood of the University of South Carolina School of Law concluded that it was unclear as to whether the General Assembly had other subpoena powers and, if so, for what purposes.

Ferguson Applies for Law License

Former Circuit Court Judge Tee Ferguson asked the South Carolina Supreme Court to reinstate his license to practice law in South Carolina. He filed his petition on May 12, 1997.

At the time of his conviction of corruption and drug violations, he was the first judge in South Carolina's history to be forced from office for conviction of a crime. Ferguson had taken a hostile attitude toward the Lost Trust prosecutions and found some comfort since in March, 1997, when Judge Hawkins had dismissed the cases of the final five Lost Trust defendants. Ferguson remarked, "What the judge has now come to realize, I knew from day one."

The South Carolina Supreme Court normally asked for public comment on applications for reinstatement, but Bart Daniel said he had no plans to comment on the Ferguson application, remarking "That's between him and the Supreme Court."

Ferguson resigned his Judgeship and was reprimanded by the South Carolina Supreme Court in 1993. After a term in prison, Ferguson thought it was time to apply for return of his law license.

Sen. Thurmond Intercedes For Daniel

Sen. Strom Thurman (R-S.C.) directly contacted the U.S. Department of Justice in late May, 1997, asking that the department provide Bart Daniel with an attorney to defend himself if he was sued by any of the legislators for his prosecution of Lost Trust on grounds of civil rights claims.

Daniel had filed a request with the Justice Department asking that the department provide him with a government defense lawyer if he was sued because of his prosecution of legislators for corruption in the Lost Trust scandal. "I have a right, as a former Department of Justice employee, to representation," Daniel asserted.

Thurmond's office explained that they had contacted the Clinton Justice Department because Daniel could not get information from the DOJ he requested about legal assistance. Daniel claimed to have sent five faxes to Justice with no response. Thurmond's office told the media, "The Sen. feels that since (Daniel) was the U.S. Attorney, it is appropriate for him to have the DOJ representation." DOJ soon told Daniel he would get a lawyer only if he was, in fact, sued.

Political Money Flows In 1997

The 1991 Ethics Act was not designed to stop the flow of political money but rather to put some limits on sources, amounts, recipients, uses, and disclosures of campaign donations and lobbying expenses. In the 1997 session of the South Carolina General Assembly interest groups spent $3.4 million on lobbying to push their agendas at the State House. Businesses fighting over deregulation of electricity and managed healthcare spent $1 million in the first quarter of 1997. Insurance, video poker, property rights, and lending institutions also spent a total of $1 million.

A total of 342 lobbyists were registered for the 1997 session. 379 lobbyists' principals spent $125,000 in campaign donations, with $60,000 each given to the Republican Caucus and the Democratic Caucus. Principals also spent $100,000 on meals given to legislators.

The power of money at the State House was still very strong seven years after Lost Trust broke. The chairman of the South Carolinians for Competitive Electricity said the group had to spend to get the attention of legislators. It spent $149,000.

The insurance industry spent $285,000 and medical providers spent $163,000. Video poker spent $306,000. One of the lobbyists for video poker was John Lindsay, Jr.

Justice Appeals Dismissal

The fact that the U.S. Department of Justice appealed Judge Falcon Hawkins dismissal order of February 28, 1997, and asked that all charges be reinstated did not surprise attorney Jack Swerling who was representing Bud Long. Swerling said, "I think they're going to vigorously defend what the whole office did. They'll take a fall-back approach that if there was misconduct, the remedy should not have been dismissal with prejudice." Commenting on June 11, 1997, Swerling thought the dismissal order had merit, observing that, "I thought the judge's opinion was well-reasoned. It was done with painstaking research and a lot of soul-searching."

The appeal filed by Justice caused those who might be adversely affected by the order to file arguments with the 4th Circuit Court of Appeals. The Appeals Court told Dick Greer, Bart Daniel, and Dale Du Tremble that they could not join the appeal, but could, in opposition, file friend-of-the court briefs in the case. Attorney Gedney Howe, representing Greer, told the media that the Appeals Court would rule that even if Judge Hawkins' statements of fact were true, the judge still acted improperly. Daniel said, "We're optimistic that the judge's order is incorrect, and it will be overturned."

On June 9, 1997, Hawkins denied Dick Greer's attorney access to the court's evidence room. Howe remarked, that he was surprised by Hawkins' denial of access, saying, "We have very limited documents."

B.J. Gordon Dies

B.J. Gordon (D-Williamsburg) the former House member still in criminal jeopardy as one of the final five dismissed defendants in Lost Trust, died on July 12, 1997. He had been cleared of all charges when Judge Falcon Hawkins ordered dismissal of such charges on February 28, 1997, although the dismissal was being appeal by the U.S. Department of Justice which wanted the charges reinstated. Gordon, 64, died of stomach cancer after having undergone surgery in 1996 for the disease.

Probe of Prosecutorial Conduct Drags On

In late 1997, the allegations of prosecutorial misconduct filed by defense attorneys led by Joel Collins, attorney for Luther Taylor who had died during the appeal process in 1997, dragged on in the hands of the Inspector General of the U.S. Department of Justice. Collins said that he did not know if anything was really being done about his complaints.

The Justice Department had conducted something of an investigation into similar charges in 1994 and had cleared the prosecutors in Lost Trust. But Collins, in 1997, had restated the complaints. Judge Hawkins criticized the 1994 probe as too limited and Collins had asked for a second review. However, in 1997 the Inspector General, Michael R. Bromwich, said that the Deputy Attorney General had instructed the Inspector to review allegations of misconduct in the Lost Trust prosecutions. As of early September, 1997, Collins had received no further contact and wrote the Inspector another letter on September 8, 1997, but without immediate response.

Attorney Jack Swerling, for Bud Long, said that the complaint should be investigated and resolved but that federal agencies usually moved slowly on such matters. A schedule of filings on the appeals of the five remaining defendants was suspended after two of them, Luther Taylor and B.J. Gordon, died in March, 1997, and July, 1997, respectively.

Sting Defendants' Estates' Law Suits Blocked

The estates of the late Rep. Luther Taylor (D-Richland) and Rep. B.J. Glover (D-Williamsburg) were dismissed as plaintiffs in late December, 1997, when they attempted to sue prosecutors in Lost Trust cases against the two which had been dismissed by Judge Falcon Hawkins.

The estates complained of the prosecution withholding evidence, presenting false testimony, and making false statements in the cases. The order of dismissal was filed on the public record by the 4th Circuit Court of Appeals in Richmond, Va. The order denied standing.

Taylor had complained that he was convicted and in federal prison when he finally found out about 201 videotapes and 484 FBI documents that related to his case which was not revealed by the government in 1990.

The attorneys of Taylor and Gordon pursuing the civil rights actions for the estates were Joel Collins and Lionel Lofton who had handled the criminal defenses and appeals of both legislators from 1990 until their deaths.

CHAPTER FORTY FOUR

1998—CRIMINAL AND CIVIL PROCEEDINGS CONTINUE

Justice Asks Reinstatement of Charges

The U.S. Department of Justice appealed Judge Falcon Hawkins' February 28, 1997, dismissal of charges against the final defendants in the Lost Trust cases. The appeal asserted that even though the prosecution had made mistakes in the cases they were not bad enough to warrant complete dismissals of all charges which Hawkins had ordered in 1997.

The appeal contained a total of 141 pages alleging that Hawkins' dismissal was in error and that all charges against the remaining defendants should be reinstated and set for retrial. The government said the defendants' rights to a fair trial remained.

The appeal by the U.S. Department of Justice seeking to reinstate charges against the remaining Lost Trust defendants was filed in Columbia but the appeal was to the 4th Circuit Court of Appeals in Richmond, Va. The DOJ appeal alleged that Judge Falcon Hawkins had exceeded his authority in dismissing all charges remaining in the Lost Trust cases. The appeal claimed, "The appropriate remedy is a retrial, not dismissal of the indictments, because the defendants now have the information that they contend was improperly withheld." The appeal was written by Justice Department attorney Elizabeth Collery.

Collery's appeal further read: "Even if the district court possessed authority to dismiss the indictments purely as a sanction for government misconduct, that authority would not have been appropriately exercised here because the record contains no evidence that the attorney's office in South Carolina has a history of prosecutorial misconduct that is systemic and pervasive."

The Justice Department appeal rebutted all of the reasons given by Judge Falcon Hawkins for dismissing the last charges in the Lost Trust cases, alleging that the misconduct which the Hawkins' order of February 28, 1997, presented was addressed by the prosecution when the Justice Department turned over 11 boxes of records to the defense prior to Hawkins' order and that only ten pages of documents in the boxes were ruled by the courts as evidence to which the defense was entitled access.

The appeal for reinstatement filed by Justice Attorney Elizabeth Collery alleged that "[t]he court's criticism...constitutes an inappropriate effort by the district court to supervise and control the investigative activities of the U.S. Attorney's office." Collery also claimed that there was "no evidence that the government intentionally withheld relevant evidence."

Collery argued, on the contrary, that the prosecution had gone overboard to provide "vast quantities of other materials rarely, if ever, disclosed in criminal trials."

Former Prosecutors Support Reinstatement Appeal

Two foremost attorneys involved in prosecuting the Lost Trust cases filed papers in opposition to Hawkins dismissal order of February 28, 1997. Former U.S. Attorney Bart Daniel and his former assistant Dale DuTremble filed February 3, 1998, in Charleston. DuTremble's filing stated: "Under no theory does the government's conduct in this case approach outrageousness. For the district court to now decide that these events are for some unidentified and unimaginable reason now not acceptable is inappropriate and unwarranted."

Hawkins' Dismissal Order Lists Reasons

The order of February 28, 1997, dismissing all charges left in the Lost Trust cases listed Judge Hawkins' reasons for the dismissal to include the following:

- The prosecution withheld evidence of FBI interviews and tape recordings that could have helped the defendants.
- The prosecution withheld evidence that its star witness Ron Cobb had used cocaine while he worked for the FBI.
- The prosecution allowed Ron Cobb to testify that the money he gave to Sen. Jack Lindsay was not a bribe when, in fact, it was.
- The prosecution presented testimony in court that there was no FBI record of Cobb's payment to Sen. Lindsay over the capital gains tax cut bill, which was false.
- The prosecution told Judge Hawkins that there was no FBI report that Cobb had paid off Lindsay, when, in fact, there was such a report.
- The prosecution failed to properly investigate whether Gov. Carroll Campbell and his Chairman of Economic Development, Dick Greer, were involved in bribery related to the capital gains tax break bill.

The Justice Department rejected all of the judge's reasons and said that Hawkins was wrong on the law.

Defense Opposes Written Statement of Charges

Defense attorney Joel Collins, who was representing in February, 1998, seven defendants who were convicted and sentenced in Lost Trust cases, challenged the reinstatement appeal of the Justice Department branding the appeal "a continuation of the government's outrageous conduct." Collins ridiculed the Justice Department, saying "they're saying that Judge Hawkins, who presided over all but one case...over six years...called it wrong."

Collins asserted that Hawkins "was the umpire behind the plate" and knew that the prosecution had been engaged in misconduct warranting dismissal. Collins concluded that the dismissed charges against all defendants should remain dismissed.

Tax Cut Probe Finds No Violations

A total of seven legislators of both parties concluded its probe into the controversial 1988 capital gains tax cut bill on March 24, 1998, but found no illegal activities. The panel, chaired by Senator Tom Moore, had taken testimony from 30 witnesses.

Chairman Moore said that the hearing would restore credibility in state government but Harvey Peeler (R-Cherokee) dismissed the proceeding as a waste of time. The issue had been aggravated when Judge Falcon Hawkins alleged that federal prosecutors had not fully probed the 1988 tax cut in the Lost Trust series of cases.

At the end of the Senate panel hearing, two aides to Gov. Carroll Campbell said they did not know about the tax cut bill until a senator raised the issue on the Senate floor in May, 1989. The two witnesses were Campbell's former Chief of Staff, Warren Tompkins, and Campbell's legislative lobbyist, Graham Tew.

The previous week sting agent Ron Cobb testified to the panel that Tompkins had helped to get the tax cut bill passed by diffusing opposition from some Republican senators.

It was known that $30,000 was paid to Sen. Jack Lindsay and Rep. Jack I. Rogers to move the tax break bill.

Attorney Joel Collins said on March 24, 1998, that the FBI in May, 1989, knew about the capital gains tax cut bill and related allegations but failed to open a file until 15 months later.

Estates File Appeals

The attorney for the estate of former Rep. Luther Taylor filed a criminal appeal on April 29, 1998, alleging that prosecutors illegally convicted Taylor in October, 1990. Joel Collins, attorney for Luther Taylor's estate, charged that as to the prosecution, "the Taylor case is one where they really threw the book out the window because they really needed to win that case."

The Taylor case had become an estate case when Taylor died in March of 1997 of cancer. The same was true of the case of B.J. Gordon who died while the charges against him were still under appeal in July, 1997. At the time Judge Hawkins' order dismissing all charges was still being contested by the Justice Department.

The Gordon estate was approved to litigate the charges against Gordon on the criminal side while the estate was moving to file a civil suit alleging that the prosecution of Gordon by federal authorities violated the law.

The 4th Circuit Court of Appeals indicated on April 23, 1998, that the estate of former Rep. B.J. Gordon could join with the litigation of the late former Rep. Luther Taylor, whose estate sought to take civil action against the federal government for prosecutorial misconduct in the Taylor case.

Oral arguments in the civil cases were set for both the estates of Taylor and Gordon for May 7, 1998, in the courtroom of the 4th Circuit Court of Appeals in Richmond, Va. At issue was Judge Hawkins' 1997 dismissal of criminal charges.

However, the U.S. Supreme Court had denied a request by the estate of B.J. Gordon to contest criminal charges against Gordon which had resulted in his conviction in his original trial but which had been overturned and ordered for a new trial.

Association Claims Bias

The National Association of Criminal Defense Lawyers filed a motion to be heard in the May 7, 1998, proceedings before the 4th Circuit Court of Appeals over whether that the dismissal of all charges remaining in the Lost Trust cases as ordered by trial Judge Falcon Hawkins in 1997 would be allowed to stand or whether the U.S. Justice Department's motions to reinstate the criminal charges would be granted.

The Association's filing complained of the fact that the court had scheduled a total of 30 minutes for interested parties Dick Greer, Dale DuTremble, and Bart Daniel to make their presentations in addition to another 30 minutes given to the Department of Justice to argue that the charges should be reinstated. Furthermore, the Association complained that Greer, DuTremble, and Daniel were given free access to the prosecution's evidence room, including evidence not in the court record of the cases.

The Association's papers were filed by attorney Marvin Miller who asked to address the hearing on the appeal to reinstate criminal charges which Hawkins had dismissed.

Dismissals at Issue on Appeal

The 4th Circuit Court of Appeals convened in Richmond, Va., on May 7, 1998, to hear argument on the U.S. Department of Justice's appeal seeking to reinstate all charges dismissed by Judge Hawkins in the final Lost Trust cases. Justice asked the court to provide new trials for all five of the former legislators whose charges had been dismissed.

A three-judge panel heard the prosecution's appeal. The panel seemed to indicate by its questions that the best course would be to reinstate the criminal charges and grant new trials to the five final defendants whose cases had been in litigation for nearly a decade at that point. One of the attorneys for the defendants, Jack Swerling, concluded after hearing the remarks of the judges that they would probably grant new trials but not affirm dismissals which had been ordered by Judge Hawkins.

The two hour hearing included arguments by Justice Department attorney Elizabeth Collery urging reinstatement of charges. She said that dismissals were far too lenient and that new trials would remedy any prosecutorial misconduct or other irregularities in the cases.

The three judges on the panel were Paul V. Niemeyer, J. Michael Luttig, and H. Emory Widener. At the May 7, 1998, hearing they repeatedly asked defense attorneys why the court's awarding of new trials to all five defendants would not be sufficient remedy rather than dismissals.

Attorney Joel Collins for seven defendant former legislators pointed to the fact that Judge Falcon Hawkins had handled the Lost Trust cases involving 27 out of the 28 total defendants ever since 1990 and that Hawkins knew about the irregularities in the cases better than anyone. Collins argued that dismissals should stand as a warning to prosecutors that their misconduct with not be tolerated by the court.

Defense attorney Jack Swerling for Sen. Bud Long, and Lionel Lofton for the estate of B.J. Gordon, argued that the dismissal order should stand. Attorney Marvin Miller of the National Association of Criminal Defense Attorneys was allowed on motion to argue that the dismissal should be affirmed as a warning against prosecutorial misconduct. Miller said, "making these defendants suffer through a new trial is to reward their misconduct." But Judge Niemeyer countered by saying, "If prosecutors misbehave, does that mean (that defendants) get off, or do we remove the prosecutors, take care of them in another way and then have a retrial?"

Former assistant U.S. Attorney Dale DuTremble of South Carolina was allowed to argue at the May 7, 1998, hearing in Richmond, Va., that Judge Falcon Hawkins erred in dismissing all charges against the final five defendants in the Lost Trust cases. DuTremble said that, if the Appeals Court ordered new trials, that would result in a determination of whether the allegations of prosecutorial misconduct were accurate.

DuTremble was allowed to appear on behalf of former U.S. Attorney Bart Daniel who had prosecuted most of the first round of trials and most of the guilty pleas for the eight defendants who went to trial and the twenty defendants who decided to plead guilty in the Lost Trust cases.

<u>Defendants Challenge Appeals Judge</u>

Attorneys Joel Collins and Lionel Lofton alleged that the 4th Circuit Court of Appeals Judge Michael Luttig made remarks at a hearing on May 7, 1998, which indicated that he had already decided before the hearing how he would rule in the Justice Department appeal seeking to reinstate charges against five defendants in the Lost Trust cases. In a motion filed on May 29, 1998, Collins and Lofton cited rulings by Luttig in favor of the prosecution. The motion alleged that Luttig was biased in favor of the Justice Department where he worked for a year in 1991 before he became a judge

New Trials Ordered for Final Defendants

On November 28, 1998, a three Judge panel of the 4th Circuit Court of Appeals in Richmond, Va., ruled that the charges against only three of the final five defendants in the Lost Trust cases should be reinstated and retried. The cases of the late Luther Taylor and late B.J. Gordon had been reversed and would not appear on Taylor's or Gordon's records. The appeals court reversed an order by trial Judge Hawkins dated February 28, 1997. The court found that the prosecutor had not engaged in intentional misconduct and the dismissal was unwarranted and therefore that the three surviving defendants—Paul Derrick, Larry Blanding, and Bud Long—should be retried.

The defense indicated an intention to appeal the ruling directing that the charges be retried. The defense said it would ask all the judges of the 4th Circuit to reverse the reinstatement of charges by the three judge panel. The Justice Department welcomed the decision. Justice spokesman John Russell told the media, "We see the opinion as a vindication." Gov. Carroll Campbell welcomed the decision, saying, "I'm tickled to death the court did what I thought it would do." In fact, the reinstatement continued the cases until 1999.

Charges Reinstated Under Protest

The decision of a three judge panel of the 4th Circuit on November 23, 1998, ordering the reinstatement of charges against the three surviving defendants in the Lost Trust cases was little more than a provocation to the defense attorneys Joel Collins and Lionel Lofton. At the time Collins also represented one of the last three defendants, Paul Derrick, and also represented the estate of Luther Taylor who had died in 1997 before he could be retried.

Collins and Lofton objected to one of the judges who was on the panel but had not received any notice of the decision on their objections to that judge, J. Michael Luttig. Collins and Lofton wondered why the three judge panel allowed Luttig to write the unanimous November 23, 1998, order while the defense had objections to him pending.

Collins raised questions about abnormalities in the handling of the Justice Department's appeal seeking to reinstate criminal charges. Collins said that before the formal hearing on May 7, 1998, at the 4th Circuit Courthouse in Richmond, Va., there was one-sided contact between Judge Luttig and Justice Department lawyer Dan Butler in the form of a car phone conversation. Ex parte communication with judges is normally improper.

Retrials Cause Problems

The order of November 23, 1998, issued by the three judge panel directed new trials for defendants Paul Derrick, Larry Blanding, and Bud Long. But it was unclear what would actually happen in the three cases. Not only did the defense lawyers announce their intentions to ask the full bench of the 4th Circuit to review the order of the panel, but the prospect of actually trying the cases again raised difficult issues. One was whether Judge Falcon Hawkins would be the trial judge after he had presided over the original trials in 1990 and 1991 and after he had ordered dismissal on all charges in February, 1997, only to have them reinstated on November 23, 1998. If Hawkins did not handle the retrials, who would?

Another problem of the retrials was whether an impartial jury could be drawn. So much publicity had been lavished on the Lost Trust scandal that finding jurors without bias would be difficult, said University of South Carolina law professor Richard Seamon. Perhaps, Seamon speculated, new jurors might feel that the cases were too old and that the defendants had been punished enough already and treat them with lenience.

Editorial on Lost Trust

Brad Warthen, editorial page editor of *The State*, weighed in on the final events of the Lost Trust cases in an essay of November 29, 1998.

Warthen started by quoting the 4th Circuit ruling in *U.S. v. Derrick* in which the court wrote that, "This kind of protracted, zealously prosecuted and defended, record-intensive litigation would challenge the most encyclopedic of minds and try the patience of even the most tolerant." Warthen pointed to the dismissal order of 1997 issued by Judge Hawkins and the tangled appeal to the 4th Circuit which had reversed the dismissals and reinstated the criminal charges against the only three living defendants with unresolved cases pending.

Warthen then quoted the reaction of former U.S. Attorney Bart Daniel who had started the first prosecutions in 1990 and 1991. Daniel said of the cases, "But this is one of those rare cases.... This is black and white." Then Warthen cited defense attorney Joel Collins' view that the dismissal order clearly indicated prosecutorial misconduct, noting that Hawkins' dismissal had alleged the misconduct was so bad as "to perpetrate a fraud upon the court."

Warthen's editorial pointed out that Lost Trust "made the public more aware than ever that relations were far too cozy between lawmakers and lobbyists. That led to the nation's toughest ethics law."

Warthen covered the unending legal proceedings from the original convictions at trial and then the appeals and then to the Hawkins' order of dismissal. Last, the appeals court ruling reinstating the criminal charges was recounted by Warthen.

The editorial noted the role of defense attorney Joel Collins who kept tenaciously fighting the case long after the first client he had in Lost Trust, former Rep. Luther Taylor, was convicted at trial and ran out of money. Collins kept going and filed appeals even though he said that he lost over a million dollars in legal fees he could had earned if he was not spending his firm's time and money repeatedly appealing Taylor's case and battling what he believed was serious prosecutorial misconduct, even after Taylor died in 1997.

Warthen also noted his conversations with Bart Daniel who expressed his outrage at Judge Hawkins' dismissal of the last defendants, noting that Hawkins had a long-standing personal relationship with Daniel and his family.

Appeals Oppose Reinstatement of Charges

Attorneys for the last three defendants facing new trials in the Lost Trust cases filed a motion to ask the full 4th Circuit Court of Appeals to reconsider its decision of November 23, 1998, to reinstate criminal charges dismissed by Judge Falcon Hawkins. The defendants filed a request on December 7, 1998, that the reinstatement order of the three judge panel be reviewed by all of the judges on the 4th Circuit bench, sitting en banc, that is, as one group.

The appeal filed on behalf of Paul Derrick, Larry Blanding, and Bud Long claimed that the three judge panel had set a new low standard for judicial review by disregarding every factual finding of the trial judge, Falcon Hawkins. Furthermore, the panel retried the case without hearing any witnesses and assessing their credibility.

The motion also alleged that if "Hawkins' conclusions were plausible when viewing the evidence in its entirety, the Court of Appeals could not reverse even if it would have weighed the evidence differently had it been the trier of fact."

Blanding's attorney, Ed Bell, filed a separate motion saying his defense was weakened because three key witnesses had died, including former lobbyist Elliott Thompson who had written the bill on which Blanding had allegedly traded his vote for cash.

Editorial Backs Retrial Order

The State published another editorial December 2, 1998, in support of the ruling of the Court of Appeals ordering the retrials of the final defendants in the Lost Trust cases. The editors argued that the ruling corrected "a terrible wrong that was done in early 1997" when trial judge Falcon Hawkins had dismissed all charges against the final five. Noting that the rule was unanimous, *The State* welcomed the prospect of retrial of the only three Lost Trust defendants having cases at issue who were still alive.

Speaker Wilkins Focuses on Soft Money

House Speaker David Wilkins on December 1, 1998, called for more disclosure of secret money spent to influence elections at the state and local levels in South Carolina. Wilkins delivered on Organization Day a speech in the newly renovated State House in which he complained of the massive amounts of money spent by undisclosed sources to oppose the re-election of Gov. David Beasley in November, 1998. Beasley was defeated and much of the money to oppose him came from covert video poker interests because Beasley wanted to abolish video poker in South Carolina. Rep. Jim Hodges (D-Lancaster) had defeated Beasley on November 3, 1998, in a race which had the issue of video poker as one of the main points of contention.

Bemoaning the masses of dark money for Hodges in the campaign, Wilkins stated that, "While we should not infringe on First Amendment rights, we have an obligation to clearly mark the money trail for all to follow." Wilkins then appealed to the legislators to support a bill which he called the Campaign Reform Act of 1999 which, he said, "will expose the sources of independent expenditures and put some teeth in reporting requirements."

Hodges Urges Campaign Finance Reforms

Responding to Speaker David Wilkins' speech to the organizational session of the South Carolina General Assembly on December 3, 1998, at the State House, newly elected governor Jim Hodges agreed with Speaker Wilkins' argument that new campaign finance legislation was needed to force disclosure of so-called soft money, or indirect undisclosed expenditures to support candidates for election to state and local offices. Hodges called for a comprehensive campaign finance reform. Hodges told the media that campaign spending limits and soft money spending limits should be considered.

Wilkins had orated that "Never again should we have an election in South Carolina when one industry can spend untold dollars to affect the outcome of an election without any disclosure as to where the money came from or where it was spent." It was known that the video poker industry had spent lavishly to help Hodges' campaign by buying billboards, television, and radio ads which attacked Beasley with telling consequences. Wilkins clearly stated that he wanted the House under his leadership to move forward new legislation to improve the campaign finance provisions of the 1991 Ethics Act which Wilkins helped to frame and pass as Chairman of the House Judiciary Committee and a member of the conference committee which wrote the 1991 Ethics Act.

CHAPTER FORTY FIVE

1999—THE LAST YEAR OF OPERATION LOST TRUST

The year 1999 marked the final phase of the Operation Lost Trust prosecution. By that time a decade had passed since Ron Cobb had been caught in a federal cocaine sting in 1989, and by the end of 1999 the last three prosecutions of a total of 28 defendants had been disposed of by either guilty pleas, trials or retrials.

Whittled down by the deaths of Reps. Taylor and Gordon in 1997, there were only three defendants left to be dealt with in 1999 by the prosecutions—former Reps. Paul Derrick and Larry Blanding and former Sen. Bud Long.

Derrick and Blanding opted to go to retrial. Derrick was convicted in one retrial, but Blanding's first retrial ended with a hung jury; his second retrial ended with a conviction. Bud Long cut a deal with the U.S. Attorney's Office and pled to a misdemeanor charge of giving false information to federal officials in exchange for the dismissal of the only felony charge still left, that of extortion in taking money from Ron Cobb.

FBI Admits Paying Cobb $250,000

On May 10, 1999, the media published information which the prosecution had released to the defense in late April, 1999, that the FBI had paid Ron Cobb a total of $250,000 by September 28, 1999, for his services. The information was released by the government to the attorneys for Paul Derrick, Larry Blanding, and Bud Long who were preparing for retrials of their cases.

At the time the FBI disclosed its payment of $250,000 to Cobb, the trial of Paul Derrick was set to start on May 24, 1999, according to federal prosecutor Richard Pilger of the U.S. Justice Department's Public Integrity Section. Pilger gave the information to John Hardaway, attorney for Derrick. Attorney Joel Collins who had fought relentlessly, often pro bono, for nearly a decade representing as many as seven Lost Trust clients at a time, remarked of the FBI's announcement that, "Now we're shocked to find that they gave him $250,000. This payment by the government to Cobb certainly raises in a lot of questions."

Derrick Retrial Begins

The jury for the Derrick retrial included six women and six men. The trial was held in Charleston, S.C. The prosecutors Robert Meyer and Richard Pilger, were new attorneys sent in by the Department of Justice to finish the job. John Hardaway appeared for Derrick.

At trial former Rep. Bob Kohn testified on May 25, 1999, that Derrick liked to shake down lobbyists. The prosecution also put up a videotape of Kohn talking to Ron Cobb about Derrick dated from before the Lost Trust scandal broke and became public. But by the time of Derrick's retrial the government had just admitted that Ron Cobb had actually received a total of $471,000 in payments and tax relief from the prosecution in return for his cooperation. This huge amount was nearly double what the FB I had told attorneys for Derrick, Blanding, and Long just a few days before Derrick's trail begin.

Bob Kohn put up some of the most damning testimony against Derrick, telling the court that Derrick had belonged to the notorious "Fat and Ugly Caucus" in the South Carolina House in the 1980s which made a practice of shaking down lobbyists for free food, drinks, and gifts. Kohn described the caucus as "just a cynical, fun loving crowd that initially was not corrupt." However, Kohn, who had served as an FBI informant in 1990, said that "Over time, we became quite corrupt. If the lobbyists didn't play the game right, we could be quite punitive." Even so, "The lobbyists enjoyed it as much as we did. They fleeced someone else for what we were fleecing them for."

Kohn told the court that he could have forced $50,000 out of the lobbyists by using the Fat and Ugly Caucus to shake down those having business at the State House. Kohn went on to admit that at the time of the FBI sting he was an alcoholic and drug addict who used cocaine. Kohn testified that Derrick took handouts from the lobbyists and "was quite receptive to it. We definitely had him down as a likely score." By this remark Kohn indicated that he and the FBI thought that Derrick would take a bribe.

After being caught by the FBI for his own corruption and drug abuse during the early days of operation Lost Trust, of course, Kohn secretly turned into an informant for the FBI to save his own skin. But he also made money off of his work for the FBI. Kohn told the court that the FBI paid him $45,000 for his help and that he received a lenient seven month sentence in a federal prison camp in Butner, N.C., because federal prosecutors intervened in his case in two instances to get his punishment reduced. Kohn also helped the government with another corruption sting operation in Kentucky.

The Derrick retrial brought out even more new details about how much Cobb was paid in the Lost Trust sting and prosecutions. FBI special agent Mike Clemens admitted to the court that Cobb received not only a lump sum payment of $250,000 in 1998 but also was given $118,000; in addition, the FBI got the Internal Revenue Service to cut Cobb's tax debt from $213,000. In total Cobb got $496,000. This information was elicited by defense attorney John Hardaway in his examination of federal witnesses, especially Clemens, the FBI special agent in Columbia.

<u>Prosecution Strategy vs Derrick</u>

The new federal prosecutors handling the Derrick case were special lawyers from the U.S. Department of Justice Public Integrity Section rather than the prosecutors of the U.S. Attorney for South Carolina as in all previous cases. The new staff attorneys sent in from Washington, D.C., were the result of repeated appeals and complaints by the defense attorneys that the prosecutors from the U.S. Attorney's Office had engaged in misconduct which Judge Hawkins ultimately thought justified the complete dismissal of all remaining charges in early 1997.

The prosecution made the point that Derrick had a reputation of being at the State House trying to feed off of the lobbyists. The government also stressed the fact that the videotapes which it presented to the jury clearly showed Derrick taking $1,000 in cash from Ron Cobb.

The prosecution pointed out that Derrick had a history of opposing the pari-mutuel betting idea until 1990, when suddenly he both took the $1,000 from Cobb and voted 6 six times for the betting bill. Finally, the government pointed out that Derrick had never reported any money or gifts from lobbyists until the day after the FBI finally asked Derrick about the money he took from Cobb.

Derrick Retrial Hears Cobb

The prosecution put up Ron Cobb as a witness against Derrick on May 26, 1999. Cobb admitted on the witness stand that he was not sure that Derrick knew the $1,000 that Cobb gave to Derrick was a bribe and not a campaign contribution. Cobb further admitted that the $1,000 that Derrick took from Cobb was not given by Cobb himself, but by former Rep. Bob Kohn as an FBI sting agent.

"Because of my conversations with Kohn, I considered it a bribe. What Mr. Derrick considered it, I don't know." Cobb said. Cobb testified that he gave Derrick ten $100 bills for his votes on the betting bill. The prosecutor told the jury that the videotape showed Derrick taking $1,000 from Cobb and that even if Derrick took the $1,000 in cash as a campaign contribution for his vote and not as a bribe it was still a crime of public corruption to sell votes.

Videotapes Hurt Derrick

The fact that the prosecution had video and audiotapes of Derrick taking $1,000 in cash from Ron Cobb was a decisive factor in the case pushing the jury toward conviction. The tapes showed Ron Cobb handing 10 $100 bills to Derrick while Derrick made self-incriminating remarks to Cobb which clearly showed Derrick's devious personality. Derrick told Cobb while on tape taking the money in Cobb's room that "If anybody ever says, 'Well, didn't you ever help him,' you can always say, 'Yeah, I bought him some stamps.' Does that suit you? I feel better about doing that."

Prosecutors said Derrick really planned to use the $1,000 from Cobb not for his campaign in which he had no opposition in the November,, 1990, election but for the purpose of buying an expensive set of golf clubs for himself. The prosecution also asserted that Derrick had suggested that he would accept more money from Cobb in the 1991 session of the General Assembly. Cobb told Derrick on tape, "I hope you'll be right in there with us again." And Derrick responded, "I'm sure I'll have another birthday coming up."

The videotapes presented to the jury in the Paul Derrick retrial were persuasive evidence. The pictures of Cobb handing $1,000 in cash to Derrick and the remarks made by Derrick in taking the money in Cobb's motel room in June, 1990, were suicidal for the defendant.

Derrick hurt himself badly by saying on tape that he would lie on his campaign finance report forms and file them with the House Ethics Committee saying that the $1,000 he took from Cobb was really only no more than $250 for the purchase of postage stamps to mail newsletters to his constituents, and he told Cobb, "It protects both of us. "

Defense attorney John Hardaway stressed the point that neither Cobb nor Derrick came right out and said that $1,000 was a bribe, saying "Why don't they have a...tape of Cobb saying...'Here's $1,000 for your vote.' It's not there. And because it's not there its reasonable doubt." Hardaway said there was no clear evidence that the $1,000 was a payoff for Derrick's vote and therefore not evidence on which to convict.

Prosecution Attacks Derrick

The leading prosecutor in the Derrick retrial, Richard Pilger from Washington, told the jurors to believe what they saw and heard on the 19 video and audiotapes the prosecution had presented in evidence. Admitting that the chief prosecution witnesses Bob Kohn and Ron Cobb were unsavory characters, Pilger explained "The government can't wait for a minister or a priest to come in and offer evidence of bribery.... So what you have to do is make deals with people like Ron Cobb."

The government presented two FBI witnesses who testified that Derrick told them on July 18, 1990, that he had not taken any cash from a lobbyist during the legislative session. The prosecution said that caused Derrick to scramble to report the money he took from Cobb on his ethics disclosure forms on July 19, 1990. Derrick also quickly called lobbyists to try to find out about Cobb's role in the sting and asked lobbyists what he should do about the $1,000.

Derrick then deposited the $1,000 in his campaign account, but back-dated the deposit slip to July 17, 1990, the day before the FBI came to Derrick. His filing of a disclosure form on July 19, 1990, was the first time he reported a contribution from the lobbyist, according to the prosecution.

Lobbyist Randy Lee, himself entangled in a drug prosecution in Lost Trust, testified that Derrick was conflicted over the money in late July, 1990. In mid-August, Lee recorded a telephone call from Derrick in which Derrick said, "I'm prepared if...I'm indicted." The tape was played for the jury.

Derrick Defense Strategy

Led by attorney John Hardaway, the defense of Paul Derrick stressed the point that the prosecution witnesses Bob Kohn and Ron Cobb were low-life political parasites wallowing in drug abuse and public corruption. The jury was given every reason to believe anything that Kohn and Cobb said in court was bought testimony by paid criminals trying not only to save their own skins but also to financially profit from their association with crimes.

In his testimony Kohn spouted profanities and even admitted that he lied to Cobb about drugs. Hardaway made it crystal clear that neither Kohn nor Cobb were worthy of belief and were compromised by naked self-interest.

For his part Derrick's lawyers characterized the $1,000 he took from Cobb as a legal campaign contribution permitted by the weak 1975 Ethics Act, even though Derrick had no opposition in the 1990 election year in his efforts to return to the House. Derrick's defense also claimed that Cobb, the FBI, and the U.S. Attorney's Office tried to lure Derrick into taking the $1,000 in spite of the fact that there was no evidence that Derrick had sold his vote in the past. However, prosecutors alleged that Derrick had voted for the pari-mutuel betting bill a total of six times in 1990, even though he had previously opposed to bill.

Derrick did not testify in retrial, unlike in his first trial which resulted in convictions in 1991.

Derrick Convicted

The case against Paul Derrick went to the jury on May 28, 1999. The jury deliberated for two hours, stopping once to review a videotape of Derrick accepting $1,000 in cash and talking about how he would disclose part of the money on his ethics reports. The same day that it took the Derrick case for deliberation, the jury returned a guilty verdict causing Bart Daniel who had prosecuted the first case to remark, “Sometimes justice is a long time coming.”

The trial Judge Charles Haden said that Derrick had met all conditions of his bond.

Reflections on Derrick Conviction

After the jury convicted Paul Derrick of corruption on May 28, 1999, the reactions were, of course, mixed. Derrick reflected on the fact that the verdict came nine years after his implication in Lost Trust was revealed, imposing a heavy burden on him. But when the verdict was announced in court he remained under control.

Defense attorney John Hardaway said that no decision to appeal had been made. Ed Bell, attorney for Larry Blanding, who had watched the Derrick trial, commented on the verdict, “I'm just shocked.” Bell said, “It's just shocking to me that someone would find Kohn believable.” Sen.

Long's attorney, Jack Swerling, thought the fact that jurors found out that Cobb was paid nearly $500,000 and Kohn got $64,700 might have undermined their credibility.

The prosecution took a victory lap. "We are pleased with the jury's verdict and we look forward to the second trial (Blanding's) June 7," said Robert Meyer, the corruption prosecutor sent in by the Justice Department to finish the final three cases in the Lost Trust sequence. Bart Daniel reflected on the fact that he had convicted 16 legislators, seven lobbyists, and four others, saying, "I think there's clearly some sense of vindication for the Justice Department, the FBI and the agents and prosecutors." Daniel went on to call Lost Trust, "the most successful public corruption case in the nation."

The State Publishes Editorial on Retrials

The State wrote an editorial in the June 9, 1999, edition and said that the "Lost Trust retrials offer lessons on the justice system." Pointing to the first of the three trials, that of Paul Derrick which ended in conviction on May 28, 1999, *The State* argued "the re-conviction of former state Rep. Paul Derrick is not important because he and two other former legislators being tried pose any threat to the body politic. Operation Lost Trust purged them from our political system and prodded the Legislature to toughen our ethics laws." *The State* admitted that "They will not return, and our new laws make a return to the too-cozy relationship between legislators and lobbyists unlikely."

Larry Blanding's First Retrial

The first retrial of Larry Blanding began June 7, 1999. Opening with special emphasis on the tapes, the prosecution told the jury it would produce tapes to show Blanding taking cash as bribes from Cobb. The government introduced as evidence on the first day of trial the campaign finance disclosure documents which Blanding had on file with the House Ethics Committee. The documents did not include any evidence that Blanding had reported the $1,300 he took from Cobb as a contribution to his election campaign in the year 1990 when he sought re-election to his seat in the House.

Prosecutor Robert Meyer told the jury that the case against Blanding involved two pledges that Blanding had made: (1) the pledge he had made to his constituents when he took the office of representative and (2) the promise that he made to Ron Cobb to vote for the betting bill. "The only pledge honored by the defendant was the one he made to the lobbyist," Meyer alleged.

At the time of the first retrial Blanding had served seven months in prison on his conviction in 1991 for bribery before his charges were overturned by the 4th Circuit and then later in 1997 dismissed by Judge Falcon Hawkins prior to being reinstated in 1998 and sent back for retrial by the 4th Circuit again.

Jurors began hearing testimony on June 8, 1999, in the first retrial of Blanding after the opening arguments of the prosecution and defense. In opening, the prosecution promised to present FBI videotapes of Blanding taking money from Ron Cobb. Prosecutor Robert Meyers said the tapes showed Blanding taking bribes "red-handed" to vote for the betting bill.

Attorney Ed Bell opened by telling the court that Blanding had supported the betting bill and helped to write the legislation to legalize betting on horses well before he took any money from Ron Cobb. Bell asked the jury the rhetorical question, "Why would Larry Blanding after 14 years in the legislature, why would he take a bribe on a bill he wrote?" Bell urged the jurors to consider other evidence aside from the tapes. Bell said that Blanding thought the $1,300 he took from Ron Cobb was a campaign contribution. Bell pointed out that in 1990 South Carolina was operating under one of the most lax campaign finance laws in the nation.

Prosecution In First Retrial Spars with Defense

The prosecution opened its presentation of evidence with videotapes of Ron Cobb handing Blanding cash which the prosecution then alleged to be bribes for the betting bill. Witness Ron Cobb said the money was intended as a bribe.

The prosecution tried to debunk Blanding's defense that the $1,300 he took from Cobb was a campaign donation by showing that Blanding had not deposited any of the money from Cobb in his official campaign account during the period from January to July, 1990. The prosecution showed that Blanding did not report any of the Cobb money on his official campaign finance documents on file with the House Ethics Committee. Witnesses told the court that there was no evidence of either a deposit or of a disclosure on file which might have indicated the money was a contribution.

On cross-examination Blanding's attorney Ed Bell asked Cobb why he did not clearly tell Blanding that the money handed to Blanding in cash was a bribe. Cobb responded that he intended the payment of the $1,300 as a bribe, saying "I knew what was in my mind. I can't say how other folks felt." Cobb then added, "I tried to be as specific as I could without saying point blank what we were doing."

Cobb testified that he did not seek out Blanding to bribe but that Rep. Luther Taylor (D-Richland) who had taken money from Cobb brought Blanding to Cobb. Cobb told the jury, "My understanding based on the conversations with Luther Taylor and Mr. Blanding was that Mr. Blanding would be supporting pari-mutuel and be paid for his vote."

Closing Arguments In First Retrial Of Blanding

The federal prosecutor Richard Philger had told the jury that Blanding had been "caught red-handed on videotape taking money, not once, but twice." Pilger in closing arguments said

Blanding's taking of two payments from Ron Cobb was "a crime to undermine democracy.... It's a crime to undermine the rights of the voters for money."

But defense attorney Ed Bell told the jurors that the money Cobb gave to Blanding was a legal campaign contribution and that the jury should acquit him. "Larry Blanding believed what he did at that time was innocent. He believes that he got a campaign contribution." Bell also told the jury in closing that the prosecution had been devious in giving the $1,300 to Blanding because it did not make it clear that the money was intended as a bribe. Bell said, "If the federal government is going to set up a sting operation, don't you think they should give you that one opportunity to say, 'No. I'm an honorable man.'"

The defense also argued that the betting bill would only have allowed voters to vote on a constitutional referendum to legalize betting which would have to be approved by the Legislature.

Prosecutor Pilger countered the defense argument in closing that Blanding had taken a legal campaign contribution of $1,300 and not a bribe. Pilger pointed to the fact that the evidence showed that Blanding was first offered $500 but then he requested an additional $500 for total first payment of $1,000. Pilger argued that such corrupt deals are not completely explicit, saying "It's not like a real estate closing—the party of the first part will sell his vote for this amount of money."

The evidence showed that Blanding had taken $1,000 in March, 1990, from Ron Cobb, and then another $300 in May, also from Cobb. Prosecutor Robert Meyer dismissed the defense argument that the $1,300 was a campaign contribution as "a smokescreen." Meyer said that even if the $1,300 was given as a campaign contribution in return for Blanding's vote the money was still a bribe: "even a campaign contribution is illegal if you take it in return for an explicit promise."

Jury Deliberations Begin

After the closing arguments the first retrial case of former Rep. Larry Blanding went to the jury in the early afternoon on June 11, 1999. After the deliberations began the jury requested videotape and audiotape recording playing machines and a copy of the judge's instruction to the jury. The jury also returned to the courtroom to hear from the judge an explanation of what the law in the case meant by an "official act."

The jury deliberated for a total of seven hours before recessing on its first day of deliberations.

Blanding's First Retrial Fails

The jury deliberated for a total of twelve hours on two days, starting on the afternoon of Friday, June 11, 1999, and concluding on Saturday without reaching a verdict in the first retrial of Larry Blanding. Thus ended the second trial of Blanding, the first having ended in 1991 with a conviction later overturned and order for new trial. In the first trial the jury had only deliberated 90 minutes before voting unanimously to convict, and in the first trial Blanding had elected to present no defense.

As the mistrial was declared, Blanding left the courthouse and referred all questions from the media to his attorney, Ed Bell. Bell responded by saying "Clearly some folks on the jury saw it differently than the way the government did.... Because of Larry Blanding's stellar background, it's so inconsistent with his character for this to happen to him in this case."

The jury struggled hard in the first retrial case and tried to avoid a mistrial. After meeting for seven hours on Friday, June 11, 1999, the jury met for two hours on Saturday morning before telling the trial judge, Charles Haden, that they could not agree on a verdict. The jury consisted of four blacks, seven whites and one Asian. The judge then sent them back to the jury room to try to reach a verdict but after three more hours they failed again to find Blanding either guilty or not guilty of the three charges against him—one count of conspiracy and two counts of extortion.

Blanding Mistrial Declared

As the jury could not agree on the charges of conspiracy and extortion, trial Judge Charles Haden declared a mistrial on June 12, 1999, and said that he would reschedule the case for a second retrial as soon as possible and before the end of the summer.

Prosecutor Robert Meyer told the media, "We're disappointed they were unable to reach a verdict and look forward to coming back and trying this case again." The prosecution's determination to continue its attack on Blanding presented him with the third trial of his case on the same facts and law. This raised the question of whether the prosecutors were going to unreasonable and excessive lengths to convict Blanding and whether in such a relatively minor corruption case based on a somewhat dubious sting operation the government should have instead chosen to move to dismiss the charges rather than put Blanding through still another expensive and oppressive third trial with the possibility that the third trial would fail as the first two trials had ended with no sustainable convictions.

Blanding's Second Retrial

The second retrial of Blanding began on August 16, 1999, and ended on August 20, 1999. The defense said there was no new evidence.

As in the first trial in 1991 and the first retrial in June, 1999, the chief prosecution witness was again Ron Cobb. He took the stand to recite the same story as in the first two trials, saying again that he had given Blanding a total of $1,300 and that he thought the payment was a bribe and telling the court, "I knew it was. I assume he did." Cobb again admitted that the sting had deliberately tried to avoid a clear and convincing statement that would have explicitly indicated to the recipient of the money that it was intended as a bribe paid to Blanding to buy his vote on the betting bill.

Both the prosecution and the defense presented the same arguments in the second retrial as in the first retrial, the government saying that Cobb gave $1,300 to Blanding as a bribe to vote for the betting bill while the defense said the money was a legal campaign donation.

Cobb told the court that he used the late former Rep. Luther Taylor as the recruiter to bring him legislators who would take money from Cobb who was asking their support on the betting bill. Cobb did not say for sure that Taylor had told Blanding that the money he would be offered by Cobb was supposed to be a bribe, but Cobb thought Taylor had told Blanding the money was a bribe.

Cobb admitted that at the direction of the FBI he intentionally had never said or implied to Blanding that the $1,300 in cash he gave to Blanding was an illegal transaction as a bribe. Cobb testified, "I was instructed not to do anything that would send up red flags with the people I was dealing with. That certainly would have sent up a red flag."

Blanding Second Retrial Hears Taylor from Grave

Cobb told the court that he never told Blanding to not tell anybody about the cash $1,300 he took from Cobb and that Blanding never agreed to enter into a conspiracy to commit a crime. This evidence seemed to mitigate Blanding's conduct.

Aged testimony the late Luther Taylor had given in Blanding's first trial in 1991 was given in transcript form to the jury for their consideration in the second retrial. In his 1991 testimony, Taylor had said that he contacted several legislators who already supported the pari-mutuel betting bill and told them all to contact Ron Cobb. Taylor said that he considered the money which Cobb was handing out to be campaign contributions and not actually as bribes. Taylor said that in his view bribery would have to cause an official to change his position on an issue and to vote differently than he intended before he took the money. Taylor said, "If a person was to buy a vote or a person was to sell a vote, they would have to change their position. You can't buy something that is not for sale." This line of argument had failed Luther Taylor in 1990 and would fail again in Blanding's second retrial.

Blanding Second Retrial Hears Kohn

The prosecution again showed the court the same videotapes of Cobb handing Blanding cash payments of $1,000 in March, 1990, and $300 in May, 1990, as had been shown in the first trial in 1991 and the first retrial in June, 1999.

Former Rep. Robert Kohn again appeared on the witness stand as he had in previous Lost Trust trials and told the same story that Blanding had voted with other pari-mutuel betting bill supporters. Kohn also testified about a series of procedural votes in April, 1991, when supporters of the betting bill tried to convince the House to debate the betting bill. The effort to move the bill failed in the House, Kohn admitted. Kohn, who had served seven months in prison for his vote-buying actions in Lost Trust, admitted on cross-examination that some of the procedural votes he cited as efforts to move the betting bill might had been, in fact, efforts to move other legislation, not the betting bill.

Blanding's Second Retrial Closes

In closing remarks the chief federal prosecutor argued that the defense statement that the $1,300 given by Cobb to Blanding was a campaign donation was nothing more than a "bald, transparent, ridiculous fraud," said Richard Pilger. "You saw the tapes and you heard the tapes," Pilger argued to the jury, adding "What you personally witnessed shows he's guilty."

The defense countered by arguing that the prosecutors' statements about Blanding's alleged guilt were not material evidence but rather that Blanding's intent was the real issue as to the criminal liability. Defense attorney Ed Bell told the jury that "It's not what these people, these government lawyers—it's not what they believe but what Larry Blanding believed at the time."

Bell pointed to witness testimony as to Blanding's reputation for honesty and integrity. He again argued that the $1,300 was a legal campaign donation to Blanding, not a bribe.

Blanding Convicted In Second Retrial

The second retrial of former Rep. Larry Blanding ended with his conviction on August 20, 1999, on charges of taking cash from Ron Cobb to support the pari-mutuel betting bill. But the jury deadlocked on a third conspiracy count and the trial judge, Charles Haden, struck the charge of conspiracy from the indictment.

In his 1991 trial and first and second retrials in 1999, the defense had used different tactics. In his failed 1991 trial, Blanding had not testified. But in the first and second retrials he had taken the stand and testified that he had supported the betting bill before he took the $1,300 from Cobb and that the cash was, in fact, just a legal campaign donation and not a sale of vote.

Blanding's attorney, Ed Bell, expressed his reaction, saying of the conviction "We are extremely disappointed." He then expressed his confidence in Blanding saying, "The kind of man he is will follow him notwithstanding the verdict."

Blanding Sentenced

The three final defendants remaining in the Lost Trust series of trials were all sentenced the same day on December 13th, 1999, before U.S. District Court Judge Charles Haden in Columbia. Haden was a West Virginia federal judge who had been sent to South Carolina to preside over the cases of Rep. Paul Derrick, Rep. Larry Blanding, and Sen. Bud Long and dispose of them.

Judge Haden sentenced Blanding to 30 months in prison for conviction on two counts of bribery involving a payment of $1,300 from lobbyist Ron Cobb to Blanding in two separate transactions. Haden gave Blanding credit for eight months time served in prison before his second retrial which ended on August 20, 1999. Blanding had been first convicted of corruption in August, 1991, and sentenced to 37 months in prison.

Derrick Sentenced

On December 13, 1999, Judge Charles Haden sentenced former Rep. Paul Derrick to a total of 24 months in prison based on his conviction in his first retrial for extorting $1,000 from an FBI informant in June, 1990. Videotapes presented as evidence in the trial showed Derrick taking ten $100 bills.

Derrick had been convicted in 1991 in his first trial and had been sentenced to 34 months in prison.

Long Admits To Lying

Former Sen. Bud Long came to court to plead on June 30, 1999, and told the judge that he had lied under oath to FBI agents investigating his role in the Lost Trust scandal. Long's appearance was pursuant to his decision to plead guilty to a lesser misdemeanor charge in return for the prosecution's willingness to drop charges against Long of felony extortion.

Long told the court that, "I stand before this court and tell you that..the statement I made that I cannot recall accepting cash from a lobbyist was untrue." Reading from a prepared statement, Long continued to tell U.S. District Judge Charles Haden that "I made that oral representation knowing that it was untrue, when in fact, I had accepted $2,800 from Ron Cobb on May 22, 1990."

Long's attorney, Jack Swerling, told the media that federal prosecutors offered Long a deal to drop the bribery charge if Long would plead to a lesser crime. "It was an offer he couldn't refuse," Swerling remarked. The deal was revealed by Swerling on June 24, 1999.

Long appeared later for sentencing on December 13, 1999, before Judge Charles Haden; Haden sentenced Long to probation for three years, a fine of $1,000, and no incarceration. The sentencing of Sen. Long concluded the disposition of Lost Trust cases. The Derrick, Blanding, and Long cases were the final three prosecutions.

Conclusion

Operation Lost Trust had started in 1989 with the arrest of Greenville, South Carolina, lobbyist Ron Cobb by the FBI for dealing cocaine. It ended in December 13, 1999, with the imposition of sentence on the last three criminal defendants.

The arrest of Cobb triggered an investigation of corruption in South Carolina state government and a probe of drug use by lobbyists, government employees, state legislators, and one private businessman which became public in mid-July, 1990, when the FBI served the first of a series of subpoenas on members of the South Carolina House of Representatives. Although 20 defendants entered guilty pleas, a total of eight legislators went to trial. All were convicted except Rep. Tim Wilkes. The sentences imposed varied widely and included federal prison time, incarceration in a halfway house, fines, and probation.

The criminal prosecutions resulted in successful appeals and motions by five of those convicted at trial, all of them legislators, which resulted in the convictions being reversed and ordered for retrial. Two of the five awarded new trials died in 1997 before retrial. Two were convicted on retrial, and one entered a guilty plea to a lesser crime.

The conduct of the U.S. Attorney of South Carolina came in for severe criticism by those who were convicted at trial and their lawyers. In addition, the judge who tried most of the Operation Lost Trust cases, Falcon Hawkins, also chastised the prosecution and even dismissed all criminal charges in 1997 against the final five criminal appellants who had been granted new trials. The 4th Circuit Court of Appeals reinstated charges on three defendants who were convicted in 1999. The allegations of prosecutorial misconduct made by appellants and Judge Hawkins were investigated by both federal and state authorities who found no such misconduct.

Operation Lost Trust proved to be the most expansive public corruption prosecution in the history of South Carolina. However, as a drug prosecution it was not especially large in terms of the number of persons convicted and the magnitude of the drug violations.

The Ethics Act passed in 1991 in response to the scandal greatly modified the political culture of state and local government by decisively imposing unprecedented standards of ethical behavior on public officials at both the state and local levels of government in South Carolina. It created strict regulations on campaign finance, lobbying, disclosure, and conflicts of interest. The new ethical standards were later applied to Governor Mark Sanford, Lt. Gov. Ken Ard, Speaker Bobby Harrell, and Sen. Robert Ford.

CHAPTER FORTY SIX

QUESTIONS ABOUT LOST TRUST

Was Sting a Rigged Game?

The way in which the sting in Operation Lost Trust was conducted raises serious issues about the wisdom and integrity of the scheme. Given the fact that a substantial number of the legislators charged with bribery had been committed to the idea of legalizing horse and dog racing and betting in South Carolina for a time before the money given to them was delivered by Ron Cobb acting for the FBI, the most serious question was whether the whole concept of trying to bribe legislators to do what they were already committed to do looks like a setup. This game was clearly designed to make it as easy as possible for the FBI to get the legislators to take the money. It was virtually inevitable that some would take the money to vote for a bill they already strongly favored.

If the money handed out by Ron Cobb had been explicitly presented as a clear-cut offering to buy votes and if the defendants had clearly expressed and explicitly indicated that they were selling their vote in return, then perhaps even the idea of offering money to persuade legislators to do what they intended to do anyhow might have been at least marginally plausible as actual bribery. However, the FBI instructed Cobb and Rep. Kohn as sting agents not to tip off the targets by using explicit and blunt language about bribery.

If, on the other hand, the money had been offered by Ron Cobb to the same legislators who took his money to instead change their positions and to oppose the betting bill, then the results might have been different and, probably, would have been different. It is more than a possibility that the money would have been refused or even if it was taken the legislators might not have, in fact, tried to stop the betting bill, and might even have voted for the bill in spite of taking the money to oppose the bill.

If Cobb had offered money to legislators who supported the betting bill to not vote for the betting bill then it is quite likely that a number of the legislators who took Ron Cobb's money would not have done so. They might even have reported the offers to law enforcement and, therefore, there would have been fewer indictments and convictions for extortion, bribery, and conspiracy under the Hobbs Act. Perhaps there would have been none based on the sting but there might have indictments related to the tax break bill.

It could even be argued that the FBI and the U. S. Attorney's office manufactured crimes and created the biggest corruption scandal in the history of the State of South Carolina which would not otherwise have ever occurred at all. Perhaps the people of South Carolina were put through an ordeal lasting from 1989 to 1999 which would not have happened had it not been for federal law enforcement using the betting bill as bait.

Was Lost Trust More About Drug Crimes?

It can also be argued that, in fact, a large part of what was subsumed as Operation Lost Trust and postured as a mass public corruption prosecution was in large part not about public corruption but about drugs. Some of the defendants charged at the time and lumped in with the bribery defendants were not, in fact, involving in bribery and were not charged with any violations of the Hobbs Act. Only one (Rep. Donna Moss) of the 18 legislators charged was charged with drug violations, not bribery. And none of the lobbyists, the two state employees, and the one business man was charged with bribery, but all with drug violations. Of the total of 28 persons charged in association with the bribery scandal, only 14 of them were convicted of public corruption, the others were not.

Did Lost Trust Target Blacks?

Another issue raised by Operation Lost Trust at the time was whether the large number of black legislators charged with bribery was the result of a deliberate federal strategy of targeting black public officials. Some black leaders alleged that it was and the issue was raised by defendants and their lawyers.

There is no persuasive evidence that the FBI and the U.S. Attorney's office intentionally set out to target black politicians and there is no evidence as to what would motivate such a scheme to target black officials. Given the fact that no black senators were charged and given the fact that the districts from which black House members came were deliberately and heavily gerrymandered to include large black majorities, it was almost inevitable that any convicted and removed black House member would have been replaced after conviction by a black. In fact, every black removed from office, all eight of them, was replaced by another black. For example the black judge, Tee Ferguson, was soon followed by the election of Rep. Danny Martin as a black judge.

However, the selection of the betting bill as the bill for which the FBI would offer money was very problematic because so many blacks were committed to legalizing horse and dog racing and pari-mutuel betting as a way of creating new jobs, especially for low-income blacks. Legislative Black Caucus members had been committed to the betting bill well before Ron Cobb began to ply black legislators with money to support it. Therefore, it was inevitable that some black legislators offered money would be inclined to support the bill and accept money which did not affect their official conduct in any substantive way.

Was Corruption Rampant In South Carolina Before Lost Trust?

It can be argued that the legislators caught up in Lost Trust were already corrupt and were finally getting what they deserved. Ron Cobb certainly indicated that he had previously corrupted a large number of both black and white legislators in South Carolina during his short career as a big spending lobbyist at the State House. Cobb claimed that he could had paid off half of the whites and bribed nearly all black legislators. If this was true then the FBI and the U.S. Attorney had good reasons to investigate persons suspected of corruption, but some other means could had been used other than the betting bill to create the sting. Even if the sting was necessary, another bill to which no sting target was previously committed could have been used, and, better yet, a bill to which legislators were clearly opposed could have been used to elicit a major change of position and action which would not otherwise have been taken and which would clearly show the effect of bribery.

It can also be argued that Operation Lost Trust belatedly and finally alerted the people of South Carolina that state government was rotted out with corruption and filled with small time hustlers and crooks. The scandal did that. But it might have been even more convincing if the culprits had been caught in clear-cut bribery where their actions could be seen as a direct product of a payoff only, not as actions they were going to take anyway because they liked the betting bill.

It can also be argued that the scandal produced the political demand from an angry public for drastic ethics reform in a state in which the only ethics law, the 1975 Ethics Act, was a pious fraud and an open invitation to corruption of every sort. And that demand resulted in the framing of a new ethics law designed to correct many problems ignored by the 1975 Act. The 1991 Ethics Act was a direct result of the scandal and opportunism of reformers.

Perhaps it can be argued that only a sting could have succeeded in exposing officials who had a long but hidden history of abuse of office and corruption. This is quite possibly true, but even if a sting was justified and necessary, the sting could have been framed to make the bait less than irresistible and more demonstrative of criminal intent and corruption motivated only by the goal of taking illegal money.

Was Lost Trust A Melodrama?

Another issue raised by the sting was the dramatic staging of the presentation of the money given out by Ron Cobb to the sting targets. There is no question that on the videotapes Cobb was playing to the camera and was producing a theatrical drama designed to make the sting targets look as greedy and criminous as possible. Cobb not only served as a chief actor in the play but he also served as the narrator of the action, telling the audience about how bad the actors in the play were, himself included.

It was not enough for Cobb to do the wrongful acts; he also framed them visually and verbally as much as possible to look evil, sinister, and exaggerated. On many tapes he fanned the money like a card dealer at Las Vegas, commented on how much it was, suggested that more money was available as payoffs, and even crackled the paper bills for sound effects. All the while he kept up a constant chatter framing the handling of the money play-by-play as a bribery transaction. The videotapes were also grainy, black and white, and the audio was scratchy and gravely to make the whole scheme look like it was filmed in hell and in the film noire genre.

Was Sting Unfairly Staged to Convince Jury?

The staging of the scenes in which Cobb gave out the money was all designed to create a prejudice in the minds of the judge and jury that the whole transaction was inherently corrupt and completely evil. Cobb was also clever in using hyper-macho talk and bombast with his targets, especially young black legislators, to pick up the dialogue in accord with the hyper-macho subculture of some black American men.

His use of language was also designed to ethically desensitize the target by framing the handouts of the money as part of a game widely played and widely accepted as normal and even expected at the State House. Cobb's patter was that what he and the target were doing was the way business was commonly done in the General Assembly and state agencies and that there was nothing deviant, abnormal, or criminal about it. Cobb scrupulously avoided using any words such as bribery or payoff.

Was State House Culture Sick?

The final issue in evaluating Lost Trust must be whether the political culture of South Carolina was pathological and had been perhaps for three hundred years. Ever since its foundation as a colony in 1670, a small predatory elite had fastened itself on the economic, cultural, and political life of the Carolina colony and afterward the state, exploiting it in ruthless, corrupt, and irresponsible ways and using government to enrich themselves.

Lost Trust shows that many politicians had been living off politics for their entire career and many of them had been using their public offices as a way to sell influence and official action for profit. Many lawyer-legislators had been taking retainers from big corporations for which they did no legal work, but instead served as in-house de facto corporate lobbyists at the State House. Many businessmen in the legislature were involved in conflicts of interest, were doing business with state and local government, and practicing corruption and abuse of office as a way of life.

In addition, the huge role of lobbyists at the State House in both the legislative and executive branches was far in excess of what should have been permitted in a democratic system of government. The lobbyists' use of money to buy influence and control over politicians and political decisions was based on their ability to use unlimited amounts of money to get what they wanted. And the total freedom of politicians to take unregulated cash and gifts from lobbyists and big money persons and corporations gave public officials the ability to do whatever they wanted, even to practice the shakedown and the brazen extortion of money and gratuities. The Ethics Act of

1975 was a total fraud and, if anything, a license to steal granted to officials, lobbyists, and special interests.

Were All Politicians Complicit In Corruption?

The leadership of the State, from Gov. Carroll Campbell and the General Assembly on down, was complicit in the massive system of corruption and abuse of office which plagued the state of South Carolina at the time of Lost Trust. They knew that the state had had the most permissive and predatory practices for generations. They knew that the Ethics Act of 1975 permitted unlimited amounts of cash to be given to public officials by lobbyists, rich people, big corporations and PACs, and they did nothing to stop it.

Prior to Lost Trust most state officials did not even talk about corruption as a problem afflicting state and local governments in South Carolina. Public officials and the State House crew had to know the 1975 Ethics Act would inevitably facilitate corruption. Everybody in contact with state government knew abuse of office and corruption was rampant in government, especially in the General Assembly. Law enforcement and the media averted their eyes and were accomplices in crime.

Was Federal Intervention Necessary?

The use of the betting bill and the Lost Trust sting raised serious questions about the way in which the investigation of corruption and drugs at the South Carolina State House was conducted. But it was the way in which the United States Attorney and the FBI decided to attack and expose corruption in state government in 1989 in 1990.

The law enforcement systems of South Carolina's state and local governments were, in fact, doing almost nothing about the massive corruption plaguing state officials, especially in the General Assembly and in the lobbying trade. The only notable activity of state level or local law enforcement was that of Fifth Circuit Solicitor Jim Anders, who was conducting a probe of drug and bribe dealing lobbyist Ron Cobb which, by accident, ran into the FBI Lost Trust sting operation involving Cobb in 1989 and 1990. Speaker Bob Sheheen had also suppressed the "Fat and Ugly Caucus" and reported Rep. Ennis Fant to SLED.

Even so, the Attorney General of South Carolina was not privy to the federal Lost Trust sting operation and neither was Gov. Carroll Campbell until July 17, 1990, the day before U.S. Attorney and the FBI went public and seized evidence. There appeared to be almost no interest and awareness by the Attorney General, SLED, or the local Richland County Sheriff in the massive scandal which had been growing at the Statehouse for years.

Perhaps federal action was the only way to attack the corruption. State and local government both seemed either conflicted or indifferent.

Was Lost Trust the Only Way to Reform South Carolina?

Those few persons who tried to point out the pathologies caused by unlimited political money were either ignored by most politicians or intimidated by crooked lobbyist or legislators. Speaker Bob Sheheen had talked about lobbying reform during the late 1980s but few had any interest. Secretary of State John Campbell did not even enforce the registration requirements in the 1975 Ethics Act, let alone its feeble disclosure provisions. Gov. Campbell had Dick Greer, a cocaine user, in his retinue as his campaign chairman and economic development chair and did not know about or did not care about it. David Hawkins, one of Campbell's staffers, was the former head of the "Fat and Ugly Caucus" convicted in Lost Trust.

Even legislators who were not themselves taking money from lobbyists as bribes were taking unlimited gifts and campaign contributions from lobbyists, special interests, big money donors, corporations, and PACs. And even the least culpable were culpable because they knew the system was inherently and rampantly corrupt and that the fake 1975 Ethics Act was an invitation to bribery and abuse of office, but they did almost nothing to stop it. The most outrageous abuses and conflicts of interest were placidly treated as the established and accepted political culture of the State House at the time of Lost Trust and had been seen as completely normal and ordinary for years until the sting was staged.

Operation Lost Trust revealed a system of government which was inherently corrupt and predatory. Those who were inside the State House knew it; those who are outside of government suspected it. Lost Trust for all of its questionable schemes and actions may have been an abuse of investigative and prosecutorial authority and it may have produced crimes and unjustly sacrificed lives in the process, but maybe Lost Trust was the only effective way to expose the cancer in the government and politics of South Carolina and to force the passive people and complicit politicians to perform radical surgery on the state's government and political system. Lost Trust and the ethics reform movement at long last cut out much of the cancer.

Finally, were bad means used to achieve good ends and were there any other practical alternatives? The reader can answer that question for himself.

CHAPTER FORTY SEVEN

REFLECTIONS ON LOST TRUST

The author asked officials, lawyers and lobbyists who were in service during the time of Operation Lost Trust and the ethics reform movement and who have continued to serve from 1990 to the present (2016) to reflect on the consequences of the scandal and the reforms.

Their comments and reflections are published below along with a brief biographical description of their backgrounds in politics, government, and public life.

Senator Larry A. Martin (Republican)

Sen. Martin is Chairman of the Senate Judiciary Committee, one of the most powerful of legislative committees.

Martin was elected to the House and began his public service in 1979 and continued as a state representative until 1992 when he was elected to the Senate. He has served continuously in the Senate since that time and is a member of committees, including Banking and Insurance, Education, Judiciary, and Rules.

He has received many honors from the Manufacturers Alliance, Fraternal Order of Police, South Carolina Human Services Providers, Palmetto Family Council, South Carolina Chamber of Commerce, and the South Carolina Sheriff's Association.

Reflections of Sen. Martin

February 1, 2016

Columbia, S.C.

Most big events in life have the ability to provoke recollections of where we were when we first heard the news. In the case of the scandal known as Lost Trust, I was at home, working in Pickens County on a hot July afternoon when I received a call from my House committee secretary, Ms. Dottie. She asked in a low, calm voice, that I quickly recognized was very serious, if I had received any calls from anyone regarding my campaign disclosure reports. When I answered, "no," she said that she had received calls that stated several members of the House Labor, Commerce and Industry Committee had received subpoenas for their campaign records. It appeared that the FBI was involved and rumors were beginning to run rampant indicating that lots of members were implicated in something pretty big.

At that time, there were no cell phones, no social media, and no blogs. It took months for the complete picture of Lost Trust to become clear. But, what was painfully obvious, almost immediately, was that everyone who was serving in the Legislature was under a cloud of suspicion. It was also crystal clear that a major overhaul of our state's ethics was needed moving forward.

For that reason, the first order of business when the Legislature reconvened was to reset the relationship between lawmakers, lobbyists, and the principals for which lobbyists worked. The "no-cup-of-coffee" rule was a key feature of that debate and drew a bright line in the social relationships that had previously existed. Rules were enacted that imposed restrictions concerning lobbyist principals. A complete ban on campaign contributions from a lobbyist was implemented, along with the restriction that a registered lobbyist could not facilitate a contribution. Additionally, the ban on cash contributions over $25 was also incorporated in reaction to the Lost Trust experience. In the end, there was much more to the 1991 Ethics Reform bill than just these restrictions.

Equally important to the bill, however, are the many individuals who advocated for reform. Not simply those inside the legislature, but also the advocates outside of the legislature. John Crangle, a key reform advocate, followed the development of the bill through each step of the legislative process. He testified in front of subcommittees and consistently called for the strongest possible reform.

John has continued to be a force for reform, particularly over these past three years while we have pursued the recent ethics reform agenda. We've had some very long and tedious debates in the Senate Judiciary Committee over independent investigations of legislators, disclosure of sources of income by public officials, and disclosure by third party campaign committees. I can't recall a single meeting where John wasn't sitting in the front row of the committee room. While we may not have always agreed on the particulars of a piece of legislation, I have always admired his push to make government and its officials more transparent and accountable. He knows, from the debates going back to the early 1990s that ethics reform doesn't happen quickly, that it requires commitment to see it through. But, I know that we can count on John Crangle to keep pushing.

Interview
Sen. John E. Courson

April 8, 2015
Columbia, S.C.

Sen. John E. Courson (Republican)

Sen. John E. Courson was elected to the South Carolina Senate in 1984 for District 20 (Richland and Lexington counties) and has continued in that position to the present. He was a member of the Senate during Operation Lost Trust and was major proponent of ethics reform principles incorporated in the 1991 Ethics Act. Sen. Courson is chairman of the Education Committee and former President Pro Tem of the Senate.

Interview with Sen. Courson

Sen. Courson indicated that he believed that the abuses discovered in Lost Trust were due in large part to the weaknesses of the 1975 Ethics Act which failed to limit campaign finance matters, allowing cash contributions in unlimited amounts to be used for personal expenses. He also believes that the Act's failure to ban lobbyists' gifts to legislators made it easier for lobbyists to give gratuities including cash to buy votes.

Sen. Courson said that in his opinion the 1991 Ethics Act was one of the strongest, if not the strongest, state ethics laws in the United States when it first took effect in 1992 and was a model for other states to emulate.

Sen. Courson believes the 1991 Ethics Act has worked well in South Carolina and notes that no lobbyists have been caught in corrupt dealings with public officials since the Act took effect. He attributes the strict limits and regulations imposed on lobbyists as major factors in preventing bribery of public officials by lobbyists. He also believes that the limits imposed on legislators by the Act have suppressed corruption in state government.

Sen. Courson recalled the cozy relations of lobbyists and legislators which existed when he first came to the South Carolina Senate in 1985, citing the fact that as a freshman senator he was invited to bring his wife on an all-expense-paid trip to the Caribbean if he would appear on a panel as a commentator. The trip was paid for by a big money special interest and was little more than a free vacation offered to him because he was a public official. He refused the trip.

Courson believes that the South Carolina Senate has done an effective job of policing its own members according to the standards of state law. He notes that in his tenure in the Senate over more than 30 years, several senators have been forced out due to misconduct in public office or personal violations of the law. He cites the recent Senate investigation and referral of Sen. Robert Ford (D-Charleston) for misuse of campaign funds which ended in Ford's resignation in May 2013 and his subsequent criminal convictions.

Interview
Jim Miles

January 27, 2015
Columbia, S.C.

Jim Miles (Republican)

Jim Miles was elected Secretary of State of South Carolina in November 1990. At the time of his election he was a member of the Greenville, S.C., City Council. He was reelected as Secretary of State in 1994 by a large margin. Miles retired from the position in 2003. He is a member of the Republican Party.

Interview

1. What was your official position at the time you ran for the office of Secretary of State in 1990?
   A. I was a member of the Greenville, S.C., City Council.
2. Why did you decide to run for Secretary of State?
   A. Gov. Carroll Campbell came to Greenville in 1989 and suggested that I run for Secretary of State. Campbell said that he was the only constitutional officer in South Carolina who was a Republican and it was lonely in Columbia where he was surrounded by Democrats. I told Campbell that I wanted to run for Attorney General but he said that the Democratic incumbent Travis Medlock had too much money to be defeated. I did not know about the office of Secretary of State so I read up on the office and found out about the duties of the position. I then met with Gov. Campbell in Columbia and talked with him about the duties. I also went over to the Secretary of State's office on the State House grounds and asked for the reports filed there by lobbyists. The staff provided me with the reports which did not provide the information required by law and were very short on financial detail. Reports were not complete nor itemized as required by state law. I also found that SCANA was a common employers of lobbyists.
3. What was your reaction to reading the reports?
   A. I not only found that the lobbyists' reports lacked information required by law but that incumbent Secretary of State John Campbell was taking campaign donations from cemetery operators who he was supposed to regulate. I decided I should run for the office to compel lobbyists to comply with the law.
4. When did you declare your candidacy?
   A. I came forward as a candidate in early 1990 and made the conduct of the lobbyists and John Campbell's failure to supervise them my major issue. Then Henry Eichel of *The Charlotte Observer* wrote an article on the failure of Campbell to regulate the lobbyists

and that gave my major campaign issue much more credibility. I then commented in public about the issue during my campaign speeches and stops.

5. What was your strategy as a candidate?
   A. Frankly, I did not think I could win the election even up to the time of the election. But I was indignant about the lobbyists issue and was determined to go ahead. I put in $200,000 of my own money and ended up spending more money on my campaign than John Campbell, who was taking donations from not only the cemetery operators but the lobbyists too.
6. How did you conduct your campaign?
   A. My focus was on the lobbyists and Campbell's failure to make them file complete reports. I talked about that issue at every opportunity. It was tough going. On July 18, 1990, I was in Orangeburg, S.C. meeting with the staff of the *Times Democrat* newspaper of that city. It was part of my campaign strategy to visit every major newspaper and town in South Carolina and discuss my candidacy; and, I might say, I was very cordially received by the newspaper editors and staffers wherever I want. They liked to have candidates come in to see them and talk politics. Anyway, while I was at the *Times Democrat* office a woman staffer came up to me and handed me a news bulletin, saying she thought I would be interested. The bulletin was about the first FBI raids on the offices of South Carolina House members. The exposure of Operation Lost Trust and the role of lobbyists such as Ron Cobb in the scandal really helped to focus public attention on the lobbyists' unregulated conduct and excessive influence at the State House. Operation Lost Trust also angered me and made me even more determined to win the election and get the lobbyists under control.
7. As the election of November, 1990, drew near what was your thinking about your chances of victory?
   A. Until the election I thought I was going to be defeated. But I was determined to expose the problems at the Secretary of State's office and the self-serving behavior of John Campbell. I did feel confident about Greenville County, my home county, and I got positive feedback from the newspapers I was visiting as part of my campaign plan. I made it a point at each newspaper office I visited to have a picture taken of myself with a copy of the newspaper held up for the camera and such pictures often got published along with the story of my visit to the newspaper and my campaign issue of the need to regulate the lobbyists. I got real good media coverage at a low cost with my visits to the newspapers. Even so, Whit Ayres was doing polling for Gov. Carroll Campbell's re-election campaign in the fall of 1990 and told me that my poll numbers were bad. So I did not expect to win. But on election night I won by a 52% margin and won some black votes in the process. For a Republican I always got more votes than other Republicans in my campaigns from the black voters of South Carolina.

8. After you won the election, what was your game plan as the incoming Secretary of State?
   - A. I had Bob Knight, my campaign manager, in mind to take a position in the Secretary of State's office. So I asked Bob to go through the lobbyists' reports in detail and identify those who were not filing complete and accurate reports and he found many such reports. I held a meeting with lobbyists after I took office and told them that under my watch they must file and comply with the law. Most of the lobbyists then complied. Jerry Beasley, lobbyist of the South Carolina Textile Manufacturers Association, at first refused to comply and disclose as I required but after I sent a letter to Attorney General Travis Medlock about Beasley, asking for action, then Beasley capitulated and did what he was supposed to do.
9. The ethics reform effort in the South Carolina General Assembly produced a bill to move jurisdiction over lobbyists from the Secretary of State to the State Ethics Commission. What was your opinion on that proposal?
   - A. I opposed the move. I thought and still think that the responsibility to regulate lobbyists should have remained under the Secretary of State as an elected official accountable to the voters. I did not agree with institutionalizing oversight of the lobbyists.
10. What do you think were the long term consequences of your efforts as Secretary of State?
   - A. I think that the mandatory disclosure of lobbyists' spending had a major impact on their behavior and caused them to follow the law ever since 1991 when I took office.

Interview
Sen. Tom Moore

By John V. Crangle
February 4, 2015

<u>Tom Moore</u> (Democrat)

Sen. Tom Moore served in the South Carolina Senate from 1981 representing Aiken County. Moore was chair of the conference committee that wrote the final draft of the 1991 Ethics Act. He later was the Democratic candidate for governor in 2006. He resigned from the Senate in 2007 to return to private employment.

Interview

1. What were the roots causes of the Operation Lost Trust scandal in 1990 and 1991?
   A. The laws at that time allowed cash contributions to candidates for state office and there were no limits on the amounts and uses of campaign funds. The only legal requirement was that the money be reported on disclosure forms filed with the Ethics Commission or legislative ethics committee but the law was not enforced. This allowed lobbyists to give cash to legislators in unlimited amounts and avoid detection.
2. Tell me about your role as chairman of the conference committee.
   A. The President Pro Tem of the Senate Marshall Williams (D-Orangeburg) and several other senators picked three senators to serve on the conference committee to finalize the ethics bill in 1991. I was picked to serve as chairman of the committee. The House picked three conferees.
3. What were the major issues before the conference committee?
   A. One of the major disputes was over how much campaign contributions should be limited. There was really no disagreement at the point that contributions should be limited but only by what amounts. Democrats on the conference committee in addition to myself were Sen. McKinley Washington (D-Charleston) and Reps. Wes Hayes (D-Rock Hill) and Candy Waites (D-Richland). They favored an across-the-board limit on all campaign donations of $250 per election cycle. (An election cycle was counted as a primary, run-off primary, or general election.) Republicans on the committee were Sen. Sam Stilwell (R-Greenville) and Rep. David Wilkins (R- Greenville). They favored higher limits of $3,000 for each election cycle whether for state-wide office such as governor or legislative or local office. The conference committee compromised on limits of $1,000 for legislative and local candidates and $3,500 for statewide candidates. These are the limits still in effect today in 2015.
4. What was Gov. Carroll Campbell's role in ethics reform legislation?
   A. Gov. Campbell did not play a major leadership role on ethics reform legislation. He seemed most concerned that campaign finance laws not be too tightly written and he either wanted no limits or high limits on contribution amounts. The Republican senator on the conference committee, Sen. Stilwell, favored limits as an essential part of a comprehensive ethics reform package.
5. What was your view on limits?
   A. I wanted limits of $250 on all contributions for all offices. The committee debated the issue and agreed on compromise limits above what I thought best.
6. What about the issue of lobbyists and lobbying in the conference committee?
   A. Even as the committee convened and began its deliberations there was a consensus of both Democrats and Republicans that the lobbyists needed to be controlled in the con-

text of the Operation Lost Trust scandal involving bribes to legislators. The committee looked at limits on lobbyists in effect in other states as examples of what could be done in South Carolina. It quickly became apparent that lobbying reform required a complete ban on lobbyists' gratuities to legislators and other officials.

7. What resistance did lobbyists put up to the committee's efforts to regulate lobbyists and lobbying?
   A. The lobbyists did not put up much opposition to a complete ban on lobbyists gratuities and neither did they really try to stop our efforts to ban lobbyists from giving campaign contributions to candidates for state and local offices, including governor. In the end the "no-cup-of-coffee" rule was adopted in the final bill signed by Gov. Campbell in 1991.
8. What is your evaluation and opinion of the 1991 Ethics Act as of the year 2015?
   A. I think the "no-cup-of-coffee" rule has improved the integrity of state and local politicians and government officials since the Ethics Act took effect in 1992. It stopped the use of money by lobbyists to try to influence legislators and it has actually saved the lobbyists a great deal of money since they have been banned from giving gratuities and donations for nearly a quarter of a century now. And you will note that in the midst of the recent and current scandals in state and local governments, no lobbyists have been implicated in criminal activity related to their lobbying work. Today no single lobbyist is a dominating figure. It is also interesting that when in 2011 the Senate tried to ban leadership PACs, the House did not ban them. This was a mistake. Leadership PACs should have been banned in the 1991 Ethics Act. (The House banned leadership PACs in 2015 when Rep. Jay Lucas became the new Speaker.)

Interview
Samuel Stilwell

By John V. Crangle
February 10, 2015
Greenville, S.C.

Samuel Stilwell (Republican)

Samuel Stilwell served as a Republican senator from Greenville County from 1987 until he was elected as a Circuit Court judge in 1995. He later served on the South Carolina Court of Appeals until his retirement.

Sen. Stilwell served on the conference committee chaired by Sen. Tom Moore which wrote the final version of the legislation which was passed by the General Assembly on September 23, 1991, and signed into law as the 1991 Ethics Act.

He returned to private practice of law in Greenville, South Carolina where he currently resides.

Interview

1. When did you serve in the South Carolina Senate?
   A. I was elected to the South Carolina Senate in a special election in 1987 and served until I was elected as a Circuit Court judge in 1995. I then served on the South Carolina Court of Appeals.
2. What was the environment in the Senate when you served?
   A. There were virtually no laws which regulated the behavior of either lobbyists or legislators. I was amazed at what was going on in Columbia in relation to the conduct of both legislators and lobbyists. When I first came into the Senate, I was surprised when I went to dinner at Beau's Restaurant and Bar at the Carolina Hotel on the corner of Assembly and Pendleton Streets in Columbia across from the State House and after dinner and drinks I was told by a woman lobbyist that legislators did not have to pay because the lobbyists had an open tab for legislators and paid all of their bills. I did not know which lobbyists were actually paying the bills or who their clients were. Nobody was getting credit with legislators for paying their bills.
3. What was your view of the lobbyists when you were in the Senate?
   A. I thought that lobbyists liked to be able to give legislators gratuities such as free meals, free trips, and free drinks because it allowed the lobbyists themselves to live high on the hog and splurge while giving public officials free food and free drinks and trips out of state. The lobbyists enjoyed the same benefits at the expense of their employers.
4. Did lobbyists' gratuities have any effect on the actions and voting of legislators?
   A. Lobbyists' gratuities had no effect on my voting in the Senate. But some legislators who came from small towns were probably dazzled by the high life in Columbia and the gratuities at restaurants, bars, and other such places.
5. With regards to ethics reform, what was your early experience?
   A. I was appointed to a sub-committee of the Senate which dealt with campaign finance matters after Operation Lost Trust broke. There were three persons on the sub-committee, including Sen. Isadore Lourie and myself. We discussed the limits and restrictions which should be imposed on lobbyists and legislators and agreed that new rules were needed to stop the abuse of campaign funds by candidates. We agreed that the

use of campaign funds for personal use was bad and that limits on the use of surplus funds after an election were also needed.

6. What proposals did the sub-committee present regarding campaign finance reform?
   A. The sub-committee proposed a limit of $3,500 on contributions to state-wide candidates such as governor and that limit was adopted by the conference committee which finalized the 1991 Ethics Act. I also proposed that the transfer of campaign funds from the account of one candidate to the account of another candidate be banned and it was later banned in the Ethics Acts. Sen. Kay Patterson (D-Richland) wanted to legalize the use of campaign funds to buy gifts for constituents of a value of not more than $25. And we agreed that such gifts should be permitted under some circumstances.
7. What were the weaknesses of the 1991 Ethics Act?
   A. It distresses me that critics say that the 1991 Ethics Act is weak because at the time it was passed it was one of the strongest in the country. What has happened since 1991 is that a number of schemes have been devised to evade the Act. For example, leadership PACs did not exist in 1991. They have been created since then as slush funds by some legislators.
8. While the 1991Ethics Act was being written and finalized by the Senate-House conference committee on which you served, did you get any outside pressure to try to affect your voting and actions?
   A. Yes, the chief lobbyist (Jerry Beasley) for the South Carolina Textile Manufacturers Association made a veiled threat to me to ease up on my efforts to restrict lobbyists and their gratuities. He suggested that the Textile Manufacturers would not look with favor on me as a candidate for re-election if I tried to ban lobbyists from giving gratuities. I disregarded his warning and it had no effect on my actions as a member of the conference committee. The fact of the matter is that I knew Beasley while we were both students at the University of South Carolina and he always loved to party and had the reputation of being a big spender. My wife also knew him as they were both from the same hometown.
9. What were the main issues in contention in the conference committee?
   A. The committee was pretty much agreed from the start on the need to ban lobbyists' gratuities and we adopted the "no-cup-of-coffee" rule without any dispute. The main issue was not whether campaign donations should be limited but at what amounts.
10. What was the dispute over the amounts?
    A. The Democrats on the conference committee wanted to limit campaign contributions to $250 per donor per election cycle and the Republicans favored a higher amount. We compromised on the amounts of $3,500 for statewide office and $1,000 for all other offices including legislators and local officials such as city council. Those limits were then adopted and passed as part of the 1991 Ethics Act signed by Gov. Carroll Campbell.

11. What is your view of the 1991 Ethics Act from the perspective of the year 2015?
    A. The Act was very advanced in the United States at the time. Perhaps it was the best ethics act in the nation along with that of Wisconsin. The Act did not go far enough but we did not foresee the creation of leadership PACs in South Carolina and other schemes to raise political money and exploit public office.
12. What is your view of the Lost Trust Sting Operation?
    A. The problem with the sting was that it used the betting bill as the basis for vote-buying. In fact, a number of legislators were in favor of the betting bill before they took money from Ron Cobb. I doubt they were guilty of taking bribes. Furthermore, I think the sting operation was illegal and should not have been done. The sting preyed on legislators who favored betting and they should not have been targeted and indicted.

Interview
Hemphill P. Pride, II
Attorney at Law

by Rick Bundrett, *The Greenville News,* and John V. Crangle
July 3, 2014
Columbia, S.C.

Hemphill P. Pride, II, Attorney at Law

Hemphill P. Pride, II, represented Judge Tee Ferguson in an Operation Lost Trust case charging Ferguson with public corruption while a member of the South Carolina House of Representatives in 1990. Mr. Pride attended Johnson C. Smith University in Charlotte, North Carolina, before enrolling at Florida A&M School of Law where he graduated in 1962. He was admitted to the South Carolina Bar in 1964. He has been a member of the South Carolina Bar and practiced in Columbia, South Carolina, since that time.

Interview

"Quite frankly, I've always thought there was a culture of corruption in government—period," Pride said. (Response to question about whether he believed a culture of corruption was evident during period of Operation Lost Trust.)

Pride acknowledged that weak ethics laws then—e. g., lobbyists were allowed to offer cash, trips and other gifts to lawmakers—aggravated the situation. "It breeds that climate of corruption," Pride said.

"I was the only African-American lawyer that went to trial during Operation Lost Trust," Pride said.

"From a purely African-American standpoint, African-American legislators, first of all, had no business sponsoring a betting bill," Pride said, noting the prior support of the Legislative Black Caucus for a betting bill and South Carolina's deep-rooted poverty. "Everybody knew they were in the wrong place in the first place."

"I raised as a legitimate defense that it was a selective prosecution on the part of the government," Pride said. (Response to question whether he believed there was selective prosecution of black lawmakers.) "I was the only lawyer who raised that it was selective prosecution [by] the government."

Pride noted that Kay Patterson and Nelson Rivers testified about the issue of selective prosecution by the government.

"It plays into the overall scheme that black people are thieves and crooks and dishonest, most of all, can't be trusted," Pride said. (Response to question about why he believed black lawmakers were targeted.)

"I thought they were trying to get a disproportionate number of African-American legislators," Pride said, adding that Judge Hawkins "summarily dismissed" that argument.

"The Supreme Court made up and promulgated rules and removed him.... He was defrocked." Pride said, noting the court relied on vague language—"inherent powers of the court." (Response to question about whether he believed the Supreme Court had the authority then to sanction Ferguson.)

"Ron Cobb played the role of "I'm a brother, too," Pride said. (Response to question about whether he believed the government used Cobb to entrap Ferguson.) "He entrapped them, and he baited them into the conversation. The intent for a level of criminality was never initiated by Ferguson; it was initiated by Cobb. He (Ferguson) didn't go in there with his hand out."

"They exceeded their authority and went beyond their borders in terms of baiting, luring and planting the seeds of criminal intent," Pride said. (Response to questions about whether he believed the government abused its authority in Operation Lost Trust.)

"We're not to be trusted—that they're just basically involved in graft," Pride said. (Response to question about perception of African Americans following Operation Lost Trust.)

Pride said he didn't believe Operation Lost Trust was a deterrent against public corruption in state government, noting, "It was just business as usual" after Operation Lost Trust. He did acknowledge, though, that it was right to ban, through the State Ethics Act, lobbyists from offering money, free trips and other gifts to lawmakers.

APPENDIX A

SUMMARY OF PROSECUTION RESULTS

Legislators

Legislators Convicted on Guilty Pleas.................... 10
Legislators Convicted at Trial.................... 06
Legislators Acquitted.................... 01
*Judge/Legislator Convicted at Trial (Ferguson).................... 01
*Judge/Legislator Convicted on Nolo Plea (Ferguson).................... 01
Total.................... 18

Lobbyists

Lobbyists Convicted on Guilty Plea.................... 06

Executive Branch Officials

Convicted on Guilty Pleas.................... 02

State Employees

Convicted on Guilty Plea.................... 01

Businessmen

Convicted on Guilty Pleas.................... 01

Total Convicted.................... 27

Total Acquitted.................... 01

Total Prosecuted.................... 28

*Note: Judge Tee Ferguson was convicted at trial for bribery and pleaded guilty to drug violations. A total of 17 sitting legislators were indicted. Ferguson had left the House, but was indicted for crimes committed while in the House.

APPENDIX B

DISPOSITION OF CASES

Legislators Convicted by Guilty Plea (11)	Convictions	Sentences
Rep. Robert Brown (D-Marion)	Selling Vote	6 months halfway house 5 months probation 200 hrs. community service
Rep. Donna Moss (D-Cherokee)	Cocaine Possession	3 years probation $2,500 fine
Rep. Ennis Fant (D-Greenville)	Selling Vote	3 years probation 200 hrs. community service 20 months in prison
Rep. Jim Faber (D-Richland)	Selling Vote	1 year prison 200 hrs. community service 3 years probation
Rep. Danny Winstead (R-Charleston)	Selling Vote	2½ years in prison 3 years supervised release $25,000 fine
Rep. Thomas Limehouse (R-Dorchester)	Witness Tampering Selling Vote	20 months in prison 3 years probation $15,000 fine 200 hrs. community service
Rep. Frank McBride (D-Richland)	Selling Vote	1 year in prison 3 years probation
Rep. Jack I. Rogers (D-Marlboro)	Racketeering (Extorting Lobbyists)	46 months in prison 3 years probation 300 hrs. community service

Judge Tee Ferguson (D-Spartanburg) (Convicted by pleas of nolo contendere) (Also convicted of corruption at trial prior to nolo plea)	2 counts cocaine possession 1 count conspiracy to possess cocaine 3 counts possession of cocaine	7 months in prison concurrent
Sen. Rick Lee (R-Spartanburg)	Selling Vote	6 months halfway house 5 years probation $3,000 restitution
Rep. Bob Kohn (R-Charleston)	Selling Vote	15 months in prison
Sen. Bud Long (D-Horry)	Lying to the FBI (1999)	3 years probation $1,000 fine

Legislators Tried and Convicted

Defendants Convicted at Trial (7)	Convictions	Sentences
Rep. Luther Taylor (D-Richland)	Selling Vote Conspiracy	6½ years in prison Overturned on appeal No Retrial (Died in 1997)
Rep. Paul Derrick (R-Lexington)	Selling Vote Retrial (1999)	24 months in prison
Rep. Larry Blanding (D-Sumter)	Selling Vote Retrial (1999)	30 months in prison
Rep. B.J. Gordon (D-Williamsburg)	Selling Vote	Overturned (Died in 1997) No Retrial
Rep. Ken Bailey (D-Orangeburg)	1 count conspiracy to violate Hobbs Act to extort a bribe 1 count taking bribe	26 months in prison
Sen. Bud Long (D-Horry)	Selling Vote	Conviction overturned
Judge Tee Ferguson (D-Spartanburg) (Also pleaded to cocaine violations)	Selling Vote	33 months in prison

Legislator Tried and Acquitted

Rep. Tim Wilkes (D-Fairfield)	Selling Vote	No sentence

Lobbyists Pleaded Guilty (6)

Defendants	Client	Convictions	Sentence
Ronnie Crow	S.C. Highway Commission	Extortion	6 months halfway house $17,411 fine
Randy Lee	Health Care Association	Marijuana possession	3 years probation $2,500 fine 150 hrs. community service
James Brown, V	S .C. Credit Union	Illegal Drugs	Deceased prior to sentencing (1990)
Ron Cobb	Alpha Group (FBI front) FBI sting agent	Cocaine possession	2 months halfway house
Tom Collins	Hitachi salesman	Cocaine possession	1 year prison-suspended 2 years probation 150 hrs. community service
Martin Guy Rohling	Household International, Inc.	Cocaine possession	3 years probation $1,000 fine 100 hrs. community service

Others Convicted By Pleas (4)

	Convictions	Sentences
James Hopkins (Clemson University Administrator)	Cocaine possession	3 years probation $1,000 fine 150 hrs. community service
David Hawkins (Aide to Gov. Campbell)	Obstruction	6 months house arrest 2 years probation
David D. Little, III (Businessman)	Cocaine possession	3 years probation 150 hrs. community service
Dick Greer (Chairman S.C. Development Board)	Cocaine	2 months halfway house 3 years probation plus fine

APPENDIX C

PROSECUTORS OF LOST TRUST CASES

The terms of the U.S. Attorneys who served during the period of 1989 to 1999 while the Lost Trust era cases were being investigated, processed in the federal grand juries, indicted, tried, and appealed were as follows:

Name	Appointed By	Term of Office
Bart Daniel	President George H.W. Bush	1989-March, 1992
John S. Simmons	President George H.W. Bush	March, 1992-April, 1993
Pete Strom, Jr.	President Bill J. Clinton	April, 1993-January, 1996
Daniel Butler	U S. Department of Justice	January 20, 1996-1999
Richard Pilger	U.S. Department of Justice	January 20, 1996-1999

APPENDIX D

MAJOR CASES—CLIENTS AND ATTORNEYS

Clients	Attorneys	Disposition
Bailey, Ken	Charles Williams Brad Hutto	Convicted at Trial
Blanding, Larry	Danny Martin	Convicted at Trial Retrial Conviction
Brown, Robert	Cam Littlejohn	Pled Guilty
Derrick, Paul	Jim Lengel John Hardaway	Convicted at Trial Retrial Conviction
Faber, James	I.S. Leevy Johnson	Convicted on Plea
Fant, Ennis	B.O. Thomason	Convicted on Plea
Ferguson, Tee	Hemphill Pride, III Donnell Jennings John Hardaway Gaston Fairey	Convicted on Pleas of Drugs Convicted at Trial on Corruption
Greer, Dick	Gedney Howe	Pled Guilty
Gordon, B.J.	Leonel Lofton	Convicted at Trial Overturned on Appeal Died before Retrial
Lee, Rick	Mike Spears	Pled Guilty
Limehouse, Tom	Andy Savage	Pled Guilty
Long, Bud	Jack Swerling Tommy Brittain	Convicted at Trial Overturned on Dismissal Pled to Misdemeanor
McBride, Frank	I.S. Leevy Johnson	Pled Guilty
Rohling, Martin Guy	Ralph Hoisington	Pled Guilty
Rogers, Jack I.	Tim Rogers Robert Simpson	Pled Guilty

Taylor, Luther	Joel Collins	Convicted at Trial Overturned on Appeal Died Before Retrial
	Arthur Aiken	Civil Suit
Wilkes, Tim	Gedney Howe	Acquitted by Jury
Winstead, Danny	Lee Bowers John Weaver	Pled Guilty

APPENDIX E

MAJOR PROVISIONS OF JUDICIAL MERIT SELECTION ACT OF 1996

<u>Section</u>

2.19.10	Created Judicial Merit Selection Commission
2.19.20	Required Commission to announce vacancies and investigate candidates for judicial offices
2.19.25	Authorizes Commission to solicit information from S.C. Bar about candidates
2.19.35	Provided criteria for evaluating candidates
2.19.80	Provided for nomination of candidates to General Assembly
2.19.90	Provided for approval of candidates by General Assembly
2.19.120	Provided for Citizens Committee on Judicial Qualifications and for Membership of Committee

APPENDIX F

PERSONS WITH SAME LAST NAMES

Brown

James – Lobbyist Convicted of drug violations
Robert – State Representative convicted of corruption

Collins

Joel – Columbia attorney who represented Rep. Luther Taylor
Tom – Lobbyist convicted of drug violations

Hawkins

David – Legislative aide to Gov. Campbell convicted of obstruction
Falcon – U.S. District Court Judge who presided over Lost Trust cases

Lee

Randy – Lobbyist convicted of drugs in Lost Trust
Rick – State Senator convicted of corruption

Lindsay

Jack – State Senator who died in 1991
John – son of Jack Lindsay who failed as a candidate to replace Jack

Rogers

Jack I. – Speaker Pro Tem convicted of racketeering
Tim – State Representative from Columbia who promoted reform
Michael – candidate who opposed Sen. Hugh Leatherman in 1992

Taylor

Levola – Richland County Councilwoman elected to House
Luther – State Representative convicted of corruption

Williams

Charles – Orangeburg attorney who represented Ken Bailey
Marshall – President of the Senate, Pro Tem

APPENDIX G

SUMMARY OF LOST TRUST CASES AS OF DECEMBER 31, 1999

Final Toll of Lost Trust

As of the end of 1999 the final results of the Operation Lost Trust criminal cases were as follows:

Tried and convicted—seven (7) (1990–1991, 1999)

Rep. Paul Derrick—convicted on retrial (1999)

Rep. Luther Taylor—overturned, died before retrial (1997)

Rep. Larry Blanding—overturned, convicted on retrial (1999) Blanding Conviction Overturned in 2001. No Reprosecution.

Rep. B.J. Gordon—overturned, died before retrial (1997)

Rep. Ken Bailey—appeal denied

Rep. Judge Tee Ferguson (also pleaded guilty to drug charges)—appeal denied

Sen. J.M. "Bud" Long—felony overturned, pleaded to misdemeanor (1999)

Tried and acquitted—one (1) (1991)

Rep. Tim Wilkes

Total Guilty Pleas—eleven (11) (1990–1991)

Rep. Tee Ferguson (also convicted on one count at trial)

Sen. Rick Lee

Rep. Danny Winstead

Rep. Robert Brown

Rep. Robert Kohn

Rep. Tom Limehouse

Rep. Donna Moss

Rep. Ennis Fant

Rep. James Faber

Rep. Frank McBride

Rep. Jack I. Rogers

State Development Board—one (1)

Dick Greer, Chairman

Businessman—one (1)

David D. Little, III

Clemson University Administrator—one (1)

James Hopkins

Aide to Governor—one (1)

David Hawkins

Lobbyists—six (6)

James Brown, V (deceased)

Martin Guy Rohling

Randy Lee

Ron Cobb

Ronnie Crow

Tom Collins

APPENDIX H

TOTAL CONVICTION BY CRIME TYPE

Public Corruption—seventeen (17)

Tee Ferguson (drugs)

Luther Taylor—Overturned. Died 1997.

Rick Lee

Paul Derrick—Convicted on retrial 1999.

Danny Winstead (obstruction)

Larry Banding—Convicted on retrial 1999.

Blanding Conviction Overturned in 2001. No Reprosecution.

Robert Brown

B.J. Gordon—Overturned. Died 1997.

Robert Kohn (drugs)

Ken Bailey

Tom Limehouse

Ronnie Crow

Ennis Fant

James Faber

Frank McBride

Jack I. Rogers

J.M. "Bud" Long. Overturned.

Illegal Drugs—eleven (11)

Dick Greer

David Little, III

James Hopkins

Rep. Donna Moss

James Brown, V

Martin Guy Rohling

Randy Lee

Ron Cobb

Tom Collins

Rep. Tee Ferguson (corruption)

Robert Kohn (corruption)

Other Crimes

David Hawkins (obstruction)

Bud Long (lying to federal agent)

Thomas Winstead (obstruction)

Thomas Limehouse (tampering)

Jack I. Rogers (racketeering)

APPENDIX I

TOTAL CONVICTIONS BY POLITICAL PARTIES

Legislators:

Republicans—five (5)

Lee, Rick

Winstead

Kohn

Limehouse

Derrick

Democrats—twelve (12)

Bailey

Brown, Robert

Fant

Gordon

McBride

Rogers

Wilkes (acquitted)

Blanding

Faber

Ferguson

Long

Moss

Taylor

Executives:

Republicans—two (2)

Greer

Hawkins

Lobbyists:

Unknown affiliation—J. Brown, R. Lee, Collins, Rohling

Known affiliation—Cobb (Democrat), Crow (Democrat)

Businessman:

Unknown affiliation—Little

Administrator:

Unknown affiliation—Hopkins

APPENDIX J

TOTAL CONVICTIONS BY RACE

Black—eight (8)

Bailey

Blanding

Faber

Fant

Ferguson

Gordon (Overturned)

McBride

Taylor (Overturned)

White—twenty (20)

Brown, James

Brown, Robert

Cobb

Collins

Crow

Derrick

Greer

Hawkins

Hopkins

Long

Lee, Randy

Lee, Rick

Limehouse

Little

Kohn

Moss

Rogers

Rohling

Wilkes (acquitted)

Winstead

Operation Lost Trust

Chronology of Major Events

Jan. 1988 – March 1989	Rep. Tee Ferguson possessed cocaine five times
April 1989	Ron Cobb arrested and agrees to cooperate
April 1989	Rep. Donna Moss possessed cocaine
Sept. 1989	Lobbyist James Madison Brown, V. arrested
Oct. 17, 1989	Rep. Bob Kohn and Ron Cobb plan to pass bill
Jan. 10, 1990	Kohn told Rep. Taylor Cobb would pay for votes
Jan. 11, 1990	Kohn and Cobb agree on $2,500 to vote for bill
Jan. 11, 1990	Rep. Limehouse discussed money for bill
Jan. 16, 1990	Kohn accepted $2,500 from Cobb to vote for bill
Jan. 16, 1990	Rep. Taylor said he would vote for bill for $2,500
Jan. 18, 1990	Kohn told Cobb he could recruit votes for bill
Jan. 19, 1990	Rep. Taylor took $2,500 from Cobb for bill
Jan. 25, 1990	Rep. Limehouse said he would accept suits for bill
April 10, 1990	Sen. Lee denies corruption exists at Senate hearing
April 19, 1990	Rep. Robert Brown takes $2,000 from Cobb on bill
April 25, 1990	Effort to move betting bill in House fails
May 8, 1990	Rep. Larry Blanding accepts $300 from Cobb on bill
May 8, 1990	Rep. Taylor accepts $500 from Cobb on bill
May 9, 1990	Rep. Fant accepts $300 from Cobb on bill
May 24, 1990	Sen. Lee accepts $2,000 from Cobb on bill
June 21, 1990	Rep. Winstead accepts $1,000 from Cobb on bill
July 18, 1990	Limehouse warns Cobb not to tell FBI about crimes
July 18, 1990	FBI served subpoenas on 16 target legislators
July 20, 1990	Rep. Winstead tells Kohn not to tell FBI
August 16, 1990	Kohn announced his cooperation with FBI
August 23, 1990	Rep. Robert Brown resigned
August 23, 1990	Judge Tee Ferguson takes voluntary suspension
August 24, 1990	Sen. Lee and Reps. Taylor, Winstead, Brown, Kohn indicted
August 28, 1990	Sen. Lee resigned
Sept. 4 – 10, 1990	Reps. Brown, Gordon, Limehouse, Fant plead
September 21, 1990	Rep. Blanding, Gordon, Limehouse, Fant indicted
September 21, 1990	Rep. Moss and lobbyist Brown indicted
September 26, 1990	Rep. Kohn pleads
October 12, 1990	Rep. Moss pleads
October 25, 1990	Rep. Taylor convicted by jury
November 6, 1990	Jim Miles elected Secretary of State
November 6, 1990	Gov. Campbell reelected
November 29, 1990	Lobbyist James Brown, V. died
December 4, 1990	Rep. Jack I. Rogers reelected as Speaker Pro Tem
December 4, 1990	Rep. Taylor sentenced to 6½ years in prison
December 5, 1990	House adopts "no cup of coffee" rule
December 7, 1990	Rep. Limehouse pleads
December 9, 1990	Sen. Lee sentenced to 6 months in Halfway House

January 11, 1991	Sen. Jack Lindsay dies
February 20, 1991	Reps. Derrick, Faber, and McBride indicted
February 20, 1991	Rohling, Collins, Randy Lee indicted
February 22, 1991	Fant pleads
March 21, 1991	McBride and Faber plead
April 10, 1991	Dick Greer indicted
April 10, 1991	Dick Greer, Randy Lee, Cobb plead to cocaine
May 8, 1991	Jack I. Rogers pleads
May 18, 1991	Lobbyist Ronnie Crow pleads
May 21, 1991	Judge Ferguson indicted
May 22, 1991	Judge Hawkins rules blacks not target in sting
May 23, 1991	Rep. Tim Wilkes and Ken Bailey indicted
May 23, 1991	David Hawkins charged
May 23, 1991	David Little, III, indicted
May 23, 1991	James Hopkins indicted
May 30, 1991	Tom Collins pleads to three (3) misdemeanors
June 7, 1991	Judge Ferguson convicted at trial
August 20, 1991	Sen. Bud Long indicted
August 24, 1991	Rep. Ken Bailey convicted at trial
August 26, 1991	Judge Ferguson resigns
August 28, 1991	Bart Daniel announces indictments ended
August 31, 1991	Sen. Rick Lee released
September 23, 1991	Ethics Act passed. October 1, 1991 signed
September 24, 1991	Rep. Wilkes acquitted
November 23, 1991	Sen. Bud Long convicted at trial
March 26, 1992	Conviction of Long overturned
March 26, 1992	Convictions of Taylor, Blanding, Gordon, and Derrick all reversed
April 8, 1992	Bill to expand jurisdiction of state grand jury passed to include public corruption.
November 3, 1992	43 new legislators elected
August 9, 1993	Donna Moss fails in reelection campaign
August 9, 1994	Retrials ordered for Taylor, Gordon, Derrick, Blanding, and Sen. Long
July 25, 1995	Jack I. Rogers completed sentence
February 28, 1997	Judge Hawkins dismisses all charges against Taylor, Gordon, Derrick, Blanding, and Sen. Long
March 23, 1997	Luther Taylor dies
July 12, 1997	B.J. Gordon dies
November 23, 1998	Fourth Circuit reinstates all charges
May 8, 1999	Derrick convicted on retrial
June 12, 1999	Blanding's first retrial hangs jury
June 30, 1999	Sen. Long pleads to misdemeanor
August 20, 1999	Blanding convicted on second retrial
	Lost Trust prosecutions ends

NOTES